STUDENT SERVICES

STUDENT SERVICES

A Handbook for the Profession

FIFTH EDITION

John H. Schuh, Susan R. Jones, Shaun R. Harper, and Associates

JOSSEY-BASS
A Wiley Imprint
www.josseybass.com

Published by Jossey-Bass
A Wiley Imprint
One Montgomery, Ste. 1200, San Francisco, CA 94104—www.josseybass.com

Jossey-Bass books and products are available through most bookstores. To contact Jossey-Bass directly call our Customer Care Department within the U.S. at 800-956-7739, outside the U.S. at 317-572-3986, or fax 317-572-4002.

Jossey-Bass also publishes its books in a variety of electronic formats. Some content that appears in print may not be available in electronic books.

Library of Congress Cataloging-in-Publication Data
Student services : a handbook for the profession. — 5th ed. / [edited by] John H. Schuh, Susan R. Jones, Shaun R. Harper, and associates.
      p. cm. — (The Jossey-Bass higher and adult education series)
    Rev. ed. of: Student services / Susan R. Komives, Dudley B. Woodard, Jr., and associates. 4th ed. c2003.
    Includes bibliographical references and indexes.
    ISBN 978-0-470-45498-5
    ISBN 978-0-470-77050-4 (ebk); ISBN 978-0-470-87214-7 (ebk); ISBN 978-0-470-87215-4 (ebk)
      1. Student affairs services—United States—Handbooks, manuals, etc.   2. College student development programs—United States—Handbooks, manuals, etc.   3. Counseling in higher education—United States—Handbooks, manuals, etc.   I. Schuh, John H.   II. Jones, Susan R., 1955–   III. Harper, Shaun R., 1975–   IV. Komives, Susan R., 1946– Student services.
  LB2342.92.K65   2011
  378.1'97—dc22

2010034869

Printed in the United States of America
FIRST EDITION
HB Printing   10 9 8 7

The Jossey-Bass Higher and
Adult Education Series

CONTENTS

Preface   xi

About the Authors   xvii

PART ONE: HISTORICAL AND CONTEMPORARY CONTEXT   1

1 Historical Overview of American Higher Education   3
John R. Thelin and Marybeth Gasman

2 Institutional Variety in American Higher Education   24
Kimberly A. Griffin and Sylvia Hurtado

3 Campus Climate and Diversity   43
Mitchell J. Chang, Jeffrey F. Milem, and anthony lising antonio

PART TWO: PROFESSIONAL FOUNDATIONS AND PRINCIPLES   59

4 The Development of Student Affairs   61
Gwendolyn Dungy and Stephanie A. Gordon

5 Philosophies and Values   80
Robert D. Reason and Ellen M. Broido

6 Ethical Standards and Principles   96
Jane Fried

7 Selected Legal Issues 120

Gary Pavela

PART THREE: THEORETICAL BASES OF THE PROFESSION 135

8 The Nature and Uses of Theory 149

Susan R. Jones and Elisa S. Abes

9 Psychosocial and Cognitive-Structural Perspectives
   on Student Development 168

Nancy J. Evans

10 Perspectives on Identity Development 187

Vasti Torres

11 Student Learning 207

Patricia M. King and Marcia B. Baxter Magolda

12 Organizational Theory 226

Adrianna Kezar

13 Campus Ecology and Environments 242

Kristen A. Renn and Lori D. Patton

14 Student Success 257

George D. Kuh

**PART FOUR: ORGANIZING AND MANAGING PROGRAMS
AND SERVICES** 271

15 Framing Student Affairs Practice 273

Kathleen Manning and Frank Michael Muñoz

16 Strategy and Intentionality in Practice 287

Shaun R. Harper

17 Financing Student Affairs 303

John H. Schuh

18 Assessment and Evaluation 321

Marilee J. Bresciani

PART FIVE: ESSENTIAL COMPETENCIES 335

19 Multicultural Competence 337

Raechele L. Pope and John A. Mueller

20 Leadership 353

Susan R. Komives

21 Staffing and Supervision 372

Joan B. Hirt and Terrell L. Strayhorn

22 Teaching in the Co-Curriculum 385

Peter M. Magolda and Stephen John Quaye

23 Counseling and Helping Skills 399

Amy L. Reynolds

24 Advising and Consultation 413

Patrick Love and Sue Maxam

25 Conflict Resolution 433

Larry Roper and Christian Matheis

26 Community Development 448

Dennis C. Roberts

27 Professionalism 468

Jan Arminio

28 Academic and Student Affairs Partnerships 482

Elizabeth J. Whitt

PART SIX: THE FUTURE 497

29 Using Research to Inform Practice: Considering the
    Conditional Effects of College 499

Linda J. Sax and Casandra E. Harper

30 Student Technology Use and Student Affairs Practice 515

Ana M. Martínez Alemán and Katherine Lynk Wartman

31 Shaping the Future 534

Susan R. Jones, Shaun R. Harper, and John H. Schuh

Name Index 547

Subject Index 557

We dedicate this book to those who served as editors and authors of the editions that preceded this one. Ursula Delworth and Gary Hanson edited the first handbook and its resounding success led to a second edition, also edited by Ursula and Gary. Susan Komives and Dudley (Doug) Woodard edited the third and fourth volumes of this book. They built on the foundations of the first two editions and skillfully crafted volumes that made significant contributions to the literature of student affairs. It has been our privilege to continue in the traditions of our predecessors. We trust that we have honored their work by developing this volume and hope that it will be of value to those who use it to inform their practice.

PREFACE

Precisely when student affairs practice began in the United States is difficult to pinpoint. It may have been when a student was subjected to institutional discipline at Harvard College in the seventeenth century. Alternately, Mueller (1961) has claimed that personnel work (the phrase of the day) was a twentieth-century phenomenon. Dr. James Rhatigan (2009) identified several sources that indicated that deans of women were appointed before the turn of the twentieth century and that LeBaron Russell Briggs of Harvard (citing Cowley, 1937) and Thomas Arkle Clark of the University of Illinois were the first deans of men. Exactly who was the first student affairs practitioner and what role this person played are less significant in our view than that people have been engaged in student affairs practice in one form or another for around one hundred years even though the roots of the field can be traced to the beginning of higher education in colonial times.

Since its beginning, student affairs practice has moved forward dramatically. At first, student personnel work, as it was known at the time, had a great deal to do with monitoring and reacting to student behavior, both good and bad. Today, student affairs practice is challenging, complex, and sophisticated, and it touches students from before they apply for admission to when they graduate and beyond. Various titles have been used to characterize the work including, but not limited to, *student personnel, student services, student development, student affairs administration*, and just plain *student affairs*. The titles of the day are probably less important than it is to recognize that it would be an unusual institution that did not have staff members dedicated to the growth and development of students outside of the formal curriculum. These staff form the audience for this volume. Although our primary audience consists of graduate students and student affairs staff who are in the early stages of their careers, we also hope that our ideas will resonate with senior leaders in student affairs as well as with those who teach courses in the preparation of student affairs practitioners.

Whether or not student affairs practice has reached full maturity as a profession (see Stamatakos, 1981), it is important in our view that the literature base of the field be refreshed on an ongoing basis. Toward that end we offer the fifth edition of this volume. It is designed to advance our field, to offer new ideas about student affairs practice, and to remind readers that the focus of our work has been and always will be on students—their growth and their development.

The Green Book

This is the fifth edition of the "Green Book." The first edition was edited by Ursula Delworth and Gary R. Hanson in 1980, and revised editions were released in 1989, 1996, and 2003. Is there a need to release new editions of this volume every few years? Obviously, we think so, but consider this: the traditional, eighteen-year-old students who are entering college in fall 2011 were not born when the first and second editions were published. They were three years old when the third volume was released, and they were in about fifth grade when the most recent edition was published. Our view is that students, in addition to institutions of higher education, curriculum, and the external environment affecting higher education, have changed dramatically since 2003, as has our profession. Accordingly, we think it is time to update this volume through a discussion of contemporary theories and practices, and our guess is that toward the end of this decade it will be time to do that again.

Ursula Delworth and Gary Hanson were the pioneers of this series, editing the first two volumes. They were pioneers in other respects, too, also having served as the inaugural editors of the *New Directions for Student Services* sourcebook series. The third and fourth editions were edited by Susan R. Komives and Dudley B. Woodard Jr., also exceptional scholars. Susan and Doug have upheld the high standards set by Ursula and Gary. When they decided they did not want to take on producing the fifth edition, it became our turn to take a crack at crafting a new edition of The Green Book. Our predecessors set the bar high, and their commitment to excellence guided our work.

The Title

The title of this book has been a concern for the editors for at least three editions, including this one. *Student services* is a dated term to describe the work of contemporary student affairs practitioners and probably has been so for several decades. Clearly some of the work of student affairs practitioners involves providing services, but it is far more complex than that. Nevertheless, we wish to be true to the roots of this series of books, and we have thus retained the title for this edition.

Focus of the Fifth Edition

As we move into the second decade of this century, the focus of this volume, as has been the case in previous editions, is on college students and how to provide the very best educational experiences for them.

We think it is interesting to note that the contributors to previous editions in this series have turned over completely. None of the authors who contributed to the first edition contributed to the fourth edition or to this one, and only three authors who contributed chapters to the second edition have contributed to all of the succeeding volumes, including this one. This group includes Jane Fried, George Kuh, and John Schuh. Just six authors who were contributors to the third edition have contributed to this one. This volume includes the work of twenty-three new lead authors as well as some new coauthors. Having multiple authors for chapters is a new concept for this edition, at least compared with the third and fourth editions. Although many of the titles of the chapters remain the same as those included in the fourth edition, the vast majority of contributors to this volume are new, and we trust they have provided a fresh treatment of their subject matter.

Contents of the Fifth Edition

The organization of this volume is similar to that of the fourth edition. It explores the roots of our practice, discusses selected theories that inform our practice, and describes administrative practices that are necessary to provide a foundation for our work. Essential competencies and techniques are discussed in detail. The competencies and techniques are not listed in any particular order nor should the reader infer that some are more important than others. Our view is that all of the competencies and techniques we discuss are essential elements in the portfolio of the contemporary student affairs practitioner. We conclude by looking forward with a glance into our crystal ball. How well have we predicted the future? We'll know that when it comes time to prepare the sixth edition!

More specifically, in Part One, Chapter One, John R. Thelin and Marybeth Gasman provide a history of higher education in the United States. Recognizing that the history of U.S. higher education encompasses more than 370 years, they identify highlights that have provided a foundation for student affairs practice. In Chapter Two, Kimberly A. Griffin and Sylvia Hurtado provide an overview of the distinctions between institutions of higher education with a focus on institutional mission and type. American higher education is complex and diverse, with institutions ranging from those that almost exclusively focus on their teaching mission to those that are research oriented. Also in the mix are those that are private but not-for-profit, those that are private and for-profit, and those that are supported by state governments. Chapter Three focuses on the diversity of students. Mitchell Chang, Jeffrey F. Milem, and anthony lising antonio share their thoughts on this increasingly complex topic.

Gwen Dungy and Stephanie Gordon begin Part Two by providing an overview of the development of student affairs from its early roots to the establishment of positions called deans of women and deans of men. They discuss the professionalization of student affairs, and the profession's current focus on student learning, success, and institutional accountability in Chapter Four. Bob Reason and Ellen M. Broido explore the philosophies and values of the student affairs profession in Chapter Five, drawing a connection between the philosophies and values of student affairs and the work we do on our campuses. In Chapter Six, Jane Fried examines professional ethics, exploring current topics in addition to providing a foundation for this aspect of our work. Gary Pavela discusses contemporary legal issues in Chapter Seven, with a focus on protecting and promoting civility, working with troubled students, and risk management.

Part Three provides a theoretical foundation for the profession. Susan Jones and Elisa Abes explore the nature of theory in Chapter Eight, concluding that the profession has a rich array of theories that can be used to inform our work. In Chapter Nine, Nancy J. Evans discusses families of theories, specifically psychosocial and cognitive-structural theories that focus on student development. Vasti Torres provides an introduction to the theoretical foundations of identity development in Chapter Ten. Pat King and Marcia Baxter Magolda discuss student learning in Chapter Eleven. Specifically, they focus on linking learning and development in their chapter. In Chapter Twelve, Adrianna Kezar explores organizational theory. Organizational theory influences the daily work of student affairs practitioners in her view and she provides perspectives on the good—and the bad—of higher education organizations. Kris Renn and Lori Patton describe the influence of the campus environment on students in Chapter Thirteen, and also explore how students experience their environment. In Chapter Fourteen, George Kuh identifies promising policies and programs that can lead to student success. Kuh includes in this chapter seven sets of activities that student affairs educators can emphasize to foster higher levels of student success.

Part Four of this volume includes four topics that are foundational to student affairs practice. In Chapter Fifteen, Kathleen Manning and Frank Muñoz use the six cultures of the academy to frame their discussion of student affairs practice. They maintain that understanding these cultures is important in thinking about how staff "fit" in their student affairs organization. Shaun Harper discusses strategy and intentionality in student affairs practice in Chapter Sixteen. The focus of Chapter Seventeen, written by John Schuh, is budgeting and financing student affairs. This chapter examines sources of revenues and expenditures in regard to these central elements of student affairs practice. This section concludes with Marilee Bresciani's discussion of assessment in student affairs. In an environment where accountability is increasingly sought by higher education's stakeholders, Chapter Eighteen provides concepts and ideas related to outcomes assessment.

Part Five provides what we think are essential competencies for student affairs practitioners. In Chapter Nineteen, Raechele Pope and John Mueller address multicultural competence. They assert that the increasingly diverse communities on college campuses present both opportunities and challenges, and argue that developing multicultural competence is important in achieving effectiveness in student affairs practice. In Chapter Twenty, Susan Komives, reviews not only historic and conventional understandings of organizational leadership but also the contemporary relational approaches valued in complex, networked organizations. In Chapter Twenty-One, Joan Hirt and Terrell Strayhorn examine the importance of staffing patterns in student affairs organizations, and then describe models of supervision and staffing practices. They conclude by discussing the role that staffing practices play in the vitality of the student affairs profession. Peter Magolda and Stephen John Quaye focus on how student affairs educators can facilitate student learning in the co-curriculum in Chapter Twenty-Two. Amy L. Reynolds explores counseling and helping skills in Chapter Twenty-Three. She examines the specific and unique awareness, knowledge, and skills necessary for student affairs practitioners to be effective and ethical in their roles as helpers and caregivers. In Chapter Twenty-Four, Patrick Love and Sue Maxam explore current issues facing individual and group advisors and they also address serving as an organizational consultant as an institutional advisor. In Chapter Twenty-Five, Larry Roper and Christian Matheis provide an introduction to conflict theory, conflict management skills, and strategies and processes for engaging conflict, and offer general observations to support effective leadership. Dennis Roberts explores community development in Chapter Twenty-Six, discussing the origins of community building, contrasting philosophies and purposes of programming, theories that inform community development, special conditions that influence community development, and competencies required to enhance community development. In Chapter Twenty-Seven, Jan Arminio describes the general characteristics that define a profession, professionals, and professionalism, as well as specific characteristics of professionalism in the context of student affairs. Elizabeth J. Whitt addresses academic and student affairs partnerships in Chapter Twenty-Eight. This chapter examines why such partnerships are established, considers evidence of their advantages and disadvantages, and offers some practical suggestions for those who seek to form effective partnerships for student learning.

In Chapter Twenty-Nine in Part Six, Linda Sax and Casandra Harper address the "conditional effects" of college, or the ways in which college environments might affect students differently based on race, class, gender, or other unique characteristics. Ana Martínez Alemán and Katherine Lynk Wartman explore technology's influence on and use in student affairs practice in Chapter Thirty. In Chapter Thirty-One, we conclude this volume with our own guesses, hunches, and musings about the future of student affairs practice.

References

Mueller, K. H. (1961). *Student personnel work in higher education*. Boston, MA: Houghton Mifflin.

Rhatigan, J. J. (2009). From the people up. In G. S. McClellan, J. Stringer, & Associates, *The handbook of student affairs administration* (2nd ed., pp. 3–18). San Francisco: Jossey-Bass.

Stamatakos, L. C. (1981). Student affairs progress toward professionalism: Recommendations for action. Part 1. *Journal of College Student Development, 22*, 105–113.

ABOUT THE AUTHORS

Elisa S. Abes is an assistant professor in the Student Affairs in Higher Education Program at Miami University in Oxford, Ohio. She earned her B.A. and Ph.D. at the Ohio State University and her J.D. at Harvard Law School. Prior to teaching at Miami University, she was an assistant professor at the University of South Florida and an attorney at Frost & Jacobs LLP. Dr. Abes was named an American College Personnel Association (ACPA) Emerging Scholar and also received the ACPA Annuit Coeptis award for an emerging professional. She is on the editorial board for the *Journal of College Student Development.*

Ana M. Martínez Alemán is an associate professor and chair of the Educational Administration and Higher Education Administration Department at the Boston College Lynch School of Education. Her research focuses on philosophy and theory of higher education; teaching and learning, particularly the impact of race, culture, and gender on college teaching and learning; and feminist theory and pedagogy. Martínez Alemán is coauthor of *Online Social Networking on Campus: Understanding What Matters in Student Culture* (Routledge, 2009) and coeditor of *Women in Higher Education: An Encyclopedia* (ABC-CLIO Press, 2002). Her scholarship has appeared in the *Journal of Higher Education, Teachers College Record, Educational Theory*, the *Teacher Educator, Feminist Interpretations of John Dewey, Educational Researcher*, and the *Review of Higher Education.* Martínez Alemán presently serves as editor of *Educational Policy*, a peer-reviewed journal.

anthony lising antonio is an associate professor of education at Stanford University and associate director of the Stanford Institute for Higher Education Research. He is also a resident fellow—a faculty member living in an undergraduate residence— working with student staff to address the academic, psychological, and emotional needs of residents. antonio has served on the editorial board of the *Journal of College*

Student Development for six years and is a member of the executive board of the *Journal of College and Character*. His primary research interests include student development in diverse environments, higher education access, and faculty of color. His research has been published in the *Journal of Higher Education, Review of Higher Education, Research in Higher Education, About Campus*, and *Academe*. antonio received the Early Career Award from the Association for the Study of Higher Education (ASHE) in 2004.

Jan Arminio worked in student affairs for over fifteen years after earning her master's degree at Bowling Green State University in Ohio in 1978. After completing her doctorate in college student personnel at the University of Maryland-College Park, Dr. Arminio became a faculty member in 1996 in the Department of Counseling and College Student Personnel at Shippensburg University, where she currently serves as professor and chair. She also chairs the Senior Scholars of the American College Personnel Association and served on the Council for the Advancement of Standards in Higher Education (CAS) from 1986 to 2009, including being elected president in 2004. She frequently writes, consults, and makes presentations about inclusion and assessment. For example, she coauthored *Negotiating the Complexities of Qualitative Research* (Routledge, 2006).

Marilee J. Bresciani is an associate professor of postsecondary education at San Diego State University and faculty coordinator of the master's and doctoral programs in postsecondary educational leadership. Bresciani previously served as the assistant vice president for institutional assessment at Texas A&M University and as director of assessment at North Carolina State University. Her areas of research focus on organizational evaluation of student learning and development. Bresciani has written five books, contributed multiple chapters, and refereed journal articles and other publications. In addition, she often facilitates workshops and conversations across the globe pertaining to evaluating student learning centeredness.

Ellen M. Broido is an associate professor of college student personnel and higher education administration at Bowling Green State University. She earned her A.B. at Columbia College of Columbia University, her M.S.Ed. at Indiana University, and her Ed.D. at the Pennsylvania State University. Previously, she was an assistant professor of university studies and coordinator of university studies–student affairs partnerships at Portland State University in Oregon, and resident director and director of judicial affairs in the department of residence life at the University of Massachusetts at Amherst. Dr. Broido has served as the editor and chair of the books and media board of ACPA-College Student Educators International, and as a member of the editorial board of the *Journal of College Student Development*.

Mitchell J. Chang is a professor of higher education and organizational change at the University of California, Los Angeles (UCLA). Chang's research focuses on the educational efficacy of diversity-related initiatives on college campuses. He has written over fifty articles and book chapters, and served as the lead editor of the book *Compelling Interest: Examining the Evidence on Racial Dynamics in Colleges and Universities*. This book was cited in the U.S. Supreme Court ruling of *Grutter v. Bollinger*. Professor Chang received a National Academy of Education/Spencer Postdoctoral Fellowship in 2001 and was awarded the Outstanding Outcomes Assessment Research Award in 2000 by

ACPA. He was also profiled in 2006 as one of the nation's top ten scholars under forty by *Diverse Issues in Higher Education*, and in 2008 he received the ACPA Asian Pacific American Network Outstanding Contribution to Research Award.

Gwendolyn Dungy is executive director of the National Association of Student Personnel Administrators (NASPA)-Student Affairs Administrators in Higher Education. She received her B.S. and M.S. degrees from Eastern Illinois University, her M.A. from Drew University in New Jersey, and her Ph.D. from Washington University in St. Louis. Prior to joining NASPA, Dr. Dungy was associate director of the Curriculum and Faculty Development Network and coordinator of the National Diversity Network at the Association of American Colleges and Universities. Previously she was a senior administrator in both academic and student affairs at community colleges. Dr. Dungy has served on various governing boards, has authored numerous articles in higher education journals and magazines, and has contributed to several books.

Nancy J. Evans is professor of higher education and coordinator of the master's program in student affairs at Iowa State University. She earned her B.A. at State University of New York (SUNY), College at Potsdam, her M.S.Ed. at Southern Illinois University-Carbondale, her M.F.A. at Western Illinois University, and her Ph.D. at the University of Missouri-Columbia. She has served as assistant dean of students at Tarkio College, residence counselor and program advisor at Stephens College, counseling psychologist at Bowling Green State University, assistant professor at Indiana University, assistant and associate professor at Western Illinois University, and associate professor at the Pennsylvania State University. She served as president of ACPA-College Student Educators International and has been honored by ACPA with the Contribution to Knowledge Award. She was named an ACPA Annuit Coeptis Senior Professional and Senior Scholar. She is a member of the *Journal of College Student Development* editorial board and past editor of *ACPA Books and Media*.

Jane Fried earned her B.A. from Harpur College, her M.A. in education from Syracuse University in New York, and her Ph.D. from the Union Graduate School. She has chaired the ACPA Ethics Committee, the Standing Committee on Women, and the Affirmative Action Committee. She was director of housing at the University of Hartford, was coordinator of staff training for the University of Connecticut residence halls, and is currently a professor and coordinator of the master's degree program in student development in higher education at Central Connecticut State University. She serves on the national board of the NASPA Undergraduate Fellows Program and is past chair of the Spirituality and Religion Knowledge Community. Her publications include *Shifting Paradigms in Student Affairs, Understanding Diversity, Ethics for Today's Campus, Learning Reconsidered, Learning Reconsidered 2*, and numerous chapters on ethics and spirituality in higher education.

Marybeth Gasman is an associate professor of higher education at the University of Pennsylvania. She is a historian whose work focuses on African American higher education, including historically Black colleges and universities, African American leadership, and Black philanthropy. She has published, in addition to many peer-reviewed journal articles, several books, including *Envisioning Black Colleges: A History of the United Negro College Fund* (Johns Hopkins University Press, 2007) and *Understanding Minority-Serving Institutions* (State University of New York Press, 2008). Gasman received the Early Career Award from ASHE in 2006.

Stephanie A. Gordon is the senior director of educational programs at NASPA. She received her B.A. in English literature and political science at Simmons College and earned her Ed.M. in higher education administration at the Harvard Graduate School of Education. Prior to joining NASPA, Ms. Gordon served as director of residence life at Chatham College, assistant director of residence life at Colgate University, and assistant director of undergraduate admissions at Simmons College.

Kimberly A. Griffin is an assistant professor of college student affairs and higher education at the Pennsylvania State University. She is also a research associate in the Center for the Study of Higher Education. Before completing her Ph.D. in higher education and organizational change at UCLA, Griffin earned a B.A. in psychology from Stanford University and an M.A. in education policy and leadership with a focus on higher education from the University of Maryland-College Park. Griffin has previously worked in undergraduate advising, orientation, admissions, and diversity recruitment, notably serving as assistant dean for graduate education at the Stanford University School of Medicine. She is a recipient of the 2010 ACPA Emerging Scholar Award

Casandra E. Harper is an assistant professor of higher and continuing education at the University of Missouri-Columbia. She earned her B.S. and M.A. at the University of Arizona, and her M.A. and Ph.D. at UCLA. Harper's research agenda focuses on the diversity of individual students' experiences. She has paid particular attention to race, ethnicity, gender, ability, and class across key experiences and outcomes: multiracial identity development, openness to diversity, the influence of student-faculty and student-parent interactions, perceptions of campus climate, and financial aid literacy as it relates to college access. Her research has been published in *Research in Higher Education*, the *Journal of College Student Development*, *NASPA Journal*, and the *Journal of College Orientation & Transition*. Previously, she was principal research analyst for UCLA's Student Affairs Information and Research Office (SAIRO). Harper serves on the editorial board of the *Journal of Student Affairs Research and Practice*, and her dissertation was awarded Research of the Year by ACPA's Multiracial Network.

Shaun R. Harper is on the faculty in the Graduate School of Education, Africana Studies, and Gender Studies at the University of Pennsylvania. He maintains an active research agenda that examines racism, racial inequities, and gender disparities in American higher education; Black male college access and achievement; the effects of education policies and campus environments on college student outcomes; and gains associated with educationally purposeful student engagement. Harper has published nine books and more than sixty peer-reviewed journal articles, book chapters, and other academic publications. He received the 2005 Emerging Scholar and the 2006 Annuit Coeptis awards, both from ACPA. In 2008 ASHE presented him with its Early Career Award. Additionally, Harper received the 2010 NASPA Outstanding Contribution to Research Award and the 2010 Early Career Award from AERA Division G (Social Context of Education). He received his Ph.D. in higher education administration from Indiana University.

Joan B. Hirt is a professor of higher education administration at Virginia Tech. She earned her B.A. at Bucknell University, her M.A.Ed. at the University of Maryland, and her Ph.D. at the University of Arizona. Prior to assuming her faculty role, she served as a student affairs administrator at universities in Maryland, California, and Arizona. Her past research focused on the nature of administrative life at different types of institutions, work that catalyzed her current interest in administrator productivity. She has received numerous professional, teaching, and advising awards from Virginia Tech, the University of Maryland, ACPA, NASPA, the Association of Fraternity Advisors, and the Association of College and University Housing Officers-International.

Sylvia Hurtado is professor and director of the Higher Education Research Institute at UCLA. She has published numerous articles, chapters, and books related to campus climates, the impact of college on student development and educational outcomes, and diversity in higher education. She has also coordinated several national research projects, including a U.S. Department of Education–sponsored study of how colleges are preparing students to achieve the cognitive and social skills to participate in a diverse democracy. In addition, Hurtado has published extensively from her NIH- and NSF-funded research on students in science, technology, engineering, and mathematics. She serves on numerous editorial boards for journals in education and is past president of ASHE. Hurtado earned her Ph.D. in higher education and organizational change from UCLA, an Ed.M. from the Harvard Graduate School of Education, and an A.B. in sociology from Princeton University.

Susan R. Jones is associate professor in the higher education and student affairs program at The Ohio State University. Prior to Ohio State, she was associate professor in the college student personnel program at the University of Maryland-College Park. She earned her B.A. from St. Lawrence University, her master's degree from the University of Vermont, and her Ph.D. from the University of Maryland. Dr. Jones's research focuses on multiple social identities, intersectionality, and service-learning. She is also a co-author of a book entitled *Negotiating the Complexities of Qualitative Research in Higher Education*. Dr. Jones is an associate editor for the *Journal of College Student Development* and recipient of a number of awards including NASPA's Robert H. Shaffer Award for Academic Excellence as a Graduate Faculty Member, ACPA's Senior Scholar and Ohio State's Distinguished Teaching Award.

Adrianna Kezar is an associate professor for higher education at the University of Southern California. Dr. Kezar holds a Ph.D. and M.A. in higher education administration from the University of Michigan and a B.A. from UCLA. Previously, she was an administrative associate for the vice president for student affairs (1992–1995) and coordinator for the Center for Research on Learning and Teaching (1995–1996), both at the University of Michigan. Her research focuses on change, leadership, public purposes of higher education, organizational theory, governance, access, and diversity and equity issues in higher education. Dr. Kezar was editor of the ASHE-ERIC Higher Education Report Series from 1996 to 2004, and also serves as a board member for the American Association for Higher Education, the *Journal of College Student Development*, the Association of American Colleges and Universities' Peer Review and Knowledge Network, the National TRIO Clearinghouse, and the *Journal of Higher Education*.

Patricia M. King is a professor in the Center for the Study of Higher and Postsecondary Education at the University of Michigan. She earned her B.A. at Macalester College and her Ph.D. in educational psychology at the University of Minnesota. She is the author or coauthor of over sixty articles and chapters on college student development, and also coauthored *Developing Reflective Judgment: Understanding and Promoting Intellectual Growth and Critical Thinking in Adolescents and Adults* with Karen Strohm Kitchener and coedited *Learning Partnerships: Theory and Models of Practice to Educate for Self-Authorship* with Marcia B. Baxter Magolda. She served as a cofounder and editor of *About Campus: Enriching the Student Learning Experience* from 1995 to 2002. She is a coprincipal investigator in the Wabash National Study of Liberal Arts Education, focusing on educational experiences that lead to the achievement of liberal arts outcomes and self-authorship.

Susan R. Komives is a professor of college student personnel at the University of Maryland. Previously, she was vice president for student development at the University of Tampa, was vice president and dean of student life at Stephens College, was associate dean of students at Denison University, and held residence life positions at the University of Tennessee. She is president of the Council for the Advancement of Standards in Higher Education and a former president of ACPA. She is a cofounder of the National Clearinghouse for Leadership Programs and coprincipal investigator for the international Multi-Institutional Study of Leadership. She and Dudley Woodard Jr. were the coeditors of the third and fourth editions of *Student Services*. She is the recipient of the ACPA Contribution to Knowledge Award and the National Association of Student Personnel Administrator's Contribution to Literature and Research Award.

George D. Kuh is Chancellor's Professor of Higher Education at Indiana University Bloomington, where he directs the Center for Postsecondary Research. A founding director of the widely used National Survey of Student Engagement (NSSE), Kuh has written extensively about student engagement, assessment, institutional improvement, and college and university cultures, and has consulted with more than two hundred colleges and universities in the United States and abroad. His two most recent books are *Student Success in College: Creating Conditions That Matter* (2005) and *Piecing Together the Student Success Puzzle: Research, Propositions, and Recommendations* (2007). In 2001 he received Indiana University's prestigious Tracy Sonneborn Award for a distinguished career of teaching and research. Kuh received his B.A. from Luther College, his M.S. from the St. Cloud State University, and his Ph.D. from the University of Iowa.

Patrick Love is associate provost for student success at Rutgers University in New York City and Westchester County. He earned his M.S. in counseling psychology and student development at SUNY Albany and his Ph.D. in higher education and student affairs at Indiana University. Before joining Pace, he taught in higher education programs at New York University, Kent State University, and Syracuse University. He is coauthor with Sandra M. Estanek of *Rethinking Student Affairs Practice* (2004). He is also the coauthor with Doug Woodard and Susan Komives of *Leadership and Management Issues for the New Century* (2000), with Vicki Guthrie of *Understanding and Applying Cognitive Development Theory* (1999), and with Anne Goodsell Love of *Enhancing Student Learning: Intellectual, Social, and Emotional Integration* (1995). In 2005 ACPA named him a Diamond Honoree for career contributions to student affairs.

Marcia B. Baxter Magolda is Distinguished Professor of Educational Leadership at Miami University in Ohio. She received her master's and Ph.D. from the Ohio State University. Her research addresses the evolution of learning and development in college and young adult life, the role of gender in development, and pedagogy to promote self-authorship. Her books include *Development and Assessment of Self-Authorship: Exploring the Concept Across Cultures, Authoring Your Life, Developing an Internal Voice to Meet Life's Challenges, Learning Partnerships: Theory and Models of Practice to Educate for Self-Authorship, Making Their Own Way: Narratives for Transforming Higher Education to Promote Self-Development, Creating Contexts for Learning and Self-Authorship: Constructive-Developmental Pedagogy*, and *Knowing and Reasoning in College*. She received the ASHE Research Achievement Award, NASPA's Robert H. Shaffer Award, and ACPA's Contribution to Knowledge Award.

Peter M. Magolda is a professor in Miami University's Student Affairs in Higher Education Program. He received a B.A. from LaSalle College, an M.A. from the Ohio State University, and a Ph.D. in higher education administration from Indiana University. Professor Magolda teaches educational anthropology and research seminars; his scholarship focuses on ethnographic studies of collegians and critical issues in qualitative research. His recent research centers on the political actions of college students. Prior to joining the Miami University faculty in 1994, Magolda worked in the division of student affairs at Miami University, the Ohio State University, and the University of Vermont.

Kathleen Manning is a professor of higher education and student affairs at the University of Vermont. She holds a Ph.D. in higher education from Indiana University; an M.S. in counseling and student development from SUNY Albany; and a B.A. from Marist College. In 2003, 2004, and 2005 she traveled to China and Hong Kong on Fulbright Fellow and Fulbright Senior Specialist awards. NASPA honored her in 2005 as a Pillar of the Profession and in 2007 with the Outstanding Contribution to Literature/Research Award. She is the author and coauthor of numerous articles and several books, most recently, *One Size Does Not Fit All: Traditional and Innovative Models of Student Affairs Practice*. Manning is currently executive editor of the *Journal of Student Affairs Research and Practice*.

Christian Matheis, student advocate at Oregon State University, has served the campus since 2007 as political advisor and community organizer for the Associated Students of Oregon State University (ASOSU). This includes teaching courses on grassroots, direct-action, and community organizing, and political identity development and political agency. He previously served as the assistant director of the LGBTA Student Resource Center at Penn State's University Park campus, and as instructor of bio-behavioral health teaching on sexuality and gender. From 2004 to 2006 Christian served at Oregon State University in both student affairs and academic affairs as program advisor for the Office of LGBT Outreach & Services, and as program coordinator for the Difference, Power, and Discrimination Program. He holds a B.S. in psychology and an M.A. in applied ethics, with minors in ethnic studies and sociology; both degrees are from Oregon State University. His research interests include ethics, political philosophy, epistemology, philosophies of community, feminist critical social theory, models of applied leadership and organizational development, pedagogy, and curriculum development.

Sue Maxam is university director for student success at Pace University, where she has worked for the past twenty years, primarily in advising leadership roles. She has codeveloped a number of highly successful, university-wide advising initiatives involving the use of technology in advising; advisor training, support and development; and the promotion of holistic, developmental, and comprehensive faculty advising. Maxam holds a B.A. from Friends World College and an M.A. from New York University, and is the recipient of the following awards: Carol Russett Award for Women Leaders in Higher Education, Jefferson Gold Award for Public Service, Pace President's Award for Staff Excellence, Future Educators of America's Commitment to Inspirational Teaching Award, Pace Outstanding Service Award for Student Centeredness, and Pace Outstanding Service Award for Teamwork.

Jeffrey F. Milem is the Ernest W. McFarland Distinguished Professor in Leadership for Education Policy and Reform at the University of Arizona. He is also associate dean for academic affairs in the College of Education and has an appointment in the Department of Medicine. Milem is past president of ASHE. Prior to joining the faculty at Arizona, he served as an associate professor and graduate program director for the higher education administration program at the University of Maryland, where he also served as director of the Provost's Research Collaborative, a longitudinal research program that examined ways in which students' experiences with diversity while at Maryland influenced learning outcomes. Milem received his B.A. in political science from Michigan State University, his M.Ed. from the University of Vermont, and his Ph.D. from UCLA.

John A. Mueller is an associate professor in the Student Affairs in Higher Education Department at Indiana University of Pennsylvania. He earned his Ed.D. in higher education at Teachers College, Columbia University and his M.S. in counseling psychology at Illinois State University. Mueller has been in higher education for over twenty years, with experience at multiple institutions. His publications and presentations have focused primarily on social identity, diversity, and multicultural issues. He has served the profession through work on editorial boards, numerous ACPA-College Student Educators International committees, and as a trainer for ACPA's Cultural Diversity, Campus Violence, and Beyond Tolerance road shows. Mueller is a recipient of ACPA's Annuit Coeptis, Emerging Scholars, and Diamond Honoree awards.

Frank Michael Muñoz received his M.Ed. in higher education and student affairs administration at the University of Vermont and his B.A. in Afro-American and African studies from the University of Virginia. His professional interests lie in student union management and its intersections with social justice work and environmental stewardship. He writes about critical race theory, campus planning and architecture, sense of place, and the experiences of historically underrepresented students in higher education.

Lori D. Patton is associate professor, Higher Education Program, University of Denver. She earned her B.S. in speech communication at Southern Illinois University at Edwardsville, her M.A. in college student personnel at Bowling Green State University, and her Ph.D. in higher education at Indiana University. She has prior professional experience in admissions, student activities, Greek life, and multicultural affairs. She is a member of ACPA, for which she served on the governing board and was recognized as an Emerging Scholar and Annuit Coeptis recipient. She maintains active involvement in NASPA and ASHE, from which she received the Council on Ethnic Participation Mildred E. Garcia Award for Exemplary Scholarship. Dr. Patton is an editorial board member of the *Journal of College Student Development*, the *Journal of Student Affairs Research and Practice*, and the *College Student Affairs Journal*.

Gary Pavela is director of academic integrity at Syracuse University, and serves on the board of the Kenan Institute for Ethics at Duke University. He is a "Fellow" of the National Association of College and University Attorneys (Fellows of the Association are identified as individuals who have "brought distinction to higher education and to the practice of law on behalf of colleges and universities across the nation.") He was also the winner of the NASPA Outstanding Contribution to Literature and Research Award. He is the author of *Questions and Answers on College Student Suicide* (2006) and of the weekly law and policy newsletter the *Pavela Report*.

Raechele L. Pope is an associate professor of higher education at the University at Buffalo. She earned her doctorate from the University of Massachusetts at Amherst. With nearly thirty years of experience in college student affairs, she has worked at several institutions in a variety of functional areas, including residential life, academic advising, and diversity education and training. In 2009 she received the NASPA Robert H. Shaffer Award for Academic Excellence as a Graduate Faculty Member. She has also received ACPA's Annuit Coeptis award, the Outstanding Contribution to the Profession of Higher Education award from the College Student Personnel Association of New York, and the Outstanding Contribution to Multicultural Education Award from the ACPA Standing Committee for Multicultural Affairs. She has served as a reviewer or as a member of the editorial board for the *Journal of College Student Development*, *ACPA Books and Media*, and the *Journal of College Student Retention*.

Stephen John Quaye is an assistant professor in the College Student Personnel Program at the University of Maryland and a department editor for *About Campus*. He earned his bachelor's degree in psychology from James Madison University, his master's degree in college student personnel from Miami University, and his Ph.D. in higher education from the Pennsylvania State University. He is the author of various book chapters, peer-reviewed articles, and other scholarly publications, some of which have appeared in the *Journal of College Student Development*, the *Review of Higher Education*, the *Journal of Research Practice*, and *Liberal Education*. In 2009 NASPA presented him with the Melvene D. Hardee Dissertation of the Year Award and ACPA recognized him as an Emerging Scholar for early career achievement. His previous experience in student affairs includes work in residence life, multicultural affairs, and learning assistance.

Robert D. Reason is an associate professor in the college student affairs and higher education programs and currently serves as the professor in charge of the M.Ed. program in college student affairs at the Pennsylvania State University. He also serves as senior research associate at Penn State's Center for the Study of Higher Education. Reason earned his Ph.D. in education at Iowa State University, his M.S. in counseling and student personnel from Mankato State University, and his B.S. in economics from Grinnell College. He has been honored with an Emerging Scholar and the Annuit Coeptis awards from ACPA and the Iowa State University Research Excellence Award.

Kristen A. Renn is an associate professor of higher, adult, and lifelong education at Michigan State University. A graduate of Mount Holyoke College, she earned her Ph.D. in higher education at Boston College. For ten years she was a dean in the office of student life at Brown University. She is associate editor for international research and scholarship of the *Journal of College Student Development*, and serves on the editorial boards of the *Journal of Higher Education* and *Educational Researcher*. She has received a research achievement award for research on lesbian, gay, bisexual, and transgender issues from the ACPA Standing Committee for Lesbian, Gay, Bisexual, and Transgender Awareness and the GLBT Knowledge Community's Service to NASPA Award.

Amy L. Reynolds is an assistant professor of counseling, school, and educational psychology at the University at Buffalo. She earned her master's and doctorate from the Ohio State University. Previously she was a counseling center psychologist at Buffalo State College and the University of Iowa. Dr. Reynolds served as chair of the Standing Committee for Lesbian, Gay, Bisexual, and Transgender Awareness and secretary for ACPA. She received Outstanding Contribution to the Profession of Higher Education from the College Student Personnel Association of New York State and the Outstanding Contribution to Multicultural Education Award from the ACPA Standing Committee for Multicultural Affairs. She has also been on the editorial boards for the *Journal of College Counseling* and the *Journal of College Student Development*. She is a coauthor for *Multicultural Competence in Student Affairs* and the author of *Helping College Students: Developing Essential Support Skills for Student Affairs Practice*.

Dennis C. (Denny) Roberts is assistant vice president for faculty and student services of the Qatar Foundation. This role involves working with six current partner universities, each providing its top academic program on the Education City campus in Doha, Qatar. The universities are Virginia Commonwealth University, Weill Cornell Medical College, Texas A&M University, Carnegie Mellon University, the Georgetown University School of Foreign Service, and Northwestern University. He earned his bachelor's and master's degrees from Colorado State University and his Ph.D. from the University of Maryland. Prior to arriving in Qatar in November 2007, Dr. Roberts served as associate vice president for student affairs at Miami University in Ohio. He is a past president of ACPA, the 2006 recipient of the Esther Lloyd-Jones Professional Service Award, and an ACPA Senior Scholar (2005–2010).

Larry Roper is vice provost for student affairs and professor of ethnic studies at Oregon State University. From June 2007 to September 2008 he served as interim dean of the College of Liberal Arts. He currently serves on the board of directors of NASPA. Previously he served a four-year term as editor of the *NASPA Journal*, was a Senior Scholar with ACPA, was a member of the board of directors of the National Association of State Universities and Land-Grant Colleges, and served on the Northwest Commission on Colleges and Universities. Roper has numerous publications and is coeditor of the book *Teaching For Change: The Difference, Power and Discrimination Model* (2007).

Linda J. Sax is a professor of higher education and organizational change at UCLA, where she also serves as faculty director of the Master's in Student Affairs Program. An author of more than fifty publications, Sax's research focuses on gender differences in college student development, specifically how institutional characteristics, peer and faculty environments, and forms of student involvement differentially affect male and female college students. She is the author of *The Gender Gap in College: Maximizing the Developmental Potential of Women and Men* (Jossey-Bass, 2008). Sax is also principal investigator on a national study of the effects of single-sex secondary education. She is a fellow with the Sudikoff Family Institute for Education & New Media, as well as the recipient of the 2005 Scholar-in-Residence Award from the American Association of University Women. ASHE presented her with the Early Career Award in 1999.

John H. Schuh is Distinguished Professor of Educational Leadership and Policy Studies Emeritus at Iowa State University. Previously he held administrative and faculty assignments at Wichita State University, Indiana University Bloomington, and Arizona State University. He received his B.A. from the University of Wisconsin-Oshkosh and his M.C. and Ph.D. degree from Arizona State University. Among his books are *Assessment Methods for Student Affairs; One Size Does Not Fit All: Traditional and Innovative Models of Student Affairs Practice* (with Kathleen Manning and Jillian Kinzie); and *Student Success in College* (with George D. Kuh, Jillian Kinzie, and Elizabeth J. Whitt). Schuh has received the Research Achievement Award from ASHE, the Contribution to Knowledge Award from ACPA, the Contribution to Research or Literature Award and the Robert H. Shaffer Award for Academic Excellence as a Graduate Faculty Member from NASPA, and two Fulbright awards.

Terrell L. Strayhorn is an associate professor in the higher education and student affairs program at The Ohio State University. He earned his B.A. at the University of Virginia, his M.Ed. from the Curry School of Education at the University of Virginia, and his Ph.D. at Virginia Tech. Dr. Strayhorn is director-elect of research and publications for ACPA, from which he received the Emerging Scholar Award and Annuit Coeptis Award for early career achievement. Strayhorn is author of four books; over sixty refereed journal articles, chapters, and papers; and over one hundred scholarly presentations, and is principal investigator of major research grants funded by the National Science Foundation, the U.S. Department of Education, and state agencies. He serves on several editorial boards, including those of the *Journal of College Student*

Development, the *Journal of Student Affairs Research and Practice*, and the *College Student Affairs Journal*. In 2009 he received the ASHE's Early Career Award.

John R. Thelin is University Research Professor in the Department of Educational Policy Studies at the University of Kentucky. His focus is on the history of higher education and public policies. Thelin received his A.B. from Brown University in 1969 with a concentration in European History and was elected to Phi Beta Kappa. His graduate degrees from the University of California, Berkeley, include an M.A. in American History (1972) and a Ph.D. in the History of Education (1973). He was Chancellor Professor at the College of William & Mary and a professor of higher education and philanthropy at Indiana University. He is author of *A History of American Higher Education* (2004) and *Games Colleges Play* (1994), both published by the Johns Hopkins University Press. A past president of ASHE, Thelin has received two major grants from the Spencer Foundation and the 2007 American Educational Research Association (AERA) award for outstanding research in higher education.

Vasti Torres is a professor of higher education and student affairs administration at Indiana University Bloomington. She earned her B.A. from Stetson University and her M.Ed. and Ph.D. from the University of Georgia. Prior to her faculty work she served as associate vice provost and dean at Portland State University in Oregon. Dr. Torres's research focuses on how the ethnic identity of Latino students influences their college experiences. From 2007 to 2008 she served as the first Latina president of a national student affairs association—ACPA. Among her honors is the NASPA Contribution to Literature and Research Award.

Katherine Lynk Wartman has a Ph.D. in higher education from Boston College, an Ed.M. in higher education from Harvard University, and an A.B. in English from Bowdoin College. Her scholarly interests include parental involvement, the first-year experience, college access, and campus culture. She is coauthor of *Online Social Networking on Campus: Understanding What Matters in Student Culture* (Routledge, 2009) and *Parental Involvement in Higher Education: Understanding the Relationship Among Parents, Students, and the Institution* (Jossey-Bass, 2008). Wartman has worked in student affairs at Dartmouth College, Harvard University, Colby-Sawyer College, and Simmons College.

Elizabeth J. Whitt is director of student success initiatives in the Office of the Provost and professor in the graduate programs in student affairs at the University of Iowa. She is also codirector of the Center for Research on Undergraduate Education (CRUE). Professor Whitt received her B.A. from Drake University, her M.A. from Michigan State University, and her Ph.D. from Indiana University. A graduate faculty member since 1988, she has also worked in residence life and student affairs administration at Michigan State University, the University of Nebraska-Lincoln, and Doane College. In 2007 Professor Whitt received the Outstanding Contribution to Knowledge Award from ACPA-College Student Educators International; she also is an ACPA Senior Scholar Diplomate and a member of the Iowa Academy of Education. She serves as the associate editor of the *New Directions for Student Services* sourcebook series and on the editorial board of the *Journal of College Student Development*.

STUDENT SERVICES

PART ONE

HISTORICAL AND CONTEMPORARY CONTEXT

This handbook is for current professionals as well as those who are preparing to become educators and administrators on college and university campuses. As is the case in other professions, familiarity with the contextual underpinnings of student affairs practice is essential. Newcomers benefit from understanding why particular techniques and perspectives are deemed normal and how they have been reshaped by various social forces over time. Also important is an understanding of the context in which a profession has evolved and negotiated its identity, legitimacy, and longevity. In addition, recognizing the range of settings in which professional activity occurs enables one to see beyond the narrow boundaries of limited, firsthand experience. Conversely, those who believe the practices of a profession began on the eve of their entry are likely to commit workplace errors that could have been anticipated or avoided through some meaningful engagement of history. Anyone who erroneously thinks the methodologies employed on one particular campus are the same everywhere else surely has much to learn about the complex landscape of practice in higher education.

An awareness of contextual factors that have influenced and continue to drive student affairs practice is required to develop expertise. Knowing how postsecondary education started in America and what led to its expansion is important, as is consciousness of the range of institutional options for enrollment and employment opportunities. For sure, there is tremendous value in knowing both the general and the specific regarding the setting in which one performs the work of education. Although student affairs practice occurs outside the classroom, it can be enhanced by an understanding of what occurs in classrooms and other parts of the campus where students interact, develop, and learn. Chapters in Part One offer a necessarily broad view of higher education in general, the range of institutional settings in which teaching and learning occur, and the needs of various types of students who enroll.

In Chapter One, John Thelin and Marybeth Gasman offer a historical overview of American higher education. They describe how institutions emerged, how student demographics shifted, and how access for diverse populations changed over time. Thelin and Gasman tell a rich yet concise story of the English influence on colonial colleges and how a distinctive "American Way" emerged. They also discuss the development of the university model, the introduction of diverse institutional types, and curricular changes in higher education. After exploring the three decades between World Wars I and II, their analysis moves to more modern perspectives on American higher education, from 1960 to the present. This chapter affords readers a baseline level of understanding about the historical evolution of the context in which their work is primarily performed—that is, college and university campuses.

Kimberly Griffin and Sylvia Hurtado cover the landscape of American higher education in Chapter Two. They summarize and articulate the benefits and shortcomings associated with using the latest version of the popular Carnegie system for classifying institution types in U.S. higher education. They also acknowledge institutions with distinctive missions dedicated to serving specific student populations, highlighting how students, educators, and administrators typically experience the unique attributes of these environments. Whereas Griffin and Hurtado highlight the diversity of institutions, Chang, Milem, and antonio's chapter focuses on student diversity. In Chapter Three, they describe the educational benefits accrued when students interact across difference. They also present a framework for understanding how campus climates differently affect diverse student populations, and recommend several practical strategies for student affairs educators who endeavor to foster and maintain inclusive educational environments for all students.

Together, these three chapters engender a deeper understanding of how postsecondary contexts and students have evolved over time. Few student affairs professionals spend their entire careers at a single institution or even in one institution type. Thus, being familiar with the diversity that exists across the landscape of higher education will make them more employable and effective once they switch between contexts. Moreover, those who are familiar with the history of higher education are able to speak accurately about the context in which their work is performed. Likewise, long gone are the days when all students enter a college or university with the same demographic characteristics. Campus environments must be designed to meet the needs of those who differ in race, socioeconomic background, ability, age, sexual orientation, and gender. Professionals who understand this and respond accordingly are most likely to be appreciated and praised by the students with whom they work. More important, they are better skilled at making sense of modern-day problems of practice by juxtaposing them with historical forces that have shaped postsecondary institutions and student affairs practice over time.

CHAPTER ONE

HISTORICAL OVERVIEW OF AMERICAN HIGHER EDUCATION

John R. Thelin and Marybeth Gasman

A historical profile of American higher education is in large part a story of structures, not just bricks and mortar but also legal and administrative complexities that reflect our nation's social and political history. Whether in the eighteenth, nineteenth, twentieth, or twenty-first century, the U.S. tradition in higher education has always espoused a strong commitment to undergraduate education. Maintaining this tradition has required vigilance, however, because many universities added graduate degree programs, research centers, and other activities far removed from the bachelor's degree curriculum. A good way to chart the history of higher education is to keep in mind that quantitative shifts have signaled qualitative changes. For example, from 1700 to 1900, less than 5 percent of Americans between the ages of eighteen and twenty-two enrolled in college. Between World Wars I and II, this figure increased to about 20 percent, rising to 33 percent in 1960 and dramatically expanding to more than 50 percent in the 1970s. These numbers define the transformation of American higher education from an elite to a mass activity, a trend that continued during the final decades of the twentieth century, as the prospect for universal access to postsecondary education emerged as part of the American agenda (Trow, 1970). Hence, tracing the history of American higher education involves no less than the interesting task of interpreting this blend of continuity and change.

To attempt to grasp the 370-year history of American higher education in a single glimpse is both unwieldy and unwise. Therefore, this chapter first considers the legacy of the English influence on colonial colleges and then shifts to how America wrestled with the question of creating a distinctive "American Way" in higher education during the new national period. Next, the discussion highlights the emergence of the "university" model from 1880 to about 1914, with the reminder that other institutional forms also flourished during this period. After considering higher education in the three decades between World Wars I and II, the historical analysis moves to the problems of abundance and prosperity in the 1960s, whereas the decades of 1970 to 1990 are analyzed as an era bringing further adjustment and accountability. Finally, analysis of some of the demographic and structural trends since 1990 to the present provides a way to make sense of the transition into the twenty-first century. Having completed this narrative account, the chapter then aims to bring coherence to the history of American higher education by considering the implications for professional practices and policies brought on by trends in research and scholarship within a variety of related disciplines.

The Colonial Period: Sorting Out the English Legacy

Although the ideal of an intense undergraduate education by which young adults are prepared for leadership and service is a distinctively American tradition, it owes much to the example set by the English universities of Oxford and Cambridge in the sixteenth and seventeenth centuries. These institutions earned a reputation for their unique practice of arranging several residential colleges within a university structure, all located in a pastoral setting. This so-called "Oxbridge" model departed from the patterns of academic life and instruction found in the urban universities of the late middle ages on the European continent. At Paris, Salerno, Heidelberg, and Bologna, scholars banded together for protection and to set standards for teaching, pay, and tuition—but gave little attention to building a permanent campus or supervising student life (Haskins, 1923). In sharp contrast, by the seventeenth century Oxford and Cambridge had developed a formal system of endowed colleges that combined living and learning within quadrangles. This model consisted of an architecturally distinct, landscaped site for an elaborate organizational culture and pedagogy designed to build character rather than produce expert scholars. The college was an isolated "total" institution whose responsibilities included guiding both the social and academic dimensions of undergraduate life. The Oxford-Cambridge model not only combined these elements, it integrated them within a coherent philosophy of residential education. This approach eventually influenced college builders in the New World.

Rudolph (1962) called this adopted educational tradition the "collegiate way" (pp. 86–109). Even when the realities of the American wilderness set in or when college officials ran out of money for building, the "collegiate way" persisted as an aspiration in the colonial and later, national culture. The most telling legacy of the early college founders is their combination of optimism and caution in their quest to create what historian James Axtell (1974) has called the "school on a hill." The American colonists built colleges because they believed in and wished to transplant and perfect the English idea of an undergraduate education as a civilizing experience that ensured a progression of responsible leaders for both church and state. Their plans reflected a deliberate attempt to avoid the problems and mistakes associated with a loss of control over curriculum and governance, problems that sometimes characterized their

European counterparts. Ironically, this meant that the two groups most central to their plan—students and teachers—were from the start restricted from holding official academic authority in matters of external institutional governance. Ultimate power was vested in a college lay board to maintain discipline and accountability—an antidote to the sloth and indulgence attributed to autonomous masters and scholars at the English universities. By incorporating a tight connection between the college board and its host civil government, the colonial colleges fostered both responsible oversight and a source of government funding from taxes, tolls, and lotteries. The importance of colleges to colonial life is suggested by their proliferation and protection—starting with Harvard, founded in the Massachusetts Bay Colony in 1636, and followed by The College of William & Mary in Virginia in 1693, Yale in Connecticut in 1701, and six more colleges by the start of the Revolutionary War in 1775.

Tensions between students and faculty characterized colonial college life. Indeed, the residential college was as much a recipe for conflicts as for harmony. Numerous consumer complaints ranging from bad food in the dining commons to dissatisfaction with the curriculum often sparked student riots and revolts. Although relatively homogeneous in its restriction to White, Christian young men, the student body still institutionalized the nuances of social class. College rosters listed students by social rank. Furthermore, following the Oxford tradition, academic robes reflected socioeconomic position, delineating the "commoners" (those who dined at college commons) from the "servitors" (those who waited on tables).

Religion was an important part of the fabric of American culture, including its colleges. Religious concerns and sectarian competition often fueled the creation of new colonial colleges. A majority of these institutions developed denominational ties, and most college presidents were men of the cloth. However, emphasis on Christian values and discipline (more specifically, Protestant values) did not preclude preparation for secular and civil life. As relatively young students matriculated, colleges embraced the role of *in loco parentis*, with the faculty and president offering supervision of student conduct and moral development. While colonial colleges did educate future ministers, that purpose was only one of many among the undergraduate bachelor of arts curriculum (Handlin & Handlin, 1974).

Few written records are available to help reconstruct the colonial collegiate curriculum. The best estimate is that oral disputations provided the most rigorous hurdles, subject to the immediate critical evaluation of both masters and fellow undergraduates. The motivation to study classical texts or to solve complex mathematical problems was to avoid the ridicule and jeers from classmates that greeted a student's poor public speaking, flawed logic, or faulty Latin translations. One puzzling characteristic of the colonial college is that there was little emphasis on completing degrees. Many students matriculated, then left college after a year or two, apparently with none of the stigma now associated with dropping out. Enrollments at each college were modest, typically seldom as much as a hundred students. At William & Mary, so few undergraduates petitioned for graduation that the new governor of Virginia offered commencement prize money as an incentive for students to complete their degree requirements.

American higher education in the eighteenth century did include some precedents for diversity—and the associated challenges of that commitment. Periodically colonial colleges attempted to expand their missions but often encountered only weak or even disastrous results. One of these episodes caused Benjamin Franklin (1784) to recount how after a group of Native American students returned from their scholarship studies at The College of William & Mary, their chieftain fathers complained that the sons had become unhealthy, lazy, and unable to make good decisions. As a result, tribal elders politely refused the college's offer to renew the scholarship program, suggesting instead that perhaps the colonial leaders would like to send *their* sons to the Native Americans for an education that would make the Anglo boys into strong and wise men.

The novelty (and high failure rate) of such experiments underscores the fundamental limits of the colonial colleges' scope and constituency. Enrollment in college courses was confined to White males, mostly from established, prosperous families and members of the colony's dominant protestant denomination. College attendance tended to ratify or confirm existing social standing rather than provide social mobility. The curriculum primarily provided for an analytical or intellectual edge in the discourse and writing associated with public life, such as in the practice of law (Handlin & Handlin, 1974). In plain terms, the college mission was to ensure the preparation and disciplined seasoning of a future leadership cohort. Certainly this was an "elite" student group. This exclusiveness, so contrary to contemporary notions of equity and social justice, does not negate the important fact that in the eighteenth century a college education served the serious, albeit limited, societal function of transforming a potentially indolent, self-indulgent group of privileged, young, White men into a responsible, literate elite committed to serving their colony and, later, the nation.

The aim of the colonial college, then, was the rigorous education of the "gentleman scholar." If the colonial colleges were limited in their constituency and their mission, they were at least remarkably effective in their education of an articulate and learned leadership group, as suggested by the extraordinary contributions of their alumni (including Thomas Jefferson and James Madison) to the political and intellectual leadership of the American Revolution and the creation of the new United States.

Creating the "American Way" in Higher Education: The New National Period

During the new national period following American independence in 1776 and extending into the mid-nineteenth century, the small college persisted as the institutional norm, despite scattered attempts to create a modern comprehensive university. On closer inspection, continual innovations and experimentation in American higher education existed, as indicated by the curriculum Thomas Jefferson proposed at the new University of Virginia. An undeniable fact of American life well into the late nineteenth century was that going to college was not necessary for "getting ahead" economically, although a college degree did confer some prestige. Colleges had to compete incessantly for the attention of both donors and paying students. Campaigns to create a truly "national" university were unsuccessful. However, the establishment of the United States Military Academy at West Point in 1802 and, later, the United States Naval Academy at Annapolis did provide the new nation with two educational institutions that were attractive to students from every state and that would prepare generations of American leaders.

New state governments showed relatively little inclination to fund higher education, although granting college charters was a popular and easy way for legislators to repay political debts. State universities in Georgia, North Carolina, and South Carolina were chartered by the early nineteenth century, but they enjoyed only sparse support from their respective legislatures and often took years to get around to the business of actually enrolling students and offering instruction. That the American college was not universally supported—either by legislators, donors, or paying students—did not mean it was unimportant. Letters from fathers corresponding with their sons in college in the early 1800s indicate that established families took college education very seriously. Parents wanted assurance that their sons were acquiring the values and skills requisite for responsible, effective participation as adults in public affairs and commerce (Wakelyn, 1985). Also, the fervor generated by the Second Great Awakening seemingly caused every religious group to want to build its own college for propagating its doctrines and for reinforcing its distinctive orthodoxy among members who were growing from adolescence into adulthood. The interesting result was a boom in college building in the first half of the nineteenth century. Whereas in 1800 there were probably 25 colleges offering instruction and conferring degrees, by 1860 this number had increased almost tenfold to 240—not including numerous institutions that had opened and then gone out of business (Burke, 1982).

Higher education, although clearly a growth industry, relied heavily on continual, grassroots efforts at recruiting undergraduates and raising money. Thus college marketing and student recruiting were peculiar during the new national period. The impoverished colleges often scrounged to survive by lowering their charges to attract more students as the start of the autumn term approached. This typically disastrous strategy, however, perpetuated the idea that pursuing a college education was not necessarily a worthwhile endeavor. Today's historians, with the benefit of hindsight, emphasize two reasons colleges lacked qualified students during the period from 1800 to 1860. First, American education was top-heavy and overextended; there were literally hundreds of colleges, but most of them had inadequate operating funds or endowments. Second, the country lagged in providing secondary education, the obvious and necessary source for college applicants. In a display of American ingenuity, however, colleges responded to this void by creating preparatory programs to serve the dual purpose of providing both sources of operating income and a flow of students who eventually could pass the college entrance examination.

The image of a stagnant campus has been modified by evidence of considerable curricular innovation at many colleges, as the pragmatic will to survive led some presidents and boards to approve new courses in engineering, the sciences, and modern languages while also experimenting with dual-track curricula. The public did not always respond favorably to such curricular shifts, however. The result was an erratic record of survival and mortality among new curricula and programs in the first half of the nineteenth century. Novel programs may not always have succeeded, but claiming there were no attempts at innovation has proven to be quite incorrect.

In addition, historians have looked beyond the formal courses of study in these universities to their extracurricular activities, such as literary societies, debating clubs, and service groups. Their research has revealed dramatic innovations and the foundations of lasting change. Here scholars identified the roots of the extensive university library of today, with readings in modern fiction, journalism, and such new fields as political economy and the natural sciences. Furthermore, even though most college presidents were drawn locally from the ranks of ordained ministers, the scholarly and intellectual life of the faculty and students frequently included connection with the Scottish Enlightenment, as found in the works of Adam Smith, David Hume, and John Locke, along with the popular philosophical and academic trends in Europe. In addition, analysis of extracurricular activities of the time shows that students exerted great influence on the life of their college and determined which activities and values were emphasized (Rudolph, 1962). This leverage required tenacity and strong fellowship, and college officials who feared activities that departed from the formal curriculum often attempted to discourage or even prohibit the various student literary and social groups.

Although attending college remained impractical for most Americans, a gradual change in the socioeconomic makeup of many student bodies occurred. A mix of students from a wide range of family incomes replaced—or, rather, joined—the more homogeneous group in what has been called a convergence of "paupers and scholars." What this meant was that at some of the newly established "hilltop colleges," such as Amherst, Williams, Bowdoin, and Dartmouth, first-generation college students often were men from modest farming families. Many of these were older than the customary seventeen to twenty-one year-olds (Allmendinger, 1975). Typically they worked their way through college, often taking time out to teach elementary school or perform a variety of subsistence jobs. Furthermore, the creation of a number of charitable trusts and scholarship funds helped colleges provide financial aid for able yet poor young men who looked forward to joining the clergy or teaching (Peterson, 1963).

Elsewhere, some colleges innovated by affiliating themselves with freestanding professional schools of medicine, law, and commerce, most of which (contrary to contemporary assumptions) did not require any undergraduate education or a bachelor's degree for admission. Despite the popularity of the new "scientific" courses of study at some colleges in the nineteenth century, a certain intellectual snobbery marked the traditional curriculum. At daily chapel, for example, students from the "scientific school" (who tended to be bright and from modest income families) were required to sit in the rear pews, conspicuously apart from the prestigious liberal arts students.

Between 1860 and 1900, such historically excluded constituencies as women, African Americans, and Native Americans gained some access to higher education. By the mid-nineteenth century, women in particular had become formal participants in advanced studies. One educational innovation was the founding of the "female academies" and "female seminaries"—institutions that offered a range of courses and instructional programs beyond elementary and secondary schooling. In part, curricula included home economics and, at some institutions, the social graces and deportment associated with a "finishing school." It is important to keep in mind that the curriculum also included formal instruction in the sciences, mathematics, foreign languages, and composition—subjects associated with undergraduate collegiate curricula. Even though such studies did not officially lead to the bachelor's degree for women, they often rivaled the academic excellence of the men's colleges of the era. Over time, especially by the 1860s and 1870s, many of the female seminaries became degree-granting colleges in their own right (Horowitz, 1984). In the late nineteenth century a few colleges, such as Oberlin and later Cornell, pioneered coeducation, enrolling both men and women—a policy that would soon gain a wide following in the Midwest and on the Pacific Coast (Gordon, 1990).

Although a few Northern Black colleges had been established by free Blacks and White abolitionists prior to the end of the Civil War, between 1865 and 1910 additional provisions were made for African American students to pursue higher education, with the founding of many small Black colleges in the South. The first impetus for financial support for these colleges came from Northern philanthropic groups, such as the Peabody Foundation. The colleges also benefited from the financial support of Black churches, state governments, and the federal government through the Freedmen's Bureau. Many of these institutions, such as Booker T. Washington's Tuskegee Institute, began as combined elementary and secondary schools that eventually offered a college-level curriculum. In this respect, newly established institutions for African Americans followed familiar patterns of nineteenth-century American colleges, displaying an array of curricular emphases ranging from liberal arts at Fisk, Howard, Spelman, and Morehouse to industrial arts and normal schools at Hampton Institute in Virginia and in historically Black state colleges in numerous Southern states. The second Land-Grant Act of 1890 also provided funding for Black colleges in sixteen states in the South, leading them to offer studies in agriculture and the mechanical arts. The historically Black colleges and universities, despite differences in curricula, religious affiliation, and leadership, shared a widespread condition of uncertain and inadequate funding. Furthermore, well into the twentieth century many of these institutions were prohibited by state governments from offering graduate programs, advanced work, or first professional degree programs, such as law (Wright, 1988). Illustrative of the impediments the Black colleges and universities faced in the South was that they were not admitted to full membership in the Southern Association of Colleges and Schools until 1957. Despite the double burden of not having large endowments or being able to charge more than modest tuitions, these colleges have been disproportionately effective in the enrollment and graduation of a large number and percentage of African American students (Drewry & Doermann, 2001). In effect, Black colleges and universities are responsible for the education of the Black middle class as we know it today. An often overlooked fact is that federal monies and private foundations of this era also supported some higher education for Native Americans—whether as part of such campuses as Virginia's Hampton Institute or at distinct institutions, such as California's Sherman School for Indians, Pennsylvania's famous Carlisle School for Indians (Jenkins, 2007), or the University of North Carolina at Pembroke.

The cumulative impact of the innovations and experiments in American higher education in the nineteenth century generated an interesting social change: by 1870, "going to college" had come to capture the American fancy. The growing number and diversity of students and institutions illustrated the variety of American higher education. There were multiple models, ranging from comprehensive institutions with diverse student bodies to special-purpose colleges serving separate, distinct groups defined, for example, by gender, race, or religious affiliation.

University Building and More: 1880 to 1914

As higher education became more and more popular, the emergence of the modern university in America dominated press coverage. At one extreme, the ideal of advanced, rigorous scholarship and the necessary resources of research libraries, laboratories, and Doctor of Philosophy programs were epitomized by the great German universities. Emulating and transplanting the German model to the United States became the passion of The Johns Hopkins University in Baltimore, Clark University in Massachusetts, and the University of Chicago. At the same time, a commitment to applied research and utility gained a following at the emerging land-grant institutions, ranging from the Midwestern, rural University of Wisconsin to the urban Massachusetts Institute of Technology. Between 1870 and 1910, America was the setting for a dramatic "university movement," which created hybrid institutions undergirded by large-scale philanthropy and widespread construction of new campus buildings (Veysey, 1965). As editor of *The Independent*, Edwin Slosson (1910), wrote, "The essential difference between a college and a university is how they look. A college looks backward, a university looks forward" (p. 374). But when historians examined the situation, they found complications and exceptions to Slosson's typology. Although the university was news, the ideal of the undergraduate college also soared in popularity. Even in the age of university building, the undergraduate—not the doctoral student or professor—became the object of praise, even envy. On balance, the building of great universities in America contributed to the advancement of cutting-edge scholarship. At the same time, however, this "cutting edge" remained marginal to the central purpose of undergraduate education. Although the ideals of research and utility were conspicuous, they were tempered to varying degrees by the value traditionally placed on a liberal education and, often, on piety. The best evidence of this claim is that no American university, including the pioneering examples of Johns Hopkins and Clark, was able to survive without offering an undergraduate course of study. Furthermore, in contrast to higher education in the twenty-first century, American universities of 1910 remained relatively underdeveloped and small. Only a handful of institutions, such as the urban universities of Harvard, Columbia, and Pennsylvania, enrolled more than five thousand students.

Even thirty years after passage of the 1862 Morrill Land-Grant Act, public higher education remained relatively underdeveloped and meagerly funded. After 1900, however, public higher education ballooned in prominence along with the burgeoning of the private universities. Legislatures in the Midwest and West started to embrace and financially support through taxation the idea of a great university as a symbol of state pride. Applied research, a utilitarian and comprehensive curriculum, not to mention the public appeal of spectator sports and the availability of federal funds for such fields as agriculture and engineering, led to the growth and maturation of the state university. Many states also utilized funding provided by the Second Land Grant Act of 1890 which created the historically Black land grant institutions along with agricultural extension services (Wright, 1988). It should be noted that Southern states did not voluntarily create Black land grant institutions; instead, the federal government refused to disperse funds to these states unless they provided higher education to Blacks as well as Whites. In addition, by World War I, the move to increase the accessibility of study beyond high school was further signaled by the founding of a distinctive American institution: the junior college (Diener, 1986).

Higher Education After World War I: 1915 to 1945

Historian David Levine (1986) charted the rise of American colleges and the concomitant "culture of aspiration" (p. 14) in the three decades between World Wars I and II. The most salient feature of this period was the stratification of American higher education into institutional layers, indicating that distinctions were drawn between prestige and purpose in pursuing a college education. The emergence of public junior colleges, an increase in state normal schools and teachers colleges, and the creation of new technical institutes all revealed this trend (Diener, 1986; Levine, 1986). The great state universities of the Midwest and West finally started to fulfill the promise of the Morrill Act to serve the statewide public, with enrollment at typical large campuses reaching fifteen thousand to twenty-five thousand. However, depictions of popular access to state universities must be analyzed carefully to avoid exaggeration. Many institutions regarded today as large state universities were still relatively limited in size and curricular offerings in the first half of the twentieth century. As late as 1940, many state universities had a total enrollment of less than five thousand students each and offered little in the way of advanced programs or doctoral studies.

Enrollments rose during the Great Depression due, in part, to widespread unemployment. Universities received little federal support, although some government involvement in selected scientific research programs existed. A few campuses, especially those with strong scientific and engineering departments, pioneered working relations with corporations and industry in contractual research and development. But these exceptional ventures remained something of a rehearsal. On balance, they did not flourish in any sustained way until the emergence of government-sponsored projects during World War II.

Perhaps the greatest puzzle facing American higher education in the early twentieth century is what may be termed the "dilemma of diversity." Individuals at the most heterogeneous institutions often encountered the most glaring conflicts, hostilities, and discrimination *within* the campus life. Coeducation, for example, deserves to be hailed as a positive change in promoting equity and access for women. At the same time, however, such celebration needs to be tempered with careful historical analysis of how female students were actually treated once admitted. Gordon (1990) found that at the University of California, the University of Chicago, and Cornell, women undergraduates encountered discrimination both academically and in student activities. A comparable pattern of discrimination occurred at those universities that enrolled ethnic, racial, and religious minorities. Historian Helen Horowitz (1987) traced the effects of this discrimination, noting how student subcultures developed over time, with "insider" groups tending to dominate the rewards and prestige of campus life. Maresi Nerad's (1999) historical case study of the University of California from the 1890s into the early 1960s documented a lamentable feature of coeducation in the twentieth century: gender equity was seldom achieved, and women as students, faculty, and administrators tended to be confined to what was called the "academic kitchen." Conversely, Helen Horowitz's (1984) account of the founding of new women's colleges from 1860 to 1930 suggests that special-purpose colleges provided distinctive educational benefits for their students and alumni.

In the 1920s some colleges enjoyed the luxury of choice. For the first time they had more applicants than student places, allowing administrators to implement selective admissions policies. They looked to testing programs of the United States military for models and inspirations of how to administer and process standardized tests. Ultimately the Educational Testing Service (ETS) was developed as an appendage of the College Entrance Examination Board (CEEB). Creation and refinement of the Scholastic Aptitude Test (widely known as the SAT) gained both stature and infamy among education-minded young Americans as a rite of passage from high school to college (Lehman, 2000). Unfortunately, these various admissions tools and practices were often used to exclude some students on the basis of race, ethnicity, gender, or other criteria unrelated to academic merit (Karabel, 2005). Marcia Synnott's (1979) study of admissions at Harvard, Yale, and Princeton suggested that selective admissions was at best a "half opened door." On balance, American higher education's capacity to provide access ran ahead of its ability to foster assimilation and parity within the campus. The result was a complex dilemma for campus officials and policy analysts: How to best serve minority groups and new participants in higher education? Often these issues of social justice were brushed aside, and the customary American response was to provide no single, and certainly no clear answer or consistent policy, relying instead on a laissez-faire arrangement of student choice and institutional autonomy. More often than not, American higher education achieved diversity through colleges dedicated to serve special constituencies, whether defined by race, gender, or religious affiliation. Accommodation with segregation was in the American grain.

Higher Education's "Golden Age": 1945 to 1970

Oscar Wilde noted that nothing is so permanent as a temporary appointment. Certainly this describes the dramatic changes in student recruitment after 1945. The federal government intended that the Servicemen's Readjustment Act, popularly known as the GI Bill, provide a short-term measure by which the federal government could mitigate the pressure of hundreds of thousands of returning war veterans becoming job seekers in a saturated national labor market. The strategy was to make federal scholarships for postsecondary education readily available to veterans. But the GI Bill had unexpected long-term consequences: first, it was far more attractive than legislators anticipated; second, it set a precedent for making portable government student aid into an entitlement; and, third, it provided a policy tool for increasing the diversity of students at American colleges and universities. In retrospect, the unexpected success of the bill also revealed some dysfunctions in the ideals of expanded opportunity. First, even though thousands of women were veterans of war service, they were underrepresented as recipients of the GI Bill scholarships. Second, the bill's well-intentioned provisions to scholarship recipients, who had a wide range of choices of programs and institutions, exposed the lack of standards or accountability in matters of institutional quality and legitimacy. This latter weakness opened the gates for regional accreditation associations to provide legislators and taxpayers with some reasonable thresholds of academic integrity among institutions approved to receive federal scholarship funds. Third, the influx of new students on many campuses, including Black colleges and universities, caused great stress on the physical plant of the institutions, causing institutions to create makeshift classrooms and residence halls.

The popularity of the GI Bill underscores the importance of higher education to the nation's long-term adjustment to a new economy and postwar democracy. A 1947 report authorized by President Harry S. Truman brought to Congress and the American public the bold proposition of permanently expanding access to and affordability of higher education. This egalitarian impulse coincided with effective lobbying for the expansion of government- and foundation-sponsored research grants for scholars at universities. The convergence of the two trends resulted in what has been called higher education's "Golden Age," one marked by an academic revolution in which colleges and universities acquired unprecedented influence in American society (Freeland, 1992; Jencks & Riesman, 1968). Growing states, such as California and New York, faced the attractive problem of whether they could build sufficient classrooms to accommodate the influx of new students graduating from high school who now had great expectations about attending college. Some state policy decisions made in these years would have long-term consequences on student choice, learning, and retention. For example, Alexander Astin in his landmark study, *Four Critical Years* (1977) noted that after 1950 most states tended to favor the construction of new commuter institutions such as community colleges and junior colleges. Although this approach succeeded in accommodating growing enrollments, the new institutions made little provision for full-time residential education—a significant departure from the traditional notion of the "collegiate way." Furthermore, because the new commuter institutions often enrolled a large percentage of first-generation college attendees, the consequence was that those students probably most in need of academic support and immersion were less likely to receive it (Brint & Karabel, 1989). It also pointed to signs of "tracking" in the American higher education system in that community colleges showed a student profile skewed disproportionately toward enrollment of African Americans and Hispanic students. At worst, the ease of admission into community colleges was followed by ease of departure, as community college students who were underprepared or unfamiliar with navigating academic institutions were susceptible to the syndrome of what sociologist Burton Clark (1970) called "the revolving door" abbreviated college experience, characterized by an institutionalized "cooling out" system with high attrition and low degree completion rates.

The emergence of the multicampus university system also developed during this era of expanding enrollments. In place of one or two flagship universities, many states now joined numerous branches into a centrally administered network or system. Although the seventy-five or so great research universities commanded the most attention in this era, equally noteworthy were the growth and curricular changes in numerous regional campuses and teachers colleges. Most of these added selected master's degree and graduate professional programs over time to supplement their customary base of bachelor degree and entry-level professional courses of study. Also, public community college systems often became partners with the state universities. The compact or articulation agreement was that the junior colleges offered the first two years of undergraduate studies and provided students with a smooth transfer to the state university for upper-level work and completion of the bachelor's degree. By the 1970s freshmen enrolled at community colleges represented more than one-fourth of all first-year college students. Such were the coalitions that characterized this era of state coordinating commissions, master plans, and accrediting agencies, with campus officials working to build a measure of coherence and quality to accompany the system's growth. The most significant change in the 1960s was the large, enduring presence of the federal government through a complex cluster of programs, ranging from the 1964 Civil Rights Act to the provisions for student financial aid provided by the Higher Education Act of 1965. All institutions, public and private, were cognizant of the growing federal presence of incentives and regulations.

Problems During a Time of Prosperity: The 1960s

Ironically, the prosperity of the 1960s actually created new problems for higher education. Freeland's study (1992) of universities in Massachusetts during the years 1945 to 1970 recounted an era of ruthless competition among colleges and universities, especially in the greater metropolitan Boston area, in pursuit of students, research grants, donors, and external funds. Most troubling for those concerned with the quality of undergraduate education was the strong temptation for all universities to use undergraduate enrollments as a convenient means of subsidizing new graduate programs and research institutes. In many states, policy proposals included discussions between university officials and legislative subcommittees over teaching strategies. For example, faculty and administrators haggled over issues such as the efficiency and legitimacy of teaching in large halls as opposed to the value of personalized instruction in seminars and small class sections.

The prestigious title used to describe the idealized institutions of the era was "multiversity," which corresponded with what Clark Kerr (1964) called the "federal grant university" (p. 46). These institutions consisted of a flagship campus with advanced degree programs whose enrollment usually exceeded twenty thousand students and whose budgets relied heavily on the "soft money" of external research and development projects funded by the federal government and private foundations. Despite the predominance of these schools, enrollments in other kinds of institutions—small independent colleges, religious colleges, private universities, community colleges, regional campuses, and technical institutes—were also healthy, often beyond enrollment capacity. As sociologist Burton Clark (1970) documented, at the same time that the "multiversity" gained prominence, the private, distinctive liberal arts colleges also flourished. Curricular innovations at all of these types of institutions added honors programs and freshman seminars. Testimony to the strength of the "collegiate ideal" for American educators of the late twentieth century was that even the large public universities came full circle to ponder ways in which mass higher education might provide a modern equivalent of the old New England hilltop college. Clark Kerr (1964), famous as the president of the University of California and featured on the cover of *Time* magazine, summed up the challenge for undergraduate education at the prestigious, large state universities of the mid 1960s with the rhetorical question: How do we make the university seem smaller as it grows larger? (pp. 104–105). He then proceeded to answer his own query by supporting an interesting innovation known as the "cluster college"—separate residential units within a large university which restored the colonial ideal of bringing living and learning together within an Oxford-Cambridge model of higher education transplanted to the late twentieth century United States. However, such experiments were exceptional and expensive. Despite their best efforts, Americans still had not resolved the dilemma of how to ensure expansive access, high retention, plus personalized attention in higher education at an affordable cost.

Expansion of such relatively young institutions as community colleges; state systems; regional state colleges; and tribal colleges created a complex umbrella arrangement pulled together in the new concept of "postsecondary education" in the three decades of growth after World War II. The ledger sheet around 1960 suggested that American postsecondary education demonstrated remarkable success in providing access to higher education. However, it remained uncertain in its ability to perfect the process and experience of a college education for all that it accommodated. Ultimately this gap between ideal and reality fanned a growing discontent among undergraduates. A landmark event, both for higher education and for student services, was the publication in 1962 of an interesting volume edited by psychologist Nevitt Sanford, *The American College*. It was a significant work on two counts: first, its research findings by behavioral and social scientists provided an early warning of problems that would surface later in the decade; second, it marked the emergence of higher education as an increasingly systematic field of study with implications for campus administrators, planners, and policymakers.

The history of higher education is often the story of unexpected consequences. For college and university administrators of the 1960s, the boom in construction and enrollments tended to mask problems and tensions among students that would emerge between 1963 and 1968 and violently erupt between 1968 and 1972. Two distinct yet related sources of undergraduate discontent existed. First, discontented students complained about large lecture classes, impersonal registration, crowded student housing, and the psychological distance between faculty and students caused by the expanded size of campuses. Second, student concerns about external political and societal events—notably the Vietnam war, the military draft, the counterculture movement, and the Civil Rights Movement—kindled a visible and eventually widespread student activism. This activism not only preoccupied, but also strained the real and symbolic foundations of higher education, affecting universities' internal and external conduct. National media, including both television news coverage and print journalism of newspapers and magazines, gave foremost attention to the student activism at the University of California, Berkeley, which was followed in the late 1960s by additional protests at Harvard, Columbia, University of Wisconsin, University of Michigan, and Michigan State University. In fact, much of the more compelling and effective initiatives came from the movement groups and strategies pioneered by students at the historically Black colleges and universities in North Carolina and elsewhere in the South. Students at both North Carolina A&T State University and Bennett College for Women participated in a sit-in at the local Woolworth in Greensboro on February 1, 1960, in effect igniting a spark among Black college students throughout the South. The most dramatic landmark event—student protests in May 1970—included student killings at Jackson State University in Mississippi along with the more publicized tragic events at Kent State University in Ohio. All told, the legacy of the decade was that by 1970 the national media portrayed the American campus less as a sanctuary and more as a battleground in a protracted generational war between college students and the established institutions associated with adult society. Outspoken student activists became symbols of a new popular culture and acquired high visibility in television, radio, and newspaper coverage.

An Era of Adjustment and Accountability: 1970 to 1990

Years of student unrest contributed to several negative effects on American higher education, not the least of which was declining confidence on the part of state governments and other traditional sources of support. No longer did public officials assume that a university president or a dean of students could keep his or her "house in order." By 1972 the federal government exerted its presence within higher education by dictating an increased commitment to social justice and educational opportunity on university and colleges campuses. The national government's action emerged with large-scale entitlements for student financial aid—an alphabet soup of funding including Basic Educational Opportunity Grants (BEOG) (later known as Pell Grants) and the Supplementary Educational Opportunity Grants (SEOG). These generous programs embodied the ideal that affordability should not circumscribe students' choices in making college plans. Enactment of further loan programs and work-study opportunities combined with increased institutional funding for scholarships to create a formidable change in access to higher education from 1972 to 1980. The traditional image of the student as "Joe College" was supplanted by women, Native Americans, African Americans, Asian Americans, Hispanics, and Americans older than twenty-five as integral members of the higher education student profile. During the same years, new legislation prohibiting discrimination in educational programs through the 1972 federal Title IX allowed women and other underrepresented constituencies to gain access gradually yet persistently to academic fields such as business, law, medicine, and a host of Ph.D. programs. By 1990, Section 504 of the Vocational Rehabilitation Act had further encouraged diversity and access by providing guidelines and advocacy for students with disabilities who sought admission to higher education institutions.

How did these new programs and policies shape campus life? The best way to approach that question is to fuse historical analysis with sociology and anthropology. Anthropologist Michael Moffatt's (1989) account of undergraduate life at Rutgers University in the late 1980s, *Coming of Age in New Jersey*, suggested that students had become increasingly resourceful at navigating the complexities of large institutions. Cohesion, however, was an increasingly uncertain dimension of the campus and curriculum. Critics continually asked whether academic standards were becoming diluted as the number of students attending college grew. Obviously, no definitive answer to that complex question existed. However, Moffatt's study included a historical analysis comparing student life of 1880 to that of a century later. His surprising finding was that undergraduates of the earlier era did not necessarily study more hours per week than the students of 1980. Rather, they simply devoted more entries in their daily logs and journals to commenting on their intention to study—or expressing their remorse over not having studied more.

The history of higher education during the 1970s and 1980s included other puzzles and uncertainties. For example, economists of the early 1970s accurately predicted to college presidents and trustees a forthcoming "new depression" in funding. By 1978 the financial hard times were even worse than had been anticipated. Campuses and other nonprofit institutions encountered ten consecutive years of double-digit inflation along with soaring heating and oil prices. Rounding out the gloomy picture, demographers projected a substantial decline in the number of high school graduates. All of this signaled a future marked by campus cutbacks and closings.

The early 1980s also was a period in which a succession of commission reports, including *A Nation at Risk* (National Commission, 1983), criticized American public education as uncertain and incoherent. Initially the focus was on primary and secondary schooling—a focus which gave higher education a temporary reprieve. However, this changed when the Study Group on the Conditions of Excellence in American Higher Education released its report *Involvement in Learning: Realizing the Potential of American Higher Education* (U.S. Department of Education, 1984). Its call for scrutiny of and reform in higher education was reinforced by numerous other reports, especially periodic studies on the college curriculum, the college as a community, and reconsideration of scholarship that the Carnegie Foundation for the Advancement of Teaching published under the leadership of Ernest Boyer. Consequently, by 1985 colleges and universities, especially public institutions, were increasingly expected by governors and state legislators to demonstrate efficiency and effectiveness. One state strategy was to tie a portion of state appropriations to performance measures, as part of a larger assessment movement that caught on in numerous states, including Tennessee, Arizona, Kentucky, and New York.

The problems were real, and the concerns were warranted, but American higher education demonstrated a great deal of innovation and resiliency. Enrollment declines were muted as colleges recruited new constituents, including older students and more students from such traditionally underserved such as women and minorities. Campus administration underwent a managerial revolution in two ways. First, administrators increasingly relied on systematic data analysis from national and institutional sources, which helped colleges make informed decisions that promoted budget accountability. Second, new government incentive programs prompted colleges to shift resources to marketing, fundraising, and student recruitment in order to seek and retain new student constituencies—and to develop new programs to serve them. Thus the period 1979 to 1989, which supposed to have been a grim winter for American colleges and universities, turned out to be an extended summer of unexpected recovery and abundance.

History, however, always includes seasonal changes, and ultimately American colleges and universities could not evade financial problems. By 1990, reports from virtually every governor's office in the country indicated severe shortfalls in state revenues, in addition to other sustained indications of a depressed economy. At the same time, federal support for university-based research tapered, making even the most prestigious universities vulnerable to budgetary problems and cutbacks. If an apt motto existed for the situation facing higher education in the final decade of the twentieth century, it was the admonition, "Do more with less." Paradoxically, going to college remained a valued experience in American life, with rising enrollments and student demand increasing at the very time that adequate funding for higher education was allegedly uncertain or inadequate.

The rub was that the increased demand for higher education coincided with increased government obligations for road construction, health services, prison systems, eldercare, and reforms in elementary and secondary education, all during a period of scarce resources. Parents worried that their children might not have access to the same quality of higher education that they enjoyed in the prosperous decades after World War II. By 1990, changing financial and demographic circumstances prompted educational leaders and critics to consider the need for a fundamental shift in attitudes toward higher education and the collegiate structure in the United States. The optimism which had emerged in the 1960s had waned. Higher education no longer necessarily aimed for unlimited diversity and choice. Perhaps one consolation in this continuous dilemma is the fact that the present still reflects the past—colleges and universities remain integral to the significant issues of American life associated with opportunity, equity, social justice, and mobility. As such they have often developed in the past innovative solutions to deal with seemingly unsolvable financial and practical dilemmas.

The Twentieth to the Twenty-First Century: 1990 to 2010

Between 1990 and 2000 most colleges and universities were prosperous and had robust enrollments that erased the harsh memories of declining state appropriations and dismal endowment portfolios of 1989. This recovery, however, did not spare colleges—including student affairs officers—from persistent concerns about how to rethink the college campus and the college experience so as to acknowledge the qualitative and quantitative changes of the recent past. Patricia Cross (1981), a pioneering dean of students and renowned researcher, forewarned her colleagues of the presence of a generation of "new learners" and of another constituency, "adults as learners." Developments at the end of the twentieth century reaffirmed her research findings and projections from the 1970s and 1980s. Furthermore, even though both parents and institutions enjoyed prosperity in the 1990s, concerns about rising college costs and their subsequent high prices persisted (Ehrenberg, 2000). Vice presidents and deans of student affairs had to face the fact that the services for which they were responsible accounted for a substantial portion of rising college costs. Increased costs were partially due to the demands and expectations of undergraduates and their parents a few decades earlier. Whatever luxuries American higher education of the 1950s or 1960s claimed, closer inspection finds them modest and frugal in comparison to contemporary expectations with regard to such obvious services as career planning, campus security, residence hall wiring to accommodate computers, health and wellness programs, and numerous new, expanded programs and facilities for students. Nevertheless, in making sense out of the nation's investment in higher education, important to note is that while costs of student services increased in actual dollars in the 1980s and 1990s, these remained fairly constant as a percentage of a college's total annual operating budget—that is, about 4 to 6 percent (Woodard, Love, & Komives, 2000, pp. 73–75).

By 2000 the certainty and coherence of the undergraduate campus experience had been diffused and diluted. The diversity of students in American higher education eventually influenced the shape and structure of institutions. One intriguing doctoral dissertation charted the ways in which a public comprehensive university altered its student services and assumptions about who was attending the college—resulting in the designation as "the commuter's Alma Mater" (Mason, 1993). However, for some higher education analysts the effort to include all students at all institutions as part of the "collegiate experience" ceased to make good sense. Alexander Astin, for example, opted to exclude community college students from his 1993 research on the college experience, *What Matters in College?* This categorical determination was bold but troubling, given that by 1990 about 40 percent of freshman enrollments were in the nation's two-year community colleges.

Also during this time, women became a decisive majority of student enrollments at numerous independent and public institutions. Nowhere was this change reflected more than in the character and composition of women's intercollegiate athletics and other student activities. Despite some gains, it appears that even by 2008, women in coeducational institutions still received less than their fair share of resources and opportunities in all activities. Still, changes in access and admissions altered student organizational life.

At several colleges and universities, and in particular, historically Black colleges and universities, women as a percentage of total undergraduate enrollments had become the majority constituency. Within the campus at several state universities data indicated that first-generation college students, including women and students of color, participated in student government and campus elections. This participation had resulted in the emergence of new leadership groups among students—and, in some cases, signs of decline of the influence of such traditionally powerful groups as fraternities in campuswide activities.

Adults, often placed in the category of "nontraditional students," continued to gain in numbers and as a percentage of enrollments at all levels of academic degree programs. Likewise, women and students of color continued to increase the diversity of graduate and professional programs. This not only changed configurations within institutions but also increased options among campuses. Some women's colleges that had resisted the invitation to adopt coeducation in the 1970s now enjoyed a resurgence of enrollments and revitalization of their special missions and constituencies. Tribal colleges and universities, especially in the Far West, gained autonomy and funding after numerous deliberations with state and federal governments. And, Hispanic-serving institutions, which were established under the Higher Education Act of 1965, grew at enormous rates—a reflection of the increasing presence of Latinos in the United States population (Gasman, Baez, & Turner, 2008).

Finally, American consumerism combined with technological advances to provide a generation of students with opportunities to study via distance learning courses, Internet curricula, "virtual universities," and off-campus sites. These options could be mixed and matched in conjunction with the traditional residential campus. These innovations led nontraditional students, especially adults, to show unprecedented interest in a new segment of postsecondary education—the for-profit education sector. The proprietary sector previously had been ignored or underestimated by established colleges and universities. However, as the proprietary institutions acquired eligibility for federal student financial aid, combined with their enterprising use of new electronic technologies, they became a substantial force within the ranks of degree-granting institutions nationwide.

Profiles of the typical college experience also faced challenges and changes due to the impact of changing student aid policies. Federal programs expanded substantially in terms of allotted dollars—yet increasingly were characterized by an emphasis on student loans rather than scholarships or grants. The prospect of indebtedness as a student meant that many undergraduates extended their length of time to degree completion from four years to six years, often because of the need to work at off-campus jobs to meet rising college prices. By 2007, student and parental concerns about the hegemony of student loans led to inquiries and investigations by the U.S. Congress about reforming federal programs and regulating the student loan industry (Thelin, 2007).

The net result of these cumulative changes was a continued decline of a dominant, discernible "collegiate culture." And, to the extent that this diversification and diffusion reflected the influences of new or previously underserved student constituencies, it was healthy. Perhaps one troubling sign was that older forms of American undergraduate life no longer had much ability to shape and elevate the standards and tastes of young Americans. Whereas in 1910, 1950, or 1960, high school students could look forward and aspire to being part of "college life," by 1990 there had been a cultural reversal: the student culture of junior high school and high school now set the tone for college life, signaling a reversal of the customary pattern of influence. The dilemma for student affairs leaders, then, was not so much how to accept and work with this change but rather how to embrace the changes in the nation's popular culture yet still provide a campus experience that was substantive and distinctive. One intriguing response of student affairs professionals was to advance by word and deed a new approach in which what had once been called the "extracurriculum" (out-of-class experiences being viewed as supplemental) now came to be called the "co-curriculum" (a seamless integration of classroom and out-of-class learning).

Conclusion

Any attempt to present a brief survey of American higher education over four centuries risks superficiality. A good resolution to carry away is to see the history of American colleges and universities less as a compendium of facts and more as a description of the lively process by which each generation of college students, administrators, donors, and legislators has wrestled with the issue of who shall be educated and how. Central to this is the idea of a "useful past," in which the history of higher education is understood as essential and applicable to one's work in student affairs and student services. Recently, the most interesting historical research on higher education has incorporated concepts from the related disciplines of sociology, anthropology, economics, and political science (Gasman, 2010; Goodchild & Wechsler, 1989). Sociologist Burton Clark (1970), for example, developed the notion of a "campus saga" to explain how some colleges acquired over time a sense of heritage and mission that they effectively transmit to new students, administrators, and faculty, as well as to alumni. Much work remains to be done in order to apply Clark's concept to numerous understudied and unexamined community colleges, colleges, and universities. Intensive case studies of individual institutions are a good way for higher education professionals to make sense of their own experiences and campuses in terms of preceding generations and national trends.

The issues of access, accountability, social justice, equity, and excellence are pressing—but they are not completely new. They were exciting in 1908 and are still so today in the twenty-first century. Higher education professionals ought to recognize that understanding the history of distant eras remains an unfinished task. Today we take for granted readily available statistical data on aspects of student life, such as retention and degree completion rates, along with sophisticated analyses of where money comes from and goes in university budgets. Statistics and other compilations from the past, linked with present data, can be integral to thoughtfully analyzing whether colleges are changing – and if so, how much in matters of efficiency and effectiveness. At the same time, we have not given adequate attention to the fiction and memoirs of student life from our own era. Also, oral history is a wonderful, flourishing part of many college and university archives—and it is useful for remembering and listening to the many voices of past and present campuses. The ultimate challenge for a lively history of higher education, then, is to be aware of landmark events that offer information and inspiration that can be useful for responding to contemporary issues on college and university campuses.

References

Allmendinger, D. (1975). *Paupers and scholars: The transformation of student life in nineteenth-century New England*. New York: St. Martin's Press.

Astin, A. W. (1977). *Four critical years*. San Francisco: Jossey-Bass.

Astin, A. W. (1993). *What matters in college? Four critical years revisited*. San Francisco: Jossey-Bass.

Axtell, J. (1974). *The school upon a hill: Education and society in colonial New England*. New Haven. CT: Yale University Press.

Brint, S., & Karabel, J. (1989). *The diverted dream: Community colleges and the promise of educational opportunity in America, 1900–1985*. New York: Oxford University Press.

Burke, C. B. (1982). *American collegiate populations: A test of the traditional view*. New York: New York University Press.

Clark, B. R. (1970). *The distinctive college: Antioch, Swarthmore, & Reed*. Chicago: Aldine.

Cross, K. P. (1981). *Adults as learners*. San Francisco: Jossey-Bass.

Diener, T. (1986). *Growth of an American invention: A documentary history of the junior and community college movement*. New York: Greenwood Press.

Drewry, H. N., & Doermann, H. (2001). *Stand and prosper: Private black colleges and their students*. Princeton, NJ: Princeton University Press.

Ehrenberg, R. G. (2000). *Tuition rising: Why college costs so much*. Cambridge, MA: Harvard University Press.

Franklin, B. (1784). *Remarks concerning the savages of North America*. New Haven, CT: Yale University, The Franklin Papers Project.

Freeland, R. (1992). *Academia's golden age: Universities in Massachusetts, 1945–1970*. New York: Oxford University Press.

Gasman, M. (Ed.). (2010). *The history of U.S. higher education: Methods for understanding the past*. New York: Routledge.

Gasman, M., Baez, B., & Turner, C.S.V. (Eds.). (2008). *Understanding minority-serving institutions*. Albany: State University of New York Press.

Goodchild, L., & Wechsler, H. (1989). *ASHE Reader on the history of higher education*. Needham, MA: Ginn Press.

Gordon, L. (1990). *Gender and higher education in the progressive era*. New Haven, CT: Yale University Press.

Handlin, O., & Handlin, M. (1974). *The American college and American culture*. New York: McGraw-Hill.

Haskins, C. H. (1923). *The rise of the universities*. Ithaca, NY: Cornell University Press.

Horowitz, H. L. (1984). *Alma mater: Design and experience in the women's colleges from their 19th century beginnings to the 1930s*. New York: Knopf.

Horowitz, H. L. (1987). *Campus life: Undergraduate cultures from the end of the eighteenth century to the present*. New York: Knopf.

Jencks, C., & Riesman, D. (1968). *The academic revolution*. New York: Doubleday.

Jenkins, S. (2007). *The real all Americans: The team that changed a game, a people, a nation*. New York: Doubleday.

Karabel, J. (2005). *The chosen. The hidden history of exclusion at Harvard, Yale, and Princeton*. New York: Houghton Mifflin.

Kerr, C. (1964). *The uses of the university*. Cambridge, MA: Harvard University Press.

Lehman, N. (2000). *The big test: The secret history of American meritocracy*. New York: Farrar, Straus, and Giroux.

Levine, D. (1986). *The American college and the culture of aspiration, 1915–1940*. Ithaca, NY: Cornell University Press.

Mason, T. (1993). *The commuter's alma mater: Profiles of college student experiences at a commuter institution*. Unpublished doctoral dissertation, The College of William & Mary, Williamsburg, VA.

Moffatt, M. (1989). *Coming of age in New Jersey: College and American culture*. New Brunswick, NJ: Rutgers University Press.

National Commission on Excellence in Education. (1983). *A nation at risk: The imperative for educational reform*. Washington, DC: U.S. Department of Education.

Nerad, M. (1999). *The academic kitchen: A social history of gender stratification at the University of California, Berkeley*. Albany: State University of New York Press.

Peterson, G. (1963). *The New England college in the age of the university*. Amherst, MA: Amherst College Press.

Rudolph, F. (1962). *The American college and university: A history*. New York: Knopf.

Sanford, N. (Ed.). (1962). *The American college*. New York: Wiley.

Slosson, E. E. (1910). *Great American universities*. New York: Macmillan.

Synnott, M. G. (1979). *The half-opened door: Discrimination and admissions at Harvard, Yale, and Princeton, 1900–1970*. Westport, CT: Greenwood Press.

Thelin, J. R. (2007). Higher education's student financial aid enterprise in historical perspective. In F. M. Hess (Ed.), *Footing the tuition bill: The new student loan sector*. Washington, DC: American Enterprise Institute.

Trow, M. (1970). Reflections on the transition from elite to mass to universal higher education. *Daedalus, 99*(1), 1–42.

U.S. Department of Education. (1984). *Involvement in learning: Realizing the potential of American higher education*. Washington, DC: Author.

Veysey, L. R. (1965). *The emergence of the American university*. Chicago: University of Chicago Press.

Wakelyn, J. L. (1985). Antebellum college life and the relations between fathers and sons. In W. J. Fraser, R. F. Sanders, & J. L. Wakelyn (Eds.), *The web of southern social relations: Women, family, and education*. Athens, GA: University of Georgia Press.

Woodard, D. B., Love, P., & Komives, S. R. (2000). *Leadership and management issues for a new century* (New Directions for Student Services No. 92). San Francisco: Jossey-Bass.

Wright, S. (1988). Black colleges and universities: Historical background and future prospects. *Virginia Humanities, 14*(1), 1–7.

CHAPTER TWO

INSTITUTIONAL VARIETY IN AMERICAN HIGHER EDUCATION

Kimberly A. Griffin and Sylvia Hurtado

One of the hallmarks of American higher education is the sheer number and variety of institutions offering educational opportunities. In the 2006–2007 academic year, approximately 6,700 postsecondary institutions participating in federal financial aid programs reported institutional data to the Integrated Postsecondary Education Data System (IPEDS). The U.S. secretary of education recognizes approximately 4,500 of these as accredited, degree-granting higher education institutions, distinguished by their missions, structures, sizes, types of students they enroll, and distinct cultures defined by history and tradition. Institutions have been founded and reshaped to satisfy an array of public purposes, and students choose to attend the schools for which they feel they are the best suited (Clark, 1983; Kerr, 2001). No single institution could begin to respond to the full range of interests expressed by students and society. Therefore, having many different types of colleges and universities allows the American higher education system to simultaneously meet students' demands, be accessible, promote excellence, and provide a wide array of educational opportunities (Birnbaum, 1991).

While American colleges and universities are diverse in many ways, an overview of the distinctions between institutions with a focus on institutional mission and type is presented in this chapter. It could be argued that postsecondary institutions are often similar in their attention to the three principle functions of higher education: teaching, research, and service (Astin, 1995; Bowen, 1997). However, how these functions are embodied and emphasized within each institution's individual mission varies substantially and certainly shapes the context for student learning and the workplace environment for faculty and staff.

Examining institutions' missions provides a framework for understanding modes of operation, the students who attend particular institutions, and the need for specific kinds of academic support and student service programs. Colleges and universities with similar missions can be organized into broader categories, representing a particular institutional type. The diversity of institutional types is most frequently discussed using the Carnegie Classification system as a framework. This chapter presents and discusses the newest version of the Carnegie Classification system, offering a word of caution about its use and noting other aspects of mission that are important when considering institutional diversity in higher education. Particular attention is given to institutions with unique missions dedicated to serving specific student populations, highlighting the environments created on these campuses and the experiences of the students enrolled and professionals employed. In her 2006 book, *Where You Work Matters: Student Affairs Administration at Different Types of Institutions,* Joan B. Hirt describes ways in which contextual factors shape the complexity of practice as well as a student affairs professional's fit within a particular institutional type. Our aim here is not to replicate these efforts, but instead to offer an introductory overview of ways in which postsecondary institutional types have been formally differentiated.

Carnegie Classification of Institutions of Higher Education

Using empirical data on degrees conferred, academic fields of emphasis, and amount of federal research dollars received, the Carnegie Foundation for the Advancement of Teaching (CFAT) first developed what is now known as the Carnegie Classification of Institutions of Higher Education in 1973. The first classification system included five institutional categories: doctoral granting institutions; comprehensive colleges; liberal arts colleges; all two-year colleges and institutes; and professional schools and other specialized institutions (McCormick & Zhao, 2005). Revisions in 1976, 1987, 1994, 2001, and 2005 allowed the Carnegie Foundation to hone and adjust their classification into six categories: doctoral and research universities, master's colleges and universities, baccalaureate colleges, associate's colleges, specialized institutions, and tribal colleges.

Researchers in higher education have made great use of the Carnegie Classification system to examine institutional differences, study the effects of different types of environments on student development and long-term outcomes, describe the enrollment of students in higher education, and select similar types of institutions that may be regarded as "peer institutions" for further study or program comparison. The friendly "competition" among peer institutions ensures not only a continued focus on institutional improvement but also an emphasis on each institution's unique history, traditions, and culture. More important, comparison among peer institutions on key issues (such as student retention, public service, and technology use) can lead to innovation in programs and initiatives. Unfortunately, there have also been many unintended uses of the classification system over the years. It was not intended to be a ranking system; however, many have viewed it as such. For example, researchers have documented a marked increase in research emphasis among faculty working at many institutional types over the years, indicating that institutions may seek to emulate the mission of the research university to increase institutional prestige (Dey, Milem, & Berger, 1997).

In response to these concerns, the most recent edition of the Carnegie Classifications includes substantial changes. First, instead of categorizing on one dimension, several parallel dimensions were created to organize institutions based on what is taught (undergraduate and graduate instructional program classifications); student enrollment (enrollment profile and undergraduate profile); and the campus physical environment (size and setting) (Carnegie Foundation for the Advancement of Teaching [CFAT], 2007). Furthermore, the classifications have been traditionally based on an analysis of existing national data on postsecondary institutions. Elective classifications were introduced, which allow institutions to provide the Carnegie Foundation with data illustrating unique institutional attributes (CFAT, 2007; Driscoll, 2008). Unlike other dimensions, elective classifications are not based on national assessments; they are also not intended to be a ranking system. Institutions interested in participating in the first elective classification category, community engagement, submitted institutional data and information and were assessed in 2006. Although the list is certainly not comprehensive or inclusive of all institutions with significant ties to their communities, a total of 119 institutions completed the steps necessary to be classified in the community engagement category, recognized as having significant engagement with their surrounding communities through curriculum, institutional outreach, and partnership efforts (CFAT, 2007; Driscoll, 2008). Other institutions beyond the initial 119 will likely pursue and achieve this designation.

Carnegie Basic Classifications

In addition to these broad categorical changes, the Carnegie Foundation has substantially revised its Basic Classification system, which allows researchers to organize institutions by degree level and specialization. The Basic Classification dimension most closely resembles the classification systems of the past, categorizing a total of 4,391 institutions into six major types: associate's institutions, doctorate-granting universities, master's colleges and universities, baccalaureate colleges, special focus institutions, and tribal colleges. By deemphasizing institutional resources, reorganizing the presentation of institutional types based on enrollment rather than perceived prestige, and searching for alternative sources of information about institutional differences, the developers of the Carnegie Classification system have attempted make the information less vulnerable to interpretation as a ranking system and more amenable to wide use and to promoting an understanding of American higher education in the future (McCormick & Zhao, 2005).

Figure 2.1 shows the distribution of institutional categories across American higher education as organized by the Carnegie Basic Classification system. This provides an overview of the predominance of institutions that may be quite different from the perspective developed while working or receiving an education in only one or two of these categories of institutions. In slight contrast, Figure 2.2 illustrates where students attending accredited higher education institutions are enrolled. Each of the institution

FIGURE 2.1.   DISTRIBUTION OF INSTITUTIONAL TYPES AND MISSIONS BY CARNEGIE BASIC CLASSIFICATION.

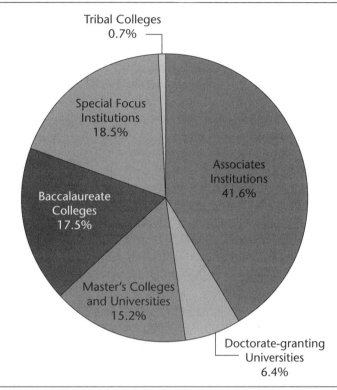

Tribal Colleges
0.7%

Special Focus
Institutions
18.5%

Baccalaureate
Colleges
17.5%

Master's Colleges
and Universities
15.2%

Associates
Institutions
41.6%

Doctorate-granting
Universities
6.4%

Source: Adapted from the Carnegie Foundation for the Advancement of Teaching, 2007.

types may require a different approach to both academic support and student service programs and have distinctive organizational configurations to deliver student services. Furthermore, since emphasis on fields and degree awards differ, it stands to reason that outcomes may differ for students. The following sections of this chapter detail each institutional type in the Basic Classification system, describing the key characteristics, institutional emphases in terms of mission, and environments relevant to the outcomes of community members.

Associate's Colleges

Institutions fall within this classification if the associate's degree is the highest degree conferred, or if fewer than 10 percent of students on campus obtain bachelor's degrees (CFAT, 2007). They constitute 41.6 percent of all accredited higher education institutions and served 38.1 percent of all students enrolled in accredited, degree-granting higher education institutions in 2004 (see Figures 2.1 and 2.2). Most maintain open admissions policies that provide students with access to postsecondary education regardless of high school preparation and performance. In addition

FIGURE 2.2.   STUDENT ENROLLMENT BY CARNEGIE BASIC CLASSIFICATION.

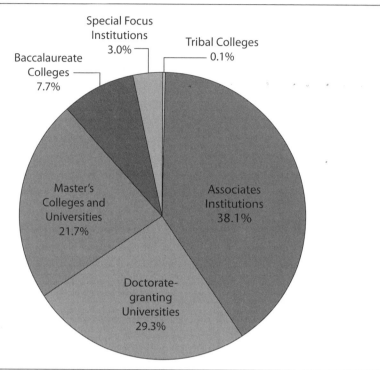

Source: Adapted from the Carnegie Foundation for the Advancement of Teaching, 2007.

to offering classes on campus, many associate's colleges offer online learning opportunities (as do some doctorate-granting and master's institutions). Associate's colleges offer students opportunities to complete the general education requirements of many baccalaureate-granting institutions, awarding associate's degrees, and also create opportunities for students to gain access to vocational courses, academic remediation, and occupational training.

The mission of two-year colleges is much broader than awarding associate's degrees and facilitating transfer to four-year institutions. Many two-year institutions perceive themselves as being in service to local community learning needs—duplicating missed opportunities at previous levels of education as well as introducing new subject matter that is practically oriented or technical in nature. These campuses also create opportunities for community members to participate in leisure activities, prepare for specialized employment and vocational areas, and gain access to instruction in newly emerging topics essential to the job market. Community colleges can also be more accessible than four-year institutions, offering cross-racial interaction and community building (Dougherty, 2002).

Because of their diverse educational goals as well as their open admissions policies, sheer numbers, low cost, and convenience, these institutions tend to attract the most diverse student bodies in terms of age, race and ethnicity, ability, and career aspirations. They seek to deliver their student services and academic support programs in ways that serve a highly mobile and diverse population. Offering support to heterogeneous populations entails busy lives for student affairs professionals. They are expected to offer a wide array of programs to students and the wider community, and they frequently must wear many hats and collaborate with each other across campus to compensate for a small student affairs staff and the need to meet a wide array of student needs (Hirt, 2006).

Doctorate-Granting Universities

The category of doctorate-granting universities, also known as research universities, includes institutions that awarded at least twenty doctoral degrees in the 2003–2004 academic year. Institutions falling within this designation are often seen as responsible for managing and integrating all three of higher education's principle functions (Gumport, 1991; Kerr, 2001). The service mission is often embedded in the teaching and research functions (Zusman, 1999); research universities are expected to train and educate undergraduate and graduate students to be productive and civically engaged members of society, as well as to conduct research that will add to human knowledge and benefit the wider public good (Checkoway, 2001; Gumport, 1991; Kerr, 2001).

Doctorate-granting universities serve large populations of students and are segmented into many schools for both professional and graduate education, in addition to offering undergraduate education. A developing trend is for individual schools within large research universities to hire professional advisors, recruiters, and their own student service personnel, in addition to their own admissions and fundraising staff (Guentzel & Elkins Nesheim, 2006). This duplication of professional and administrative roles suggests that there are many units and departments in which skilled higher education professionals can be employed on these campuses, creating a variety of opportunities for professionals to gain experience and advance their careers.

Although serving large populations of undergraduates, doctorate-granting universities have often come under criticism for a perceived lack of attention to undergraduate education (Boyer Commission, 1998; Checkoway, 2001; Zusman, 1999). Undergraduate teaching, advising, and mentoring have been increasingly reassigned to graduate students and adjunct faculty, while full-time faculty focus their attention on research. Graduate students are often used to assist faculty in grading and leading small discussion groups to minimize the impersonal nature of learning in large lecture halls, which are present and widely used on many university campuses.

Although doctoral and research universities make up only 6.4 percent of all institution types, they enroll a disproportionately large segment of students, specifically 29.3 percent of all enrolled at accredited institutions. This reflects the fact that many doctorate-granting universities have large campuses that enroll a sizeable student body. Students enrolled at large institutions are less likely to interact with faculty, get involved in student government, participate in athletics or honors programs, or have opportunities to speak up during class; and as a result, are also much less satisfied with faculty relationships or classroom instruction than students attending smaller campuses (Astin, 1979).

An interesting paradox as it relates to size is that at the same time that large campuses can hinder individual involvement in particular activities, these are places of tremendous activity, with hundreds of student organizations that address a variety of social and academic interests. There is some evidence that students on large campuses are able to adjust well (socially, academically, and emotionally) to college, once they learn to navigate the social and physical geography of a campus (Hurtado, Carter, & Spuler, 1996). For example, students use organization memberships to achieve personal goals, make sense of large environments, and engender a sense of belonging to the campus community (Hurtado & Carter, 1997).

In addition to influencing student outcomes, institution size and enrollment have implications for individuals seeking employment at these institutions. First, higher education professionals are likely to work in more highly specialized units or programs at large institutions like doctorate-granting institutions, and coordinating efforts across units can be challenging (Hirt, 2006). Second, finding ways to create a greater sense of campus community becomes an implicit goal on campuses where it is not possible for everyone to know each other. Campus administrators are often asked to design and employ initiatives to make large campuses operate like small college environments through residence hall programming, undergraduate research programs through which students develop relationships with faculty, first-year seminars with limited enrollments, and orientation programs that help students navigate complex environments.

Master's Colleges and Universities

Institutions within this designation are somewhat similar to doctorate-granting universities in that they have a research function and confer doctoral degrees. However, these institutions have less of a research emphasis; the category includes institutions awarding fewer than twenty doctoral degrees per year but at least fifty master's degrees. Also similar to doctorate-granting institutions, master's colleges and universities are typically large, enrolling 21.7 percent of all students in higher education (see Figure 2.2). Thus they face challenges similar to those seen at doctorate-granting universities in managing large enrollments and creating community among students on campus. Interestingly, master's colleges are distinctive from major research universities in that they are often not as bureaucratically complex or decentralized. This may be partially due to the fact that these campuses are something of a hybrid between baccalaureate institutions and doctorate-granting universities. Collaborations among professionals also appear to be more common on these campuses than among student affairs officers employed at doctorate-granting universities (Hirt, 2006).

Baccalaureate Colleges

Institutions are classified as baccalaureate colleges if they award fewer than fifty master's degrees, and at least 10 percent of conferred degrees are bachelor's degrees. In contrast to doctorate-granting and master's universities, there are many baccalaureate colleges (17.5 percent of all institutions), but they enroll a small proportion of students in postsecondary education (7.7 percent). Accordingly, these campuses tend to serve smaller student bodies and offer more intimate environments for teaching and learning.

Small four-year colleges were the norm in the United States until the 1950s, established in an entrepreneurial manner similar to the settlements and communities across America. Although some of the initial baccalaureate colleges evolved into more complex higher education organizations, some closed due to financial problems; still others remain strong liberal arts colleges at which students acquire the values of a liberal education. Although faculty at liberal arts institutions are increasingly expected to engage in research and scholarly work, with some institutions even offering limited graduate programs, these institutions are known for being small, largely residential schools that focus on the teaching function of higher education (Altbach, 2001; Keohane, 2001). The goals of liberal arts institutions focus on developing the critical thinking, writing, quantitative reasoning, and inquisitiveness of its students through exposure to a wide range of subjects (Keohane, 2001).

Scholars have chronicled the positive influence the environment at these institutions has on student learning and development. For example, liberal arts institutions are more effective in fostering several good practices in undergraduate education linked to student learning and development, including student-faculty contact, active learning, cooperation among students, and teaching quality (Pascarella, Cruce, Wolniak, & Blaich, 2004). Some of these outcomes are likely due at least in part to baccalaureate colleges' smaller, more manageable environments, which enable deeper levels of student engagement (Chickering & Reisser, 1993). However, they are also brought forth by the culture of these institutions (Pascarella et al., 2004). An emphasis on developing relationships with students extends from the faculty to student affairs professionals, and all are expected to work closely with students in an effort to foster their academic, emotional, and physiological development. In addition to expectations of high quality relationships, student affairs professionals are expected to maintain a high quantity of interactions with students. Due to relatively small student enrollments, baccalaureate colleges usually maintain relatively small student affairs staffs, and the administrators on these campuses find themselves engaging closely with students, fulfilling multiple roles on campus (Hirt, 2006).

Special Focus Institutions

In contrast to institutions offering a broad liberal arts curriculum, small, specialized institutions focus on specific careers and vocations. Specialized institutions in the Carnegie Classification are further differentiated into many categories, which include theological seminaries; medical schools; separate health profession schools; schools of engineering and technology; schools of business and management; schools of law; teachers colleges; schools of art, music, and design; as well as a generic category of other specialized institutions. Many of these institutions enroll students in professional or graduate programs, and student affairs practice in service to students enrolled in such programs is an emerging area of growth and research.

Tribal Colleges

The "Tribal College" designation is unique in the Carnegie Basic Classification system. It represents a group of institutions united in their mission to teach and serve a specific community of students: Native Americans. The American Indian Movement in the 1960s and its goals for "self-determination" gave birth to organized efforts to counter problems associated with education for Native Americans, including attempts to eradicate native cultures and assimilate students in schools and colleges. The goal of preserving culture and pride in identity remains central at tribal colleges. Founding leaders believed that postsecondary education could be a primary vehicle for improving conditions on reservations that have high rates of poverty, sustaining native cultures, and advancing the progress of Native Americans without assimilation (Boyer, 1997). The primary mission of tribal colleges is to offer culturally based education, addressing the whole person (mind, body, spirit, and family), and advance local economic and other pressing needs of the native community (White House Initiative on Tribal Colleges and Universities, 1996).

The first tribally controlled college, now called Diné College, was established by the Navajo Nation in 1968 (American Indian Higher Education Consortium [AIHEC], 1999). AIHEC was founded by the presidents of the first six tribal colleges and is jointly governed by the participating tribal colleges. Today, AIHEC recognizes 37 tribal colleges. These institutions enroll students from over 250 tribal nations and are located in 12 states. Tribal colleges focus on assisting students to meet their goals in overcoming social and economic barriers, foster a family-like atmosphere, and build strong relations between students and faculty (Guillory & Ward, 2008; Tierney, 1992). Compared to other institution types, they are typically small with an average of 550 students per institution (CFAT, 2007). All offer two-year degree programs, several award baccalaureate degrees, and a few offer master's degrees. The colleges offer courses on tribal languages and cultures that could disappear if not preserved, their libraries serve as repositories for cultural artifacts and oral histories from Indian elders, and American Indian role models constitute 30 percent of the teaching faculty and 79 percent of the full-time staff (AIHEC, 1999). In terms of service, tribal colleges provide technical assistance that is vital to rural communities, offering adult education and distance education for nontraditional students.

Student affairs divisions at tribal colleges are often smaller and have fewer resources and more intense workloads than do divisions at other types of institutions (Fox, Lowe, & McClellan, 2005). Budgets are stretched, and many of these colleges face financial challenges because they receive little or no state funding. Tribal colleges mostly serve areas in extreme poverty and require improved facilities and technology to accomplish their educational mission of preserving the cultures and advancing the economic progress of Native American communities (Guillory & Ward, 2008). Contrary to popular assumptions, only five tribal colleges are eligible to receive a small and unstable income from casinos—very few tribes actually operate gaming facilities (American Indian College Fund, 2006). Federal legislation intended to provide funds for core operations, the 1978 Tribally Controlled and University Assistance Act, has only provided half of the funds committed.

These institutions were recently made eligible for funds under Title III of the Higher Education Act, an initiative to strengthen minority-serving institutions that include historically Black colleges and universities (HBCUs) and Hispanic-serving institutions (HSIs). Given chronic funding problems, Presidents Clinton and Bush issued their own respective executive orders to strengthen the infrastructure of tribal colleges, to encourage partnerships, and to strengthen and sustain quality education in these culturally based institutions. Because the majority of Native American students (55 percent) in higher education are enrolled in two-year colleges, finding ways to increase access to other levels of higher education and support their success in baccalaureate institutions may require higher education professionals to develop partnerships with tribal colleges in the future.

Serving Specific Populations in Higher Education

Other than the identification of tribal colleges as relatively unique institutions, the Carnegie Classification system does not differentiate institutions with missions that address the goal of educating specific student populations. Although these institutions do not constitute a large segment of higher education, they are important. They continue to serve specific populations that have often been excluded from higher education throughout history. These institutions today include approximately 70 women's colleges, 103 HBCUs, 268 HSIs, 6 Asian American–serving institutions, and 3 institutions serving the differently abled.

It is important to note that institutions that began with a history of service to underserved populations often did not restrict their admission of other groups, although the majority of students they serve continue to be from the population group for whom the institution was established. For example, although HBCUs never engaged in race-exclusive policies and, although they have faculty and students of all races, they continue to serve a unique function in primarily educating Black students (Allen, Jewell, Griffin, & Wolf, 2007). The majority of HBCUs and women's colleges today enroll many other types of students as part-time, evening, or graduate students, as well as students who seek degrees in unique academic programs.

Women's Colleges

The majority of women's colleges were established between 1850 and the beginning of the twentieth century; fewer than 10 percent were founded since World War II. The women's colleges flourished as a result of the Civil War casualties and the need for labor, including the need for women to support themselves financially and the expansion of educational institutions that needed teachers. Women's colleges initially proliferated in those states where there was high resistance to coeducation—primarily eastern U.S. states with private education for men, and fewer in the West, where there was the rapid expansion of public institutions (Rudolph, 1965). From the close of World War II, American higher education experienced accelerated growth, with the highest number of women's four-year colleges (214) reported in 1960 (Tidball, 1977). Various social movements increased awareness and demands for equal opportunity, equal pay, and equal status during the 1960s and early 1970s. Coupled with landmark federal legislation for women, minorities, and low-income students, these events lowered resistance to coeducation and opened the doors for entry of these diverse groups of students into higher education.

Finding themselves in competition with many coeducational institutions in recruiting the best students and attempting to meet costs, many women's colleges closed, merged, or became coeducational. Many of the prestigious colleges for men (such as Yale, Princeton, and the University of Virginia) also relented in the face of pressure to become coeducational. Although there were only 125 women's colleges by 1976, it was a historic turning point. Many women's colleges chose to reaffirm their roles and "asserted their autonomy and their inherent value as entities distinct from other forms of higher education and unique in their concerns for the education of women" (Tidball, 1977, p4395). They created new methods to assist in the development of women, provided opportunities for many women to return to college for training, initiated cross-registration opportunities to take advantage of resources from neighboring institutions, and stimulated scholarship on gender-related topics. Some institutions were also able to maintain their historic missions because of large endowments and active alumnae—an important benefit of generations of student satisfaction with the educational environment.

Most of the research on college students indicates that women's colleges have been successful in their mission, counting many women leaders and professionals among their alumnae. This success is not only demonstrated in terms of the accomplishments of their students, but also in the special environment of support they create (Smith, 1989). For example, students attending women's colleges are more likely to perceive personal support for their success than are students attending coeducational institutions (Kinzie, Thomas, Palmer, Umbach, & Kuh, 2007). Women are more likely to find strong role models on these campuses; compared with other institutions in the same Carnegie Classification category (that is, baccalaureate and master's institutions), women's colleges employ women in faculty and administrative leadership roles at substantially higher rates (Harwarth, Maline, & DeBra, 1997). This fosters an environment in which faculty and staff inherently believe in the abilities and potential of women, setting high expectations and requiring high levels of academic commitment and involvement (Kinzie et al. 2007).

The supportive environments created on these campuses lend themselves to more positive outcomes for female students than those observed among women attending coeducational institutions. Women's college students are more satisfied with the faculty, academic requirements, individual support services, and the overall quality of instruction (Astin, 1993). Moreover, their satisfaction with college persists five years after graduation (Langdon, 1999). Women's colleges were also found to have positive effects on students' overall academic development, baccalaureate completion, cultural and self-awareness, engagement, writing skills, critical thinking ability, and foreign language skills (Astin, 1993; Kinzie et al., 2007). A relatively higher proportion of students from women's colleges eventually complete doctoral degrees compared to those at other institutions, even after controlling for entering academic credentials (Tidball, 1999). These outcomes attest to the relative success of women's colleges in achieving key liberal education goals.

Historically Black Colleges and Universities

The earliest of the HBCUs were established in 1830 when the education of Blacks was prohibited, as most were still slaves and considered the property of White landowners. A few colleges were established before the Civil War by Black communities for self-education, but organized efforts to educate former slaves occurred primarily after the Civil War through the work of the Freedmen's Bureau (a federal assistance program), the Black community, and philanthropic and religious organizations (Hoffman, Snyder, & Sonnenberg, 1996). Most of the public support for the establishment of Black colleges, as well as the general growth in the public sector of institutions, came in the form of funds to states from the sales of public lands in the National Land-Grant Colleges Act also known as the Morrill Act (1862). Despite a call for land-grant colleges to be accessible to all students, many states in the South chose to build institutions for White students only. To counter resistance to the education of African Americans and sustain the development of public higher education nationally, Congress passed the Second Morrill Act (1890), requiring states with dual systems of higher education to provide land-grant assistance to both Black and White institutions, eventually leading to the development of nineteen public institutions for Black students (Hoffman, Snyder, & Sonnenberg, 1996).

To overcome the effects of discrimination and strengthen institutional capacity, several generations of American presidents have signed executive orders in support and recognition of the work of HBCUs. In addition, further litigation persisted well into the 1980s in an attempt to correct inadequate funding of public HBCUs, to increase minority student access to predominantly White institutions, and to deseg-regate eighteen states with a history of dual systems of higher education. In the 1992 *United States v. Fordice* case, the Supreme Court ruled that the states had not done enough to rectify the effects of segregation and must justify or revise their current practices. While there was some initial concern that the ruling does not preserve the HBCUs, states appear to be planning to provide more choice and opportunities for Black and White students to encourage more diverse student bodies, both at public HBCUs and at predominantly White institutions (PWIs).

An unusual mix of private and public support over time has resulted today in many different types of HBCUs that span six of the Carnegie Basic Classification categories. Most HBCUs remain rather small when compared to other campuses of the same institution type; have lower tuition; and continue to attract a relatively high percentage of disadvantaged students, who view these institutions as places of opportunity for African Americans. Further, many HBCUs maintain open access missions, and students entering with disadvantages in academic preparation find support for their educational goals. The results of education at these institutions are impressive. Although they represent approximately 3 percent of all colleges and universities, HBCUs enroll just under one-fifth of all Black students and are responsible for educating approximately 30 percent of all Black bachelor's degree recipients (Allen & Jewell, 2002; Nettles & Perna, 1997). They have made significant contributions in educating Black students in the sciences, granting over 40 percent of bachelor's degrees in agriculture and natural resources, physical sciences, mathematics, and biological sciences (Hoffman et al., 1996). HBCUs are also known for fostering students' postgraduate aspirations, producing a disproportionately high number of Black students who complete graduate and professional degrees (Allen et al., 2007; Solórzano, 1995). In addition, some of the most prominent leaders in the African American community were educated at HBCUs. Impressive alumni include many famous academics, political leaders, scholars, writers, judges, and entertainers.

Research across many studies indicates that Black college attendance is significantly associated with students' cognitive development, baccalaureate attainment, and level of educational attainment (Pascarella & Terenzini, 2005). African American students who attend historically Black public universities reported more favorable relationships with professors, more support and concern for their welfare, better academic performance, greater social involvement, and higher occupational aspirations than Black undergraduates at predominantly White universities (Allen,1992; Nelson Laird, Bridges, Morelon-Quainoo, Williams, & Salinas Holmes, 2007). In contrast, Black students reported more concerns with the racial climate at predominantly White universities and a lack of integration. However, some of these climate issues may also be the result of impersonal environments and a lack of a student-centered focus at some predominantly White universities. Students reported favorable racial climates at predominantly White institutions where there was a high concern for students and their development, regardless of size or type of institution or the race or ethnicity of the student (Hurtado, 1992). Lessons learned from education at an HBCU suggest that a student-centered environment, high expectations for students, affirmation for racial or ethnic identity, and interactions with faculty make a positive environment for learning and student development (Hurtado, Milem, Clayton-Pederson, & Allen, 1999; Smith, 1989).

Hispanic-Serving Institutions

Few institutions have been established with the express purpose of responding to the educational needs of Hispanic/Latino students, including Hostos Community College and Boricua College (both located in New York); St. Augustine in Illinois, which offers bilingual higher education; and National Hispanic University in California. The majority of Hispanic-serving institutions (HSIs) began as predominantly White institutions located in regions that have experienced significant demographic growth in terms of Hispanic births and immigration over time. HSIs are defined primarily by enrollment: at least 25 percent of their full-time equivalent undergraduate student enrollment must be of Hispanic or Latino ethnicity (see the White House Initiative on Excellence in Education for Hispanic Americans, www.ed.gov/offices/OIIA/ Hispanic). The Higher Education Act also requires that HSIs be institutions where the student body is composed of at least 50 percent low-income students. Finally, to be distinguished as an HSI, an institution must file a five-year plan focused on addressing the needs of students from Hispanic or low-income backgrounds (Hurtado, 2006).

In 1992, Congress formally recognized the role of HSIs as minority-serving institutions, allowing campuses to become eligible for federal appropriations to support the educational progress of their Hispanic students. There are 268 institutions that meet the federal enrollment criteria to be defined as Hispanic-serving institutions. These campuses are located in twelve states and Puerto Rico and serve almost half of all Hispanic, full-time equivalent students in higher education (Hurtado, 2006). Many first-generation college students are of Hispanic origin, and HSIs enroll a large share of these students as well (Horn & Nunez, 2000). The majority of HSIs are public (68 percent) and are located near urban areas where large increases in the college-age, Hispanic/Latino population have occurred. Although there is much more variety among HSIs in terms of institutional type compared to tribal colleges, approximately 51 percent of the HSIs are two-year institutions that enroll large numbers of Hispanic students. Fourteen percent of HSIs offer bachelor's degrees, about 18 percent offer master's degrees, and 12 percent offer doctorates. It is important to note that there are over twice as many proprietary institutions (for-profit institutions with specialized academic programs) that have Hispanic enrollments over 25 percent, but these institutions are not officially recognized as HSIs.

In terms of student outcomes, a comparison of Latino students attending HSIs and PWIs revealed that student outcomes were surprisingly similar across institutional type. Students at both institutional types expressed similar levels of higher order thinking, satisfaction with college, and perceptions of a supportive campus environment. This trend may be linked to HSIs' relatively short history of serving Latino students. Many have not yet fully adopted this designation as a core part of their respective missions, and are in the midst of making the transition from being PWIs to their new focuses and goals as HSIs (Contreras, Malcom, & Bensimon, 2008; Hurtado, 2006). As HSIs engage in this process, it is important that they attend to the climate for diversity on campus. Climate is key to successful Latino student adjustment at four-year colleges, as is providing sensitive support staff and peer support (Hurtado, 1994; Hurtado, Carter, & Spuler, 1996). As HSIs and other institutions become more attuned to their growing Latino student populations, we are likely to learn more about factors that contribute to the success of these students in the future.

Asian American– and Pacific Islander–Serving Institutions

Frustrated with unequal education attainment and misunderstandings of Asian American students and their needs, there were several calls for more attention to the issues of these students throughout the late 1990s and early 2000s (Park & Teranishi, 2008). In response to assumptions of uniform success and a discrimination-free experience, Congressman Robert Underwood proposed an amendment to the Higher Education Act in 2002 to establish an institutional type much like HBCUs and HSIs that would meet the unique educational needs of Asian American and Pacific Islander (AAPI) students. The bill was reintroduced in different forms several times in subsequent years, refining the criteria for institutional designation as an Asian American Pacific Islander–serving institution (AAPISI) and detailing how funds administered should be used. Eligible institutions must have an AAPI enrollment of at least 10 percent, and have either half of their student bodies receiving financial aid or a proportion of Pell Grant recipients in the student body above the national median (Park & Teranishi, 2008).

In August 2008, the Asian American– and Pacific Islander–Serving Institution program became a component of the Higher Education Opportunity Act. Six institutions were designated AAPISIs, including four associate's colleges (City College of San Francisco, Foothill-De Anza Community College, Guam Community College, and Seattle Community College), one bachelor's college (University of Hawaii at Hilo), and one doctorate-granting institution (University of Maryland-College Park). The campuses were awarded a total of $10 million to develop programs and initiatives to meet the needs of Asian American and Pacific Islander students on their campuses, particularly those from low-income backgrounds. As these campuses institute their programs, it will be interesting to observe whether and how these institutions shape the access, experiences, and outcomes of the students who attend.

Institutions Serving Students Who Are Deaf and Blind

In addition to institutions serving students who are members of historically underrepresented, underserved, or marginalized ethnic minorities, there is also a well-known college established initially for deaf and blind students. Galludet University was established in 1817 as a for-profit college, and is now one of three nonprofit higher education institutions focused specifically on the education of deaf and hard-of-hearing students. Along with the National Technical Institute for the Deaf (part of the Rochester Institute of Technology) and the Southwest Collegiate Institute for the Deaf (a community college), it is one of the three nonprofit higher education institutions dedicated to the education of deaf students.

Reconsidering Diversity in American Higher Education

If a small group of strangers were asked to describe what an American college is like, it is likely that most would begin to describe a familiar archetype. They might start by describing old stately buildings and walls draped in ivy. They may paint a mental picture of students walking across a large, grassy quad from their residence halls to their classes, carrying their books and talking about what types of jobs they will get when they complete their four-year degrees. This is what we often see in the media, when television and movie executives depict their visions of what an American college should be. But not all postsecondary institutions fit into this depiction or are the same. Some campuses are larger than others, many students do not have opportunities (or the desire) to reside on campus, and a significant proportion of institutions offer two-year rather than four-year degrees. Campuses vary according to a wide array of characteristics, including size, selectivity, cost, location, governance structure, instructional delivery (in person versus virtual), and academic focus.

The diversity of American institutions and their international reputation for quality remain key advantages for the social and economic development of our society. The diversity in missions and functions among institutions in particular permits them as a group to target areas of specialization to advance knowledge in their unique ways, as well as join together in consortia to achieve common goals. Institutional diversity ensures stability in sustaining time-honored traditions at some institutions, which can simultaneously exist alongside the more "experimental" practices and policies at others. Despite fears of excessive "institutional imitation," with institutions tending toward incorporating research in their missions to increase prestige and quality assurances through the accreditation process, which can lead to uniformity of educational standards, it should be noted American colleges and universities continue to strive for unique identities that will attract students, faculty, and professionals.

We appreciate the diversity present in American postsecondary institutions and the uniqueness it lends to our system of higher education. As we applaud this heterogeneity, it is also important to acknowledge that it has real consequences, not only for students but also for the professionals who work on college campuses. Although there is often serious consideration of geographic location when choosing a position, the ways in which an institution fulfills its commitment to the primary functions of higher education often receive less attention. An institution's mission is easily found on most campus Web sites, and how a commitment to teaching, research, and service is embodied within that mission can provide insight into students' potential needs and experiences on a given campus. A college or university's mission can serve as a good indicator of what an institution does and does not value, and misalignment between individual and institutional values can certainly lend to frustration and disappointment as new professionals transition into their roles.

The U.S. Department of Education's Integrated Postsecondary Education Data System (IPEDS) and the Carnegie Foundation for the Advancement of Teaching provide helpful information on institutional mission, size, selectivity, resources, student demographics, and other important details for most community colleges and four-year institutions in America. Moreover, carefully examining mission statements, organizational charts, and other characteristics on college and university Web sites can also furnish instructive insights into the work environments new professionals will enter. But perhaps nothing is more revealing than actually visiting a campus and talking with students, faculty, academic affairs administrators, alumni, and of course colleagues who work in the student affairs division. As Hirt (2006) notes, thoughtfully considering an institution's culture, administrative norms and practices, and priorities can have profound effects on a student affairs professional's satisfaction and retention within that particular job, institution, or institution type. Thus it is important to employ as many strategies as possible to understand the full landscape of American higher education as well as the specific institutional environments one hopes to enter as an educator or administrator.

References

Allen, W. R. (1992). The color of success: African American college student outcomes at predominately White and historically Black public colleges and universities. *Harvard Educational Review, 62*(1), 26–44.

Allen, W. R., & Jewell, J. O. (2002). A backward glance forward: Past, present, and future perspectives on historically Black colleges and universities. *Review of Higher Education, 25*(3), 241–261.

Allen, W. R., Jewell, J. O., Griffin, K. A., & Wolf, D. (2007). Historically Black colleges and universities: Honoring the past, engaging the present, touching the future. *Journal of Negro Education, 76*(3), 263–280.

Altbach, P. G. (2001). The American academic model in comparative perspective. In P. G. Altbach, P. J. Gumport, & D. B. Johnstone (Eds.), *In defense of American higher education* (pp. 11–37). Baltimore, MD: Johns Hopkins University Press.

American Indian College Fund. (2006). About us. Retrieved January 19, 2009, from www .collegefund.org/about/main.html.

American Indian Higher Education Consortium (AIHEC). (1999). *Tribal colleges: An introduction.* Alexandria, VA: Author.

Astin, A. W. (1979). *Four critical years.* San Francisco: Jossey-Bass.

Astin, A. W. (1993). *What matters in college? Four critical years revisited.* San Francisco: Jossey-Bass.

Astin, A. W. (1995). *Achieving educational excellence.* San Francisco: Jossey-Bass.

Birnbaum, R. (1991). Value of different kinds of colleges. In J. L. Bless (Ed.), *Foundations of American higher education* (pp. 111–129). Needham Heights, MA: Simon & Schuster.

Bowen, H. R. (1997). *Investment in learning: The individual and social value of American higher education.* Baltimore, MD: Johns Hopkins University Press.

Boyer, P. (1997). *Native American colleges: Progress and prospects.* Princeton, NJ: Carnegie Foundation for the Advancement of Teaching.

Boyer Commission on Educating Undergraduates in the Research University. (1998). *Reinventing undergraduate education: A blueprint for America's research universities.* Stony Brook, NY: Carnegie Foundation for the Advancement of Teaching. (See also www.sunysb.edu/boyerreport)

Carnegie Foundation for the Advancement of Teaching (CFAT). (2001). *The Carnegie Classification of Institutions of Higher Education, 2000 edition: A technical report.* Menlo Park, CA: Author.

Carnegie Foundation for the Advancement of Teaching (CFAT). (2007). The Carnegie Classifications of Institutions of Higher Education. Retrieved January 15, 2009, from www .carnegiefoundation.org/classifications/index.asp.

Checkoway, B. (2001). Renewing the civic mission of the American research university. *Journal of Higher Education, 72*(2), 125–147.

Chickering, A., & Reisser, L. (1993). *Education and identity* (2nd ed.). San Francisco: Jossey-Bass.

Clark, B. R. (1983). *The higher education system: Academic organization in a cross-national perspective.* Berkeley, CA: University of California Press.

Contreras, F. E., Malcom, L. E., & Bensimon, E. M. (2008). An equity-based accountability framework for Hispanic serving institutions. In M. Gasman, B. Baez, & C. S. V. Turner (Eds), *Understanding minority-serving institutions* (pp. 71–90). Albany: State University of New York Press.

Dey, E. L., Milem, J. F., & Berger, J. B. (1997). Changing patterns of research productivity: Accumulative advantage or institutional isomorphism? *Sociology of Education, 70*(4), 308–323.

Dougherty, K. J. (2002). The evolving role of the community college: Policy issues and research questions. In J. C. Smart & W. Tierney (Eds.), *Higher education: Handbook of theory and research* (Vol. 17, pp. 295–348). Bronx, NY: Agathon Press.

Driscoll, A. (2008). Carnegie's community engagement classification: Intentions and insights. *Change, 40*(1), 38–41.

Fox, M.J.T., Lowe, S. C., & McClellan, G. S. (Eds.). (2005). *Serving Native American students* (New Directions for Student Services No. 109). San Francisco: Jossey-Bass.

Guentzel, M., & Elkins Nesheim, B. (Eds.). (2006). *Supporting graduate and professional students: The role of student affairs* (New Directions for Student Services No. 115). San Francisco: Jossey-Bass.

Guillory, J. P., & Ward, K. (2008). Tribal colleges and universities: Identity, invisibility, and current issues. In M. Gasman, B. Baez, & C. S. V. Turner (Eds.), *Understanding minority-serving institutions* (pp. 91–110). Albany: State University of New York Press.

Gumport, P. J. (1991). Built to serve: The enduring legacy of public higher education. In P. G. Altbach, P. J. Gumport, & D. B. Johnstone (Eds.), *In defense of American higher education* (pp. 85–109). Baltimore, MD: Johns Hopkins University Press.

Harwarth, I., Maline, M., & DeBra, E. (1997). *Women's colleges in the United States: History, issues, and challenges.* Washington, DC: U.S. Department of Education.

Hirt, J. B. (2006). *Where you work matters: Student affairs administration at different types of institutions.* Lanham, MD: University Press of America.

Hoffman, C. M., Snyder, T. D., & Sonnenberg, B. (1996). *Historically Black colleges and universities 1976–1994.* Washington, DC: National Center for Education Statistics.

Horn, L., & Nunez, A. M. (2000). *Mapping the road to college: First generation college students' math track, planning strategies and context of support* (Report No. 2000-153. Washington, DC: U.S. Department of Education.

Hurtado, S. (1992). The campus racial climate: Contexts of conflict. *Journal of Higher Education, 63*, 539–569.

Hurtado, S. (1994). The institutional climate for talented Latino students. *Research in Higher Education, 35*, 21–41.

Hurtado, S. (2006). *Realizing the potential of Hispanic-serving institutions.* Commissioned paper presented at the Hispanic Association of Colleges and Universities (HACU) Hispanic Higher Education Research Conference, San Antonio, TX.

Hurtado, S., & Carter, D. F. (1997). Effects of college transition and perceptions of campus racial climate on Latinos' sense of belonging. *Sociology of Education, 70*(4), 324–345.

Hurtado, S., Carter, D. F., & Spuler, M. (1996). Latino student transition to college: Assessing difficulties and factors in successful college adjustment. *Research in Higher Education, 37*(2), 135–157.

Hurtado, S., Milem, J. F., Clayton-Pederson, A., & Allen, W. (1999). *Enacting diverse learning environments: Improving the climate for racial/ethnic diversity in higher education* (ASHE-ERIC Report Series, Vol. 26, No. 8). San Francisco: Jossey-Bass.

Keohane, N. O. (Ed.). (2001). *The liberal arts and the role of elite higher education.* Baltimore: Johns Hopkins University Press.

Kerr, C. (2001). *The uses of the university* (5th ed.). Cambridge, MA: Harvard University Press.

Kinzie, J., Thomas, A. D., Palmer, M. M., Umbach, P. D., & Kuh, G. D. (2007). Women students at coeducational and women's colleges: How do their experiences compare? *Journal of College Student Development, 48*(2), 145–165.

Langdon, E. (1999). Who attends a women's college today and why she should: An exploration of women's college students and alumnae. In I. B. Harwarth (Ed.), *A closer look at women's colleges.* Washington, DC: U.S. Department of Education. (See also www.ed.gov/pubs/WomensColleges)

McCormick, A. C., & Zhao, C. (2005). Rethinking and reframing the Carnegie Classification, *Change, 37*(5), 51–57.

Nelson Laird, T. F., Bridges, B. K., Morelon-Quainoo, C. L., Williams, J. M., & Salinas Holmes, M. (2007). African American and Hispanic student engagement at minority serving and predominantly White institutions. *Journal of College Student Development, 48*(1), 39–56.

Nettles, M. T., & Perna, L. W. (1997). *The African American education data book: Vol. 1. Higher and Adult Education.* Fairfax, VA: Frederick D. Patterson Research Institute.

Park, J. J., & Teranishi, R. T. (2008). Asian American and Pacific Islander serving institutions. In M. Gasman, B. Baez, and C.S.V. Turner (Eds.), *Understanding minority-serving institutions* (pp. 111–126). Albany: State University of New York Press.

Pascarella, E. T., & Terenzini, P. T. (2005). *How college affects students: A third decade of research* (2nd ed.). San Francisco: Jossey-Bass.

Pascarella, E. T., Cruce, T. M., Wolniak, G. C., & Blaich, C. F. (2004). Do liberal arts colleges really foster good practices in undergraduate education? *Journal of College Student Development, 45*(1), 57–72.

Rudolph, F. (1965). *The American college and university: A history.* New York: Knopf.

Smith, D. G. (1989). *The challenge of diversity: Involvement or alienation in the academy?* (ASHE-ERIC Higher Education Report Series No. 5). Washington, DC: George Washington University School of Education and Human Development.

Solórzano, D. G. (1995). The doctorate production and baccalaureate origins of African Americans in the sciences and engineering. *Journal of Negro Education, 64*, 15–32.

Tidball, E. (1977). Women's colleges. In A. S. Knowles (Ed.), *The international encyclopedia of higher education* (p. 4395). San Francisco: Jossey-Bass.

Tidball, M. E. (1999). What is this thing called institutional productivity? In I. B. Harwarth (Ed.), *A closer look at women's colleges.* Washington, DC: U.S. Department of Education. (See also www .ed.gov/pubs/WomensColleges)

Tierney, W. G. (1992). *Official encouragement, institutional discouragement: Minorities in academe—the Native American experience.* Norwood, NJ: Ablex.

White House Initiative on Tribal Colleges and Universities. (1996). Retrieved July 16, 2002, from www.ed.gov/offices/OPE/TribalColleges/index.html.

Zusman, A. (1999). Issues facing higher education in the 21st century. In P. G. Altbach, R. O. Berdahl, & P. J. Gumport (Eds.), *American higher education in the twenty-first century: Social, political, and economic challenges* (pp. 109–148). Baltimore, MD: Johns Hopkins University Press.

CHAPTER THREE

CAMPUS CLIMATE AND DIVERSITY

Mitchell J. Chang, Jeffrey F. Milem,
and anthony lising antonio

Students are influenced in a number of ways by the colleges and universities they attend. Many of these influences, of course, are intentional and planned. Most colleges and universities, however, make little formal effort to shape student values, in spite of general agreement about the need for higher education to do so. But if colleges and universities do not typically organize themselves to shape attitudes and values, how are outcomes in this area produced? (Dey, 1997, p. 398)

The late Eric L. Dey spent much of his career studying the relationship between students and the college environment. This was especially important to him because he firmly believed that colleges and universities should do more than prepare students for the workforce; they should also prepare students to be good stewards of our nation's democratic principles and ideals. He rejected the view that students are simply resources or products, instead advocating an ecological perspective based on rigorous research, others' as well as his own. This perspective reconceptualizes the relationship between students and the college environment as both reciprocal and dynamic. Through a series of empirical studies (e.g., Dey & Hurtado, 1995; Hurtado, Dey, Gurin, & Gurin, 2003; Mayhew, Grunwald, & Dey, 2005), Dey and his colleagues demonstrated the impact of the dynamic interconnections between human and interpersonal environments on a range of student outcomes.

Dey's work proved to be essential for understanding the educational benefits associated with enrolling a diverse student body. He was recruited to serve on the University

Portions of this chapter were published with permission in 2005 as Making Diversity Work on Campus: A Research-Based Perspective by the Association of American Colleges and Universities (Milem, Chang, antonio).

of Michigan's expert social science research team shortly after the university decided to contest two lawsuits that challenged the use of affirmative action in admissions. The team's work resulted in an expert witness report submitted to the U.S. Supreme Court Expert Report of Patricia Gurin: *Gratz et al. v. Bollinger et al.*, No. 97–75321 [E.D. Mich.]; *Grutter et al. v. Bollinger et al.*, No. 97–75928 [E.D. Mich.]). The report, drawing from Dey's ecological perspective and other social psychological and educational research, offered a theoretical model that explained how a diverse student body within an institution can produce far-reaching educational benefits for all college students. The report, which also included extensive analytical work, contended that students in diverse educational environments learn more and are better prepared to become active participants in a pluralistic, democratic society when they leave higher education. The report was foundational in the Supreme Court's decision, which ruled that the educational benefits of diversity "are not theoretical but real" and that diversity is a compelling interest in higher education.

We begin with an emphasis on Dey's work not only as a tribute to him and his important contributions to diversity research but also to illustrate how as a community of scholars and practitioners we have come to understand better the ways to more effectively engage diverse student populations. For sure, he has deeply influenced our lives and our work in this area. The publications associated with the Michigan team's research are now seminal for understanding the educational value of diversity in the college environment (see, for example, Gurin, Dey, Gurin, & Hurtado, 2003; Gurin, Dey, Hurtado, & Gurin, 2002; Gurin, Lehman, & Lewis, 2004; Gurin, Nagda, & Lopez, 2004; Hurtado, Dey, Gurin, & Gurin, 2003). Even though the team members showed that higher education has a compelling interest to enroll a racially diverse student body, they also showed that the educational benefits associated with diversity are not assured, but conditional. In other words, student affairs professionals play significant roles and can either advance or undermine the impact of diversity on students. Because space constraints do not allow for an exhaustive review of related research, we will only highlight a few key insights in this chapter based largely on Dey's contributions.

The aim of this chapter leans more toward a broader conceptualization of diversity with an eye toward application as opposed to a description of contemporary shifts and detailed practices. Our goal here is not to furnish an overview of the current state of diversity in higher education, but instead to provide a conceptual understanding of the many key internal and external forces that potentially can facilitate or undermine efforts related to addressing students' learning and experiences in diverse educational settings. Thus we contend that for student affairs professionals, the importance of understanding student diversity rests in an understanding of the relationship between campus diversity and student outcomes. Based on this understanding, we offer some recommendations for engaging diversity on campus. Our overarching hope is that readers will better recognize that there are no easy solutions for serving a diverse student body effectively and reaching their diversity-related campus goals, in large part because there are many moving parts shaped by multiple forces that can affect the outcomes of even the best initiatives. However, we believe that by developing an empirically based, conceptual understanding of those key forces, student affairs educators will be better positioned to reach their desired goals.

Throughout the chapter we use the term *diversity* to refer to the broad range of differences (in gender, language fluency, sexual orientation, socioeconomic status, geographic origin, religion, ability, and so on) encountered on college campuses, even though most of our discussion draws from empirical research that tends to focus more specifically on racial diversity. Although we carefully considered this limitation in crafting the chapter, readers should still keep this in mind when considering our recommendations. Because we base our discussion largely on Dey's work, much of which did not focus exclusively on race, our discussion will have relevance for a fuller consideration of diversity beyond race.

Diversity in Higher Education: Dey's Legacy

When it comes to conceptually understanding the potential impact that student affairs professionals can have on students, one of the most important insights that Eric Dey's research illustrated is the tight interconnections between individual change, institutional change, and social change or what was referred to earlier as his ecological perspective. In his 1996 study, for example, Dey showed not only that undergraduate students' political orientations during college change in ways that align with general social trends but also that institutional contexts can conditionally influence those orientations by either reinforcing or buffering against larger social influences. In a subsequent study, Dey (1997) statistically modeled the influence of college peers on students' political orientations across distinct social and political eras to better assess the unique effects of institutional context and the larger social context. He found that students consistently are influenced by their campus peers, regardless of the social norms of the era in which they attend college. In other words, there is a tendency for students to change in the direction of institutional peer norms. At the same time, however, he also found that the larger social context had a significant effect on students above and beyond the influence of the campus. These findings suggest that it is important to examine both societal trends as well as the campus context when considering how students' college experiences might shape their attitudes and values. Dey contended: "Because the influences of general campus context and the larger social context operate independently, these contextual factors can work in concert with or in opposition to one another, depending upon institutional and historical circumstances" (1997, p. 410). Dey's ecological perspective is foundational for an effective approach to engaging a diverse campus. His perspective suggests that we start with a multidimensional framework for understanding the campus context.

A Campus Climate Framework

Diversity is most often considered in racial and ethnic dimensions, certainly due to the stark change from almost exclusively White campuses in the early twentieth century to the multicultural campuses of today. Although racial minorities historically have been denied access to higher education through policies and practices of colleges and universities as well as the K–12 education system (Harper, Patton, & Wooden, 2009; Weinberg, 1977; Yosso, Parker, Solórzano, & Lynn, 2004), representation in postsecondary institutions is now about 13 percent African American, 11 percent Latino/a, 6.7 percent Asian Pacific Islander, and 1 percent Native American (Snyder, Dillow, & Hoffman, 2009). Colleges and universities, however, increasingly recognize that a student body with a burgeoning range of attributes poses both challenges and opportunities to their educational objectives. More than ever, the current era requires the student affairs educator to consider the campus climate in every dimension of his or her work. Campus climate is centrally important as it encompasses the dynamics of diversity inherent in every student interaction. It provides an important conceptual context for understanding the ecological approach Dey advocated.

Dey's work empirically identified key forces that have an impact on students, and Hurtado, Milem, Clayton-Pedersen, and Allen (1998, 1999) advanced this ecological perspective more specifically to understanding campus diversity by turning their attention to campus constituents' attitudes, perceptions, and observations about the environment. In so doing, they focused on variations among campus constituents, especially with respect to racial differences. For example, when it comes to engaging with diversity, White students tend to view this as an opportunity to be exposed to different cultures, whereas African American students tend to view this as an opportunity to enhance their institution's capacity for inclusion. However, Hurtado et al. did not consider these differences as being necessarily in conflict with one another, and they maintained that individual attitudes and perceptions tend to be more malleable and, as a result, can be differentiated from the more stable institutional norms and beliefs that are used to characterize an organization's culture. The institutional culture, by comparison, can magnify group differences in ways that aggravate the racial climate and intensify racial antipathy. Also, in the framework offered by Hurtado et al. (1998, 1999), climate is not limited to perceptions and attitudes (what they term the "psychological climate"), but also includes the institution's structure and history as well as people's interactions across differences. Moreover, this framework assumes that students are educated in contexts that vary from campus to campus, and, similar to Dey's perspective, that variations in climate are shaped by a range of external and internal forces. Hurtado et al. (1998, 1999) identified four distinct dimensions in their campus climate framework, to which we recently added a fifth dimension to understanding the key forces that can shape the impact of campus diversity efforts (Milem, Chang, & antonio, 2005). We briefly review these dimensions below.

External Forces

Key external forces that shape campus climate include governmental policies, programs, and initiatives, as well as sociohistorical forces. Some governmental factors that influence the campus climate are financial aid policies and programs, state and federal policies regarding affirmative action, court decisions related to access and equity in higher education, and the manner in which states provide for institutional differentiation within public systems of higher education. Examples of sociohistorical forces that influence campus climate include events or issues in the larger society that relate to the ways in which people view or experience various forms of diversity. Although these forces occur "outside" of college campuses, they often serve as stimuli for discussions or other activities that occur on campus. The ongoing debate over same-sex marriage, for example, has had a noticeable impact on the climate for lesbian, gay, bisexual, and transgender (LGBT) persons on college and university campuses across the country. Likewise, our country's responses to the tragic events of 9/11 are sociohistorical forces that have had a profound effect on campus climate for Muslims and international students from the Middle East.

Internal Forces

As noted by Hurtado et al. (1998, 1999), external forces interact with internal forces to produce the climate for students on college and university campuses. To describe these internal forces, they highlight four dimensions that result from the educational programs and practices at an institution: (1) compositional diversity, (2) historical legacy of inclusion or exclusion, (3) psychological climate, and (4) behavioral climate. We would add a fifth dimension of climate—organizational/structural diversity— which was originally conceptualized by Milem, Dey, and White (2004).

Compositional Diversity. This dimension of diversity refers to the numerical and proportional representation of various student populations on a campus. Much of the recent research on campus climate and the educational outcomes of diversity describes this dimension of climate as *structural diversity*. However, Milem et al. (2004) recently argued that the term *compositional diversity* is a more accurate descriptor of the phenomenon that it represents. Milem and colleagues assert that using the term *structural diversity* to represent the numerical and proportional composition of the campus can result in confusion with another important dimension of campus climate that is absent from the framework as originally described by Hurtado et al. (1998, 1999). This "fifth dimension" of campus climate represents various organizational-structural aspects of the campus climate. Institutional programs and policies that increase the compositional diversity of a campus play an important symbolic role by communicating to interested internal and external constituents that diversity is a priority for the campus and its leaders. Hence, it is not surprising that Hurtado et al. (1998, 1999) argue that compositional diversity is the single dimension of the climate that most campus leaders think about when they consider creating programs and initiatives targeted at improving the climate. However, there is also a tendency for educators, institutional leaders, and policymakers to focus *only* on this dimension. In fact, a frequently claimed assertion is that a "critical mass" of people from different groups must be present if diversity is to work on our campuses. In forwarding the idea of a "critical mass," student affairs professionals and other campus officials must be prepared to respond to questions about how much diversity is enough to achieve desired educational benefits. Moreover, when the focus is solely or primarily on compositional diversity, there is a tendency to focus on diversity as an end in itself, rather than as an educational *process* that, when properly implemented, has the potential to produce many important educational outcomes.

Clearly, increasing the compositional diversity of a campus is an important first step in efforts to enhance these outcomes. However, this cannot be the only aspect of climate that student affairs educators address when planning and implementing campus diversity initiatives. Although diverse campuses provide important opportunities for teaching and learning that more homogeneous campuses do not offer, they also present significant challenges that must be addressed if the educational benefits of campus diversity are to be achieved. It is for this reason that student affairs educators and others must learn to think and act more multidimensionally about the learning that can be derived from campus diversity.

Historical Legacy of Inclusion or Exclusion. This dimension points to the historical vestiges of segregated schools and colleges, which continue to affect the climate for racial and ethnic diversity on college campuses (Hurtado et al., 1998, 1999). We find evidence of this in the resistance to desegregation in some communities and campus settings; in the maintenance of policies that benefit a homogeneous population (mostly White, Christian, heterosexual, and male); and in the prevalence of attitudes and behaviors that impede or prevent interactions across communities of difference. It is important to note that most predominantly White colleges and universities have a much longer history of exclusion than they do of inclusion, and that this history continues to shape group dynamics on our campuses. One byproduct of a history of exclusion is that, on many campuses, benefits sustained for particular groups go unrecognized and often work to the detriment of groups that have been historically excluded by the institution.

It is important for educators to be clear about any history of exclusion that has occurred on their campus, to talk about efforts over time to be more inclusive, and to address any persistent negative consequences of this history. If this dimension is properly addressed, we believe support is more likely to be garnered for diversity initiatives and other programs that are designed to improve the campus climate. Moreover, those who acknowledge their institution's history of exclusion demonstrate to internal and external constituents that the institution is willing to acknowledge its prior transgressions and is indeed making efforts to redress its exclusionary past.

Psychological Climate. Hurtado et al. (1998, 1999) describe the psychological dimension of campus climate as including views held by individuals about intergroup relations as well as institutional responses to diversity, perceptions of discrimination or conflict among groups, and attitudes held toward individuals from different backgrounds. We know from many studies of campus climate (i.e., Harper & Hurtado, 2007; Hurtado, 1992) that administrators, students, and faculty from different backgrounds are likely to view the campus climate in dramatically different ways. Hurtado et al. (1998, 1999) assert that who people are and where they are positioned in an institution affect the ways in which they experience and view the campus, its mission, and its climate. It is therefore critical that educators neither dismiss nor underestimate the significance of these perceptual differences. These perceptions are products of the environment, and they influence the decisions people make about their future interactions with others in the environment as well as the outcomes that result from these interactions (Astin, 1968; Berger & Milem, 1999; Milem & Berger, 1997; Tierney, 1987).

Behavioral Climate. The behavioral dimension of campus climate consists of the status of social interaction on the campus, the nature of interactions between and among individuals from different backgrounds, and the quality of intergroup relations (Hurtado et al., 1998, 1999). A commonly held view is that campus race relations are poor, and that segregation has increased on college campuses—usually as the result of students of color isolating themselves from the rest of the campus (antonio, 2004; Harper & Hurtado, 2007). However, the empirical research that examines student interactions reveals that students of color are much more likely than White students to report that they interact across racial and ethnic groups (Hurtado, Dey, & Treviño, 1994; antonio, 2001; Chang, Denson, Saenz, & Misa, 2006). In addition, research indicates that students from different racial and ethnic groups view same-group inter-actions differently. For example, Loo and Rolison (1986) found that White students viewed ethnic group clustering as an example of racial segregation or separation, whereas students of color viewed this clustering as a means for finding cultural support within a larger environment that they felt was unsupportive.

At the same time, the absence of contact across difference does affect students' views toward others, their support for campus diversity initiatives, and their development of key educational outcomes (Hurtado et al., 1998, 1999). Clearly, same-group and intergroup contact need not be mutually exclusive—what matters is the quality of interaction. Students who have the opportunity to engage with peers from different backgrounds in regular, structured interactions are more likely to show growth in a number of critical educational outcomes.

Organizational/Structural Diversity. Although Hurtado and colleagues argue that the historical legacy of exclusion at higher education institutions influences insti-tutional policies and practices, they do not fully elaborate on this important idea (Hurtado, 1992; Hurtado et al., 1998, 1999). We concur with the recent assertion of Milem et al. (2004) that there is a "fifth dimension" of climate that is necessary to consider and that can serve as an important source of influence in shaping the cam-pus climate. Specifically, this dimension represents ways in which benefits for some groups become embedded in institutional structures and organizational processes. The organizational-structural dimension of climate is reflected in the curriculum and campus activities; in decision-making practices related to budget allocations, admissions, staffing, and reward structures; and in other important structures and processes that guide the day-to-day "business" of our campuses. For example, recent research by Smith, Turner, Osei-Kofi, and Richards (2004) indicates that racially homogeneous search committees are not likely to hire candidates from different racial groups unless deliberate steps are taken to require the committees to seriously consider such candidates.

FIGURE 3.1.   CAMPUS CLIMATE FRAMEWORK.

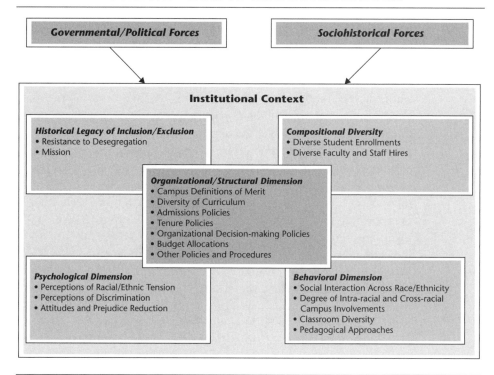

Source: Milem, Chang, & antonio (2005, p. 18).

Figure 3.1 summarizes the five dimensions that shape campus climate and affect the degree to which diversity efforts will confer educational benefits for students. These dimensions are interconnected, but at the same time each dimension is unique and must be intentionally addressed if the associated benefits are to be realized. To clarify how educators can address these dimensions, we highlight a set of promising practices in the next section.

Applying the Framework

In this section, we introduce a few guidelines as well as some practical recommendations for engaging diversity. We do this to illustrate how approaching diversity-related work based on a multidimensional framework, such as the one we proposed above, can lead to an intentional and coherent process of planning, developing, and implementing institutional policies and practices explicitly designed to help students attain the benefits that can be gained from attending a diverse college or university. Also, our ongoing discussion is informed by the most current available research, and we hope to strengthen the connection between academic scholarship on diversity and student affairs practice. The following discussion is not intended to serve as a plan or strategy for action, but instead to provide examples of some basic approaches and considerations to help student affairs professionals address diversity on campus in more comprehensive ways. We preface these recommendations with four general principles for practice:

1. *Take a multidimensional approach.* Specific policies may not be effective with all students in the same way. Therefore, it would be wise for educators to employ a multidimensional approach to diversity and anticipate that the effects of diversity policies may differ. For example, Duster (1992) found that at the University of California, Berkeley, White students preferred informal opportunities to engage diversity, whereas African Americans desired formal campus programs. Similarly, students of color benefit educationally from same-race interaction in ways that White students do not. The same is likely true for LGBT students and their interactions with nonheterosexual peers. Orchestrating multiple and varied initiatives is a central principle of strong diversity practices.

2. *Engage all students.* The benefits derived from diversity cannot be reserved for White students, residential students, students in certain majors, or the most actively engaged students on campus. All students should be considered when developing a multidimensional approach, so that everyone pursues cultural "border crossing." It is especially important that no single group of students—especially one that is in the minority on campus—be unintentionally burdened as "the diversity" with whom all others should interact.

3. *Focus on process.* Diversity is a means toward achieving important educational outcomes, not an end in itself. When educators view diversity as the end goal, they often fail to see the contextual dynamics that surround interactions among different groups, which can limit the effectiveness of certain practices. For example, diversity dialogues are counterproductive when the goal of mere participation outweighs the goals of developing empathy and understanding among participants. This can occur when well-intentioned institutions require dialogues but staff them with poorly trained facilitators.

4. *Doing diversity right requires difficult and sustained effort.* It is clear that engaging diversity to improve students' educational outcomes is an ever-changing and demanding process that must account for multiple facets of a campus community and employ a wide range of interventions. Not all campus interventions will be designed to reach all students; some may instead strategically focus on particular groups of students. Even broad interventions will benefit different groups of students in different ways. Campuses are dynamic communities; interventions and their corresponding outcomes are rarely stable—and thus engagement with diversity will likely remain a work in progress.

These four overarching principles should be kept in mind when creating policies and enacting practices that are intended to enhance the campus climate. Next, we present five areas related to our conceptual framework that serve as examples to help student affairs educators and campus leaders apply these principles of good practice.

Institutional History

An institution's historical legacy of inclusion and exclusion serves as the backdrop for the campus climate. Actively engaging students in the school's history—be it positive or negative—communicates to the campus community that local issues of discrimination, exclusion, and injustice are acknowledged and understood, and that current understandings benefit from historical context. Institutions can draw upon their histories to address campus climate in several ways. The University of Texas, for example, hosts an annual symposium on civil rights named for Heman Sweatt, an African American who was denied admission to its law school in 1946 on the basis of race and later gained admission following a Supreme Court ruling. Dartmouth's annual Pow-Wow marks both the institution's poor commitment to Native Americans early in its history as well as its more recent accomplishments. Some campuses also highlight moments of inclusion, such as the admission of the first gay and lesbian students, women, or Native Americans, in histories placed on their Web sites.

Encouraging and Fostering Cultural Border Crossing

Although the presence of visible clustering among students by race and gender on campus may not be directly related to institutional policy and practice, it does present a formidable barrier to cross-cultural interaction if left unaddressed. The relevant policy area for institutions here is research and dissemination. Careful monitoring of the campus climate through surveys; interviews; and systematic, ethnographic methods can generate valuable data on the actual extent of interaction across student groups and can indicate whether such behaviors are at odds with surface-level perceptions. Communication of these data through articles in the student newspaper and official statements can help dispel negatively perceived images of the campus climate and replace them with information more consistent with students' actual experiences.

A key finding across the research on diversity is that student-student interaction is essential for realizing the assorted educational benefits (Denson & Chang, 2009). The development of interracial and intercultural friendships is particularly important because friendship represents the interaction context that is most likely to be characterized by equal status between individuals. Many structural aspects of an institution can strongly influence this behavioral aspect of the campus climate. The setting for student interaction that a campus fosters, for example, creates a pool of peers for friendship selection, establishes the patterns and terms of contact among peers, and determines the types of friendship roles that are important within that setting (antonio, 2001). Consequently, the local environment in which a student most often interacts plays the critical role of determining the diversity of a student's potential friends.

Institutions need to recognize how different policies and practices create social structures that limit or broaden students' access to the full diversity of a campus community. On a diverse residential campus, for instance, residence halls are extremely important sites for the development of friendships with students from diverse backgrounds. In contrast, common barriers to broad interaction generally and interaction across difference specifically include exclusionary fraternity and sorority systems, off-campus work, and commuting (Chang & DeAngelo, 2002; Perna, 2010). Institutions with a student population of traditional age can minimize the impact of these barriers with policies focused on first-year students, because the first year is the period when friendship selection is the dominant aspect of a student's social life. Proximity is a strong determinant of friendship selection, and this proximity can influence interaction across difference.

Diversity as Policy

To improve campus climates for diversity, colleges and universities must have policies that govern their educational efforts. Ideally, the institution's commitment to diversity should permeate policy in all areas of campus life. A first step in signaling an institution-wide commitment to diversity is for educators and administrators (including the president and cabinet-level leaders) to issue statements of support, purpose, and action regarding the important role that diversity plays in the educational mission of the institution. These statements establish principles for diversity education, and in some cases they set forth goals for creating a welcoming and safe environment for interaction across groups and for diversifying the curriculum, faculty, and student body. A survey of these statements revealed that they are often linked to university mission statements that espouse commitments to democracy, social justice and educational opportunity, values regarding openness, tolerance and acceptance, or the centrality of diversity in achieving the learning outcomes of college (antonio & Clarke, forthcoming). Because these statements will provide an organizing framework for specific diversity programs and activities, it is crucial that they reflect all of these multiple missions. Omitting the social justice mission, for example, may render diversity commitments hollow with respect to access and equity goals. Statements of diversity provide philosophical direction for the development of initiatives that communicate to students in a tangible, unambiguous way that institutional commitment to diversity is strong, steady, and proactive. The campus community can also use these statements to hold their institutional leaders accountable for keeping their diversity-related promises.

Another particularly important area of institutional policy for diversity is the recruitment, retention, and promotion of a diverse faculty and staff. Faculty and staff serve as an institution's front-line representatives, and in the academic realm, faculty are also the embodiment of authority on campus. Students are painfully aware when there is discrepancy in diversity between the student body and the faculty and staff on their campus, and failure to actively and publicly pursue a more diverse faculty and staff sends a message of insincere commitment to diversity.

Retention and Student Support

A key responsibility for institutions is to keep diverse student populations enrolled and to help them reach levels of high academic achievement and accrue a wide array of educational outcomes that will be useful post-graduation. Underrepresented students typically have lower retention rates, and therefore campuses should develop and support programs shown to increase their retention and educational outcomes. These may include plans to identify inequities in educational outcomes by analyzing disaggregated data on student success indicators (e.g., GPA and major migration) and, further, to address those inequities by targeting their underlying causes through policy and practice. Also necessary are retention programs that offer tutoring, academic advising, and financial aid counseling; cultural centers that serve as physical homes and central gathering places for students, thus providing social anchors for those students most at risk of dropping out; and population-specific resources, organizations, and offices that provide opportunities for identity development, cross-cultural learning, and peer support. Of course, decisions to implement these approaches are subject to legal considerations at particular institutions and in particular states.

Creating a Culture of Evidence Regarding Diversity and Its Impact on Campus

Our final recommendation here is for student affairs educators to plan and implement an ongoing program of assessment that allows them to determine the impact that diversity has on important institutional and individual outcomes. However, based upon the work that we have done as scholars and as consultants to campus leaders, we are troubled by our observations of how little most campus leaders know about the impact that diversity has on their campuses—especially as it relates to the learning and developmental outcomes of their students. It is important that we focus our efforts on creating a culture of evidence regarding the important role that diversity plays on our college campuses.

In large part, the University of Michigan was able to successfully argue that diversity was a compelling interest because of the availability of empirical evidence that substantiated claims made regarding the important role of diversity on the campus. Our appraisal regarding the status of diversity assessments indicates that too few institutions are in the position to be able to do what Michigan did in support of its claims. Before engaging in these important assessment activities, student affairs educators must recognize that they will, in addition to learning about what their campus is doing well in regard to its diversity mission, learn about what their campus is not doing well. Such information can be used to make the changes necessary to achieve the desired educational outcomes.

The Diversity Agenda: Time for Sustained Action

To fully appreciate the concept of diversity and its educational potential in higher education, it is important to understand that achieving greater diversity on college campuses is a painstaking work in progress. Over the course of four decades, the concept of diversity and the diversity agenda have evolved to encompass a broad set of purposes, issues, identity groups, and initiatives on college campuses

(Chang 2002). The earliest initiatives to increase minority access to predominantly White campuses and later to enhance gender equity were prompted by desegregation mandates as well as social justice concerns grounded in democratic principles of equal opportunity and equality. Ongoing incidents of racial and ethnic hostility and the need for what Levine (1996) terms "a more eclectic, open, culturally diverse, and relevant curriculum" (p. 171) have become important concerns in a rapidly expanding diversity agenda. Such trends have not only centered on race and ethnicity but also encompassed other forms of difference (e.g., gender, class, sexual orientation, religion, and ability).

This oversimplified historical account makes clear several crucial points about campus diversity. First, the concept of diversity has evolved to now encompass a range of issues related to democratizing nearly every aspect of higher education. Second, the diversity agenda is closely linked to a broad and varied set of campus activities and initiatives. Third, diversity-related efforts are not limited to simply improving the proportional representation of students of color; they also seek to address multiple aspects of campus life and climate. Subsequently, this chapter attempts to provide student affairs professionals with a conceptual framework that they can apply toward their diversity-related work. We realize that our discussion lacks a level of specificity that can translate better to practice, but we also believe that those who are engaged with this work on their individual campuses are in the best position to specify the details of their particular initiatives. Although our goals for this chapter have been general and modest, however, we hope that it will at the very least convince practitioners to pursue their work in a broader context, thereby increasing the probability that their efforts will have a positive and sustained long-term effect.

Over the past two decades, a large body of scholarly work on diversity has illustrated the empirical connections between diversity and educational outcomes (Milem, 2003). Although this work has helped to establish the legitimacy of diversity as a central value in higher education, the scholarship has provided little concrete direction for achieving institutional change (Clarke & antonio, 2009). We have become increasingly concerned that the notion of diversity is turning into simply a fashionable slogan in higher education, whereby those who celebrate its educational benefits divorce the notion from any effort to transform institutions by first remedying the present effects of past discrimination.

Chang, Chang, and Ledesma (2005) argued that when diversity is decoupled from those interests advanced by the modern civil rights movement, the educational benefits associated with diversity are expected to accrue as if by magic. They employed the term "magical thinking" to describe the shortcomings associated with promoting diversity without coupling it with efforts to address systematic discrimination and exclusion on college campuses. An "education-only" rationale, they argued, fails to acknowledge the fact that a campus's capacity to remedy the present effects of past discrimination is instrumental in maximizing the educational benefits associated with a diverse student body. Failure to intervene at the basic, remedial level not only reduces the chances of realizing the benefits associated with a diverse student population but also can fuel alienation, antipathy, higher rates of departure, and students' dissatisfaction with their overall college experience.

When it comes to shaping students' attitudes and values, Eric Dey claimed that a campus can work either in concert with or in opposition to social trends. However, as he also noted, campuses seem to make no formal effort to do this. We agree with Harper and antonio (2008) that a passive approach to engaging diversity (in other words, a lack of intentionality) can be counterproductive and, indeed, educationally negligent. Given the dramatic demographic shifts of the last decade, we cannot afford to squander this opportunity, thereby underpreparing graduates to engage in a society that is becoming increasingly more diverse. To do so would fail our students and the democratic principles that most institutions of higher education so strongly espouse. Hence student affairs educators and administrators cannot simply sit on the sidelines and cheer for diversity as if its associated educational benefits are going to accrue magically. Instead, these colleagues must work to intentionally and systematically enact and assess diversity on our college campuses.

References

antonio, a. l. (2001). Diversity and the influence of friendship groups in college. *Review of Higher Education, 25*(1), 63–89.

antonio, a. l. (2004). When does race matter in college friendships? Exploring men's diverse and homogeneous friendship groups. *Review of Higher Education, 27*(4), 553–575.

antonio, a.l., & Clarke, C. G. (forthcoming). Equity or ideas? The official organization of diversity in American higher education. In L. M. Stulberg and S. L. Weinberg (Eds.), *Critical Issues in Diversity in Higher Education.* New York: Routledge.

Astin, A. W. (1968). *The college environment.* Washington, DC: American Council on Education.

Berger, J. B., & Milem, J. F. (1999). The role of student involvement and perceptions of integration in a causal model of student persistence. *Research in Higher Education, 40*(6), 641–664.

Chang, M. J. (2002). Preservation or transformation: Where's the real educational discourse on diversity? *Review of Higher Education, 25*(2), 125–140.

Chang, M. J., Chang, J., & Ledesma, M. C. (2005). Beyond magical thinking: Doing the real work of diversifying our institutions. *About Campus, 10*(2), 9–16.

Chang, M. J., & DeAngelo, L. (2002). Going Greek: The effects of racial composition on white students' participation patterns. *Journal of College Student Development, 43*(6), 809–823.

Chang, M. J., Denson, N., Saenz, V., & Misa, K. (2006). The educational benefits of sustaining cross-racial interaction among undergraduates. *Journal of Higher Education, 77*(3), 430–455.

Clarke, C., & antonio, a.l. (2009, November). *Re-thinking research on the impact of racial diversity in higher education.* Paper presented at the meeting of the Association for the Study of Higher Education, Vancouver, Canada.

Denson, N., & Chang, M. J. (2009). Racial diversity matters: The impact of diversity-related student engagement and institutional context. *American Educational Research Journal, 46*(2), 322–353.

Dey, E. L. (1996). Undergraduate political attitudes: An examination of peer, faculty, and social influences. *Research in Higher Education 37*(5), 535–554.

Dey, E. L. (1997). Undergraduate political attitudes: Peer influence in changing social contexts. *Journal of Higher Education, 68*(4), 398–413.

Dey, E. L., & Hurtado, S. (1995). College impact, student impact: A reconsideration of the role of students within American higher education. *Higher Education, 30,* 207–223.

Duster, T. (1992). *The Diversity Project: Final report.* Berkeley: University of California, Institute for the Study of Social Change.

Gratz v. Bollinger, 123 S. Ct. 2411 (2003).

Grutter v. Bollinger, 123 S. Ct. 2325 (2003).

Gurin, P., Dey, E. L., Gurin, G., & Hurtado, S. (2003). How does diversity promote education? Western Journal of Black Studies, 27(1), 20–29.

Gurin, P., Dey, E. L., Hurtado, S., & Gurin, G. (2002). Diversity and higher education: Theory and impact on educational outcomes. *Harvard Educational Review, 72(3),* 330–366.

Gurin, P., Lehman, J. S., & Lewis, E. (2004). *Defending diversity: Affirmative action at the University of Michigan.* Ann Arbor: University of Michigan Press.

Gurin, P., Nagda, B. A., & Lopez, G. (2004). The benefits of diversity in education for democratic citizenship. *Journal of Social Issues, 60*(1), 17–34.

Harper, S. R., & antonio, a. l. (2008). Not by accident: Intentionality in diversity, learning, and engagement. In S. R. Harper (Ed.), *Creating inclusive campus environments for cross-cultural learning and student engagement* (pp. 1–18). Washington, DC: National Association of Student Personnel Administrators.

Harper, S. R., & Hurtado, S. (2007). Nine themes in campus racial climates and implications for institutional transformation. In S. R. Harper & L. D. Patton (Eds.), *Responding to the realities of race on campus* (New Directions for Student Services No. 120, pp. 7–24). San Francisco: Jossey-Bass.

Harper, S. R., Patton, L. D., & Wooden, O. S. (2009). Access and equity for African American students in higher education: A critical race historical analysis of policy efforts. *Journal of Higher Education, 80*(4), 389–414.

Hurtado, S. (1992). The campus racial climate: Contexts for conflict. *Journal of Higher Education, 63*(5), 539–569.

Hurtado, S., Dey, E. L., Gurin, P., & Gurin, G. (2003). College environments, diversity, and student learning. In J. C. Smart (Ed.), *Higher education: Handbook of theory and research* (Vol. 18, pp. 145–190). UK: Kluwer Academic.

Hurtado, S., Dey, E. L, & Treviño, J. (1994, April). *Exclusion or self-segregation? Interaction across racial/ethnic groups on college campuses.* Paper presented at the meeting of the American Educational Research Association, New Orleans, LA.

Hurtado, S., Milem, J. F., Clayton-Pedersen, A., & Allen, W. R. (1998). Enhancing campus climates for racial/ethnic diversity through educational policy and practice. *Review of Higher Education, 21*(3), 279–302.

Hurtado, S., Milem, J. F., Clayton-Pedersen, A., & Allen, W. R. (1999). *Enacting diverse learning environments: Improving the campus climate for racial/ethnic diversity in higher education* (ASHE-ERIC Higher Education Report, Vol. 26, No. 8). San Francisco: Jossey-Bass.

Levine, L. W. (1996). *The opening of the American mind.* Boston: Beacon.

Loo, C. M., & Rolison, G. (1986). Alienation of ethnic minority students at a predominately white university. *Journal of Higher Education, 57*(1), 58–77.

Mayhew, M. J., Grunwald, H. E., & Dey, E. L. (2005). Curriculum matters: Creating a positive climate for diversity from the student perspective. *Research in Higher Education, 46*(4), 389–412.

Milem, J. F. (2003). The educational benefits of diversity: Evidence from multiple sectors. In M. J. Chang, D. Witt, J. Jones, & K. Hakuta (Eds.), *Compelling Interest: Examining the Evidence on Racial Dynamics in Colleges and Universities.* Stanford, CA: Stanford University Press.

Milem, J. F., & Berger, J. B. (1997). A modified model of college student persistence: The relationship between Astin's theory of involvement and Tinto's theory of student departure. *Journal of College Student Development, 38*(4), 387–400.

Milem, J. F., Chang, M. J., & antonio, a. l. (2005). *Making diversity work on campus: A research-based perspective.* Washington DC: Association of American Colleges and Universities.

Milem, J. F., Dey, E. L., & White, C. B. (2004). Diversity considerations in health professions education. In B. D. Smedley, A. S. Butler, & L. R. Bristow (Eds.), *In the nation's compelling interest: Ensuring diversity in the health care workforce* (pp. 345–390). Washington, DC: National Academies Press.

Perna, L. W. (Ed.). (2010). *Understanding the working college student: New research and its implications for policy and practice.* Sterling, VA: Stylus.

Smith, D. G., Turner, C. S., Osei-Kofi, N., &, Richards, S. (2004). Interrupting the usual: Successful strategies for hiring diverse faculty. *Journal of Higher Education, 75*(2), 133–160.

Snyder, T. D., Dillow, S. A., & Hoffman, C. M. (2009). *Digest of Education Statistics 2008* (NCES 2009-020). National Center for Education Statistics, Institute of Education Sciences, U.S. Department of Education. Washington, DC.

Tierney, W. G. (1987). Facts and constructs: Defining reality in higher education organizations. *Review of Higher Education, 11*(1), 61–73.

Weinberg, M. (1977). *Minority students: A research appraisal.* Washington, DC: Government Printing Office.

Yosso, T. J., Parker, L., Solórzano, D. G., & Lynn, M. (2004). From Jim Crow to affirmative action and back again: A critical race discussion of racialized rationales and access to higher education. *Review of Research in Education, 28*(1), 1–25.

PART TWO

PROFESSIONAL FOUNDATIONS AND PRINCIPLES

In Part One our authors provided the historical context for higher education in the United States, and then discussed diversity from two perspectives: the diversity of our students and of our institutions. Clearly, over time our enrollments have increased and the number of institutions in the United States has grown. For example, in 1979–1980, around the time the first Green Book was released, total fall enrollment was 11,538,899 in 3,152 degree-granting institutions. By 2006–2007, the most current data available at the time of this writing, enrollment had grown to 17,758,870 in 4,314 institutions. Another way to look at this growth is to note that enrollment grew by approximately 53 percent, and the number of institutions grew by nearly 37 percent in a period of fewer than thirty years. Although it is true that the growth of the post–World War II era has been characterized as extraordinary, higher education as an enterprise has continued to grow and diversify. And this time period is not unique. For every decade beginning with 1869–1970 enrollment has grown. Within this period of constant growth, student affairs practice has evolved and developed.

Part Two examines the foundations and principles of student affairs practice. Four elements are examined in this section: the development of the profession, the philosophy and values of the profession, ethical principles and standards, and legal issues. Each of these topics could easily fill a volume on its own. Accordingly, the treatments of these topics are only cursory here. Our hope is that the reader's interest will be piqued such that you review additional readings to explore the topics in greater depth.

In Chapter Four, Gwen Dungy and Stephanie Gordon provide a historical look at the development and evolution of student affairs practice. The practice of student affairs has evolved from an *in loco parentis* oversight of students' lives to complex, sophisticated work undergirded by theories of student growth and learning as well as by organizational and leadership theory. They also trace the development of professional associations and the contemporary emphasis on outcomes assessment. They posit that student affairs practice will continue to be influenced by change, and that one of the challenges to practitioners is to anticipate and respond to both internal and external change in higher education.

Bob Reason and Ellen Broido explore the philosophies and values that undergird student affairs practice in Chapter Five. Among the issues they address is the matter of whether or not student affairs has a guiding philosophy. They provide a framework to understand philosophies and then address the philosophical legacy of student affairs. They then move on to the enduring principles and values of the profession, concluding with a discussion of the student development and student learning movements.

In Chapter Six, Jane Fried discusses ethical standards. She provides a description of Eurocentric beliefs regarding ethics and reminds us that we have multiple ethical obligations in our practice. She notes the ethical codes of our professional organizations as well as ethical principles and virtues. Jane also identifies and discusses ethical themes and fundamental principles, and concludes with cases for analysis.

Part Two concludes with Gary Pavela's examination of three selected legal issues in Chapter Seven. The law of higher education in general and student affairs in particular is very complex. Accordingly, Gary has chosen to address three important, contemporary issues: protecting and promoting civility, working with troubled students, and risk management. The reader is cautioned to seek professional counsel when legal issues arise and is reminded that the legal environment is ever changing. Consequently, what might serve as sound legal advice one day may be poor advice the next.

These chapters—the development of student affairs as a profession and its philosophical, ethical, and legal foundations—remind the reader of the complexity of student affairs practice, and they also position the reader for a series of chapters related to how students learn and grow. One set of chapters sets the stage for the next, and we trust that this set of chapters positions the reader well for the discussion of theory that follows.

CHAPTER FOUR

THE DEVELOPMENT OF STUDENT AFFAIRS

Gwendolyn Dungy and Stephanie A. Gordon

This chapter provides an overview of the development of student affairs, from its early roots to the establishment of such positions as deans of women, deans of men, and personnel workers. It addresses the professionalization of the discipline and the profession's current focus on student learning, student success, and institutional accountability. Professionals in student affairs take into consideration a student's academic learning and healthy maturation—in other words, the whole student. A strength of student affairs professionals is their anticipation of the environment's impact on students and their ability to address students' academic and personal needs. A hallmark of student affairs is to anticipate the winds of change and the impact they may have on student success.

Founding and Early Years: 1636–1850

The challenges student affairs educators experience today—for example, students' activism against institutional policies, alcohol abuse, mental health needs—were present in the colonial colleges and throughout higher education. Student affairs professionals in various incarnations have been addressing these issues since Harvard College was founded "to advance learning and perpetuate it to prosperity" (New England's First Fruits, 1998). In the early years of higher education, college faculty, tutors, and presidents were not only charged with achieving the academic mission of their colleges but also expected to manage the seemingly inconsequential at the time social, athletic, and co-curricular lives of students.

We acknowledge the research assistance of Keith B. O'Neill, Bowling Green State University.

The college president, faculty, and tutors strictly ruled students' lives with heavy institutional regulations. Students had very structured daily activities, which included required meetings, chapel services each morning, and evening study hours. Colonial college presidents and faculty were empowered to act *in loco parentis*. Although increasing academic rigor and students' successful graduation into public service were the college's primary goals, the college also ensured that the social, moral, and intellectual aspects of a student's life were in line with the Christian faith of the community. During the Federal Period, roughly 1780-1820, college staff's administration of the dormitories, monitoring of the welfare of enrolled individuals, and disciplining of the students were the fundamental beginnings of the student affairs profession of today (Leonard, 1956).

By the mid-1700s and early 1800s, college environments shifted due to changes in American society, the religious environment and the Great Awakening, and the aftermath of war in the colonial states. Seven of the nine established colleges were taken over and physically disrupted by the Revolutionary War. The faculty, presidents, and tutors had little control over their institutions and even less over the actions of the small number of students who remained enrolled. Students began to use graduation as a forum and organized into various groups on campus—those supporting the war and those who were loyalists to the British government. The dilemma of church versus state and reconciling the traditional, elitist university life with the increasingly egalitarian public also took a toll on the social environment on campus (Lucas, 1994).

In addition to divisions within student populations, students also began to have more organized conflict with the administration (Lucas, 1994). Students often disciplined themselves based on student organization rules and regulations, although the charters of the individual colleges and universities still governed the major discipline issues. The changes in discipline included a focus on morality, rather than just conduct (Leonard, 1956). Tensions between church and state, old curriculum and practical curriculum, pious students and nonreligious students, and students and administration began to erode the established authoritarian system.

The earliest organized student groups were literary and debating societies, which focused on the academic pursuits of the undergraduate students (Harding, 1971). Fraternity and secret society organizations began in 1825 with Kappa Alpha at Union College (although Phi Beta Kappa was founded in 1776), and by 1850 many New England colleges and midwestern state colleges had fraternal organizations. Unlike literary societies, these were small, self-selected groups of men who pledged their loyalty, secrecy, and support of their hierarchical organizations. A number of college presidents tried to ban fraternities because they had little control over such organizations. The bans did not work, however, because loyal students refused to divulge who the members of the secret societies were (Lucas, 1994). As higher education was pressed to implement reforms, reform was pressed upon higher education, presidents and faculty evaluated their focus as it related to the student experience. With the founding of fraternal organizations, individuals in college and university administration began to realize that there was more to campus life than the academic classroom. However, there was no significant movement to appoint administrators to assist students with their co-curricular activities.

Diversification: 1850–1900

As American higher education matured, classical colleges were reformed into liberal arts colleges, land-grant institutions, women's colleges, technical institutes, and research universities. The expanding roles of the faculty and the growing demands on the time of university presidents created a need for student personnel administrators to take responsibility for student welfare, discipline, housing, and activities (Leonard, 1956; Nuss, 2003; Rudolph, 1965).

With the passage of the Morrill Act of 1862, the government gave states federal land and funds to support programs in agricultural sciences, what is today known as engineering, and military officer training, and emphasized the practical benefits of knowledge. There were several Morrill Acts, but the 1862 act began the trend of providing education at the public's expense and helped to begin the modern concept of equal access (Nuss, 2003). The second Morrill Act of 1890 provided regular appropriations to land-grant colleges. States with racially segregated education only received money if they provided the same education to Black students as they did to Whites. The creation of land-grant institutions accelerated a new form of education and access to individuals; also, educators began to articulate an ideology that public education would create engaged citizens, provide social mobility, and foster students' commitment to democracy and service.

As colleges and universities began to diversify, so too did the need to employ educators who would handle student unrest, discipline issues, housing administration, and other duties that the college president and the faculty could not. President Charles Eliot of Harvard appointed the first student dean of higher education in 1870, Professor Ephraim Gurney, who in addition to his teaching performed such administrative functions as maintaining student records and managing registration. Although Gurney was primarily an academic dean, Eliot created this role in order to release him (Eliot) from his responsibilities as disciplinarian (Garland, 1985; Nuss, 2003; Stewart, 1985).

Although it is unclear when the first dean of men was appointed, W. H. Cowley postulated that that the first dean of men was LeBarron Russell Briggs of Harvard, who assumed this position in 1890 (Cowley, 1940). The deans of men were charged with the development of students, which included attending to students' indiscretions. The dean of men's position evolved from simply focusing on student discipline to handling student life as it changed with the social and political nature of the surrounding environment (Rhatigan, 1978; Secretarial Notes, 1929). With the increase of women in higher education during this period, there were additional needs within college environments to address the health and welfare of female students, including their housing and boarding needs (Geiger, 2000; Leonard, 1956; Nidiffer, 2001; Nuss, 2003; Rudolph, 1965). The University of Chicago is considered the first institution to use the title of Dean of Women, which was given to Alice Freeman Palmer in 1892, although Marion Talbot performed most of the duties of the dean of women because Palmer traveled often (Fley, 1979; Horowitz, 1987). Talbot eventually founded the Association of Collegiate Alumnae (ACA), which was the predecessor to the American Association of University Women (AAUW) (Isaac, 2007).

Modern Developments: 1900–1950

By the early twentieth century, student life had evolved into more than just receiving classroom teaching and improving oratory skills. Students had a wide array of potential experiences, in and outside of the classroom. The concepts of educating the whole student and of establishing the connection between the curriculum and extracurricular activities provided the basis for the student personnel movement (Brubacher & Rudy, 1976; Nuss, 2003). The basis or foundation of the profession was the original concept of higher education concerned with the development of the individual to be a well-rounded, balanced citizen who had a foundation in education and social and moral convictions. This concept was prominent in early-twentieth-century roles of the deans of men and women. Thomas Arkle Clark, for example, was an influential dean of men who assumed his role at the University of Illinois in 1909. Clark was well regarded as an expert in student life and the challenges that college men face. He assumed that positive character development was a natural part of higher learning (Fley, 1979). An example of character development was the implementation of honor systems. By 1915 there were at least 123 colleges and universities that had implemented an honor code or system. (Nuss, 2003) It was also at this time that many of the student affairs practices in place today became more widespread, with funded, regulated student activities and a point system for participation, minimum grade point averages in order to participate, and the establishment of a student government association structure (Nuss, 2003; Williamson, 1961).

There were differences, however, between the roles of a dean of men and a dean of women. The challenges that the early deans of women experienced were often related to how women were treated in society and the understanding that many women who attended universities were either preparing for teaching or learning how to be good wives for their educated men. Some presidents who appointed deans of women immediately gave these individuals administrative and disciplinary functions that were unlike the counseling and advising functions of deans of men (Mueller, 1961). There were boarding houses for women early on, despite a widespread sentiment that women were not able to adapt to and assimilate the higher education environment. Oberlin and Antioch colleges were first to employ female chaperones to protect the students from the "dangers" of male students (Nidiffer & Bashaw, 2001, p. 136). Positions and responsibilities of the early deans of women varied from campus to campus (Bashaw 1992; Nuss, 2003). In 1928, Anna Eloise Pierce, dean of women at the New York State College for Teachers in Albany, provided a list of over one hundred activities for which the dean of women position holder would be responsible. The dean of women was to provide guidance on vocational preparation, educate students on moral and religious issues, chaperone and provide discipline, and act as a mother away from home for the women on campus. Lulu Haskell Holmes (1939) put it best when she wrote, "The 'whole life' of the women students is still the primary concern for of the Dean of Women and her assistants; the coordination of all the interests and activities of the women students into a balanced system of living for the college years continues to be their chief task" (p.133).

As the co-curricular life of students became more complex, the dean of men and dean of women positions soon became dual roles of managing the administration of the multiple services available on the college campus while simultaneously focusing on the overall development of students. Due to the breadth of student life services on a college campus, the dean became one of the more influential positions on campus, and anyone who assumed the role began to shape the foundation of the student affairs profession.

Student Personnel Point of View

The 1937 *Student Personnel Point of View (SPPV)* was a report from a conference held under the auspices of the American Council on Education (ACE), (1994). This report would serve as a guide not only for understanding the nature and extent of student personnel work but also to future developments in a field that was changing rapidly. Upon approval of the 1937 report, the ACE established a Committee on Student Personnel Work to continue to examine specific practices in accomplishing the goals of higher education. These practices would be embedded in a total education program with a focus on the whole student, and committee members encouraged institutions to give equal emphasis to the development of the person and the development of the mind. In addition to a set of desired developmental outcomes for students, ranging from forming ethical values to choosing a vocation, what became the 1949 *SPPV* drew attention to the development of the student in the context of the student's relationship with society. The 1949 *SPPV* was prescient in its attention to the college's "urgent responsibility for providing experiences which develop in its students a firm and enlightened belief in democracy, a matured understanding of its problems and methods, and a deep responsibility for individual and collective action to achieve its goals" (Williamson, 1949, p. 20). Following World War II, the 1949 *SPPV* advocated for broader educational goals, which included democracy, international understanding, and using higher education to solve social problems.

Student affairs professionals today strive to achieve similar goals. In order to achieve the balance among developmental, ethical, and career preparation skills in the context of a student's relationship to society, that professionals must assume responsibility for their knowledge and conduct, be open to change in the application of skills and knowledge, adopt a spirit of experimentation, and evaluate programs against standards of excellence (Creamer, 1988).

Professional Associations

Some assert that the variety of associations serving the professional development needs of student affairs are the profession's strength and weakness. Whereas some professions can tie all of their roles and functions clearly and directly to a single, narrow focus, the breadth of the work encompassed by student affairs makes this cohesion difficult. The diverse roles and functions of the student affairs profession have led to the creation of a number of specialized associations that address specific skill needs of increasingly specialized workers. Sandeen and Barr (2006) write about the "proliferation of student affairs associations, each claiming to represent a special constituency or agenda in the field," which has made it "very difficult for student affairs to speak with an effective voice in higher education" (p. 190).

After the turn of the twentieth century, professionals in student affairs began to organize: for example, the Association of College Unions International (ACUI), established in 1910; the American Association of Collegiate Registrars and Admissions Officers (AACRAO), established in 1910; and the National Association of Deans of Women (NADW), organized from the American Association of University Women (AAUW) in 1916. NADW became the National Association of Women Deans and Counselors (NAWDC) in 1956; in 1973, NAWDC became the National Association of Women Deans, Administrators, and Counselors (NAWDAC); and in 1991, NAWDAC became the National Association of Women in Education (NAWE). The American College Health Association (ACHA) was established in 1920; and the National Orientation Directors Association (NODA) was established in 1937 (Cowley, 1937/1994; Nuss, 2003). There are a number of additional student affairs associations that were also founded in the early to mid-twentieth century, including those for housing, student activities, student conduct, counseling, and academic advising. As with many other professions in the United States, organizing associations around commonalities provided venues for discussion, research, and professional development.

The two generalist associations in student affairs are the American College Personnel Association (ACPA) and the National Association of Student Personnel Administrators (NASPA). What has become NASPA was created at a conference of deans and advisors of men in 1919. The first name of the association was the National Association of Deans and Advisers of Men (NADAM). In 1951, it adopted its current name. NASPA has been the association for administrators who see their roles broadly, for the most part, in being part of college or university leadership teams. NASPA's members hold every description and level of position in student affairs. Group membership provides an opportunity for interdisciplinary learning and networking (Nuss, 2003).

ACPA, which has become ACPA-College Student Educators International, was founded in 1924 and adopted its name in 1931 (Bloland, 1983; Johnson, 1985; Sheeley, 1983; Nuss, 2003). ACPA began as the National Association of Appointment Secretaries (NAAS) in 1924, and changed its name to the National Association of Placement and Personnel Officers (NAPPO) in 1929. It was instrumental in the formation of the American Personnel and Guidance Association (APGA) in 1952, and withdrew its affiliation with APGA in 1991 in order to establish ACPA as a separate association in 1992. ACPA, like NASPA, attracts professionals from every student affairs discipline (Nuss, 2003).

Professional associations for student affairs were founded during a time of strict racial segregation in the U.S., and some were slow to give women a voice in the associations. Of particular note are the efforts made by certain African Americans in student affairs who created a professional association because of segregation. Accepting the tenets of the *Student Personnel Point of View*, deans and advisors at historically Black colleges and universities merged two organizations separated by gender, the National Association of Deans of Women and Advisors of Girls in Colored Schools (DOWA), founded in 1929, and the National Association of Personnel Deans of Men in Negro Educational Institutions (DOMA), founded in 1935, in order to form the National Association of Personnel Workers (NAPW) in 1954. Today, the association born from this merger is known as the National Association of Student Affairs Professionals (NASAP) (L. W. Watson, personal communication, April 7, 2009).

For African Americans forced to form their own professional association because of segregation, NASAP served a need both to focus on problems of Black students and to assist in the smooth transition from a segregated society to the current higher education environment. Ironically, during the first years of desegregation, NASAP had to defend its existence. Despite gains in integration, members of NASAP saw a continuing need to help Black students confront problems that related directly to their cultural, economic, and social backgrounds (L. W. Watson, personal communication, April 7, 2009). NASAP continues as a professional association for student affairs professionals in historically Black institutions; however, the association has strong, collaborative ties with both NASPA and ACPA, and most members of NASAP belong to and have prominent leadership roles in other professional associations for student affairs.

Expanding Student Life: 1950–1970

The student affairs profession grew dramatically during the post–World War II period, in concert with rapid growth in enrollments at institutions of higher education. Increasing specialization among student affairs professionals marked this time period.

Student Development Concepts and Theories

Student development concepts and theories have influenced change in the practice of student personnel work. Common among them is the foundational perspective of supporting a comprehensive education that includes attention to both students' cognitive acquisition of knowledge and their development and maturation.

In Loco Parentis. During the early years of the profession, student personnel workers were seen as the caretakers who looked after the welfare needs of students. They were expected to serve in place of the parents, ensuring that students adhered to rules that would continue their development and encourage behaviors and values appropriate for a college-educated individual.

Student Services/Personnel. As the number of students attending colleges and universities increased, and as students brought an increasing variety of needs that did not fall within the purview of classroom faculty, student services or student personnel staff provided such services for students as recruiting students, providing financial aid, housing them, feeding them, and providing health services and services for students with disabilities, all the while continuing to discipline students as necessary. Walter Dill Scott published the first book on the application of psychology to personnel management. Scott was appointed president of Northwestern University in 1919 and applied this theory to training individual students for the needs of the current society, thus beginning the first student personnel point of view (Barr, Keating, & Associates, 1985). This concept of a personnel worker in higher education differed from that of the dean, in that the personnel worker was focused more on the guidance of students than on their discipline and management.

Student Development. Some have asserted that the reconceptualization of the roles of student affairs personnel from acting *in loco parentis* and providing student services was a consequence of the student activism of the 1960s and 1970s. Paul Bloland (1991) cites three seminal documents as the beginning of the student development movement: "Student Development Services in Higher Education," issued in 1972 by the Council of Student Personnel Associations in Higher Education (COSPA); "Student Development in Tomorrow's Higher Education—A Return to the Academy," written by Robert D. Brown in a 1972 ACPA monograph; and the 1972 statement by the Higher Education Project, "A Student Development Model for Student Affairs in Tomorrow's Higher Education," published through ACPA in 1975. The two premises upon which the student development movement rest, according to Paul Bloland, are that "university staff should intentionally introduce proactive programs called interventions, to promote development; and the nature and content of these interventions and the outcome could be specified by designing them in conformance with an appropriate theory of human development" (Bloland, 1991). Miller and Prince (1976) offer a process on the implementation of student development and connect adult development to college student learning. The decade of the 1970s was the height of debates about the differences between student development and student affairs (Nuss, 2003). Although the conversation still continues today, student affairs educators must be concerned with the learning and success of the students in their charge: the education of the whole student is still at the forefront of the daily work on campus.

Community Colleges and Student Services

Community colleges traditionally provide the associate's or two-year degree for technical or career programs, as well as the first two years of general education courses, which students can apply toward the bachelor's degree at four-year colleges or universities. The number of community colleges more than doubled between 1950 and 1970, and enrollment increased from 217,000 to 1,630,000 (Kirst, 2009). With the recession of 2008, enrollment pressures increased as community colleges became the alternative for workers who lost their jobs and sought training to retool their careers. Enrollments peaked in community colleges during the recession at 3.4 million students (Fry, 2009). President Barack Obama's goal of every American's attaining at least one year of higher education or career training by 2020 only added to the enrollment pressure. To help community colleges accept this challenge, government stimulus funds and large private foundation grants were directed at community colleges. When a community college leader, Martha Kanter, was appointed as the undersecretary of education for the U.S. government, community colleges celebrated their recognition for their important role in higher education.

Student affairs professionals are rising to the challenge posed by the increases in student enrollment and presumably many first-generation students out of the workforce, and are keeping a focus on student learning outcomes and collaboration with their academic colleagues. The work at St. Louis Community College provides one example of the attention to outcomes. The college, which has a dedicated team of more than thirty faculty, staff, and administrators, has implemented a "mission-based approach to using assessment to improve student learning outcomes and institutional effectiveness." The regional accrediting agency for the Midwest, the Higher Learning Commission, recognized their work by granting the college a ten-year accreditation (Cosgrove & McDoniel, 2009, paragraph 4).

The metaphor of the revolving door in reference to the lack of student retention is no longer tenable, and student affairs professionals have a major role to play in assessment of learning and support services at community colleges.

Professional Preparation and Standards

The first formal program of study in vocational guidance for student affairs practitioners began at Columbia University's Teachers College (Nuss, 2003). The first professional diploma for an "advisor of women" was awarded in conjunction with the master's degree in 1914 (Nuss, 2003; Bashaw, 1992; Gilroy, 1987; Teachers College, 1914). Over one hundred graduate preparation programs in student affairs are listed in both the *Directory of Graduate Programs in Student Personnel* (Barratt & Collins, 2008) and the *NASPA Graduate Program Directory* (Daver, 2008). By the middle of the 1960s, college student personnel had become a professional field. An applied science, the professional preparation programs require knowledge drawn from psychology, sociology, education, organizational development, and personnel management (Barr et al., 1985; Rhatigan, 2009).

In 1979, the Council for the Advancement of Standards in Higher Education (CAS) was established to provide standards and ethical guidelines that would both inform the work of graduate preparation programs and student affairs educators and guide the self-assessment of programs. The five guiding principles of CAS include the following:

- Students and their institutions
- Diversity and multiculturalism
- Organization, leadership, and human resources

- Health-engendering environments
- Ethical considerations

There are thirty-five functional area standards that are regularly reviewed and revised by the CAS board of directors, which represents the thirty-six professional associations that are members of CAS. (Council for the Advancement of Standards in Higher Education, 2006) New standards evolve as the profession advances, but the fundamental principles underlying CAS standards provide a foundation for these discussions. NASPA and ACPA have created opportunities for student affairs professionals to document their continuing education.

Policy Perspectives—Early Federal Involvement, Legal Challenges, and Student Activism

With the landmark Supreme Court decision *Brown v. the Board of Education* in 1954, the college and university system changed dramatically. Not only were there concerns about access and affordability but the challenges of student activism and diversity on campus demanded even more from the student affairs role. Student affairs administrators were on the front lines during this period and often intervened as educators and mentors during times of conflict (Wolf-Wendel, Twombly, Nemeth Tuttle, Ward, & Gaston-Gayles, 2004).

As the challenges of integration evolved through the late 1950s and 1960s, student affairs administrators continued to educate students on how to advocate effectively for themselves, while simultaneously managing the needs and wishes of college and university presidents and boards of trustees. *In loco parentis* was challenged and abolished, and in 1961, in *Dixon v. Alabama State Board of Education*, the Supreme Court declared that due process requires notice and some opportunity for a hearing before students at a tax-supported college could be expelled for misconduct (Ardiaolo, 1983; Ratliff, 1972; Nuss, 2003). Following the 1961 case, the Supreme Court rendered a series of student rights decisions that reflected their recognition that persons above the age of eighteen are legally adults, and that students at public colleges do not relinquish their fundamental constitutional rights by accepting student status (Bickel & Lake, 1994).

Policymakers were inspired by the success of the GI Bill to create broader programs that were not related to military service but provided opportunity for equal access to higher education. The National Defense Education Act of 1958 provided the first low-interest loans to college students and offered debt cancellation for those who became teachers (Gladieux & King, 1999). The federal government continued to provide increased support for higher education throughout the 1960s. As part of President Lyndon B. Johnson's Great Society, the Higher Education Act of 1965 was one of the most significant changes to address the social inequities of American higher education, having been established to further the social cause of providing equal opportunity to the neediest students (Keppel, 1987). With expanded access, student affairs administrators were needed to help campus communities prepare and manage the challenges of serving first-generation college students, economically challenged students, and racially and ethnically underrepresented students.

Impact of the Environment on Student Life: 1970–1990

Federal Legislation Affecting Race and Gender

During the 1970s, race and gender equity became focal points for the federal government, and therefore for college administrators. In 1972, Congress passed Title IX and Title VII. Title IX specifically addressed student athletics and protection against sexual harassment in higher education, and Title VII amended the 1964 Civil Rights Act to address the rights of all employees at educational institutions. Student affairs administrators and others were called upon to ensure adherence to these laws. In 1978, the Supreme Court's decision in *Regents of the University of California v. Bakke* became the pivotal affirmative action case in college and university admissions. The decision did not allow universities to designate numbers of spaces or establish quota systems, but it did provide latitude for programs that give equal access to minority students. Although the decision was a landmark case for affirmative action, however, it did not necessarily have an impact on all colleges and universities (Bok & Bowen, 1998). These federal changes, which emphasized women's rights and procedures for admissions decisions regarding minority students, provided some guidance for future years of changing demographics on campuses and began to suggest how university administrations would handle the new rules and regulations.

During the 1980s, enrollments in higher education remained at approximately twelve million students annually. Whereas the number of traditional-age students declined in the 1980s, older students attended college in higher numbers. Older students often were not traditional, full-time students, and did not participate in campus activities at the same rate (Altbach, 1993). Student affairs had to account for these enrollment changes and provide services for these new adult learners, who had very different needs than traditional-age students.

Winds of Change and Contemporary Student Life: 1990 to the Present

Increasing Diversity of Students with Unique Needs and Technological Breakthroughs Define Contemporary Student Life

According to the Organization for Economic Cooperation and Development (OECD), the United States continues to be the most popular destination for international students (2007). These students expect and deserve high-quality services that address their unique psychological, academic, sociocultural, general-living, and career-development needs (Harper & Quaye, 2009). As more U.S. students are encouraged to study abroad, moreover, a current challenge is to prepare them to adjust to the shock of being a minority within foreign cultures.

In the 2000–2001 academic year, 56 percent of colleges and universities offered distance education courses (National Center for Education Statistics, 2003). Current technology allows students to take classes online from multiple campuses or blend their on-campus courses with online education, posing a challenge that student affairs will need to meet by providing adequate services and by understanding when and how online students become fully engaged in their academic pursuits.

A majority (over 61 percent) of U.S. college students self-identify as Christian (NASPA Center for Research, 2009). Although the percentage of non-Christian students is small, equity issues are important. Student affairs professionals will need to work to accommodate unique religious practices while guarding against appearing to espouse a religious preference on nonsectarian campuses.

Enrollment of veteran students will continue to increase. The first wave of veteran students eligible for benefits from the new, post-9/11 GI Bill faced many administrative barriers in accessing their benefits. These were added stresses for those who returned with severe physical injuries, with serious mental health problems, and with a need for assistance in making the transition from the military to college (DiRamio, Ackerman, & Mitchell, 2008). Understanding that veteran students today need more than financial aid upon their entry or reentry into college, student affairs professionals at each college are convening work groups with representatives from offices across campus to address support needs of veteran students. Prominent members of the work groups are veterans. As important as these efforts are, however, there is a need for research-based organizational models to support this student population.

NASPA's 2009 survey of 11,500 students from 35 demographically diverse colleges and universities captured some specific characteristics of students in addition to information about race and ethnicity: 14 percent are first-generation students, 11 percent transferred from a two-year to a four-year college, and 10 percent transferred from a four-year college to their current college. The systematic collection, analysis, and sharing of such data are essential as campuses become more diverse (NASPA Center for Research, 2009).

Student Learning Outcomes and Assessment

The student affairs profession makes frequent adjustments in its emphases as students—and the conditions in which they are learning—change. As students become more international in their worldviews, and as they face the global competition that is evident in the outsourcing of jobs, they will become acutely aware of the need to distinguish themselves by how much they have learned and what they can do with that learning. As the costs of a college education continue to outpace the ability of families to pay for college without incurring huge debts, families, the voters, and Congress want accountability from educators about the value institutions provide in terms of the quality of student learning.

In 2004, ACPA and NASPA published *Learning Reconsidered: A Campus-Wide Focus on the Student Experience* (Keeling, 2004). It emphasized the philosophical foundation of student affairs: emphasizing the whole student and working effectively with faculty to create a coherent curriculum in which specified learning outcomes are achieved through collaboration. *Learning Reconsidered* defines learning broadly as a "comprehensive, holistic, transformative activity that integrates academic learning and student development" (Keeling, 2004, p. 2). Accepting the premise of the interaction of learning and development marks a high point in embracing assessment as essential in measuring students' acquisition of learning and institutional accountability.

Most important, *Learning Reconsidered* (Keeling, 2004) expands, builds upon, and further illuminates previous documents that have recognized the need to reconsider learning in terms of educational goals and learning outcomes. The 1994 document the *Student Learning Imperative* (American College Personnel Association, 1994) emphasized the role of student affairs professionals as educators whose primary goal is to affirm student learning and personal development and to work collaboratively with students, faculty, academic administrators, and others to accomplish the goal of learning. In 1996, graduate preparation program faculty and student affairs administrators from ACPA and NASPA teamed to write *Principles of Good Practice for Student Affairs* (American College Personnel Association & National Association of Student Personnel Administrators). It outlines ten principles that support effective learning and collaborative action.

In 1998, the American Association of Higher Education (AAHE), ACPA, and NASPA established criteria for effective collaborations between academic and student affairs that would "deepen student learning." (American Association for Higher Education, American College Personnel Association, NASPA: Student Affairs Administrators in Higher Education, 1998) The resulting product, *Powerful Partnerships: A Shared Responsibility for Learning*, looked beyond the typical partners of academic and student affairs to include all constituent and stakeholder groups within the academic and surrounding off-campus community.

In 2006 ACPA and NASPA, in collaboration with partner student affairs professional associations, published *Learning Reconsidered 2* (Keeling, 2006). The publication, discussion, and use of the works discussed in this section influence professionals in student affairs in ways that emphasize their roles as educators in partnership with faculty and the rest of the academic community.

Federal Mandates and Stakeholder Expectations

When the then secretary of education Margaret Spellings convened a nineteen-member Commission on the Future of Higher Education in fall 2005, with the goals of achieving open hearings for public testimony and making recommendations on access, affordability, accountability, and quality in higher education, there were many who were skeptical about the motivation behind the commission. Because Secretary Spellings had been instrumental in the creation of the federal mandate No Child Left Behind, some were predicting that the commission's final report would recommend standardized testing for college students. The major themes of the commission's report centered on reducing the variation among regional accrediting agencies and creating more transparency and accountability among colleges and universities (Ewell, 2008). Responding to the call for greater accountability, student affairs professionals have continued their focus on learning outcomes and assessment in order to demonstrate student affairs programs and services' valuable contributions to the development of the whole student.

When the seventh reauthorization of the Higher Education Opportunity Act was passed by Congress and signed by President Clinton in 1998, the plan was to have the bill reauthorized in five years. The reauthorization was finally passed in fall 2008. Key provisions of the bill, which required compromise, included mandates to create a national watch list of the most expensive colleges, to bar the U.S. Education Department from dictating to colleges how to measure student learning, to punish states that fail to maintain spending on higher education, to require colleges to do more to crack down on students' illegal sharing of music and video files, more transparency of their preferred-lender list for financial aid, and to require textbook publishers to divulge more information about prices (Field, 2008, p. A1). Regulations in the 2008 Higher Education Opportunity Act that will have the most direct impact on the interaction of student affairs and students include those pertaining to critical incident notification, missing students notification, and campus fire safety. A concern expressed by some in higher education is that the regulations will reduce flexibility of campuses to critically analyze and respond to campus emergencies using their best professional judgment. The regulations also raise expectations of parents that campus personnel can monitor the comings and goings of students. With an increase in violent deaths on campus through school shootings of students by students, the federal emphasis on campus safety regulations has greatly increased. Reporting requirements about campus crime, safety precautions and security alert systems have increased in the Higher Education Opportunity Act of 2008. The impact on student affairs will be felt in every area of responsibility.

Looking Forward to Continuing Change

New ways of attending college with the advent of the Internet and online learning, the education community's acceptance of the relationship between student engagement and academic success, and the increasing calls for evidence-based research to measure outcomes of learning demand that theories of student development continue to evolve.

Student affairs, in collaboration with academic affairs, will continue to see more engagement in political activities among students. "Only 16.2 percent of the 1996 freshmen say that they had frequently 'discussed politics' during the past year." (Astin, Parrott, Korn, & Sax, 1997). When asked about "keeping up with political affairs, only 24.4 percent of the freshmen said this was an important goal in life" (Astin et al., 1997). By 2008, this percentage had increased to 39.5 percent (The Chronicle of Higher Education, 2009, p. 18). Although political engagement has seen peaks and valleys, however, student participation in service learning has climbed steadily since the late 1980s (Astin, et al., 1997).

Assumptions about college enrollment are usually based on the number of students available who are of college age, from the recent high school graduate to the senior adult. One variable that must be considered now, in the first part of the twenty-first century, is whether or not college-eligible students can afford the cost of attendance. For years, Congress and its constituencies have asserted that the costs of college exceed the financial capabilities of middle-class families. For decades, liberal loan requirements and student aid helped close the gap between the costs of college and a family's ability to pay. During a serious economic downturn or recession, however, students will be challenged to afford college, and loans may not be readily available. Not only students but also some colleges and universities may face serious financial problems in the future. College attendance patterns are expected to change, in that students and families who might have selected a more expensive and elite college in previous years may opt for "less expensive institutions, regardless of 'fit,' and faculty members nearing retirement may decide to keep teaching for more years than they had planned, increasing the financial burden on institutions" (Breneman, 2008, p. A112). Student affairs professionals will act according to the greatest needs of colleges and universities. Students and families will require support and resources, which student affairs professionals will provide to assist students in their degree and education attainment.

The concept of *in loco parentis* has been discarded; parents now continue to be highly involved in the daily lives of their students. Highly involved parents have accompanied each succeeding generation of students since those who entered college in 2000, frequently referred to as *millennials*. Student affairs has developed partnerships with parents to provide the support students need for academic and personal success. These partnerships will continue to evolve as the current financial recession causes more stress on the parent-family relationship.

There is no going back. The foundational philosophy of student development is becoming the accepted and preferred way of conceptualizing how students learn. The whole-systems approach to learning will enhance the efforts at collaboration between academic and student affairs as we become more transparent in our work, pursuing intentional learning outcomes and using assessment to hold student affairs staff and the institution accountable for student success.

Conclusion: Student Affairs at the Forefront of Change

As noted in the beginning of the chapter, the development of the student affairs profession tracks the development of higher education and American society. From the early beginnings of *in loco parentis*, to the sometimes hostile environments created by activist students evolving from the diversification of types of institutions and the changing nature of students, the student affairs profession has been nimble and has adapted to institutional missions and the needs of students. These adaptations, however, continued to adhere to the founding perspective of focusing education on the whole student. The changing student population and the growing societal fascination and expectation of one-to-one customization creates challenges for student affairs in particular. Challenges for student affairs are not new. With demands for accountability for student learning and continuing calls for collaboration across and within colleges and universities, graduate preparation programs and professional associations must be prepared to provide opportunities for research, scholarship, practice, and assessment. As the country deals with the financial recession acknowledged in 2008, and as President Obama calls for an educated nation, student affairs must rise to the challenge, think differently about the services that could help move society forward, and continually evolve to provide a stable and motivating force for the collegiate environment.

Student affairs professionals, as emphasized at the early beginnings of the profession and still today by James Rhatigan (2009) in the new edition of *The Handbook of Student Affairs Administration*, must continually educate themselves, conduct research, and produce scholarship concerning the profession that we hold dear. Addressing a wealth of new areas of emphasis as well as traditional areas of support, student affairs will continue to contribute to student learning as it is defined by students themselves and by other stakeholders within and beyond the boundaries of higher education.

References

Altbach, P. G. (1993). Students: Interests, culture and activism. In A. Levine (Ed.), *Higher learning in America, 1980–2000* (pp. 203–221). Baltimore: Johns Hopkins University Press.

American Association for Higher Education, American College Personnel Association, & National Association of Student Personnel Administrators: Student Affairs Administrators in Higher Education. (1998). *Powerful partnerships: A shared responsibility for learning.* Washington, DC: Authors. Retrieved May 18, 2010 from http://www.naspa.org/career/sharedresp.cfm.

American College Personnel Association. (1994). *The student learning imperative.* Washington, DC: Author.

American College Personnel Association (ACPA) & National Association of Student Personnel Administrators (NASPA). (1996). *Principles of good practice for student affairs.* Washington, DC: Authors.

American Council on Education. (1994). The student personnel point of view. In A. L. Rentz (Ed.), *Student affairs: A profession's heritage* (2nd ed., American College Personnel Association Media Publication No. 40, pp. 66–77). Lanham, MD: University Press of America. (Original work published 1937)

Ardiaolo, F. P. (1983). What process is due? In M. J. Barr (Ed.), *Student affairs and the law* (New Directions for Student Services No. 22, pp. 13–16). San Francisco: Jossey-Bass.

Astin, A. W., Parrott, S. A., Korn, W. S., & Sax, L. J. (1997). *The American freshman: Thirty-year trends.* Los Angeles: Higher Education Research Institute, University of California, Los Angeles.

Barr, M. J., Keating, L.A., & Associates. (1985). *Developing effective student services programs: Systematic approaches for administrators.* San Francisco: Jossey-Bass.

Barratt, W., & Collins, D. (2008). *Directory of graduate programs in student personnel.* Retrieved November 30, 2008, from www.acpa.nche.edu/c12/directory.htm.

Bashaw, C. T. (1992). *We who live off on the edges: Deans of women at southern coeducational institutions and access to the community of higher education, 1907–1960.* Unpublished doctoral dissertation, University of Georgia.

Bikel, R. D., & Lake, P. T. (1994). Reconceptualizing the university's duty to provide a safe learning environment: A criticism of the doctrine of *in loco parentis* and the restatement (second) of torts. *Journal of College & University Law, 20*, 261–293.

Bloland, P. A. (1983). Ecumenicalism in college student personnel. In A. A. Belson & L.E. Fitzgerald (Eds.), *Thus we spoke: ACPA-NAWDAC, 1958–1975* (pp. 237–254). Alexandria, VA: American College Personnel Association.

Bloland, P. A. (1991, March). *A brief history of student development.* Paper presented at the Annual Convention of the American College Personnel Association, Atlanta, GA.

Bok, D., & Bowen W. G. (1998) *The shape of the river: Long-term consequences of considering race in college and university admissions.* Princeton, NJ: Princeton University Press.

Breneman, D. (2008, October 10). What colleges can learn from recessions past. *Chronicle of Higher Education, 55*(7), A112.

Brown v. Board of Education of Topeka, 347 483 (1954).

Brubacher, J. S., & Rudy, W. (1976). *Higher education in transition: A history of American colleges and universities, 1636–1976.* New York: Harper & Row.

Cosgrove, J., & McDoniel, L. J. (2009). Assessment is more than keeping score: Moving from inquiry, through interpretation to action. *Learning Abstracts, 12*(2). Retrieved May 18, 2010 from http://www.league.org/blog/post.cfm/assessment-is-more-than-keeping-score-moving-from-inquiry-through-interpretation-to-action.

Council for the Advancement of Standards in Higher Education. (2006). *CAS professional standards for higher education* (6th ed.). Washington, DC: Author.

Cowley, W. H. (1940). The history and philosophy of student personnel work. *Journal of the National Association of Deans of Women, 3*(4), 153–162.

Cowley, W. H. (1994). Reflections of a troublesome but hopeful Rip Van Winkle. In A. L. Rentz (Ed.), *Student affairs: A profession's heritage* (2nd ed., American College Personnel Association Media Publication No. 40, pp. 66–77). Lanham, MD: University Press of America. (Original work published 1937)

Creamer, D. G. (1988). *Key issues in the practice of college student personnel: A commitment to excellence.* Blacksburg: Virginia Polytechnic Institute and State University. (ERIC Document Reproduction Service No. ED284088)

Daver, Z. (2008). *NASPA graduate program directory.* Retrieved November 30, 2008, from www.naspa.org/career/gradprograms/default.cfm.

DiRamio, D., Ackerman R., & Mitchell, R. L. (2008). From combat to campus: Voices of student-veterans. *NASPA Journal, 45*, 73–102.

Dixon v. Alabama Board of Education, 294 F.2d 150 (4th Cir. 1961), cert. Denied 368 U.S. 930 (1961).

Ewell, P. T. (2008). *U.S. accreditation and the future of quality assurance.* Washington, DC: Council for Higher Education Accreditation (CHEA).

Field, K. (2008, August 8). A bill that took longer than a bachelor's degree. *Chronicle of Higher Education, 54*(8), p. A1.

Fley, J. (1979). Student personnel pioneers: Those who developed our profession. *NASPA Journal, 17*, 22–31.

Fry, R. (2009, October 29). *College enrollment hits all-time high, fueled by community college surge.* Washington, DC: Pew Research Center Publications.

Garland, P. (1985). *Serving more than students: A critical need for college student personnel services.* Washington, DC: Association for the Study of Higher Education.

Geiger, R. L. (2000). College as it was in the mid-nineteenth century. In R. L. Geiger (Ed.), *The American college in the nineteenth century* (pp. 80–90). Nashville, TN: Vanderbilt University Press.

Gilroy, M. (1987). *The contributions of selected teachers of college women to the field of student personnel.* Unpublished doctoral dissertation, Columbia University Teachers College, New York.

Gladieux, L. E., & King, J. E. (1999). The federal government and higher education. In P. G. Altbach, R. O. Berdahl, & P. J. Gumport (Eds.), *American higher education in the twenty-first century: Social, political, and economic challenges* (pp. 151–182). Baltimore: Johns Hopkins University Press.

Harding, T. S. (1971). *College literary societies: Their contribution to higher education in the United States, 1815–1876*. New York: Pageant.

Harper, S. R., & Quaye, S. J. (2009). *Student engagement in higher education*. New York: Routledge.

Holmes, L. H. (1939). *A history of the position of dean of women in a selected group of co-educational colleges and universities in the United States*. New York: Columbia University Teachers College.

Horowitz, H. L. (1987). *Campus life: Undergraduate cultures from the end of the eighteenth century to the present*. New York: Knopf.

Issac, C. (2007). *Women deans: Patterns of power*. Lanham, MD: University Press of America.

Johnson, C. S. (1985). The American College Personnel Association. *Journal of Counseling & Development, 63*, 405–410.

Keeling, R. P. (Ed.). (2004). *Learning reconsidered: A campus-wide focus on the student experience*. Washington, DC: American College Personnel Association & National Association of Student Personnel Administrators.

Keeling, R. P. (Ed.). (2006). *Learning reconsidered 2: A practical guide to implementing a campus-wide focus on the student experience*. Washington, DC: American College Personnel Association, Association of College and University Housing Officers-International, Association of College Unions International, National Association for Campus Activities, National Academic Advising Association, National Association of Student Personnel Administrators, & National Intramural-Recreational Sports Association.

Keppel, F. (1987). The Higher Education Acts contrasted, 1965–1986: Has federal policy come of age? *Harvard Educational Review, 57*, 27–43.

Kirst, M. W. (2009). *Community colleges move away from K–12 and students suffer*. A college success blog, Stanford University. Retrieved May 18, 2010 from http://thecollegepuzzle.blogspot.com/.

Leonard, E. A. (1956). *Origins of personnel services in American higher education*. Minneapolis: University of Minnesota Press.

Lucas, C. J. (1994). *American higher education: A history*. New York: St. Martin's Griffin.

Miller, T. K., & Prince, J. S. (1976) *The future of student affairs: A guide to student development for tomorrow's higher education*. San Francisco: Jossey-Bass.

Mueller, K. H. (1961). *Student personnel work in higher education*. Cambridge, MA: Riverside Press.

NASPA Center for Research. (2009). *Profile of today's college student*. Washington, DC: Author. Retrieved May 18, 2010 from http://www.naspa.org/divctr/research/profile/results.cfm.

National Center for Education Statistics. (2003). *Distance education at degree-granting postsecondary institutions: 2000–2001*. Washington, DC: Author. Retrieved May 18, 2010 from http://nces.ed.gov/surveys/peqis/publications/2003017/.

New England's first fruits. (1998). In S. R. Morison (Ed.), *The founding of Harvard College* (pp. 419-447). Cambridge, MA: Harvard University Press. (Original work published 1643)

Nidiffer, J., & Bashaw, C. T. (2001). *Women administrators in higher education*. Albany: State University of New York Press.

Nuss, E. M. (2003). The development of student affairs. In S. R. Komives, D. B. Woodard Jr., & Associates (Eds.), *Student services: A handbook for the profession* (4th ed., pp. 65–88). San Francisco: Jossey-Bass.

Organization for Economic Cooperation and Development (OECD). (2007). *StatExtracts, Foreign/ international students enrolled*. Retrieved on November 29, 2009, from http://stats.oecd.org/index.aspx.

Pierce, A. E. (1928). *Deans and advisers of women and girls*. New York: Professional & Technical Press.

Ratliff, R. C. (1972). *Constitutional rights of college students*. Metuchen, NJ: Scarecrow Press.

Regents of the University of California v. Bakke, 438 U.S. 265 (1978).

Rhatigan, J. J. (1978). A corrective look back. In J. Appleton, C. Briggs, & J. J. Rhatigan (Eds.), *Pieces of eight: The rites, roles, and styles of the dean by eight who have been there* (pp. 9–41). Portland, OR: NASPA Institute of Research and Development.

Rhatigan, J. J. (2009). From the people up: A brief history of student affairs administration. In G. S. McClellan, J. Stringer, & Associates (Eds.), *The handbook of student affairs administration* (pp. 3–18). San Francisco: Jossey-Bass.

Rudolph, F. (1965). *The American college and university: A history*. New York: Knopf.

Sandeen, A., & Barr, M. J. (2006). *Critical issues for student affairs*. San Francisco: Jossey-Bass.

Secretarial notes on the annual conferences of deans and advisers of men of midwestern institutions. (1929). *Senior Student Affairs Officer 2009 Executive Report*. Washington, DC: National Association of Student Personnel Administrators.

Sheeley, V. L. (1983). NADW and NAAS: 60 years of organizational relationships (NAWDAC-ACPA: 1923–1983). In B. A. Belson & L. E. Fitzgerald (Eds.), *Thus we spoke: ACPA-NAWDAC, 1958–1975* (pp. 179–189). Alexandria, VA: American College Personnel Association.

Stewart, G. M. (1985). *College and university discipline: A moment of reflection, a time for new direction*. Unpublished manuscript, Catholic University of America, Washington, DC.

Teachers College. (1914). *Columbia University School of Education announcement*. New York: Author.

The Chronicle of Higher Education. (2009). *Almanac of higher education, 2009-10*, vol. LVI, no. 1.

Williamson, E. G. (1961). *Student personnel services in colleges and universities*. New York: McGraw-Hill.

Williamson, E. G., Blaesser, W. W., Helen D. Bragdon, H. D., Carlson, W. S., Cowley, W.H., Feder, D. D., Fisk, H. G., Kirkpatrick, F. H., Lloyd-Jones, E., McConnell, T. R., Merriam, T. W., Shank, D. J. (1949). *The student personnel point of view* (American Council on Education Studies, Series VI: Student Personnel Work in Colleges and Universities, Vol. 13, No. 13). Washington, DC: American Council on Education.

Wolf-Wendel, L. E., Twombly, S. B., Nemeth Tuttle, K., Ward, K., & Gaston-Gayles, J. L. (2004). *Reflecting back, looking forward: Civil rights and student affairs*. Washington, DC: National Association of Student Personnel Administrators.

CHAPTER FIVE

PHILOSOPHIES AND VALUES

Robert D. Reason and Ellen M. Broido

In 1984, Stamatakos and Rogers posed the question: Is the student affairs profession in need of a professional philosophy? These authors presented a strong case for the practical importance of a professional philosophy. They argued that a professional philosophy would allow us as student affairs professionals to articulate what we believe; what we value; what we do; and, ultimately, who we are—four questions they believed could not be answered in the early 1980s.

A strong philosophy would allow us as student affairs practitioners to assume ourselves to be professional, as opposed to working in a constant state of questioning our own worth (Stamatakos & Rogers, 1984). Further, a strong philosophy, widely understood within the academy, would discourage our faculty colleagues from questioning our professionalism. And, perhaps most important, a strong professional philosophy would allow for purpose-driven work by student affairs professionals. It makes sense that if we know what we believe, what we value, what we do, and who we are, then it becomes easier to make a purposeful decision when forced to choose between multiple courses of action.

Complaints about the lack of a philosophical rationale for the work of student affairs have a long tradition; such criticism dates at least as early as 1938. That year Lloyd-Jones and Smith, in the first edition of *A Student Personnel Program for Higher Education*, reviewed the debates within higher education as a whole about the purposes of higher education and, specifically, whether higher education should concern itself solely with intellectual development or with "intellectual, physical, emotional, spiritual" development (Wriston, 1930, as cited in Lloyd-Jones & Smith, 1938, p. 4). These tensions reflect, in part, the similarly long-standing conflict within higher education between "(a) Those who interpret 'preparation for life' predominantly in a vocational, professional, utilitarian sense [and] (b) those who interpret 'preparation for life' from a broader standpoint as including properly one's ability to function successfully in nonvocational activities and relationships; those who believe that there is an 'art of living' which is as important as the 'business of earning a living'" (Lloyd-Jones & Smith, 1938, p. 7).

Joined by Bloland ten years after their initial discussion, Stamatakos and Rogers (Bloland, Stamatakos, & Rogers, 1994) concluded, "It is fair to say that we in the profession have been denied a Hegelian 'zeitgeist' through which to put our entire house into rational order because we have failed to resolve the essential question of which [philosophical] statement best represents the philosophy and foundations of the student affairs profession." (p. 18)

But are we still a profession in search of a philosophy? If, as Bloland and his colleagues implied, our profession requires a single, coherent, comprehensive statement to serve as our philosophy, then we are still in need. We do, however, have a series of documents which, taken together, address Stamatakos and Rogers's four questions. Building on the ideas of John Dewey, these thirteen documents reviewed by Evans and Reason (2001) widely acknowledged and read in our profession, provide our philosophical foundation. Furthermore, the widely accepted idea of student development theory as the educational foundation of our profession, although not without critics, informs our principles and values. The same is true for the more recent "student learning" movement in student affairs. Although not neatly packaged in a single document, we believe a shared sense of philosophy and values is not absent from student affairs.

A Framework for Understanding Philosophies

In their critique of student affairs, Stamatakos and Rogers (1984) argued that professional philosophies, regardless of profession, contain four common elements: (1) an articulation of the basic principles that underlie the profession; (2) clarity about the values that arise from and sustain those basic principles; (3) statements of the roles, functions, and standards of practice of a profession "that are congruent with what the profession believes and values" (p. 401); and (4) an awareness of what the profession is and what it means to be a professional in that field in a way that is consistent with and builds upon the previous three components.

Basic Principles

Stamatakos and Rogers (1984) and later Bloland, Stamatakos, and Rogers (1994) applied these four criteria to student affairs, arguing that our basic or first principles were found in the answers to the three-part question, What does the student affairs field believe to be "the role and purpose of institutions of higher education, the human nature of students, and the educational relationship between the two, i.e., learning" (Bloland et al., p. 19). Without a shared understanding of the purpose of higher education, of students, and of how learning (or development) occurs, we lack the foundation for a professional philosophy. Although Bloland et al. asserted that the answers to these particular questions would identify our first principles, there is no consensus within the student affairs profession as a whole that these are the questions with which we should be grappling. A review of the history of student affairs indicates that other questions and answers seem to have formed our foundational beliefs, and that we do indeed have a well-defined set of basic principles that are widely shared.

Values

A profession's values derive from and are consistent with its basic principles. Whereas principles speak to what is, values speak to what should be. Values are what "we hold to be a preferable state" (Bloland et al., 1994, p. 20), or what Young (1993a) defined as "beliefs that guide action toward desirable ends" (p. 1). Bloland et al. argued that our values are the answers to the following questions: What do we believe the purpose of higher education should be? What aspects of human nature are desirable in students? and How should we best help students acquire those traits? Other writers have identified different sets of values as fundamental to and commonly shared by student affairs practitioners. Young and Elfrink (1991), for example, found that student affairs practitioners with overwhelming consensus identified the following seven values as essential to the profession:

- *Altruism*, or concern for the welfare of others
- *Equality*, or ensurance that all people have the same rights, privileges, or status
- *Aesthetics*, or qualities of objects, events, and persons that provide satisfaction
- *Freedom*, or the capacity to exercise choice
- *Human dignity*, or the inherent worth and uniqueness of an individual
- *Justice*, or the upholding of moral and legal principles
- *Truth*, or faithfulness to fact or reality (Young, 1993a, p. 1)

Adding to this list of seven, Young (1993a) and Roberts (1993) argued that *community* was and historically has been an additional, essential value of student affairs, a perspective shared by other writers.

Roles and Functions

Articulation of the roles and functions of the profession is the third aspect of a professional philosophy, according to Stamatakos and Rogers (1984). In a very pragmatic way, professionals must understand how their work has been carried out historically and currently as well as what standards and training are necessary to be effective. Common roles and functions of student affairs professionals are covered in Parts Four and Five of this volume. It should be noted here, however, that the influence of institutional types and contexts on what is under the purview of student affairs is strong (Dungy, 2003). Admissions, academic advising, intercollegiate athletics, and campus safety, for example, may (or may not) fall under the auspices of the student affairs division at any particular institution. We would certainly argue that professionals in these areas undertake student affairs functions, regardless of their organizational placement.

Stamatakos and Rogers (1984), however, likely would argue that the lack of consensus about which functional areas fall under student affairs in an organizational chart hinders the development of a clear professional philosophy for student affairs. Recent work within the profession to identify essential competencies for all student affairs professionals, however, begins to provide some coherence to the skills necessary to be a student affairs professional (American College Personnel Association [ACPA], 2007). This work, along with the commonly agreed-on criteria set forth by the Council for the Advancement of Standards in Higher Education (CAS, 2009), identifies standards and training necessary to be an *effective* student affairs professional. Although the student affairs profession may never have the level of consensus about necessary professional competencies, roles, and functions that would allow for certification or entry exams (e.g., CPA exam or bar exam), an understanding of shared competencies moves us closer to the professional philosophy Stamatakos and Rogers (1984) envisioned.

A Profession's Identity

Stamatakos and Rogers (1984) noted that "the integration and well-developed congruence among what a profession believes, what it values, and what it does surely results in clarity and integrity—if not self-actualization—regarding who it is" (p. 401). They suggested that given clarity about the initial three questions, questions of professional identity in student affairs would be limited to those relating to admission to and criteria for membership in the profession. However, concerns and questions about whether student affairs is a *real* profession have plagued it from its start. These questions continue today in the form of concerns about whether it is necessary to have a degree in student affairs or higher education to be an effective practitioner. If so, is a master's degree sufficient? Must one have a doctorate to advance to senior levels? Should graduate preparation programs be accredited, or should individual practitioners meet licensing or certification requirements? Should there be requirements for ongoing professional development? In part, these questions and concerns about what constitutes a professional student affairs practitioner arise because we conduct our work in a setting in which another professional group, the faculty, sees itself as having the primary responsibility for students' education. Criticisms of student affairs professionals' contributions to student success have played out in the national media (e.g., National Association of Scholars, 2008) and in daily battles for funding on individual campuses. Although at many institutions student affairs work is valued, this is often not the case, and questions about the value and importance of student affairs' contribution to student learning and success are an ongoing concern.

The Philosophical Legacy of Student Affairs

One of the strengths of student affairs has been its willingness to draw from a variety of sources for its ideas and practices, and the philosophical assumptions underlying our work share this eclecticism. Beliefs about the nature of people's capacities for and inclinations in work and learning shaped the measurement movement, perhaps the first philosophical influence on the student personnel profession, in the years immediately following World War I (Caple, 1998). This focus on assessment and the use of data concerning students has been on ongoing theme in student affairs work.

By 1931, Clothier (1931/1986) laid out sixteen principles of student personnel work, the first of which stated, "Every student differs from every other student in aptitudes . . . ; in interests . . . ; [and] in character traits. . . . The college must know these qualifications so far as it is possible to do so and must utilize that knowledge in planning his [*sic*] college course, both within and without the curriculum" (pp. 12–13). This first principle was an early indicator of our profession's ongoing concern with the uniqueness of each student; the other fifteen principles dealt with specific functions student personnel workers were to assume in ensuring that diverse students were to be successful.

Cowley (1936/1986) placed basic assumptions about students within a tradition dating back to the Greek philosophers, noting that student personnel's concern with the development of the whole student was not "the private concern of personnel workers." He argued instead that "personnel people are merely subscribing to the point of view of a long line of philosophers dating at least from Socrates and leading to John Dewey and his adherents" and that "the psychology of individual differences from which many personnel activities have directly grown is but a verification by science of an age-old philosophical insight" (pp. 69–70).

Many of the guiding principles and values of today's student affairs work can be traced back through our profession's historical documents, beginning with The Student Personnel Point of View in 1936, and prior to that to ideas advocated by the educational philosopher and theorist John. Dewey has been described as "an internationally known educational theorist, as well as a philosopher and psychologist" (Murphy, 1990, p. 60). Although his major influence on higher education has been in debates about the nature of the curriculum (Taylor, 1952; Thelin, 2004), and although his main focus was primary and secondary education (Fuhrman, 1997), Dewey's ideas also shaped the ideas of early student affairs practitioners.

Many authors (e.g., Cowley, 1936/1986; Young, 1996) have noted Dewey's influence on early leaders in student affairs, and specifically the significance of his philosophy of pragmatism. Although this claim may be overstated in that writers are vague about the specific links between ideas of pragmatism and Dewey's more general views about education that have been embraced by student affairs, there is no question that many of his ideas shaped student affairs practice.

Education for Democracy

Dewey believed that the primary function of education in a democratic society was to enable citizens to participate fully and effectively in that democracy. For Dewey, democracy was not merely a form of government but a way of living in community, a way of interacting that affected all aspects of life, a way of making decisions. Dewey believed that education was the primary means by which societies shape the values of their citizens, and he had a profound belief that education should promote particular democratic values: "cooperation, tolerance, critical mindedness, and political awareness" (Hlebowitsh, 2006, p. 74). Perhaps Dewey's most frequently cited statement is his definition of *democracy*. He wrote, "A democracy is more than a form of government; it is primarily a mode of associated living, of conjoining communicated experience. The extension in space of the number of individuals who participate in an interest so that each has to refer his own action to that of others, and to consider the action of others to give point and direction to his own, is equivalent to the breaking down of those barriers of class, race, and national territory which kept men [*sic*] from perceiving the full import of their activity" (1916/1964, p. 87).

Dewey believed that students learned to be effective members of democratic societies by attending democratic schools. Noddings (2007), summarized Dewey's perspective, noting that "learning to participate in democratic life involves living democratically—students working together on common problems, establishing the rules by which their classrooms will be governed, testing and evaluating ideas for the improvement of classroom life and learning, and participating in the construction of objectives for their own learning" (p. 36). This belief in the importance of democracy meant that students should have a voice in the direction of their own education. Dewey wrote, "There is, I think, no point in the philosophy of progressive education which is sounder than its emphasis upon the importance of the participation of the learner in the formation of the purposes which direct his activities in the learning process" (Dewey, 1938, p. 77). The idea that students should direct their own learning is clearly echoed in early student affairs writings. Lloyd-Jones and Smith (1938) cited Dewey's 1933 volume *How We Think* when they argued, "Only when a student is free to make choices is it possible to enlist his [*sic*] whole intelligence and his initiative in the situation" (p. 122).

Education for Everyone

Another of Dewey's ideas that had significant influence on student affairs was his belief that everyone could and should benefit from education, and that education should be tailored for each student (Martínez Alemán, 2001). Dewey believed that "education should develop the intellectual capacities of all individuals, regardless of race, gender, or socioeconomic standing" (Fuhrman, 1997, p. 90). Writing about Dewey's educational philosophies, Orrill (1997) stated, "The social purpose of genuinely democratic and liberal education . . . was not to convey that 'genius' is exceptional and far above the common lot, but rather . . . to bring to full realization the natural fact that resourcefulness and intelligence are widespread. If varied in their outward appearance, these human capacities nonetheless are possessions owned by all and are endowments from which each can contribute to the betterment of associated living and common enterprise" (p. xix).

Problem-Based Learning

Dewey believed that the goal of education is the growth of people's capacity to solve problems, skills he called *inquiry*, not simply the transmission of existing knowledge.

Dewey "argu[ed] that learning should be an active and collaborative enterprise that is firmly rooted in the students' personal life experiences. Dewey's philosophy of education, with its emphasis on inquiry rather than the regurgitation of facts, is an early expression of his pragmatism" (De Waal, 2005, p. 110). Thus, Dewey believed that education should be grounded in real-world problems of interest to and experienced by the student. Dewey would have seen a student's experiences working in the university library or participating in a committee within a sorority or fraternity as having as much (if not more) educational potential as what she or he learned in the classroom. As Fuhrman (1997) wrote, "Dewey contributed to our thinking the concepts of active, experiential, and problem-based learning" (p. 90). Dewey "believed that to be educative, an experience has to be built on or be connected to prior experience" (Noddings, 2007, p. 31), and "the experience itself must have meaning for students here and now" (p. 32).

Dewey's focus on grounding learning in students' lived experiences and on the importance of learning through problem solving are constitutive elements of today's student affairs work. Grounding learning in students' experiences and treating knowledge as something that can be developed by all people are fundamental aspects of college students' growth and development (Baxter Magolda, 1992), and are widely accepted principles of many statements of exemplary student affairs practice (e.g., Keeling 2004, 2006).

Dewey's ideas are most often seen in student affairs work in contemporary writing about service-learning (Kezar & Rhoads, 2001; Rhoads, 1998). Kezar and Rhoads tied the founding of service-learning to Dewey's emphasis on the importance of grounding learning in real experience, erasing the dualism of learning and doing. Rhoads saw service-learning as a way of achieving the kinds of understandings of others required to fulfill Dewey's definition of democracy. Hlebowitsh thought Dewey believed "inculcating students in the attitudes, habits of mind and methods of scientific inquiry could not only give students, as Dewey phrased it, 'freedom from control by routine, prejudice, dogma, unexamined tradition, [and] sheer self-interest' but 'also the will to inquire, to examine, to discriminate, to draw conclusions only on the basis of evidence after taking pains to gather all available evidence' (Dewey, 1938)", as cited in Hlebowitsh, 2006, p. 75). This set of assumptions clearly leads to the view that education should be problem based, focusing on methods of inquiry rather than memorization of existing knowledge.

The profession of student affairs has a wide and varied philosophical framework, which is to be expected of a field with a history of more than one hundred years. Nevertheless, certain core principles have continued from our profession's origin through to the present day. Although the next section will cover values that arose as student personnel work entered its more formalized history, during which it has published several statements of philosophies and values, it is clear that early beliefs about students, how they learn, and to what ends that learning should be directed influence us to this day.

Enduring Principles and Values of Student Affairs

After reviewing thirteen philosophical documents of our profession, Evans and Reason (2001) concluded that the student affairs profession has consistently maintained four broad guiding principles: a focus on students as the primary purpose of our work; a recognition of the role of the environment in a student's collegiate experience; an acknowledgement of the importance of intentional, empirically grounded practice; and a belief that student affairs professionals are responsible to the broader society. These authors also acknowledged that one important student affairs principle was noticeably absent from the philosophical literature. The literature does not explicitly address the role that student affairs professionals have in advocating for, and encouraging others to advocate for, social justice.

The principles identified by Evans and Reason (2001) are reflected in and reinforced by the values of the profession, as articulated by the two major professional associations, the American College Personnel Association (ACPA) and the National Association of Student Personnel Administrators (NASPA), and the work of other scholars (Young, 1993c; Young & Elfrink, 1991). If we accept the proposition that the values articulated by ACPA and NASPA are the overarching values of the student affairs profession, then by juxtaposing these values with the principles identified by Evans and Reason we see even more clearly the congruence within our professional philosophy and values.

Lest we leave the reader with any sense that philosophical principles and professional values are erudite matters for academics, the discussion below provides tangible examples of how each principle and value influences the daily functioning of student affairs professionals. In this way we agree with Stamatakos and Rogers (1984): a professional philosophy that comprises guiding principles and thoughtful values provides purpose for professionals and guides daily practice. We also enact Dewey's (1938) assertion that theory must guide and be informed by practice.

Focus on Students

The philosophical documents throughout our professional history call for a holistic view of students, a respect for individual differences, and an appreciation for the agency students bring to their own learning (Evans & Reason, 2001). These understandings focus our work directly on students and students' development and learning as the most prominent aspects of student affairs works.

These early and consistent understandings of our profession's focus on students hold true today. More recent works, such as *Learning Reconsidered* (Keeling, 2004, 2006), continue the call for a holistic view of students, emphasizing the importance of engaging students in their own learning processes. These principles are further reinforced by the values forwarded by the two major professional organizations. ACPA, for example, lists the "education and development of the total student" and "diversity, multicultural competence, and human dignity" as primary values (n.d.). NASPA's stated core values also include "diversity" (National Association of Student Personnel Administrators [NASPA], n.d.). The connection between today's values and the historical focus on students is clear and consistent.

In their book addressing the foundations of student affairs practice, Hamrick, Evans, and Schuh (2002) identified key outcomes for higher education students and the role that student affairs professionals play in student achievement of those outcomes. These authors demonstrated this holistic approach to helping students, including in their comprehensive list outcomes related to psychosocial development (self-awareness, interpersonal sensitivity); intellectual development; and life-skills development (workforce and life-management skills).

The Educative Role of the Environment and Context

Evans and Reason (2001) found that the philosophical documents of our profession contained a consistent call to harness the educational potential of campus environments. Lewin's *interactionist perspective* (1936), in which behavior is assumed to be the result of the interaction between a person and the environment, was an unstated assumption underlying each document reviewed by Evans and Reason and is a foundation for most student development theories that guide our profession (Evans, Forney, & Guido-Dibrito, 1998). Concurrent with Lewin, Dewey (1916/1964, 1933) suggested that most, if not all, of education was mediated through the environment. Our understanding of the importance of environment and the component parts of a positive learning environment have grown over the years since Lewin's and Dewey's work (Strange & Banning, 2001).

ACPA cites as a core value of the association the "free and open exchange of ideas in a context of mutual respect," a value that directly relates to the educative role of the college environment (n.d.). This statement reveals the value student affairs professionals place on the education process and on educational environments.

Student affairs professionals influence the learning environment in many ways, and they take this role seriously. Lovell and Kosten (2000), for example, found that "milieu management" (p. 561) was rated consistently over thirty years as an essential skill for student affairs administrators. Environments, according to Strange and Banning (2001), can be managed to facilitate learning through physical structures, human aggregates, and organizational characteristics. For example, one needs look only so far as the increase of living-learning communities (organizational characteristic) to recognize how student affairs professionals have adapted residence halls (physical structures) to encourage students and faculty (the human aggregate) to engage around educational topics.

Intentional, Empirically Grounded Work

Despite the long-held belief that the student affairs profession is anti-intellectual, our philosophical documents reveal a deep-rooted belief in the importance of research-driven, intentional practice. Careful reading of various histories of the student affairs profession (for example, Bashaw, 1999; Nidiffer, 2000), including the biographical treatments of student affairs professionals (for example, Jablonski, Mena, Manning, Carpenter, & Siko, 2006; Wolf-Wendel, Twombly, Tuttle, Ward, & Gaston-Gayles, 2004), reveal a profession built on "scholar-practitioners." Even prior to the widespread development of student affairs graduate programs, the professional leaders of student affairs were making decisions based on disciplinary study and empirically grounded research.

This focus on intentional and empirically grounded work continues today, an emphasis that both ACPA and NASPA reinforce through their values. NASPA upholds a "spirit of inquiry," supporting research and scholarly efforts to inform the practice of the administration of student affairs (n.d.); ACPA propounds the "continuous professional development" of student affairs practitioners. ACPA has assumed as one of its major roles the "advancement and dissemination of knowledge relevant to college students and their learning and to the effectiveness of student affairs professionals and their institutions" (n.d.). ACPA's journal, the *Journal of College Student Development*, is considered a top journal within all of higher education.

The principle of intentional, empirically grounded work and its constituent values of inquiry and scholarship manifest themselves directly in the continued, growing focus on assessment in student affairs. In recent years, both ACPA and NASPA have focused their professional development efforts on assessing students' experiences and outcomes. Numerous books, monographs, webinars, and training opportunities reveal how this principle influences our work on a daily basis.

Responsibility to Society

Student affairs professionals take seriously their role in preparing college students to be fully functioning members of a democratic society (Evans & Reason, 2001; Hamrick, 1998; Hamrick et al., 2002). Although this was the least consistent principle identified by Evans and Reason, a sense of responsibility to society has been of growing importance in our professional literature for the last twenty years. The increasing focus on accountability has influenced our profession lately, but a sense of responsibility to educate democratic citizens is grounded in the philosophical history of student affairs. Dewey (1916/1964) wrote: "A society which makes provision for participation in its good of all members on equal terms and which secures flexible readjustment of its institutions through interaction of the different forms of associated life is insofar democratic. Such a society must have a type of education which gives individuals a personal interest in social relationships and control, and the habits of mind which secure social changes" (p. 95). Hamrick (1998) found further support for Dewey's call, citing at least three major philosophical documents that call for educating students for engaging with a democratic society.

It is clear that our sense of responsibility to society translates into a value placed upon democratic citizenship broadly defined (Hamrick et al., 2002). Hamrick and her colleagues define citizenship as "actively attending to the well-being, continuity, and improvement of society through individual action or actions or civic and social collectives" (p. 183). Facilitating citizenship education through programming, advising student leaders, and engaging students in service-learning activities are manifestations of this value in our professional practice.

Social Justice Advocacy

Evans and Reason (2001) noted that social justice advocacy was conspicuously absent from the historical documents they reviewed. However, after comparing these documents with the stated values of the profession, Evans and Reason concluded that student affairs practitioners should consider social justice advocacy a guiding principle of the profession. As stated previously, both ACPA and NASPA indicate a value placed on diversity. ACPA goes further to include the language of multicultural competence, human dignity, and inclusion as stated values, which we believe inform an activist perspective within the profession. Moreover, ACPA directly addresses advocacy as a value, calling for, "Outreach and advocacy on issues of concern to students, student affairs professionals and the higher education community, including affirmative action and other policy issues" (n.d.). ACPA's statement is broader than social justice advocacy (speaking directly to advocacy on behalf of students), but the specific mention of affirmative action certainly grounds the discussion in social justice issues.

Robert Young's work (1993c; Young & Elfrink, 1991) on the values of our profession reinforces the focus on social justice advocacy. Young and Elfrink (1991), in a study of professional leaders and senior administrators, found almost unanimous support for eight professional values, which Young (1993b) later grouped into three broad categories: human dignity, equality, and community. The connection between these three categories of values and social justice advocacy and activism seems readily apparent, and these values underscore the central role of advocacy and activism in student affairs work proposed by Evans and Reason (2001)

Hamrick (1998) crafted a compelling argument that student affairs professionals should value social justice advocacy as a form of democratic engagement—a form of citizenship. Hamrick ties together the principles of responsibility to society and social justice advocacy with the values of democracy, human dignity, equality, and community. Understanding a citizen's responsibilities to include "critique, dissent, and reform of the status quo" also allows student affairs professionals to advise students about appropriate, peaceful activism (Hamrick et al., 2002, p. 187).

Student Development and Learning

The previous discussion revealed long-held professional principles and values identified in several historical and contemporary documents. More recently, two movements have begun in student affairs: a student development movement and a student learning movement. We turn now to these contemporary movements in order to more fully refine our understanding of the philosophy and values of the student affairs profession.

The Student Development Movement

Bloland et al. (1994) labeled the acceptance of student development theories as the foundation of the student affairs profession a "movement," implying that the wholesale acceptance of these theories was more closely related to a conversion experience than a reasoned decision. These authors went on to critique student development theories and their application to student affairs work, as if these theories constituted a new philosophical principle for the profession. Although we disagree with Bloland et al.'s assertion that the student development perspective constitutes a philosophical principle, we recognize that student development influences the constituent parts of a philosophy—what we believe in, what we value, what we do, and who we are as professionals.

Evolving since the early 1970s, the movement toward accepting student development as the theoretical foundation of the profession has its roots in the need for establishing legitimacy within the academy (Bloland, Stamatakos, & Rogers, 1994); the need to understand, anticipate, and address an increasingly complex set of student issues (Evans, Forney, & Guido-Dibrito, 1998); and the need to ground professional practice in disciplinary theory (Evans, Forney, & Guido-Dibrito). Student development theories guide the work of student affairs professionals, describing how students change and grow during college and what activities or experiences best influence that growth (Evans, 2003). Student development theories attempt to explain the process of human development in college students and, as such, do serve as the educational foundation of the student affairs profession.

Bloland et al. (1994) critiqued student development as a philosophy for the profession, claiming that "student development emphasizes the student to the exclusion of the other institutional purposes [and] ignores or deems as unimportant the collegiate institution's responsibilities for preserving, transmitting, and enriching the culture, for creating new knowledge, or for educating students toward being responsible participants in society" (p. 20). Although Bloland and his colleagues base this conclusion on the review of a single document, *Student Development Services in Post-Secondary Education* (Council of Student Personnel Associations, 1975), limiting greatly their understanding of student development, it behooves us to examine their perspective closely.

In keeping with our professional principles and values, student development theories do emphasize a student's growth toward a more complex and integrated whole (Evans et al., 1998). But do they do so at the expense of other important purposes? We think not. Recent advances in student development theories reinforce the importance of cultures (not a singular culture as Bloland and his colleagues imply, however). Cognitive development theories focus on intellectual skill development and knowledge acquisition (King, 2003). More recent attempts to integrate cognitive development with interpersonal and intrapersonal development (see, for example, Baxter Magolda, 1999, 2002, 2003) begin to build a holistic understanding of student development, inclusive of creating knowledge of and responsibility toward others. In this manner, student development reinforces the principles and values of the student affairs profession.

The student development movement also has allowed us as student affairs professionals to understand what we do and who we are professionally, the final two components of a professional philosophy (Stamatakos & Rogers, 1984). The student development movement has pushed us as student affairs professionals to see ourselves as educators concerned about holistic student growth and development (Evans et al., 1998). We might argue that the educator identity that grew out of the student development movement foreshadowed the student learning movement in student affairs, to which we now turn.

The Student Learning Movement

Komives and Schoper (2006) suggested that, beginning in the 1980s, a series of reports calling for a renewed focus on learning and learning outcomes in higher education began the student learning movement in student affairs. The evolution of the movement from *student development* to *student learning* as the primary focus of student affairs work focused much attention on the concept of learning both within and outside of student affairs. Student affairs scholars responded to this evolution in 1994 with the *Student Learning Imperative* (ACPA, 1994), which clearly put learning in the forefront of our professional practices.

More recently, documents produced in collaboration among many student affairs professional organizations continued and furthered the profession's focus on learning. *Learning Reconsidered* (Keeling, 2004) and *Learning Reconsidered 2* (Keeling, 2006) serve as a call and a how-to manual to focus on learning in student affairs work, respectively. Learning, according to the authors in these two documents, is inseparable from development. Learning is also something larger and transformative, incorporating both intellectual and personal growth and resulting in a qualitative change in *who* a learner is (i.e., identity development).

The student learning movement places student affairs practice in the center of the learning environment. According to the authors of *Learning Reconsidered*, "Student affairs, in this conceptualization, is integral to the learning process because of the opportunities it provides students to learn through action, contemplation, reflection and emotional engagement as well as information acquisition" (Keeling, 2004, p. 11). Student affairs professionals thus assume a proactive and coprimary role with faculty members in the education of college students.

The increased attention on learning emphasizes many of the previously held beliefs of student affairs professional. In fact, we would argue that the student learning movement is congruent with all of the principles identified by Evans and Reason (2001). Interestingly, although some view the focus on student learning as new, we argue that it simply reinforces and re-centers an emphasis on learning that has been part of student affairs since the beginning (Evans & Reason, 2001; Rentz, 2004). The movement does, however, change what we do and how we see ourselves professionally. Student affairs professionals now focus on learning outcomes (Bresciani, Zelna, & Anderson, 2004; Komives & Schoper, 2006) and creating curricula to guide the achievement of those outcomes.

Conclusion

In this chapter we have drawn a connection between the philosophies and values of student affairs and the work we do on our campuses. But have we answered the initial question, Is the student affairs profession still in need of a philosophy? As a profession, we do not have a single document to "put our entire house into rational order" (Bloland et al., 1994, p. 18), but we are not without a strong, coherent, and consistent professional heritage.

The philosophical roots of our profession, grounded in the guidance movement of the 1920s, the works of John Dewey in the 1930s, and other writings of the twentieth century, still inform our values in the twenty-first century. Our values inform our practice. We would argue that a single document is not needed to put our house in order, but rather the multiple documents, written over decades, add to the strength of our professional philosophy. Although our philosophy has evolved slightly with the changing times, our profession has held true to a coherent set of principles and values; we know what we believe, what we value, what we do, and who we are.

References

American College Personnel Association (ACPA). (n.d.). *About ACPA.* Retrieved November 24, 2008, from www.myacpa.org/au/au_index.cfm.

American College Personnel Association (ACPA). (1994). *The student learning imperative: Implications for student affairs.* Washington DC: Author.

American College Personnel Association (ACPA). (2007). *Professional competencies: A report of the steering committee on professional competencies.* Retrieved February 9, 2009, from www.myacpa.org/au/governance/docs/ACPA_Competencies.pdf.

Bashaw, C. T. (1999). *"Stalwart women": A historical analysis of deans of women in the South.* New York: Teachers College Press.

Baxter Magolda, M. B. (1992). *Knowing and reasoning in college.* San Francisco: Jossey-Bass.

Baxter Magolda, M. B. (1999). Defining and redefining student learning. In E. J. Whitt (Ed.), *Student learning as student affairs work: Responding to our imperative* (NASPA Monograph Series Vol. 23, pp. 35–49). Washington, DC: National Association of Student Personnel Administrators.

Baxter Magolda, M. B. (2002). Helping students make their way to adulthood: Good company for the journey. *About Campus, 6*(6), 2–9.

Baxter Magolda, M. B. (2003). Identity and learning: Student affairs' role in transforming higher education. *Journal of College Student Development, 44,* 231–247.

Bloland, P. A., Stamatakos, L. C., & Rogers, R. R. (1994). *Reform in student affairs: A critique of student development.* Greensboro: NC: ERIC Counseling and Student Services Clearinghouse.

Bresciani, M. J., Zelna, C. L., & Anderson, J. A. (2004). *Assessing student learning and development: A handbook for practitioners.* Washington, DC: National Association of Student Personnel Administrators.

Caple, R. B. (1998). *To mark the beginning: A social history of college student affairs.* Lanham, MD: University Press of America.

Clothier, R. C. (1986). College personnel principles and functions. In G. L. Saddlemire & A. L. Rentz (Eds.), *Student affairs: A profession's heritage* (pp. 9–20). Alexandria, VA: ACPA Media. (Reprinted from *The Personnel Journal,* pp. 9–17, 1931.)

Council for the Advancement of Standards in Higher Education. (2009). *CAS professional standards for higher education* (7th ed.). Washington, DC: Author.

Council of Student Personnel Associations. (1975). Student development services in post-secondary education. *Journal of College Student Personnel, 16,* 524–528.

Cowley, W. H. (1986). The nature of student personnel work. In G. L. Saddlemire & A. L. Rentz (Eds.), *Student affairs: A profession's herit*age (pp. 47–73). Alexandria, VA: ACPA Media. (Reprinted from *Educational Record,* pp. 3–27, 1936).

De Waal, C. (2005). *On pragmatism.* Belmont, CA: Thompson Wadsworth.

Dewey, J. (1933). *How we think: A restatement of the relation of reflective thinking to the educative process.* New York: D. C. Heath.

Dewey, J. (1938). *Experience and education.* New York: Macmillan.

Dewey J. (1964). *Democracy and education: An introduction to the philosophy of education.* New York: Macmillan. (Original work published 1916)

Dungy, G. J. (2003). Organization and functions of student affairs. In S. R. Komives, D. B. Woodard Jr., & Associates (Eds.), *Student services: A handbook for the profession* (4th ed., pp. 339–357). San Francisco: Jossey-Bass.

Evans, N. J. (2003). Psychosocial, cognitive, and typological perspectives on student development. In S. R. Komives, D. B. Woodard Jr., & Associates (Eds.), *Student services: A handbook for the profession* (4th ed., pp. 179–202). San Francisco: Jossey-Bass.

Evans, N. J., Forney, D. E., & Guido-Dibrito, F. (1998). *Student development in college: Theory, research, and practice.* San Francisco: Jossey-Bass.

Evans, N. J., & Reason, R. D. (2001). Guiding principles: A review and analysis of student affairs philosophical statements. *Journal of College Student Development, 42,* 359–377.

Fuhrman, B. (1997). Philosophies and aims. In J. G. Gaff, J. L. Ratcliff, & Associates (Eds.), *Handbook of the undergraduate curriculum* (pp. 86–99). San Francisco: Jossey-Bass.

Hamrick, F. A. (1998). Democratic citizenship and student activism. *Journal of College Student Development, 39,* 449–460.

Hamrick, F. A., Evans, N. J., & Schuh, J. H. (2002). *Foundations of student affairs practice: How philosophy, theory, and research strengthen educational outcomes.* San Francisco: Jossey-Bass.

Hlebowitsh, P. S. (2006). John Dewey and the idea of experimentalism. *Education and Culture, 22,* 73–76.

Jablonski, M. A., Mena, S. B., Manning, K., Carpenter, S., & Siko, K. L. (2006). Scholarship in student affairs revisited: The summit on scholarship, March 2006. *NASPA Journal, 43,* 182–200.

Keeling, R. P. (Ed.). (2004). *Learning reconsidered: A campus-wide focus on the student experience.* Washington, DC: American College Personnel Association & National Association of Student Personnel Administrators.

Keeling, R. P. (Ed.). (2006). *Learning reconsidered 2: A practical guide to implementing a campus-wide focus on the student experience.* Washington, DC: American College Personnel Association, Association of College and University Housing Officers-International, Association of College Unions International, National Association for Campus Activities, National Academic Advising Association, National Association of Student Personnel Administrators, & National Intramural-Recreational Sports Association.

Kezar, A. & Rhoads, R. A. (2001). The dynamic tensions of service learning in higher education. *Journal of Higher Education, 72*(2), 148–171.

King, P. M. (2003). Student learning in higher education. In S. R. Komives, D. B. Woodard Jr., & Associates (Eds.), *Student services: A handbook for the profession* (4th ed., pp. 234–268). San Francisco: Jossey-Bass.

Komives, S. R., & Schoper, S. (2006). Developing learning outcomes. In R. P. Keeling (Ed.), *Learning reconsidered 2: A practical guide to implementing a campus-wide focus on the student experience.* Washington, DC: American College Personnel Association, Association of College and University Housing Officers-International, Association of College Unions International, National Association for Campus Activities, National Academic Advising Association, National Association of Student Personnel Administrators, & National Intramural-Recreational Sports Association.

Lewin, K. Z. (1936). *Principles of topological psychology.* New York: McGraw-Hill.

Lloyd-Jones, E., & Smith, M. R. (1938). *A student personnel program for higher education.* New York: McGraw-Hill.

Lovell, C. D., & Kosten, L. A. (2000). Skills, knowledge, and personal traits necessary for success as a student affairs administrator: A meta-analysis of thirty years of research. *NASPA Journal, 37,* 553–572.

Martínez Alemán, A. M. (2001). Community, higher education, and the challenge of multiculturalism. *Teachers College Record, 103*(3), 485–503.

Murphy, J. P. (1990). *Pragmatism from Peirce to Davidson.* Boulder, CO: Westview.

National Association of Scholars. (July 16, 2008). *Rebuilding campus community: The wrong imperative.* Retrieved November 30, 2008, from www.nas.org/polArticles.cfm?Doc_Id=251.

National Association of Student Personnel Administrators (NASPA). (n.d.). *About us.* Retrieved November 24, 2008, from www.naspa.org/about/default.cfm.

Nidiffer, J. (2000). *Pioneering deans of women: More than wise and pious matrons.* New York: Teachers College Press.

Noddings, N. (2007). *Philosophy and education.* Boulder, CO: Westview.

Orrill, R. (1997). Editor's prologue. In *Education and democracy: Re-imagining liberal learning in America* (pp. xxi–xxvi). New York: College Entrance Examining Board.

Rentz, A. L. (2004). Student affairs: An historical perspective. In F.J.D. McKinnon & Associates (Ed.), *Rentz's student affairs practice in higher education* (3rd ed., pp. 27–57). Springfield, IL: Charles C. Thomas.

Rhoads, R. A. (1998). In the service of citizenship: A study of student involvement in community service. *Journal of Higher Education, 69,* 277–297.

Roberts, D. C. (1993). Community: The value of social synergy. In R. B. Young (Ed.), *Identifying and implementing the essential values of the profession* (New Directions for Student Services No. 61, pp. 35–45). San Francisco: Jossey-Bass.

Stamatakos, L. C., & Rogers, R. R. (1984). Student affairs: A profession in need of a philosophy. *Journal of College Student Personnel, 25,* 400–411.

Strange, C. C., & Banning, J. H. (2001). *Educating by design: Creating campus learning environments that work.* San Francisco: Jossey-Bass.

Taylor, H. (1952). The philosophical foundations of general education. In N. B. Henry (Ed.), *The fifty-first yearbook of the National Society for the Study of Education: Part 1. General education* (pp. 20–45). Chicago: University of Chicago Press.

Thelin, J. (2004). *A history of American higher education.* Baltimore: Johns Hopkins University Press.

Wolf-Wendel, L. E., Twombly, S. B., Tuttle, K. N., Ward, K., & Gaston-Gayles, J. L. (2004). *Reflecting back, looking forward: Civil rights and student affairs.* Washington, DC: National Association of Student Personnel Administrators.

Young, R. B. (1993a). Editor's notes. In R. B. Young (Ed.), *Identifying and implementing the essential values of the profession* (New Directions for Student Services No. 61, pp. 1–3). San Francisco: Jossey-Bass.

Young, R. B. (1993b). Essential values of the profession. In R. B. Young (Ed.), *Identifying and implementing the essential values of the profession* (New Directions for Student Services No. 61, pp. 5–14). San Francisco: Jossey-Bass.

Young, R. B. (Ed.). (1993c). *Identifying and implementing the essential values of the profession* (New Directions for Student Services No. 61). San Francisco: Jossey-Bass.

Young, R. B. (1996). Guiding values and philosophy. In S. R. Komives, D. B. Woodard Jr., and Associates (Eds.), *Student services: A handbook for the profession* (pp. 83–105). San Francisco: Jossey-Bass.

Young. R. B. (2003). Philosophies and values guiding the student affairs profession. In S. R. Komives, D. B. Woodard Jr., & Associates (Eds.), *Student services: A handbook for the profession,* (4th ed., pp. 89–106). San Francisco: Jossey-Bass.

Young, R. B., & Elfrink, V. L. (1991). Essential values of student affairs work. *Journal of College Student Development, 32*(1), 47–55.

CHAPTER SIX

ETHICAL STANDARDS AND PRINCIPLES

Jane Fried

Ethical beliefs and standards represent a community's most deeply held and widely accepted values. Therefore, these standards and beliefs are inseparable from the communities that create them. The ethical systems that shape most Eurocentric beliefs reflect Aristotelian thinking. Aristotle emphasized the connection between community values and ethics when he wrote that the purpose of ethical inquiry was to determine which good most benefits both the individual and the society (as cited in McKeon, 1941). Ethical discourse addressed both private virtue and public behavior, and an ethical citizen was expected to habitually behave in a manner that contributed to the public welfare. The world has become vastly more complex and interconnected since Aristotle's era. Our ethical thinking has come to rely almost exclusively on the application of universal principles to particular situations and has diminished the emphasis on the interaction between individual, private good and the collective, public good. *Cosmopolitanism: Ethics in a World of Strangers* (Appiah, 2006) presents us with situations in which the common good may be impossible to discern because of conflicting beliefs about what is considered "good" in different contexts. Multiple ethical systems are constantly in play. Some systems privilege principled thinking; some privilege relationships; some look to religious beliefs for guidance; and some are purely utilitarian, relying on assessments of power and beneficial outcomes for specific groups.

Any discussion of ethical standards for the profession of student affairs requires a conversation about the interactions between personal belief systems and the obligations that individual members of the profession have to one another, to the profession at large, and to the range of communities that the profession serves. The student affairs profession is working in a "world of strangers," both within the profession and on individual campuses. After more than two decades of efforts to draw members of nondominant groups into student affairs, our profession has begun to reflect the population of the larger society. The increasing globalization of higher education makes highly questionable any assumptions about which ethical system is in use in any particular situation. When one system dominates or remains invisible, there may be unintended consequences for people who subscribe to nondominant belief systems. In order to update ethical thinking and decision-making in the student affairs profession, practitioners must become cognizant of a range of ethical beliefs and skilled in conducting the dialogues necessary to bring different beliefs into a coherent approach to particular problems as they arise.

Higher education often considers itself a community, but is it is also filled with divisions between faculty and administration and between the professional staff and the clerical and maintenance staffs. Student groups are also split in a process that Levine and Cureton (1998) call *mitosis*, a phenomenon that involves groups' splitting into increasingly smaller segments based on increasingly narrower definitions of what members have in common. In addition to internal interest groups there are also external groups that have strong interests in what goes on in colleges and universities—families of students; alumni; donors; corporate sponsors; and, in the case of public universities, state legislators. In every college community there is a local government that is also concerned about the ways in which the institution does business and the ways in which it handles disruptions of community order. Some of these groups may have codes of ethics. Many do not. All have members who try to advance their own individual and collective ideas about the good at the point where their interests intersect with that of some element of the university. We do not have to look beyond local constituents to find our own world of strangers and to begin to grapple with differing ideas about the good in particular situations.

The final consideration in this discussion of ethics is the interconnectivity of the planet and its inhabitants. According to Albert Einstein, "No problem can be solved from the same level of consciousness that created it" (as cited in Lazlo and Currivan, 2008, p. 173). Less formally, Margaret Barr has observed that we can no longer say, "The hole is in your end of the canoe" (personal conversation). Our reliance on principles for ethical decision making is connected to positivist epistemology, with its assumptions that observer and observed are not connected and that truth can be discerned by identifying what facts are true, regardless of time, space, or context. Positivist epistemology has been extremely important for science and the development of rational, evidence-based inquiry in Western culture. Positivism currently has less utility for ethics, however, because of its emphasis on objectivity and universality. In our world of strangers, constructivist epistemology may lead to more fruitful conversations because it does not require that all participants agree on "the facts," and it acknowledges that perspective affects interpretation. Many of the ethical issues that our campuses are facing have to do with interconnected concerns: environmental sustainability; contracts with manufacturers that employ people in substandard conditions; access for all qualified students; equity for speakers of many languages; and policies that support equitable treatment of students who practice different religions, express different gender identities and sexual orientations, and have different family circumstances. We must therefore move our ethical thinking to a different level of consciousness as well as address these concerns.

Levels of Ethical Inquiry

Ethics can be considered a continuing discussion that explores questions about the highest good to be achieved in particular situations. Kitchener (1985) has divided ethical inquiry into three levels: principles, theories, and codes of conduct. Principles are the most fundamental, articulating a set of ideas about "the good," which are considered binding on their face or *prima facie*. Varied emphases on different fundamental principles, such as love, justice, duty, or caring, can lead to differing ethical approaches. Ethical theories provide the rationale for making decisions when two or more ethical principles come into conflict. When ethical principles conflict in a particular situation, this is called an ethical dilemma. Ethical codes are the most specific and provide the clearest guidelines for behaving ethically and resolving ethical dilemmas when they occur. Professions generally have ethical codes and expect their members' behavior to conform to those codes. The American College Personnel Association (ACPA) and the National Association of Student Personnel Administrators (NASPA) have both published ethical codes that are discussed more in depth later in this chapter. The National Orientation Directors Association (NODA) and the Association of College and University Housing Officers-International (ACUHO-I) also have ethical codes and guidelines that are specific to practice in their respective areas. The Council for the Advancement of Standards in Higher Education (CAS) has a brief statement of ethical principles that is a repetition of the 1985 Kitchener principles. Ethical codes apply only to members of the profession that subscribes to them, and more specifically to members of the association that has published each code. This chapter will discuss ethical principles, virtues that are considered characteristic of ethical practitioners, ethical codes, and a multidimensional approach to ethical analysis that adds several new dimensions for consideration. In addition, this chapter describes two decision-making models and explores the role of justice in decision making pertaining to ethical conflicts among groups (Young, 1990). All of these frameworks will be applied to specific cases and issues that are typical of those facing the student affairs profession.

Knowing Right from Wrong: Principles and Virtues

In this section we examine a number of principles and virtues that provide a foundation for ethical behavior.

Principles

Student affairs has based its ethical frameworks on a set of five principles: respecting autonomy, doing good, doing no harm, being faithful, and being just (Kitchener, 1985). In this chapter, the additional principle of veracity, or truth telling, is also suggested. Principles have provided the fundamental elements of ethical decision making in Western culture for the past two hundred years. They are presumed to reflect universal values and to remain consistent across time and place. The study of ethics in student affairs has traditionally consisted of applying principles to specific cases, balancing the relative significance of each principle to the particular case, and then deciding on the most ethical response to the problem. These six principles are considered equal in overall significance, and deciding which principle or principles are most relevant to a specific situation is the task of the decision maker. Because autonomy is of high value in the United States, respecting autonomy is often considered the primary principle to be considered in decision making.

Autonomy. Autonomy involves respecting the right of each person to make his or her own choices with as little interference from outside influences as possible. The principle of respecting autonomy is fundamental to American values and is closely connected to First Amendment rights such as freedom of speech and assembly and the right to self-determination. The principle of respecting autonomy has become difficult to apply in dealings with students who come from cultures that are more collectivist and less individualistic than the United States. Southeast Asian, Native American, African American, and Latino students often understand freedom of choice differently from the ways that Anglo-Americans understand it. Student affairs professionals must first understand how students see themselves as decision makers in their own lives and what responsibilities families expect those students to fulfill. After making the effort to understand students' worldviews, we as professionals must fully explore the notion of autonomy as we help students from collectivist cultures decide how to make life choices. In a world of strangers, respecting autonomy requires that prior to any decision making there be a conversation in which participants from collectivist societies define the term and its consequences for their freedom of choice.

This caveat stated in the previous sentence also applies to student affairs policy. Student affairs professionals no longer work in an environment of unmitigated *in loco parentis*. The laws and regulations that govern communication among parents, guardians, students, and the institution have become a patchwork that depends on particular issues at hand, the age of the student, the student's status as a dependent, and the institutional policies regarding communication with responsible parties. We are responsible for maintaining a safe, civil, and educationally supportive environment on our campuses, but we are not necessarily responsible for controlling student life so completely that students do not have the opportunity to learn from their own mistakes, either personal errors or errors made by student organizations. Walking this line is a delicate balance, particularly in an era of heightened security when families may wish to keep their college students in a cocoon of apparent safety. In addition, student affairs professionals often are expected to help resolve conflicts between groups over issues such as use of space, free speech versus harassment or hate speech, and allocation of limited funds among different student organizations for different purposes. In this setting, the role of student affairs professionals may not be to render an ethical decision but rather to establish norms of ethical decision making among the groups involved in the conflict. This "justice approach" to decision making requires that professionals use these kinds of conflicts to teach students how to make ethical decisions in which all groups with an interest in the outcomes have opportunities to participate in the process, using norms of "reciprocity and mutual toleration of difference" (Young, 1990, p. 34). All groups should "have an effective voice in its consideration and be able to agree without coercion" (p.34).

Do No Harm. Doing no harm is generally considered the fundamental principle of all helping professions. "Above all, hurt no one," is the foundation of the Hippocratic Oath. Doing no harm has become as complex as respecting autonomy. It is relatively easy to avoid hurting people physically. We put up barriers to keep people out of areas that are physically unsafe. We conduct fire inspections and drills. We interfere with or stop harassment and punish harassers. But what kind of harm do we do when we tell students from a collectivist culture to make their own decisions and "follow your dream"? We may well be setting those students up for serious, potentially harmful conflicts with their families.

Benefit Others. Benefiting others is the positive way to express the previous principle. Student affairs professionals typically choose this career because they want to help other people. Once again, it is very important to be sure that the help is perceived as helpful and can be accepted as such. Benefiting others can best be carried out in the context of understanding how a student or group of students defines *good*. It is also important to examine one's motivation and to be sure that our understanding of what might be good for somebody does not emerge from an excess of well-intentioned authoritarianism. For example, a student activities advisor might suggest that a student group choose a date for its event that does not conflict with several other events that appeal to the same population, but that advisor should not tell the group when to hold their event.

Be Just. Justice implies fairness, impartiality, quality and reciprocity. "Equals are to be treated equally and unequals may be treated unequally if the source of the inequality is relevant to the circumstances" (Fried, 2001). During registration, residence hall staff, athletes and members of various traveling groups are often permitted to choose courses before the rest of the student body. Is this unfair, or is it a reflection of groups' being unequal because of unequal responsibilities and therefore eligible for different treatment? A huge area of debate around the justice principle is access and equity. Are there certain circumstances under which some groups should be give access to a university because of historical exclusion, low family income, having attended substandard high schools, or having served in the military? Affirmative action for underserved groups has been drastically redefined in the past decade, but there are always groups who request differential treatment because of a wide range of circumstances. How does a society that pledges "liberty and justice for all" make decisions about access to higher education? All these questions relate to the issue of unequal circumstances justifying unequal treatment.

Be Faithful. Fidelity "is at the core of relationships between people. If people were not faithful to each other, no meaningful human bonds could exist" (Kitchener, 1985, p. 25). "The foundation of the student affairs profession, as all other helping professions, is the creation of bonds of trust between people" (Fried, 2001a). Being faithful requires that we recognize the interdependence of human beings. When we commit to keeping promises, we also have to take into account the effect that the promise will have on the welfare of the other, both as an individual and as a family member (Dalai Lama, 1999). Therefore we must keep appointments and commitments with students and colleagues while simultaneously recognizing that some students may have a different sense of "promptness." We must be honest about explaining to students when we don't completely understand how to answer a question or present a policy while simultaneously recognizing that some students may be distressed when an authority figure doesn't have an immediate answer. We must honor confidentiality and not gossip, while simultaneously recognizing our obligation under the "duty to warn" mandate. Finally, we must live up to the ethical codes of our profession by confronting colleagues when we believe that they are not keeping their promises, while recognizing that we rarely know the whole story. The Golden Rule is represented in most of the world's religions, and it contains the most significant promise we can make—to treat others as we wish to be treated.

Veracity. Truth telling is quite problematic in a postmodernist era that has learned to respect multiple perspectives. We now know that what one person thinks is true (small "t") is often a function of that person's perspective, which always limits what each person can see or understand. Multiple truths coexist whenever multiple persons are involved in a situation. Nevertheless, operational understandings of truth can usually be agreed upon in the context of respectful listening, honest speaking, and nondefensive understanding. Student affairs professionals should honor the principle of speaking accurately and making clear distinctions between reporting facts and making inferences.

Virtues

Virtues complement principles. While principles are presumed to remain constant across time and context, virtues vary with the situation. Every culture and most contexts have slightly different ideas of what types of behavior and what personality characteristics are considered virtuous. "A virtue is a trait of character that is socially valued and a moral virtue is a trait that is morally valued" (Beauchamp & Childress, 1994, p. 63). The research on counselors, psychologists, and other helping professionals suggests that there are four essential virtues for anyone in the helping professions: prudence, integrity, respectfulness, and benevolence (Meara, Schmidt, & Day, 1996). Virtues describe a person's typical ways of behaving and thinking. Rather than serving as principles that one thinks about as a guide to action, virtues are predispositions or habits that tend to shape one's responses to specific situations. A person could think through an ethical dilemma on the basis of principles. However, that person might know what to do but still be unable to carry out the ethical response to the problem because of a failure to develop appropriate virtues.

Self-Regarding Virtues: Prudence and Integrity. Self-regarding virtues primarily benefit the person who acquires and uses them. They are marks of the character strength of people who possesses them. Prudence suggests a habitual tendency to think carefully and act cautiously when faced with ethical conflicts. Prudent people do not leap into action as soon as one side of the problem becomes apparent. They consider all sides, take time to reflect, and consider potential outcomes before making a decision or taking action. The habit of prudence also leads to development of integrity. Integrity suggests internal consistency and wholeness. People of integrity are what they appear to be and are generally consistent in behavior and decision making. Needless to say, developing integrity is the work of a lifetime.

Other-Regarding Virtues: Respectfulness and Benevolence. Other-regarding virtues are "oriented toward producing moral good for others or providing for the good of the community in general" (Meara et al., 1996, p. 37). They are intertwined with the self-regarding virtues. If a person is characteristically prudent, it is easier to treat others with respect. Many Americans of European descent are now challenged to become more respectful of their Arab and Muslim neighbors and to become better informed about the beliefs and practices of Islam. When the United States became the target of terrorist attacks, the imprudent response was to attack persons in the local environment who appeared to be connected in some way to the perpetrators. Fortunately, political, religious, and civic leaders spoke out immediately and presented a more prudent response. Information about Islam has become more widely available to the non-Islamic public, and interfaith, intercultural dialogues have become widespread. Anger is an understandable response to assault. Although prudent people acknowledge anger, they give thought to the situation before responding ethically and constructively. Respectfulness generally leads to benevolence. If one treats another with respect, taking that person's welfare into account becomes habitual. "True compassion is not just an emotional response but a firm commitment founded on reason. Therefore a truly compassionate attitude toward others does not change even if they behave negatively" (Dalai Lama, 1998, p.40).

Patterns of Meaning and Ethical Perspectives

Our campuses and the larger environment around them have become incredibly complex places in which people from all over the world study, work, and interact socially on a daily basis. Principles provide consistency when making ethical decisions. Virtues describe patterns of behavior that are considered exemplary in particular settings. There remains a need for a broader framework that will bring coherence to these two dimensions and integrate them with a sense of context. Fried and Malley (2002) have created a three-dimensional model, shown in Figure 6.1, that incorporates consideration of virtues and principles in a broader context that includes culture, phenomenology, time frame and dynamic interaction among all segments of the three dimensions.

FIGURE 6.1.   ETHICS WHEEL.

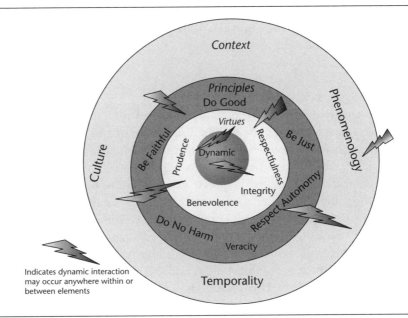

Source: Fried & Malley (2002). Not to be reproduced without permission.

Cultural Values

Values that pertain to any specific ethical dilemma include the cultural perspectives and values of individuals from various ethnic groups as well as cultures related to identity groups such as gender and sexual orientation, faith groups, athletes, persons with disabilities, and so forth. Campus culture and the culture of the surrounding community are also relevant. A racial incident that occurs on a public urban campus in the Northeast, for example, might have different ramifications than a similar incident that occurs in a private college in a rural area. Students from different cultures may have dramatically different reactions to the same event.

Despite the potential conflicts among different cultural values, Appiah (2006) offers several ideas that seem to transcend most conflicts and have the potential to bring coherence when addressing particular situations. "If you are the person in the best position to prevent something really awful and it won't cost you much to do so, do it. . . . Our obligation is not to carry the whole burden (of solving any particular problem.) Each of us should do our fair share, but we cannot be required to do more" (pp.161, 164). Appiah asserts an overarching, cosmopolitan approach to praxis, the implementation of principles in different situations. "Whatever our basic obligations, they must be consistent with our being . . . partial to those closest to us: to our families, our friends, our nations; to the many groups that call upon us through our identities, chosen and unchosen; and, of course, to ourselves" (p.165). In a world of strangers, we should not expect ourselves to live according to principles that violate our basic sense of connection, but neither should we put at a disadvantage those among us who are connected in more distant ways than those who are closer. This approach provides a challenging scale on which to balance competing interests and values.

Phenomenology

Phenomenology refers to individual points of view that are based on the interaction of cultural and personal perspectives. Talking about and reflecting on life experiences develops these perspectives. Every person's individual phenomenology is slightly different. For example, a patient and easygoing person might not get too upset about having to wait in line for forty-five minutes to check out at the bookstore. A less patient person might get angry or decide to come back tomorrow or buy the books online. A student with an anti-authoritarian bent might become very angry if a professor calls on her in class and makes a sarcastic comment if she can't answer the question. A student with a different phenomenology might react to the same put-down by admitting that he hadn't done the reading and couldn't really blame the professor for getting upset with him. Phenomenology shapes the kinds of reactions people have to events that contain ethical dilemmas and influences what kinds of events people choose to react to.

Temporality

Temporality refers to all the timing elements that are relevant to any particular dilemma. Has the situation been going on for months, or did it just develop recently? Are there deadlines for resolving this issue? Has a major event occurred while this problem was in process to change perspectives of those involved? Has the event occurred among friends who have known each other for a long time or among strangers who don't know each other very well? Phases of the academic calendar are also relevant to some situations—whether an event occurred at the beginning of the year or in midwinter may change the outcome. Finally, the spirit of the times in which a dilemma arises can also influence the resolution of that dilemma. Veterans returning from the wars in Iraq and Afghanistan are treated quite differently than those who returned from Vietnam, because the public memory of the abuse the Vietnam vets received is still raw. A GI bill containing educational benefits was passed in 2008, but nothing similar was extended to veterans of the first Iraq War or the Vietnam War.

Dynamic Interactions

Dynamic considerations involve the elements of a situation that are in flux. The wheel in Figure 6.1 is intended to convey a picture of a fluid system where all of the elements interact and coevolve as time goes on and perspectives shift. The lightening bolts around the wheel signify the dynamic elements of the ethical process. Dynamic systems are "open to the environment, exchanging matter, energy and information" (Caine & Caine, 1997, p. 58). Universities are dynamic systems in which information circulates. Information may attract or repel resources at any given time. Energy can move into the system when people are hopeful and flow out of the system when people are depressed, such as in times of budget cuts or campus crises like fires, floods, or shootings. When systems are close to equilibrium, in times of little change and adequate resources, small problems do not provoke big changes. When systems are far from equilibrium, in times of great change and social disruption, any small event may provoke enormous and unanticipated consequences. A swastika spray painted on the side of a building may simply be painted over in times of stability. The day after a threat is made to kill all Jews and Americans, that event will provoke a very different reaction. The campus bookstore may use a camera-based security system to prevent theft when students have enough money to buy books. However, the manager may decide that use of a uniformed or undercover security officer is necessary when loan money disappears, part-time jobs are hard to find, and scholarships are cut. What ethical issues should the bookstore manager be thinking about under these conditions?

The Ethics Wheel in Figure 6.1 can be used to analyze ethical dilemmas. The reader should imagine that each circle turns independently of the others, and that the key issues can be lined up in order to imagine which elements interact and their relative importance in the situation. Some suggested questions to consider are as follows:

1. Are there cultural concerns involved in this situation? Are there values held by specific groups that are being challenged? Are there considerations that affect various cultural groups on campus differentially? What is the time frame that is relevant to this situation? Do we have months to investigate or does something have to be done in the next few hours or days? Is anyone in danger?
2. Are there radically different perspectives about the importance of the problem? Does the vice president for student affairs see things very differently from the vice president for academic affairs?
3. Do the people who have to address this problem share an ethical framework that guides their thinking, or are there conflicting ethical perspectives in the decision-making group? Are these people open to listening to each other or attempting to gain advantage for their approach? Are there dialogic approaches that might be used in conversation to use the controversy constructively and find common ground? (Young, 1990; Yankelovich, 1999)

The Ethics Wheel should be used in an atmosphere of community engagement and authentic dialogue. Its use will engender understanding and communication in difficult, dynamic situations.

Community as Context for Dialogue

In the information-saturated environments where most student affairs work is accomplished, the dimensions of ethical analysis interact constantly. Creating a culture in which ethical concerns can be discussed is a project that must be undertaken by the entire campus community, not simply the division of student affairs (Brown, 1985). A sense of community emerges from an attitude of respect rather than simply from physical proximity. Parker Palmer considers community a place where the person you never want to see again moves in next door and the subsequent work that developing a relationship with that person involves (personal communication, March, 1995). Peck describes community as a safe place where a "group can fight gracefully" (1987, p. 70). The community process focuses on dialogue—the exchange of perspectives for the purpose of creating shared meaning on subjects of mutual concern. Community is not easily achieved in this period of global tension. It must be created constantly in response to the endless conflicts that seem to make consensus a hypothetical goal beyond a constantly receding horizon. Unless community is seen as a value and a practice, addressing ethical dilemmas becomes a process of resolving conflicts among competing interests, with few if any agreed-on priorities and principles. Young (1990) asserts that the notion of impartiality in these dialogues is an illusion, and that the community is best served when all of the particular interests are discussed in a public conversation. Transparency of particular interests replaces the previous notion of an ideal good, or the greatest good for the greatest number.

Communities must be committed to dialogue if they wish to create frameworks within which ethical dilemmas can be addressed. Dialogue is "thinking together in a coherent way. . . . (it) does not require people to agree with each other. Instead it encourages people to participate in a pool of shared meaning that leads to aligned action" (Jaworski, 1998, p. 111). Dialogue encourages the development of prudence, benevolence, respect, and integrity within a community. Brown (1985) considered community as fundamental to the creation of ethical practice in student affairs. He suggested that establishment of an ethical environment in which dialogue could occur as essential to the mission of education for student development and citizenship.

Developmentally, students have frequently conflicting personal needs—to make friends, to choose majors and pursue careers, to learn group and leadership skills, and to achieve academically. Students are attempting to make sense out of their lives and learn how to live in relation to others in ways that are meaningful and satisfying. Student affairs administrators help students learn ethical behavior, not by talking about it but by modeling it in conversation and behavior. This practice exposes students to increasing levels of cognitive complexity that are necessary for the comprehension and resolution of ethical dilemmas. We now know that cognitive development occurs in a social context, and that "individual, social partners and the cultural milieu are inseparable contributors to the ongoing activities in which cognitive development takes place" (Love & Guthrie, 1999, p. 54). If students do not experience the real-life struggles with problems that have no simple solutions, we will all remain trapped in dualism (Perry, 1970). We will continue to hear slogans like "America—love it or leave it." We will be trapped in situations where we continue to think in "us and them" terms that make conflict resolution extremely difficult. Our history of assuming that there is a universal good, discernable by rational means, supports the notion that simple solutions can be created for complex problems. All of us need practice in managing emotions (Chickering, 1969). Struggling with ethical issues in a world of strangers can help us learn this skill. We must continually attend to our own ethical practice, to the creation of communities that support ethical dialogue, and to the process of ethics education that we conduct with students on a daily basis. None of this can be divided.

Ethical Themes and Fundamental Principles

As soon as student affairs professionals begin to integrate the ethical framework of the profession into their work, ethical dilemmas become visible. This multidimensional exploration of ethics can provide opportunities to address dilemmas. Three overarching questions are significant: (1) How shall we treat each other, both as colleagues and as people who have fiduciary responsibilities to students? (2) How and what shall we help students learn? and (3) How shall we steward the resources we are responsible for managing?

How Shall We Treat Each Other?

Relational ethics constitutes one school of ethical thinking (Gilligan, 1982; Noddings, 1984). Caring is the fundamental principle that guides this approach. The principle of caring asserts that taking the well-being of the other person into account should be the supreme consideration in ethical relationships. Guthrie (1997) refers to Noddings's concept of "ethical affect," which "acknowledges the interaction of cognition and feeling in the creation of an ethical response to the other" (Guthrie, p. 33). Thinking about a relationship or a problem within it serves the higher goal of understanding how to care about a particular person in a specific situation. Gilligan, who writes descriptively about moral development, struggles with the same type of integration. Her model of female moral development has three stages: (1) caring about self, (2) caring about others, and (3) balancing care for self with care for others. Although Gilligan discusses moral rather than cognitive development, it is clear that increasingly complex thinking capacities are necessary for people to think through moral dilemmas when they are trying to take the needs of both people into account, as they do in stage three of her framework.

Cultural and institutional complexity highlight some of the challenges an ethical person faces when trying to understand how to demonstrate caring for another person. These challenges are particularly difficult for Americans from the dominant culture, given the historical American belief in the "melting pot" approach and a general unwillingness to adapt to the expectations of members of nondominant cultures in the United States (Fried & Associates, 1995). A simple American gesture of caring, a hug for example, can be considered incredibly rude to a Japanese person. A hug from an American woman to a Muslim man is a violation of prescribed behavior between unrelated males and females. Direct feedback about behavior to many persons from East Asia is insulting, although such feedback often represents a gesture of caring to Americans. Directness, which is valued in American culture, is considered tactless in many other cultures. These same cultures often prefer to send messages of distress through a third party in a very subtle way, assuming that the message will get to the person for whom it is intended. An American might receive such a message with confusion or see it as a request to spread gossip.

The Dalai Lama (1999) also has discussed the complexities of caring for others as well. "We all desire happiness and wish to avoid suffering. We have no means of discriminating between right and wrong if we do not take into account others' feelings. . . . One of the things that determines whether an act is ethical or not is its effect on others' experience or expectation of happiness. An act which harms or does violence to this is potentially an unethical act" (p. 28). The Dalai Lama points our thinking to the inescapable reality that everyone and everything is connected to everyone and everything else.

How and What Shall We Help Students Learn?

The traditional "curriculum" of student affairs is widely understood among members of our profession, but rarely resembles a formal academic curriculum. The student affairs approach to teaching and learning tends to be less formal than traditional academic instruction. Student affairs pedagogy is typically experiential, relying on an action-reflection cycle (Kolb, 1984). We often call our teaching "training" because a lot of it is included in our responsibilities for training students to do specific kinds of jobs on campus, including paraprofessional work in residence halls and career centers and leadership in student organizations. Our teaching combines counseling; training and coaching; and engaging intellect, emotions, and behavior. Methods used in student affairs education are more closely related to the neurological processes that humans use to learn than is the traditional, highly verbal approach used in most classrooms. We help people learn to live their own lives and get along with others in one-to-one conversations that occur in counseling and disciplinary discussions. Much of the teaching that student affairs professionals do on campus does not carry academic credit and is not part of any academic department.

Nevertheless, the curriculum of student affairs is central to the mission of most colleges. It includes interpersonal communication, conflict resolution, personal life planning, financial planning, career planning, leadership and participation in small and large groups, public speaking, and developing the necessary skills to live and work in a culturally diverse democracy (Fried, 2002). In some cases, it also includes guiding students through the process of deepening and personalizing their faith and their capacity to behave ethically. Academically this learning is below the radar screen although it is integrated into every segment of student life. These skills and capacities represent the glue that allows college graduates to use whatever else they have learned in college to create productive and satisfying lives for themselves and their families. Recent research in cognitive science indicates that action/reflection learning is more likely than traditional learning to transform the perspectives of the learners, because the holistic approach engages all segments of the brain and the connections among the parts. Transformative approaches allow students to reclaim or develop a sense of personal wholeness as well as a connection to increasingly wider groups of people—and ultimately to their own sense of purpose and meaning in the world (O'Sullivan, 1999). From this perspective, the learning that is supported and stimulated by the student affairs segment of any institution provides the opportunity to reflect on all dimensions of their learning and to create a sense of meaning and purpose.

Ethically we are obligated to provide whatever types of training and education in these areas that the policy makers on each campus expect us to provide or that we believe students need. If a college president asked a dean of students to create a career development office, the dean would not be at liberty to refuse. In times of crisis, such as the death of a student, a hate crime, or a national catastrophe, student affairs professionals are ethically obligated to participate in or lead the effort to help students understand and respond. If we handle these responsibilities well, our students finally resume their daily lives with some sense of equanimity. If we handle these situations effectively, students also learn about the situation, themselves, others in their community, and the world in which the agonizing incident occurs. We help students learn powerful lessons, often under excruciating circumstances. Ethically we are obligated to do this. The ACPA code of ethics is quite clear: "Student development is an essential purpose of higher education and the pursuit of this aim is a major responsibility of student affairs. Development is complex and includes cognitive, physical, moral, social, career, spiritual, personal and educational dimensions. Professionals must be sensitive to the variety of backgrounds, cultures and personal characteristics evident in the student population and use appropriate theoretical perspectives to identify learning opportunities and to reduce barriers that inhibit development." (American College Personnel Association [ACPA], 2006, p. 91)

In addition, student affairs professionals also teach in more formal settings, such as new student orientations; first-, second-, third-, and fourth-year experience courses; leadership programs; and peer helper courses.

The ethical issue that arises in this discussion is about professional integrity. If the type of learning for which student affairs professionals are responsible is so significant in student life, how have we, as a profession, let this work be undervalued or ignored by our academic and administrative colleagues? Why is student development education often a marginalized function, even though its learning outcomes are highly visible in the mission statements of most colleges and universities? What ethical mandates must our profession honor in order to move the work of student affairs from the margin of our educational institutions to the center, where students live and learn as integrated human beings? We must learn to discuss our work, both in terms of student learning and learning outcomes and in terms of services and activities (for further discussion, see Keeling, 2004, 2006).

How Shall We Steward the Resources We Are Responsible for Managing?

The ethical issues present in this huge area of responsibility—serving as stewards of resources—are sometimes obvious, sometimes subtle. They often involve the use of funds, oversight of facilities, and responsible attention to the details of planning and supervising events. All of our ethical guidelines address the issues that responsible stewardship raises. Stealing and mishandling funds are obviously violations of trust. Failure to provide for proper security at a campus event is unfair to the students who plan and attend the event and may bring harm to these people. A discussion of more nuanced dilemmas follows in the next section.

In many ways, our responsibilities for managing the physical and fiscal elements of our work are the easiest and most obvious ones to analyze when it come to making ethical choices. In these cases the biggest challenge may be determining the difference between ethical behavior and common practice. Much of the time, common practice falls in the domain of the ambiguous-subtle, apparently not harming anyone yet not quite right. Learning how to tell the difference between right and wrong in resource management and stewardship is one of the most difficult challenges a new professional faces. Stealing has become "misappropriation." Lying has become "misrepresenting." Not getting caught seems to have replaced doing the right thing. "Everybody does it" and "I didn't hurt anybody" seem to have replaced our sense of right and wrong in many situations.

Today's Ethical Issues

Ethical issues on today's campuses reflect the complexity of the world in which we live. The dilemmas flow from many sources that were unanticipated even twenty years ago. A few of the major dilemmas are described below

Access

Access is often a financial issue, but it can also be an issue of language for first-generation status. Public financial support for higher education has been decreasing for a generation, although some improvements have occurred with the creation of the recent GI Bill for returning veterans of the Iraq War era. Individual students must assume more debt because fewer grants and scholarships are available. This issue will become increasingly prominent as the United States moves through a transition period under the Obama administration. The privatization of payment for higher education took on credibility and strength in the Reagan era and seems to have run its course. What has been considered a "private good," or education as personal property will probably be transformed into a public good, or "education as investment" in the skills and knowledge of the American people. This change in approach has been cyclic throughout the past century, and we seem to be at the pivot point of a swinging pendulum in the early part of the twenty-first century (Levine, 1980). New policies will, therefore, be made, and ethical issues of access should be part of the conversation. How do we maintain access for students who do not want to burden their lives with debt, keep our costs manageable, and still provide quality experiences in the student affairs domain? How high should private institutions raise their tuition in order to fund scholarships for students with fewer financial resources? Should information for new students be provided in the dominant languages of the student body, or should everybody be required to achieve English competence before beginning school? What kinds of supports and information must be provided for first-generation students in order to enhance their chances of success in postsecondary education?

We also face the question of allocation of institutional resources. How does a vice president for student affairs manage faculty relations when members of the faculty have decided that too much money is being spent on student affairs programs at the expense of academic priorities? In this gap is an especially explosive issue – how do we define eligibility for "affirmative action" programs and scholarships? Is diversity a function of race and ethnicity or class? Who pays for academic support programs for underprepared students? This question cuts to the heart of the university's mission: What is higher education? Is remediation part of the mission of colleges and universities, or should that mission be served by community colleges and special preparatory "academies"? In this era of redrawing boundaries and questioning assumptions that have dominated the discourse about higher education for the past generation, it is critical that we raise ethical concerns as new policies are created.

Personnel

There have always been serious ethical dilemmas in the domain of hiring and supervising staff. How are an applicant's ethical standards and past behavior assessed during the process of hiring and checking references? How does a supervisor convey the ethical standards of the institution to new staff members? What are the ethics of "caring confrontation" between two staff members when one of them thinks that the other has violated some element of professional ethics? What is a reasonable time lapse between the moment when a supervisor discovers that a staff member has done something inappropriate, committed an ethical lapse, or simply behaved incompetently, and the moment when the supervisor confronts that individual? What ethical issues arise when a supervisor cannot reduce staff responsibilities, even though the staff has been "downsized"? This is a fine line to walk, and an understanding of the ethical guidelines of the profession must support judgments made in this domain.

Crisis Intervention and Threats to the Community

Student affairs divisions are generally responsible for the physical and emotional well-being of students on their campuses. Crises have become less predictable and seem more frequent, and psychological pressure has increased on our campuses. Students in the military reserves are being called to active duty. Muslim students, including but not limited to those whose ancestry may be traced to the Middle East, Pakistan, or Afghanistan, have become targets of hostile and dangerous behavior. Some of these students have also exhibited this kind of behavior. Students continue to become infected with HIV/AIDS and spread it to others. Increasing numbers of students with mental illnesses are able to attend college because of the benefits of psychotropic medications, but some of those students discontinue their medications and manifest symptoms that had been controlled. The most horrific examples of recent campus crises include the suicide and murder incidents at Virginia Tech in 2007 and Northern Illinois University in 2008. We have no way of knowing how people will handle these stresses and who will act out their fears in dangerous ways. Student affairs divisions are ethically obligated to review crisis protocols on a regular basis and to imagine what new crises might develop. Albert Einstein is quoted on bumper stickers as believing that "Imagination is more important than knowledge." This is one area where we must use imagination to meet ethical obligations.

Information Oversight

Information is not a thing but a process, and the process presents us with ethical dilemmas every day, both electronically and interpersonally. Wheatley calls information "a dynamic element . . . that gives order, that prompts growth, that defines what is alive" (1994, p.102). She calls information "the key source of structuration—the process of creating structure" (p.104). Organizations thrive when information flows freely. The ethical dilemmas we face concerning information involve what to communicate and how to determine credibility of a source. When do we choose to use the information we have to work with colleagues to solve institutional problems, and when do we keep our information close to the chest in order to look like heroic problem solvers or to protect privacy? In the domain of electronic communication on campus, information oversight becomes a policy issue similar to the one raised by crisis protocols. Are institutional policies current and responsive to the endless creativity of Web users, some of whom use this vehicle to harass, intimidate, steal, or lie?

In the crisis that occurred at Virginia Tech, numerous people had identified Cho Seung Hui as a student who was difficult, unhappy, and the author of violent stories who never spoke in class. He had spent some time in an institution because of his behavior. Because people who were aware of the situation were constrained by confidentiality expectations, none of the information about Cho was shared. Cho's explosive assault can be seen as a failure of communication among concerned parties, but every one of the parties seems to have honored the ethical mandate of respecting autonomy. This incident highlights the absolute need to extend ethical examination to institutional policies and communication across departments and agencies. This incident highlighted a profound conflict between two different aspects of autonomy—the individual's right to confidentiality and the expectation that administrators maintain a safe environment so that each person can pursue his or her goals in attending the institution.

Ethical Management of External Financial Resources

In a time of diminished budgets, numerous opportunities for partnering with external agencies appear possible. Money comes into budgets from external vendors, auxiliary services, companies that recruit on campus and provide in-kind or financial support for programs in career development, and other organizations that benefit from doing business on campus. Outside grants have formulas for determining overhead costs, and some of this money may be channeled to in ways that state money cannot be used. Privatized housing and other facilities may not appear as costs in the budget of university departments, but long-term maintenance remains a responsibility of the institution. Even when there is allegedly "no money," there is some discretionary money in a budget somewhere. Determining how to manage financial resources remains a constant ethical challenge.

Athletics and Other Independent Power Centers

Relationships between the athletic department and the division of student affairs on campuses where athletics play an important role are a serious challenge to ethical decision making. In almost any situation where student athletes violate university policy there is some hidden or obvious source of pressure to be more lenient with athletes than with other students. The more money the athletic program generates, the more difficult this problem can become. Major private donors cannot be easily ignored. Donors can also be the source of vague pressure to ignore the rules for student behavior, to change a room or grant a single room to a student not ordinarily eligible for one, or to pay for damage but not punish the vandal. In public institutions, this pressure may also come from members of local or state government. When the university president receives a phone call requesting a favor from a member of the state legislature who will vote on the university budget, the president listens; when the president listens, the staff may be expected to listen as well.

Presenting the Value of Student Affairs Ethically

Student affairs is generally considered an auxiliary function, focusing on management of student behavior rather than contributing to learning. While behavior management remains an important part of student affairs work, the field has expanded its responsibilities dramatically. In terms of our responsibilities to attend to the welfare of the "whole student," it remains very important that chief student affairs officers and any relevant designees describe the work of student affairs and the level of responsibility that student affairs staff members carry whenever appropriate or whenever it appears that these contributions are being overlooked in policy decisions.

Professional Codes and Communities

This brief review of ethical themes and current issues illustrates the complexity of the ethical environment in which student affairs professionals work. Professional codes provide one very valuable source of guidance in ethical decision making. Student affairs has two profession-wide organizations and numerous other associations that focus on such specific areas of practice as activities, housing, career development, and academic advising. The two generalist organizations in student affairs, ACPA and

NASPA, both have ethical codes, each of which springs from a community of values that forms the foundation for its respective association. Although both groups have a great deal in common, each has a slightly different area of professional emphasis. This chapter will address the major elements of the ACPA and NASPA ethical codes as well as aspects of institutional review boards.

ACPA has been associated with counseling and the provision of services and education for individuals and small groups of students. Its code of ethics (American College Personnel Association [ACPA], 2006) reflects a strong emphasis on student development and the connections between professional competence and responsibilities to students, the institution, and the society at large. The ACPA "Statement of Ethical Principles and Standards" is preceded by Kitchener's five ethical principles (1985). The code also includes a description of the process for using the statement in relationship to colleagues (2006). The entire code is quite specific about obligations and prohibitions, including such issues as avoidance of dual-role relationships, maintaining institutional loyalty, refraining from actions that impinge on personal privacy, representing one's institution and one's competencies accurately, supporting student development, avoiding discrimination and harassment, and preparing students for the responsibilities of citizenship.

NASPA's historical origins are connected to administration and organizational leadership. Its ethical statement (National Association of Student Personnel Administrators [NASPA], 1993) emphasizes the relationship between student affairs professionals and the institutions that employ them. It is composed of eighteen brief statements that stipulate expectations for ethical behavior, addressing such issues as management of institutional resources, agreement with institutional mission and goals, hiring practices, job evaluations, responsibility for promoting a sense of community on campus, obligations for continuing professional development, and accurate representation of personal competence. NASPA's statement also mandates respect for confidentiality, integrity of information and research, and fostering responsible student behavior (1993). More attention is paid to institutional obligations in the NASPA statement and more to student development and education in the ACPA statement, but both statements cover similar areas of practice.

In addition to professional codes of ethics, student affairs practitioners are obligated to comply with institutional review boards (IRBs) whenever they conduct research with human subjects. These boards have been established to provide oversight that ensures the safety of any living being included in any kind of research. Student affairs professionals are often involved in assessment activities, and the line between assessment and research is occasionally difficult to define. Therefore, all student affairs professionals should familiarize themselves with the IRBs on their own campuses.

All of the issues that have been described in this section come from the author's experience. Since college students, institutions of higher education, and the larger social context continue to change, the ethical dilemmas we face also change endlessly. No one knows how to handle every issue that she or he confronts as a professional. It is important to create a sense of ethical community on each campus and to be aware of which associations also provide ethical support for their members. ACPA has a formal Ethics Committee which provides programs at national conferences, conducts research about ethical practices and supports columns in the ACPA newsletter, *Developments*. This committee is available for consultation with members about specific concerns. NASPA has no formal ethics committee.

Processes for Ethical Decision Making

There is no universally accepted set of procedures to follow in addressing an ethical dilemma. Most approaches have common characteristics, such as careful data gathering, analysis, consultation, and decision making. Resolutions of ethical dilemmas are usually controversial. Use of the ethical virtues of prudence and integrity are essential in the review process. In all cases, the person who is concerned about a possible ethical violation is obligated to speak with the person or persons believed to be in violation of the code.

The Interactive Process for Social Construction of a Response

Cottone (2001) suggests that ethical decision making cannot yield objective decisions based on absolute values. The decision-making process must be built on the construction of a social consensus among the concerned parties about what ethical concerns exist and the relative priority of standards in deciding on a course of action. Ethical decisions should be consensualized if possible and arbitrated if necessary. This process includes:

1. Gathering information from all involved in the problem. Determining who is involved and who is potentially affected may provide an additional dilemma.
2. Assessing the nature of the relationships among the parties involved. Are there conflicting opinions and adversarial relationships, or do the persons share similar values?
3. Consulting with valued colleagues and experts in the community, and reviewing the pertinent ethical standards and codes.

After these steps are taken, a social process must occur in which meaning and values are discussed and negotiated in order to achieve a consensus. If consensus building fails, interactive reflection is suggested in order to determine if arbitration is necessary. Interactive reflection is "a process of conversation with trusted individuals to come to an agreement as to whether arbitration should be sought or whether a position needs to be modified to reenter negotiations" (Cottone, 2001, p. 43).

Kocet, McCauley, and Thompson (2008) have suggested a twelve-step process for student affairs professionals to follow when they are faced with decisions that have ethical consequences.

1. Develop an ethical worldview.
2. Identify the ethical dilemma or problem.

3. Weigh competing ethical principles.
4. Select relevant ethical guidelines and professional standards.
5. Examine potential cultural and contextual issues that have an impact on the ethical dilemma.
6. Investigate applicable laws, campus regulations, policies, procedures, handbooks, Web sites, and so on.
7. Search for ethical, legal, and professional precedence.
8. Collaboratively consult and brainstorm.
9. Evaluate possible options and consequences of action or inaction.
10. Choose a course of action.
11. Implement the selected course of action.
12. Reflect on the experience as it relates to future ethical decisions.

In the tradition of counseling and development that shapes the student affairs profession, the Kocet et al. model begins and ends with personal responsibility and reflection.

Conclusion

The days when professionals could confidently and easily resolve ethical dilemmas are long gone, if indeed they ever existed. Ethical standards, values, norms, and codes are created by communities that share certain beliefs about good and bad and the relative importance of the individual and the community. Our campuses' populations include members of ethnic communities from all over the globe, from all of the major religious traditions, and from many different professions and societies, each of which has its own code of ethics. In addition, there are numerous belief systems about acceptable behavior that students, faculty, and administrators hold on personal levels as well as other, less formal group identities that shape students' personal perspectives. When ethical issues arise, they almost automatically evoke ethical perspectives from many different groups. In most cases, no person and no single point of view dominates. The process by which we resolve ethical dilemmas must incorporate elements of the approaches described throughout this chapter. We must reflect on our own personal ethics and the ways we adapt to both the ethical codes of our profession and the ethical expectations of the institutions at which we work. Each of us must identify the stakeholders in these dilemmas and decide how to construct solutions to our problems that all can live with. We must learn to listen carefully and accurately to all persons involved so that we stretch to understand perspectives and values that we have never before considered. None of this is easy or simple. However, unless we continually review our own ethical standards and behaviors, we will undermine our ability to call student affairs a profession. Ethics provides the foundation for a coherent approach to professional practice, and continuing ethical dialogue is essential.

Cases

1. The campus Gay Pride group wants to hold a rally at noon on the quad in support of gay marriage. Your campus is public but has a significant population of students from various religious groups that oppose gay marriage. A coalition of students from several different organizations oppose the Gay Pride rally and want to hold an opposition rally on the quad at the same time. The anti–gay marriage coalition has a lot more members than the Gay Pride group. Both groups want their rallies to use the space in front of the administration building, where there is more traffic and a better backdrop for the TV cameras that are sure to attend. Your president would rather not have any rallies on this subject. Your vice president knows she can't stop this process but wants to attract as little attention as possible from the public. As director of student activities, how do you manage the needs for autonomy specific to each of the parties involved in this dilemma?

2. A White male student whose great grandfather fought for the Confederacy hangs up a Confederate flag in his residence hall room. Several of the African American students on the floor ask him to remove it. At a staff meeting the RA brings up the problem with the hall director and the area coordinator. They are all concerned that the continued presence of the flag might lead to a serious confrontation. The hall director is concerned about autonomy and free speech. The area coordinator is concerned about doing no harm. Is there a prudent response to this issue—or more than one?

3. You are a residence hall director. You have one student in your building who has "aged out" of the foster care system and has no place to go for the break between semesters. You are allowed to remain in your apartment during that time. You also have several relatives who are very poor and have had to live with your family from time to time. You know what this student is feeling. You could invite the student to spend the break in your apartment, but there are many ethical issues to consider. What are those issues?

4. You are an administrator at a catholic college, and you have been working closely with a student lesbian, gay, bisexual, and transgender (LGBT) organization. For a second time, the group has worked diligently to gain support across the campus to have sexual orientation added to the college's nondiscrimination policy and, for the second time, their request has been denied. As an administrator of the college, you feel as though you need to support the college's decision; however, you absolutely disagree with it. In addition, you are faced with many questions from an angry and dejected student group who feels even more isolated from the college community. How should you best respond as a college administrator and as a student advocate?

5. You are a member of a student government committee that buys such items as T-shirts, plaques, statues, and other paraphernalia each year to promote its work and reward students and their organizations. Your committee can get a price that is 15 percent lower if you purchase from a business that imports everything from Bangladesh.

If you buy from a business that produces its own items in the United States, the prices will be higher, but you know that the workers have good working conditions and health benefits. You are responsible for managing the money in the best interests of the students. What ethical issues and principles does this require you to consider?

6. The student government is the official voice of students and also oversees student fees for activities for all student groups. This involves fair distribution of more than two million dollars to student groups. Detailed funding guidelines govern these decisions. As part of a weeklong set of programs, the Progressive Campus Group requested funding for a performer, Immortal Technique. Members of the student senate thought that his lyrics were sexist, misogynist, vulgar, and insensitive to such issues as sexual assault. The campus had recently experienced two very violent sexual assaults, and the student government had been pressing the faculty to cancel classes for one day to hold an educational teach-in to create a more civil community. Some senators thought funding Immortal Technique would completely oppose all of their efforts to change campus climate. Others thought it should be funded if the funding guidelines were met, arguing that the student government had funded a very controversial speaker several years previously that they did not support, but had done so because the guidelines were followed. Should the student government evaluate whether a speaker or performer adds to or works against a positive campus climate? What ethical and practical considerations are involved in this decision?

7. You coordinate transfer initiatives on your community college campus (including guaranteed admission articulation agreements but excluding program-to-program agreements). There is an increasing trend to create pathways to four-year colleges of which transferability of courses for credit is a huge component. A new program, created by faculty and the dean without consultation with the transfer counselors, is now in the catalogue. You notice that several courses in the program will not transfer to the corresponding institutions. The faculty think these courses are necessary, but the receiving college does not. You ask the faculty to add comments in the catalogue indicating which courses are not transferable, but they will not change the requirements or make the comments. You are the newest staff member in the office and are continuously working on building good relationships across departments. However, you believe that without the necessary changes you will be giving students bad advice. What are the ethical issues involved in this situation?

References

American College Personnel Association (ACPA). (2006). *Statement of ethical principles and standards.* Retrieved October 19, 2009, from http://www2.myacpa.org/ethics/statement.php.

Appiah, K. (2006). *Cosmopolitanism: Ethics in a world of strangers.* New York: Norton.

Beauchamp, T., & Childress, J. (1994). *Principles of biomedical ethics* (4th ed.). New York: Oxford University Press.

Brown, R. (1985). Creating an ethical community. In H. Canon & R. Brown. (Eds.), *Applied ethics in student services* (New Directions for Student Services No. 30, pp. 67–79). San Francisco: Jossey-Bass.

Caine, R., & Caine, G. (1997). *Education on the edge of possibility.* Alexandria, VA: Association for Supervision and Curriculum Development.

Chickering, A. W. (1969). *Education and identity*. San Francisco: Jossey-Bass.

Cottone, R. (2001). A social constructivism model of ethical decision-making in counseling. *Journal of Counseling & Development, 79,* 39–45.

Dalai Lama. (1998). *The path to tranquility*. New York: Penguin Books.

Dalai Lama. (1999). *Ethics for the new millennium*. New York: Penguin Putnam.

Fried, J. (2001a, September). Keeping our promises. *Developments*. Washington, DC: American College Personnel Association.

Fried, J. (2001b, December). When justice rocks the boat. *Developments*. Washington, DC: American College Personnel Association.

Fried, J. (2002, April 30) Transforming higher education: Learning how we really learn. *NetResults*. www.naspa.org.

Fried, J., & Associates. (1995). *Shifting paradigms in student affairs: Culture, context, teaching and learning*. Lanham, MD: American College Personnel Association/University Press of America.

Gilligan, C. (1982). *In a different voice*. Cambridge, MA: Harvard University Press.

Guthrie, V. (1997). Cognitive foundations of ethical development. In J. Fried (Ed.), *Ethics of today's campus: New perspectives on education, student development, and institutional management* (New Directions for Student Services No. 77, pp. 23–44). San Francisco: Jossey-Bass.

Jaworski, J. (1998). *Synchronicity: The inner path of leadership*. San Francisco: Berrett Kohler.

Keeling, R. P. (Ed.). (2004). *Learning reconsidered: A campus-wide focus on the student experience*. Washington, DC: American College Personnel Association & National Association of Student Personnel Administrators.

Keeling, R. P. (Ed.). (2006). *Learning reconsidered 2: A practical guide to implementing a campus-wide focus on the student experience*. Washington, DC: American College Personnel Association, Association of College and University Housing Officers-International, Association of College Unions International, National Association for Campus Activities, National Academic Advising Association, National Association of Student Personnel Administrators, & National Intramural-Recreational Sports Association.

Kitchener, K. (1985). Ethical principles and ethical decisions in student affairs. In H. Canon and R. Brown (Eds.), *Applied ethics in student services* (New Directions for Student Services No. 30, pp. 17–30). San Francisco: Jossey-Bass.

Kolb, D. A. (1984). *Experiential learning: Experience as the source of learning and development*. Englewood Cliffs, NJ: Prentice Hall.

Lazlo, E., & Currivan, J. (2008). *CosMos: A co-creator's guide to the whole world*. Carlsbad, CA: Hay House.

Levine, A. (1980). *When dreams and heroes died*. San Francisco: Jossey-Bass.

Levine, A., & Cureton, J. S. (1998). *When hope and fear collide*. San Francisco: Jossey-Bass.

Love, P., & Guthrie, V. (1999). *Understanding and applying cognitive development theory* (New Directions for Student Services No. 88). San Francisco: Jossey-Bass.

McKeon, R. (Ed.). (1941). *The basic works of Aristotle*. New York: Random House.

Meara, N., Schmidt, L., & Day., J. (1996). A foundation for ethical decisions, policies and character. *Counseling Psychologist, 24,* 4–77.

National Association of Student Personnel Administrators (NASPA). (1993). *Standards of professional practice. Member Handbook 1993–1994*. Washington, DC: Author.

Noddings, N. (1984). *Caring: A feminine approach to ethics and moral education*. Berkeley: University of California Press.

O'Sullivan, E. (1999). *Transformative learning: Educational vision for the 21st century*. New York: Zed Books.

Peck, S. (1987). *The different drum: Community making and peace*. New York: Simon & Schuster.

Perry, W. (1970). *Forms of intellectual and ethical development in the college years: A scheme*. Austin, TX: Holt, Rinehart and Winston.

Wheatley, M. (1994). *Leadership and the new science*. San Francisco: Berrett-Koehler.

Yankelovich, D. (1999). *The magic of dialogue*. New York: Simon & Schuster.

Young, I. (1990). *Justice and the politics of decision-making*. Princeton, NJ: Princeton University Press.

CHAPTER SEVEN

SELECTED LEGAL ISSUES

Gary Pavela

The legal system in the United States has evolved over more than two hundred years, through a combination of laws passed and judicial decisions in an ever-changing environment as well as policies and practices adopted by various governmental agencies and other bodies charged with oversight of higher education. Legal issues influence institutions of higher education in many aspects of their endeavors from admissions practices to contractual relationships with faculty and staff to oversight for various aspects of student life.

Student affairs practitioners should be aware of some of the rudimentary aspects of the law but above all are well advised to make themselves aware of legal resources available from their institutions. Most colleges and universities have in house legal counsel or a legal advisor available on retainer. In some cases state universities have legal counsel available from their state government, such as through the attorney general's office. When legal issues arise student affairs practitioners should seek help rather than make judgments that ultimately could be wrong and could expose them and their institutions to unpleasant consequences.

The array of issues that potentially could affect student affairs practice is substantial (see, for example, Areen, 2009; Kaplin & Lee, 2009). This chapter explores three important legal concepts, including protecting and promoting civility, working with troubled students, and risk management. These concepts reflect contemporary concerns on campus that, because of our dynamic legal environment, may change in the future. But for now, these issues are central to the work of student affairs practitioners and, accordingly, are discussed below.

This chapter is based on articles previously written for the *Pavela Report* (http://collegepubs.com/the_pavela_report) and the *Law and Policy Report* (http://www.theasca.org/en/cms/?38).

Protecting and Promoting Civility

Civility (usually the perceived lack of it) remains a pressing issue on most campuses. The topic overlaps with student academic freedom and classroom disruption, which we address in another section of this chapter. Our goal in this section is to define civility and to suggest ways to make civil dialogue a component of active learning and student engagement on your campus.

What Does Civility Mean?

Visualizing images evoked by a word can help us define that word. I'll show you my mental image of civility, drawn from a great piece of art. However, before I do so, please take a moment and create your own mental image of civility. I wonder if we're not tempted to see civility as something akin to ducks floating serenely on a pond. But civility is not the same thing as serenity. If serenity is your goal, you were born in the wrong species. Nor is civility properly understood simply as good manners—like learning how fold a napkin or eat asparagus properly. Colleges and universities that define civility in that narrow sense are relegating themselves to the role of finishing schools.

According to the *Oxford English Dictionary (OED)*, the word *civility* has ancient Latin roots in the word *civilitas*, meaning "community" or "city" (Simpson & Weiner, 1989, p. 256). The *OED* further explains that *civility* was "connected with citizenship" and the "behavior befitting a citizen" (p. 256). Civility in this sense implies a recognition of duty, action, and engagement, not simply "politeness." The *OED* also says civility can refer to "training in the humanities" (p. 256). More on that in my conclusion.

Here's my visual image of civility. In the centerpiece of his famous fresco *The School of Athens*, Raphael depicted Plato (whose arm is uplifted to point at heavenly forms) in earnest and affectionate debate with his prized pupil, Aristotle (whose arm is extended downward to emphasize what can be categorized on earth). This is the idealized image of Plato's Academy, from which schools and colleges have claimed lineage throughout the ages. The instructional method of the Academy was dialogue. The aim of dialogue was closer approximation of truth. The following words seem to fit Raphael's artistic depiction of teacher (Plato) and student (Aristotle) actively seeking to discover truth together:

- Truth seeking and truth loving
- Candid
- Courageous
- Devoted
- Affectionate
- Risk taking
- Assertive
- Challenging
- Free thinking
- Creative

These words imply action, engagement, and relationship. The word *serenity* doesn't seem to fit.

Raphael's fresco crystallizes the idea of civility, because dialogue constitutes civility in practice. This idea was expressed by law professor James White (1983) in his article "The Ethics of Argument: Plato's Gorgias and the Modern Lawyer":

> Rhetoric naturally treats others as means to an end, while dialectic treats others as ends in themselves. . . . Dialectic . . . proceeds not by making lengthy statements . . . but by questioning and answering in one-to-one conversation. Its object is to engage each person *at the deepest level*, and for this it requires utter frankness of speech on each side. . . . This is not a competition to see who can reduce the other to his will, but mutual discovery by mutual refutation. . . . The object of it all is truth, and its method is friendship. [emphasis supplied, pp. 849, 870–871]

Understanding "uncivil" behavior helps us define "civility." Rather than participating in dialogue, Plato could have responded to Aristotle in several ways we might regard as "uncivil." Three come to mind, all combined in one hypothetical internal Academy memorandum:

> Memorandum
>
> FROM: Plato
>
> TO: Aristotle
>
> SUBJECT: Your Insufferable Impertinence
>
> I'm in charge of this Academy. Sit down and shut up!
>
> Debate is welcome except on matters of fundamental truth. I've discovered truth (perfect forms in a mathematical world are faintly reflected in this one). Disagree on this point and you're guilty of heresy. The penalty for heresy is expulsion.
>
> You've hurt my feelings by challenging my fundamental beliefs in an open and demonstrative way. Hurting people's feelings is insensitive. It silences them. You, Aristotle, have created a hostile learning environment for every teacher and student in my Academy. The penalty for creating a hostile learning environment is expulsion.

Imagining uncivil behavior helps sharpen our definitions. I think a workable definition of *incivility* is that which inhibits engagement, dialogue, and learning. Consequently, in the college and university context, the core definition of *civility* is active engagement in creating, protecting, and participating in a learning community.

Formalistic Politeness and "Speech Codes" as Incivility

Can uncivil behavior be polite behavior? Yes. Politeness as an end in itself, or formalistic politeness, creates distance; it seems expressly designed to preclude engagement "at the deepest level." This is probably the most common form of incivility—grounded in indifference—that we and our students inflict on each other.

Can we be uncivil in the guise of protecting civility? Yes again. The college speech code movement actively discouraged engagement while claiming to promote it. This was a point made years ago by Pulitzer Prize winning reporter Barry Siegel (1993) in his analysis of the failed University of Wisconsin speech code:

> Beyond the desired diversity of color and gender, surely there was also an enforced orthodoxy of thought and expression. [And] amid all this talk of the [UW] code's value as symbol, it was a bit unclear just whom the symbol was meant to protect—minority students from harassment by racists or UW leadership from denunciation by minorities.

> Siegel reported that one of the initial supporters of the code, Associate Dean of Students John Howard, was dismayed to find that "[p]eople were perfectly willing to restrict speech when it served their agendas . . ." Another problem Howard eventually saw in the code was its inhibiting impact on genuine dialogue: "No one knew what the code covered," he said. "I've heard of students saying 'shhh—don't say anything about affirmative action, the university will punish you.' There was a McCarthy-esque venue. I think there was a chilling effect." Howard concluded: "I absolutely have come to the conclusion that it's better policy not to have a code. The human instinct—or the American instinct—for censorship is just too strong." [cited in Siegel, 1993]

Looking beyond disruption, Is active engagement possible? Certainly there's a role for discipline when students disrupt classes or otherwise seek to inhibit learning. But punishment should not be inflicted as the first resort. A wonderful example of good educational judgment in this regard can be found in University of Virginia English professor Mark Edmundson's book *Teacher: The One Who Made the Difference* (2002). The teacher referenced in the title, Franklin Lears, taught for a year in Edmundson's high school and transformed Edmondson's life. The following passage describes Lears's response to an incident of classroom disruption, when a group of African American students stormed into Lears's classroom to conduct an unscheduled teach-in on the life of Malcolm X:

> Lears would make use of whatever came his way. . . .

> "Sit down, sit anywhere you like," [Lears said]. "Perhaps we could talk about Malcolm some." And the group did, and suddenly they were no longer a gang but part of a seminar. They were there with something to teach. "Now tell us," Lears said softly, "what we need to know about Malcolm X. He lived here in Boston for awhile didn't he? He worked at the dance hall in Roxbury."

> Thurston [the teach-in leader who then spoke] about Malcolm's greatness . . . seemed to be blown away—proud and astonished at once—that White people (and the class was all White) would take something like this so seriously. But of course we probably would not have, at least on our own. Lears had shown us what it was to disarm someone's aggression and then, rather than gloating at your little rhetorical win, listen—genuinely listen—to what he had to say. [pp. 221–222]

Respectful listening is the essence of dialogue. Turning incidents of disruption into dialogue should be the educator's art, both in and outside of the classroom.

Columnist Nat Hentoff described one example in a 1991 *Washington Post* article about the response of four Black women at Arizona State University (ASU) to a racially offensive flyer posted on a residence hall door (also described in my *Chronicle of Higher Education* essay on this topic, Pavela, 2006a). Instead of seeking to invoke ASU's speech code, the women told the occupants why they objected to the flyer—which was promptly taken down. Then, with the support of ASU administrators, they helped organize a series of campus forums and discussions, as well as a residence hall program on African American history. Lively correspondence continued in the campus newspaper, culminating in a letter to the editor ("names withheld upon request") that read: "We would like to extend our sincerest and deepest apologies to anyone and everyone who was offended by the tasteless flyer that was displayed on our front door. We did not realize the hurt that would come from this flyer. We now know that we caused great distress among many different people, and we would like again to apologize" (Pavela, 2006a, p. B14).

A Concluding Suggestion

My primary aim has been to advance what might be regarded as an unconventional definition of civility. That definition implies a specific and practical response: promote active engagement in a learning community. At the core of this response is a demonstrable style—a style that encourages dialogue at the deepest level and dispenses with detachment, aloofness, or the artificial barriers created by specialization and hyperprofessionalism.

Student development practitioners are rightly concerned about applications and technique. But we're educators as well as technicians. Our first responsibility is to think. Thinking deeply and clearly about what civility means will prompt us to:

- Be more attentive to our own educational development as lifelong learners
- Learn and practice skills in dialogue and "respectful listening"
- Treat students more like partners in learning, not children in need of supervision
- Seize more opportunities (usually in the context of campus controversies) to promote active engagement in learning
- Candidly discuss our doubts, mistakes, and deficiencies—all with the aim of encouraging conversation with students and colleagues at the deepest level

The first goal identified above, to be more attentive to our own educational development as lifelong learners, reveals my bias about an apparent deficiency in the training of our new student development practitioners. Most know something about possible stages of moral development, but few have grappled with serious texts, such as Aristotle's *Nichomean Ethics*. This deficiency not only deprives them of engagement with singularly powerful minds but also prevents them from participating in knowledgeable discourse with faculty colleagues likely to be assigned to work on cross-functional committees created to enhance student life and ethical development. This point brings us back to the *OED* definition of civility as "training in the humanities." To the degree that training has been denied to student development practitioners, they have been subject to a manifest form of incivility. We can understand in this context that incivility may be passive as well as assertive; it encompasses inaction as well as action. Perhaps the greatest form of incivility has been the failure to engage ourselves and our students in the great play of ideas occurring at the heart of our best colleges and universities.

Teaching Troubled Students

The April 16, 2007, massacre at Virginia Tech University confronted college administrators with many of the realities faced by school principals after Columbine. What is the best way to identify and respond to troubled students? To what degree can violence be predicted and prevented? Is there an association between mental illness and violence? What legal issues arise, including the scope of federal privacy laws and laws protecting people with mental disabilities?

College administrators should continue to expect multiple inquiries from faculty members about how to respond to troubled students in the classroom. It's particularly important to provide emergency contact information; reliable data about the statistical risks of violence on campus; the tenuous connection between violence and mental illness; the limits of "profiling" possible shooters; and suggestions for talking with students about conduct that seems threatening or disruptive.

What follows is a suggested memorandum to the faculty, which is designed to be refined and augmented for use on your campus.

Memorandum to the Faculty

You will find pertinent data and general advice in this memorandum.

1. *What should I do if I have concerns about a student?*

What is most important to remember is that trained colleagues are standing by to help. The campus police will respond to any act or threat of violence. Administrators responsible for student conduct are authorized to impose an immediate suspension (pending a hearing) if a student engages in threatening or disruptive behavior. Finally, mental health professionals can initiate a mandatory evaluation process or even invoke procedures to dismiss students who pose a "direct threat" to self or others.

Students must be treated fairly and responsibly—just as administrators and faculty members would expect if they were the subjects of comparable inquiry—but the campus is not powerless or reluctant to act decisively when threats arise. The campus Incident Response Team [or other appropriate title] manages our overall process. You may reach the team by contacting [name and telephone number]. In emergencies, call the campus police first [emergency number].

2. *How frequent are homicides and other violent crimes on campus?*

According to data from the U.S. Department of Education, the Census Bureau, and the FBI, "The murder rate on college campuses was 0.28 per 100,000 people, compared with 5.6 per 100,000 nationally" (Kingsbury, Brush, Greene, & Schulte, 2007, p. 49). The magnitude of the Virginia Tech shootings (32 people killed) is highlighted by the fact that the total number of murders on American college campuses (approximately 4,200 institutions enrolling 16 million students) from 1997 to 2004 ranged from 9 to 24 (Virginia Youth Violence Project, 2009). In terms of other types of violent crime (robbery, aggravated assault, and simple assault against students), a 2005 U.S. Department of Justice study reported that:

> For the period 1995 to 2002, college students ages 18 to 24 experienced violence at average annual rates lower than those for nonstudents in the same age group (61 per 1,000 students versus 75 per 1,000 nonstudents). Except for rape/sexual assault, average annual rates were lower for students than for nonstudents for each type of violent crime measured. . . . Rates of rape/sexual assault for the two groups did not differ statistically. . . . Between 1995 and 2002 rates of both overall and serious violence declined for college students and nonstudents. The violent crime rate for college students declined 54% (41 versus 88 per 1,000) and for nonstudents declined 45% (102 versus 56 per 1,000). [Baum & Klaus, 2005, p. 1]

Among the "characteristics of violent victimizations of college students," Baum and Klaus reported that "93% of crimes occurred off campus, of which 72% occurred at night" (p. 1).

3. *How dangerous is college teaching?*

A 2001 Bureau of Justice Statistics (BJS) report (the latest available in the series) on data for 1993 through 1999 from the National Crime Victimization Survey shows that employees of colleges and universities have a violent crime victimization rate of 1.6 per 1,000, compared to 16.2 for physicians; 20 for retail sales workers; 54.2 for junior high teachers; 68.2 for mental health professionals; and 260.8 for police officers. The BJS report states that "among the occupational groups examined . . . college teachers were victimized the least" (Duhart, 2001, p.1).

4. *School shootings are often suicides. How widespread is suicide among college students?*

Multiple studies have found that college students commit suicide at half the rate of their nonstudent peers. One of the most cited surveys "found an overall student suicide rate of 7.5 per 100,000, compared to the national average of 15 per 100,000 in a sample matched for age, race and gender" (Silverman, Meyer, Sloane, Raffel, & Pratt, 1997, p. 285).

Generally, the national suicide rate for teenagers and young adults has been declining—after an extraordinary increase since the 1950s. More baseline studies pertaining to college students are needed, but experts believe the suicide rate in that group has been declining as well.

5. *Are more students coming to college with mental disorders?*

Probably yes. Caution is required because increases in counseling center visits and use of psychotropic medications may mean contemporary students are more willing to seek help for mental illness. In any event, college health center directors have been calling particular attention to larger numbers of students reporting the characteristics of clinical depression. A 2004 American College Health Association study found that 45 percent of the students surveyed "felt so depressed" that it was "difficult to function."

Nearly 1 in 10 students reported that such feelings occurred "9 or more times" in the past school year. Likewise, about 10 percent of college students reported that they "seriously considered suicide," and about 1.4 percent reported that they had *attempted* suicide (Silverman, as cited in Association for Student Judicial Affairs, 2007, n.p.).

6. *Shouldn't we routinely remove depressed students, especially if they report suicidal ideation?*

No, unless a threat or act of violence is involved. A 2006 article by Paul S. Appelbaum, professor and director of the Division of Psychiatry, Law, and Ethics at the Columbia University College of Physicians and Surgeons (and a past president of the American Psychiatric Association) highlights some the practical issues involved:

> No matter how uncommon completed suicides are among college students, surveys suggest that suicidal ideation and attempts are remarkably prevalent. Two large scale studies generated nearly identical findings. Roughly 10 percent of college student respondents indicated that they had thought about suicide in the past year, and 1.5 percent admitted to having made a suicide attempt. Combining data from the available studies suggests that the odds that a student with suicidal ideation will actually commit suicide are 1,000 to 1. Thus policies that impose restrictions on students who manifest suicidal ideation will sweep in 999 students who would not commit suicide for every student who will end his or her life—with no guarantee that the intervention will actually reduce the risk of suicide in this vulnerable group. And even if such restrictions were limited to students who actually attempt suicide, the odds are around 200 to 1 against the school's having acted to prevent a suicidal outcome. [p. 915]

Aside from unjustified removal of thousands of individuals—including some of our best and most creative students—routine dismissals for reported depression or suicidal ideation would also discourage students from seeking professional help. Good policy, good practice, and adherence to state and federal laws protecting people with disabilities require professional, individualized assessment and a fair procedure before students or employees can be removed on the ground that they have a mental disability that poses a "direct threat" to themselves or others.

7. *Is there an association between mental illness and violence?*

Research shows some association between severe mental illness and violence, especially when mental illness is accompanied by substance abuse. The 1998 American Psychiatric Association *Fact Sheet: Violence and Mental Illness* contains the following observation:

> People often fear what they do not understand, and for many of us, mental illnesses fall into that category. This fear . . . [often] stems from the common misconception that the term "mental illness" is a diagnosis, and that all mental illnesses thus have similar symptoms, making all people who suffer with them equally suspect and dangerous. . . . Recent research has shown that the vast majority of people who are violent do not suffer from mental illnesses. However, there is a certain small subgroup of people with severe and persistent mental illnesses who are at risk of becoming violent. [n.p.]

The U.S. Department of Heath and Human Services (2007) observes that "compared with the risk associated with the combination of male gender, young age, and lower socioeconomic status, the risk of violence presented by mental disorder is modest" (n.p.). Such a "modest" correlation won't be sufficient to draw conclusions about the future behavior of any particular student. Again, individualized assessment will be imperative, focusing on a specific diagnosis, demonstrable behavior, compliance in taking prescribed medications, patterns of substance abuse, and any recent traumatic events or stresses, among other factors.

8.   *How can I identify potentially violent students?*

This is not a task to be undertaken alone. Expertise is available on campus to help. See the contact information below and in our first answer.

It's important to resist the temptation to try to "profile" potentially violent students based on media reports of past shootings. The 2003 National Research Council (NRC) report *Deadly Lessons: Understanding Lethal School Violence* contains the following guidance:

> One widely discussed preventive idea is to develop methods to identify likely offenders in instances of lethal school violence or school rampages. . . . The difficulty is that . . . [t]he offenders are not that unusual; they look like their classmates at school. This has been an important finding of all those who have sought to investigate these shootings. Most important are the findings of the United States Secret Service, which concluded . . . [t]here is no accurate or useful profile of "the school shooter."

- Attacker ages ranged from 11–21.
- They came from a variety of racial and ethnic backgrounds. In nearly one-quarter of the cases, the attackers were not White.
- They came from a range of family situations, from intact families with numerous ties to the community to foster homes with histories of neglect.
- The academic performance ranged from excellent to failing.
- They had a range of friendship patterns from socially isolated to popular.
- Their behavioral histories varied, from having no observed behavioral problems to multiple behaviors warranting reprimand and/or discipline.
- Few attackers showed any marked change in academic performance, friendship status, interest in school, or disciplinary problems prior to their attack. [Moore et al., pp. 332–333]

A more promising approach is "threat assessment" based on analysis of observable behavior compiled from multiple sources and reviewed by a trained threat assessment team. The report *Threat Assessment in Schools: A Guide to Managing Threatening Situations and to Creating Safe School Climates* (developed by the U.S. Secret Service and U.S. Department of Education) contains the following overview:

- Students and adults who know the student who is the subject of the threat assessment inquiry should be asked about communications or other behaviors that may indicate the student of concern's ideas or intent. The focus of these interviews should be factual: What was said? To whom?

- What was written? To whom?
- What was done?
- When and where did this occur?
- Who else observed this behavior?
- Did the student say why he or she acted as they did?

Bystanders, observers, and other people who were there when the student engaged in threatening behaviors or made threatening statements should be queried about whether any of these behaviors or statements concerned or worried them. These individuals should be asked about changes in the student's attitudes and behaviors. Likewise, they should be asked if they have become increasingly concerned about the student's behavior or state of mind. However, individuals interviewed generally should not be asked to characterize the student or interpret meanings of communications that the student may have made. Statements such as "I think he's really dangerous" or "he said it with a smile, so I knew that he must be joking" may not be accurate characterizations of the student's intent, and therefore are unlikely to be useful to the threat assessment team. [Fein et al., 2002, p. 52]

Proper threat assessment is a team effort requiring expertise from experienced professionals, including law enforcement officers. Threat assessment on our campus is done by [name of the team or committee], headed by [name and telephone number]. Faculty members should contact the threat assessment team whenever they believe a student may pose a risk of violence to self or others. If in doubt, seek a threat assessment. In an emergency, contact the campus police immediately through [emergency telephone number].

9. *Should I talk with a student about my concerns?*

Exercise judgment on a case-by-case basis, preferably after consultation with colleagues, perhaps including the threat assessment team. An effort at conversation is generally advisable. Students are often oblivious to the impressions they make. Careful listening and courteous dialogue—perhaps with participation by a department chair or student conduct administrator—will often resolve the problem. At a minimum, the discussion may prove valuable in any subsequent threat assessment process. Please do not give assurances of confidentially. A student who appears to pose a threat to self or others needs to be referred for help and supervision. College teachers should not abrogate their traditional roles as guides and mentors, but they must not assume the responsibilities of therapists or police officers.

◆ ◆ ◆

One danger in the aftermath of the Virginia Tech shootings is the potential for creating a climate of fear and distance between teachers and students—especially students who seem odd, eccentric, or detached. Research on violence prevention suggests that schools and colleges need more cross-generational contact, not less. The NRC report stated that:

In the course of our interviews with adolescents, we are reminded once again of how "adolescent society," as James S. Coleman famously dubbed it 40 years ago, continues to be insulated from the adults who surround it. . . . The insularity of adolescent society serves to magnify slights and reinforce social hierarchies; correspondingly, it is only through exchange with trusted adults that teens can reach the longer-term view that can come with maturity. . . . [W]e could not put it better than the words of a beloved long-time teacher [at one of the schools studied]: "The only real way of preventing [school violence] is to get into their heads and their hearts. [Moore et al., 2003, p. 160]

Getting into the "heads and hearts" of students goes beyond individual conversations. It entails fostering a community of engagement, defined not by codes of silence or barriers of indifference but by an active sense of mutual responsibility. This critical endeavor depends upon the faculty. Now more than ever faculty must demonstrate skills in reaching outward rather than retreating inward.

Risk Management and the Brain's Fear System

In this third component of our chapter I examine legal issues from a physiological perspective. Strange as that may sound, most of us are well aware that decision making draws upon the complex neural architecture of the human brain. An important component of that architecture is the capacity for fear. Although fear served us well in the days when leopards jumped from the bush, it is more likely in contemporary society to prevent us from taking reasonable risks to pursue worthy goals.

The role of fear in risk management is evident in the proliferation of warning labels on commercial products. Examples cited in the national press include a fishing lure with the caution "harmful if swallowed"; solemn announcements that sleeping pills may "cause drowsiness"; and warnings on bottles of dried bobcat urine (used as rodent repellent): "Not for human consumption." Aside from their entertainment value, a profusion of bizarre warning labels highlights a preoccupation with litigation in American society. Sometimes fear of litigation is justified, but the pervasiveness of fear suggests a contagion that may be feeding on itself. Perhaps the way human brains are wired has something to do with the phenomenon.

A part of the primate brain called the *amygdala* appears to be the site of the fear response. In evolutionary terms the amygdala is old, but hardly primitive. It seems to have formed complex interactions with the prefrontal cortex—a more recently evolved part of the human brain that relies, in part, on cognition to evaluate the nature and seriousness of a perceived threat.

What is the relevance of this short anatomy lesson to the world of higher education law? Please weigh your emotional responses to the words "lawsuit," "summons," "subpoena," "discovery," and "deposition." They evoke fear—and fear is a devilishly difficult feeling to manage well.

Consider this observation published by the Center for Neural Science at New York University (NYU):

> Many of the most common psychiatric disorders that afflict humans are emotional disorders, and many of these are related to brain's fear system. According to the Public Health Service, about 50% of mental problems reported in the U.S. (other than those related to substance abuse) are accounted for by the anxiety disorders, including phobias, panic attacks, post-traumatic stress disorder, obsessive compulsive disorder, and generalized anxiety. Research into the brain mechanisms of fear help us understand why these emotional conditions are so hard to control. Neuroanatomists have shown that the pathways that connect the emotional processing system of fear, the amygdala, with the thinking brain, the neocortex, are not symmetrical—the connections from the cortex to the amygdala are considerably weaker than those from the amygdala to the cortex. This may explain why, once an emotion is aroused, it is so hard for us to turn it off at will [LeDoux Laboratory, n.d.]

The implications for college administrators are many and varied. I'd like to stress three:

1. *Our heightened attention to threats may limit access to information.* The mind seems to focus on future dangers, even if the dangers are largely imaginary. The media are well aware of this trait and pay special attention to threats of lawsuits; preliminary findings that point to possible liability (e.g. a "duty of care"), and predictions from lawyers, consultants, and risk management experts about the next wave of litigation certain to engulf us all. It's not that the facts or data are necessarily wrong, but the predisposition of reporters and readers is to stress the negative. Most college administrators, for example, are well aware of the Shin case at the Massachusetts Institute of Technology (MIT), and the preliminary finding of a "duty of care" when a student is known to be at risk of suicide (*Shin v. Massachusetts Institute of Technology et al.*, 2005). Fewer administrators are conversant with equally viable opinions pointing in different, less ominous directions. For example, a judicial decision and jury verdict (both favorable to the college) in student suicide litigation at Allegheny College just a few months after the Shin decision received far less attention (*Mahoney v. Allegheny College*, Crawford County Court of Common Pleas; December 22, 2005).

The importance of gathering evidence includes making more data-driven decisions about how institutions should define and respond to "dangerous" conditions or behavior. Again, as suggested earlier, many college administrators equate suicidal ideation with high rates of completed suicide. However, research published in the July 2004 issue of *Psychiatric Times* reported that "suicidal ideation occurs in about 5.6% of the U.S. population, with about 0.7% of the population attempting suicide. The incidence of completed suicide is far lower, at 0.01%. This rarity of suicide, even in groups known to be at higher risk than the general population, contributes to the impossibility of predicting suicide" (Kanapaux, 2004, n.p.).

In short, before acting on anecdotes or media reports about alarming legal trends—or the latest crisis affecting America's youth—college administrators should make a deliberate, thoughtful effort to examine a broader array of information and perspectives. The rush to regulate (or to find creative ways to dismiss "troubled" students) may end up causing more legal problems than it solves.

2. *Disproportionate attention to threats may slant the interpretation of information we do receive.* Nuances and caveats in judicial opinions are sometimes swept aside by the exclusive focus on an unfavorable result. In the Shin case, for example, the court focused on "numerous reports" from students, administrators, and mental health administrators indicating that Elizabeth Shin was at immediate risk of suicide. I wrote in my 2006 book *Questions and Answers on College Student Suicide*: "There is no indication [after Shin that] courts in Massachusetts . . . will impose a requirement that colleges randomly screen and predict which students will commit suicide and make timely interventions to save their lives. Nor will administrators or counselors (who are not mental health professionals) be expected to know and respond to all of the evolving and frequently ambiguous "warning signs" of suicide. Instead, institutions of higher education may face heightened risk of liability for suicide when they ignore or mishandle known suicide threats or attempts" (Pavela, 2006b, p. 8).

Those caveats were lost on college administrators who concluded that one lower court in Massachusetts had transformed all of American law by holding that educators had a blanket responsibility to prevent student suicide.

3. *Fear may disguise and displace educational priorities.* A popular adage used by management consultants is: "Having lost sight of our objective we redoubled our efforts." The point, of course, is that mindless activity fills the void left by a lack of vision. Fear can accomplish the same harmful result. Consider again this observation from the NYU brain researchers: "Neuroanatomists have shown that the pathways that connect the emotional processing system of fear, the amygdala, with the thinking brain, the neocortex, are not symmetrical—the connections from the cortex to the amygdala are considerably weaker than those from the amygdala to the cortex" (LeDoux Laboratory, n.d., n.p.).

In other words, the neural wiring for fear is more efficient than the wiring for cognition. Fear readily dominates cognition—often with bad results in contemporary social environments. Avoiding this phenomenon requires discipline, training, and advance preparation. These traits draw upon the cognitive capacity of the brain to define goals worth taking risks to achieve.

◆ ◆ ◆

A critical goal for student development administrators is the maturation of young adults. Maturation is grounded in the development of skills in self-regulation, including the insights that come from encountering failure. There will be instances, for example, when we give students considerable autonomy—knowing they're likely to fail. Our objective is to use failure to help students develop self-insight. University of

Virginia psychologist Jonathan Haidt (2006) advises parents in this regard: "Shelter your children when young, but if the sheltering goes on through the child's teens and twenties, it may keep out wisdom and growth as well as pain" (p. 153).

College administrators preoccupied by the fear of litigation will replay their own variation of the "helicopter parents" phenomenon: ever-increasing reliance upon supervision and control, combined with the added ingredient of "zero tolerance" policies designed to eliminate any exercising of discretion. By these means the illusory pursuit of a risk-free environment (without any effort to balance risks and educational objectives) undermines one of the fundamental reasons why we formed educational communities in the first place.

Summary

This chapter has examined three particularly important aspects of student affairs practice, including protecting and promoting civility, working with troubled students, and risk management. Beyond the information provided herein, student affairs practitioners are advised to make use of legal resources as they are available at their institution. Finally, it is important to remember that these and other legal issues are fluid. That is, they will change as courts hand down decisions and state legislatures, and as the national government passes new legislation or promulgates new rules and regulations.

References

American Psychiatric Association (APA). (1998). *Fact sheet: Violence and mental illness*. Washington, DC: Author.

Appelbaum, P. S. (2006). Depressed? Get out! *Psychiatric Services, 57*(7), 914–916.

Areen, J. (2009). *Higher education and the law*. New York: Thomson.

Association for Student Judicial Affairs. (2007, May 11). ASJA law and policy report no. 254. Retrieved April 22, 2009, from www.ferris.edu/htmls/studentlife/personalcounseling/vtu.pdf.

Baum, K., & Klaus, P. (2005). *Violent victimization of college students, 1995–2002*. Washington, DC: U.S. Department of Justice, Bureau of Justice Statistics.

Duhart, D. T. (2001). *Violence in the workplace, 1993–1999*. Washington, DC: U.S. Department of Justice, Bureau of Justice Statistics.

Edmundson, M. (2002). *Teacher: The one who made the difference*. New York: Vintage.

Fein, R. A., Vossekuil, B., Pollack, W. S., Borum, R., Modzeleski, W., & Reddy, M. (2002). *Threat assessment in schools: A guide to managing threatening situations and to creating safe school climates*. Washington, DC: U.S. Secret Service & U.S. Department of Education.

Haidt, J. (2006). *The happiness hypothesis: Finding modern truth in ancient wisdom*. New York: Basic Books.

Kanapaux, W. (2004, July 1). Guideline to treatment of suicidal behavior. *Psychiatric Times, 24*(4). Retrieved April 22, 2009, from www.psychiatrictimes.com/suicidal-behavior/article/10168/47561#.

Kaplin, W. A., & Lee, B. A. (2009). *A legal guide for student affairs professionals*. San Francisco: Jossey-Bass.

Kingsbury, A., Brush, S., Greene, E. W., & Schulte, B. (2007, April). Toward a safer campus. *U.S. News and World Report, 142*, 48–52.

LeDoux Laboratory. (n.d.). *Overview: Emotion, memory and the brain.* New York: New York University, Center for Neural Science. Retrieved April 13, 2009, from www.cns.nyu.edu/home/ledoux/overview.htm.

Mahoney v. Allegheny College (Crawford County Court of Common Pleas, 2005).

Moore, M. H., Petrie, C. V., Braga, A. A., & McLaughlin, B. L. (Eds.). (2003). *Deadly lessons: Understanding lethal school violence.* Washington, DC: National Research Council.

Pavela, G. (2006a, December 1). Only speech codes should be censored. *Chronicle of Higher Education, 53,* B14.

Pavela, G. (2006b). *Questions and answers on college student suicide.* St. Johns, FL: College Administration Publications.

Shin v. Massachusetts Institute of Technology, et al. (Superior Ct., Mass., 2005).

Siegel, B. (1993, March 28). Fighting words. *Los Angeles Times Magazine,* p. 14. Cited in Synfax Weekly Report, 93.86, The politics of the Wisconsin speech code.

Silverman, M. M., Meyer, P. M., Sloane, F., Raffel, M., & Pratt, D. M. (1997). The Big Ten suicide study: A 10-year study of suicides on midwestern university campuses. *Suicide and Life Threatening Behavior, 27(3),* 285–303.

Simpson, J., & Weiner, E. (Eds.). (1989). *Oxford English Dictionary* (2nd ed., Vol. 3). New York: Oxford University Press.

U.S. Department of Health and Human Services. (2007, April 20). *Understanding mental illness: Fact sheet.* Washington, DC: Author. Retrieved April 13, 2009, from http://www.samhsa.gov/MentalHealth/understanding_Mentalllness_Factsheet.aspx.

Virginia Youth Violence Project. (2009). *College violence.* Charlottesville, VA: University of Virginia, School of Education. Retrieved April 9, 2009, from http://youthviolence.edschool.virginia.edu/violence-in-schools/collegecampus.html.

White, J. B. (1983). The ethics of argument: Plato's Gorgias and the modern lawyer. *University of Chicago Law Review, 50(2),* 849–895.

PART THREE

THEORETICAL BASES OF THE PROFESSION

Long ago, social psychologist Kurt Lewin declared that there is "nothing so practical as a good theory"; and indeed, the rich theoretical bases that serve as a foundation for practice contribute to the professional vigor and resilience of student affairs. As suggested in Parts One and Two, the development of a body of theories guiding student affairs practice is integrally related to the history of higher education and the evolution of student affairs as a profession. In fact, as the chapters in Part Three demonstrate, theories are socially constructed in that they reflect both the historical, societal, political, and cultural contexts in which they evolved and the perspectives of those who generated them. However, although theories have evolved over time and new theoretical perspectives have been offered, those in student affairs remain concerned with understanding the whole student; that is, how individual students develop and learn and come to construct their identities; the role of the environment in promoting or deterring

development; the influence of organizations and campus climate on students' experiences and outcomes; and what contributes to student success, broadly defined.

The chapters in Part Three discuss both foundational theories with which all in student affairs should be familiar and newer theoretical perspectives for understanding college students, their experiences, and their environments. It is impossible in a text of this nature to cover all theories in great depth. Instead, we tried to strike an artful balance in discussing those foundational theories that have not only served the profession well over time but also been extended to broaden the focus, expanded to be more inclusive, or reconceptualized to pose new theorizations of important concepts and ideas integral to contemporary student affairs practice. We also provide here the updated and revised Theories about College Students, Environments, and Organizations, initially developed by Marylu McEwen, which first appeared in the fourth edition of *Student Services*, revised by Susan R. Jones, Elisa S.

Abes, and Kristan Cilente for this volume. This chart is not intended to be exhaustive, however, nor is it representative of all the possibilities for understanding college students. In revising this chart, we erred in the direction of only including *theories*: frameworks grounded in empirical research that describe abstract representations of the relationships among variables and that describe a phenomenon of interest. The chart provides sources for several foundational theories in each area, as well as newer work contributing to the development of theory. We were also aware of those areas in which very little work exists or in which boundaries for categories are not clear. A careful review will reveal that the box for social class is empty, because we were unable to locate any theories related to social class identity. In addition, the categories of faith, religion, and spirituality demonstrate the limitations of organizing theories in this way. Finally, we did include primary sources for several new theoretical perspectives (not theories per se), such as critical race theory, queer theory, and intersectionality, because they are gaining currency in student affairs as significant lenses for exposing and understanding the experiences of historically marginalized student populations and the influence of structures of inequality on education, including student affairs practice.

In Chapter Eight, Susan R. Jones and Elisa S. Abes discuss the nature of theory and theories in student affairs. They provide an overview of the current conceptualization of families of theories, with an emphasis on what distinguishes these families from one another. Addressing theory construction and evolution, they also examine paradigmatic perspectives on the creation of theory and how different worldviews yield different results. In Chapter Nine, Nancy Evans provides an overview of psychosocial and cognitive structural development, with a discussion of the foundational theories within each of these two families of student development. In Chapter Ten, Vasti Torres focuses on identity development, particularly social identities such as race, gender, ethnicity, and sexual identity. Her review captures both the evolution of identity theories as well as the influence of newer conceptualizations, such as critical race theory. The challenge of inclusivity is particularly apparent in this chapter, given that it was impossible to include detail on the full range of possible social identities. In a nearly new Chapter Eleven on Student Learning, Patricia King and Marcia Baxter Magolda situate their discussion of student learning in the context of self-authorship theory and research. They also offer specific suggestions for designing educational environments that promote transformative learning and self-authorship.

In Chapter Twelve, Adrianna Kezar moves the discussion from the individual to organizations, providing an overview of several influential theories that address organizations and organizational change. Kezar helps student affairs educators both analyze the organizations in which they work and learn how to use multiple frameworks for understanding issues within organizations in order to create change. In Chapter Thirteen, Kristen Renn and Lori Patton describe campus ecology theory and its application to an understanding of how campus environments influence student learning and development. Their chapter includes a discussion of differing institutional types in relation to institutional identities and campus climate. Finally, in Chapter Fourteen, George Kuh takes a view of student success that goes beyond the more typical focus on student retention and persistence by focusing on a broad array of student outcomes. In particular, he offers seven strategies student affairs educators may utilize to foster student success.

The discussion of the relationship of theories to practice is as old as the profession itself. In this age of accountability and documenting outcomes, it behooves those more comfortable in the world of theories to ground their theories in the realities of practice; and for those more at ease in the world of practice to guide their practice in theories generated from a quest to understand the experiences of students. The chapters in Part Three provide a good foundation of those theories useful to student affairs practice. We encourage readers to broaden their knowledge of theories by studying those not included in these chapters given the limitations of space and to also deepen their understanding by reading primary sources.

THEORIES ABOUT COLLEGE STUDENTS, ENVIRONMENTS, AND ORGANIZATIONS
By Susan R. Jones, Elisa S. Abes, and Kristan Cilente

Theory Family	Subcategory	Focus of Theory	Specific Theories
Psychosocial Development (see Chapter Nine)	General psychosocial development	Foundational theory	Erikson, E. H. (1968). *Identity: Youth and crisis.* New York: Norton.
		Challenge and support	Sanford, N. (1962). *The American college.* New York: Wiley. Sanford, N. (1967). *Why colleges fail: A study of the student as a person.* San Francisco: Jossey-Bass.
		Vectors of development	Chickering, A. W., & Reisser, L. (1993). *Education and identity* (2nd ed.). San Francisco: Jossey-Bass.
		Crisis and commitment	Marcia, J. E. (1966). Development and validation of ego-identity status. *Journal of Personality and Social Psychology, 3,* 551–559.
		Women's development	Josselson, R. (1987). *Finding herself: Pathways to identity development in women.* San Francisco: Jossey-Bass. Josselson, R. (1996). *Revising herself: The story of women's identity from college to midlife.* New York: Oxford University Press.
		Career development	Super, D. E. (1990). A life-span, life-space approach to career development. In D. Brown, L. Brooks, & Associates (Eds.), *Career choice and development: Applying contemporary theories to development* (2nd ed., pp. 197–261). San Francisco: Jossey-Bass.
	Adult development	Life stage	Levinson, D. J. (1978). *The seasons of a man's life.* New York: Ballantine. Levinson, D. J. (1996). *The seasons of a woman's life.* New York: Ballantine. Vaillant, G. (1977). *Adaptation to life.* Boston: Little, Brown.
		Life events	Goodman, J., Schlossberg, N. K., & Anderson, M. L. (2006). *Counseling adults in transition* (3rd ed.). New York: Springer.
		Life course	Arnett, J. J. (2004). *Emerging adulthood: The winding road from the late teens through the twenties.* New York: Oxford University Press. Ferraro, K. F. (2001). Aging and role transitions. In R. H. Birnstock & L. K. George (Eds.), *Handbook of aging and the social sciences* (pp. 313–330). San Francisco: Jossey-Bass. Kroger, J. (2004). *Identity in adolescence: The balance between self and other* (3rd ed.). London: Routledge. Neugarten, B. L. (1979). Time, age, and the life cycle. *American Journal of Psychiatry, 136,* 887–894.

Development of Social Identities (see Chapter Ten)	General identity development	Racial identity	
			Deaux, K. (1993). Reconstructing social identity. *Personality and Social Psychology Bulletin, 19*, 4–12.
		Black racial identity	Cross, W. E. (2001). Encountering nigrescence. In J. G. Ponterotto, J. M. Casas, L. A. Suzuki, & C. M. Alexander (Eds.), *Handbook of multicultural counseling* (pp. 371–393). Thousand Oaks, CA: Sage.
			Helms, J. E., & Cook, D. A. (1999). *Using race and culture in counseling and psychotherapy: Theory and process.* Boston: Allyn & Bacon.
		White racial identity	Helms, J. E., & Cook, D. A. (1999). *Using race and culture in counseling and psychotherapy: Theory and process.* Boston: Allyn & Bacon.
		Asian American racial identity	Kim, J. (2001). Asian American identity development theory. In C. L. Wijeyesinghe & B. W. Jackson III (Eds.), *New perspectives on racial identity development: A theoretical and practical anthology* (pp. 67–90). New York: New York University Press.
			Kodama, C. M., McEwen, M. K., Liang, C.T.H., & Lee, S. (2002). An Asian American perspective on psychosocial student development theory. In M. K. McEwen, C. M. Kodama, A. Alvarez, S. Lee, & C.T.H. Liang (Eds.), *Working with Asian American college students* (New Directions for Student Services No. 97, pp. 45–59). San Francisco: Jossey-Bass.
		Native American racial identity	Horse, P. G. (2001). Reflections on American Indian identity. In C. L. Wijeyesinghe & B. W. Jackson III (Eds.), *New perspectives on racial identity development: A theoretical and practical anthology* (pp. 91–107). New York: New York University Press.
			Laframboise, T. D., Trimble, J. E., & Mohatt, G. V. (1990). Counseling intervention and American Indian tradition: An integrative approach. *Counseling Psychologist, 18(4),* 628–654.
		Latino racial identity	Ferdman, B. M., & Gallegos, P. I. (2001). Racial identity development and Latinos in the United States. In C. L. Wijeyesinghe & B. W. Jackson III (Eds.), *New perspectives on racial identity development: A theoretical and practical anthology* (pp. 32–66). New York: New York University Press.
			Torres, V. (2004). Familial influences on the identity development of Latino first year students. *Journal of College Student Development, 45(4),* 457–469.

(continued)

THEORIES ABOUT COLLEGE STUDENTS, ENVIRONMENTS, AND ORGANIZATIONS (continued)
By Susan R. Jones, Elisa S. Abes, and Kristan Cilente

Theory Family	Subcategory	Focus of Theory	Specific Theories
		Biracial identity	Kerwin, C., & Ponterotto, J. G. (1995). Biracial identity development: Theory and research. In J. G. Ponteretto, J. M. Casas, L. A. Suzuki, & C. M. Alexander (Eds.), *Handbook of multicultural counseling* (pp. 199–217). Thousand Oaks, CA: Sage.
			Kich, G. K. (1992). The developmental process of asserting a biracial, bicultural identity. In M.P.P. Root (Ed.), *Racially mixed people in America* (pp. 304–417). Newbury Park, CA: Sage.
			Poston, W.S.C. (1990). The biracial identity development model: A needed addition. *Journal of Counseling & Development, 69,* 152–155.
		Multiracial identity	Renn, K. A. (2004). *Mixed race students in college: The ecology of race, identity, and community.* Albany, NY: SUNY Press.
			Renn, K. A. (2008). Research on biracial and multiracial identity development: Overview and synthesis. In K. A. Renn & P. Shang (Eds.), *Biracial and Multiracial Students.* (New Directions for Student Services No. 123 (pp. 13-21)). San Francisco: Jossey-Bass
			Root, M.P.P. (Ed.). (1996). *The multiracial experience: Racial borders as the new frontier.* Thousand Oaks, CA: Sage.
			Wijeyesinghe, C. L. (2001). Racial identity in multiracial people: An alternative paradigm. In C. L. Wijeyesinghe & B. W. Jackson III (Eds.), *New perspectives on racial identity development: A theoretical and practical anthology* (pp. 129–152). New York: New York University Press.
	Ethnic identity	Crisis and commitment	Phinney, J. S. (1993). A three-stage model of ethnic identity development in adolescence. In M. E. Bernal & G. P. Knight (Eds.), *Ethnic identity formation and transmission among Hispanic and other minorities* (pp. 61–79). Albany, NY: State University of New York Press.
			Ruiz, A. S. (1990). Ethnic identity: Crisis and resolution. *Journal of Multicultural Counseling and Development, 18*(1), 29–40.

Sexual identity	Gay and lesbian identity	Abes, E. S., & Jones, S. R. (2004). Meaning-making capacity and the dynamics of lesbian college students' multiple dimensions of identity. *Journal of College Student Development, 45*(6), 612–632.
		Bilodeau, B. L., & Renn, K. A. (2005). Analysis of LGBT identity development models and implications for practice. In R. L. Sanlo (Ed.), *Gender Identity and Sexual Orientation: Research, Policy, and Personal Perspectives,* (New Directions for Student Services No. 111, pp. 25–39) San Francisco: Jossey-Bass.
		Cass, V. C. (1979). Homosexual identity formation: A theoretical model. *Journal of Homosexuality, 4,* 219–235.
		D'Augelli, A. R. (1994). Identity development and sexual orientation: Toward a model of lesbian, gay, and bisexual development. In E. J. Trickett, R. J. Watts, & D. Birman (Eds.), *Human diversity: Perspectives on people in context* (pp. 312–333). San Francisco: Jossey-Bass.
		Fassinger, R. E., & Arseneau, J. R. (2007). "I'd rather be wet than be under that umbrella": Experiences and identities of lesbian, gay, bisexual, and transgender people. In K. J. Bieschke, R. M. Perez, & K. A. DeBord (Eds.), *Handbook of counseling and psychotherapy with lesbian, gay, bisexual, and transgender clients* (pp. 19–49). Washington, DC: American Psychological Association.
		McCarn, S. R., & Fassinger, R. E. (1996). Revisioning sexual minority identity formation. *Counseling Psychologist, 24*(3), 508–534.
	Bisexual identity	Klein, F., Sepekoff, B., & Wolf, T. J. (1990). Sexual orientation: A multi-variable dynamic process. In T. Geller (Ed.), *Bisexuality, a reader and sourcebook* (pp. 64–81). Ojai, CA: Times Change Press.
		Parker, B. A., Adams, H. L., & Phillips, L. D. (2007). Decentering gender: Bisexual identity as an expression of a non-dichotomous worldview. *Identity: An International Journal of Theory and Research, 7*(3), 205–224.
	Heterosexual identity	Mueller, J. A., & Cole, J. C. (2009). A qualitative examination of heterosexual consciousness among college students. *Journal of College Student Development, 50*(3), 320–336.
		Worthington, R. L., Savoy, H. B., Dilon, F. R. & Vernaglia, E. R. (2002). Heterosexual identity development: A multidimensional model of individual and social identity. *Counseling Psychologist, 30,* 496–531.

(continued)

THEORIES ABOUT COLLEGE STUDENTS, ENVIRONMENTS, AND ORGANIZATIONS (*continued*)
By Susan R. Jones, Elisa S. Abes, and Kristan Cilente

Theory Family	Subcategory	Focus of Theory	Specific Theories
		Queer identity	Abes, E. S., & Kasch, D. (2007). Using queer theory to explore lesbian college students' multiple dimensions of identity. *Journal of College Student Development, 48*, 619–636.
	Gender identity	Feminist identity	Downing, N. E., & Roush, K. L. (1985). From passive acceptance to active commitment: A model of feminist identity development for women. *Counseling Psychologist, 13*, 695–709.
		Womanist identity	Ossana, S. M., Helms, J. E., & Leonard, M. M. (1992). Do "womanist" identity attitudes influence college women's self-esteem and perceptions of environmental bias? *Journal of Counseling & Development, 70*, 402–408.
		Men's identity	Davis, T. L. (2002). Voices of gender role conflict: The social construction of college men's identity. *Journal of College Student Development, 43*, 508–521. Edwards, K. E. & Jones, S. R. (2009). "Putting my man face on": A grounded theory of college men's gender identity development. *Journal of College Student Development, 50*(2), 210–228. Harper, S. R., & Quaye, S. J., (2007). Student organizations as venues for Black identity expression and development among African American male student leaders. *Journal of College Student Development, 48*(2), 127–144. Kimmel, M. (2008). *Guyland: The perilous world where boys become men.* New York: HarperCollins.
		Transgender identity	Beemyn, B., Curtis, B., Davis, M., & Tubbs, N. J. (2005). Transgender issues on college campuses. In R. L. Sanlo (Ed.), *Gender Identity and Sexual Orientation: Research, Policy, and Personal Perspectives,* (New Directions for Student Services No. 111, pp. 49–60). San Francisco: Jossey-Bass. Carter, K. A. (2000). Transgenderism and college students: Issues of gender identity and its role on our campuses. In V. A. Wall & N. J. Evans (Eds.), *Toward acceptance: Sexual orientation issues on campus* (pp. 261–282). Lanham, MD: University Press of America.

	Social class and background	
	Religious identity	Peek, L. (2005). Becoming Muslim: The development of a religious identity. *Sociology of Religion, 66*(3), 215–242.
	Abilities and disabilities	Gibson, J. (2006). Disability and clinical competency: An introduction. *California Psychologist, 39*, 6–10. Jones, S. R. (1996). Toward inclusive theory: Disability as a social construction. *NASPA Journal, 33*, 347–354. Sherry, M. (2004). Overlaps and contradictions between queer theory and disability studies. *Disability & Society, 19*(7), 769–783.
	Multiple oppressions	Reynolds, A. L., & Pope, R. L. (1991). The complexities of diversity: Exploring multiple oppressions. *Journal of Counseling & Development, 70*, 174–180.
	Multiple identities	Abes, E. S., Jones, S. R. & McEwen, M. K. (2007). Reconceptualizing the Model of Multiple Dimensions of Identity: The role of meaning-making capacity in the construction of multiple identities. *Journal of College Student Development, 48*, 1–22. Jones, S. R. (2009). Constructing identities at the intersections: An autoethnographic exploration of multiple dimensions of identity. *Journal of College Student Development, 50*(3), 287–304. Jones, S. R., & McEwen, M. K. (2000). A conceptual model of multiple dimensions of identity. *Journal of College Student Development, 41*, 405–414. Stewart, D. L. (2009). Perceptions of multiple identities among Black college students. *Journal of College Student Development, 50*(3), 253–270.
Cognitive–Structural Development (see Chapters Nine and Eleven)	Foundational theory	Piaget, J. (1950). *The psychology of intelligence*. San Diego, CA: Harcourt Brace Jovanovich. Piaget, J. (1977). *The moral judgment of the child* (M. Gabain, Trans.). Harmondsforth, England: Penguin. (Original work published 1932)
	Intellectual and ethical development	Perry, W. G., Jr. (1970). *Forms of intellectual and ethical development in the college years: A scheme.* New York: Holt, Rinehart and Winston.
	Women's ways of knowing	Belenky, M. F., Clinchy, B. M., Goldberger, N. R., & Tarule, J. M. (1986). *Women's ways of knowing: The development of self, voice, and mind.* New York: Basic Books.

(continued)

THEORIES ABOUT COLLEGE STUDENTS, ENVIRONMENTS, AND ORGANIZATIONS (continued)
By Susan R. Jones, Elisa S. Abes, and Kristan Cilente

Theory Family	Subcategory	Focus of Theory	Specific Theories
		Reflective judgment	King, P. M., & Kitchener, K. S. (2002). The reflective judgment model: Twenty years of research on epistemic cognition. In B. K. Hofer & P. R. Pintrich (Eds.), *Personal epistemology: The psychology of beliefs about knowledge and knowing* (pp. 37–61). Mahwah, NJ: Erlbaum.
		Epistemological reflection	Baxter Magolda, M. B. (1992). *Knowing and reasoning in college: Gender-related patterns in students' intellectual development.* San Francisco: Jossey-Bass.
	Moral development	Justice and rights	Kohlberg, L. (1976). Moral stages and moralization: The cognitive-developmental approach. In T. Lickona (Ed.), *Moral development and behavior: Theory, research, and social issues* (pp. 31–53). New York: Holt, Rinehart and Winston.
		Care and responsibility	Gilligan, C. (1982). *In a different voice: Psychological theory and women's development.* Cambridge, MA: Harvard University Press.
		Moral reasoning	Rest, J. R., Narvaez, D., Bebeau, M. J., & Thoma, S. J. (1999). *Postconventional moral thinking: A neo-Kohlbergian approach.* Mahwah, NJ: Lawrence Erlbaum.
	Faith development	Faith	Fowler, J. (2000). *Becoming adult, becoming Christian: Adult development and Christian faith* (Rev. ed.). San Francisco: Jossey-Bass.
		Spirituality	Parks, S. D. (2000). *Big questions, worthy dreams: Mentoring young adults in their search for meaning, purpose, and faith.* San Francisco: Jossey-Bass.
			Stewart, D. L. (2002). The role of faith in the development of an integrated identity: A qualitative study of Black students at a White college. *Journal of College Student Development, 43*(4), 579–596.
		Maturity	Heath, D. H. (1968). *Growing up in college.* San Francisco: Jossey-Bass.
Holistic development (See Chapter Eight)		Self-evolution	Kegan, R. (1982). *The evolving self: Problem and process in human development.* Cambridge, MA: Harvard University Press. Kegan, R. (1994). *In over our heads: The mental demands of modern life.* Cambridge, MA: Harvard University Press.

			References
		Self-authorship	Baxter Magolda, M. B. (2001). *Making their own way: Narratives for transforming higher education to promote self-development*. Sterling, VA: Stylus.
			Pizzolato, J. E. (2003). Developing self-authorship: Exploring the experiences of high risk college students. *Journal of College Student Development, 44*(6), 797–812.
			Torres, V., & Hernandez, E. (2007). The influence of ethnic identity on self-authorship: A longitudinal study of Latino/a college students. *Journal of College Student Development, 48*(5), 558–573.
Typologies and Student Learning (see Chapters Nine and Eleven)	Personality	Temperament and development	Heath, R. (1964). *The reasonable adventurer*. Pittsburgh, PA: University of Pittsburgh Press.
			Jung, C. G. (1971). *The collected works of C. G. Jung: Vol. 6. Psychological types*. Princeton, NJ: Princeton University Press. (Original work published 1923).
		Psychological type	Myers, I. B. (1980). *Gifts differing*. Palo Alto, CA: Consulting Psychologists Press.
		Vocational personality types	Holland, J. L. (1985). *Making vocational choices: A theory of vocational personalities and work environments* (2nd ed.). Englewood Cliffs, NJ: Prentice Hall.
		Learning styles	Kolb, D. (1976). *Learning styles inventory technical manual*. Boston: McBer.
	Learning	Transformative learning	Mezirow, J. (Ed.). (2000). *Learning as transformation: Critical perspectives on a theory in progress*. San Francisco: Jossey-Bass.
		Intercultural learning	King, P. M., & Baxter Magolda, M. B. (2005). A developmental model of intercultural maturity. *Journal of College Student Development, 46*(6), 571–592.
Organizational Approaches (see Chapter Twelve)	Organizational Theories		Baldridge, J. V. (1971). *Power and conflict in the university: Research in the sociology of complex organizations*. New York: Wiley.
			Bergquist, W. (1992). *The four cultures of the academy*. San Francisco: Jossey-Bass.
			Bolman, L., & Deal, T. (2008). *Reframing organizations: Artistry, choice, and leadership*. San Francisco: Jossey-Bass.
			Cohen, M., & March, J. (1974). *Leadership and ambiguity*. Boston: Harvard Business School Press.
			Morgan, G. (1997). *Images of organization*. Thousand Oaks, CA: Sage.
			Weick, K. E. (1995). *Sensemaking in organizations*. Thousand Oaks, CA: Sage.nal.

(continued)

THEORIES ABOUT COLLEGE STUDENTS, ENVIRONMENTS, AND ORGANIZATIONS (continued)
By Susan R. Jones, Elisa S. Abes, and Kristan Cilente

Theory Family	Subcategory	Focus of Theory	Specific Theories
Campus environments (see Chapter Thirteen)	Human aggregates	Environmental press	Moos, R. H. (1979). Evaluating educational environments: Procedures, measures, findings, and policy implications. San Francisco: Jossey-Bass.
	Organized environments	Campus culture	Kuh, G. D., & Whitt, E. J. (1988). The invisible tapestry: Culture in American colleges and universities (ASHE-ERIC Higher Education Report No. 1). Washington, DC: Association for the Study of Higher Education.
	Constructed environments	Inclusion and safety, involvement, and community	Strange, C. C. (2003). Dynamics of campus environments. In S. R. Komives, D. B. Woodard Jr., and Associates (Eds.), Student services: A handbook for the profession (4th ed., pp. 297–316). San Francisco: Jossey-Bass.
			Strange, C. C., & Banning, J. H. (2001). Educating by design: Creating campus learning environments that work. San Francisco: Jossey-Bass.
	Design for educational success	Campus ecology	Banning, J. H., & Kaiser, L. (1974). An ecological perspective and model for campus design. Personnel and Guidance Journal, 52, 370–375.
			Bronfenbrenner, U. (1993). The ecology of cognitive development: Research models and fugitive findings. In R. H. Wozniak & K. W. Fischer (Eds.), Development in context: Aging and thinking in specific environments (pp. 3–44). Hillsdale, NJ: Erlbaum.
			Moos, R. H. (1986). The human context: Environmental determinants of behavior. Malabar, FL: Krieger.
	Environmental impact	Outcomes	Astin, A. W. (1993). What matters in college? Four critical years revisited. San Francisco: Jossey-Bass.
			Pascarella, E. T., & Terenzini, P. T. (2005). How college affects students: A third decade of research. San Francisco: Jossey-Bass.
	Involvement	Student involvement	Astin, A. W. (1984). Student involvement: A developmental theory for higher education. Journal of College Student Development, 25, 297–308.
	Mattering and marginality	Building community	Schlossberg, N. K. (1989). Marginality and mattering: Key issues in building community. In D. C. Roberts (Ed.), Designing campus activities to foster a sense of community (New Directions for Student Services No. 48, pp. 5–15). San Francisco: Jossey-Bass.

Student Success (see Chapter Fourteen)	Student departure	Braxton, J. M., Hirschy, A. S., & McClendon, S. A. (2004). *Understanding and reducing college student departure.* (ASHE-ERIC Higher Education Report, Vol. 30, No. 3.) Washington, DC: Graduate School of Education and Human Development, The George Washington University.
	Student persistence	Tinto, V. (1993). *Leaving college: Rethinking the causes and cures of student attrition* (2nd ed.). Chicago: University of Chicago Press.
	Modified model of student persistence	Milem, J. E. & Berger, J. B. (1997). A modified model of college student persistence: Exploring the relationship between Astin's model of student involvement and Tinto's theory of student departure. *Journal of College Student Development, 38*(4), 387–400.
	Student success	Kuh, G. D. (2008). *High-impact educational practices: What they are, who has access to them, and why they matter.* Washington, DC: Association of American Colleges and Universities.
		Kuh, G. D., Kinzie, J., Schuh, J. H., Whitt, E. J., & Associates (2005). *Student success in college: Creating conditions that matter.* San Francisco: Jossey-Bass.
		Perna, L. W., & Thomas, S. L. (2008). *Theoretical perspectives on student success.* (ASHE-ERIC Higher Education Report, Vol. 34, No. 1.) San Francisco: Jossey-Bass.
Emerging Theoretical Perspectives (see Chapters Eight and Ten)	Critical race theory	Delgado, R., & Stefancic, J. (2001). *Critical race theory: An introduction.* New York: New York University Press.
		Delgado Bernal, D. (2002). Critical race theory, Latino critical theory, and critical raced-gendered epistemologies: Recognizing students of color as holders and creators of knowledge. *Qualitative Inquiry, 8*(1), 105–126.
		Ladson-Billings, G. (1998). Just what is critical race theory and what's it doing in a nice field like education? *Qualitative Studies in Education, 11*(1), 7–24.
	Queer theory	Sullivan, N. (2003). *A critical introduction to queer theory.* New York: New York University Press.

(continued)

THEORIES ABOUT COLLEGE STUDENTS, ENVIRONMENTS, AND ORGANIZATIONS (continued)
By Susan R. Jones, Elisa S. Abes, and Kristan Cilente

Theory Family	Subcategory	Focus of Theory	Specific Theories
	Intersectionality		Dill, B. T., McLaughlin, A. E., & Nieves, A. D. (2007). Future directions of feminist research: Intersectionality. In S. N. Hesse-Biber (Ed.), *Handbook of feminist research* (pp. 629–637). Thousand Oaks, CA: Sage.
			Dill, B. T., & Zambrana, R. E. (Eds.). (2009). *Emerging intersections: Race, class, and gender in theory, policy, and practice.* Piscataway, NJ: Rutgers University Press.
	Latino/a critical theory		Villalpando, O. (2003). Self-segregation or self-preservation? A critical race theory and Latino/a critical theory analysis of a study of Chicano college students. *Qualitative Studies in Education, 16,* 619–646.
	Critical race feminism		Wing, A. K. (Ed.). (2003). *Critical race feminism* (2nd ed.). New York: New York University Press.
Theoretical Critiques (see Chapter Eight)	Multiple theoretical perspectives		Abes, E. S. (2009). Theoretical borderlands: Using multiple theoretical perspectives to challenge inequitable power structures in student development theory. *Journal of College Student Development, 50,* 141–156.
			Lather, P. (2007). *Getting lost: Feminist efforts toward a double(d) science.* Albany, NY: SUNY Press.
			Lincoln, Y. S., & Guba, E. G. (2000). Paradigmatic controversies, contradictions, and emerging confluences. In N. K. Denzin & Y. S. Lincoln (Eds.), *Handbook of qualitative research* (2nd ed., pp. 163–188). Thousand Oaks, CA: Sage.
			Tanaka, G. (2002). Higher education's self-reflexive turn: Toward an intercultural theory of student development. *Journal of Higher Education, 73*(2), 263–296.

Based on McEwen, M. (2003). The nature and uses of theory. In S. R. Komives, D. B. Woodard Jr., & Associates (Eds.), *Student services: A handbook for the profession* (4th ed., pp. 153–178). San Francisco: Jossey-Bass. Adapted and updated with permission.

CHAPTER EIGHT

THE NATURE AND USES OF THEORY

Susan R. Jones and Elisa S. Abes

Students who are involved in student organizations and leadership positions are more satisfied with their overall college experiences.

First-generation students struggle with their transition from high school to college because they have parents who do not understand what they are going through.

Black students hang out together in the cafeteria because the campus climate is a chilly one for them.

Living on campus, especially in living-learning communities, improves retention of students participating in these programs.

Introduction: "Nothing as Useful as a Good Theory"

The preceding statements each represent a point of view that a student affairs educator may have about students. But are they theories? Student affairs educators may hold perspectives grounded in their own experiences and informed by observations that clearly influence their practice. Indeed, we all carry with us explicitly stated or implicitly implied ideas, beliefs, and prior experiences that directly influence how we make sense of ourselves and the students with whom we interact. Do these constitute theories? What "theories" do you have about college students? And from where do these "theories" come? What questions about college students do your "theories" address—are they questions about college student development, about campus environments, about institutions and organizations? These are all questions that may require considerations using theories as a guide.

Although well-known social psychologist Kurt Lewin (1951) suggested that there is nothing so practical as a good theory, theories represent more than common sense or a particular point of view based upon one's own experiences, assumptions, and beliefs. As student affairs educators, it is important for us to distinguish between informal assumptions we hold (such as those noted at the beginning of the chapter) and more formal theories that attempt to explain complex phenomena related to the college student experience. Theories have long served and equipped the student affairs profession. Whether focused on individual college student development, campus environments, student learning, student engagement, or organizational functioning, theories are thought to provide a "common language" (Knefelkamp, 1982, p. 379) for those interested in understanding college students and their experiences on campus. However, it is also important to note that the content of this "common language" has shifted over the years. Although many of the early theories of the 1950s and 1960s continue to serve as guiding principles, newer theories have emerged that shift the discourse of theory in student affairs and influence how we understand both the process and content of student development and the student experience.

Our hope in this chapter is to illuminate the more traditional approaches to theory, focusing on families of theories in particular, while also introducing readers to newer theoretical conceptualizations that extend or reframe foundational theoretical perspectives. More specifically, the purposes of this chapter are the following: (1) to provide the foundation for the theory-based chapters that follow by defining *theory* and distinguishing formal theory from the informal assumptions we use in our daily practice; (2) to explore current conceptualizations of families of theories and the characteristics of each family, including emerging theoretical conceptualizations; (3) to describe paradigmatic influences on the construction of theories, with attention to how and why theories evolve; and (4) to consider the relationship between theories and student affairs practice.

What Is Theory?

Noted author Robert Coles (1989) recounts an anecdote about himself as a young medical resident eager to treat a psychiatric patient. After spending a short amount of time with the patient and asking specific questions related to her medical history, he quickly diagnosed her condition. Still, the patient neither responded to him nor improved. Under the tutelage of a supervisor, Coles learned the importance of not only using medical shorthand to diagnose and categorize the condition of his patient but also truly listening to the patient's story in order to understand her and relate to her experiences. When he understood her unique story, he found that the patient was more than a medical category. And consequently they developed a caring connection that allowed him to help her more effectively.

Through this anecdote, Coles (1989) illustrates the relationship between a theory and a story. How often do student affairs professionals quickly try to make sense of students by assigning theoretical language (in Coles's case, medical shorthand) based on brief observations or experiences rather than listening to stories? When we do this, are we "diagnosing" students and categorizing them with broad theories rather than honoring their individuality? Is it possible to learn, plan for, and respond to numerous and diverse students' individual stories without the benefit of theories to inform our understanding? Coles's anecdote asks us to think about the meaning of theory. What is a theory? How do we both honor individual stories and apply the abstract theories upon which they are based? These questions are woven throughout this chapter, but it is up to each of us to determine how to strike this artful balance.

Theories help to simplify and make sense of the complexities of life, representing "an attempt to organize and integrate knowledge and to answer the question 'why?'" (Patterson, 1986, p. xix). Although this is generally also true of our informal assumptions, the theories we describe in this book are different from the informal assumptions we carry about students and student affairs practice. Rodgers (1980) defined formal theory as "a set of propositions regarding the interrelationship of two or more conceptual variables relevant to some realm of phenomena. It provides a framework for explaining the relationship among variables and for empirical investigations" (p. 81). Strange and King (1990) defined a theory as "an abstract representation based on a potentially infinite number of specific and concrete variations of a phenomenon" (p. 17).

Starting with the Greek origin of the word *theory*, meaning "I behold," Coles (1989) explained that just as we behold a scene at a theater, when working with people we "hold something visual in our minds; presumably the theory is an enlargement of observation" (p. 20). Theory also offers a framework for understanding more than what is obvious from our observations. As Rabbi Abraham Heschel (n.d.) illuminated, "It is far easier to see what we know than to know what we see." In essence, theories in student affairs are grounded in the particularities of individual stories and experiences and serve as a way to make sense of the diversity and complexity of phenomena by reducing many aspects of a phenomenon into a more integrated representation (McEwen, 2003).

Although we try to construct theories that are true to the stories upon which they are based, empirical research does not entail the objective creation of theory. Coles (1989) recollected: "Remember, what you are hearing . . . is to some considerable extent a function of *you*, hearing" (p. 15, emphasis in original). Indeed, Knefelkamp suggested that all theory is autobiographical—that is, "theory represents the knowledge, experience, and worldviews of the theorists who construct it" (McEwen, 2003, p. 165). As socially constructed ideas, theories are developed within changing sociological, historical, and political contexts (McEwen). Depending on the worldview of the theorist, therefore, theory can reinforce the status quo or societal power relationships, such as racism, heterosexism, and classism.

When applied with the understanding that theories are socially constructed and do not capture the diversity of all stories, theories serve at least six purposes. Theory is used to describe, explain, predict, influence outcomes, assess practice, and generate new knowledge and research (Knefelkamp, Widick, & Parker, 1978; McEwen, 2003; Moore & Upcraft, 1990). Sometimes one theory is appropriately applied in some respects for all six purposes, although some theories might serve some of these six purposes more effectively than they do others. For example, Cross's (1995) theory of Black racial identity, an example of a student development theory, *describes* several stages that

African American students experience as they develop complex understandings of their racial identity. Through its description of developmental stages, this theory also *explains* why students might behave in certain ways; for instance, why some African American students might frequent Black cultural centers or prefer to sit together in the cafeteria (Tatum, 2003). Through this description and explanation, student affairs professionals can *predict* behavior and provide educational contexts that allow for this intentional gathering that Cross's theory espouses as integral to Black racial identity development. In this way, the theory can also be used to *influence outcomes* by encouraging particular educational contexts that intentionally foster the development of a student's Black identity, often with the assumption that a more complex identity is beneficial to the student. The theory can then be used to *assess* the educational contexts that are intended to foster development by determining whether or not they are indeed promoting development toward the more complex stages. Finally, scholar-practitioners might see limitations to the stages Cross uses to describe Black racial identity development and choose to conduct research that builds upon his theory, thus *generating new knowledge and research.*

Student affairs professionals have numerous theories from which to choose, yet not all theories are of the same value or usefulness. Patterson (1986) described criteria to evaluate the value of a theory. Accordingly, theories should be: (1) important and relevant to everyday life; (2) precise and understandable; (3) simple and parsimonious; (4) comprehensive; (5) able to be operationalized; (6) empirically valid or verifiable; (7) able to generate new research and ideas; and (8) useful to practitioners (McEwen, 2003; Patterson). When determining a theory's value, it is also important to ask upon what population that theory is based. For example, does the theory apply only to individuals with those characteristics or more generally to other individuals (Knefelkamp et al., 1978)? This last point is especially important for considering how theories apply to diverse students and learning contexts. Indeed, Coles (1989) reminds us that theories need to be true to the stories of the individuals and situations upon which they are based.

Theories in Student Affairs

A diverse array of theories provide the foundation for student affairs practice and are typically grouped together in what are referred to as "families" of theories or "theory clusters" (Knefelkamp et al., 1978, p. xi). This umbrella term incorporates those theories that are developmental and focus on the individual, including social identities; those that examine students in the collegiate context such as student success, engagement, and learning; theories that explain the relationship of campus environments to student development and success; and those focused on organizations and institutions of higher education.

The chapters that follow reflect this conceptualization of families of theories, and each explores more fully a particular family and representative theories within each family. Although this conceptualization of theories as families is useful as an organizing heuristic, newer theories provide alternative theoretical explanations for understanding students, such as critical and poststructural approaches to student development (e.g., critical race theory and queer theory), or those grounded in a more holistic conception of overlapping theory families and intersecting theories (e.g., self-authorship and intersectionality). These theoretical frameworks push the boundaries of the more traditional template and offer new lenses through which to interpret student development and the student experience.

What follows is a brief summary of each of the theory families, including newer theories that were not represented in the original conceptualization of theory families. Because student development theories are foundational to the profession of student affairs and central to our philosophical commitment to the development of the whole person, we emphasize these in the next section.

Developmental Theories

Theories of student development serve as a foundation for student affairs practice. The term *student* refers to one who is enrolled in a higher education setting, and *development* suggests that some kind of positive change occurs in the student (e.g., cognitive complexity, self-awareness, racial identity, or engagement). One of the earliest contributors to the scholarship on student development, Sanford (1967) defined development as the "organization of increasing complexity" (p. 47); Rodgers (1990) extended this definition to focus on students, defining student development as: "the ways that a student grows, progresses, or increases his or her developmental capabilities as a result of enrollment in an institution of higher education" (p. 27). The focus of developmental theories gives us a lens for examining both the content of development (e.g., psychosocial theories) and the process of development (e.g., cognitive-structural theories). A few concepts that are central to developmental theories are briefly introduced here.

Challenge and Support. One of the most fundamental theories of student development is Sanford's (1966) theory of challenge and support. Sanford suggested that students need an optimal balance of challenge and support for development to occur. That is, too much support and students are able to stay comfortable with what they know and experience, too much challenge and the student becomes overwhelmed. In articulating the need for both challenge and support, Sanford implies that the campus environment interacts with the individual student either by employing people and implementing policies and programs that support students' development or by impeding student development with the imposition of too much challenge. As the scholarly base of student development theory has evolved, we have come to understand that what constitutes challenge and support for different populations of students may vary. For example, what constitutes support for first-generation college students may be distinct from that for students with parents who attended college. Further, differing cultural backgrounds among first-generation students may also influence how support is constructed and perceived.

Dissonance. Nearly all developmental theories suggest that for development to occur, the individual must experience dissonance or crisis. This crisis, as Widick, Parker, and Knefelkamp (1978) pointed out, "is not a time of panic or disruption: It is a decision point—that moment when one reaches an intersection and must turn one way or the other" (pp. 3–4). The individual's resulting interest in resolving the dissonance or crisis creates the conditions for development to occur. Dissonance may emerge from environmental forces, internal processes, or a combination of these.

Stages, Phases, Statuses, Vectors. Many of the theories most often utilized in student affairs practice include terminology that places or locates individuals along a continuum or on a map. Some of the language to convey these locations includes *stages* (e.g., Erikson, 1959), statuses (e.g., Helms, 1995), vectors (e.g., Chickering, 1969), positions (e.g., Perry, 1968), perspectives (e.g., Belenky et al., 1986), types (e.g., Holland, 1966), frames (e.g., Bolman & Deal, 1991), dimensions (e.g., Jones & McEwen, 2000), or elements (e.g., Baxter Magolda, 2008). The differential language used signals the categorization of theories into specific "families," but also conveys underlying ideas about the process of development and worldviews about how students and their experiences are best understood. For example, Helms (1995) revised the terminology she used for her racial identity theories from *stage* to *status* in order to more adequately capture the fluid and dynamic nature of development. Likewise, poststructural theorists resist the use of terminology that suggests the possibility of categorizing or compartmentalizing something as complex as identity.

Regardless of the terminology used, the intent of these theorists was never to posit that the totality of a student's experiences and development could be understood through knowledge only of one's stage or dimension. Each stage or status, for example, is intended to capture some defining feature of an individual. Presumably if a student affairs educator is able to assess where a student is cognitively or in one's racial identity, for example, then the educator knows something about how that student understands himself or herself and the environment. Similarly, organizations or campus environments can be examined for central characteristics, such as culture or climate, and be defined accordingly. For example, a campus culture that is described as highly engaged or one determined to possess a chilly climate for women will provide clues to student affairs professionals about key areas for attention. Thus, the intersection of student development and campus environments is also important to explore.

Epigenetic Principle and Developmental Trajectory. One of the foundational principles in Erikson's work on identity development (1959/1980) is the epigenetic principle, or the idea that "anything that grows has a ground plan . . . and out of this ground plan the parts arise, each part having its time of special ascendancy until all parts have arisen to form a functioning whole" (p. 52). During the traditional college years, according to Erikson's theory, the epigenetic plan calls for the individual to address such core identity questions as Who am I? (Widick et al., 1978). Although Erikson's work is specific to psychosocial development, the idea of a "ground plan" is consistent across and embedded in many theories of student development, in that development occurs along a trajectory of simple to complex and in predictable stages or sequences. The content of development and the process of development will look different depending on the actual theory (e.g., cognitive, racial identity, psychosocial), but developmental movement is characterized by sequential movement along a trajectory. Newer theoretical frameworks for understanding student development, particularly the influence of the larger structures of privilege and oppression, question the centrality of a trajectory, who names the trajectory, and the role of context in defining progress.

What follows is a brief overview of what we consider to be the major clusters of theories within the family of developmental theories. It is important to note that some of the theories that focus on social identities (e.g., race, ethnicity, and sexuality) are developmental (e.g., GLBT identity), but not all are (e.g., queer theory); and newer conceptualizations suggest the importance of viewing social identities as intersecting and representing the overlap of psychosocial and cognitive domains of development.

Psychosocial Development Theories (See Chapter Nine)

Psychosocial development theories are rooted in the work of Erik Erikson and, as the term *psychosocial* implies, focus on the interaction of the individual with his or her social world. Psychosocial theories examine the content of development, in particular what individuals are most concerned about in different time periods of the life cycle. These concerns include values, identity, relationships, career and work, and family. Because of the emphasis on development across the life span, psychosocial theories include those that focus on adolescents, college students, and adults (for example, Arnett, 2004; Chickering & Reisser, 1993; Erikson, 1959/1980; Josselson, 1987, 1996; Levinson, 1986; Marcia, 1966).

Cognitive Development Theories (See Chapters Nine and Eleven)

Cognitive-structural theories, anchored in the work of Jean Piaget (1952), focus on the structure of thinking applied to the content of those psychosocial issues identified above. This structure provides an information processing filter that enables the individual to make sense of experiences and new encounters in the world and evolves from more simple to increasingly complex (King, 1978; McEwen, 2003). Most cognitive-structural theories are hierarchical and sequential, with each stage representing a more complex way of making meaning. Perry's (1968) work serves as the foundation for many of the cognitive-structural theories used in student affairs. Theories of moral development and faith development are also considered cognitive-structural (e.g., Fowler, 1981; Gilligan, 1993; Kohlberg, 1975).

Social Identity Theories (See Chapter Ten)

Social identity theories focus on "those roles *or* membership categories that a person claims as representative" (Deaux, 1993, p. 6). These include theories of racial identity (e.g., Helms, 1995), ethnic identity (e.g., Phinney, 1990; Torres, 2003), cultural identity (e.g., Yon, 2000); sexual identity (e.g., Cass, 1979; Fassinger & Arseneau, 2007), gender identity (e.g., Downing & Roush, 1985; Kimmel, 2008); religion (e.g., Parks, 2000), disability (e.g., Fine & Asch, 2000; Gibson, 2006), and social class (e.g., hooks, 2000). A number of these particular social identities are insufficiently researched; however, theoretical frameworks that incorporate the influence of structures of power and oppression on student development and experience have yielded new insights into social identities. Further, a number of social identity scholars are emphasizing the importance of examining social identities in relation to one another, rather than as discrete units of analysis (e.g., Dill, McLaughlin, & Nieves, 2007; Weber, 2001).

Emerging Theoretical Perspectives (See Chapter Ten)

Several emerging theoretical perspectives, although not created with college students in mind, are useful to new interpretations of college student development and the college experience. Examples of these include critical race theory (e.g., Delgado & Stefancic, 2001), queer theory (e.g., Sullivan, 2003), and intersectionality (Dill et al., 2007). Each new perspective may be used to both critique and reconceptualize existing theoretical frameworks. These theories have in common an interest in problematizing the "grand narratives" (Lyotard, 1984) and the taken-for-granted dimensions of the college experience. They also emphasize the centrality of power and the importance of social change. For example, an intersectional approach emphasizes the individual's simultaneous location in multiple social identities, such as race, class, and gender, and suggests that individuals can operate within systems of both privilege and oppression (e.g., Dill et al.). Understanding the experience of a White male student with a disability, for example, requires examining both the privilege associated with gender and the oppression attached to disability, as well as the interplay between the two. Intersectionality both illuminates the individual lived experience and necessarily situates the individual within larger structures of inequality.

Theories Emphasizing Holistic Development (See Chapter Eleven)

Extending the work of Robert Kegan (1982, 1994) Baxter Magolda (2001, 2008), based upon extensive longitudinal research, crafted a theory of self-authorship that is defined as "a developmental capacity" (Baxter Magolda, 2008, p. 269). This theory is considered holistic because of its interrelated domains of interpersonal, identity, and cognitive development (Baxter Magolda, 2008). Additional research using diverse samples (e.g., Abes, Jones, & McEwen, 2007; Torres & Hernandez, 2007) highlights the promise of conceptualizing development holistically in order to illuminate the importance of such contextual influences as privilege and oppression (Jones, 2009). In these studies, confronting racism as a developmental task that is integral to holistic development (Torres & Hernandez),; the role of context in prompting a more fluid and complex intersection of cognitive, interpersonal, and identity domains of development; (Abes, Jones, & McEwen), and the interaction of privileged and oppressed identities in relation to holistic development (Jones, 2009) all emerged as significant findings.

Theories of Organizations and Campus Environments (See Chapters Twelve and Thirteen)

Theories that focus on organizations, organizational behavior, and campus environments (e.g., Banning, 1989; Bolman & Deal, 1991; Strange & Banning, 2001) emphasize the influence of these larger entities on the relationships between student development and the student experience. For example, the ways in which campus policies are created reflect particular views of organizations and come together to create a campus environment and culture that promote or impede student success.

Student Success Theories (See Chapter Fourteen)

New research builds on what is known about student involvement (e.g., Astin, 1984) and student success (e.g., Braxton, 2003; Perna & Thomas, 2008; Tinto, 1993) to illuminate student engagement (e.g., Kuh, Kinzie, Schuh, & Whitt, & Associates, 2005). Student success theories can be used to understand what institutions can do to promote student success along outcomes determined to be central to the student experience, such as student development.

Typology Models

Typology models (covered only very briefly in this text) differ from many of the other theories useful in student affairs practice because they emphasize what are considered to be more persistent individual traits and characteristics, such as personality type (e.g., Jung, 1923/1971); learning style (e.g., Kolb, 1984); and vocational choice (e.g., Holland, 1966). Although it is tempting to identify a person by his or her "type," typology models are nonevaluative (Evans, 2003) and not meant to suggest rigidity in type.

Paradigmatic Influences on the Construction and Application of Theory

How is it that we move from the particularities of individual stories to the construction of the formal theories used in student affairs practice? Unlike our informal assumptions, empirical research, both qualitative and quantitative, is used to generate and validate formal theories. For instance, using grounded theory methodology is one qualitative approach to constructing a theory (Strauss & Corbin, 1990). The art and science of grounded theory, which is an inductive approach to theory creation that uses stories gathered through interviews and other sources, is to create a theory that is general enough to describe the experiences of all of the participants but also stays true to the particularities of each of the individual's story. Quantitative research, which relies on statistical analysis of numerical data that is typically accessed through surveys or questionnaires, is a more deductive approach and can also be used to generate theory. Derived usually from large samples, these theories offer a broad perspective on college students and their experiences.

Regardless of the research method used to create theory, our identities, experiences, and worldviews, also known as subjectivities (Fine, 1994), influence theory construction. To the extent possible, theorists should be aware of this influence and, although they cannot entirely know the influence of their subjectivities, since we are all often unaware of perspectives beyond our field of vision (much like a fish unaware of the water in which it swims), there are certain subjectivities about which it is important to be explicit. Specifically, it is important to make clear the research paradigm that guided the theory construction. In this section we not only review paradigms that have traditionally been used in the creation of student affairs theories but also emphasize paradigms that address social inequities in student affairs and move toward intercultural theories (Tanaka, 2002).

A paradigm, often referred to as a worldview, is a "set of interconnected or related assumptions or beliefs" that guides thinking and behavior (Jones, Torres, & Arminio, 2006, p. 9). Every research paradigm consists of assumptions about the nature of reality (ontology), knowledge (epistemology), and how knowledge is accessed (methodology) (Guba & Lincoln, 2005). Depending on the content of these assumptions, a paradigm influences the questions guiding the research from which a theory is created; whose stories are included in the research; how the researcher hears the stories; and how the researcher retells the stories. In his notable work *The Structure of Scientific Revolutions*, Kuhn (1962) describes how new paradigms emerge as the limitations of previous ones become apparent. With the emergence of new paradigms, contemporary student affairs theorists are diversifying the assumptions behind theory construction, which results in more inclusive theories that challenge dominant or normative understandings of students and student affairs practice.

We briefly review and provide examples of a few of the traditional and emerging paradigms that have been used to create theories about college students. Whether creating theory, applying theory in practice, or developing and refining one's own professional philosophy, it is important to be aware that the worldviews guiding theory creation are not merely scholarly terms saved for rigorous research but rather philosophical beliefs that shape our practice as we apply theory to understand diverse student populations. Theory construction is a dynamic process that informs and is informed by practice, and that therefore matters to all who work with college students.

Two of the paradigms that have traditionally been used in the context of student affairs are positivism and constructivism. We will begin this section by reviewing some of their basic elements as well as the strengths and limitations that are important to consider when creating and applying theories.

Positivism

Positivism assumes the existence of one reality and that knowledge is objectively knowable, measurable, and predictable through inquiry in which the researcher is removed from the object of study (Lincoln & Guba, 2000). For instance, in the early phases of her longitudinal study, Baxter Magolda used a positivist framework as she began her study of epistemological development (Baxter Magolda, 2004). She assumed an objective stance separate from the research participants in order to categorize students into developmental stages. She put the theory in the foreground and students in the background, seeking to fit the participants into an unchanging theory. Although this framework offers predictability, consistency, and a timeless nature in research results (which some consider a strength), it does not allow for differences in interpretation based on diverse identities and perspectives, nor does it allow for the influence of changing contexts on interpretation.

Constructivism

In later phases of her longitudinal research, Baxter Magolda (1992, 2001) transitioned to a constructivist paradigm. She explained that constructivism allowed her to understand students' experiences and ways of making meaning in more depth than did positivist approaches that boxed students into preexisting categories (2004). Constructivism, also sometimes referred to as interpretivism, is grounded in the notion that multiple realities exist, and that knowledge is co-constructed between the researcher and participants (Lincoln & Guba, 2000). In terms of methodology, constructivist research typically seeks to understand reality through dialogue (Lincoln & Guba). Using a constructivist approach, Baxter Magolda (2004) put the students' stories before existing theories, allowing her to see multiple possible interpretations of students' stories based on their individuality, changing contexts, and her own subjectivities. She found that she was able to reshape existing theory rather than only testing it. With the limitations of positivism becoming more apparent, much of the contemporary research on student development is grounded in constructivist perspectives.

Although constructivist theories allow for the participants' voices to more prominently make their way into theory, this paradigm does not intentionally address how such power structures as racism, classism, and heterosexism have shaped theory. Here we review how two theoretical frameworks that address these concerns have emerged as a way to interpret student experiences and deconstruct theories used in student affairs.

Critical Theory

Critical perspectives uncover how invisible power structures shape whose stories are told and how they are heard in the construction of student affairs theories. Critical theory calls for a "radical restructuring [of] society toward the ends of reclaiming historic cultural legacies, social justice, the redistribution of power and the achievement of truly democratic societies" (Lincoln & Denzin, 2000, p. 1056). The goal of critical theory is "a society in which all people, regardless of their economic and cultural backgrounds have a voice in decisions affecting their lives" (Rhoads & Black, 1995, p. 416). An important element of critical theory is its praxis component, meaning that research should be tied into action that changes society in a socially just way. Examples of the use of critical theory to critique student affairs practice include work that unpacks the power dynamics associated with service-learning (Butin, 2005); fraternities (Rhoads, 1995); and the rituals associated with campus tours (Magolda, 2000).

One critical perspective especially worth noting is critical race theory. Critical race theorists seek first to illuminate how society is structured along racial lines, and then to transform this condition. Some of the central tenets of critical race theory are that racism is an inherent part of society, that race is a social construction, and that addressing racism depends on hearing the narratives of people of color (Delgado & Stefancic, 2001). Examples of the use of critical race theory to understand student affairs practice include a study of Chicana and Chicano student peer groups (Villalpando, 2003) and facilitating dialogues about racial realities (Quaye, 2008), both of which demonstrate the centrality of race in daily practices and interactions.

Poststructural Theories

Poststructural theories explore how the power structures that are invisibly woven into society construct reality and the meaning of "normal" (Lather, 2007). Unlike critical theorists who seek to transform society in a particular way, poststructuralists assume that there are multiple possibilities for how society ought to be structured (Rhoads & Black, 1995). Poststructural theories therefore describe identity as a fluid process (Sullivan, 2003). Furthermore, they suggest that it is impossible to tell a single story of development and, in fact, that "refusing definition is part of the theoretical scene" (Lather, p. 5).

Queer theory is one example of a poststructuralist theory. Queer theory brings poststructural concerns to sexuality studies and is effective for addressing power dynamics because of its focus on challenging the heteronormativity in identity constructions. Heteronormativity is the unexamined and prevalent societal assumption that "normal" is defined through heterosexuality (e.g., Britzman, 1997). Still an emerging perspective, queer theory has been used to challenge heteronormative assumptions about how college students develop, suggesting multiple and fluid possibilities for how development might be conceptualized (Abes & Kasch, 2007).

How Theories Evolve

All paradigms are incomplete in that they each represent one worldview (Kuhn, 1962). The use of emerging paradigms or even multiple paradigms is therefore one way in which theories evolve to more effectively help us understand college students (Abes, 2009). As the nature of college students evolve, so too must theories used in student affairs. New research questions must be asked and new methodological approaches utilized, both as critiques of the limitations of existing theories and as ways to build upon these theories as new insights are generated. Not only are students and student affairs practice changing, but also are the identities of the theorists. Researcher subjectivities drive the nature of the research questions asked, and the identities of those applying these theories in practice reveal both strengths and limitations in theory development, prompting the need for continuous inquiry into this complex field.

Relationships of Theories to Student Affairs Practice

Student affairs educators are frequently faced with complex decisions in their daily practice. Consistent with the goals of student affairs, our roles often include overlapping responsibilities and obligations to promote student development, design campus environments that are educationally purposeful, and understand higher education as an organization (McEwen, 2003). Theories provide an important and necessary lens through which to engage our roles and responsibilities and make decisions. Theories do not inform us about what exactly to do, but they do provide us with ways to make decisions and to think about how to interpret individuals, environments, and organizations. Although some may argue that student affairs educators could be effective without using theory to guide their practice, an important indicator of professional competence is knowledge of the field's theoretical foundation (Pope & Reynolds, 1997).

When applying theory to practice in student affairs it is important to remember, as Perry (1981) cautioned, that students always remain larger than their categories. Theories are meant to provide an interpretive lens for what a student affairs educator is anticipating, witnessing, or planning. Let's look at an example:

Scenario

During the weeklong resident assistant (RA) training, one session on "appreciating diversity" utilized the well-known Privilege Walk activity. The facilitator, a White woman and new residence hall director fresh out of graduate school, believed it was a great way to help students understand the concepts of privilege, racism, and oppression. Lining up the RAs, she instructed the group to take steps forward or backward to represent their responses to a series of statements. She begins:

  If your ancestors were forced to come to the United States, take one step back.
  If you were raised in a rented apartment or house, take one step back.
  If you were ever called names because of your race, ethnicity, or sexual orientation, take one step back.
  If you were taken to plays or art galleries by your parents, take one step forward.

As she moved through her list, the resident director noticed that the RAs who were members of underrepresented racial and ethnic groups appeared to stop paying attention and to be chatting about other things. Meanwhile, the White males were competing with one another for "first place." At the conclusion of the activity, the resident director began processing the Privilege Walk, and almost immediately conflict in the group erupted.

(continued)

An American Indian male began:

I don't know why we need yet another activity to remind students of color of "their place" in this world. This activity seems designed to reinforce all kinds of stereotypes and assumptions about who I am and where I come from.

To which a White female RA responded:

I think you are taking this way too personally. I think it is so good that we are talking about these issues.

And a Latina student retorted:

Well, this is easy for you to say. You have the luxury of obliviousness. I do take this personally, because it is personal, it is my life!

Source: Adapted from Jones, 2008.

How might a student affairs educator use theories to make sense of what took place in this scenario, and then develop an appropriate response? First, it is very important for a practitioner to evaluate the assumptions brought to an interpretation of a particular situation. When thinking about identifying theories and applying them to practice, it behooves student affairs educators to look inward and consider how their own experiences, biases, and assumptions may predispose them to one set of theories over another. This scenario might be interpreted through the theoretical lenses of racial or ethnic identity theory. However, an emphasis given to individuals alone may miss the larger consideration of the organizational culture in residence life that perpetuates training activities that promote learning for some at the expense of others.

Second, because of the complexity of much of our work, it is rare that one theory will carry enough explanatory power for a particular phenomenon so that when applying theory to practice, theories often are used in combination. In this scenario, a student affairs educator might begin by considering the racial identity of each individual (e.g., Helms's theories of White Racial Identity and People of Color Racial Identity [1995]) as well as the other social identities that may be salient for each individual (using, for, example, Jones and McEwen's Model of Multiple Dimensions of Identity [2000]). This might help explain why the White woman was not attuned to the emotional impact for some of the Privilege Walk activity, and why the American Indian man was perceived as lashing out. The educator might glean further understanding from adding a cognitive theory dimension to the application as the White woman appears to be viewing this situation in a less cognitively complex way than are the students of color, which may be the result of differing lived experiences. In addition, an organizational analysis might also be useful, in that this activity may both be reflective of a particular organizational culture and have an impact on the climate among the RAs. Drawing from a critical race theory interpretation necessitates an analysis of this situation in relation to the omnipresence of racism and discrimination in the United States. It is important to recognize that in practice, as in this scenario, student affairs educators rarely possess all there is to know about a particular situation, individual, or dilemma. Therefore, theories guide us toward potential and plausible interpretations, but none of these should ever be viewed as *the* one way to understand what is going on. Consulting with trusted colleagues is very helpful in applying theories to practice, especially when doing so with someone who might not share the same social identities or background experiences.

Third, applying theories to practice takes practice. Because no situation or individual is ever exactly the same, no precise recipes exist for determining which theories to use under which set of circumstances. To be sure, there are clear indicators of fit and mismatch, but each theory applied to a particular phenomenon will illuminate a different part of the story. Furthermore, theories evolve, so staying current with theory generation and scholarly literature is also important when applying theory to practice. Student affairs educators now have a far greater and deeper repertoire of theories from which to choose than was the case twenty years ago.

Conclusion

The chapters that follow provide more in-depth descriptions of theories that provide the foundation for the student affairs profession. We have a rich and varied body of theory from which to draw, and it is important to read primary sources rather than to rely on summaries of these theories. As noted in this chapter, theories continue to evolve because of new questions, new students, new methodological approaches, and in relation to who is developing and applying theories. However, we need not completely discard those early theories that guided the field. As you continue to study, understand, and apply theories and theoretical perspectives that inform student affairs research and practice, you will discern those constructs and themes that are enduring and that serve as important points of departure. Finally, as your knowledge of theories becomes more robust, you will see that indeed there is nothing as useful as a good theory.

References

Abes, E. S. (2009). Theoretical borderlands: Using multiple theoretical perspectives to challenge inequitable power structures in student development theory. *Journal of College Student Development, 50,* 141–156.

Abes, E. S., Jones, S. R., & McEwen, M. K. (2007). Reconceptualizing the Model of Multiple Dimensions of Identity: The role of meaning-making capacity in the construction of multiple identities. *Journal of College Student Development, 48,* 1–22.

Abes, E. S., & Kasch, D. (2007). Using queer theory to explore lesbian college students' multiple dimensions of identity. *Journal of College Student Development, 48,* 619–636.

Arnett, J. J. (2004). *Emerging adulthood: The winding road from the late teens through the twenties.* New York: Oxford University Press.

Astin, A. W. (1984). Student involvement: A developmental theory for higher education. *Journal of College Student Personnel, 25,* 297–308.

Banning, J. (1989). Creating a climate for successful student development: The campus ecology manager role. In U. Delworth, G. Hanson, & Associates, *Student services: A Handbook for the profession* (2nd ed., pp. 304–322). San Francisco: Jossey-Bass.

Baxter Magolda, M. B. (1992). *Knowing and reasoning in college: Gender-related patterns in students' intellectual development.* San Francisco: Jossey-Bass.

Baxter Magolda, M. B. (2001). Making their own way: Narratives for transforming higher education to promote self-development. Sterling, VA: Stylus.

Baxter Magolda, M. B. (2004). Evolution of a constructivist conceptualization of epistemological reflection. *Educational Psychologist, 39*(1), 31–42.

Baxter Magolda, M. B. (2008). Three elements of self-authorship. *Journal of College Student Development, 49*, 269–284.

Belenky, M. F., Clinchy, B. M., Goldberger, N. R., & Tarule, J. M. (1986). *Women's ways of knowing: The development of self, voice, and mind.* New York: Basic Books.

Bolman, L., & Deal, T. (1991). *Reframing organizations.* San Francisco: Jossey-Bass.

Braxton, J. M. (2003). Student success. In S. R. Komives, D. B. Woodard Jr., & Associates (Eds.), *Student services: A handbook for the profession* (4th ed., pp. 317–335). San Francisco: Jossey-Bass.

Britzman, D. P. (1997). What is this thing called love? New discourses for understanding gay and lesbian youth. In S. de Castell & M. Bryson (Eds.), *Radical in(ter)ventions: Identity, politics, and difference/s on educational praxis* (pp. 183–207). Albany: State University of New York Press.

Butin, D. W. (2005). Disturbing normalizations of service-learning. In D. W. Butin (Ed.), *Service-learning in higher education* (pp. vii–xx). New York: Palgrave Macmillan.

Cass, V. C. (1979). Homosexual identity formation: A theoretical model. *Journal of Homosexuality, 4*, 219–235.

Chickering, A. W. (1969). *Education and identity.* San Francisco: Jossey-Bass.

Chickering, A. W., & Reisser, L. (1993). *Education and identity* (2nd ed.). San Francisco: Jossey-Bass.

Coles, R. (1989). *The call of stories: Teaching and the moral imagination.* Boston: Houghton Mifflin.

Cross, W. E., Jr. (1995). The psychology of nigrescence: Revising the Cross model. In J. G. Ponterotto, J. M. Casas, L. A. Suzuki, & C. M. Alexander (Eds.), *Handbook of multicultural counseling* (pp. 93–122). Thousand Oaks, CA: Sage.

Deaux, K. (1993). Reconstructing social identity. *Personality and Social Psychology Bulletin, 19*, 4–12.

Delgado, R., & Stefancic, J. (2001). *Critical race theory: An introduction.* New York: New York University Press.

Dill, B. T., McLaughlin, A. E., & Nieves, A. D. (2007). Future directions of feminist research: Intersectionality. In S. N. Hesse-Biber (Ed.), *Handbook of feminist research* (pp. 629–637). Thousand Oaks, CA: Sage.

Downing, N. E., & Roush, K. L. (1985). From passive acceptance to active commitment: A model of feminist identity development for women. *Counseling Psychologist, 13*, 695–709.

Erikson, E. H. (1980). *Identity and the life cycle.* New York: W. W. Norton & Company. (Original work published 1959)

Evans, N. J. (2003). Psychological, cognitive, and typological perspectives on student development. In S. R. Komives, D. B. Woodard Jr., & Associates (Eds.), *Student services: A handbook for the profession* (4th ed., pp. 179–202). San Francisco: Jossey-Bass.

Fassinger, R. E., & Arseneau, J. R. (2007). "I'd rather get wet than be under that umbrella": Experiences and identities of lesbian, gay, bisexual, and transgender people. In K. J. Bieschke, R. M. Perez, & K. A. DeBord (Eds.), *Handbook of counseling and psychotherapy with lesbian, gay, bisexual, and transgender clients* (pp. 19–49). Washington, DC: American Psychological Association.

Fine, M. (1994). Working the hyphens: Reinventing self and other in qualitative research. In N. K. Denzin & Y. S. Lincoln (Eds.), *Handbook of qualitative research* (pp. 70–82). Thousand Oaks, CA: Sage.

Fine, M., & Asch, A. (2000). Disability beyond stigma: Social interaction, discrimination, and activism. In M. Adams, W. J. Blumenfeld, R. Castaneda, H. W. Hackman, M. L. Peters, & X. Zuniga (Eds.), *Readings for diversity and social justice* (pp. 330–339). New York: Routledge.

Fowler, J. (1981). *Stages of faith: The psychology of human development and the quest for meaning.* New York: Harper & Row.

Gibson, J. (2006). Disability and clinical competency: An introduction. *California Psychologist, 39*, 6–10.

Gilligan, C. (1993). *In a different voice: Psychological theory and women's development.* Cambridge, MA: Harvard University Press. (Original work published in 1982)

Guba, E. G, & Lincoln, Y. S. (2005). Paradigmatic controversies, contradictions, and emerging confluences. In N. K. Denzin & Y. S. Lincoln (Eds.), *The Sage handbook of qualitative research* (pp. 191–215). Thousand Oaks, CA: Sage.

Helms, J. E. (1995). An update of Helms's white and people of color racial identity models. In J. G. Ponterotto, J. M. Casas., L. A. Suzuki, & C. M. Alexander (Eds.), *Handbook of multicultural counseling* (pp. 181–198). Thousand Oaks, CA: Sage.

Holland, J. (1966). *The psychology of vocational choice.* Waltham, MA: Blaisdell.

hooks, bell. (2000). *Where we stand: Class matters.* New York: Routledge.

Jones, S. R. (2008). Student resistance to cross-cultural engagement: Annoying distraction or site for transformative learning? In S. R. Harper (Ed.), *Creating inclusive campus environments* (pp. 67–85). Washington, DC: National Association of Student Personnel Administrators.

Jones, S. R. (2009). Constructing identities at the intersections: An autoethnographic exploration of multiple dimensions of identity. *Journal of College Student Development, 50*, 287–304.

Jones, S. R., & McEwen, M. K. (2000). A conceptual model of multiple dimensions of identity. *Journal of College Student Development, 41*, 405–414.

Jones, S. R., Torres, V., & Arminio, J. (2006). *Negotiating the complexities of qualitative research in higher education: Fundamental elements and issues.* New York: Routledge.

Josselson, R. (1987). *Finding herself: Pathways to identity development in women.* San Francisco: Jossey-Bass.

Josselson, R. (1996). *Revising herself: The story of women's identity from college to midlife.* San Francisco: Jossey-Bass.

Jung. C. (1971). *The collected works of C. G. Jung: Vol. 6. Psychological types.* Princeton, NJ: Princeton University Press. (Original work published 1923)

Kegan, R. (1982). *The evolving self: Problem and process in human development.* Cambridge, MA: Harvard University Press.

Kegan, R. (1994). *In over our heads: The mental demands of modern life.* Cambridge, MA: Harvard University Press.

Kimmel, M. (2008). *Guyland: The perilous world where boys become men.* New York: HarperCollins.

King, P. M. (1978). William Perry's theory of intellectual and ethical development. In L. L. Knefelkamp, C. Widick, & C. A. Parker (Eds.), *Applying new developmental findings* (New Directions for Student Services No. 4, pp. 35–51). San Francisco: Jossey-Bass.

Knefelkamp, L. L. (1982). Faculty and student development in the '80s: Renewing the community of scholars. In H. F. Owens, C. H. Witten, & W. R. Bailey (Eds.), *College student personnel administration: An anthology* (pp. 373–391). Springfield, IL: Charles C. Thomas.

Knefelkamp, L. L., Widick, C., & Parker, C. (Eds.). (1978). *Applying new developmental findings* (New Directions for Student Services No. 4). San Francisco: Jossey-Bass.

Kohlberg, L. (1975). A cognitive-developmental approach to moral education. *Phi Delta Kapan, 56*, 670–677.

Kolb, D. A. (1984). *Experiential learning: Experience as the source of learning and development.* Englewood Cliffs, NJ: Prentice Hall.

Kuh, G. D., Kinzie, J., Schuh, J. H., Whitt, E. H., & Associates (2005). *Student success in college: Creating conditions that matter.* San Francisco: Jossey-Bass.

Kuhn, T. S. (1962). The structure of scientific revolutions. Chicago: University of Chicago Press.

Lather, P. (2007). *Getting lost: Feminist efforts toward a double(d) science.* Albany: State University of New York Press.

Levinson, D. J. (1986). A conception of adult development. *American Psychologist, 41*, 3–13.

Lewin, K. (1951). *Field theory in the social sciences.* New York: HarperCollins.

Lincoln, Y. S., & Denzin, N. K. (2000). The seventh movement: Out of the past. In N. K. Denzin & Y. S. Lincoln (Eds.), *Handbook of qualitative research* (2nd ed., pp. 1047–1065). Thousand Oaks, CA: Sage.

Lincoln, Y. S., & Guba, E. G. (2000). Paradigmatic controversies, contradictions, and emerging confluences. In N. K. Denzin & W. S. Lincoln (Eds.), *Handbook of qualitative research* (2nd ed., pp. 163–188). San Francisco: Sage.

Lyotard, J-F. (1984). *The postmodern condition: A report on knowledge* (Theory and History of Literature, Vol. 10). Manchester, England: Manchester University Press.

Magolda, P. M. (2000). The campus tour ritual: Exploring community discourses in higher education. *Anthropology and Education Quarterly, 31*(1), 24–36.

Marcia, J. E. (1966). Development and validation of ego-identity status. *Journal of Personality and Social Psychology, 3*, 551–558.

McEwen, M. K. (2003). The nature and uses of theory. In S. R. Komives, D. B. Woodard Jr., & Associates (Eds.), *Student services: A handbook for the profession* (4th ed., pp. 153–178). San Francisco: Jossey-Bass.

Moore, L. V., & Upcraft, M. L. (1990). Theory in student affairs: Evolving perspectives. In L. V. Moore (Ed.), *Evolving theoretical perspectives on students* (New Directions for Student Services No. 51, pp. 3–23). San Francisco: Jossey-Bass.

Parks, S. D. (2000). *Big questions, worthy dreams: Mentoring young adults in their search for meaning, purpose, and faith.* San Francisco: Jossey-Bass.

Patterson, C. H. (1986). *Theories of counseling and psychotherapy* (4th ed.). New York: Harper & Row.

Perna, L. W., & Thomas, S. L. (2008). *Theoretical perspectives on student success: Understanding the contribution of the disciplines* (ASHE Higher Education Report, Vol. 34, No. 1). San Francisco: Jossey-Bass.

Perry, W. G., Jr. (1968). *Forms of intellectual and ethical development in the college years: A scheme.* New York: Holt, Rinehart and Winston.

Perry, W. G., Jr. (1981). Cognitive and ethical growth: The making of meaning. In A. W. Chickering & Associates (Eds.), *The modern American college: Responding to the new realities of diverse students and a changing society* (pp. 76–116). San Francisco: Jossey-Bass.

Phinney, J. S. (1990). Ethnic identity in adolescents and adults: Review of research. *Psychological Bulletin, 108*, 499–514.

Piaget, J. (1952). *The origins of intelligence in children.* New York: International Universities Press.

Pope, R. L., & Reynolds, A. L. (1997). Student affairs core competencies: Integrating multicultural awareness, knowledge, and skills. *Journal of College Student Development, 38*, 266–277.

Quaye, S. J. (2008). *Pedagogy and racialized ways of knowing: Students and faculty engage racial realities in postsecondary classrooms.* Unpublished doctoral dissertation, The Pennsylvania State University.

Rhoads, R. A. (1995). Whale tales, dog piles, and beer goggles: An ethnographic case study of fraternity life. *Anthropology and Education Quarterly, 26*, 306–323.

Rhoads, R. A., & Black, M. A. (1995). Student affairs practitioners as transformative educators: Advancing a critical cultural perspective. *Journal of College Student Development, 36*, 413–421.

Rodgers, R. F. (1980). Theories underlying student development. In D. G. Creamer (Ed.), *Student development in higher education* (pp. 10–95). Cincinnati, OH: American College Personnel Association.

Rodgers, R. F. (1990). Recent theories and research underlying student development. In D. G. Creamer & Associates, *College student development: Theory and practice for the 1990s* (pp. 27–79). Alexandria, VA: American College Personnel Association.

Sanford, N. (1966). *Self and society.* New York: Atherton Press.

Sanford, N. (1967). *Where colleges fail: A study of the student as a person.* San Francisco: Jossey-Bass.

Strange, C. C., & Banning, J. (2001). *Educating by design: Creating campus learning environments that work.* San Francisco: Jossey-Bass.

Strange, C. C., & King, P. M. (1990). The professional practice of student development. In D. G. Creamer (Ed.), *College student development: Theory and practice for the 1990s* (pp. 9–24). Alexandria, VA: American College Personnel Association.

Strauss, A., & Corbin, J. (1990). *Basics of qualitative research: Grounded theory procedures and techniques.* Newbury Park, CA: Sage.

Sullivan, N. (2003). *A critical introduction to queer theory.* New York: New York University Press.

Tanaka, G. (2002). Higher education's self-reflexive turn: Toward an intercultural theory of student development. *Journal of Higher Education, 73*(2), 263–296.

Tatum, B. D. (2003). *Why are all the Black kids sitting together in the cafeteria?* (2nd ed.). New York: Basic Books.

Tinto, V. (1993). *Leaving college: Rethinking the causes and cures of student attrition* (2nd ed.). Chicago: University of Chicago Press.

Torres, V. (2003). Influences on ethnic identity development of Latino college students in the first two years of college. *Journal of College Student Development, 44*, 532–547.

Torres, V., & Hernandez, E. (2007). The influence of ethnic identity on self-authorship: A longitudinal study of Latino/a college students. *Journal of College Student Development, 48*, 558–573.

Villalpando, O. (2003). Self-segregation or self-preservation? A critical race theory and Latina/o critical theory analysis of a study of Chicano college students. *Qualitative Studies in Education, 16*, 619–646.

Weber, L. (2001). *Understanding race, class, gender, and sexuality: A conceptual framework.* New York: McGraw-Hill.

Widick, C., Parker, C., & Knefelkamp, L. L. (1978). Erik Erikson and psychosocial development. In L. L. Knefelkamp, C. Widick, & C. A. Parker (Eds.), *Applying new developmental findings* (New Directions for Student Services No. 4, pp. 1–17). San Francisco: Jossey-Bass.

Yon, D. (2000). *Elusive culture: Schooling, race, and identity in global times.* New York: State University of New York Press.

CHAPTER NINE

PSYCHOSOCIAL AND COGNITIVE-STRUCTURAL PERSPECTIVES ON STUDENT DEVELOPMENT

Nancy J. Evans

Jessie recently accepted a new position as an academic advisor at an urban community college. Previously she was a hall director at a small private college, and she is amazed at how different the students are in her new setting. How is Jessie to make sense of the differences in ages, backgrounds, perspectives, concerns, and interests she sees in these students?

As Jones and Abes noted in the previous chapter, student development theory provides a useful guide for student affairs educators like Jessie. In this chapter, I discuss two major classifications of theory—psychosocial and cognitive-structural—that focus on student development. I also highlight specific theories within each category that have particular utility in student affairs practice.

Other theories that help to explain differences among students include typological theories that examine (1) personality types based on how individuals perceive the world around them, how they make judgments about the information they take in, and how they relate to the external world (Myers, 1980), and (2) people's vocation-related interests, corresponding characteristics of various work environments, and the impact each has upon the other (Holland, 1997). Another very useful theory is Kolb's (1984) theory of experiential learning, in which learning is viewed as a cyclical process involving the use of concrete experience, reflective observation, abstract conceptualization, and active experimentation. Unfortunately, space limitations preclude discussing these theories in greater detail.

Psychosocial Perspectives

Jillian is a nineteen-year-old, White sophomore at the private college where Jessie previously worked. She is trying to identify a career direction and discover what matters to her as a person. Jillian has always looked to her parents for guidance, but now she finds it important to strike out on her own. Elicia, also a second-year student, attends the urban community college where Jessie currently works. She is a thirty-five-year-old, African American single parent who enrolled in college to create a better life for her family. Her main goals are to be a good role model for her children and to make a positive contribution to her community.

Although they are both sophomores, these two women face very different challenges. Psychosocial theories focus on issues that individuals face as they mature psychologically and experience contextual challenges that trigger dissonance, including issues such as defining self-concept, determining how to relate to others, deciding on life directions, and establishing belief systems. Psychosocial theorists examine the developmental issues that arise at different points during the life span and how they are resolved. The major concepts associated with this approach derive primarily from the work of Erikson (1959/1980, 1968). Erikson suggested that development occurs within a series of age-linked, sequential stages that arise during an individual's lifetime. Within each stage, particular issues, called developmental tasks, become preeminent and must be addressed. In the example above, Jillian is dealing with the developmental tasks of determining a vocational direction and identifying a personal set of beliefs and values. Elicia is revisiting her previous life decisions in these arenas, while also focusing on the developmental tasks of actively nurturing her children and contributing to society.

According to Erikson (1959/1980), each new stage occurs when internal psychological and biological changes interact with external social demands to create a developmental crisis, or turning point, in a person's life. For Jillian, the maturation associated with young adulthood, along with the societal expectation that college students must choose a career, has contributed to a developmental crisis: establishing her identity. Each such crisis offers heightened opportunity as well as vulnerability for the individual (Erikson, 1968).

End goals of psychosocial development are individuation, or becoming the best self one can be (Gardner, 1961)—and differentiation becoming a unique person (Young, 2003). A successful resolution of each developmental crisis leads to the student's development of new skills or attitudes that contribute to these outcomes. A less successful resolution, however, contributes to a negative self-image and restricts the individual's ability to successfully address future crises. Regression to previous stages and recycling of developmental issues frequently occur as individuals attempt to more successfully resolve previous crises. To work through the issues associated with making a contribution to her community, for example, Elicia is revisiting issues associated with earlier stages, such as developing a sense of accomplishment and acquiring skills and knowledge.

Although Erikson (1959/1980, 1968) did not specifically address issues facing college students, theorists who built on his work did examine this population. They include Marcia (1966, 1980), Josselson (1987, 1996), and Chickering and Reisser (1993). Other theorists have expanded on Erikson's (1959/1980, 1968) belief that development is a lifelong process, introducing different ways of viewing adult development. Finally, Super (1990) delineated a career development model based on the propositions of psychosocial theory.

Identity Development: Marcia and Josselson

James Marcia (1966, 1980) was the first theorist to empirically investigate the identity development process in young adults. He was specifically interested in the identity versus identity diffusion stage of Erikson's (1959/1980, 1968) model, which occurs in adolescence. Focusing on the role of exploration and commitment, Marcia (1966) studied the experiences of college men as they related to identity formation. He defined *exploration* as a "crisis, defined in terms of the presence or absence of a decision-making period" (Marcia, 1980, p. 161). Commitment occurred when individuals made a decision in which they were personally invested. Marcia (1966) found that identity resolution was based on the extent to which the individual (1) had experienced crises related to vocational choice, political values, or religion, and (2) made commitments in these areas. Based on a later study involving college women, Schenkel and Marcia (1972) added sexual values and standards as a fourth area in which exploration and commitment occur.

Marcia (1966) posited that the presence or absence of exploration and commitment led to four styles of identity resolution, which can change over time and are not linear:

1. *Identity diffusion.* Individuals have neither experienced a crisis nor made a commitment; they appear unconcerned with their lack of direction.
2. *Foreclosure.* Individuals have experienced no crises, but have made commitments based on the desires or role modeling of others, particularly their parents.
3. *Moratorium.* Individuals in this status are actively experiencing a crisis and attempting to resolve it; this is a volatile state in which a great deal of dissonance is experienced.
4. *Identity achievement.* Having experienced crises and worked through them, individuals in this status have made decisions independent of others and committed to their choices.

Marcia's work (1966, 1980) suggests that not all students approach the identity resolution process similarly, and that they may need different types of interventions to progress.

Marcia (1980) has had an important influence on other theorists. Of particular note is the use of Marcia's model as a basis for Phinney's (1993) model of ethnic identity development, as well as the heterosexual identity development model of Worthington, Savoy, Dillon, and Vernaglia (2002). Additional research has examined race, ethnicity, and gender differences in identity formation as well as the statuses in adult development (see Evans, Forney, Guido, Patton, & Renn, 2010).

Building on the work of Marcia (1966, 1980), Josselson (1987, 1996) studied identity development in a group of women for over twenty years, interviewing them during their college years (Jillian's age) and again at midlife (Elicia's age). Josselson's theory is helpful as Jessie considers challenges of identity development in college faced by both Jessie and Elicia. Social, sexual, and religious values, more than occupational and political values, were found to be significant areas of crisis and commitment for the women in young adulthood. Crisis in relationships, more than in any other area, led to growth and change for the women (Josselson, 1987, 1996). The degree to which the women deviated from or remained connected to the value systems of their parents—especially their mothers—largely determined their identities.

Josselson (1987) identified four styles of identity resolution similar to those Marcia delineated (1966). Josselson (1996) used the following labels to describe women exhibiting each of the four styles: *drifters* (identity diffusion), *guardians* (foreclosure), *searchers* (moratorium), and *pathmakers* (identity achievement). Drifters were characterized by a lack of direction both when they graduated from college and at midlife. Guardians also changed little over the course of the twenty-year study, living lives similar to those they experienced during their childhoods. Women who left college as searchers continued to explore and question their decisions as they moved through their lives, often coming to tentative resolutions by midlife with which they were relatively satisfied. The significant aspect of the lives of pathmakers is their ability to make autonomous decisions as their circumstances or desires change. They face challenges and effectively resolve them without undo anxiety. Josselson's longitudinal research (1987, 1996) provides important information about how women construct their identities and underscores the importance of the college years in determining how women will approach their later years.

Vectors of Development: Chickering and Reisser

The first theorist to explicitly examine the psychosocial development of college students was Arthur Chickering (1969). His theory expanded upon Erikson's (1968) notions of identity and intimacy and suggested that the establishment of identity is the central developmental issue during the college years. In 1993, working with Linda Reisser, Chickering revised his theory to incorporate new research findings. Jessie will find this theory helpful in understanding the different areas of growth her students are experiencing.

Chickering and Reisser (1993) proposed seven vectors of development that contribute to the formation of identity (see Exhibit 9.1). Chickering (1969) chose the term *vectors* to describe the developmental tasks students experience "because each seems to have direction and magnitude—even though the direction may be expressed more appropriately by a spiral or by steps than by a straight line" (p. 8). Chickering and Reisser noted that students move through these vectors at different rates, that vectors can interact with one another, and that students often find themselves reexamining issues they had previously addressed. Although not rigidly sequential, Chickering and Reisser's vectors do build on each other and lead to greater complexity, stability, and integration. The work of these authors incorporates emotional, social, and intellectual aspects of development.

Chickering and Reisser (1993) argued that educational environments exert a powerful influence that helps students move through the seven vectors of development. Key factors in this process include institutional objectives, institutional size, faculty-student interaction, curriculum, teaching practices, diverse student communities, and

EXHIBIT 9.1.   CHICKERING AND REISSER'S VECTORS OF DEVELOPMENT.

1. *Developing Competence.* This vector focuses on the tasks of developing intellectual, physical and manual, and interpersonal competence. In addition, students develop confidence in their abilities within these arenas.

2. *Managing Emotions.* In this vector, students develop the ability to recognize and accept emotions, as well as to appropriately express and control them. This vector includes a broad range of feelings such as depression, anger, guilt, caring, optimism, and happiness.

3. *Moving Through Autonomy Toward Interdependence.* At this stage, students develop increased emotional independence, self-direction, problem-solving ability, persistence, and mobility, as well as recognition and acceptance of the importance of interdependence.

4. *Developing Mature Interpersonal Relationships.* Tasks addressed in this vector include the development of acceptance and appreciation of differences as well as the capacity for healthy and lasting intimate relationships.

5. *Establishing Identity.* A positive identity includes (1) comfort with body and appearance, (2) comfort with gender and sexual orientation, (3) a sense of one's social and cultural heritage, (4) a clear conception of self and comfort with one's roles and lifestyle, (5) a secure sense of self in light of feedback from significant others, (6) self-acceptance and self-esteem, and (7) personal stability and integration. Chickering and Reisser (1993) acknowledged differences in identity development based on gender, ethnicity, and sexual orientation.

6. *Developing Purpose.* This vector consists of developing clear vocational goals, making meaningful commitments to specific personal interests and activities, and establishing strong interpersonal commitments.

7. *Developing Integrity.* In this vector, students progress from rigid, moralistic thinking to a more humanized, personalized value system that acknowledges and respects the beliefs of others. Values and actions become congruent.

Source: Adapted from Chickering and Reisser, 1993. Reproduced with permission.

student affairs programs and services. Furthermore, three principles underscore these factors: integration of work and learning, acknowledgement of and respect for differences, and recognition of the cyclical nature of learning and development.

Researchers examining the applicability of Chickering's original theory (1969) and its later revision (Chickering & Reisser, 1993) to various student populations, including women, African American, Asian American, international, and lesbian, gay, and bisexual students, have found gender and cultural differences in the ordering and importance of various vectors (for a summary of this research, see Evans et al., 2010). Pope (1998) argued that psychosocial theories, particularly Chickering's, may be "insufficient" (p. 274) to explain the development of students of color because of cultural and experiential differences in their lives. In addition, racial identity development interacts with other aspects of psychosocial development and therefore must be taken into consideration in facilitating the development of students of color (Pope, 2000). Kodama, McEwen, Liang, and Lee's (2002) explication of the identity development of Asian American students is a particularly good example of such differences.

Adult Development

Psychosocial theorists following Erikson have used different perspectives to examine development across the lifespan, an important consideration when working with adult students like Elicia. Theories of adult psychosocial development can be categorized into three major groups based on the extent to which they emphasize psychological versus sociological factors in development. Moving from internally focused to externally oriented, these models are life stage, life events and transition, and life course approaches. In addition, integrative models, which account for biological, sociological, and psychological aspects of development, such as those of Baltes (1987), Magnusson (1995), and Bronfenbrenner (2005), are gaining popularity. Good introductions to adult development theories are provided by Clark and Caffarella (1999) and Merriam, Caffarella, and Baumgartner (2007).

Life Stage Perspectives. This approach suggests that individuals become unique and complex as they progress through life, with later developmental tasks building on earlier tasks in a predictable pattern. Developmental change occurs according to an internal timetable, influenced to some extent by environmental forces. Some theories in this category suggest that development is linked to age (for example, Levinson, 1978; Levinson, 1996), whereas others present sequential stages that are not necessarily tied to specific ages (for example, Howell & Beth, 2002; Vaillant, 1997).

Life Events and Transition Perspectives. These theorists, including Fiske and Chiriboga (1990) and Goodman, Schlossberg, and Anderson (2006), focus on the timing, duration, spacing, and ordering of individual and cultural life events (such as having a child or experiencing an economic downturn) over the course of human development, and they explore how individuals handle the transitions they experience as a result of these events. Unlike the life stage theorists, theorists associated with this perspective do not see life events as necessarily occurring in predictable stages. Life events theorists focus on how individuals make meaning of the events they experience and how they negotiate them. The manner in which they accomplish these tasks is seen as contingent on both internal variables, such as personality and attitude, and external variables, such as available support networks and outside resources.

Life Course Perspectives. Stressing the variability of human development and the importance of environment in growth and change, life course theorists focus on the social roles that individuals assume during their lives (Ferraro, 2001; Hughes & Graham, 1990); the timing of life events (Bengston, 1996; Neugarten, 1979); and the ways in which individuals construct and respond to their environments (Elder, 1995). More so than life stage or life events theorists, theorists in this group stress the variability of human development and the importance of environment in growth and change. Constructivist in nature, life course theories focus on the socially constructed beliefs that people hold about the roles they assume, such as about what it means to be a parent, worker, partner, or friend (Hughes & Graham). These theorists also consider the impact on the individual of such factors as the modification of roles (for example, redefining the parent role when a child leaves home); assumption of new roles (for example, getting married); and loss of certain roles (for example, having a parent die) (Ferraro).

Life course theorists view the timing of events in a person's life as particularly important. People develop "social clocks" that tell them when certain events are supposed to occur in their lives. When events are "off-time" (Neugarten, 1979, p. 888), as with Elicia's starting college at age thirty-five, stress results. Elder (1995) argued that in dealing with life events, people have agency—they plan and make choices about how to respond. Their decisions alter the courses of their lives. He also noted that individuals' lives are linked; persons' actions affect the lives of their significant others. Elder further examined the influence of social forces, place, and historical time, noting that the individual life course exists within the context of the society.

Career Development: Super

As Jillian's and Elicia's stories suggest, vocational decision making is an important consideration during college. In his psychosocial theory, Super (1990) identified five age-linked stages of career development, influenced by both personal and social variables, through which individuals progress. In the first stage, *growth* (ages zero to fourteen), children try out various experiences and develop an understanding of work. In the second stage, *exploration* (ages fourteen to twenty-four), individuals investigate possible career options, become aware of their interests and abilities, and develop the skills necessary to enter a career. The third stage, *establishment* (ages twenty-five to forty-four), consists of becoming competent in a career and advancing in it. In the fourth stage, *maintenance* (ages forty-five to sixty-five), persons continue to enhance their skills to remain productive while making plans for retirement. The final stage, *decline* (age sixty-five and older), involves adjusting work to one's physical capability and managing resources to remain independent. Super suggested that recycling of stages occurs during periods of transition, allowing for additional growth, exploration, and establishment. Super also noted that individuals can be successful in a variety of occupations and that, over time, individuals' preferences, self-concepts, and settings evolve, which may affect their satisfaction with the choices they have made and possibly lead to career shifts.

Using Psychosocial Theories in Practice

At this point you may be wondering what all these developmental tasks, vectors, and crises have to do with student affairs practice. Revisiting Jessie, the new academic advisor at an urban community college, may provide some suggestions. Certainly, psychosocial theories give Jessie a better understanding of the issues that may be important to the students with whom she works. For instance, Elder's (1995) theory of life course development suggests that lives are linked together, with significant events in one person's life influencing the lives of significant others. As an example, what is happening in the lives of Elicia's children will affect Elicia's ability to function effectively in college. This knowledge can increase Jessie's sensitivity as she helps Elicia plan her schedule to allow for attendance at her children's school events. Understanding psychosocial development helps educators be more proactive in anticipating student issues and more responsive to and understanding of concerns that may arise as they work with students.

Psychosocial theory is also helpful in program development. Whether planning orientation, educational sessions for Greek chapters, or staff development for resident assistants, student affairs professionals can use their knowledge of the timing and content of developmental stages to guide the selection of topics for presentation. For instance, at the private college where Jessie previously worked, most first-year students were probably dealing with Chickering and Reisser's (1993) early vectors. Programming in the first-year residence hall, then, might have focused on academic and social skills (vector 1) and managing the stresses of college (vector 2).

In addition, psychosocial theory can guide the formation of policy. For example, Ferraro's (2001) life events theory suggests that adults must balance many roles at the same time. Knowing that most students at the community college at which Jessie is now working are older adults who are working and attending evening classes will raise her awareness that they may be unable to find the time to accomplish routine tasks, such as registering for classes during regular business hours. Policies could be adjusted to allow for online registration as a support for them.

Cognitive-Structural Perspectives

Jessie is facing a dilemma. Noreen, a Muslim student who is one of her advisees, has come to her with a concern about her food science class. In this class, students are expected to sample foods to assess such qualities as sweetness, texture, and bitterness. However, during the holy month of Ramadan, Muslims must fast from sunrise until sundown. Noreen has spoken to her instructor about this problem, but the instructor was not sympathetic, suggesting that Noreen drop the class if she can't fulfill the requirements. Noreen needs the class to graduate on time and can't afford to stay an extra semester. Jessie believes that Noreen is being treated unfairly by a professor who is insensitive to Noreen's religious beliefs, and her first impulse is to intervene on Noreen's behalf with the department chair. However, Jessie's supervisor cautions her not to "rescue" her advisees and to think twice before criticizing the actions of faculty members without first getting both sides of the story.

How both Jessie and Noreen are processing this dilemma can be better understood through the lenses of cognitive-structural theories. Rooted in the work of Piaget (1952), cognitive-structural theories examine how people think and make meaning out of their experiences. The mind is thought to have structures—sets of assumptions people use to adapt to and organize their environments. Structures determine *how* people think but not *what* they think. Structures change, expand, and become more complex as a person develops. Younger students, like Noreen, are less likely to see the complexities of the dilemmas they face than are individuals like Jessie who are further along in their cognitive development.

Cognitive-structural stages are viewed as arising sequentially, regardless of cultural conditions. The age at which each stage appears and the rate of speed with which the person passes through it are variable. Each stage derives from the previous one, incorporating aspects of it, and is qualitatively different and more complex than earlier stages (Wadsworth, 1979).

According to cognitive-structural theorists, change takes place as a result of assimilation and accommodation. Assimilation is the process of integrating new information into existing structures—a quantitative change. Accommodation is the process of creating new structures to incorporate stimuli that do not fit into existing structures—a qualitative change (Wadsworth, 1979). Disequilibrium, or cognitive conflict, occurs when expectations are not confirmed by experience. When an individual experiences conflict, he or she first tries to assimilate the new information into the existing structure; if assimilation is not possible, then accommodation occurs in order to regain equilibrium (Wadsworth). Encountering an instructor who would not adjust the class requirements was a conflict for Noreen; trying to decide how to handle her student's problem was likewise a conflict for Jessie. Each first attempted to use strategies that were familiar to her: Noreen went to an authority for a solution; Jessie's first impulse was to intervene on behalf of her student. If these approaches do not work, they will search for new, more effective, approaches.

Piaget (1952) stressed the importance of heredity in cognitive development but also noted the role played by the environment in presenting experiences to which the individual must react. Social interaction with peers, parents, and other adults is especially influential in cognitive development. The interaction between Noreen and Jessie, for example, has the potential to influence the manner in which each of them comes to understand this and similar situations in the future.

Many theories applicable to college students are based in the cognitive-structural tradition. This section includes an examination Perry's (1968) theory of intellectual and ethical development and a brief review of some of the later theories that expanded his work (Baxter Magolda, 1992; Belenky, Clinchy, Goldberger, & Tarule, 1986; King & Kitchener, 1994). I then discuss moral development theories (Gilligan, 1982; Kohlberg, 1976; Rest, Narvaez, Bebeau, & Thoma, 1999; Rest, Narvaez, Thoma, & Bebeau, 2000) and theories of spiritual and faith development (Fowler, 1981, 2000; Parks, 2000), topics that are receiving increasing attention in higher education.

Theories of Intellectual and Epistemological Development

Perry's (1968) work established a foundation for later theorists interested in the intellectual and epistemological development of students. These included Belenky et al. (1986), who studied women's "ways of knowing," Baxter Magolda (1992); who explored gender differences in epistemological development; and King and Kitchener (1994), who introduced the concept of reflective judgment.

Intellectual Development. Based on a longitudinal study of undergraduates at Harvard and Radcliffe Colleges in the 1950s, Perry's (1968) theory of intellectual and ethical development identified structures that determine how individuals view their life experiences, such as the situation that Noreen faced in her food science class.

EXHIBIT 9.2.   PERRY'S SCHEME.

1. *Dualism* (positions 1 and 2). The student believes that right answers exist to all questions and that authorities have these answers. The world is viewed in absolute, right-wrong terms. In position 3 some uncertainty is recognized, but it is viewed as a challenge set by authorities for students to learn to find the answers on their own.
2. *Multiplicity* (positions 3 and 4). Uncertainly is now viewed as temporary in areas in which authorities have yet to find the answers. In position 4 uncertainty is seen as so extensive that all opinions are equally valid, and students begin to rely less on authorities.
3. *Relativism* (positions 5 and 6). A major shift in thinking occurs at position 5 as the student comes to view knowledge as contextual and relative and is able to make judgments based on evidence and the merits of an argument.
4. *Commitment in Relativism* (positions 7 to 9). Students test out and evaluate various commitments leading to the development of a personalized set of values, lifestyle, and identity.

Source: Evans, 1996. Reprinted with permission.

In Perry's scheme, individuals move through a series of positions, starting with simple forms of interpretation and ending with complex forms. Each of the nine positions he identified represents a different way of looking at the world. Although they form a continuum, the positions are not of fixed duration. It is in the transition between positions that development actually occurs. The nine positions in Perry's scheme (1968) are often grouped into four levels, which are delineated in Exhibit 9.2.

Although individuals typically move through these positions in order, Perry (1968) noted three deflections from growth that can occur: *temporizing* is a period in which movement out of a particular position is postponed, *escape* involves an abnegation of responsibility accompanied by alienation, and *retreat* is a temporary regression back to a dualistic position.

Although Perry (1968) did not address application of his theory in much detail, others interested in facilitating the cognitive development of students have used his concepts extensively. Of particular note is the developmental instruction model developed by Knefelkamp and Widick (as cited in Knefelkamp, 1999), which suggested ways in which students' cognitive development can be enhanced through the use of challenge and support. The strategies Knefelkamp and Widick advocated involve use of varying degrees of structure, diversity, experiential learning, and personalism (see Evans et al., 2010, for a more detailed discussion of this model).

Women's Ways of Knowing. In response to the lack of attention given to the intellectual development of women in Perry's (1968) study, Belenky, Clinchy, Goldberger, and Tarule (1986) undertook a study in the late 1970s that examined the intellectual development of women. Their participants, unlike Perry's, came from diverse socioeconomic backgrounds and were recruited from social service agencies as well as educational settings, allowing the authors to identify similarities among women regardless of their backgrounds. Belenky and her colleagues identified five different "ways of knowing" that they referred to as "perspectives" rather than "stages." Within each of their perspectives, the development of a voice, self, and mind were intertwined

(Belenky et al.). Retrospectively, women who had previously used the first way of knowing, *silence*, described themselves at that time as mindless, voiceless, and totally subject to external authority. These were women at the lowest socioeconomic level who were recruited at social services agencies. Women who used the next perspective, *received knowing*, incorporated knowledge provided by external authorities and were able to reproduce it when called on. Users of the third perspective, *subjective knowing*, viewed knowledge as an intuitive process that was personal and private. Women using *procedural knowing* made an investment in learning and looked for objective procedures for obtaining knowledge and determining if it was valid. Some women using this perspective demonstrated an impartial, impersonal approach to learning, labeled *separate knowing*, whereas others used an approach that was relational in nature and based on personal experiences, labeled *connected knowing*. Women who used the final perspective identified by Belenky and her colleagues, *constructed knowing*, valued both subjective and objective learning, saw knowledge as contextual, and understood that they had the ability to create knowledge. Later studies (e.g., Goldberger, 1996) suggested that these five perspectives are not experienced similarly by all women and are influenced by women's cultural backgrounds. For instance, Noreen's Islamic culture is likely to influence how she approaches her teacher and her advisor.

Epistemological Development. In 1992, Baxter Magolda initiated a longitudinal study comparing the epistemological development (that is, assumptions about learning) of men and women during college (discussed in greater detail in Chapter Eleven). Based on her findings, Baxter Magolda (1992) developed the Epistemological Reflection Model, which consists of four increasingly complex stages. In the first stage, *absolute knowing*, students consider all knowledge as certain; they expect authorities to provide answers to every question; and they believe that they must memorize and reproduce information that authorities provide. Learners in stage two, *transitional knowing*, understand that knowledge is sometimes uncertain and that authorities may not have the answers for all questions. In this stage, learners view themselves as understanding and being able to use information. In stage three, *independent knowing*, students accept the fact that most knowledge is uncertain. They value instructors who create a positive learning environment in which students can engage in independent thinking and share their opinions. The final stage of Baxter Magolda's model, *contextual knowing*, is generally not achieved until after students complete college and begin jobs or enter graduate school. Individuals who reach this stage recognize that they must consider context when determining if knowledge is valid and that they must provide evidence to support the positions they take. Baxter Magolda found gender-related differences in the first three stages in her model, with women more often using patterns of knowing that were relational and men using patterns that were impersonal. Noreen and Jessie both exhibited relational patterns as they sought out others to help them process Noreen's situation. Data from Baxter Magolda's ongoing study (1995) suggested that these two patterns come together in the fourth stage, where greater complexity in reasoning allows more flexibility in choice of the most appropriate pattern for a given situation.

Reflective Judgment. King and Kitchener (1994) undertook a research program to better understand the relationship between epistemology and judgment. They explored how individuals address *ill-structured problems*—those without clear answers (for example, Jessie's dilemma of how to assist Noreen). In their Reflective Judgment Model, King and Kitchener (1994) identified seven stages of development that they grouped into three levels. At each stage, individuals understand differently what knowledge is, how knowledge is acquired, and how ill-structured problems are resolved. Thinking becomes more complex as individuals move through the seven stages. In King and Kitchener's first level, *prereflective thinking* (stages one through three), individuals view knowledge as certain, see every problem as having a correct answer, and do not understand the role of evidence in reaching a conclusion. *Quasi-reflective thinkers* (those in stages four and five) recognize the existence of ill-structured problems and are aware that conclusions can sometimes be uncertain. They use evidence in making arguments but don't always come up with persuasive reasoning for the judgments they put forth. Individuals who are *reflective thinkers* (stages six and seven) are aware that knowledge is constructed rather than preexisting and that context is an important factor in coming to conclusions. They understand that evidence must be provided to support judgments and that the introduction of new data warrants the reevaluation of conclusions. Individuals are capable of using more than one stage of reflective judgment; which stage they use is contingent on the support and feedback they receive while making judgments (Kitchener, Lynch, Fischer, & Wood, 1993).

Exposure to controversial issues and opportunities to work through complex concerns encourage the development of reflective judgment (King & Kitchener, 1994). Individuals also benefit from intentional training in how to use evidence when making judgments (King, 2003). Furthermore, extensive research supports the validity and value of the Reflective Judgment Model in college settings (King & Kitchener, 1994, 2002).

Theories of Moral Development

Moral development is the process by which individuals go about making decisions that affect themselves and others. Clearly the decisions that Jessie makes about how to address Noreen's dilemma in her food science class will affect her, Noreen, the class instructor, and possibly Jessie's supervisor. Kohlberg's (1976) work focusing on moral reasoning, the cognitive component of moral behavior, provided the foundation for later work by Gilligan (1982) and Rest et al. (1999).

Kohlberg. Based on a series of studies, Kohlberg (1976) developed a six-stage model of moral development centered around the concept of justice, which he defined as "the primary regard for the value and equality of all human beings, and for reciprocity in human relations" (Kohlberg, 1972, p. 14). He grouped his stages into *preconventional; conventional;* and *postconventional* levels, based on the individual's relationship with the rules of society (Colby, Kohlberg, & Kauffman, 1987; Kohlberg, 1976). His model is outlined in Exhibit 9.3.

EXHIBIT 9.3.   KOHLBERG'S STAGES OF MORAL REASONING.

Preconventional Level

The individual's thinking is concrete and self-focused. Societal rules and expectations are not yet understood. This level has two stages.

Stage 1. Heteronomous Morality
The direct consequences of actions determine right and wrong. The individual acts to avoid being punished. The rights and concerns of others are not recognized.

Stage 2. Individualistic, Instrumental Morality
Decisions are made pragmatically, based on equal exchange. "You scratch my back and I'll scratch yours" sums up this position.

Conventional Level

The rules of society and the opinions of others take precedence in decision making. Being a good citizen is an important criterion for action. This level also has two stages.

Stage 3. Interpersonally Normative Morality
Good behavior is defined as that which pleases those to whom one is close and gains their approval. Individuals adhere to stereotypes images of "right" behavior.

Stage 4. Social System Morality
Actions are based on upholding the system and obeying the rules of society. Showing respect for authority and maintaining the social order for its own sake are seen as important.

Postconventional, or Principled Level

Reasoning is based on self-determined principles and values. Individuals choose their own directions rather than following a prescribed path. This level has two stages as well.

Stage 5. Human Rights and Social Welfare Morality
Right action is determined by the standards that have been agreed upon by society, but an awareness exists that rules can be reevaluated and changed. Individuals are bound by the social contracts into which they enter.

Stage 6. Morality of Universalizable, Reversible, and Prescriptive General Ethical Principles
Self-chosen ethical principles, including justice, equality, and respect for human dignity, guide behavior. Principles take precedence over laws.

Source: Adapted from Colby, Kohlberg, and Kauffman, 1987; Evans, 2003; and Kohlberg, 1976.

The ability to reason logically and to see the point of view of others is necessary, but not sufficient, to achieve more advanced levels of moral reasoning (Kohlberg, 1976). Moral development occurs in response to cognitive conflict that disrupts one's current way of thinking. It is enhanced by chances to confront situations that have moral implications (Kohlberg, 1972), such as the dilemma Noreen faces.

Gilligan. Gilligan (1977, 1982) asserted that Kohlberg's theory, with its focus on justice and rights, did not take into account the concern that women have with care and responsibility for others. Based on her findings from several studies involving real-life moral dilemmas, such as whether or not to have an abortion, Gilligan (1977) proposed an alternative model of moral development with three levels and two transition periods. In the first level, which Gilligan called *orientation to individual survival,* decisions center on the self and one's own desires and needs. In the first transition, *from selfishness to responsibility*, the desire to take care of oneself remains but is in conflict with a growing sense that the right thing to do is to take care of others. In the second level, *goodness as self-sacrifice*, acceptance by others becomes the primary criterion. This goal is achieved by caring for others and protecting them, a tendency Jessie demonstrates in the scenario. One's own desires are relegated to a secondary position. As persons begin to question the logic of always putting themselves second, the second transition, *from goodness to truth*, begins, and the concept of responsibility is reconsidered in an effort to include taking care of oneself as well as others. In the third level, *the morality of nonviolence*, the individual "asserts a moral equality between self and other" (Gilligan, 1977, p. 504) and comes to understand that the prohibition against hurting also includes not hurting oneself, a position Jessie's supervisor seems to take. This principle of nonviolence becomes the person's main guiding force.

While evidence supports the existence of at least two bases for moral decision-making—one being justice and rights and the other being care and responsibility (see Evans et al., 2010)—research suggests that they are gender-related rather than gender-specific. While men and women have been found to use both styles, men use justice and rights arguments more often, while women more frequently base their judgments on responsibility and care (Jones & Watt, 2001; Liddell, Halpin, & Halpin, 1992).

Rest. Rest and his associates have actively pursued research on moral development for over twenty-five years (Rest et al., 1999). Based on their research, they introduced a neo-Kohlbergian approach to understanding moral reasoning (Rest et al., 2000). Like Kohlberg's (1976) approach, Rest et al.'s (2000) model is both cognitive-structural and developmental, in that reasoning is seen to increase in complexity over time. Both approaches also focus on how individuals attempt to make meaning out of their social experiences and emphasize the shift from conventional to postconventional thinking in early adulthood. However, unlike Kohlberg (1976), Rest et al. (2000) viewed moral reasoning as fluid and used concrete definitions of stages; they addressed both content and structure as aspects of moral reasoning; and they did not assume their theory was universal (in other words, it did not fit everyone).

Rest et al. (2000) postulated three structures in moral reasoning, based on how the person interprets and responds to societal obligations: the *personal interest schema*, the *maintaining norms schema*, and the *postconventional schema*. They defined *schemas* as "general knowledge structures residing in long-term memory" that develop as individuals "notice similarities and recurrences in experiences" (p. 389). The personal interest schema predominates in childhood and becomes less prominent in reasoning as the person moves into adolescence. This type of reasoning involves analysis of what each individual has to gain or lose and does not acknowledge the importance of society-wide cooperation. The emphasis is on the concerns of the individual and those to whom he or she is close. As can be seen in Exhibit 9.3, this schema includes elements of Kohlberg's second and third stages. The maintaining norms schema is similar to Kohlberg's fourth stage. Individuals using this type of reasoning recognize and abide by established societal norms, believe that all norms must be obeyed, and acknowledge the legitimate roles of authorities. Noreen's instructor might be using this type of reasoning in that he is concerned about applying the same policies to all of his students. Postconventional schema thinking, in contrast, interprets moral obligations as "based on shared ideals," "fully reciprocal," and "open to scrutiny" (p. 388). This schema contains aspects of Kohlberg's postconventional stages five and six.

Spiritual Development

Spirituality, defined by Parks (2000) as a personal search for purpose and meaning in life, is an important yet sometimes neglected aspect of student development. Two prominent theorists have addressed this topic: Fowler (1981, 2000) looked at faith development across the life span and Parks (2000) focused on the development of spirituality in college.

Fowler. Fowler (1981) viewed faith as a process of making meaning out of life's experiences. Although he assumed that faith is a universal construct, he also noted that the manner in which it is expressed is unique for each person (Fowler, 1981, 2000). Stressing the relational nature of faith, he focused on the interaction of self, others, and a larger center of meaning and purpose, which some call "God" (Fowler, 1981). Fowler (2000) saw faith as taking the form of unconscious structures that make up six stages of faith development, which describe how beliefs and values come to be important to the individual rather than the specific beliefs and values the individual adopts. Thus Fowler's theory (1981, 2000) could be applied to the development of Noreen's faith as a Muslim as well as the evolution of Jessie's Catholic beliefs. Fowler (1981) adhered closely to traditional cognitive-structural assumptions, describing his stages as sequential, hierarchical, and generalizable across cultures. Crises in the lives of individuals lead to movement from one stage to the next. Each stage is more complex than the one it follows, with later stages being more mature expressions of faith than earlier ones.

Parks. Parks's (2000) work builds on Fowler's theory (1981), adding a stage of young adulthood that she felt was missing from his approach. Parks (2000) identified four interacting components of faith: self, other, world, and God. The manner in which each of these elements is viewed and relates to the others undergoes change as the person's faith develops. She proposed a four-stage model emphasizing the contributions of affective, cognitive, and sociocultural factors in faith development. Most college students are in the *young adulthood stage*, at which individuals make and learn from tentative commitments. They begin to develop a sense of independence from others. At this point, they need a compatible mentoring community in which to explore. Some college students, particularly older students, may be in the *tested adult stage*, which is characterized by more secure commitments and confident inner dependence. Individuals in this stage seek out communities that have compatible belief systems.

Parks (2000) stressed the role of imagination in faith development, identifying five steps in acts of imagination. *Conscious conflict* involves recognizing that something in one's life is out of balance. *Pause* is a time of reflection and examination. *Image (or insight)* is the moment when everything comes together. *Repatterning and release of energy* consists of letting go of tension and reorganizing the phenomena under consideration. The last step, *interpretation*, involves openly trying out new perspectives. Parks suggested that colleges are communities of imagination that can affect faith development either positively or negatively. For positive development to occur, students need to be introduced to new ideas and have opportunities to reflect on them and to try out new positions. Noreen, for example, seems to be experiencing conscious conflict as a result of her interactions with her instructor. Jessie might suggest to Noreen that a period of pause could help her come to a moment of insight that will enable her to repattern her thinking about the event and make sense of it within her belief system.

Using Cognitive-Structural Theories in Practice

Cognitive-structural theories can help to explain dilemmas that persons such as Jessie and Noreen are facing. Understanding how a student thinks about a situation can guide a student affairs professional in working with the student. For instance, Perry's theory (1968) can help Jessie to understand the struggle that Noreen is having in resolving the issue with her food science professor: if Noreen has not yet reached a relativistic level of reasoning and relies on authorities for answers, she may be caught between the two conflicting positions that authorities in her life are maintaining: her professor is telling her she must participate fully in the class by consuming food, whereas her religious leaders are telling her that she cannot eat during Ramadan.

In examining her own response to the situation from a moral development perspective, being aware of Gilligan's theory (1977) may help Jessie see that she is functioning at the second level of moral reasoning by putting her students' needs before her own as a professional. She may come to understand that solving Noreen's problem for her by taking Noreen's concern to the department chair without first hearing the professor's side of the issue may harm her professional reputation. Thinking about where Noreen is in her own development may also lead Jessie to reconsider what will be most helpful for encouraging Noreen's development. A more appropriate approach might be to coach Noreen about how to approach her professor and possibly the department chair.

Cognitive-structural theories are also very helpful in deciding how to structure classes and workshops. For example, if Jessie decides to offer a class for students attending her community college who are planning to transfer to a four-year college or university, she might recall Knefelkamp and Widick's Developmental Instruction Model (Knefelkamp, 1999) and incorporate appropriate levels of structure, diversity, experiential learning, and personalism to meet the needs of students at various levels of cognitive development. Cognitive-structural theories can also guide policy decisions. For instance, younger learners, who are often prereflective or quasi-reflective learners as defined by King and Kitchener (1994), will be encouraged to develop reflective judgment by being placed in situations in which they must confront complex issues and make their own decisions. Student affairs professionals can guide such individuals through the process of identifying and evaluating evidence for various positions they might take, rather than leaving faculty and administrators to make decisions for these students.

Conclusion

As can be seen from the examples presented, each theoretical perspective adds a piece to the puzzle of student development. Psychosocial theories provide information on the issues and concerns facing students in college, and cognitive-structural theories explain how students make meaning of their experiences and come to conclusions about how to approach them. Hopefully, the examples and connections provided in this chapter have demonstrated ways in which these types of theories can be used effectively in the daily activities of student affairs practice and have encouraged readers to become theory-based practitioners. Obviously, however, reading a few paragraphs on each of the many theories mentioned here will not make anyone an expert. The main goal of this chapter, then, has been to pique your interest in further reading and ongoing study of the valuable student development theories introduced here.

References

Baltes, P. B. (1987). Theoretical propositions of life-span developmental psychology: On the dynamics between growth and decline. *Developmental Psychology, 23*, 611–626.

Baxter Magolda, M. B. (1992). *Knowing and reasoning in college: Gender-related patterns in students' intellectual development.* San Francisco: Jossey-Bass.

Baxter Magolda, M. B. (1995). The integration of relational and impersonal knowing in young adults' epistemological development. *Journal of College Student Development, 36*, 205–216.

Belenky, M. F., Clinchy, B. M., Goldberger, N. R., & Tarule, J. M. (1986). *Women's ways of knowing: The development of self, voice, and mind.* New York: Basic Books.

Bengston, V. L. (Ed.). (1996). *Adulthood and aging: Research on continuities and discontinuities.* New York: Springer.

Bronfenbrenner, U. (Ed.). (2005). *Making human beings human: Bioecological perspectives on human development.* Thousand Oaks, CA: Sage.

Chickering, A. W. (1969). *Education and identity.* San Francisco: Jossey-Bass.

Chickering, A. W., & Reisser, L. (1993). *Education and identity* (2nd ed.). San Francisco: Jossey-Bass.

Clark, M. C., & Caffarella, R. S. (Eds.). (1999). *An update on adult development theory* (New Directions for Adult and Continuing Education No. 84). San Francisco: Jossey-Bass.

Colby, A., Kohlberg, L., & Kauffman, K. (1987). Theoretical introduction to the measurement of moral judgment. In A. Colby & L. Kohlberg (Eds.), *The measurement of moral judgment: Vol. 1. Theoretical foundations and research validation* (pp. 1–67). New York: Cambridge University Press.

Elder, G. H., Jr. (1995). The life course paradigm: Social change and individual development. In P. Moen, G. H. Elder Jr., & K. Lüscher (Eds.), *Examining lives in context: Perspectives on the ecology of human development* (pp. 101–139). Washington, DC: American Psychological Association.

Erikson, E. H. (1968). *Identity: Youth and crisis.* New York: Norton.

Erikson, E. H. (1980). *Identity and the life cycle.* New York: Norton. (Original work published 1959)

Evans, N. J. (1996). Theories of student development. In S. R. Komives, D. B. Woodard Jr., & Associates (Eds.), *Student services: A handbook for the profession* (3rd ed., pp. 164–187). San Francisco: Jossey-Bass.

Evans, N. J. (2003). Psychosocial, cognitive, and typological perspectives on student development. In S. R. Komives, D. B. Woodard Jr., & Associates (Eds.), *Student services: A handbook for the profession* (4th ed., pp. 179–202). San Francisco: Jossey-Bass.

Evans, N. J., Forney, D. S., Guido, F., Patton, L. D., & Renn, K. A. (2010). *Student development in college: Theory, research, and practice* (2nd ed.). San Francisco: Jossey-Bass.

Ferraro, K. F. (2001). Aging and role transitions. In R. H. Birnstock & L. K. George (Eds.), *Handbook of aging and the social sciences* (pp. 313–330). San Francisco: Jossey-Bass.

Fiske, M., & Chiriboga, D. A. (1990). *Change and continuity in adult life.* San Francisco: Jossey-Bass.

Fowler, J. W. (1981). *Stages of faith: The psychology of human development and the quest for meaning.* New York: Harper & Row.

Fowler, J. W. (2000). *Becoming adult, becoming Christian: Adult development and Christian faith* (Rev. ed.). San Francisco: Jossey-Bass.

Gardner, J. (1961). *Excellence.* New York: Harper & Row.

Gilligan, C. (1977). In a different voice: Women's conception of self and morality. *Harvard Educational Review, 47,* 481–517.

Gilligan, C. (1982). *In a different voice: Psychological theory and women's development.* Cambridge, MA: Harvard University Press.

Goldberger, N. R. (1996). Cultural imperatives and diversity in ways of knowing. In N. R. Goldberger, J. M. Tarule, B. M. Clinchy, & M. F. Belenky (Eds.), *Knowledge, difference, and power* (pp. 335–371). New York: Basic Books.

Goodman, J., Schlossberg, N. K., & Anderson, M. L. (2006). *Counseling adults in transition* (3rd ed.). New York: Springer.

Holland, J. L. (1997). *Making vocational choices: A theory of vocational personalities and work environments* (3rd ed.). Odessa, FL: Psychological Assessment Resources.

Howell, L. C., & Beth, A. (2002). Midlife myths and realities: Women reflect on their experiences. *Journal of Women and Aging, 14*(3/4), 189–204.

Hughes, J. A., & Graham, S. W. (1990). Adult life roles: A new approach to adult development. *Journal of Continuing Higher Education, 38*(2), 2–8.

Jones, C. E., & Watt, J. D. (2001). Moral orientation and psychosocial development: Gender and class standing differences. *NASPA Journal, 39*(3), 1–13.

Josselson, R. E. (1987). *Finding herself: Pathways to identity development in women.* San Francisco: Jossey-Bass.

Josselson, R. E. (1996). *Revising herself: The story of women's identity from college to midlife.* New York: Oxford University Press.

King, P. M. (2003). Student learning in higher education. In S. R. Komives, D. B. Woodard Jr., & Associates (Eds.), *Student services: A handbook for the profession* (4th ed.). San Francisco: Jossey-Bass.

King, P. M., & Kitchener, K. S. (1994). *Developing reflective judgment: Understanding and promoting intellectual growth and critical thinking in adolescents and adults.* San Francisco: Jossey-Bass.

King, P. M., & Kitchener, K. S. (2002). The Reflective Judgment Model: Twenty years of research on epistemic cognition. In B. K. Hofer & P. R. Pintrich (Eds.), *Personal epistemology: The psychology of beliefs about knowledge and knowing* (pp. 37–61). Mahwah, NJ: Erlbaum.

Kitchener, K. S., Lynch, C. L., Fischer, K. W., & Wood, P. K. (1993). Developmental range of reflective judgment: The effect of contextual support and practice on developmental stage. *Developmental Psychology, 29,* 893–906.

Knefelkamp, L. L. (1999). Introduction. In W. G. Perry Jr. *Forms of ethical and intellectual development in the college years: A scheme* (pp. xi–xxxvii). San Francisco: Jossey-Bass.

Kodama, C. M., McEwen, M. K., Liang, C.T.H., & Lee, S. (2002). An Asian American perspective on psychosocial student development theory. In M. K. McEwen, C. M. Kodama,

A. Alvarez, S. Lee, & C.T.H. Liang (Eds.), *Working with Asian American college students* (New Directions for Student Services No. 97, pp. 45–59). San Francisco, Jossey-Bass.

Kohlberg, L. (1972). A cognitive-developmental approach to moral education. *Humanist, 6,* 13–16.

Kohlberg, L. (1976). Moral stages and moralization: The cognitive-developmental approach. In T. Lickona (Ed.), *Moral development and behavior: Theory, research, and social issues* (pp. 31–53). New York: Holt, Rinehart and Winston.

Kolb, D. A. (1984). *Experiential learning: Experience as the source of learning and development.* Englewood Cliffs, NJ: Prentice Hall.

Levinson, D. J. (1978). *The seasons of a man's life.* New York: Ballantine.

Levinson, D. J. (1996). *The season of a woman's life.* New York: Ballantine.

Liddell, D. L., Halpin, G., & Halpin, W. G. (1992). The measure of moral orientation: Measuring the ethics of care and justice. *Journal of College Student Development, 33,* 325–330.

Magnusson, D. (1995). Individual development: A holistic, integrated model. In P. Moen, G. H. Elder, & K. Lüsher (Eds.), *Examining lives in context: Perspectives on the ecology of human development* (pp. 19–60). Washington, DC: American Psychological Association.

Marcia, J. E. (1966). Development and validation of ego-identity status. *Journal of Personality and Social Psychology, 3,* 551–558.

Marcia, J. E. (1980). Identity in adolescence. In J. Adelson (Ed.), *Handbook of adolescent psychology* (pp. 159–187). New York: Wiley.

Merriam, S. B., Caffarella, R. S., & Baumgartner, L. M. (2007). *Learning in adulthood: A comprehensive guide.* San Francisco: Jossey-Bass.

Myers, I. B. (1980). *Gifts differing.* Palo Alto, CA: Consulting Psychologists Press.

Neugarten, B. L. (1979). Time, age, and the life cycle. *American Journal of Psychiatry, 136,* 887–894.

Parks, S. D. (2000). *Big questions, worthy dreams: Mentoring young adults in their search for meaning, purpose, and faith.* San Francisco: Jossey-Bass.

Perry, W. G., Jr. (1968). *Forms of intellectual and ethical development in the college years: A scheme.* New York: Holt, Rinehart and Winston.

Phinney, J. S. (1993). A three-stage model of ethnic identity development in adolescence. In M. E. Bernal & G. P. Knight (Eds.), *Ethnic identity: Formation and transmission among Hispanics and other minorities* (pp. 61–79). Albany: State University of New York Press.

Piaget, J. (1952). *The origins of intelligence in children.* New York: International Universities Press.

Pope, R. L. (1998). The relationship between psychosocial development and racial identity of Black college students. *Journal of College Student Development, 39,* 273–282.

Pope, R. L. (2000). The relationship between psychosocial development and racial identity of college students of color. *Journal of College Student Development, 41,* 302–312.

Rest, J., Narvaez, D., Bebeau, M. J., & Thoma, S. J. (1999). *Postconventional moral thinking: A neo-Kohlbergian approach.* Mahwah, NJ: Erlbaum.

Rest, J., Narvaez, D., Thoma, S. J., & Bebeau, M. J. (2000). A neo-Kohlbergian approach to morality research. *Journal of Moral Education, 29,* 381–395.

Schenkel, S., & Marcia, J. E. (1972). Attitudes toward premarital intercourse in determining ego identity status in college women. *Journal of Personality, 40,* 472–482.

Super, D. E. (1990). A life-span, life-space approach to career development. In D. Brown, L. Brooks, & Associates, *Career choice and development: Applying contemporary theories to development* (2nd ed., pp. 197–261). San Francisco: Jossey-Bass.

Vaillant, G. (1997). *Adaptation to life.* Boston: Little, Brown.

Wadsworth, B. J. (1979). *Piaget's theory of cognitive development* (2nd ed.). New York: Longman.

Worthington, R. L., Savoy, H. B., Dillon, F. R., & Vernaglia, E. R. (2002). Heterosexual identity development: A multidimensional model of individuals and social identity. *Counseling Psychologist, 30,* 496–531.

Young, R. B. (2003). Philosophies and values guiding the student affairs profession. In S. R. Komives, D. B. Woodard Jr., & Associates (Eds.), *Student services: A handbook for the profession* (4th ed., pp. 89–106). San Francisco: Jossey-Bass.

CHAPTER TEN

PERSPECTIVES ON IDENTITY DEVELOPMENT

Vasti Torres

No one knows precisely how identities are forged, but it is safe to say that identities are not invented: an identity would seem to be arrived at by the way in which the person faces and uses his [sic] experiences. (Baldwin, 1985, p. 549)

This quote by noted author James Baldwin illustrates the experiences that can bring about changes in a person during college. These changes are encompassed in the concept of *identity*, describing how individuals organize their experiences within the context of the environments in which they are situated (Erikson, 1959/1994). The tasks involved in creating an identity (or self-definition) require that college students make intentional and informed decisions about vocation, relationships, influence from their families of origin, and meaningful values that allow them to enter adult life (Kroger, 2000). The need to help students through these critical developmental tasks requires student affairs practitioners to understand how identity is formed during the college years.

The formation of identity is defined at various stages of life as a balance between self and others (Kegan, 1982; Kroger, 2004). The "others" can be interpreted to include people, societal norms, or cultural expectations. It is this interplay between self and others that sets the foundation for identity as socially constructed and vulnerable to the sociocultural influences within the context (environment) in which the individual interacts (Kroger, 2004). In higher education this interplay is seen when students are drawn to different organizations, courses, or events based on their feelings about the interaction between self and the context set by the event (Torres, Jones, & Renn, 2009). As with any phenomenon that is socially constructed, it is important to raise questions about who decides what is considered typical, appropriate, or "normal." This questioning of "majority" or dominant social constructions undergirds the evolution of new perspectives on identity development and helps explain the diversity of students in higher education. Changing demographics in the student body not only create the need for practitioners to understand how different populations organize their life experiences within varying institutional contexts but also make knowledge of identity development theories a critical competency for student affairs practitioners.

This chapter provides a broad introduction to the theoretical foundations for identity development and then narrows in on several new perspectives. It is impossible to provide a complete analysis of all theories or all social identities found on a college campus; therefore, in this chapter I highlight key theorists, illustrate several common themes, and examine the interplay among theories and the ways in which these theories inform practice.

The Evolution of Identity Development Theories

Identity theories evolved from earlier theories that were considered lifespan and psychosocial in nature (see chapter Nine). These theories are typically referred to as *ego development theories*, and provide broad overviews of how different experiences are organized during one's life span. They focus on three interacting elements: biological characteristics, psychological needs, interests and defenses, as well as cultural environment (Kroger, 2000). Erikson (1959/1994), perhaps the best known of the life-span theorists, defined *ego identity* as "certain comprehensive gains which the individual, at the end of adolescence, must have derived from all of his [*sic*] pre-adult experience in order to be ready for the tasks of adulthood" (p. 108). Others who contributed to the development of identity theories include Loevinger's (1976) ego identity development theory and Kegan's (1982) evolving self. These early theorists defined *identity* at various points in the life span as "the means by which we differentiate ourselves from other people in our lives as well as from our own organic functions" (Kroger, 2004, p. 10). As identity develops individuals incorporate greater complexity into their personal and social identities (McEwen, 2003).

From these earlier theories three major themes influenced the development of new perspectives in identity theories in more recent years: role of late adolescence, influence of historical and cultural aspects, and processes beyond the adolescent years. The first theme focuses specifically on the college years and developmental tasks associated with late adolescence. The second theme considers different dimensions of identity—or what would now be referred to as social identity—and was acknowledged within the early work on ego identity as the influence of different historical and cultural aspects on identity (Erikson, 1959/1994). Erikson (1959/1994) defined ego identity as developing from "a gradual integration of all identifications, but here, if anywhere, the whole has a different quality than sum of its parts" (p. 95). In talking about a Jewish person Erikson described that the person's identity was linked "with the unique values, fostered by a unique history, of his [*sic*] people" (p. 109).

The unique history and values that influence identity development in the United States are mainly formed by the dominant group (usually defined as White and middle class within the United States) (Torres, Howard-Hamilton. & Cooper, 2003). Tatum (1997) explained, "The dominant group holds the power and the authority in society relative to the subordinates and determines how that power and authority may be acceptably used" (p. 23). Because historically subordinate groups were seen as inferior to the dominant group, oppression of subordinate groups was considered acceptable. For this reason, when subordinate, or minority groups "see things differently, their lack of control over the apparatuses of society that sustain ideological hegemony makes the articulation of their self-defined standpoint difficult" (Collins, 1989, p. 749). These socially constructed influences on how experiences are interpreted and perceived have far reaching consequences. As a result, for those in the minority, the influence of oppression on how they organize their experiences becomes a complex developmental task (Abes & Kasch, 2007; Jones, 2009; Torres et al., 2003). For those in the majority, the societal norms around privilege also influence how their identities are formed.

The third theme addresses the understanding that beyond the adolescent years, identity development researchers describe a process of re-visiting identity statuses, suggesting that identity should not be seen as linear and completed at a certain point. As the average age of college students continues to increase, it is important to consider how the years beyond adolescence can influence identity. Marcia (2002) recognized that in adults there can be an "identity reconstruction" process (p. 15). This process typically entails an experience that produces disequilibrium and prompts the individual to enter a re-formation period, which then results in reconstruction of his or her identity. This reconstruction process does not create a disintegration of identity; rather, it is a revisiting of previous developmental tasks, as adults experience changes in their lives.

Social Identity Theories

Social identities influence who we are, how we see ourselves and how we relate to others. These aspects of identity include race, social class, gender, sexual orientation, religion, language, abilities, and age, as well as other aspects of our identity (Reynolds, 2001). These characteristics are oriented toward describing a reference group and not personality variables (Cross & Vandiver, 2001). This is why social identities in this chapter refer to the individuals' relation to social group membership and in many cases to oppression of those groups (Wing & Rifkin, 2001). Hardiman and Jackson (1997) developed a social identity theory that focuses across groups. In their theory, identity development follows five stages that reflect many of the stage processes found in other identity theories. The stages include: naive or no social consciousness, acceptance, resistance, redefinition, and internalization (Hardiman & Jackson). Commonalities between these stages and the theories explained next are discussed in terms of the social identities likely to be found within the college environment: racial, ethnic, gender, and sexual identity, as well as multiple identities.

Racial Identity Theories

The meaning of the term *racial identity* is not always clear; it will be defined here as "a sense of group or collective identity based on one's perception that he or she shares a common racial heritage with a particular racial group" (Helms, 1990, p. 3). The racial identity a person develops involves continual and often conflicting messages about the "people who comprise his or her externally ascribed reference group as well as the people who comprise other racial groups" (Thompson & Carter, 1997, p. 15). These conflicting messages make the process of identifying with a particular race developmental in nature, with choices and meaning-making processes at work.

Black Identity Theories. There is no single definition of what it means to be Black (Cross, 2001). The theories focused on Black identity, therefore, attempt to describe processes that explain the way a person thinks, feels, and acts in reference to being Black (Cross & Vandiver, 2001). Among the best-known theorists on Black identity are William Cross (1971, 1995) and Janet Helms (1990; Helms & Cook, 1999), who created theories to explain the processes of developing a Black identity. Cross described *nigrescence* as "a series of experiences and that resocializes a person's preexisting non-Afrocentric identity into an Afrocentric one" (as cited in Torres et al., 2003, p. 41). In 1971 Cross originally conceived his theory with five stages; in 1995 he revised his theory to better incorporate cultural, social, psychological, and historical changes that occurred since his initial conception of the theory. The revised theory takes into account issues of race salience, reference group orientation, and social identity awareness (Cross & Vandiver, 2001).

Helms wrote about Black racial identity and in 1999 created a set of statuses for people of color (Helms & Cook, 1999). Helms (1994) chose the term *statuses* instead of *stages* because people tend to think of stages as being external to the self and stable. Instead, ego status, once manifested, is always present thus "earlier modes of coping can influence people even after they think that they have resolved their racial identity issues" (p. 302).

What is common among these theories is the process of changing from low race salience (acknowledging being Black yet race is seen as insignificant in life) to more complex understandings of race. Students with low race salience are not likely to understand the role race plays in society within the United States, and therefore accept the roles determined through ideological hegemony. The meaning of race changes when an encounter occurs; though it does not have to be a negative encounter, it can be linked to experiencing firsthand the racism that is prevalent in society and institutional contexts. Encounters often challenge the notion that race is insignificant. The meaning-making process that results from the encounter propels the individual to consider immersion and emersions by experiencing anger, guilt, and pride. Once an individual can make meaning of his or her reactions to the encounter, a more internalized and integrated sense of self emerges that promotes positive views of his or her race as well as other racial groups (Cross, 2001; Helms & Cook, 1999).

These developmental processes can be seen in students in a variety of ways. For example, African American students at a college can be attracted to attending their

Black Student Union for many reasons, some of which could be linked to their identity development. For some, the student group offers an opportunity to explore their Black identity within the context of the college environment. For others, the student group serves as a platform to help gain additional funding to help with scholarships and services for African American students. For the student wanting to explore, understanding the early stages of Cross is critical, whereas for the student wanting to use the group as a platform, it is important to perceive how the later stages can present themselves. In either case, students from different stages will be members of this student organization; therefore practitioners must understand that each stage has different developmental tasks and that helping students with these tasks supports their identity development. The presence of students in different stages will influence the dynamics of the organization. Reading these dynamics through a developmental lens, moreover, helps practitioners work with students in the organization in effective ways.

White Identity Theories. Because Whites continue to occupy the majority status within U.S. society, they tend not to question their own culture or how they express their culture. White identity theories focus on the understanding and acknowledgement of privilege that comes from being in the majority (Helms, 1990). In her model of White Racial Identity, Helms (1990, 1994) illustrates two phases, each of which has three statuses. The first phase is the Abandonment of Racism, and its statuses are Contact, Disintegration, and Reintegration. The second phase is Defining a Non-Racist White Identity, with Pseudo-independence and Immersion and Emersion as statuses. These statuses emphasize the understanding of one's own privilege and the role this privilege has played in shaping the historical and social norms that influence the social distance between the races. The final status is one of Autonomy characterized by an internalized understanding of nonracism and the value of racial diversity. In this final status, individuals seek more diversity in their lives and do not impose White culture on others (Helms, 1994).

Individuals may "express several statuses simultaneously, one of which is dominant" (Thompson & Carter, 1997, p. 25). Although resolution of issues within early statuses is important to development, this may give the statuses a linear feel to them that is not intended. Because individuals have different configurations of racial identity, some statuses may be more prominent than others. A person might return to a previous status, but would experience that status differently (Thompson & Carter, 1997).

Helping majority White students through these developmental processes can be challenging. Many diversity education programs focus mainly on educating about the "other," whereas these theoretical tasks indicate that an individual should first focus on understanding the influence of his or her own culture (Helms, 1994; Ortiz & Rhoads, 2000). Restructuring approaches to help students understand how their own cultural influences have an impact on their values and views can help students begin the process of understanding privilege.

Multiracial Theories. The last fifteen years brought an increase in the number of multiracial or biracial students and subsequent research on this population. For several years, Root (1992) was the only researcher considering multiple races, but recently the research has been more robust (Renn, 2008; Root, 2003; Wijeyesinghe, 2001). Unlike many college student development models, multiracial development theories begin with childhood and with the individual's recognition of growing up in a multiracial home. Similarly, distinct from the many college students who come to college to discover themselves, multiracial students are likely to encounter choices between racial identity much earlier in life during the early adolescent years rather than late adolescent (Renn, 2008; Root, 2003; Wijeyesinghe, 2001). Theories about multiracial students explain processes by which the individual attains a sense of self in relation to multiple races rather than only one race. This more complex integration of race leads to a different understanding of race and identity and is inclusive of multiple racial perspectives rather than only one.

It is important to understand that mixed race students may struggle with institutional requirements to pick only one race. This struggle is part of identity processes and should be seen as an educational opportunity to help the students define themselves within the context, not just within established racial boxes. Recognizing that mixed race students may resist filling in such boxes—and respond to what they perceive as limited programmatic and educational options that reflect their sense of identity—will assist practitioners in better acknowledging the needs of mixed race students.

Ethnic Identity Theories

Research focused on ethnic identity represents one of three frameworks. These frameworks revolve around social identity theory, acculturation and cultural conflict, and identity formation (Phinney, 1990). While social identity theory would interpret membership in the group as sufficient for a positive sense of belonging, the issue of who holds the power and how oppression is expressed provides some groups with potentially negative images. These negative images may encourage individuals from ethnic groups to seek out being part of the majority. The acculturation and cultural conflict framework focuses on how the minority (or immigrant) relates to the dominant majority culture. The third framework more explicitly addresses ethnic identity formation, which acknowledges the dynamic nature of ethnic identity and the influences that occur as a result of time and context (Phinney, 1990). In this chapter the frameworks of identity and social identity formation were described; therefore it is important to understand the process around acculturation as part of ethnic identity.

Acculturation. Early theories of acculturation emphasized a three-stage process of contact, conflict, and adaptation. More recent models consider the interplay between the person, his or her ethnic group, and larger societal issues within the majority culture. Berry (2005) acknowledges that pluralistic societies contain multiple groups that coexist and each brings cultural factors to the environment. As a result, Berry focuses on acculturative strategies that result from issues surrounding the individual and describes them as a preference for: (1) maintaining the culture and identity of origin, or (2) establishing contact with and participation in the larger society and with other ethnic groups (Berry, 2005). This interplay occurs when one's culture of origin has greatly different cultural aspects.

An international study looking at issues of acculturation and identity found that among adolescents aged thirteen to eighteen, those with an integration profile (bicultural) had the best psychological and sociocultural adaptation outcomes (Berry, Phinney, Sam, & Vedder, 2006). This study considered both immigrant and native adolescents, and contributes to the understanding of how adaptation mechanisms can help. It is perhaps no longer necessary to view immigrants as needing to assimilate.

The following theories illustrate the elements within these three frameworks regarding ethnic identity and add to our understanding of the meaning-making process that ethnic minority college students experience.

Asian American Identity Theories. The division between race and ethnicity is not always clear within such groups as Asian Americans. The diversity within the category allows for many Asian Americans to fit the definition of race as an "externally ascribed reference group" (Helms, 1990), whereas other members of this group are more likely to resemble definitions of ethnicity.

Asian American identity revolves around the resolution of racial conflicts faced as "Americans of Asian ancestry in a predominantly White society" (Kim, 2001, p. 67). Asian American Identity Development (AAID) theory, which has five stages, focuses on the processes Asian Americans use to achieve a positive identity (Kim, 2001). Stage one focuses on level of ethnic awareness. Family and the racial composition of the surrounding community mainly influence this stage. Stage two is White identification, and there are two variations that can occur within this stage—active or passive White identified. The third stage focuses on awakening to sociopolitical consciousness, which indicates a shifting worldview and understanding that the Asian American is not responsible for the racism against Asians. The fourth stage is redirection toward an Asian American consciousness, and the final stage is incorporation (see Table 10.1).

A recent research study found that Asian Americans viewed certain social identities, including those based on race, ethnicity, gender, age, and socioeconomic status, as assigned by society rather than self-assigned (Chen, 2005). This finding highlights the social construction of race and the importance of contextual influences on how college students from different racial backgrounds will self-identify. In addition this illustrates how values of Western culture can conflict when an individual is balancing different cultural values.

Latino Identity Theories. Several models of Latino ethnic identity use a strong acculturation framework, offering categorical types in which to place Latinos' orientation (Felix-Ortiz de la Garza, Newcomb, & Myers, 1995; Ferdman & Gallegos, 2001; Keefe & Padilla, 1987; Torres, 1999). These theories describe Latinos in categories

TABLE 10.1. COMMONALITIES AMONG RACIAL/ETHNIC IDENTITY DEVELOPMENTAL THEORIES.

	Identity diffusion	Foreclosure		Moratorium		Identity achievement	
			Encounter	Immersion-emersion		Internalization	Internalization-commitment
Marcia (1966; 1993)	Identity diffusion	Foreclosure	Encounter →	Immersion-emersion →		Internalization	Internalization-commitment
Theory of nigrescence (Cross, 1971, 1995)		Pre-encounter	Encounter	Immersion-emersion		Internalization	Internalization-commitment
People of color racial identity (Helms & Cook, 1999)		Status 1: Conformity	Status 2: Dissonance	Status 3: Immersion	Status 4: Emersion	Status 5: Internalization	Status 6: Integrated awareness
Kim (2001)		Level of ethnic awareness and White identification	Awakening to social political awareness	Redirection to an Asian American consciousness		Incorporation	
Ruiz (1990)		Causal	Cognitive	Consequences		Working through	Successful resolution
Phinney (1993)	Unexamined ethnic identity		Ethnic identity search (moratorium)			Achieved ethnic identity	

Source: Adapted from Phinney, 1993, p. 67.

by level of acculturation to the majority culture and pride in their ethnic culture of origin (Torres & Delgado-Romero, 2008). These categories represent orientations such as bicultural (cultural blending), Latino oriented (Latino identified), American identified (Anglo oriented), or marginal (not fitting in) (Torres & Delgado-Romero, 2008). The more developmental theories focus on the influences Latinos' experience in their ethnic identity formation, such as how family influences sense of identity. Ruiz (1990) conceptualized five stages from case studies in his counseling practice: causal, cognitive, consequence, working through, and successful resolution. These stages have some similarity to other racial and ethnic theories, as shown in Table 10.1, in that the individual is seen to move from negative images of being Latino to a greater acceptance of self, Latino culture, and his or her own ethnicity (Torres & Delgado-Romero, 2008).

In identifying how Latino college students situate their ethnic identity, Torres (2003, 2004) found four conditions that influence how Latino/a students make meaning of their ethnic identity when they begin their college careers. These conditions are: environments in which they grew up, family and generational statuses in the United States, self-perceptions of status in society, and the college environment. These conditions are interrelated and influence each other; therefore, they should be considered together rather than separately. The more dissonance there is between the environment in which Latinos grew up and the college environment, the more likely cultural conflicts will play a role in their self-identification.

Extending the research about the journey toward self-authorship, Torres and Hernandez (2007) found that Latino/a college students face additional developmental tasks during the college years. Perhaps the most important of these tasks is the recognition of racism and the ability to make meaning of how racism influences identity development. Although Latino/as may understand that racism exists, it is not until they have had to face racism against themselves (or their culture) that the reality of oppression truly influences their identities (Torres & Hernandez, 2007).

Student affairs practitioners are in the position to help Latino/a or Asian American students process these developmental tasks. Understanding the conditions described in the theories (e.g., environment in hometown, family composition, generation in the United States, or experiences with racism) can help the practitioner initiate conversations with students that are both culturally sensitive and focused on what is happening with the student. For example, within these two cultures, a practitioner must understand that disobeying a parent or separating from the parent may not feel like an option to a student; instead, administrators can help the student learn the skills necessary to manage and maneuver familial expectations.

American Indian-Native American Identity Theories. Despite attempts to assimilate and destroy native culture, American Indians "insist on surviving on their own terms" (Lomawaima & McCarty, 2002, p. 281). This includes maintaining their native cultures, languages, and values. At the core of Indian values are communal concerns (including adherence to tradition), responsibility for family and friends, cooperation, and tribal identification (LaFromboise, Heyle, & Ozer, 1990). These values can at times be in conflict with the majority values of individualism, competitiveness, and amassing property and titles. When working with American Indian students, a student affairs professional should recognize and understand the central roles these values play.

Like many cultures that interact with the majority White culture prevalent in the United States, American Indians possess varying degrees of acculturation to the majority culture. This level of acculturation influences both the self-identification and the development of American Indian college students. Horse (2001) discusses American Indian identity by identifying factors that influence individual and group identities. Two models emerge from the framework of acculturation and can help practitioners understand the American Indian college student. The first is the Five Categories of Indianness: traditional, transitional, marginal, assimilated, and bicultural (LaFromboise, Trimble, & Mohatt, 1990). Like the Latino identity models, these categories focus on the level of acculturation and maintenance of ethnic identity the individual exhibits. The second is the Health Model Conceptualization of Acculturation, which represents four areas of human personality that are in harmony "with the domains of the medicine wheel (a uniquely Indian means of conceptualizing the human condition based on four essential elements)" (Choney, Berryhill-Paapke, & Robbins, 1995, p. 85). The four areas of human personality are: behavioral, social-environmental, affective-spiritual, and cognitive domains. Within these areas are concentric circles, with the perimeter of each circle representing a different level of acculturation: traditional, transitional, marginal, assimilated, and bicultural. There is no value judgment "placed on any level of acculturation, nor is any dimension of personality emphasized more than another" (Choney et al., p. 85). Understanding the categories of Indianness without placing a value on them can help student affairs practitioners engage American Indian students in conversations about what is happening in the interactions between context and self.

Changing Perspectives on Racial and Ethnic Identity

Recently, researchers considering the development of college students adopted several theoretical perspectives that enrich the contextual understanding of the college environment and highlight the diversity among college students. Critical race theory (CRT), for example, helps explain the centrality of race and ethnicity while emphasizing the influence of culture on identity. Three principles underline the tenets of CRT: (1) deconstruction of structures that oppress is necessary to understand how they influence others; (2) reconstruction for the value of every human being is critical; and (3) construction of a society with equal power among all involved is valued (Ladson-Billings, 1998). A central idea in CRT is the belief that there is no such thing as color-blind research, and that not recognizing race, ethnicity as well as other social identities, furthers inequality within society (Parker, 1998). Researchers who utilize CRT as a theoretical perspective are "interested in studying and transforming the relationship among race, racism, and power" (Delgado & Stefancic, 2001, p. 2).

Critical race theory has prompted Latinos to consider a critical perspective that places Latino ethnicity at the forefront. Latino critical theory, LatCrit, provides "credence to critical raced-gendered epistemologies that recognize students of color as holders and creators of knowledge" (Delgado Bernal, 2002, p. 107). Using LatCrit as a lens to view research involves contrasting European-based perspectives with more Latino-oriented outlooks and highlighting the differences. Placing power and race at the forefront instead of the background helps highlight how power is used to oppress certain identities. By using a critical lens, more researchers are illuminating voices and experiences previously not found in the literature.

Gender Identity Theories

Although *gender* is often used synonymously with *sex*, gender and sex are very different constructs. Gender is learned through a "complex psychological process, and what it entails, varies across cultures and historical periods" (Gilbert & Rader, 2002, p. 567). This differentiation requires that gender identity development be seen as a result of "personal and societal beliefs, stereotypes, and ingrained views about the fundamental nature of women and men" (p. 567). This section of identity theories revolves around the social construction of being women, men or transgendered.

Women's Identity Development. The development of gender incorporates a variety of lenses. Josselson (1996) considered women's identity to reside between the struggle to be competent and the balance required to maintain connections. Downing and Roush (1985) considered women's development as the construction of a positive feminist identity accomplished through five stages: passive acceptance (stage 1), revelation (stage 2), embeddedness-emanation (stage 3), synthesis (stage 4), and active commitment (stage 5). Ossana, Helms, and Leonard (1992) viewed women as developing through a womanist lens that may or may not be associated with feminist beliefs. And finally, those who consider the influence of gender roles critique models that bifurcate the differences in biological sex and that do not consider the complex social variables that influence the development of gender (Gilbert & Rader, 2002). What these models have in common is their emphasis on women's development from accepting societal norms about being women, to experiencing crises that allow them to question traditional roles, and eventually to growth toward a final stage characterized by a truce between societal gender expectations and the individuals' desires to actively change the way women are seen in society. Because women have been historically oppressed, theories about women's development resemble the trajectory of other oppressed racial and ethnic groups.

Recent research conducted on the Downing and Roush model (1985) proposed two interesting aspects of their model to consider (Fischer et al., 2000). First, sufficient evidence was found that the last two stages, synthesis and active commitment, are distinguished by different behaviors. Second, research indicated that the model did not necessarily address the multiple contexts in which women's identity evolves, including race/ethnicity, culture, class, age, and sexual orientation (Fischer et al., 2000).

When considering race, class, and gender together, it is important to understand that a minority group may not see gender as salient or in the same way as women from the dominant group. This requires minority groups to create alternative means of validating their own ways of being (Collins, 1989).

As practitioners it is important to recognize that women encourage silencing behaviors among themselves, which can be a particularly sensitive in groups of all women. Although we like to think that this no longer is the case, social pressures to "fit in" can promote behaviors that silence some women around such issues as sexual assault, eating disorders, and sexual orientation. Women's identity development theories provide insight on how to empower women in these situations and the ways in which social pressure can be tied to women's developmental stages and environmental circumstances.

Men's Identity Development. Definitions of masculinity and what it means to be a man have changed over time, and it is these societal shifts that significantly influence men's identity development (Kimmel, 2006). Because today's men are growing up without a road map or blueprint that clearly illustrates what it means to be a man, practitioners who work with young men must understand the "volatile combination of anomie and entitlement that can come to characterize Guyland" (Kimmel, 2008, p.42). Recent research on men's issues acknowledges that men need guidance to navigate changing societal expectations (Kimmel, 2008), yet the culture of entitlement around men allows them not to question or think about their gender (Davis, 2002). Kimmel (2008) argues that "the only way to transform Guyland is to break the culture of silence that sustains the Guy Code" (p. 280), referring to a "code" that encourages never showing emotions or admitting weakness. Other recent theoretical understandings also support the notion of breaking the culture. Edwards and Jones (2009) set forth a theory in which men move through phases beginning with "feeling a need to put on a mask" through "wearing a mask" to "experiencing and recognizing consequences of wearing a mask" (p. 215). When college men move through these phases, according to the theory, they begin "to transcend external expectations" (p. 215), and each becomes his own man.

Additional considerations should be given to African American men. Bonner and Bailey (2006) suggest that the educational difficulties that can arise for African American men can "trigger academic disidentification" (p. 34), which is associated with the negative group stereotypes that can emerge in an academic setting. These situations may encourage men to take on "cool behaviors" as a way to cope with being unsuccessful within an academic environment. "Cool pose" behaviors provide the male with a sense of control and convey strength and security (Bonner & Bailey, 2006).

◆ ◆ ◆

Being aware of these gendered processes can assist practitioners in understanding the behaviors and struggles of college students. For example, conflicts with leadership styles among students could be viewed in terms of gendered expectations and perhaps explained in a manner that can help students address their own expectations as well as societal influences. Helping students talk to one another about gendered expectations may help expose some of the myths that both encourage the guy code and promote silence among women.

Transgender Identity. Perhaps the most misunderstood minority within higher education are transgender individuals. In using the term *transgender*, it is important to understand that the term focuses on gender expression, although it is frequently grouped with sexual minorities, as the lesbian, gay, bisexual, and transgender (LGBT) moniker implies. A transgender individual may identify as one gender or attempt to blend genders, and may exist without the dichotomous distinctions society places on gender (Carter, 2000). A variety of expressions are represented within the term *transgender* that create some misunderstandings regarding sexual orientation. For transgender individuals who desire to change their sex designation, the dichotomous view of gender prevalent in most college environments becomes difficult to navigate (Beemyn, Curtis, Davis, & Tubbs, 2005). Even institutions that include sexual orientation in their policies need also to consider gender identity or expression (Beemyn et al., 2005). A good resource to help practitioners understand related legal and policy issues is the Transgender Law and Policy Institute (www.transgenderlaw.org/).

Sexual Identity and Sexual Orientation

Earlier writings in student affairs assumed that sexual identity is synonymous with sexual orientation, but more recent discourse differentiates between these two constructs. Sexual identity is a broader construct that does include sexual orientation, but that also "reflects a person's sexual values, sexual needs, preferred modes of sexual expression, preferences for characteristics of sexual partners and preferences for sexual activities" (Worthington, 2004). This distinction helps practitioners understand that whereas sexual behavior or identity might change, sexual attraction (sexual orientation) is relatively unchallengeable (Worthington, 2004). This is consistent with the American Psychological Association's view that sexual orientation is not a choice made by the individual (Worthington, Savoy, Dillon, & Vernaglia, 2002). In looking at developmental theories, this section concentrates on sexual identity theories and highlights theories for understanding heterosexual, gay, lesbian, and bisexual identities.

Heterosexual Identity. Because heterosexuals constitute the majority, research on heterosexual identity is almost nonexistent (Worthington et al., 2002). The first developmental status associated with heterosexual identity is unexplored commitment. This status reflects familial and societal gender roles and sexual behaviors that are assumed as part of the privileged majority. The next status is active exploration, in which an individual is involved in purposeful exploration, evaluation, and experimentation (processes that can be cognitive or behavioral). If an individual does not enter active exploration, then he or she enters the diffusion status, in which goal-directed intentionality is missing. It is only when the individual moves toward making a committed choice that the deepening and commitment status occurs. The final status is synthesis, in which an individual demonstrates congruence among all aspects of his or her identity (Worthington et al., 2002). This model has been criticized for insufficiently considering gender processes that are contextually based and that shape men and women differently in relation to how heterosexual identity develops (Gilbert & Rader, 2002).

Gay, Lesbian, and Bisexual (GLB) Identity Development.

GLB individuals share a common experience of "invisibility, oppression, isolation, and marginalization" (Fassinger & Arseneau, 2007, p. 43). With these commonalities in mind, Fassinger and Arseneau propose a model that considers "identity enactment of gender-transgressive sexual minorities" (p. 22). Their model considers identity enactment as occurring within a "contextual layer of temporal influences in which identity is shaped by the interactive influence of experiences of gender and gender expression (here termed 'gender orientation'), sexuality and sexual expression (here termed 'sexual orientation'), and cultural variables such as race, ethnicity, social class, disability, and religion (here termed 'cultural orientation')" (p. 24).

Temporal influences can include either cohort, signifying historical circumstances that shape society's views as well as the legal and interpersonal context occurring within sexual minority communities.

A central tenet in gay and lesbian identity development models is an acceptance of homosexual orientation in the context of a heterosexist social environment. The three most used models include several intersecting concepts (Cass, 1979; D'Augelli, 1994; Fassinger & Miller, 1996). Both Cass and Fassinger and Miller begin with an awareness phase, and the final facet of each of these models focuses on issues of commitment and internalization of gay or lesbian orientation. D'Augelli (1994) describes the beginning of concurrent processes once the person makes the decision to exit a heterosexual identity, and incorporates the concept of *developmental plasticity*, which implies that human functioning is "highly responsive to environmental circumstances and to changes induced by physical and other biological factors" (p. 320). His theory considers identity development as "dynamic processes" (p. 324) that is influenced by context and social exchanges over time.

Among these models it should be noted that Fassinger and Miller (1996) separate processes between individual and group identities. This allows for consideration of personal issues that can be somewhat different from societal issues. Although these theorists describe the process of "coming out" in stages or concurrent processes, the actual experiences are seen as more fluid, with pauses and backtracking (Bilodeau & Renn, 2005).

The amount of research regarding the identity development of bisexual individuals is not as vast. D'Augelli (1994) incorporates bisexual orientation in his life-span model of development. Others point out the negative reactions bisexuals receive from both the heterosexual and gay and lesbian communities (Arseneau & Fassinger, 2006). More research on this sexual minority is needed to help understand the within-group issues.

Like the research concerning race and ethnicity, research pertaining to sexual orientation is being influenced by critical perspectives, such as queer theory, which considers identity and gender fluidity as normative and recognizes the historical traditions that categorize behaviors as "nonconforming" (Bilodeau & Renn, 2005; Halperin, 2003). According to Abes and Kasch (2007), "Queer theory creates complex intersections of identity through multiple strategies of resistance" (p. 622). *Resistance* refers to opposing power structures that attempt to impose what is "normal." Researchers using queer theory question the social construction of "normal behaviors" as defined by the privileged, who tend to be White, heterosexual, and from the middle class. These theories are extremely useful in understanding students' experiences and identity construction processes. However, it is also important to recognize that these are complex experiences with many consequences.

Multiple Identity Theories

Theories of multiple identities are considered last in this chapter because practitioners need to understand the different influences on identity before understanding the convergence of those influences. One of the first efforts to acknowledge multiple identities is the Multidimensional Identity Model which illustrated the complexity of being a person experiencing oppression from multiple group memberships (Reynolds & Pope, 1991). More recent research expands the understanding of how these multiple dimensions of identity influence "the dynamic construction of identity and the influence of changing context on the relative salience of multiple identity dimensions, such as race, sexual orientation, culture, and social class" (Abes, Jones, & McEwen, 2007, p. 3).

The most recent conception of the Model of Multiple Dimensions of Identity furthered the work of Jones and McEwen (2000) by illustrating how the meaning-making capacity of the individual relates to the influence of context and self-perceptions of multiple identities (Abes et al., 2007) (see Figure 10.1). The importance of this integration of cognitive capacity with perception highlights the need to understand where the student is developmentally in order to understand how he or she perceives different aspects of identity. As more complex understandings of self occur, the meaning-making filter becomes less porous, and the influence of contextual elements on the self-perception of identity decreases. The more porous the filter, the more influence context will have on identity, resulting in modifications that reflect the context rather than the person's inner self. This model assists in both understanding the interconnections between different domains of development and comprehending how the lack of development of an internal voice to guide decisions can influence every aspect of a student's identity.

FIGURE 10. 1.   RECONCEPTUALIZED MODEL OF MULTIPLE DIMENSIONS OF IDENTITY.

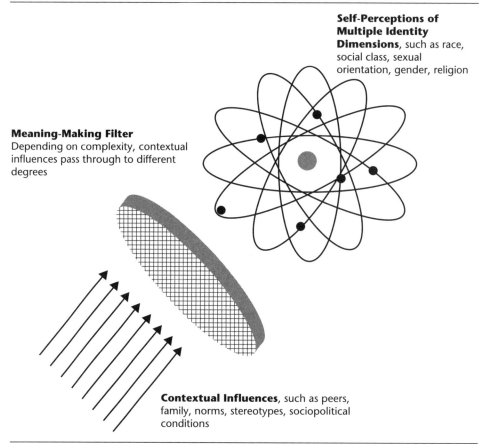

Self-Perceptions of Multiple Identity Dimensions, such as race, social class, sexual orientation, gender, religion

Meaning-Making Filter
Depending on complexity, contextual influences pass through to different degrees

Contextual Influences, such as peers, family, norms, stereotypes, sociopolitical conditions

Source: Abes et al., 2007. Reprinted with permission.

Using Identity Development Theories to Inform Practice

Helping students make meaning of their experiences within the context of higher education requires that a practitioner understand identity development theories. Today there are very few college campuses with a homogeneous student body possessing similar economic and cultural backgrounds, and therefore we cannot presume that all students experience college in the same way. The diversity of our students and the diversity of our campuses require us to understand how identity is developed.

Identity theories can assist practitioners in individual situations by helping us understand students' interpretations of their experiences. How students make meaning of their experiences, especially those interactions that are racist, sexist, or homophobic, will influence their well-being and development. Practitioners must be prepared to understand experiences outside of their own in order to assist students through these developmental tasks. It is in understanding the complexity of others' experiences that identity theories are most helpful. Applying these theories allows a practitioner to be in someone's situation for a few minutes and to consider the complex emotions and tasks that person experiences.

In group situations, identity theories help explain why one group is susceptible to "group think" and another group is not. Recognizing that individuals are driven by external environmental forces is an important tool for changing group culture. Assisting individual members to develop stronger internal definitions of self will help a group to be more responsible and to consider multiple perspectives.

Finally, identity theories help explain subcultures within our college campuses. As members of these subcultures make meaning of their experiences, they will act in ways that either protect their ways of knowing or challenge the dominant culture with different ways of knowing. Such behaviors are connected to how identity is formed and "the ways in which the person faces and uses his [*sic*] experiences" (Baldwin, 1985, p. 459). These theories provide snapshots of how students may experience the college environment and therefore give practitioners insight into the lives of many on their campuses.

References

Abes, E. S., Jones, S. R., & McEwen, M. K. (2007). Reconceptualizing the Model of Multiple Dimensions of Identity: The role of meaning-making capacity in the construction of multiple identities. *Journal of College Student Development, 48*, 1–22.

Abes, E. S., & Kasch, D. (2007). Using queer theory to explore lesbian college students' multiple dimensions of identity. *Journal of College Student Development, 48*, 619–636.

Arseneau, J. R., & Fassinger, R. E. (2006). Challenges and promise: The study of bisexual women's friendships. *Journal of Bisexuality, 6*, 69–90.

Baldwin, J. (1985). *The price of the ticket.* New York: St. Martin's/Marek.

Beemyn, B., Curtis, B., Davis, M., & Tubbs, N. J. (2005). Transgender issues on college campuses. In Sanlo, R. L. (Ed.), *Gender identity and sexual orientation* (New Directions for Student Services Series No. 111, pp. 49–60). San Francisco: Jossey-Bass.

Berry, J. W. (2005). Acculturation: Living successfully in two cultures. *International Journal of Intercultural Relations, (29)6*, 697–712.

Berry, J. W., Phinney, J. S., Sam, D. L. & Vedder, P. (2006). Immigrant youth: Acculturation, identity and adaptation. *Applied Psychology: An International Review, 55*(3), 303–332.

Bilodeau, B. L., & Renn, K. A. (2005). Analysis of LBGT identity development models and implications for practice. In Sanlo, R. L. (Ed.), *Gender identity and sexual orientation* (New Directions for Student Services Series No. 111, pp. 25–39). San Francisco: Jossey-Bass.

Bonner, F. A., II, & Bailey, K. W. (2006). Enhancing the academic climate for African American men. In M. J. Cuyjet (Ed.), *African American men in college* (pp. 24–46). San Francisco: Jossey-Bass.

Carter, K. A. (2000). Transgenderism and college students: Issues of gender identity and its role on our campuses. In V. A. Wall & N. J. Evans (Eds.), *Toward acceptance: Sexual orientation issues on campus* (pp. 261–282). Lanham, MD: University Press of America.

Cass, V. C. (1979). Homosexual identity formation: A theoretical model. *Journal of Homosexuality, 4*, 219–235.

Chen, G. A. (2005). *The complexity of "Asian American identity": The intersection of multiple social identities.* Unpublished doctoral dissertation, University of Texas, Austin.

Choney, S. K., Berryhill-Paapke, E., & Robbins, R. R. (1995). The acculturation of American Indians: Developing frameworks for research and practice. In J. G. Ponterotto, J. M. Casas, L. A. Suzuki, & C. M. Alexander (Eds.), *Handbook of multicultural counseling* (pp. 73–92). Thousand Oaks, CA: Sage.

Collins, P. H. (1989). The social construction of Black feminist thought. *Signs, 14*(4), 745–773.

Cross, W.E. (1971). The Negro-to-Black conversion experience. *Black World, 20,* 13–27.

Cross, W. E. (1995). The psychology of nigrescence: Revising the Cross model. In J. G. Ponterotto, J. M. Casas, L. A. Suzuki, & C. M. Alexander (Eds.), *Handbook of multicultural counseling* (pp. 93–122). Thousand Oaks, CA: Sage.

Cross, W. E. (2001). Encountering nigrescence. In J. G. Ponterotto, J. M. Casas, L. A. Suzuki, & C.M. Alexander (Eds.), *Handbook of multicultural counseling* (pp. 30–44). Thousand Oaks, CA: Sage.

Cross, W. E., & Vandiver, B. J. (2001). Nigrescence theory and measurement: Introducing the Cross Racial Identity Scale (CRIS). In J. G. Ponterotto, J. M. Casas, L. A. Suzuki, & C. M. Alexander (Eds.), *Handbook of multicultural counseling* (pp. 371–393). Thousand Oaks, CA: Sage.

Davis, T. L. (2002). Voices of gender role conflict: The social construction of college men's identity. *Journal of College Student Development, 43,* 508–521.

D'Augelli, A. R. (1994). Identity development and sexual orientation: Toward a model of lesbian, gay, and bisexual development. In E. J. Trickett, R. J. Watts, & Birman, D. (Eds.), *Human diversity perspectives on people in context* (pp. 312–333). San Francisco: Jossey-Bass.

Delgado, R., & Stefancic, J. (2001). *Critical race theory: An introduction.* New York: New York University Press.

Delgado Bernal, D. (2002). Critical race theory, Latino critical theory, and critical raced-gendered epistemologies: Recognizing students of color as holders and creators of knowledge. *Qualitative Inquiry, 8*(1), 105–126.

Downing, N. E., & Roush, K. L. (1985). From passive acceptance to active commitment: A model of feminist identity development for women. *Counseling Psychologist, 13,* 695–709.

Edwards, K. E., & Jones, S. R. (2009). "Putting my man face on": A grounded theory of college men's gender identity development. *Journal of College Student Development, 50,* 210–228.

Erikson, E. H. (1994). *Identity and the life cycle.* New York: W. W. Norton. (Original work published 1959)

Fassinger, R. E., & Arseneau, J. R. (2007). "I'd rather get wet than be under that umbrella": Differentiating the experiences and identities of lesbian, gay, bisexual, and transgendered people. In K. J. Bieschke, R. M. Perez, & K. A. DeBord (Eds.), *Handbook of counseling and psychotherapy with lesbian, gay, bisexual, and transgendered clients* (2nd ed., pp. 19–48). Washington, DC: American Psychological Association.

Fassinger, R. E., & Miller, B. A. (1996). Validation of an inclusive model of sexual minority identity formation on a sample of gay men. *Journal of Homosexuality, 32,* 53–78.

Felix-Ortiz de la Garza, M., Newcomb, M. D., & Myers, H. F. (1995). A multidimensional measure of cultural identity for Latino and Latina adolescents. In A. M. Padilla (Ed.), *Hispanic psychology: Critical issues in theory and research* (pp. 30–42). Thousand Oaks, CA: Sage.

Ferdman, B. M. & Gallegos, P. I. (2001). Racial identity development and Latinos in the United States. In C. L. Wijeyesinghe & B. W. Jackson III (Eds.), *New perspectives on racial identity development: A theoretical and practical anthology* (pp. 32–66). New York: New York University Press.

Fischer, A. R., Tokar, D. M., Mergl, M. M., Good, G. E., Hill, M. S., & Blum, S. A. (2000). Assessing women's feminist identity development. *Psychology of Women Quarterly, 24,* 15–29.

Gilbert, L. A., & Rader, L. (2002). The missing discourse of gender? *Counseling Psychologist, 30,* 567–574.

Halperin, D. M. (2003). The normalization of queer theory. *Journal of Homosexuality, 45,* 339–343.

Hardiman, R., & Jackson, B. W. (1997). Conceptual foundation for social justice courses. In M. Adams, L. A. Bell, and P. Griffin (Eds.), *Teaching for diversity and social justice: A sourcebook* (pp. 16–29). New York: Routledge.

Helms, J. E. (1990). *Black and white racial identity theory, research, and practice.* Westport, CT: Praeger.

Helms, J. E. (1994). The conceptualization of racial identity and other "racial" constructs. In E. J. Trickett, R. J. Watts, & D. Birman (Eds.), *Human diversity perspectives on people in context* (pp. 285–311). San Francisco: Jossey-Bass.

Helms, J. E., & Cook, D. A. (1999). *Using race and culture in counseling and psychotherapy: Theory and process.* Boston: Allyn & Bacon.

Horse, P. G. (2001). Reflections on American Indian identity. In C. L. Wijeyesinghe & B. W. Jackson III (Eds.), *New perspectives on racial identity development: A theoretical and practical anthology* (pp. 91–107). New York: New York University Press.

Jones, S. R. (2009). Constructing identities at the intersections: An autoethnographic exploration of multiple dimensions of identity. *Journal of College Student Development, 50,* 267–304.

Jones, S. R., & McEwen, M. K. (2000). A conceptual model of multiple dimensions of identity. *Journal of College Student Development, 38,* 376–386.

Josselson, R. (1996). *Revising herself: The story of women's identity from college to midlife.* New York: Oxford University Press.

Keefe, S. E., & Padilla, A. M. (1987). *Chicano ethnicity.* Albuquerque: University of New Mexico Press.

Kegan, R. K. (1982). *The evolving self: Problem and process in human development.* Cambridge, MA: Harvard University Press.

Kim, J. (2001). Asian American identity development theory. In C. L. Wijeyesinghe & B. W. Jackson III (Eds.), *New perspectives on racial identity development: A theoretical and practical anthology* (pp. 67–90). New York: New York University Press.

Kimmel, M. S. (2006). *Manhood in America: A cultural history* (2nd ed.). New York: Oxford University Press.

Kimmel, M. S. (2008). *Guyland: The perilous world where boys become men.* New York: HarperCollins.

Kroger, J. (2000). *Identity development adolescence through adulthood.* Thousand Oaks, CA: Sage.

Kroger, J. (2004). *Identity and adolescence: The balance between self and other* (3rd ed.). London: Routledge.

Ladson-Billings, G. (1998). Just what is critical race theory and what's it doing in a nice field like education? *Qualitative Studies in Education, 11*(1), 7–24.

LaFromboise, T. D., Heyle, A. M., & Ozer, E. J. (1990). Changing and diverse roles of women in American Indian cultures. *Sex Roles, 22*(7/8), 455–476.

LaFromboise, T. D., Trimble, J. E., & Mohatt, G. V. (1990). Counseling intervention and American Indian tradition: An integrative approach. *Counseling Psychologist, 18*(4), 628–654.

Loevinger, J. (1976). *Ego development: Conceptions and theories.* San Francisco: Jossey-Bass.

Lomawaima, K. T., & McCarty, T. L. (2002). When tribal sovereignty challenges democracy: American Indian education and the democratic ideal. *American Educational Research Journal, 39*(2), 279–305.

Marcia, J. E. (1966). Development and validation of ego-identity status. *Journal of Personality and Social Psychology, 3,* 551–558.

Marcia, J. E. (1993). The status of the statuses: Research review. In J. E. Marcia, A. S. Waterman, D. R. Matteson, & S. L. Archer (Eds.), *Ego identity: A handbook for psychosocial research* (pp. 22–41). New York: Springer-Verlag.

Marcia, J. E. (2002). Identity and psychosocial development in adulthood. *Identity: An International Journal of Theory and Research, 2*(1), 7–28.

McEwen, M. K. (2003). New perspectives on identity development. In S. R. Komives, D. B. Woodard Jr., & Associates (Eds.), *Student services: A handbook for the profession* (4th ed., pp. 203–233). San Francisco: Jossey-Bass.

Ossana, S. M., Helms, J. E., & Leonard, M. M. (1992). Do "womanist" identity attitudes influence college women's self-esteem and perceptions of environmental bias? *Journal of Counseling & Development, 70,* 402–408.

Ortiz, A. M., & Rhoads, R. A. (2000). Deconstructing whiteness as part of a multicultural educational framework: From theory to practice. *Journal of College Student Development, 41,* 81–93.

Parker, L. (1998). Race is...race ain't: An exploration of the utility of critical race theory in qualitative research in education. *Qualitative Studies in Education, 11*(1), 43–55.

Phinney, J. S. (1990). Ethnic identity in adolescents and adults: Review of research. *Psychological Bulletin, 108*(3), 499–514.

Phinney, J. S. (1993). A three-stage model of ethnic identity development in adolescence. In M. E. Bernal & G. P. Knight (Eds.), *Ethnic identity formation and transmission among Hispanic and other minorities* (pp. 61–79). Albany: State University of New York Press.

Renn, K. A. (2008). Research on bi- and multiracial identity development: Overview and synthesis. In K. A. Renn & P. Shang (Eds.), Biracial and multiracial college students: Theory, research, and best practices in student affairs. New Directions for Student Services, No. 123 (pp. 13–21). San Francisco: Jossey-Bass.

Reynolds, A. L. (2001). Embracing multiculturalism: A journey of self-discovery. In J. G. Ponterotto, J. M. Casas, L. A. Suzuki, & C. M. Alexander (Eds.) *Handbook of multicultural counseling* (pp. 103–112). Thousand Oaks, CA: Sage.

Reynolds, A. L. & Pope, R. L. (1991). The complexities of diversity: Exploring multiple oppressions. *Journal of Counseling & Development, 70*, 174–180.

Root, M.P.P. (1992). *Racially mixed people in America*. Newbury Park: CA: Sage.

Root, M.P.P. (2003). Racial identity development and persons of mixed race heritage. In M.P.P. Root & M. Kelley (Eds.), *Multiracial child resource book: Living complex identities* (pp. 34–41). Seattle, WA: Mavin Foundation.

Ruiz, A. S. (1990). Ethnic identity: Crisis and resolution. *Journal of Multicultural Counseling and Development, 18*, 29–40.

Tatum, B.D. (1997). *Why are all the Black kids sitting together in the cafeteria?* New York: Basic Books.

Thompson, C. E., & Carter, R. T. (1997). *Racial identity theory applications to individual, group, and organizational interventions*. Mahwah, NJ: Lawrence Erlbaum Associates.

Torres, V. (1999). Validation of a bicultural orientation model for Hispanic college students. *Journal of College Student Development, 40*, 285–299.

Torres, V. (2003) Influences on ethnic identity development of Latino college students in the first two years of college. *Journal of College Student Development, 44*, 532–547.

Torres, V. (2004) Familial influences on the identity development of Latino first year students. *Journal of College Student Development, 45*, 457–469.

Torres, V., & Delgado-Romero, E. (2008). Defining Latino/a identity through late adolescent development. In K. L. Kraus (Ed.), *Lifespan development theories in action: A case study approach for counseling professionals* (pp. 363–388). Boston: Lahaska Press Houghton Mifflin.

Torres, V., & Hernandez, E. (2007). The influence of ethnic identity on self-authorship: A longitudinal study of Latino/a college students. *Journal of College Student Development, 48*, 558–573.

Torres, V., Howard-Hamilton, M., & Cooper, D. L. (2003). *Identity development of diverse populations: Implications for teaching and practice* (ASHE/ERIC Higher Education Report, Vol. 29). San Francisco: Jossey-Bass.

Torres, V., Jones, S. R., & Renn, K. A. (2009). Identity development theories in student affairs: Origins, current status, and new approaches. *Journal of College Student Development, 50*, 577–596.

Wijeyesinghe, C. L. (2001). Racial identity in multiracial people: An alternative paradigm. In C. L. Wijeyesinghe & B.W. Jackson III (Eds.), *New perspectives on racial identity development: A theoretical and practical anthology* (pp.129–152). New York: New York University Press.

Wing, L., & Rifkin, J. (2001). Racial identity development and the mediation of conflicts. In C. L. Wijeyesinghe & B.W. Jackson III (Eds.), *New perspectives on racial identity development: A theoretical and practical anthology* (pp.182–208). New York: New York University Press.

Worthington, R. L. (2004). Sexual identity, sexual orientation, religious identity, and change: Is it possible to depolarize the debate? *Counseling Psychologist, 32*, 741–749.

Worthington, R. L., Savoy, H. B., Dillon, F. R., & Vernaglia, E. R. (2002). Heterosexual identity development: A multidimensional model of individual and social identity. *Counseling Psychologist, 30*, 496–531.

CHAPTER ELEVEN

STUDENT LEARNING

Patricia M. King and Marcia B. Baxter Magolda

Student learning in postsecondary education involves more than the acquisition of knowledge and skills; it also includes developing a frame of mind that allows students to put their knowledge in perspective; to understand the sources of their beliefs and values; and to establish a sense of self that enables them to participate effectively in a variety of personal, occupational, and community contexts. It is in such contexts that students apply their knowledge, skills, and capacities for deeper understanding to responsibilities that span work, family, and civic contexts, a point that has been noted in several recent national reports (Association of American Colleges and Universities [AAC&U], 2005, 2007; Keeling, 2004). Learning is a central mission of higher education, and these reports convey an urgency for college educators to sustain and strengthen their efforts to help students achieve these deeper learning outcomes. In this chapter we show how educators can apply concepts and principles of learning to meet this challenge.

We have chosen to explicitly link learning and development, two approaches to understanding and promoting college student success that are often separated by disciplinary and organizational boundaries. Learning has its roots in the discipline of psychology and applied educational contexts and is often viewed as the responsibility of faculty, whereas student development has its roots in the field of higher education and student affairs and is often seen as the responsibility of student affairs staff. We take issue with these boundaries (Baxter Magolda, 1996; King & Kitchener, 1994) and have argued for an integrated view of learning that spans cognitive and affective development, viewing them as related parts of one process (King, 2003; King & Baxter Magolda, 1996) and as the foundation for educational outcomes such as intercultural maturity (King & Baxter Magolda, 2005). We link learning and development by anchoring these observations in self-authorship theory (Baxter Magolda, 2001; Kegan, 1994), showing how they provide complementary perspectives for educational practice. This is consistent with calls for transformative educational practices made by Baxter Magolda (2004a), by Mezirow (2000), and in many national reports: the *Student Learning Imperative* (American College Personnel Association [ACPA], 1994); *Powerful Partnerships* (American Association of Higher Education [AAHE], ACPA, & National Association of Student Personnel Administrators [NASPA], 1998); *Learning Reconsidered* (Keeling, 2004); and the Association of American Colleges and Universities (AAC&U)'s (2002, 2005, 2007) publications on student learning.

This chapter opens with a discussion of the role of meaning making in learning, showing how the way one understands and interprets experience lays a foundation for the attainment of substantive learning outcomes that have a long-term impact and consequences. Accomplishing such outcomes requires the development of new capacities for handling a range of life demands, which we explicate through an extended discussion of self-authorship theory and research. Finally, we explore implications for designing educational experiences that promote deep learning and foster self-authorship, illustrating the application of developmentally grounded principles of practice using Baxter Magolda's (2004b) Learning Partnerships Model.

Learning as Making Meaning

When confronted with events we don't understand or with observations that startle us or pique our interest, it is common to ask, Did I hear that right? How did that happen? Being motivated to discern the meaning of events and actions can bring to the surface an awareness of assumptions that otherwise remain hidden. Mezirow (2000) noted the human penchant for meaning making: "A defining condition of being human is our urgent need to understand and order the meaning of our experience, to integrate it with what we know to avoid the threat of chaos" (p. 3). Providing students with rich opportunities to understand the world and "order the meaning" is central to higher education's learning mission. Opportunities for deep and sustained reflection are particularly conducive to this goal. In a list of what participants need to engage in reflective discourse, Mezirow (2000) includes "freedom from coercion and distorting self-deception; openness to alternative points of view; greater awareness of the context of ideas and, more critically, reflectiveness of assumptions, including their own" (p. 13). Habits of mind such as these exemplify attributes that reflect sophisticated meaning making and that underlie more general learning outcomes, for example, critical thinking or taking seriously the perspectives of others. As these attributes become more complex and well developed, they provide more adaptive ways of making meaning, which in turn enable the achievement of deep learning outcomes.

People convey changes in their meaning making through comments such as "I don't think of it that way anymore" and "I never thought I'd be saying this, but . . ." When these changes are developmentally adaptive, they result in what Mezirow (2000) calls transformative learning: "Transformative learning refers to the process by which we transform our taken-for-granted frames of reference (meaning perspectives, habits of mind, mind-sets) to make them more inclusive, discriminating, open, emotionally capable of change, and reflective so that they may generate beliefs and opinions that will prove more true or justified to guide action" (pp. 7–8).

Opportunities through which students learn to construct new frames of reference with these features make for powerful educational experiences. In addition, such experiences can cut across dimensions of development: they can help students become good critical thinkers and decision makers (epistemological development), become self-aware and appropriately confident (intrapersonal development), and socially responsible citizens (interpersonal development). In their aptly titled book *Learning That Lasts*, Mentkowski and Associates (2000) offer detailed evidence that transformative learning can occur when a college organizes itself to do so. Their conceptualization goes one step further in that they emphasize performance—what students *do* with their knowledge and understanding, which the authors call "deep and durable learning" (p. xv). Later in this chapter, we discuss the features of transformative learning environments.

Self-Authorship: A Foundation for Holistic, Transformative Learning

Transformative learning, or transforming one's frame of reference, requires growth in ways of making meaning from relying on external authorities to constructing one's own internal authority. Although many student development theories describe various strands of this developmental trajectory (see Chapters Eight, Nine, and Ten in this volume), we begin with Kegan's (1982; 1994) theory of self-evolution because it portrays development holistically. Kegan (1994) described the subject-object relationship as the "deep structure" (p. 32) of how we make meaning of our experiences. *Object* refers to elements of our knowing of which we are aware and have control. These elements are "distinct enough from us that we can do something with [them]" (Kegan, 1994, p. 32). *Subject* refers to elements of our knowing of which we are unaware and that thus have control over us. These elements are ones "that we are identified with, tied to, fused with, or embedded in. We *have* object; we *are* subject" (1994, p. 32, italics in original). Kegan described transformation from one meaning making structure to the next as "liberating ourselves from that in which we were embedded, making what was subject into object so that we can 'have it' rather than 'be had' by it" (p. 34).

Kegan's Self-Evolution Theory

Kegan's (1994) five orders of consciousness each reflect a different meaning-making structure based on a particular subject-object relationship. Each subject-object relationship constitutes an organizing principle that guides how we come to know (the epistemological dimension), how we form an identity (the intrapersonal dimension), and how we frame social relations (the interpersonal dimension). Kegan's theory thus integrates these three dimensions of development within each order of consciousness. During childhood, others' perspectives matter to us to the extent that they help us meet our egocentric needs (second order). During adolescence, others' perspectives begin to matter to us in a different way as we become socialized to be part of a larger community. Kegan describes his third order, or socializing meaning making, as orienting to others' perspectives, bringing them inside to the point that our perspective is co-constructed with others'. Thus we are embedded in or subject to these co-constructions in these relationships, and unable to stand outside of them to reflect on them. This applies to believing what others think we should believe, forming the identities we think others want from us, and behaving in relationships to acquire others' approval. This socializing way of making meaning carries with it a concern for others and commitment to relationships, yet simultaneously allows us to be consumed by others' perceptions. In contrast, the fourth order—the self-authoring way of making meaning—"is characterized by its capacity to take responsibility for and ownership of its own internal authority; its capacity to internally hold, manage, and prioritize the internal and external demands, contradictions, conflicts, and expectations of oneself and one's life" (Popp & Portnow, 2001, p. 61). Self-authoring persons generate their beliefs, values, identities, and relational roles on the basis of internal standards they have created for themselves. Kegan described the transition from socializing to self-authoring as a slow, arduous process in which people gradually recognize various elements that were subject and make them object. For example, the self-authoring person comes to see relationships as object, reflected in *having* relationships instead of *being* the relationship (subject). Inner emotional states and values become object, making it possible to reflect on them and make internal choices about them that are separate from others' expectations. Kegan's third and fourth orders are most relevant to college student learning.

Baxter Magolda's Self-Authorship Journey

Baxter Magolda's (1992, 2001, 2009) twenty-two-year longitudinal study of a group of college students and graduates from ages eighteen to forty elaborates on Kegan's self-evolution theory, offering empirical evidence for the holistic model and nuances of transition from socializing to self-authoring meaning making. Beginning with 101 students in 1986, Baxter Magolda interviewed students annually through their college years to trace their meaning making and its relationship to learning. Seventy participants agreed to continue in the study after graduation; thirty-five still participate today. Table 11.1 synthesizes three phases of the journey toward self-authorship that emerged from this study.

Participants followed external formulas throughout their college experiences, and many carried them into their post-college lives. However, they quickly discovered that the formulas either did not yield success or left them feeling dissatisfied. Recognizing the need to consider their own thinking, feelings, and needs in relationships led many to spend the majority of their twenties working through the crossroads (Baxter Magolda, 2001). Their descriptions of this phase of the journey match Kegan's transition from

TABLE 11.1. DEVELOPMENTAL JOURNEY TOWARD SELF-AUTHORSHIP.

Dimension	External Formulas	Crossroads	Self-Authorship
Epistemological	View knowledge as certain or partially certain, yielding reliance on authority as source of knowledge; lack of internal basis for evaluating knowledge claims results in externally defined beliefs	Evolving awareness and acceptance of uncertainty and multiple perspectives; shift from accepting authority's knowledge claims to personal processes for adopting knowledge claims; recognize need to take responsibility for choosing beliefs	View knowledge as contextual; develop an internal belief system via constructing, evaluating, and interpreting judgments in light of available evidence and frames of reference
Intrapersonal	Lack of awareness of own values and social identity, lack of coordination of components of identity, and need for others' approval combine to yield an externally defined identity that is susceptible to changing external pressures	Evolving awareness of own values and sense of identity distinct from external others' perceptions; tension between emerging internal values and external pressures prompts self-exploration; recognize need to take responsibility for crafting own identity	Choose own values and identity in crafting an internally generated sense of self that regulates interpretation of experience and choices
Interpersonal	Dependent relations with similar others are source of identity and needed affirmation; frame participation in relationships as doing what will gain others' approval	Evolving awareness of limitations of dependent relationships; recognize need to bring own identity into constructing independent relationships; struggle to reconstruct or extract self from dependent relationships	Capacity to engage in authentic, interdependent relationships with diverse others in which self is not overshadowed by need for others' approval; mutually negotiating relational needs; genuinely taking others' perspectives into account without being consumed by them

Source: Adapted from *Learning Partnerships: Theory and Models of Practice to Educate for Self-Authorship*, edited by Marcia B. Baxter Magolda and Patricia M. King, 2004, Sterling, VA: Stylus Publishing, LLC. Copyright 2004, Stylus Publishing, LLC. Adapted with permission.

third order, in which others' perspectives are in the foreground, to fourth order, in which one's internal authority moves to the foreground. Following the participants through their thirties revealed three elements within self-authoring: trusting the internal voice, building an internal foundation, and securing internal commitments (Baxter Magolda, 2008, 2009). Participants first learned to trust their own internal voices when they realized that despite their inability to control reality, they could control their reactions to it. As they encountered success in making internal meaning of events in their professional and personal lives, they came to trust themselves to organize their own experiences.

Using their internal voices, they began to build an internal foundation to guide their reactions to life's realities. This involved revisiting beliefs, values, identities, and relationships to align them with their internal authority. Doing so yielded a philosophy of life to use as a compass for navigating uncertainty. Living these commitments, described by participants as having them in their hearts rather than only in their heads, led to securing internal commitments. This element involved integrating internal commitments with external realities and merging knowledge and sense of self into a confident approach to life.

Self-Authorship Research with Contemporary College Students

Research with contemporary college students reveals both similarities with and differences from Baxter Magolda's participants' experiences in college in the late 1980s. The main phases of the journey toward self-authorship (shown in Table 11.1) also emerged in Torres's longitudinal study (2003; Torres & Hernandez, 2007; see chapter 10 this volume) with Latino/a students. However, the dynamics of recognizing their cultural reality, incorporating an informed Latino/a identity into their daily lives, and renegotiating their relationships with others based on their Latino/a identity were central to their development. Similarly, Abes's (2009; Abes & Jones, 2004; Abes & Kasch, 2007) longitudinal interviews with lesbian students revealed other dynamics created by forging identity in the face of heterosexist social norms as students moved from formulaic to self-authoring meaning making. In both studies, negotiating oppression prompted growth toward self-authorship during college. Pizzolato's (2003) interviews with a diverse group of high school students also indicated that resisting social norms (in this case, by attending college) could stimulate self-authorship prior to college. Research on self-authorship among diverse populations and cultural contexts is ongoing (see Baxter Magolda, Creamer, & Meszaros, 2010). Abes, Jones, and McEwen (2007) show how contextual influences relate to multiple identity dimensions and position meaning making as a filter for understanding contextual influences. Similarly, King and Baxter Magolda (2005) conceptualized the relationship of multiple dynamics in the development of intercultural maturity.

The Wabash National Study of Liberal Arts Education offers a window into students' growth toward self-authorship (Barber, 2009; Baxter Magolda, King, Taylor, & Wakefield, 2009; Kendall Brown, 2008) and the achievement of learning outcomes (Barber, 2009; Baxter Magolda, King, Taylor, & Wakefield, 2009; Kendall Brown, 2008; King, Kendall Brown, Lindsay & VanHecke, 2007; Lindsay, 2007; VanHecke, 2006). In Year 1 of this study, a sample of 315 diverse students from six campuses participated in interviews, described in Baxter Magolda and King (2007, 2008), that were to be administered annually. By Year 2, interviews from 228 of these students illustrated growth toward self-authorship for 63 percent (Baxter Magolda, King, Taylor, & Wakefield, 2009). For example, during his sophomore year, Gavin still struggled to find external formulas for what to believe. He often handled ambiguity by simply giving up:

> I get in so many conversations with people talking about whether it's a just war or like good or bad or whether they're for it or against it and I've heard so many good points, but I've gone from being for it to against it to back in the middle and so some things I just kind of give up on. I know that I'll never know everything about that situation. There's just no way and so I'm not going to pretend to make an opinion about it, so there's some things that I just try to leave alone. (Baxter Magolda, King, Taylor, & Perez, 2008, p. 19)

Gavin was unable to form an opinion because he could not find a consistent external formula. Although he was learning in class to entertain subjectivity, he reported that he found it problematic:

> Somebody one day could tell me one thing and then another, they could tell me another thing and they could both claim to be right . . . and I could spend my whole life trying to figure out who's right and what this guy meant and if I came to like [laughs], you know, I could arrive at the wrong conclusion. I mean spend my whole life analyzing something and having it ending up, be no right answer. . . . I feel like I wasted my time and [laughs] my efforts. (Baxter Magolda et al., 2008, p. 20)

Gavin's ability to learn to defend his own beliefs is clearly hindered by his reliance on others' knowledge for determining what to believe.

By contrast, Gabriella has moved into the crossroads. In discussing her experience as a member of a social organization (referred to as a society) that functions like a sorority, she commented that her parents now disapprove of her membership in this society based on some of her experiences with her society sisters. "They make judgments. And I can't blame them, because they want what's best for me, and unfortunately, that hasn't become the society anymore." When asked what she does when there is a conflict between what she wants for herself and what other people want from her, she replied:

> I think that's part of what changed. Previously I would've done what they [my parents] wanted . . . but at this point, I'm going to do what makes me happy. I feel awful about it sometimes because so much of me wants to make them happy with me and keep them being my friends, but at the same time, it's not what I want, it's not where I'm going, and in the grand scheme of things, I have two more years of this society being important in my life, and after that, five years from now, so three years after I graduate, how much is their opinion really going to affect me? So I'm going to be happier and enjoy my junior year doing what I want and seeking my own balance versus seeking their balance. . . . It is [a pretty big change]. It is. And it's hard. It's really hard, 'cause there's so many times where I'm like, "Okay, fine, well I'll do what they want instead of what I want" and I'll break down for things, but at the end of the day, I know what's best and I know what I need to do. So being determined and sticking with it is harder than I thought it would be.

Whereas Gabriella formerly would have made her decisions about how to interact with her society sisters to make her parents happy, she now has confidence in her own judgments, puts her challenges with the group into a longer-term perspective, and chooses to seek her own balance. All are signs of movement away from external authority and toward self-authorship.

Tyler's description of the criteria he uses to judge ideas reveals an internal frame of reference for meaning making:

> You compare them [new ideas or perspectives] to what you think you believe and you have to ask yourself, "Can I believe this? And what or who will I be if I start to believe this? Is it logical? Is it propaganda? I mean is it a mind game? What is it?" So when you encounter new ideas, I mean they're always good, but you have to evaluate, "Will this be sane? Is he credible? Is he an idiot? I mean, who is he, for God's sake? What he's trying to get me to take away?" And I mean if it's good stuff, why I'll take it, but if it's bad stuff, I'll criticize him, like he really shouldn't have said that or he was a terrible public speaker, he could have structured his speech better or whatever. So new ideas are definitely good and they're healthy because they help your mind grow. You just have to look at it, take it for what you know, and then [ask,] "What if I incorporate this in my life? How would I be?" So it's that type of thing, I think.

The questions Tyler uses to evaluate new ideas show that he values multiple perspectives and is open to new ideas "because they help your mind grow." He acknowledges not only that what he believes is his decision but that it has implications for the kind of person he is ("What or who will I be if I start to believe this?"). This deeper awareness of his own thinking processes, his unapologetic ownership of his beliefs, his openness to and skepticism about new ideas, and his understanding of the link between what he believes and who he is reflect the complex meaning making associated with self-authorship.

Learning Contexts That Promote Development

Both person (learner characteristics) and environment (learning context) must be considered when designing educational experiences. In this section, we show how this can be done in order to promote learning and self-authorship.

As noted in the earlier description of self-authorship and its research base, key features of developmental changes in the ways people make meaning of their experiences over time in increasingly complex and inclusive ways are now well documented. Interestingly—and not coincidentally—there is a strong correspondence between characteristics of self-authorship that reflect personal maturity and characteristics associated with the goals of higher education related to learning outcomes. As a result, the self-authorship literature provides a strong foundation for designing effective learning environments.

Educators who intentionally design learning environments for students are acknowledging (at least implicitly) that learning occurs in a context, and that contexts can be shaped and structured for that purpose. Philosopher John Dewey (1916/2004) noted this when he observed: "We never educate directly, but indirectly by means of the environment. Whether we permit chance environments to do the work, or whether we design environments for the purpose makes a great difference" (p. 18). Here we explore how to design environments for the purpose of promoting collegiate learning outcomes and self-authorship.

A plethora of practices are widely used in higher education for creating rich learning environments. For example, first-year experiences, senior capstone courses, undergraduate research programs, service-learning experiences, the use of community standards in judicial affairs, learning communities, and study abroad opportunities are popular innovations that provide or build on rich contexts for learning. Such contexts often introduce students to places or people who are unfamiliar, provide hands-on experiences for learning and practicing new skills, and orient students to standards and expectations of their collegiate communities. A key feature of such experiences is that they encourage active participation in their communities, help students develop friendships and a sense of belonging, and provide a tangible means of communicating institutional values.

Another way of thinking about rich contexts for learning is to ask how such contexts could be designed with transformative purposes in mind. That is, how could educators create learning environments that are designed to help transform students' forms of meaning making from approaches that are externally grounded to those that reflect consciously selected or affirmed criteria and values? Mezirow (2000) expressed a similar set of educational purposes in his description of his model of transformative learning as focusing on "how we learn to negotiate and act on our own purposes, values, feelings, and meanings rather than those we have uncritically assimilated from others—to gain greater control over our lives as socially responsible, clear-thinking decision makers" (p. 8). These purposes are clearly consistent with the attributes of self-authorship. King, Baxter Magolda, Barber, Kendall Brown, and Lindsay (2009) specifically focused on transformation in their study of developmentally effective experiences. These seemed to trigger developmental changes in how students made meaning, in that students interpreted their experiences in more developmentally advanced ways.

Although the mechanisms of development that reflect progress toward this transformation are not precisely understood, a large body of scholarship now informs our understanding of the kinds of learning environments that enhance this kind of personal maturity. A common attribute of these environments is that they not only give students opportunities to learn new skills but also systematically and intentionally build in opportunities to help students "make object" that to which they are currently "subject" (to use Kegan's (1994) language). Building in reflective practices (e.g., discussion questions, journal prompts) that include provocative questions and stimulate students' assessments of their own meaning making is another common attribute of programs and courses that enable students to gain the kind of control over their lives to which Mezirow (2000) refers.

Practices such as these are firmly grounded in developmental purposes in that
they reflect progress toward epistemological complexity, self-understanding, and the
ability to engage in respectful relationships with others that are characterized by mutual-
ity. They also reflect developmental principles in that they offer a balance of challenge
and support so that students can learn more adaptive responses that will serve them
in the future. Baxter Magolda (2004b) has provided a more detailed description of
developmentally grounded practices in her Learning Partnerships Model, to which
we now turn.

Learning Partnerships Model

The Learning Partnerships Model (LPM; see Figure 11.1) emerged from over one thousand interviews in which Baxter Magolda's participants described conditions in their
work, academic, and personal lives that helped them come to trust their internal voices
(Baxter Magolda, 2001, 2004b). Their insights collectively portray a philosophy of the
relationship between educator and learner and suggest a pedagogy for promoting self-
authorship and learning.

FIGURE 11.1. LEARNING PARTNERSHIPS MODEL.

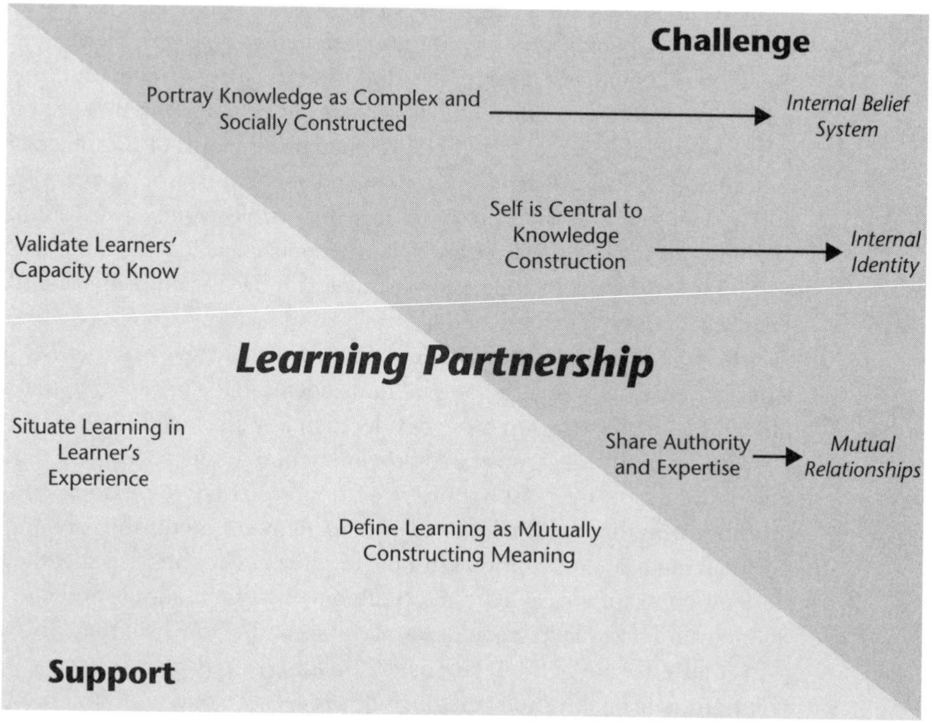

Source: Reprinted with permission from *Learning Partnerships: Theory and Models of Practice to Educate
for Self-Authorship*, edited by Marcia B. Baxter Magolda and Patricia M. King, 2004, Sterling, VA: Stylus
Publishing, LLC. Copyright 2004, Stylus Publishing, LLC.

Baxter Magolda (2001) used a tandem bicycle metaphor to explain the relationship between educator and learner, suggesting that the learner take the front "captain's seat" and the educator take the back seat to provide support and guidance, while allowing the learner to direct the journey. Specifically, educators *support* learners in developing internal authority by: validating learners' capacity to know (e.g., respecting their thoughts and feelings, thus affirming the value of their voices); situating learning in learners' experiences (e.g., using learners' experiences as the foundation for subsequent learning and growth); and defining learning as a mutual process (e.g., collaborating with learners to analyze and address problems) (Baxter Magolda, 2004b, 2009). These three forms of support help strengthen learners' internal voices by welcoming their thoughts and feelings and offering practice in refining them. These supports enable learners to bring their internal voices into conversations with others in the learning process. Simultaneously, educators *challenge* learners to develop internal authority by: portraying knowledge as complex and socially constructed (e.g., drawing learners' attention to the complexity of work and life decisions and discouraging simplistic solutions); emphasizing self as central to knowledge construction (e.g., encouraging learners to listen to their own voices when deciding what to believe); and encouraging learners to share authority and expertise (e.g., work interdependently with others to solve mutual problems) (Baxter Magolda, 2004b; 2009).

These challenges collectively engage learners in working through complex ideas and problems, helping them see the roles of their own perspectives in these tasks and the value of working collaboratively with educators and peers toward learning goals. As learners' internal voices emerge and become more prominent, educators can introduce increasing challenge in ways that lead learners to further examine, deepen, and refine their emerging internal belief systems, internal identities, and mutual relationships. The supports and challenges described in the LPM are tailored to connect to learners' current meaning-making structures, balancing challenge and support as is appropriate to the context and to learners' particular approaches to meaning making. This creates what Kegan (1994) calls an evolutionary bridge that offers "both welcoming acknowledgement to exactly who the person is right now as he or she is, and fosters the person's psychological evolution" (p. 43). Learning partnerships resonate with feminist (e.g., hooks, 1994), liberatory (e.g., Freire, 1988; Shor, 1992), and culturally relevant (e.g., Ladson-Billings, 1994) pedagogies in welcoming learners' experience and voices. Learning partnerships' unique contribution is linking learning to learners' meaning making.

The promise of learning partnerships is evident in numerous contexts. Learning partnerships in a four-year writing curriculum (Haynes, 2004); a four-course general education sequence (Bekken & Marie, 2007); a student affairs master's program (Rogers, Magolda, Baxter Magolda, & Knight-Abowitz, 2004); and a community college business course focused on diversity (Hornak & Ortiz, 2004) helped learners who use various meaning-making structures move toward increasingly complex ways of knowing, feeling, and relating socially. Learning partnerships in a semester-long cultural exchange program in El Salvador (Yonkers Talz, 2004); an urban leadership internship program (Egart & Healy, 2004); and a residential community standards model (Piper & Buckley, 2004) supported learners in facing the epistemological, intrapersonal, and interpersonal challenges involved in living and working in diverse environments. Learning partnerships in an academic advising retention program (Pizzolato & Ozaki, 2007) supported learners in moving from external formulas to considering their own experiences and values in shaping their academic success. Finally, a sustained, multiyear faculty development effort framed using the LPM generated multiple faculty and staff partnerships that in turn yielded curricular and co-curricular innovation (Wildman, 2004, 2007); and a student affairs division reorganized to focus on student learning used the LPM as a guide, in doing so generating learning partnerships among staff and with students (Mills & Strong, 2004). Thus the LPM shows substantial promise as an organizing framework for intentional design of developmentally sequenced educational practice (Baxter Magolda & King, 2004).

Using the LPM requires educators to think about the educational process and their roles in promoting learning in ways that may be unfamiliar, in that it asks educators to think through several key factors that drive decisions about how to link supports and challenges to learners' meaning-making structures. Within any selected context, the primary factor to consider is student learner characteristics (their meaning-making structures). This information guides the identification of learning outcomes and the underlying developmental goals that are appropriate to the learner characteristics; together, these provide benchmarks that map steps on the path to achieving the ultimate (not just initial or intermediary) desired educational outcomes. Using this framework, educators can then determine how to support the achievement of these goals through the activities they offer, how the activities are structured, and how they define their own priorities and educational roles when working with students. Because of the salience of learner characteristics in the LPM, it follows that each of these types of decisions about how to organize learning opportunities should take into account students' developmental characteristics. Thus, once students achieve initial learning outcomes and underlying developmental goals, they are then ready for the intermediate steps in the sequence and are prepared to tackle more advanced goals; this requires educators to shift the nature of the challenge and support they offer to accommodate changes in learner characteristics. When these decisions are made intentionally, educators can offer increasingly complex and demanding educational programs that reflect the evolving capacities associated with changing learner characteristics. Using the LPM, educators organize and coordinate developmental goals, learning outcomes, and learning activities, scaffolding students' movement from initial, to intermediate, to advanced ways of meaning making about knowledge, self, and relationships with others.

Taylor and Haynes (2008) articulate an in-depth example of how they are using the LPM to guide both the curriculum and the co-curriculum in a university honors program. There are many ways to organize one's work using the LPM; here we offer this example not as a specified template but as a clearly articulated and candid illustration of how these educators chose to use the LPM in their particular context. Their three-tiered framework (see Table 11.2) offers a comprehensive example of developmental goals, learning outcomes, faculty/staff expectations, and learning experiences that are designed and sequenced appropriately to students who follow external formulas (Tier 1), are in the crossroads (Tier 2), or are self-authoring (Tier 3).

Table 11.2 demonstrates the increased complexity of the goals, outcomes, and expectations. This three-tiered model shows how educators can intentionally link students' current meaning making, the choice of developmental goals that support incrementally ordered learning outcomes, and the design of possible learning experiences in order to achieve ends. Each tier illustrates how the components of learning partnerships take on different shapes on the developmental journey toward self-authorship.

The table starts by identifying student traits (learner characteristics) and coordinating the other factors to this approach to meaning making. For externally defined learners in Tier 1, the developmental goals focus on seeing the limitations of relying on others for their knowledge and identity. The learning outcomes focus on experiences that bring these limitations to the surface and offer initial opportunities to think through them. Creating a safe environment and validating learners' capacity to learn (e.g., by asking them to engage in critical reflection of their assumptions about learning), using their experiences as a context for learning (e.g., by inviting learners to choose relevant learning experiences to meet goals), and encouraging multiple perspectives all match the LPM's supports and challenges for students who are trying to extract themselves from reliance on external formulas. Learning experiences are organized specifically to match these developmental goals, learning outcomes, and faculty and staff expectations. Tier 2 shifts to encouraging learners to identify their own beliefs and values as a way through the crossroads, still drawing from others' views but increasingly bringing their own perspectives to this process. The learning outcomes reflect this increase in complexity, and the supports and challenges shift to emphasize working together toward mutually defined goals. Learning experiences are designed specifically to reflect these characteristics. Tier 3 focuses on developing internal belief systems and authentic relationships using self-authored meaning making. These learning outcomes and corresponding developmental goals are more challenging than those in previous tiers—and more consistent with the institutional mission and with AAC&U's (2005) essential learning outcomes.

It is important to note that Taylor and Haynes (2008) acknowledge that students enter college with different skill levels and developmental capacities; and although many students enter college with an external orientation (e.g., 86 percent, reported by Baxter Magolda et al., [2009]), these tiers are not strictly ordered by year of enrollment. Some students are ready for Tier 2 challenges, as determined through assessment data and structured advising sessions. No summary table alone can capture the richness of an ambitious and creative program like this, what Table 11.2 does do is illustrate how educators can tailor their work to intentionally foster student learning by taking seriously what we know about student development and creatively applying the LPM.

TABLE 11.2. FRAMEWORK FOR STUDENT DEVELOPMENT.

Tier 1

Student Traits	Developmental Goals	Student Learning Outcomes	Faculty/Staff Expectations	Learning Experiences
• Knowledge viewed as certain • Reliance on authorities (parents, faculty, textbooks) • Externally defined value system and identity • Relate to others for approval	• Question how authorities create knowledge and see the need to create their own knowledge • Realize the drawbacks of defining themselves based on others' perceptions and focusing on approval from others	• Communicate by presenting controlling idea, logical organization and supporting evidence • Explore contemporary or enduring question about society or environment • Think critically by identifying multiple perspectives on an issue • Identify one's strengths and areas for improvement • Interact with others to engage with provocative ideas, disciplines or cultures	• Cultivate a safe climate for honest exchange of ideas • Validate students' capacity to know and learn • Build on students' experiences; connect academic learning to their experiences • Provide multiple valid perspectives on topics • Model critical self-reflection, and offer regular feedback • Sequence material to cultivate students' research or discovery-oriented skills	• Honors seminar meeting Tier 1 outcomes • First-year seminar • Assistantship in lab or research center for one semester • Completion of weekly book or film club led by faculty/staff and upper-class student • Community service (for one year with ongoing reflection) • Summer international workshop • Learning community (e.g., students co-enroll in set of courses and create study group) • Hall council membership

Tier 2

Student Traits	Developmental Goals	Student Learning Outcomes	Faculty/Staff Expectations	Learning Experiences
• Evolving awareness of multiple perspectives and uncertainty • Evolving awareness of own values and identity and of limitations of dependent relationships	• Begin choosing their own beliefs and understand how they themselves decide what is true/valid within the context of multiple perspectives • Define and act on their own values as well as mutually negotiate with others	• Communicate in a recognizable academic or public genre (using appropriate tone, structure and argument) • Think critically by analyzing or comparing scientific, humanistic or artistic concepts or frameworks • Assess and refine one's educational goals	• Help students understand the limitations and benefits of various knowledge domains (e.g., disciplines, practices, cultures, conventions) • Assist students in processing problems and resist temptation to "rescue" or provide answers for them	• Honors seminar meeting Tier 2 outcomes • Summer or semester-long research experience • Semester-long study abroad

(continued from previous page)

Student Learning Outcomes	Faculty/Staff Expectations	Possible Experiences
• Operate effectively within a diverse team to solve a problem, address an issue or answer a question	• Help students function productively on a team (role negotiation, listening, time management) • Integrate opportunities for students to practice discovery and to make connections among their various learning experiences (in-class and out-of-class)	• Internship with additional research & reflection • Tutoring experience with training & evaluation (one yr) • Participation on Mock Trial or Forensics Team (one year) • Resident Assistantship • Independent study • Application for national fellowship or external grant with close faculty guidance

Tier 3

Student Traits	Developmental Goals	Student Learning Outcomes	Faculty/Staff Expectations	Possible Experiences
• Awareness of knowledge as contextual • Development of internal belief system and sense of self • Capacity to engage in authentic, interdependent relationships	• Consistently base their decisions and constructions of knowledge upon their internal belief system • Integrate aspects of their identity and recognize the multifaceted identities of others	• Produce work that advances an original idea and is aligned with personal philosophy, and present to a public audience • Think critically by actively engaging with, evaluating and integrating diverse knowledge • Create, critique, apply knowledge in multiple contexts • Align one's actions with one's values • Sustain and enact a commitment to creating an inclusive community	• Open up opportunities for students to construct knowledge • Share authority and expertise with students • Create opportunities for students to teach, lead and learn from and with others • Offer narrative and face-to-face evaluations on students' work • Provide opportunities for students to reflect on their undergraduate experience and apply lessons learned to career plans • Encourage students to engage with one another in respectful dialogue to explore disagreements and differences of opinions	• Honors seminar meeting Tier 3 outcomes • Student-designed and led course • Traditional thesis • Publication in peer-reviewed journal • Legacy project (project that gives back to the institution) • Presentation at national conference • Direct exchange study abroad experience at foreign institution • Student teaching with assessment project • Design competition • Business consultancy • Concert or art exhibition with explanatory notes and reflection

Source: "A framework for intentionally fostering student learning" by K. B. Taylor and C. Haynes, 2008, *About Campus: Enriching the Student Learning Experience,* 13(5), pp. 6–7. Reprinted with permission.

Conclusion

In this chapter we have argued for a view of learning in higher education that prioritizes deep learning outcomes, acknowledges the central role of meaning making as a foundation for learning, takes into account how learner characteristics evolve over time, and applies principles of learning and student development to organize learning environments in ways that maximize deep learning. Because many studies have persuasively documented the evolution in epistemological assumptions and complex identities, there is a solid foundation on which to build programs and courses of study to promote self-authored meaning making in many learning contexts (see Chapters Nine and Ten in this volume; Baxter Magolda, Creamer, & Meszaros, 2010). And there are many reasons to do so: as Baxter Magolda (2001, 2004a) and the authors of the national reports noted in the introduction to this chapter have shown, the capacities associated with self-authorship are essential for the achievement of the complex learning outcomes such a pluralistic democracy as the United States needs from its graduates.

Many developmental issues underlie educational processes; to ignore these connections is to limit the potential of collegiate experiences to fulfill their learning missions. Similarly, ignoring other factors can also impede student learning: these include gaps in the foundation of students' knowledge and skill bases, competing demands that disrupt attempts to practice and refine skills, lack of detailed and timely feedback on student performance, lack of substantive opportunities to learn new skills or deepen understanding, or administrative or cultural barriers on campus that make it difficult to link learning across campus contexts or to have substantive interactions with individuals from different backgrounds or beliefs. Although these challenges are part of the context of higher education, educators have tools to address them. Those who have an understanding of learner characteristics and can articulate complex learning goals, who can recognize students' steps toward these goals, and who can identify challenging and supportive factors in educational environments have the tools to apply this understanding to the design of educational programs that promote learning and the achievement of desired collegiate learning outcomes.

As we have shown here, the components of self-authorship are closely linked to collegiate learning outcomes, and the design of effective educational programs can be grounded in the mechanisms of student development. Students will thus be better served if college educators have a firm grounding in concepts and principles of college student learning and development.

References

Abes, E. (2009). Theoretical borderlands: Using multiple theoretical perspectives to challenge inequitable power structures in student development theory. *Journal of College Student Development, 50,* 141–156.

Abes, E. S., & Jones, S. R. (2004). Meaning-making capacity and the dynamics of lesbian college students' multiple dimensions of identity. *Journal of College Student Development, 45,* 612–632.

Abes, E. S., Jones, S. R., & McEwen, M. K. (2007). Reconceptualizing the Model of Multiple Dimensions of Identity: The role of meaning-making capacity in the construction of multiple identities. *Journal of College Student Development, 48*, 1–22.

Abes, E. S., & Kasch, D. (2007). Using queer theory to explore lesbian college students' multiple dimensions of identity. *Journal of College Student Development, 48*, 619–636.

American Association of Higher Education (AAHE), American College Personnel Association (ACPA), & National Association of Student Personnel Administrators (NASPA). (1998). *Powerful partnerships: A shared responsibility for learning.* Washington, DC: Authors.

American College Personnel Association (ACPA). (1994). *The student learning imperative: Implications for student affairs.* Washington, DC: Author.

Association of American Colleges and Universities (AAC&U). (2002). *Greater expectations: A new vision for learning as a nation goes to college.* Washington, DC: Author.

Association of American Colleges and Universities (AAC&U). (2005). *Liberal education outcomes: A preliminary report of student achievement in college.* Washington, DC: Author.

Association of American Colleges and Universities (AAC&U) (2007). *College learning for the new global century.* Washington, DC: Author.

Barber, J. P. (2009). *Integration of learning: Meaning making for undergraduates through connection, application, and synthesis.* Unpublished doctoral dissertation, University of Michigan.

Baxter Magolda, M. B. (1992). *Knowing and reasoning in college: Gender-related patterns in students' intellectual development.* San Francisco: Jossey-Bass.

Baxter Magolda, M. B. (1996). Cognitive learning and personal development: A false dichotomy. *About Campus, 1*(3), 16–21.

Baxter Magolda, M. B. (2001). *Making their own way: Narratives for transforming higher education to promote self-development.* Sterling, VA: Stylus.

Baxter Magolda, M. B. (2004a). Self-authorship as the common goal of 21st century education. In M. B. Baxter Magolda & P. M. King (Eds.), *Learning partnerships: Theory and models of practice to educate for self-authorship* (pp. 1–35). Sterling, VA: Stylus.

Baxter Magolda, M. B. (2004b). Learning Partnerships Model: A framework for promoting self-authorship. In M. B. Baxter Magolda & P. M. King (Eds.), *Learning partnerships: Theory and models of practice to educate for self-authorship* (pp. 37–62). Sterling, VA: Stylus.

Baxter Magolda, M. B. (2008). Three elements of self-authorship. *Journal of College Student Development, 49*, 269–284.

Baxter Magolda, M. B. (2009). *Authoring your life: Developing an internal voice to navigate life's challenges.* Sterling, VA: Stylus.

Baxter Magolda, M. B., Creamer, E. G., & Meszaros, P. S. (Eds.). (2010). *Development and assessment of self-authorship: Exploring the concept across cultures.* Sterling, VA: Stylus.

Baxter Magolda, M. B., & King, P. M. (Eds.). (2004). *Learning partnerships: Theory and models of practice to educate for self-authorship.* Sterling, VA: Stylus.

Baxter Magolda, M. B., & King, P. M. (2007). Interview strategies for assessing self-authorship: Constructing conversations to assess meaning making. *Journal of College Student Development, 48*, 491–508.

Baxter Magolda, M. B., & King, P. M. (2008). Toward reflective conversations: An advising approach that promotes self-authorship. *Peer Review, 10*(1), 8–11.

Baxter Magolda, M. B., King, P. M., Taylor, K. B., & Perez, R. J. (2008). *Developmental steps within external meaning making.* Paper presented at the Association for the Study of Higher Education, Jacksonville, FL.

Baxter Magolda, M. B., King, P. M., Taylor, K. B., & Wakefield, K. (2009). *Decreasing authority-dependence during the first year of college.* Paper presented at the American Educational Research Association, San Diego, CA.

Bekken, B. M., & Marie, J. (2007). Making self-authorship a goal of core curricula: The Earth Sustainability Pilot Project. In P. S. Meszaros (Ed.), *Self-authorship: Advancing students' intellectual growth* (New Directions for Teaching and Learning No. 109, pp. 53–67). San Francisco: Jossey-Bass.

Dewey, J. (2004). *Education and democracy: An introduction to the philosophy of education.* New York: Macmillan. (Original work published 1916)

Egart, K., & Healy, M. (2004). An urban leadership internship program: Implementing learning partnerships "unplugged" from campus structures. In M. B. Baxter Magolda & P. M. King (Eds.), *Learning partnerships: Theory and models of practice to educate for self-authorship* (pp. 125–149). Sterling, VA: Stylus.

Freire, P. (1988). *Pedagogy of the oppressed.* New York: Continuum. (Original work published 1970)

Haynes, C. (2004). Promoting self-authorship through an interdisciplinary writing curriculum. In M. B. Baxter Magolda & P. M. King (Eds.), *Learning partnerships: Theory and models of practice to educate for self-authorship* (pp. 63–90). Sterling, VA: Stylus.

hooks, b. (1994). *Teaching to transgress: Education as the practice of freedom.* New York: Routledge.

Hornak, A., & Ortiz, A. M. (2004). Creating a context to promote diversity education and self-authorship among community college students. In M. B. Baxter Magolda & P. M. King (Eds.), *Learning partnerships: Theory and models of practice to educate for self-authorship* (pp. 91–123). Sterling, VA: Stylus.

Keeling, R. P. (Ed.). (2004). *Learning reconsidered: A campus-wide focus on the student experience.* Washington, DC: American College Personnel Association & National Association of Student Personnel Administrators.

Kegan, R. (1982). *The evolving self: Problem and process in human development.* Cambridge, MA: Harvard University Press.

Kegan, R. (1994). *In over our heads: The mental demands of modern life.* Cambridge, Massachusetts: Harvard University Press.

Kendall Brown, M. (2008). *A mixed methods examination of college students' intercultural development.* Unpublished doctoral dissertation, University of Michigan.

King, P. M. (2003). Student learning in higher education. In S. R. Komives, D. B. Woodard Jr., & Associates (Eds.), *Student services: A handbook for the profession* (4th ed., pp. 234–268). San Francisco: Jossey-Bass.

King, P. M., & Baxter Magolda, M. B. (1996). A developmental perspective on learning. *Journal of College Student Development, 37*, 163–173.

King, P. M., & Baxter Magolda, M. B. (2005). A developmental model of intercultural maturity. *Journal of College Student Development, 46*, 571–592.

King, P. M., Baxter Magolda, M. B., Barber, J. P., Kendall Brown, M., & Lindsay, N. K. (2009). Developmentally effective experiences for promoting self-authorship. *Mind, Brain, and Education, 3*(2), 108–118.

King, P. M., Kendall Brown, M., Lindsay, N. K., & VanHecke, J. R. (2007). Liberal arts student learning outcomes: An integrated approach. *About Campus, 12*(4), 2–9.

King, P. M., & Kitchener, K. S. (1994). *Developing reflective judgment: Understanding and promoting intellectual growth and critical thinking in adolescents and adults.* San Francisco: Jossey-Bass.

Ladson-Billings, G. (1994). *The dreamkeepers: Successful teachers of African American children.* San Francisco: Jossey-Bass.

Lindsay, N. K. (2007). Enhancing perpetual learning: The nexus between a liberal arts education and the disposition toward lifelong learning. Unpublished doctoral dissertation, University of Michigan.

Mentkowski, M., & Associates. (2000). *Learning that lasts: Integrating learning, development, and performance in college and beyond.* San Francisco: Jossey-Bass.

Mezirow, J. (Ed.). (2000). *Learning as transformation: Critical perspectives on a theory in progress.* San Francisco: Jossey-Bass.

Mills, R., & Strong, K. L. (2004). Organizing for learning in a division of student affairs. In M. B. Baxter Magolda & P. M. King (Eds.), *Learning partnerships: Theory and models of practice to educate for self-authorship* (pp. 269–302). Sterling, VA: Stylus.

Piper, T. D., & Buckley, J. A. (2004). Community Standards Model: Developing learning partnerships in campus housing. In M. B. Baxter Magolda & P. M. King (Eds.), *Learning partnerships: Theory and models of practice to educate for self-authorship* (pp. 185–212). Sterling, VA: Stylus.

Pizzolato, J. E. (2003). Developing self-authorship: Exploring the experiences of high- risk college students. *Journal of College Student Development, 44*, 797–812.

Pizzolato, J. E., & Ozaki, C. C. (2007). Moving toward self-authorship: Investigating outcomes of learning partnerships. *Journal of College Student Development, 48*, 196–214.

Popp, N., & Portnow, K. (2001). Our developmental perspective on adulthood. In Adult Development Research Group (Ed.), *Toward a new pluralism in ABE/ESOL classrooms: Teaching to multiple "cultures of mind"* (pp. 43–75). Cambridge, MA: National Center for the Study of Adult Learning and Literacy, Harvard University Graduate School of Education.

Rogers, J. L., Magolda, P. M., Baxter Magolda, M. B., & Knight-Abowitz, K. (2004). A community of scholars: Enacting the Learning Partnerships Model in graduate education. In M. B. Baxter Magolda & P. M. King (Eds.), *Learning partnerships: Theory and models of practice to educate for self-authorship* (pp. 213–244). Sterling, VA: Stylus.

Shor, I. (1992). *Empowering education: Critical teaching for social change.* Chicago: University of Chicago Press.

Taylor, K. B., & Haynes, C. (2008). A framework for intentionally fostering student learning. *About Campus, 13*(5), 2–11.

Torres, V. (2003). Factors influencing ethnic identity development of Latino college students in the first two years of college. *Journal of College Student Development, 44*, 532–547.

Torres, V., & Hernandez, E. (2007). The influence of ethnic identity development on self-authorship: A longitudinal study of Latino/a college students. *Journal of College Student Development, 48*, 558–573.

VanHecke, J. R. (2006). *Responsible citizenship among college students: A study of predictive experiences and values.* Unpublished doctoral dissertation, University of Michigan.

Wildman, T. M. (2004). The Learning Partnerships Model: Framing faculty and institutional development. In M. B. Baxter Magolda & P. M. King (Eds.), *Learning partnerships: Theory and models of practice to educate for self-authorship* (pp. 245–268). Sterling, VA: Stylus.

Wildman, T. M. (2007). Taking seriously the intellectual growth of students: Accommodations for self-authorship. In P. S. Meszaros (Ed.), *Self-authorship: Advancing students' intellectual growth* (New Directions for Teaching and Learning No. 109, pp. 15–30). San Francisco: Jossey-Bass.

Yonkers Talz, K. (2004). A learning partnership: U.S. college students and the poor in El Salvador. In M. B. Baxter Magolda & P. M. King (Eds.), *Learning partnerships: Theory and models to educate for self-authorship* (pp. 151–184). Sterling, VA: Stylus.

CHAPTER TWELVE

ORGANIZATIONAL THEORY

Adrianna Kezar

Organizational theory is perhaps one of the most important frameworks for student affairs practitioners to understand in order to successfully enact their roles. Leadership, governance, organizational change, resource allocation, human resource management, organizational design, restructuring, hiring, teamwork, networking, and organizational culture are all explained and addressed through organizational theory. Most student affairs practitioners cannot imagine a workday without addressing one or more of these key areas of campus operations. In this chapter, in order to provide a broad introduction to well-known concepts, I review the following key organizational theories: Bolman and Deal's (1997) four frames synthesis of organizational theories; Birnbaum's (1988) exploration into the four frames within college and university settings; a summary of unique college characteristics; and Morgan's (1997) work on the dark side of organizations examining dysfunctional, unconscious, and oppressive systems that are often overlooked.

Student affairs practitioners sometimes seek leadership roles because they identify changes that they think are important for their campuses—they have a vision. However having a vision is very different from being able to accomplish change—one of the most elusive practices on college campuses. Understanding how to create change in the difficult college environment is an important skill. Organizational theory offers rich knowledge concerning organizational change. In order to make concrete the organizational theories presented here, I will apply them to a case of creating change—building learning communities on campus, a task on which many in student affairs are currently working. Learning communities are interdisciplinary teaching environments structured so that students learn in cohorts together and often live in the same space, blending their in-and-out of classroom experiences. After I present each theory, I will describe how that theory helps to address the challenge of moving the campus from traditional forms of lecture-based, individualistic learning toward learning communities.

Making Sense of Organizations: The Four Frames

Bolman and Deal (1997) provide one of the most comprehensive overviews of organizational theory and its implications for leaders. Morgan (1997), in his book Images of Organization, also provides an analysis of a helpful framework for understanding organizations similar to that of Bolman and Deal (1997), which uses metaphors rather than frames. The metaphors that he uses for organizations are machines, organisms, brains, cultures, political systems, psychic prisons, flux and transformation, and instruments of domination. This is also an important book for understanding how organizations operate and ways for leaders to successfully navigate subsystems of these organizations.

Bolman and Deal's (1997) book *Reframing Organizations* synthesizes thousands of studies about organizational behavior and theory and describes four major frames that help to understand how organizations operate: structural, human resource, political, and symbolic. The term *frame* could also be called a mental model, mind-set, or cognitive lens, and refers to a set of ideas or assumptions that guide behavior. Frames are important because they help leaders to understand and negotiate particular issues. Bolman and Deal also liken frames to a roadmap; if a leader is able to effectively understand the four frames, he or she will be better able to use them like a roadmap to navigate and address organizational problems. Let us examine the frames more deeply (a summary is also presented in Table 12.1).

TABLE 12.1.   OVERVIEW OF THE FOUR-FRAME MODEL.

	Structural	Human Resource	Political	Symbolic
Metaphor of the Organization	Factory or machine	Family	Jungle	Carnival, temple, or theater
Central Concepts	Rules, goals, policies, technology, and environment	Needs, skills, and relationships	Power, conflict, competition, and organizational politics	Culture, meaning, metaphor, ritual, ceremony, stories, and heroes
Image of Leadership	Social architecture	Empowerment	Advocacy	Inspiration
Basic Leadership Challenge	Attune structured tasks, technology, and environment	Aligning organizational and human needs	Develop agenda and power base	Create faith, beauty, and meaning

Source: Adapted from Bolman and Deal, 1997.

Structural Frame

The structural frame is perhaps the most commonly used framework among leaders and the most familiar to those in the general public. This frame is often epitomized by the notion of the organizational chart, with which people understand how the organization functions through definitions of a variety of roles and the relationships among those roles. The organizational chart is the underlying architecture or structure of the organization. Although individuals often mistake the notion of hierarchy as synonymous with the structural frame, these are distinct concepts. The *structural frame* is a broader term to describe the many ways organizations can be organized, from a matrix or team structure, to a network organization, to a professional bureaucracy.

Six assumptions underlie the structural frame:

1. Organizations exist to achieve established goals and objectives.
2. Organizations increase efficiency and enhance performance through specialization and a clear division of labor.
3. Appropriate forms of coordination and control ensure that diverse efforts of individuals and units mesh.
4. Organizations work best when rationality prevails over personal preferences and extraneous pressures.
5. Structures must be designed to fit an organization's circumstances (including its goals, technology, workforce, and environment).
6. Problems and performance gaps arise from structural deficiencies and can be remedied through analysis and restructuring.

The structural lens is important because it helps to identify ways that the organization might be restructured in order to maximize performance or to better meet a goal. A leader might decide to differentiate work or integrate more; work might become more autonomous or more controlled; or work might need more or less coordination—or more or fewer rules or policies.

Human Resource Frame

Many student affairs practitioners may find themselves conceptualizing organizations through the human resource frame because of their counseling or psychology backgrounds. Not surprisingly, the human resource frame emphasizes the human subsystem of the organization, focusing on the motivation, needs, commitment, training, hiring, and socialization of people within the organization and how these affect organizational functioning. The human resource frame is built on four basic assumptions:

1. Organizations exist to serve human needs rather than the reverse.
2. People and organizations need each other. Organizations need ideas, energy, and talent; people need careers, salaries, and opportunities.

3. When the fit between individual and system is poor, one or both suffer. Individuals are exploited or exploit the organization—or both become victims.
4. A good fit between individual and organization benefits both. Individuals find meaningful and satisfying work, and organizations get the talent and energy they need to succeed.

Leaders with a human resource frame are more likely to understand the importance of supporting human capital, hiring the right people, promoting from within, providing leadership that brings out the best in others, making sure to invest in and reward each individual's commitment and effort, encouraging participation, and promoting diversity, all of which enable the human resource subsystem to operate more smoothly.

Political Frame

Bolman and Deal's (1997) research identified that many people, particularly educators and often women, downplayed the political framework for understanding organizational challenges and developing solutions. Politics often gets a negative image—in terms of ambitious people climbing to the top willing to engage in unscrupulous activities in order to move their agendas forward, but this is a very limited view of politics. The political frame can help leaders understand the important ways they can build agendas or common visions for change, mobilize people, use persuasion to influence others, identify sources of power and use these to leverage change and the power of networks in order to create organizational direction. The political frame also helps many conflict-averse leaders see the value in conflict, which can help identify where people have competing interests and where negotiation and solutions lie. The political frame also challenges leaders with highly rational approaches to their work to think about other conditions that are shaping organizational behavior, such as differing interests or beliefs.

The five major assumptions of the political frame are:

1. Organizations are coalitions of diverse individuals and interest groups.
2. There are enduring differences among coalition members in values, beliefs, information, interests, and perceptions of reality.
3. Most important decisions involve allocating scarce resources.
4. Scarce resources and enduring differences make conflict central to organizational dynamics and underlie power as the most important asset.
5. Goals and decisions emerge from bargaining, negotiation, and jockeying for position among competing stakeholders.

Symbolic Frame

Perhaps the most underused frame is the symbolic perspective of the organization. Research and theory about the cultural and symbolic aspects of organizations did not emerge until the 1980s (Kezar & Eckel, 2002). Its recent emergence into academic research reflects the way that the symbolic subsystem (e.g., mission, vision, values) of an organization has been downplayed and not capitalized on in the past. People inherently need meaning, and the symbolic frame helps provide avenues for individuals to establish meaning through their work. This frame also demonstrates why mission and vision are important for providing members of the organization with a sense of purpose and an image of the future toward which they may aim. Leaders can communicate meaning through rituals and ceremonies that help people to collectively remember their purpose. An example of an important ritual that takes place on most campuses and reminds members of the organization of their purpose is the beginning-of-the-year convocation, which again centers these individuals on their work. Overall, the symbolic subsystem of an organization sheds light on the values undergirding its activities, practices, and policies, which typically go unnoticed. Bolman and Deal (1997) pointed out how the symbolic frame, more so than any other, moves leaders beyond thinking in a highly rational or only strategic manner, highlighting the importance of faith, purpose, emotions, values, and spirit for organizational functioning.

The five major assumptions of the symbolic frame are:

1. What is most important is not what happens but what it means.
2. Activity and meaning are loosely coupled; events have multiple meanings because people interpret experiences differently.
3. In the face of widespread uncertainty and ambiguity, people create symbols to resolve confusion, increase predictability, find direction, and anchor hope and faith.
4. Many events and processes are more important for what is expressed than for what is produced. They form a cultural tapestry of secular myths, heroes and heroines, rituals, ceremonies, and stories that help people find purpose and passion in their personal and work lives.
5. Culture is the glue that holds an organization together and unites people around shared values and beliefs.

Multiframe Thinking: Pulling the Frames Together

Bolman and Deal's (1997) empirical research suggests that leaders are more successful and effective when they use multiframe thinking for conceptualizing issues within organizations. Their research also suggests that leaders tend to use a single frame or a couple of frames in order to understand and analyze issues within an organization. Furthermore, studies demonstrate that leaders tend to overestimate their use of frames—they might believe they are using the symbolic frame, but none of the people they work with perceive them using this frame. Leaders are biased toward relying on the "one right answer" or the "one best way" and, as a result, are often faced with resistance and turmoil. For example, if a vice president for student affairs establishes a task force to address retention issues on campus, and if several months later that task force is experiencing significant problems in addressing their charge, the leader will likely assume that the problem can be found within her own personal way of viewing the organization. Therefore, if this vice president for student affairs tends to approach the organization through a human resource frame, she will believe that she put the wrong people on the task force and work to put new people on the committee. If she comes from a structural frame, she might believe that the charge was not clear enough and develop more explicit instructions for the task force. Bolman and Deal's research (1997) demonstrates that leaders who look at such a task force from multiple perspectives—that the wrong people might be on the task force, that task force members might need a clearer charge, that politics have emerged that are hindering interaction, or that common values are missing— are more likely to correctly diagnose problems and develop appropriate solutions. Finally, it is important to note that each frame has strengths and weaknesses. Any frame, when taken to the extreme, can jeopardize a leader's success. No frames are necessarily better for understanding or addressing problems, but leaders who use multiple frames increase their effectiveness.

One of the primary insights from Bolman and Deal's (1997) work is the importance of developing complex analysis and solutions—a task at which many leaders fail because they lack awareness about the various subsystems that operate within organizations or are guided by unacknowledged biases of looking at single frames. Bolman and Deal also note how leaders tend to value certainty, rationality, and control, and fear ambiguity or "going with the flow." Being a good leader requires engaging in the ambiguity and complexity of organizations, being willing to learn and grow as a leader, and the ability to embrace creative and nonmechanistic solutions to problems.

How can the four frames offered by Bolman and Deal (1997) help in thinking about our particular case of organizational change (the move toward learning communities)? First, from a structural perspective, the campus will need to be significantly restructured to support a set of residentially based learning communities. Leaders spearheading the initiative should probably report to both academic and student affairs so that open communication between the units is established. New faculty roles will need to be created, such as faculty in residence, and new responsibilities should be developed for these individuals. From the human resource perspective, staff members will need to be recruited and trained to work in and support the learning communities. These employees will need to be socialized to the value of in-and out-of-classroom learning and interdisciplinary approaches to teaching and knowledge construction. From a political perspective, disciplinary and departmental resistance to the idea of interdisciplinary teaching will need to be addressed. Various coalitions that support interdisciplinary teaching across campus can be mobilized to provide support for the initiative. From a symbolic perspective, leaders need to describe how the identity of the campus is changing and create new rituals and ceremonies that celebrate the move toward interdisciplinary teaching and learning on campus. The way the mission and values of the campus support the move toward learning communities should be emphasized—whether it be the liberal arts orientation, a belief in collaboration, or the importance of developing the whole student. These values can be used to get people across campus to buy into the notion of learning communities.

The Four Frames in Higher Education

Birnbaum's (1988), *How Colleges Work*, examines the four frames—structural, human resource, political, and symbolic—and describes how they operate within college campuses. Whereas Bolman and Deal (1997) think about the frames generically as interpretive lenses for viewing the subsystems of an organization, Birnbaum applies the frames as a way to view the organizational behavior of colleges and universities. Some campuses operate more from a human resource perspective and can be called collegial. Others are more managerial and hierarchical and reflect the assumptions of the structural lens. Birnbaum uses the same concepts (political, human resource, and structural), but with slightly different names (collegial for human resource, bureaucratic for structural). He also introduces a new lens—anarchical—which he sees as a unique organizational lens within colleges. Birnbaum notes that the collegial and bureaucratic organizational characteristics have long-term, historical roots in American higher education. The political and anarchical characteristics, however, are more recent adaptations that respond to modern society. Table 12.2 summarizes Birnbaum's conceptualization of the four frames and how they help explain college organizational behavior. By understanding these four organizational archetypes, which are common across higher education and within various units, leaders can better understand how to navigate the organizational environment. As Bergquist (1992) noted, "We must determine how to work with and use the strength and resources of the existing organizational culture to accomplish our goals" (p. xii).

TABLE 12.2.   ORGANIZATIONAL ARCHETYPES—SELECTED EXAMPLES.

Bureaucratic	Collegial	Political	Anarchical
Focus on aligning goals of various bureaucratic units	Agreed-upon goals	Contested goals	Ambiguous goals
Chain-of-command decision making	Consensus-based decision making	Bargaining and negotiation	Unclear decision-making processes
Top-down leadership	Distributed leadership, but with more power among certain groups	Conflict and confrontation between bottom-up and top-down leadership	Leadership emerging anywhere
Operate by directives	Operate by agreed-upon values	Operate based on negotiated agreements	Operations based more on individual decision making and professional values
Change occurs by mandates	Change occurs through dialogue and conversation	Change occurs when competing interests clash	Change occurs on the margins of the organization, based on the work of innovative individuals

For example, some campuses seem to be dominated by the rationalizing forces of the structural frame. Goals and purposes drive the way people think about their work and direct their activities. People within the organization tend to value fiscal responsibility, efficiency, and effective supervision. These more bureaucratic campuses typically are larger, and there tends to be less face-to-face interaction among faculty, staff, and students. The campus is organized into many different hierarchical and siloed units. Communication across campus and between units is often difficult, and people are often isolated in their work and responsibilities. The campuses operate from codified rules, regulations, and policies. Individuals' roles and responsibilities are defined by written job descriptions, and they have highly specialized work. When people start new jobs, they are handed binders with various directives to follow. Much of the communication that happens is in the form of memoranda that come out as mandates with new policies and practices. Written records, rather than people's recollections, drive campus operations and decision making; bureaucratic directives shape the nature of work.

Campuses highly influenced by the human resource frame, or collegial institutions, seem to possess an egalitarian ethic among different groups on campus. Insiders, however, know that faculty have more power and influence than staff and students. Faculty, staff, students, and the administration have great respect and admiration for one another; people characterize the campus as a "tight-knit community." Faculty all tend to know one another well and have formed close relationships. The administration is seen as having goals similar to those of the faculty on campus, and they have a strong system of shared governance in place. Consensus, the democratic process, shared power, common commitments and aspirations, and leadership by consultation are important to the governance of the campus. People are treated as autonomous professionals, and decision making is highly decentralized into what has been termed a loosely coupled system (Weick, 1991). People often have common backgrounds, continuous interactions, and many rituals and traditions in place that they share. Goals tend to be accomplished because of collegial agreements that are in place rather than bureaucratic directives. Disciplinary and professional values, notions of scholarship, and faculty beliefs often drive campus operations. Birnbaum (1988) found that the collegial campus is more likely to be found in liberal arts colleges, but can nevertheless be found in any type of institution. The collegial campus might even be a particular subsystem, such as the student affairs division.

In institutions that are shaped by the political frame, various interest groups and distinctive cultures exist. There are few common values, and communication happens in small circles among like-minded people. These various interest groups interact by forming coalitions, bargaining, compromising, and reaching agreements; there is a decidedly "us" versus "them" mentality on campus. Budget decisions are extremely complex and involve much competition among interest groups. Research shows that a political culture is often present on unionized campuses (Bergquist, 1992). Many campuses with a political culture have staff and faculty who feel alienated by the size and complexity of the institution. Joining a union appears to be one way to develop a professional community. Also, collegiality is not in place to bring people together and form a community. Bergquist suggested that this culture emerged out of the inability of the managerial or bureaucratic culture to meet the personal and financial needs of faculty and staff. Although collective bargaining use should be largely in the domain of community colleges, in the last ten years many other sectors of higher education have unionized, particularly with the rise of non–tenure track faculty, who make up over two-thirds of the faculty in higher education (Kezar, 2001). It is likely that the negotiating or political culture will become more prevalent in years to come.

A unique organization type emerged within higher education—the anarchical institution. Cohen and March's *Leadership and Ambiguity* (1974) was the first to identify the notion of organized anarchy and the way that many research universities tend to operate in ways that are unique from other types of organizations. The main characteristic of an organized anarchy is that there are so many different goals that it is difficult to understand and make sense of the various directions of the organization. To the outside observer, the organized anarchy looks like chaos and as if people do not know what they are doing. Certain campuses seem to be organized anarchies due in part to the independence and autonomy of faculty, the shared nature of power and authority, and the complexity of the work of faculty and staff in the teaching and learning processes. These factors relate to and grow out of a collegial context. For example, creating liberally educated students is a complex goal that is difficult to distill to a few practices or programs on campus. Ambiguity is also highly prevalent; there is ambiguity about who holds authority in higher education institutions. Even though trustees hold the formal authority, over the years, faculty and administrators have developed authority within the organization. Power is ambiguous, moreover, because in a collegial system it is unacceptable to visibly display power.

Returning to our example of fostering learning communities, how can Birnbaum's (1988) characterizations of organizational behavior through the four frames help create change? If the campus is bureaucratic in orientation, it will be important for champions of learning communities to outline the learning goals that can be achieved through this effort. Champions should provide a clear concept paper about the vision, goals, and implementation plan that outlines how roles and responsibilities will be important for obtaining buy-in. Evaluation of the program should be a priority, and data must be collected to help garner future support. Working through the chain of command to communicate and obtain buy-in and resources will enable the change to occur more easily. If the campus operates like the collegial model, then moving toward learning communities may be easier because there are already many existing relationships across campus and between units. Leaders can describe how learning communities are an extension of the way the campus already operates through relationships. However, leaders need to be aware that many faculty may see this approach as breaking down important disciplinary affiliations. Furthermore, the highly decentralized decision-making process may make the move toward learning communities happen slowly over time as various departments become familiar with the concept. Campuswide retreats that build upon, but also break down, departmental affiliations will be needed, as will much time for discussion.

Therefore, strategies and approaches will vary based on campuses' or units' different forms of operation.

Digging Deeper into Distinctive Organizational Features

Birnbaum's (1988) scholarship suggests that higher education has some unique features that, when bundled together, become distinctive cultures that differ from those of other organizations (e.g., businesses or hospitals) and that it is important to understand these features in order to lead or be an administrator within such cultures. Recent organizational theory has illustrated that leaders are more successful when they take leadership approaches that fit specific organizational contexts. In this section, I elaborate on the distinctive features that organizational scholars consider important for making decisions or approaching organizational processes.[1] Like the frames and cultures, research studies demonstrate that leaders who are cognizant of the unique organizational features, and create strategies based on those features, are more successful in decision making, change, and daily operations (Kezar, 2001).

Weick (1991) described higher education institutions as loosely coupled systems. Tightly coupled organizations are centralized, non-differentiated, and highly coordinated, with strict division of labor. Loosely coupled systems are decentralized, have a large degree of differentiation among components, are uncoordinated, and have high degrees of specialization among workers. Birnbaum (1988) associated the anarchical culture with the loosely coupled nature of many campuses.

Because higher education institutions are loosely coupled systems, decision making is decentralized through the shared governance processes. Trustees or boards of regents have ultimate governance authority in certain areas of the institution, such as finances, but the major functions and decisions of the institution are shared between the faculty and administrators (Birnbaum, 1988). Members interact as equals, minimizing status differences to allow for greater collective voice and involvement. Power also tends to be informal, through networks of influence. Broad buy-in is necessary in decision making, and veto power is exercised by a small group if they perceive that all voices have not been heard (Baldridge, Curtis, Ecker, & Riley, 1977). Shared governance is an area that varies by institutional type; for example, community colleges with collective bargaining systems tend to have less participation in institutional governance.

Commentators on the higher education system have noted that it is strongly values driven (Birnbaum, 1988; Clark, 1983). Although all organizations have belief systems that guide them, colleges and universities are noted for the complex and contrasting systems of beliefs that have been developed to guide and shape their cultures and structures (Clark, 1983). For example, each disciplinary culture has distinctive beliefs and is socialized to its particular profession: mathematicians stress logic and consistency of numbers, whereas art historians emphasize perspective and

---

1. This section draws largely from Kezar (2001).

interpretation. Although some values and beliefs are shared across the enterprise, such as integrity in research, freedom to teach what is considered appropriate, the significance of shared governance and academic freedom, belief in access to higher education, and the value in specialization, faculty and administrators tend to hold vastly different values.

Birnbaum (1988) noted that normative organizations, such as colleges and universities, rely on referent and expert power rather than coercive power (prisons), reward power (increased salary), or legitimate power (businesses). Referent power results from the willingness to be influenced by another person because of one's identification with this person. Expert power is present when one person allows himself or herself to be influenced because the other person has some special knowledge. In particular, faculty are likely to be influenced by referent power through other members of their community whom they trust; colleagues with shared values; or appeals to principles, such as ethics, rather than salary increases or administrative sanctions (Birnbaum, 1988). In addition, autonomous faculty are unlikely to be influenced by other forms of administrative influence and power, such as top-down control.

It is not just that academic institutions have unique power structures; they also have competing authority structures. *Authority* is the right of a person or office in an organization to demand action of others and expect those demands to be met (Birnbaum, 1988). Clark (1991) identified four kinds of competing authority systems: academic authority, enterprise-based authority, system-based authority, and charisma. Academic authority is maintained by the faculty and is broken up into various subgroups such as disciplinary societies, associations, and collective bargaining units, all with varying degrees of power. In contrast, enterprise-based authority, which includes trustees or institutional authority, has the legal right to act on behalf of the institution. It is essentially a position-based authority. Enterprise-based power also encompasses bureaucratic authority based on hierarchical power (whether reward based or legitimate). System-based authority comprises governmental authority; political authority; and academic oligarchy (e.g., statewide governing boards). System-based authority tends to operate on reward and legitimate power as well. Lastly, charisma, which refers to a leader's ability to garner the willingness of a group to follow him or her because of unusual personal characteristics, is often associated with a particular president, trustee, or faculty member. This occurs from time to time on campuses. Clark (1991) noted another authority that is imposed on the higher education system and that is growing in importance—the market. Market forces cannot be ignored by institutions and shape institutions because of these institutions' dependence on resources to operate. Bess (1999) provided the following example of a market force: "While faculty may wish to maintain a strong curriculum in, say, aeronautical engineering, if there are too few students willing to major in that subject, the voice of the market will win out over the voice of the faculty" (p. 9).

Another unique characteristic of higher education institutions is that the two main employment groups, administration and faculty, tend to have differing values systems (Birnbaum, 1988; Sporn, 1999). Administrative power (both academic and student affairs) is based on hierarchy, and it values bureaucratic norms and structure, power and influence, rationality, and control and coordination of activities. Professional authority (disciplinary and scholarly based), however, is knowledge based, with a values system emphasizing collegiality, dialogue, shared power, autonomy, and peer review. Faculty also have divided loyalty between disciplinary societies, professional fields, and other external groups in which they participate (Sporn). Currently, faculty and administrative values are becoming increasingly divergent. Several studies have illustrated the growing bureaucratization and corporatization of administrative staff (Gumport, 1993; Rhoades, 1995). Administrative staff are increasingly coming from the business or legal professions rather than the ranks of faculty, and they are suggesting strategies from the corporate sector, such as privatization and outsourcing.

There is minimal employee turnover in higher education, and faculty tend to stay in their jobs for their entire careers because of the tenure system. Few organizations exist with this type of employee stability. In addition, even part-time faculty and contract faculty, noted as a rising percentage in the faculty, tend to stay at institutions for long periods of time (Finklestein, Seal, & Schuster, 1999). Academic and student affairs staff have more turnover, but compared to administrative staff in some other sectors their tenure is lengthy (Donofrio, 1990).

Finally, image drives behavior in higher education institutions because there are few bottom-line measures, like profit or return on investment, for assessing an institution's standing or establishing its competitive advantage (Astin, 1993; Gioia & Thomas, 1996). *Image* is generally defined as how members believe others view their organization—and ultimately how others view individuals within the organization (Gioia & Thomas). This means that benchmarking, peer evaluations, and other comparative systems and ranks tend to influence behavior.

Returning to our example of learning communities, how can these unique organizational characteristics help shape our implementation strategy? Knowing that shared governance is an important structure on many campuses, leaders can make sure to engage key stakeholders in the shared governance process through discussions about creating learning communities. Whereas business leaders can hire new people and easily fire those who no longer fit certain roles, staff and faculty in higher education are less expendable, and training and development of longtime employees is required. Therefore, in starting up learning communities, the campus center for teaching and learning might offer a course on developing interdisciplinary courses, and staff might be trained on how their roles will change as a result of developing learning communities. Because most campuses are not fashioned in ways that support collaborative work, and people work autonomously, the campus will likely have to be restructured in order for a learning community to be effectively implemented, which will include the development of a cross-campus team representing different institutional units and decisions that would otherwise be siloed from each other. Because influential, longtime employees have great powers of persuasion, a leader can recruit respected faculty members on campus to support the learning community idea and promote the concept among various disciplines. Finally, if a leader is aware of the loose coupling of campus operations, he or she will know that it will take multiple efforts at persuasion and gaining influence among a variety of different groups throughout the system in order to implement the change toward learning communities.

The Dark Side of Organizations

Most organizational theory has focused on how to improve, change, and learn (Morgan, 1997). However, it is also important to investigate the darker or less functional sides of organizations, such as the ways that they exploit or frustrate people. The dysfunctional elements of an organization, when ignored, can cripple an organization. Even with the best and most complex decisions made by leaders, organizations may find themselves paralyzed. Leaders should try to understand ways to address such dysfunctionality. Morgan's *Images of Organization* provides two helpful metaphors for understanding the dark side of organizations: organizations as instruments of domination and organizations as psychic prisons.

Organizations are made up of policies and practices (often implicit) that negatively affect many different members. Unless they are aware of the impact of existing policies and practices, leaders are likely to replicate oppression, domination, and inequities that are embedded into organizational structures and cultures. Morgan (1997) reminded us that organizations have served the role of social domination throughout history; more-powerful groups have imposed their will on other less-powerful groups for centuries. One group's achievement, unfortunately, often comes at the price of exploiting certain other groups. Morgan used the example of the building of the great pyramids at Giza, which involved the use of ten thousand slaves over twenty years in hard labor. However, existing examples of workplace abuse range from work hazards and industrial accidents to long work hours, workaholism, unequal pay, mental and emotional stress due to bullying coworkers, exploitation of the environment, breaking of unions, and other such practices that happen daily.

Morgan (1997) pointed out that organizations do not have domination and oppression as their goals; instead, these are typically the unintended consequences of trying to meet such objectives as increased profits or surviving in hard times. In fact, oppression is usually "a consequence of rational actions through which a group of individuals seeks to advance a particular set of aims, such as increased profitability and corporate growth. If rationality has unintended negative impacts that lead even the most celebrated and excellent organizations to create problems for others, why is such action rational? . . . Actions that are rational for increasing profitability may have a damaging effect on employees' health" (p. 340).

Only by carefully weighing the values and ethics of decisions can we ensure that wise decisions are made. Organizational researchers are now beginning to examine the problem of traditional organizational research, which has ignored the role of values and ideological premises as part of decision-making processes. Leaders and organizations tend to see themselves as ideologically neutral, operating by reason rather than according to any value base. The value of profit is often seen as more central than the health of employees, for example. Leaders need to carefully evaluate the ethical underpinnings of the decisions they make.

Ethical dilemmas abound in higher education, from conflicts of interest to athletic scandals, academic integrity issues, and power differences between academic and student affairs or between staff and faculty. Student affairs employees are routinely asked to work long hours and on weekends; employees are asked to forsake their families, and female executives often forgo having families at all; racism and sexism are prevalent on most campuses; multiculturalism and the interests of diverse groups are often demonized; and gay bashing frequently occurs. These issues are often ignored and lead to further problems. Successful leaders will use the skills offered through the four frames (Birnbaum, 1988; Bolman & Deal, 1997) to present these issues to campuses, engage in constructive dialogue, and develop solutions that both include aspects of the four frames of the organization and respect the unique characteristics of higher education (Bolman & Deal, 1997; Morgan, 1997).

One of the reasons that campus employees repress the dysfunctionality of organizations is that organizations operate like people: they deny (refuse to acknowledge a fact); idealize (play up the good aspects and protect themselves from the bad); split (isolate situations, taking out the bad and focusing on the good); and rationalize (create elaborate schemes of justification that disguise underlying motives and intentions). Morgan (1997) pointed out that psychological theory can help us understand the impulse to ignore the realities of organizations. One of the reasons that these psychological issues emerge is that work environments remind people of complex family dynamics or negative situations that have caused them anxiety. For example, the hierarchical arrangements of many college campuses put leaders in positions where they are often seen as the patriarch or matriarch in a family.

If leaders realize that individuals are made up of unconscious anxieties, stereotypes, undealt with aggressions, fears and feelings of inadequacy, and unconscious projections, they are better able to navigate the psychological issues that can emerge within organizations. The structural frame of organizations tends to dominate, downplaying the role of emotions and completely ignoring unconscious processes that may be shaping organizational behavior and functioning. Although leaders cannot turn into psychologists, the organization cannot become group therapy, and people cannot "manage" each other's minds and emotions, leaders can nevertheless develop modes of practice that respect and cope with unconscious concerns and dysfunctional patterns. As Morgan (1997) noted, "It is pointless to talk about creating learning organizations or of trying to develop corporate cultures that thrive on changes if the unconscious human dimension is ignored. If underlying preoccupations and concerns are not addressed, the rhetoric of creating a new organization is almost sure to fall on deaf ears" (p. 246).

In working to create learning communities on campus, we have yet another tool in Morgan's concepts (1997), which help us understand the unconscious processes and oppressive and dominating forces that can impede change. For example, acknowledging the power differential between student and academic affairs and having open conversations about the need to respect one another as equals in developing learning communities are important for breaking down barriers to working together. Student affairs administrators often hold stereotypes of faculty members as eccentric and disruptive individuals who are unable to function as part of the community. These unconscious beliefs and stereotypes will need to be addressed if people are to work together in respectful ways. Ignoring these issues of power and unconscious stereotypes will lead to unhealthy work environments, absenteeism and turnover, and resistance to the change processes over time.

Conclusion

Organizational theory can help student affairs leaders become complex thinkers who use multiple frames, understand the unique characteristics and cultures of higher education, and delve into the rational and irrational sides of organizations. It will take years of practice to be able to sophisticatedly apply this thinking as an individual. However, creating leadership teams with people who hold different perspectives—who see the world through different frames, exist in different subcultures on campus, and possess strengths in both emotional and cognitive orientations—can help student affairs educators more quickly capitalize on complex thinking within organizations to inform decisions.

References

Astin, A. (1993). *What matters in college? Four critical years revisited*. San Francisco: Jossey-Bass.

Baldridge, J. V., Curtis, D. V., Ecker, G. P., & Riley, G. L. (1977). Alternative models of governance in higher education. In G. L. Riley & J. V. Baldridge (Eds.), *Governing academic organizations* (pp. 2–25). Berkley, CA: McCutchan.

Bergquist, W. (1992). *The four cultures of the academy*. San Francisco: Jossey-Bass.

Bess, J. L. (1999). *The ambiguity of authority in colleges and universities: Why the new managerialism is winning*. Paper presented at the annual meeting of the Association for the Study of Higher Education, San Antonio, TX.

Birnbaum, R. (1988). *How colleges work: The cybernetics of academic organization and leadership*. San Francisco: Jossey-Bass.

Bolman, L., & Deal, T. (1997). *Reframing organizations*. San Francisco: Jossey-Bass.

Clark, B. R. (1983). *The higher education system: Academic organization in cross-national perspective*. Berkley: University of California Press.

Clark, B. R. (1991). Faculty organization and authority. In M. Peterson (Ed.), *ASHE reader on leadership and governance* (pp. 449–458). Needham Heights, MA: Ginn Press.

Cohen, M., & March, J. (1974). *Leadership and ambiguity*. Boston: Harvard Business School Press.

Donofrio, K. (1990). *Compensation survey*. Washington, DC: College and University Personnel Association.

Finklestein, M., Seal, M., & Schuster, J. (1999). New entrants to the full-time faculty of higher education institutions. *Education Statistics Quarterly*, *1*(4), 78–80.

Gioia, D. A., Thomas, J. B. (1996). Identity, image, and issue interpretation: Sensemaking during strategic change in academia. *Administrative Science Quarterly*, *41*, 370–403.

Gumport, P. (1993). Contested terrain of academic program reduction. *Journal of Higher Education,* *64*(3), 283–311.

Kezar, A. (2001). *Understanding and facilitating organizational change in the 21st Century: Recent research and conceptualizations.* (ASHE Higher Education Report, Vol. 28, No. 4). San Francisco: Jossey-Bass.

Kezar, A., & Eckel, P. (2002). The effect of institutional culture on change strategies in higher education: Universal principles or culturally responsive concepts? *Journal of Higher Education,* *73*(4), 435-460.

Morgan, G. (1997). *Images of organization.* Thousand Oaks, CA: Sage.

Rhoades, G. (1995) Rethinking and restructuring universities. *Journal of Higher Education Management* *10*(2), 17–23.

Sporn, B. (1999). *Adaptive university structures: An analysis of adaptation to socioeconomic environments of US and European universities.* London: Jessica Kingsley.

Weick, K. E. (1991). Educational organizations as loosely coupled systems. In M. W. Peterson, E. E. Chaffee, & T. H. White (Eds.), *Organization and governance in higher education* (4th ed.). Needham Heights, MA: Ginn Press.

CHAPTER THIRTEEN

CAMPUS ECOLOGY AND ENVIRONMENTS

Kristen A. Renn and Lori D. Patton

Through architecture, planning, design, and technology, humans adapt physical spaces to suit their needs and accomplish their purposes. These spaces, however, also act on humans to shape the ways they live, work, and learn. Whether one multipurpose building on a city block or the sprawling buildings, green space, and farms of a land-grant university, the nature of a college campus as a collection of spaces poses challenges and opportunities for educators to create optimal learning and development. In addition to the human-built aspects of a campus are the psychological and sociocultural spaces created and occupied by students, faculty, and staff.

Knowing how people occupy and interact with campus environments—and how those environments influence people—is an important element in understanding contexts for leadership, organizational change, and student learning and development. Student affairs professionals have a long history of examining campus contexts in relation to student outcomes. For example, in the first half of the twentieth century, pioneers of the college union movement in the United States imagined a crossroads or hearth for the campus, at which students and faculty would come together (Butts, 1971). At the same time, student housing consisted of dormitories with "house parents" acting *in loco parentis*. Today, living-learning communities in which academic and student life merge have returned U.S. higher education to its seventeenth century roots.

Student affairs professionals recognize that the philosophy "if you build it, they will come" is insufficient to provide a campus climate that promotes learning and development for all students. Working in buildings and on campuses designed for homogeneous student populations (majority White, middle-class, able-bodied, Christian, and male), educators today must address historical exclusion and contemporary diversity. Campus cultures and climate are shaped by, and shape in return, psychological and sociocultural environments. Although it may be difficult or costly to adapt the physical environment (e.g., by creating worship spaces for religiously diverse students and ensuring that transgender students have access to safe restroom and locker room facilities), the needs of traditionally marginalized groups must be brought to the center of campus planning and design.

Given the substantial literature on the interactions between students and environments, we present models for understanding these interactions through an ecological lens. Drawing on research on campus climate and culture, we describe how students experience campus environments. Finally, we provide recommendations and future directions for applying environmental theory and research to student affairs practice.

Ecology of Campus Environments

Premised on biological conceptions of ecology, human ecology focuses on interactions among individuals and groups of people as nested in their human-built, sociocultural, and natural physical-biological environments (Bubolz & Sontag, 1993). A primary goal of the ecosystem is survival, which is accomplished by adapting to environments and adapting them to meet one's needs. These basic tenets form the foundation for concepts of campus ecology.

Human Ecology Theory

Bronfenbrenner (1979) introduced a human ecology model to explain development as an interaction between person and environment. The model includes interactions among process, person, context, and time. Processes take place between an individual and his or her proximal environment. The "person" element comprises individual characteristics that influence how someone elicits responses from and responds to the environment. Context has four levels: *microsystems*, or immediate settings; *mesosystems*, the interactions among microsystems; *exosystems*, interactions outside the immediate environment but exerting influence on the individual; and *macrosystems*, or broad sociocultural factors. The element of time, which Bronfenbrenner sometimes called the *chronosystem*, interacts both as general context (i.e., the era in which one lives) and specific context (i.e., the time at which an event occurred in one's life).

When combined, process, person, context, and time form a powerful model for understanding students' developmental ecosystems (Renn & Arnold, 2003). The model explains, for example, why two students with similar entry characteristics could have vastly different college outcomes, depending on the extent to which they experienced increasingly complex processes in a variety of micro- and mesosystems; what exosystem factors (e.g., financial aid policy or interruption of parents' work) came into play; and how their individual (person) characteristics led them to engage or disengage from various opportunities in college. The model also accounts for various environmental presses (Pace & Stern, 1958) and buffers, what Bronfenbrenner (1993) called a "force-resource" approach (p. 14) and Sanford (1960) described as challenges and supports. Developmental ecology does not speak to *what* aspect of the individual is being developed, but it provides a way to understand *how* and *in what contexts* that development occurs.

Campus Ecology

Campus ecology, which applies principles of human and developmental ecology to higher education settings, provides a framework for understanding, designing, and evaluating educational environments that promote learning and development (see Moos, 1979, 1986; Strange & Banning, 2001). Campus ecology "is the study of the relationship between the student and the campus environment" (Banning, 1978, p. 5). It focuses on the influences of environments on students and students on environments, as well as the design of campus environments for optimal student outcomes.

Strange and Banning (2001) advocated for designing educational environments that promoted *inclusion* and *safety*, encouraged *involvement*, and built *community*. These three goals are accomplished by attending to the physical, human aggregate, organizational, and constructed components of campus milieus. Like human ecologists Bubolz and Sontag (1993) and ecological psychologist Moos (1979, 1986), Strange and Banning emphasized human-built elements (i.e., architecture and campus planning) and natural elements (i.e., climate and geography) of the physical environment. Considering the human aggregate, they attended to both people and person-environment interactions (Strange, 2003; Strange & Banning, 2001). Organizational structures and designs played key roles in achieving the three educational goals, as did constructed environments, including environmental press, social climate, and campus culture (Strange, 2003). Strange and Banning (2001) presented a cube-shaped campus design matrix (see Figure 13.1) to illustrate the intersecting dimensions of environmental components

FIGURE 13.1.   CAMPUS DESIGN MATRIX.

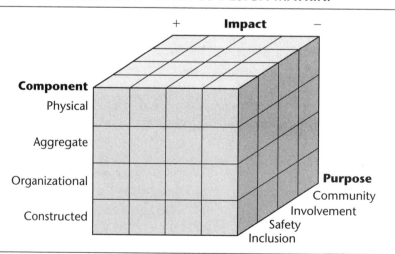

Source: Strange, C. C. (2003). Dynamics of campus environments. In S. R. Komives, D. B. Woodard Jr., & Associates (Eds.), *Student services: A handbook for the profession* (4th ed., p. 312). San Francisco: Jossey-Bass.

(physical, aggregate, organizational, constructed); purposes (inclusion, safety, involvement, community); and impacts (positive to negative).

Synthesis and Summary

Taking human and campus ecology theories together, it becomes clear that the person-environment interactions occurring in the micro- and mesosystem levels of Strange and Banning's (2001) environmental components lead to the achievement of varying degrees of inclusion, safety, involvement, and community. Bronfenbrenner's (1993) explicit attention to a person's developmentally instigative characteristics balances the detailed attention paid by Strange and Banning (2001) to the environmental characteristics of a campus. Ecological theories provide a sound foundation for understanding how and why individual students—even those who share similar backgrounds—experience campus environments and climates in substantially different ways. We turn now to a discussion of those experiences at a variety of institutional types.

Institutional Identities and Campus Climate

There is enormous diversity among colleges and universities in the United States. Every campus environment has a distinct identity that is based upon a number of factors, ranging from student subcultures and history to geographical location and traditions. Of these, two key factors are instrumental in understanding and experiencing campus environments: institutional identity and institutional culture. The manner in which institutions identify themselves is heavily situated in institutional type and mission. How individuals experience the campus environment has much to do with the role of culture and how it is fostered, as well as the climate that emanates through culture.

Institutional Types and Missions

Since the founding of Harvard in 1636, the number and diversity of postsecondary institutions has multiplied to include over four thousand institutions varying in governance and funding (public, private, for-profit); degree programs (certificate, associate's, undergraduate, graduate, professional); student populations; and curricula. Institutions have been categorized and categorize themselves in various ways, for example by the Carnegie Classification System; affiliation with athletic conferences (e.g., the Ivy League); and association memberships (e.g., the National Association of State Universities and Land-Grant Colleges). Yet these affiliations and classifications do not fully explain how students and others experience campus environments. We argue that institutional mission, type, and identity are critical to campus ecology and campus climate.

According to Lyons (1993), "Each college or university is unique, and that uniqueness derives from a distinctive mission" (p. 3). This mission serves as a public declaration of the institution's identity (Meacham & Gaff, 2006). Institutional missions evolve from a number of factors, including but not limited to history, tradition, heritage, geographical location, relationship to the state in which it resides, and culture (Lyons, 1993). Missions influence how university administrators facilitate the business of the campus, shape the behaviors that permeate the daily interactions on campus, and serve as philosophical and practical guides for carrying forth the goals and objectives of each college or university. Institutional missions serve as the crux of communal knowledge and respond to questions such as (1) Who are we? (2) What do we value? and (3) Where are we headed? How such questions are answered relies heavily on the institutional type and its culture.

Campus Culture and the Influence of Institutional Types

Kuh and Whitt (1988) referred to *culture* as the "invisible tapestry" of an institution. They defined it as "Persistent patterns of norms, values, practices, beliefs, and assumptions that shape the behavior of individuals and groups in a college or university and provide a frame of reference within which to interpret the meaning of events and actions on and off the campus" (p. iv).

As previously noted a host of different institutional types exist and are comprised of various characteristics that when combined exert a cultural milieu on campus that sets an institution apart from others. Culture is present in classrooms, the student union, and human interactions. In short, culture is conveyed in each level of Bronfenbrenner's (1993) ecology system and in the four components of the Strange and Banning (2001) campus design matrix. The following examples illustrate the unique cultures of four institutional types: community colleges, tribal colleges, historically Black colleges and universities, and women's colleges.

Community Colleges. Community colleges provide a disproportionate number of adult learners, women, and racially underrepresented populations with an opportunity to pursue postsecondary education (Hirt, 2006; Shuetz, 2005). They are essential points of entry to higher education for students who may not have other alternatives. For many, "The choice is not between the community college and a senior residential institution; it is between the community college and nothing" (Cohen & Brawer, 2003, p. 53). A major mission of community colleges is to create access to higher education for *anyone* who desires the opportunity. They also provide a pathway for students wishing to pursue vocational education, take remedial courses, or transfer to four-year institutions. Schuetz (2005) contended that studies of community colleges rarely account for the role the campus environment plays in student success and attrition. Attrition is particularly high among first-year community college students because many attend part-time, work full-time, support families, or may be academically underprepared. Although community colleges are "open-access" environments and live out their missions by providing access to affordable higher education for millions of students, they still face the daunting task of sharing the responsibility to ensure that students achieve their educational goals (Shuetz, 2005).

Tribal Colleges. Tribal colleges educate a majority of the Native American population in the United States. Tribal colleges' missions are similar to those of other community colleges in that they exist to serve students and the surrounding communities. However, what make tribal colleges unique are their service to reservation communities and their strong emphases on tribal cultures, customs, and ways of knowing: "Tribal colleges are different from mainstream community colleges in their cultural identities, which are reflected in virtually every aspect of college life" (American Indian Higher Education Consortium, 1999, p. B-1). Tribal colleges have missions of preserving their heritage while providing a quality education. Every aspect of these campuses—including artwork, physical structures, and the curriculum—is rooted in Native American cultures. Although they suffer from an extreme lack of resources, their presence is essential to cultural preservation, education, and economic development on reservations (Pavel, Inglebret, & VanDenHende, 1999).

Historically Black Colleges and Universities. Historically Black colleges and universities (HBCUs) have a mission of ensuring that African Americans receive access to higher education, support in their academic endeavors, and racial empowerment and uplift in settings that value African American culture, history, and identity (Gasman, Baez, & Turner, 2008). Existing literature suggests that HBCUs have a substantial impact on their students, specifically that African American students have experiences that are more positive overall at these institutions in comparison to predominantly White institutions (PWIs) (Allen, 1992; Fleming, 2001; Outcalt & Skewes-Cox, 2002; Roebuck & Murty, 1993). Whereas African American students at PWIs often experience feelings of isolation and discrimination, those attending HBCUs thrive due to opportunities to interact one-on-one with faculty and administrators (many of whom serve as mentors); engage in educationally meaningful activities; develop the academic and intellectual skills to succeed toward graduation; and remain consistently satisfied with their experiences.

Women's Colleges. Women's colleges have a well-known reputation for creating educationally rich environments that are central to empowering and supporting the unique needs of women college students. Collectively they are recognized for learning effectiveness and educational gains, especially in comparison to coeducational institutions (Kinzie, Thomas, Palmer, Umbach, & Kuh, 2007; Yates, 2001). Tidball, Smith, Tidball, and Wolf-Wendel (1999) identified two unique characteristics of women's colleges that are largely responsible for their ability to promote success: the student population they serve and their institutional missions. The presence of an all-women environment means that women's voices are heard and respected; issues important to women are unapologetically grounded in women's experiences; and students gain experience by serving in leadership roles on campus, many of which are traditionally held by men on coeducational campuses. There is also a strong press toward positive peer influence. Finally, the mission of a women's college is deeply interwoven, linking history to a current context in which the education of women remains at the core and intersects with every aspect of the campus environment.

◆ ◆ ◆

Community colleges, tribal colleges, HBCUs, and women's colleges exemplify institutional types committed to creating campus environments focused on student success. Through their missions they convey their institutional identities as distinct from those of thousands of other colleges and universities in the United States. Through their educational programs they aim to create campus climates that align with their missions and identities.

Campus Climate

We define *campus climate* as the overall ethos or atmosphere of a college campus, mediated by the extent to which individuals feel a sense of safety, belonging, engagement within the environment, and value as members of a community. Campus climate is a reflection of institutional mission and identity. Mission statements and related texts often reflect commitment to diversity and to fostering nondiscriminatory campus climates. Terms such as *diversity, multiculturalism,* and *social justice* are frequently noted among intended outcomes of a college education. Many mission statements also highlight the importance of students' being able to live and work in a diverse world (Roper, 2004). They also stress the importance of students' being able to acknowledge and celebrate diverse perspectives. Although it would seem that campus climate should reflect the institutional mission, but this is not always the case. Indeed, Hurtado (1992) suggested that colleges and universities have "embedded ideologies that work to preserve inequality" (p. 544). Therefore, despite institutional missions' emphasizing diversity, many colleges and universities are steeped in traditions, behaviors, assumptions, beliefs, and attitudes that reaffirm dominant paradigms that privilege the status quo rather than dismantle it.

Strange and Banning (2001) noted that the people who inhabit campus environments also construct those environments. What they construct is grounded in their experiences (in classrooms, residence halls, or administrative buildings), and how they construct the environment is their reality. Although the overall climate is typically contingent upon a shared construction of the environment, some populations on campus do not share these constructed meanings. Indeed, some groups and subcultures within the larger campus context, such as women and racially underrepresented populations, experience campus climates that are chilly at best, hostile at worst.

Scholars (Hall & Sandler, 1984; Pascarella et al., 1997; Sandler, 1986) have discussed the "chilly campus climate" for women. They described how collegiate settings foster an inherently sexist environment in which women's viewpoints and presence are ignored, devalued, and treated as invisible. Behaviors including sexist humor, sexual harassment, and encouragement of lower academic standards for women are a few examples that Hall and Sandler (1984) provided to illustrate the daily inequities that women face on college campuses.

A number of researchers have also examined factors that contribute to the campus racial climate and affect the sense of belonging and inclusion among students of color. For example, using a campus-climate assessment instrument, Rankin and

Reason (2005) explored perceptions of campus climate among students from different racial groups. Their findings were similar to earlier scholarship (Ancis, Sedlacek, & Mohr, 2000; Cabrera, Nora, Terenzini, Pascarella, & Hagedorn, 1999; Feagin, Vera, & Imani, 1996; Hurtado, 1992; Hurtado, Milem, Clayton-Pederson, & Allen, 1998) in that in comparison to White students, students from racially underrepresented groups perceived a more hostile racial climate, experienced more levels of harassment and racism, and believed that their institutions needed to implement more interventions to improve the climate.

Students who ascribe to a religious belief other than Christianity also perceive hostile campus climates. Most U.S. universities structure academic calendars, semester breaks, and even meal options around Christian traditions, with little attention given to those with different religious worldviews and cultures. For example, a Muslim student may not readily find a safe prayer space on campus. Similarly, a Jewish student may struggle to identify kosher meal options in the dining hall. Further, the holidays and celebrations of Muslim, Jewish, and other religious cultures are not present, due to an overwhelming press toward Christianity on college campuses in the United States. Across the human-built and organizationally designed campus environments, these students may experience the campus climate as unwelcoming and girded in Christian privilege.

Summary and Synthesis

These examples of campus climate based on gender, race, and religious tradition draw attention to the ways interactions with people; physical elements; and organizational structures (e.g., calendars and menus) on campus influence the learning and developmental ecologies of college students in all types of institutions. Other examples could be drawn from research on campus climate for lesbian, gay, bisexual, and transgender (LGBT) individuals, people with disabilities, students from working-class families, and so on. Our point here is that campus environments shape campus climate, and campus climate influences perceptions and experiences. Institutional mission and type set the stage for the complex human and human-environment interactions that make up the educational experience. Given all of these factors—student characteristics, the physical environment, individual sense making, and construction of campus climate—some of which are outside the control of a student affairs professional, how can campus ecology theories be used to influence learning and development?

Applications of Research and Theory to Student Affairs Practice

It is a complex task to combine the principles of ecology theory and the campus design matrix (Strange & Banning, 2001; see Figure 13.1) in the context of varying institutional types and identities, while also considering the developmentally instigative characteristics and experiences of individuals from a range of backgrounds. Two recent books—Hirt's *Where You Work Matters* (2006) and Manning, Kinzie, and Schuh's *One Size Does Not Fit All* (2006)—remind student affairs professionals that institutional mission, type, and size matter in designing and working within various higher education environments. They present compelling cases for why and how educators should maintain commitments to core professional principles, values, and theories in very different institutions. We share their conviction that research and theory can inform practice in any professional setting. To illustrate, we discuss and provide examples of applications of theory to practice in three domains of campus environments: the educational experience aimed at students living on campus; elements independent of campus residency (e.g faculty, facilities, and online learning contexts); and campus cultural centers.

Ecology Theory and Campus Living Environments

What would it look like to apply developmental and campus ecology principles to the design and implementation of residential campus settings? The student affairs literature is historically rich in this very concept; indeed, early student development research suggested that living on campus was nearly essential to positive outcomes of higher education. Once seen as a means to control student behavior around the clock, dormitories evolved into residence halls and residential colleges or living-learning centers designed to promote positive learning and developmental outcomes at four-year institutions and, increasingly, community colleges (Horowitz, 1987; Ryan, 1992). The mid-twentieth-century building boom on many campuses—financed in part by the influx of student veterans after World War II and in part by bonds in decades following—resulted in a large stock of campus housing comprising "double-loaded corridors" (with rooms for two or more students on either side of long hallways), shared bathrooms, and floor lounges. Reflecting student affairs philosophies of the time (see the *Student Personnel Point of View*, 1937), the efficient and egalitarian, largely charmless buildings (from an architectural standpoint, in any case) represent an approach to campus design that emphasized homogeneity and stability, places where children of the wealthy and the working class were accommodated in equal fashion. Societal and educational values of *in loco parentis* were carried out through a variety of parietal rules and house parents who enforced them (Horowitz, 1987). Roommate assignments at many institutions kept students of color separated from White students, and women and men in separate buildings (Horowitz, 1987). Thus, architecture, values, and policies based on those values shaped the daily lives of students in college dormitories. Just as surely, the environments influenced the developmental ecologies of these students.

The abandonment of *in loco parentis;* diversification of student populations; and emergence of student development theories emphasizing challenge and support (Sanford, 1960) and involvement (Astin, 1984) ushered in a new era in residential life, albeit primarily in the same double-loaded corridor buildings from the previous era of efficiency and control. Taking seriously the "Environment" (E) element of Astin's (1991) Input-Environment-Outcome (I-E-O) Model of campus experience, residence life professionals promote Strange and Banning's (2001) purposes of campus design: inclusion, safety, involvement, and community. Professional and paraprofessional staff, hall government, and other leadership opportunities contribute to the human aggregate, organizational, and constructed components of the residential environment, creating micro-, meso-, and exosystems in which student development and learning occur.

Ecology Theory Across Campus

Not every student lives in a residence hall, and not every member of the campus community is a student. Ecology theory can be applied to design and assess learning and developmental contexts across the institution. The human-built elements of a college or university are an obvious place to begin examining the environment, but organizational and psychological ecologies also are critical to understanding learning and developmental contexts.

With the rare exception of a new campus's being planned and built, student affairs professionals inherit architecture and geography that may have been designed to meet very different needs from those of a twenty-first-century institution. Accessibility for people with disabilities may be poor, parking and transportation may be constant complaints, the location of various student services may be disjointed or inconvenient, and space for new programs and services may be lacking. Yet principles of campus ecology can be applied to make the most of what is available and to work around existing challenges. For example, recognizing that environments shape human behavior (Bronfenbrenner, 1979, 1993; Moos, 1986), existing spaces can be used for new purposes that bring people together in different ways. Comfortable seating, Wi-Fi access, and a coffee kiosk in the little-used lobby of an academic building, for example, can transform a space into a satellite of the campus center, in which faculty, students, and staff share space. Well-lit, secure bus shelters transform cold, dark street corners into welcoming spots to wait for public transportation. Clearly marked, easy-to-locate recycling bins attract users and promote sustainability. Every campus has environmental limitations, but good examples of overcoming limitations and maximizing potential can be found and shared across departments and institutions. The human-built environment extends online as well. Certainly educators cannot know or control the extent of students' use of the Web, but it is important to understand that interactions in cyberspace are as much a part of student—and increasingly, faculty and staff's— learning and developmental ecologies as anything on campus (Martínez Alemán & Wartman, 2008). At a minimum student affairs professionals should attend to the design of departmental Web sites to ensure that they are attractive and useful, just as any physical space should be. Keeping in mind the Strange and Banning (2001) campus design matrix, professionals can examine Web sites through the eyes of users (students, parents, faculty, colleagues) to understand how they contribute to the four purposes of inclusion, safety, involvement, and community. Images are particularly important in online environments, and good design lowers barriers for access and involvement. To understand the contemporary student experience and environment, professionals should explore Web interfaces with which students interact—at a minimum, course software (e.g., BlackBoard, WebCT, and ANGEL); the library Web site; administrative offices' online resources (registrar, bursar, and financial aid); and social networking sites (Facebook, MySpace, and so on).

The combined physical and online environments shape student behavior, learning, and developmental opportunities. Ecology theory holds that environments select and favor some behaviors and personal characteristics over others, sustaining "ecological niches" that promote or inhibit certain kinds of development (Bronfenbrenner, 1993; Moos, 1986; Strange & Banning, 2001). Designing the environment so that every student finds a supportive ecological niche is the shared responsibility of academic and student affairs professionals.

Ecological Niches: The Example of Cultural Centers

In recent years campuses have taken steps to address issues of isolation that many marginalized students experience. In addition to sponsoring cultural events and increasing recruitment efforts, institutions have also enhanced the curriculum to include ethnic studies courses and departments to address the experiences of diverse groups through an academic lens. Among efforts to make the campus a more positive environment is the establishment of multicultural offices or culture centers. Since the student movements of the 1960s and 1970s, cultural centers have emerged with the purpose of providing welcoming environments for racially underrepresented groups, LGBT students, international students, and women.

Although their presence is strong and represents a solid effort to improve the campus environment, little research exists to examine the role of cultural centers. To date, Patton (2006a, 2006b) is one of few to conduct research on Black culture centers (BCCs). Key findings from her research indicated that although African American students still experience blatant and covert forms of racism, their involvement with the BCC helped to facilitate their adjustment to campus, provided academic resources that were not perceived to be readily available through other campus offices, served as a bridge connecting students to the campus, and provided a springboard to participation and involvement in larger campus activities and opportunities. Most important among the findings was that BCCs facilitated positive identity development, preserved Black culture, and served as "a home away from home" for African American students. These findings clearly suggest that the establishment of cultural centers on campus can serve as crucial interventions for students by promoting retention, engagement, and success.

As ecological niches, BCCs promote Strange and Banning's (2001) purposes of inclusion, safety, involvement, and community. They also create microsystems that promote learning and development more generally. Applying ecological theory to campus programming and design suggests that cultural centers are valuable elements of a comprehensive, inclusive campus environment.

Future Directions for Research and Practice

Campus ecology played a central role in approaches to student affairs administration through the 1970s and early 1980s (Banning, 1978; Banning & Kaiser, 1974) and persisted somewhat marginally until reinvigorated in the early 2000s (Renn & Arnold,

2003; Strange & Banning, 2001). In addition to the campus design and assessment uses discussed earlier in this chapter, ecology models offer valuable theoretical insight into current challenges facing student affairs administrators in an era of increasing accountability and emphasis on institutional "productivity." They remain valuable in examining educational environments for populations historically and disproportionately underrepresented among college graduates and new—or newly visible—student populations, especially as a means to understand and address persistent problems of chilly campus climate.

Accountability and Institutional Productivity

There has never been more attention from outside constituencies (government, public, parents, etc.) to higher education's accountability and institutional productivity, which in the twenty-first century is typically measured by such factors as number of degrees granted, student contributions to the workforce, and technology transfer (see Altbach, Gumport, & Johnstone, 2001). Abundant evidence (e.g., Cabrera et al., 1999; Hurtado, 1992; Hurtado et al., 1998) links campus climate to student retention and graduation rates, a key component of productivity. Strange and Banning's (2001) campus design matrix is ready-made for conducting environmental assessments, including those of campus climate and related outcomes. Before the matrix was presented, Moos (1979) advocated for ecological assessments of educational environments, and Banning and colleagues conducted several studies of campus climate as perceived by students from groups less likely to persist to graduation, for example commuter students (Banning & Hughes, 1986) and Hispanic/Latino students (Banning & Luna, 1992). Though not always stated, assumptions about campus ecology and the importance of physical, human, and organizational environments form the foundation for the area of campus climate assessment (e.g., Ancis et al., 2000; Cabrera et al., 1999; Feagin et al., 1996; Hurtado, 1992; Hurtado et al., 1998; Rankin & Reason, 2005). Ecological theory and environmental assessment have strong potential to contribute to demonstrating institutional efficacy in retaining and graduating diverse students, one measure of productivity.

Campus Climate for New—or Newly Recognized—Populations

Even without the productivity argument linking campus climate to institutional objectives, many student affairs professionals operate from a commitment to social justice that impels them to care about campus climate. Studies of campus climate based on gender, race, and sexual orientation have a modest history, as noted earlier. Campus climate for religious minorities, commuter students, international students, adult learners, students with disabilities, and online learners has been studied even less. It is not enough, however, to consider campus climate only for those categories of students already identified; ecology theory provides a lens through which to consider the developmental and learning environments for invisible populations and those who are anticipated but who may not yet have arrived on campus (possibly because they cannot yet see a place for themselves in the campus ecology). Examples of these groups include student veterans; immigrant students and other English language learners; students with autism and other communication disorders; student parents (in other words, parents of young children); and undocumented citizens. To be sure, students from all of these groups are already on campus, but little is known about how they experience campus climate and what ecological niches support their success.

Conclusion

Ecological theories provide insight into campus experiences, yet they also provide a way of organizing student affairs work and approaching student development that is expansive and flexible enough to account for ever-changing student demographics. The students experiencing a chilly climate today will, with some changes to the campus environment, find it welcoming tomorrow. But there will always be another group, previously unrecognized, encountering a chilly climate. Instead of working on only one group at a time, ecology theory provides a way to think about both the overall campus climate and the specific ecological niches experienced by students in varying circumstances. In a rapidly changing society, what works now is out-of-date in a few years, yet the underlying ecological principles of creating a welcoming, warm climate for all learners endures.

References

Allen, W. R. (1992). The color of success: African American college student outcomes at predominantly White and historically Black colleges and universities. *Harvard Educational Review, 62*(1), 26–44.

Altbach, P. G., Gumport, P. J., & Johnstone, D. B. (Eds.). (2001). *In defense of American higher education.* Baltimore: Johns Hopkins University Press.

American Indian Higher Education Consortium. (1999, February). Tribal colleges: An introduction. Retrieved July 6, 2005, from www.aihec.org/colleges.cfml.

Ancis, J. R., Sedlacek, W. E., & Mohr, J. J. (2000). Student perceptions of campus cultural climate by race. *Journal of Counseling & Development, 78,* 180–185.

Astin, A. W. (1984). Student involvement: A developmental theory for higher education. *Journal of College Student Personnel, 25,* 297–308.

Astin, A. W. (1991). *Assessment for excellence: The philosophy and practice of assessment and evaluation in higher education.* New York: American Council on Education/Macmillan Series on Higher Education.

Banning, J. H. (Ed.). (1978). *Campus ecology: A perspective for student affairs.* Washington, DC: National Association of Student Personnel Administrators. Retrieved April 22, 2008, from www.campusecologist.org/files/Monograph.pdf.

Banning, J. H., & Hughes, B. M. (1986). Designing campus environments with commuter students. *NASPA Journal, 24*(1), 17–24.

Banning, J. H., & Kaiser, L. (1974). An ecological perspective and model for campus design. *Personnel and Guidance Journal, 52,* 370–375.

Banning, J. H., & Luna, F. C. (1992). Viewing the campus ecology for messages about Hispanic/Latino culture. *Campus Ecologist, 10*(4), 1–4.

Bronfenbrenner, U. (1979). *The ecology of human development: Experiments by nature and design.* Cambridge, MA: Harvard University Press.

Bronfenbrenner, U. (1993). The ecology of cognitive development: Research models and fugitive findings. In R. H. Wozniak & K. W. Fischer (Eds.), *Development in context: Acting and thinking in specific environments* (pp. 3–44). Hillsdale, NJ: Erlbaum.

Bubolz, M. M., & Sontag, M. S. (1993). Human ecology theory. In P. Boss, W. J. Doherty, R. LaRossa, W. R. Schumm, & S. K. Steinmetz (Eds.), *Sourcebook of family theories and methods: A contextual approach* (pp. 419–447). New York: Plenum Press.

Butts, P. (1971). *The college union idea.* Stanford, CA: Association of College Unions International.

Cabrera, A. F., Nora, A., Terenzini, P. T., Pascarella, E., & Hagedorn, L. S. (1999). Campus racial climate and the adjustment of students to college: A comparison between white students and African-American students. *Journal of Higher Education, 70*(2), 134–160.

Cohen, A. M., & Brawer, F. B. (2003). *The American community college* (4th ed.). San Francisco: Jossey-Bass.

Feagin, J. R., Vera, H., & Imani, N. (1996). *Agony of education: Black students at white colleges and universities.* New York: Routledge.

Fleming, J. (2001). The impact of a historically black college on African American students: The case of LeMoyne-Owen College. *Urban Education, 36*(5), 597–610.

Gasman, M., Baez, B., & Turner, C.S.V. (2008). *Understanding minority-serving institutions.* Albany: State University of New York Press.

Hall, R., & Sandler, B. (1984). *Out of the classroom: A chilly campus climate for women?* (Project on the Status and Education of Women). Washington, DC: Association of American Colleges and Universities.

Hirt, J. B. (2006). *Where you work matters: Student affairs administrators at different types of institutions.* Lanham, MD: University Press of America.

Horowitz, H. L. (1987). *Campus life: Undergraduate cultures from the end of the eighteenth century to the present.* New York: Knopf.

Hurtado, S. (1992). The campus racial climate: Contexts of conflict. *Journal of Higher Education, 63*(5), 539–569.

Hurtado, S., Milem, J. F., Clayton-Pederson, A. R., & Allen, W. R. (1998). Enhancing campus climates for racial/ethnic diversity: Educational policy and practice. *Review of Higher Education, 21*(3), 279–302.

Kinzie, J., Thomas, A. D., Palmer, M. M., Umbach, P. D., & Kuh, G. D. (2007). Women students at coeducational and women's colleges: How do their experiences compare? *Journal of College Student Development, 48*(2), 145–165.

Kuh, G. D., & Whitt, E. J. (1988). *The invisible tapestry: Culture in American colleges and universities* (ASHE-ERIC Higher Education Report, Vol. 17, No. 1). Washington, DC: Graduate School of Education and Human Development, The George Washington University.

Lyons, J. W. (1993). The importance of institutional mission. In M. J. Barr & Associates, *The handbook of student affairs administration* (pp. 3–15). San Francisco: Jossey-Bass.

Manning, K., Kinzie, J., & Schuh, J. H. (Eds.) (2006). *One size does not fit all: Traditional and innovative models of student affairs practice.* New York: Routledge.

Martínez Alemán, A. M., & Wartman, K. L. (2008). *Online social networking on campus: Understanding what matters in student culture.* New York: Routledge.

Meacham, J., & Gaff, J. G. (2006). Learning goals in mission statements: Implications for educational leadership. *Liberal Education, 92*(1), 6–13.

Moos, R. H. (1979). *Evaluating educational environments: Procedures, measures, findings, and policy implications.* San Francisco: Jossey-Bass.

Moos, R. H. (1986). *The human context: Environmental determinants of behavior.* Malabar, FL: Krieger.

Outcalt, C. L., & Skewes-Cox, T. E. (2002). Involvement, interaction, and satisfaction: The human environment at HBCUs. *Review of Higher Education, 25*, 331–347.

Pace, C. R., & Stern, G. G. (1958). An approach to the measurement of psychological characteristics of college environments. *Journal of Educational Psychology, 49*, 269–277.

Pascarella, E. T., Whitt, E. J., Edison, M. I., Nora, A., Hagedorn, L. S., Yeager, P. M., et al. (1997). Women's perceptions of a "chilly climate" and their cognitive outcomes during the first year of college. *Journal of College Student Development, 38*, 109–124.

Patton, L. D. (2006a). Black culture centers: Still central to student learning. *About Campus, 11*(2), 2–8.

Patton, L. D. (2006b). The voice of reason: A qualitative examination of Black student perceptions of the Black culture center. *Journal of College Student Development, 47*(6), 628–646.

Pavel, D. M., Inglebret, E., & VanDenHende, M. (1999). Tribal colleges. In B. Townsend (Ed.), *Two-year colleges for women and minorities* (pp. 113–149). New York: Falmer.

Rankin, S. R., & Reason, R. D. (2005). Differing perceptions: How students of color and white students perceive campus climate for underrepresented groups. *Journal of College Student Development, 46*(1), 43–61.

Renn, K. A., & Arnold, K. D. (2003). Reconceptualizing research on peer culture. *Journal of Higher Education, 74*, 261–291.

Roebuck, J. B., & Murty, K. S. (1993). *Historically Black colleges and universities: Their place in American higher education.* Westport, CT: Praeger.

Roper, L. (2004, November/December). Do students support diversity programs? *Change, 36*(6) 48–51.

Ryan, M. B. (1992). Residential colleges: A legacy of living and learning together. *Change, 24*(5), 26–35.

Sandler, B. R. (1986). *The campus climate revisited: Chilly for women, faculty, administrators, and graduate students* (Project on the Status and Education of Women). Washington, DC: Association of American Colleges and Universities.

Sanford, N. (1960). *Self and society.* New York: Atherton Press

Schuetz, P. (2005). UCLA community college review: Campus environment: A missing link in studies of community college attrition. *Community College Review, 32*, 60–80.

Strange, C. C. (2003). Dynamics of campus environments. In S. R. Komives, D. B. Woodard Jr., & Associates (Eds.), *Student services: A handbook for the profession* (4th ed., pp. 297–316). San Francisco: Jossey-Bass.

Strange, C. C., & Banning, J. H. (2001). *Educating by design: Creating campus learning environments that work.* San Francisco: Jossey-Bass.

Student Personnel Point of View. (1937). Washington, DC: American Council on Education. Retrieved January 5, 2009, from www.bgsu.edu/colleges/library/cac/sahp/word/ THE%20STUDENT%20PERSONNEL.pdf.

Tidball, M. E., Smith, D. G., Tidball, C. S., & Wolf-Wendel, L. E. (1999). *Taking women seriously: Lessons and legacies for educating the majority.* Phoenix, AZ: Oryx.

Yates, E. L. (2001). Noteworthy news: Women's colleges receive high marks for learning effectiveness. *Black Issues in Higher Education, 17*(24), 22–23.

CHAPTER FOURTEEN

STUDENT SUCCESS

George D. Kuh

Jeannie Sue graduated near the top of her class of seventy-seven students at her small, rural high school. Three weeks into her first term at the state university, she is overwhelmed by its size and at times intimidated by other students who look and act differently than people she knew back home. Making matters worse, her roommate's boyfriend spends a lot of time in their residence hall room. Homesick every day, fall break can't come soon enough so she can tell her parents that college is not for her.

Felipe is the first in his family to go to college. After three years of taking community college classes, he is now enrolled at the university in his hometown. Still living with his grandmother, who raised him, he skipped the university's optional transfer student orientation program because his friends said it wasn't worth the time and money. Five weeks into the semester, he has not yet met with his major field advisor.

Miranda left college after her first year to get married. Now twenty-nine years old, divorced with a child, she works at least thirty hours a week while taking three courses a term. Her college experience is limited mostly to finding a place to park near campus and going to class.

On many campuses, students like Jeannie Sue, Felipe, and Miranda are becoming the norm. They represent the hundreds of thousands of undergraduates who deal with circumstances that make it difficult for them to earn a baccalaureate degree.

This chapter expands on ideas expressed in two papers published in 2007. The first is "How to Help Students Achieve," *Chronicle of Higher Education, 53*, B12–13. The second is "Success in College" in P. Lingenfelter (Ed.), *More Student Success: A Systemic Solution*. Boulder, CO: State Higher Education Executive Officers.

In this chapter, I identify some promising policy and programmatic levers that student affairs professionals can use to help foster student success. Success is defined broadly, encompassing academic achievement; engagement in educationally effective activities; satisfaction; acquisition of twenty-first-century knowledge, skills, and competencies, such as those explicated by the Association of American Colleges and Universities (2007); and persistence (Braxton, Hirschy, & McClendon, 2004; Kuh, Kinzie, Buckley, Bridges, & Hayek, 2007). The responsibility of student affairs to assist in fostering student success is consistent with the historical raison d'être of the field, albeit with different terms representing the concept of success from one era to another. Equally important, the espoused mission of student affairs on the vast majority of college campuses is to help students attain their educational and personal development goals. It is fairly easy, therefore, to say that student success is central to student affairs work. But enacting this purpose is much more challenging. In an era of heightened emphasis on accountability and transparency, it is imperative that student affairs professionals use policies, programs, and practices known to have desired effects on various dimensions of student performance.

There are limits as to how much student affairs educators and their colleagues can do to help students survive and thrive in college, and the research shows that the trajectory for academic success in college is established long before students matriculate (Kuh et al., 2007). Socioeconomic background, financial resources, academic preparation, and family encouragement substantially influence whether a person pursues and attains his or her educational objectives. For example, if a student does not perform well in the right kinds of courses in high school, including four years of English and advanced mathematics classes (such as algebra II, precalculus, and calculus), whatever student affairs staff do may at best have modest effects on this underprepared student's chances to complete a baccalaureate degree. In addition, changes in the American family structure are another factor, because more students have psychological challenges that, if unaddressed, can have a debilitating effect on their academic performance and social adjustment.

At the same time, a major factor in students benefitting in desired ways from the college experience is the degree to which they engage in educationally purposeful activities—those that are linked with desired outcomes of college, such as campus leadership positions, study abroad, and collaborative study groups (Astin, 1993; Kuh, 2001, 2003; Pascarella & Terenzini, 2005). At least on the margins, student affairs professionals can help shape the college environment to increase the likelihood that students like Jeannie Sue, Felipe, Miranda, and countless others will take part in productive activities and get the support they need when they need it (Kuh, Douglas, Lund, & Ramin-Gyurnek, 1995; Ortiz, 2004; Rendon, Jalomo, & Nora, 2000). Recent studies show that student engagement has compensatory effects, in that those who start college less advantaged tend to benefit more in terms of their grades, for example, than higher achieving students if they take part in effective educational practices (Cruce, Wolniak, Seifert, & Pascarella, 2006; Kuh, 2008; Kuh, Cruce, Shoup, Kinzie, & Gonyea, 2008; Kuh et al., 2007).

What can student affairs professionals do on their own and working with others to engage students more frequently in effective educational practices and provide the support they need when they need it to help more students succeed?

Creating Conditions That Matter to Student Success

A study of twenty colleges and universities with better-than-predicted graduation rates and scores on the National Survey of Student Engagement (NSSE) revealed that the factors and conditions that matter to student success are many and varied (Kuh, Kinzie, Schuh, Whitt, & Associates, 2005). Among the properties common to these high-performing institutions are a collaborative ethos and highly competent student affairs staff who are exceptional at their jobs and share operating philosophies that are congruent with their institutions' missions. In this section I discuss seven sets of activities that student affairs educators can emphasize to foster higher levels of student success. To varying degrees, all of these activities have been positively associated with different dimensions of student success.

1. Feature Student Success in the Division of Student Affairs Mission and as an Institutional Priority

To focus student affairs staff's time and energy on building the programs and practices that matter to student success, the senior student affairs officer must periodically affirm a clear, persuasive case for the importance of high-quality out-of-class experiences and articulate a compelling vision of how the daily work of student affairs contributes to student success and the institution's educational mission. Staying focused on key objectives demands that people periodically reflect on what they are trying to achieve (Senge, 1999). For example, annual public reporting of progress made on student affairs priorities, such as increased numbers of students participating in such high-impact activities as internships and study abroad, serves as a concrete reminder to student affairs professionals and others on campus about how they should be spending their time.

In addition, the senior student affairs officer and division leaders must regularly champion student success throughout the institution, reminding the campus community through annual reports about the quality of campus life; convocations; and other venues, including newsletters and events that recognize and celebrate the outstanding work by members of the division and other colleagues in the service of students and their success. Another tactic for making student success a priority is to select an annual theme for an academic year around which such events can be organized.

2. Teach New Students How to Make Good Use of Institutional Resources

Student affairs has three nonnegotiable obligations to new students. New students are those attending college for the first-time (like Jeannie Sue), those returning after stopping out for more than a year (like Miranda), and those transferring from another institution (like Felipe). Although most colleges and universities have designed programs and services with first-time, first-year students in mind, too many have done too little to effectively address the circumstances of such students as Felipe and Miranda.

The first obligation is to establish and hold students to high performance expectations outside the classroom that are consistent with students' backgrounds, abilities, and aspirations (Kuh, Schuh, Whitt, & Associates, 1991). The vast majority of students benefit more from the college experience when they are asked to put forth more effort than they would ordinarily expend. To do this, student affairs staff must first understand who their students are, what they are prepared to do academically and capable of interpersonally, and what they expect of the institution and themselves, and then share this information widely with faculty and others who work with students, such as custodians, campus security, academic advisors, and others. This requires having accurate, reliable information about student backgrounds and expectations for college, which can be generated using one or more assessment tools discussed in Chapter Eighteen, as well as information routinely provided to the institution in the form of ACT or SAT score reports. Score reports include information about students' previous educational experiences and biographical data that they provide when registering to take a college entrance examination. Unfortunately, most colleges and universities discard these treasure troves of insight into the matriculating class, which the testing firms have delivered at no cost to the institution!

The second obligation is to establish policies and practices that induce or in some instances require students to participate in activities associated with various dimensions of student success. Most institutions offer a blend of summer orientation or advising sessions and a fall welcome week. In general, the evidence suggests that students who attend these events get better grades and graduate at higher rates than their peers (Pascarella & Terenzini, 2005). For this reason, some institutions have made mandatory first-time students' participation in these anticipatory socialization activities. However, few colleges and universities require transfer students like Felipe to attend orientation events designed specifically for them or to meet with an advisor before they are allowed to take classes. There are multiple reasons for this. Many transfer students are reluctant to do things they believe they have already done or will not benefit from, especially when they must pay a fee to do so and perhaps miss work to boot. At the same time, permitting transfer students to opt out of such activities does not breed success, given that, on balance, they are less engaged after they enroll at the transfer institution than students who started their baccalaureate studies at the same campus. A major issue that must be addressed is that transfer orientation and advising programs too closely parallel those designed for first-time, first-year students, often reflecting the interests and preferences of the student affairs staff responsible for the programs and not the needs of transfers. For example, much of the information that transfer students need to make orderly, efficient, and smooth transitions to their new institutions can be delivered more effectively through the Web, such as by using the program developed by Temple University (www.temple.edu/orientation/transfers/transfer_students.html). Most transfer students are, however, willing to meet with an academic advisor (London & Shaw, 1996). Perhaps those aspects of orientation that require students to come to the campus, such as obtaining ID cards and parking permits, can be handled as part of a required academic advising session. Another step that student affairs can take is to establish remote advising centers at nearby colleges from which large numbers of students transfer, similar to what the University of Houston Main Campus is doing as part of its Achieving the Dream initiative to increase the number of transfer students who complete a baccalaureate degree.

If an institution wants to improve first-generation student success rates, it should also create ways to make it possible for more—ideally all—of those students to live on campus, at least for the first year (Pike & Kuh, 2005). Granted, students living on campus represent only about 15 percent of all undergraduates (U. S. Census, 2003). Yet the fact remains that students who live on campus are more engaged and gain more from their college experiences. They have easier access to faculty, staff, and peers, and they are more likely to take advantage of the institution's cultural and artistic venues. They also have more experiences with diversity. Requiring first-year students to live on campus will also necessitate making more financial assistance available to low-income students. Work-study or co-op living units could be created to offset cost differences between living on and off campus or at home. Of course, for returning students with families and full-time jobs like Miranda, this is not an option. In those instances, innovative approaches are needed that attract nontraditional students and their families to spend time on the campus.

Although living in a campus residence is generally associated with higher levels of student engagement relative to those who live off campus, it does not guarantee that any individual student will take advantage of academic support services, participate in co-curricular activities, interact with faculty members or friends on meaningful levels, or take part in other educationally purposeful activities. And in Jeannie Sue's case, it does not guarantee a high-quality living environment.

This brings us to the third obligation of student affairs—providing intrusive, success-oriented advice and feedback to steer students toward activities that will enrich their college experiences and increase the odds that they will persist in and benefit in the desired ways from college. The residence life staff in Jeannie Sue's residence hall should be aware of the difficulties she has adjusting to the campus, which are exacerbated by the third person who spends so much time in her room. Student affairs staff should become proficient with success-oriented "intrusive advising," such as George Mason University's academic advising office which contacts students with low grades who have not declared a major and Ursinus College where a residence life staff member or faculty advisor will meet with students who seem to be struggling academically or socially (Kuh, Kinzie, Schuh, Whitt, & Associates, 2005). Many other new students—especially those from historically underserved groups—do not fully understand and appreciate their roles as learners and are not aware of some of the most developmentally powerful, rewarding opportunities available to them. For example, fewer first-generation students like Felipe and students of color take part in high-impact activities compared with their counterparts (Kuh, 2008). Students who study abroad, conduct an independent inquiry project or work with a faculty member on research, or complete a senior culminating experience are more engaged across the board in various effective educational practices; these students also report gaining more from their college experiences. Members of athletic teams, choirs and bands, and fraternities and sororities tend to graduate at higher rates, in part because the momentum of the group carries them forward, buoying them during difficult times. They also derive personal satisfaction from being part of something larger than themselves. When students are responsible for tasks that require daily decisions over an extended period, they become invested in the activities, which deepens their commitment to the college and their studies. This is in part why working on campus, writing for the student newspaper, or completing a career-launching internship can be every bit the life changing experience for students as having studied abroad. Student affairs staff should work with their colleagues in academic affairs to make sure that all students, their socioeconomic and other background characteristics notwithstanding, have an equal opportunity to have such experiences.

3. If a Program or Practice Works, Make It Widely Available

Most institutions offer every high-impact practice mentioned above and others (Kuh, 2008). But at many colleges and universities they are in the form of small, boutique-like programs involving only small fractions of undergraduates. Student affairs professionals must champion efforts to scale up the numbers of students who take advantage of these and other demonstrably effective practices, such as discipline-based first-year seminars that are team taught by tenure-stream faculty and upper-division peer preceptors, supplemental instruction, and placement testing to ensure that students enroll in courses for which they are prepared. One increasingly common activity proven to be effective for students like Jeannie Sue is participating in a learning community. For example, first-year students in residence-based learning communities at the University of Missouri at Columbia live in the same building and take the same three core courses and an additional class focused on skills needed to succeed in college, giving them common ground both in and out of the classroom. NSSE results show that students who live in learning communities tend to interact more with their professors and diverse peers, study more, and excel at synthesizing material and analyzing problems (Zhao & Kuh, 2004). They also report gaining more from their college experiences. Moreover, the "engagement advantage" for students in learning communities lasts through senior year, suggesting that this experience—which most students have in their first college year—positively affects what they do later in college. Engstrom and Tinto (Engstrom & Tinto, 2008; Tinto & Engstrom, 2008) and researchers at the Washington Center for Improving the Quality of Undergraduate Education at Evergreen State College have found that nonresidential learning communities generally have similar conditional, salutary effects for community college students like Felipe.

It sounds heretical in an era of seemingly endless curricular options and college-attendance patterns, but if a program or learning experience has positive effects for students who engage in them, why not expect all students to participate in such an activity or something that has similarly positive effects? Left to their own devices, students (and student affairs staff, too!) do not always choose wisely, as Twigg (2005), president and CEO of the National Center for Academic Transformation, discovered in her successful experiments with technology-enriched course redesigns. She concluded that even though this generation of students is tech savvy, first-year students "don't do optional"—even when it is in their interest to do so. It therefore behooves student affairs staff committed to student success to scale up opportunities to participate in high-impact practices and find ways to induce students to do them. In many instances, this might best be done through collaborating with academic affairs, as is the case with many of the examples of effective programs discussed throughout this chapter.

4. Establish and Monitor Early-Warning Systems and Safety Nets to Support Students When They Need Help

Three-fifths of students in public two-year colleges and one-quarter of students in four-year institutions must complete at least one remedial course (Kuh et al., 2007). No wonder nine out of every ten students starting college say they intend to use an academic-assistance or learning-skills center (National Survey of Student Engagement [NSSE], 2006). But by the end of the first year, only about half as many have done so (NSSE, 2006). Because socialization to academic norms is not complete at the end of the first year of college, especially for first-generation college students like Felipe and for others like Miranda who lack tacit knowledge about what is required to succeed at the university or whose goals and aspirations are not yet clear, additional interventions may be needed for certain groups so that these students continue to engage in the kinds of activities associated with success in college.

Student affairs staff should take the lead in making sure that campus early-warning systems and safety nets are adequate to respond to students who are likely to struggle, that they are working as intended, and that students are using them. This is easier in some ways for residence life staff to do, because they are in the company of resident students many hours a week which means they should have firsthand knowledge of whether students are doing the things that will pay off, or wasting time. At some colleges, success-oriented interventions are sewn into structures to support first-year students, such as "tag teams" assigned to first-year seminars or learning communities that are composed of a combination of student affairs staff, faculty members, peer mentors, advisors, librarians, and other staff. Student affairs staff also can partner with the registrar and academic advisors to monitor class-attendance patterns, drop-add information, early semester and midterm grades, and preregistration information to identify and intervene with students who are experiencing academic difficulties. For example, instructors in Fayetteville State University's Early Alert program contact first-year student mentors to alert them about any students experiencing difficulty during the first two weeks of the semester. At Wheaton College in Massachusetts, a first-year student's advising team is made up of a faculty member, a student preceptor, and an administrative advisor, usually a student life staff member or librarian

(Kuh, Kinzie, Schuh, Whitt, & Associates, 2005). Mentors contact students to advise and refer as appropriate. Some educational consulting firms, such as EducationDynamics (www.educationdynamics.com), have developed attractive, Web-based platforms that institutions can use to stay in touch with students like Miranda who, because of their multiple obligations and prior collegiate experiences, may be at risk. These technology-based strategies periodically prompt students to talk with an advisor or use student skills centers.

The success-oriented student affairs division also recognizes that in addition to working with academic affairs, a partnership with a student's family is needed for an early-warning system to be effective. Students who are considering leaving school, like Jeannie Sue, will likely first mention this prospect with a family member. Many parents and other family members—especially those whose students are the first in their families to go to college—often lack the knowledge about campus resources that their student could use to resolve problems. While most institutions offer parent orientation programs, they have many of the same limitations as those designed for students. So much information is presented at one time that it is difficult to absorb or remember it all. Many parents, like their students, do not know where to turn when challenging circumstances arise. Some institutions are experimenting with ongoing parent communication networks, some of which are built on locally developed, Web-based platforms or those provided by educational consulting firms. While the efficacy of these approaches have not yet been determined, they promise to provide an inter-active medium through which institutions can stay in touch with students and remind them about resources, such as supplemental instruction and learning-skills centers, available to help them manage key transition points and contend with academic challenges.

5. Help Faculty Create a Sense of Community in the Classroom

Students learn more and more deeply when their experiences inside and outside the classroom are complementary and mutually reinforcing (Kuh et al., 1991; Kuh, Kinzie, Schuh, Whitt, Associates, 2005; Pascarella & Terenzini, 2005). Decades ago, when most undergraduates lived near their classmates and teachers, propinquity and serendipity established the social order and worked together to instill shared values and understandings. Today, the majority of students are like Miranda; they commute to school and work many hours a week. As a result, they spend a limited amount of time on campus, and have less contact with faculty members (NSSE, 2006).

For commuter students and transfer students like Felipe who comprise the growing majority of undergraduates, the classroom is the only venue where they regularly have face-to-face contact with their peers as well as their teachers. For these students, the classroom is also the place where they will hear about how the institution works and where they will learn most of what they know about campus culture. That makes a classroom instructor's job much more complicated. In addition to having substantive expertise in the discipline and using effective pedagogical approaches, he or she must also cultivate an atmosphere in which a group of strangers will listen attentively to others with respect and challenge and support one another to attain previously unimagined levels of academic performance (Kuh et al., 2007; Tinto, 1997).

Faculty members should not have to create such classroom learning environments alone. Student affairs professionals in partnership with faculty and others staff familiar with culture-building strategies can work together to fashion a rich, engaging classroom experience that complements the institution's academic values and students' preferred learning styles. At Indiana University-Purdue University at Indianapolis (IUPUI), for example, student affairs professionals, librarians, and other staff familiar with effective approaches to community-building work with professors to design a rich, engaging classroom experience that complements the institution's academic values and students' preferred learning styles. They emphasize active learning approaches such as group projects that sometimes take students off campus, which work well with students who prefer concrete, hands-on learning activities (Kuh, Kinzie, Schuh, Whitt, & Associates, 2005). Through this team approach, an institution can more effectively teach institutional values and traditions and inform students about campus events, procedures, and deadlines, such as registration and financial aid applications. And when instructional teams made up of faculty members and student affairs staff use cooperative learning activities to bring students together after class to work on meaningful tasks, students develop friendships built upon common intellectual experiences, making them more comfortable in the learning environment and further strengthening their commitment to attaining their educational and personal goals.

6. Focus Assessment and Improvement Efforts on What Matters to Student Success

One of the most powerful levers for institutional improvement is the use of credible data that tell an accurate, comprehensive story of students' educational experiences. The ability to prompt significant institutional change to increase student success will be severely limited unless student affairs has adequate data systems to evaluate its performance and the experiences of students with different characteristics and backgrounds, such as race/ethnicity, gender, SES, first-generation status, and transfer status. Deciding what to measure is critical, because whatever student affairs chooses to assess is what the division of student affairs will end up reporting and perhaps even devoting resources to. Along with student engagement data, other commonly used indicators of success to which student affairs should attend include student retention and graduation rates, transfer student success, student satisfaction, students' personal and professional development, and citizenship. Another critical step is making sure the programs that research shows to be potentially high impact (Kuh, 2008) actually are having the desired effects. One of the reasons so many of the college impact studies show equivocal or mixed findings is that the program or practice being evaluated was not implemented effectively.

At high-performing colleges and universities, student affairs staff periodically collect and review data about the effectiveness of policies and practices, with an eye toward ensuring that what is enacted is of acceptable quality and consistent with their institutions' espoused priorities and values (Kuh, Kinzie, Schuh, Whitt, & Associates, 2005). Such examinations are sometimes triggered by self-studies done to prepare for regional accreditation reviews. Others may be prompted by institutional strategic priorities. For example, the University of Michigan conducted six major studies between the mid-1980s and 2000 to monitor the impact of initiatives intended to improve the quality of the undergraduate experience (Kuh, Kinzie, Schuh, Whitt, & Associates).

Many campus personnel know a good deal about their first-year students and graduating seniors, those students who are highly involved in leadership positions, and those who struggle academically and socially. Not enough is known about the all-but-invisible majority with whom most student affairs staff have little or no contact students like Felipe and Miranda. Many of these students, including some who are only a semester or two away from fulfilling graduation requirements, leave college without completing their degrees. The students at greatest risk of leaving college sometime after the second year are almost identical in terms of demographic characteristics to those who leave prior to that point. It is essential that student affairs extend its data collection to the experiences of students that span all the years of baccalaureate study. As mentioned earlier, one promising approach are the Web-based templates that allow student affairs staff to send electronic prompts to students; these encourage students to take advantage and report on their use of institutional resources.

7. Reculture the Student Affairs Division

Virtually every study of high-performing organizations points to culture as a major factor in their success (Collins, 2001; Kuh, Kinzie, Schuh, Whitt, & Associates, 2005; Kuh & Whitt, 1988; Tierney, 1999). Culture is the tie that binds, the "invisible tapestry" (Kuh & Whitt) that connects and gives meaning to activities and events. Norms, values, and tacit assumptions and beliefs about students work together to provide a purpose and direction for community members and their activities and highlight institutional priorities. Thus, as with so many aspects of institutional effectiveness, the whole of the cultural properties that comprise and contribute to student success is greater than the sum of the parts.

One roadblock to student engagement and success, which is woven into the culture on scores of campuses, including small colleges, is what students call "the runaround." Variations abound, but the basic storyline is that no matter where students turn, they cannot get the information or help they need, whether from residence life administrators, financial aids, the registrar, or others. That such conditions exist today is unconscionable and stands in stark contrast to colleges marked by a sense of positive restlessness, in which people constantly are asking how they can improve what they do, and administrators regularly evaluate campus priorities, policies, and programs. Asking questions like What are we doing? and Why are we doing it this way? helps people determine not only whether established practices are still relevant to the changing needs and interests of students and evolving institutional conditions but also why and how proposed interventions would address student and institutional needs.

Reculturing a student affairs division to focus on student success is challenging, time consuming, and labor intensive. In addition, even high-performing student affairs units in which student success is an espoused and often enacted value (Kuh et al., 2005) can have contested terrain: contradictions, inconsistencies, and diverse and sometimes competing perspectives may exist concerning the division's priorities and aspirations. Such differences in views and values should not necessarily be viewed as shortcomings or as evidence of a dysfunctional culture (Kuh et al., 1991; Martin, 2002). The objective is to make student success central to the student affairs mission and to emphasize assumptions and beliefs that are congenial to this purpose. It is also essential to have in place reward systems and staff hiring and professional development practices that encourage and support staff whose contributions are demonstrably effective in promoting student success.

One way to identify aspects of the student affairs culture that may need attention is to conduct an audit that focuses on, among other things, artifacts such as traditions, stories, ceremonies, language, norms, values, and widely held beliefs about, for example, what kinds of students receive attention and resources and which do not, and the importance of certain goals, activities, and relationships (Kuh & Whitt, 1988). Central to such an undertaking is systematically answering diagnostic queries, including the following:

- To what extent is the culture of the student affairs division clearly focused on student success?
- Does the student affairs culture enhance or hinder student success?
- In what ways are the artifacts, values, and beliefs of the student affairs culture consistent with or contradictory to the educational goals of the institution and student success?
- Are there elements of the culture that need to be modified to promote a deeper sense of positive restlessness, experimentation with promising approaches, or more consistent use of effective educational practices? How might this be done?

The *Inventory for Student Engagement and Success* is a self-study guide for both assessing the extent to which campus cultures support student success and identifying policies and practices that need attention to encourage more students to survive and thrive in college (Kuh, Kinzie, Schuh, & Whitt, 2005). This approach can be adapted to audit the culture of a student affairs division.

Conclusion

We know many of the factors that facilitate and inhibit earning a bachelor's degree. And we also know a good deal about some interventions that promise to increase this number if they are implemented effectively and touch large numbers of students in meaningful ways. Certainly we need to learn more, especially about the conditional effects of student affairs programs and practices, including which interventions benefit students with certain characteristics more than others.

There are limits to what student affairs staff can do to foster student success. Student success will look different and mean different things for different types of students. Putting in place all the programs and practices outlined in this chapter will not in every case make up for students' prior inadequate academic preparation. In addition, many long-held beliefs and standard operating practices are tightly woven into the student affairs culture and embedded in the psyche of senior administrators and others, some of which may be counterproductive. Even so, student affairs in partnership with academic affairs, can do better for the likes of Jeannie Sue, Felipe, and Miranda by making it possible for them to take part in purposeful, high-impact activities that enhance their learning and personal development. The real question is whether we have the will to do so.

References

Association of American Colleges and Universities. (2007). *College learning for the new global century*. Washington, DC: Author.

Astin, A. W. (1993). *What matters in college? Four critical years revisited*. San Francisco: Jossey-Bass.

Braxton, J. M., Hirschy, A. S., & McClendon, S. A. (2004). *Understanding and reducing college student departure* (ASHE-ERIC Higher Education Report, Vol. 30, No. 3). Washington, DC: Graduate School of Education and Human Development, The George Washington University.

Collins, J. C. (2001). *Good to great: Why some companies make the leap—and others don't*. New York: Harper Business.

Cruce, T., Wolniak, G. C., Seifert, T. A., & Pascarella, E. T. (2006). Impacts of good practices on cognitive development, learning orientations, and graduate degree plans during the first year of college. *Journal of College Student Development, 47*, 365–383.

Engstrom, C., & Tinto, V. (2008). Access without support is not opportunity. *Change, 40*, 46–51.

Kuh, G. D. (2001). Assessing what really matters to student learning: Inside the national survey of student engagement. *Change, 33*(3), 10–17.

Kuh, G. D. (2003). What we're learning about student engagement from NSSE: Benchmarks for effective educational practices. *Change, 35*(2), 24–32.

Kuh, G. D. (2007). How to help students achieve. *Chronicle of Higher Education, 53*(41), B12–13.

Kuh, G. D. (2007). Success in college. In P. Lingenfelter (Ed.), *More student success: A systemic solution* (pp. 95–107). Boulder, CO: State Higher Education Executive Officers.

Kuh, G. D. (2008). *High-impact educational practices: What they are, who has access to them, and why they matter*. Washington, DC: Association of American Colleges and Universities.

Kuh, G. D., Cruce, T. M., Shoup, R., Kinzie, J., & Gonyea, R. M. (2008). Unmasking the effects of student engagement on college grades and persistence. *Journal of Higher Education, 79*, 540–563.

Kuh, G. D., Douglas, K. B., Lund, J. P., & Ramin-Gyurnek, J. (1995). *Student learning outside the classroom: Transcending artificial boundaries* (ASHE-ERIC Higher Education Report No. 8). Washington, DC: Graduate School of Education and Human Development, The George Washington University.

Kuh, G. D., Kinzie, J., Buckley, J., Bridges, B., & Hayek, J. C. (2007). *Piecing together the student success puzzle: Research, propositions, and recommendations* (ASHE Higher Education Report, Vol. 32, No. 5). San Francisco: Jossey-Bass.

Kuh, G. D., Kinzie, J., Schuh, J. H., & Whitt, E. J. (2005). *Assessing conditions to enhance educational effectiveness: The inventory for student engagement and success*. San Francisco: Jossey-Bass.

Kuh, G. D., Kinzie, J., Schuh, J. H., Whitt, E. J., & Associates (2005). *Student success in college: Creating conditions that matter*. San Francisco: Jossey-Bass.

Kuh, G. D., Schuh, J. H., Whitt, E. J., & Associates. (1991). *Involving colleges: Successful approaches to fostering student learning and development outside the classroom*. San Francisco: Jossey-Bass.

Kuh, G. D., & Whitt, E. J. (1988). *The invisible tapestry: Culture in American colleges and universities* (ASHE-ERIC Higher Education Report No. 1. Washington, DC: Graduate School of Education and Human Development, The George Washington University.

London, H. B., & Shaw, K. M. (1996). Enlarging the transfer paradigm: Practice and culture in the American community college. *Metropolitan Universities: An International Forum, 7*(2), 7–14.

Martin, J. (2002). *Organizational culture: Mapping the terrain*. Thousand Oaks, CA: Sage.

National Survey of Student Engagement (NSSE). (2006). *Engaged learning: Fostering success of all students*. Bloomington: Indiana University Center for Postsecondary Research.

Ortiz, A. M. (2004). Promoting the success of Latino students: A call to action. In A. M. Ortiz (Ed.), *Addressing the unique needs of Latino American students* (New Directions for Student Services No. 105, pp. 89–97). San Francisco: Jossey-Bass.

Pascarella, E. T., & Terenzini, P. T. (2005). *How college affects students: A third decade of research*. San Francisco: Jossey-Bass.

Pike, G. R., & Kuh, G. D. (2005). First- and second-generation college students: A comparison of their engagement and intellectual development. *Journal of Higher Education, 76(3)*, 276–300.

Rendon, L. I., Jalomo, R. E., & Nora, A. (2000). Theoretical consideration in the study of minority student retention in higher education. In J. M. Braxton (Ed.), *Rethinking the departure puzzle: New theory and research on college student retention* (pp. 127–156). Nashville, TN: Vanderbilt University Press.

Senge, P. M. (1999). *The dance of change: The challenges of sustaining momentum in learning organizations*. New York: Currency/Doubleday.

Tierney, W. G. (1999). *Building the responsive campus: Creating high performance colleges and universities*. Thousand Oaks, CA: Sage.

Tinto, V. (1997). Classrooms as communities: Exploring the educational character of student persistence. *Journal of Higher Education, 68*, 599–623.

Tinto, V., & Engstrom, C. (2008). Learning better together: The impact of learning communities on the persistence of low-income students. *Opportunity Matters, 1*, 5–21.

Twigg, C. A. (2005, July). *Improving learning and reducing costs: New models for online learning*. Keynote address at the annual meeting of the Association for Learning Technology, Manchester, England.

U. S. Census (2003). *Population in Group Quarters by Type, Sex and Age, for the United States: 2000*. Table 1. Population in Group Quarters by Type, Sex and Age, for the United States. Retrieved from http://www.census.gov/population/cen2000/phC-t26/tab01.pdf.

Zhao, C. -M., & Kuh, G. D. (2004). Adding value: Learning communities and student engagement. *Research in Higher Education, 45(2)*, 115–138.

PART FOUR

ORGANIZING AND MANAGING PROGRAMS AND SERVICES

Our experience has been that few people decide to enter the student affairs profession because they want to engage in long-range planning, craft organizational charts, mull over spreadsheets, or assess programs and student experiences. Yet these activities and functions are necessary to ensure that the division of student affairs can sufficiently provide student programs, experiences, services, and so on.

A volume such as this would be incomplete without a treatment of the administrative and managerial responsibilities of student affairs professionals. Accordingly, we have identified four chapters that are central to providing an administrative foundation for student affairs practice. These address how student affairs is organized, how plans are developed, how student affairs is financed, and how student affairs is assessed.

How student affairs is organized will depend to a great deal on institutional mission and philosophy. There is no best way to organize a division of student affairs. What is important, however, is that the organization

be crafted so that student affairs professionals are able to do their work in ways that are aligned with what the institution espouses about the student experience.

Student affairs typically develops its strategic plan to align with that of the larger institution. The plan serves as a roadmap for the division and also as a means by which decisions can be made related to adding or deleting programs and services. A typical element of a strategic plan is the mission statement, and, as is the case with the overall plan, the mission statement of the student affairs division needs to be aligned with that of the larger institution.

The economic circumstances that affect virtually all of higher education mean that financial resources are spent wisely. Just as important, as the cost of attendance has exceeded common measures of inflation, institutions and their various units, including student affairs, have had to justify increases in tuition, student fees, and fees for services.

The emphasis on the managerial dimension of student affairs practice has increased over the years, particularly with the growing emphasis on assessment that higher education has experienced. Stakeholders have expected that institutions of higher education demonstrate the potency of learning experiences, and student affairs professionals must develop assessment components for the areas of student learning for which they are responsible. Mere claims about the efficacy of student experiences will not suffice. Empirical data are necessary. In Chapter Fifteen, Kathleen Manning and Frank Michael Muñoz explore how student affairs might be organized. They use the six cultures of the academy as developed by Bergquist and Pawlak (2008), which include collegial, managerial, developmental, advocacy, virtual, and tangible cultures. Managerial and administrative practices accompany each of the cultures, and vignettes are provided for each one of the cultures of the academy. The authors assert that staff members will "fit" best in cultures with which they are most comfortable.

Shaun Harper explores strategy and intentionality in student affairs practice in Chapter Sixteen. His approach, for which he presents three case examples, focuses on how to be thoughtful, systematic, and intentional in educational practice. In Chapter Seventeen, John Schuh examines financing student affairs. The costs of higher education have risen rapidly in recent years, but if one takes the long view, the amount of money that higher education institutions have spent on students has been greater than the consumer price index for more than eighty years, with just a few exceptions. Nevertheless, past is not necessarily prologue, and institutions of higher education are under increasing pressure to control costs. This chapter looks at the sources of revenue

and the categories of expenditures for student affairs It concludes with a discussion of various approaches that institutions use in the budgeting process.

Marilee Bresciani discusses assessment and evaluation in Chapter Eighteen. These activities are central to the accountability movement in student affairs and, while they might have been seen at one time as useful activities but not necessary, they are crucial to the long-term viability of student affairs. Senior administrators have more options than ever in contemporary higher education, and they might choose to reassign functions to academic affairs, or they might choose to outsource them to private concerns. Perhaps the most important assessment activity is measuring outcomes, because outcomes are so important to the student learning experience. In the chapter outcomes-based assessment is explored in detail and a step-by-step approach is provided. It also includes a number of questions to address in implementing outcomes-based assessment.

Although the topics included in Part Four are not typically the focus of the practice of entry-level student affairs professionals (or perhaps not even of those in their second professional positions), those who aspire to more senior positions undoubtedly will have to address and master the issues presented throughout. Having at least a rudimentary understanding of the information presented here is very much a part of being a student affairs professional.

Reference

Bergquist, W. H., & Pawlak, K. (2008). *Engaging the six cultures of the academy*. San Francisco: Jossey-Bass.

CHAPTER FIFTEEN

FRAMING STUDENT AFFAIRS PRACTICE

Kathleen Manning and Frank Michael Muñoz

With education as the vision for their work, student affairs professionals must rely on a wealth of theories and concepts to guide their practice with students. Those who work in student affairs are educators who use a range of approaches, including programming, advising, environmental management, administration, and policymaking, to achieve educational goals. An interdisciplinary field, student affairs relies on human development and counseling theory from psychology, knowledge of cultures from anthropology, management and administrative theory from business, group behavior theory from sociology, ways of knowing from philosophy, and knowledge of past events from history (Manning, 1993).

In this chapter, we use Bergquist and Pawlak's (2008) six cultures of the academy (collegial, managerial, developmental, advocacy, virtual, and tangible) as a framework through which to discuss potential ways to think about student affairs practice. We illustrate each of these cultures with vignettes that help the reader link organizational theory and student affairs practice within a higher education context. As will be discussed in this chapter, each culture includes a set of accompanying management and administrative practices. We encourage you, in your work as a student affairs professional, to consider two frames: the cultural frame that best defines your work environment and that in which you are most comfortable working. If these two cultures are similar, you will feel that you "fit"; if they conflict, you will struggle to understand and be successful in your environment.

Collegial Culture

Lilliana, the new director of student activities, works in a university with a collegial culture. Because she graduated from an institution with similar values, she knows what to expect at the upcoming club advisor training. Because her invitation for involvement would most likely go unnoticed by faculty, she asked the provost to send out the notice she composed. She knew that faculty often travel for their research over semester breaks, so she planned the training for October, which she assumed would be a convenient time for them. Because the institution has several very active and successful academically oriented clubs, she invited the advisors from those groups to help her plan the training. These faculty determined what values they felt should be communicated. In turn, Lilliana introduced the participating faculty to theories of student engagement and success espoused by student affairs.

Origins of the Collegial Culture

The purpose of higher education, from the collegial culture perspective, is the generation, interpretation, and dissemination of knowledge. In colleges and universities adhering to the collegial model, nothing is more important than high-quality research, scholarship, and teaching. Collegial culture in the United States originated in the English Oxbridge (i.e., Oxford and Cambridge Universities) system (Bergquist & Pawlak, 2008) of housing students on campus in residence halls. Though perhaps odd to those of us accustomed to residence life systems, prior to this Oxbridge innovation, students lived off campus in nearby city or town residences. Intellectual and personal pursuits were separate; the institution took no responsibility for out-of-classroom life. Prior to the Oxbridge model, only the student's "life of the mind" was of interest to faculty and administrators. With the invention of residence halls, higher education embraced the purpose of fostering character, social, emotional, and moral development.

The thirteenth-century Oxbridge model of "newly invented" quadrangles, campus greens, and residence hall communities were the crux of the "whole student" philosophy of the student affairs field (American Council on Education, 1937, 1949). "In the 13th century, rioting between town and gown (townspeople and students) hastened the establishment of primitive halls of residence. These were succeeded by the first of Oxford's colleges, which began as medieval 'halls of residence' or endowed houses under the supervision of a Master. University, Balliol and Merton Colleges, which were established between 1249 and 1264, are the oldest" (Oxford, 2010). Current day living-learning centers, learning communities, and residence hall programs dotting colleges and universities originated in Oxford and Cambridge. Important sites for mentoring, counseling, and advising, these original residence halls were the precursors of our current system.

Characteristics of the Collegial Culture

When today's student affairs professionals use the collegial culture perspective to guide their work, they envision a higher education environment steeped in old-fashioned, traditional values. Meaning about university life (e.g., management assumptions, distribution of authority, how student life is viewed) originates in the academic disciplines, particularly more "traditional" areas, such as philosophy, history, physics, and other high-status subjects.

In the collegial culture, research and scholarship are valued, particularly by faculty who prize expert knowledge over administrative rank and authority. Shared governance, as represented by boards of trustees, faculty senates, student government, and staff councils, is an important part of participatory decision and policy making. Furthermore, consensus building, particularly with faculty, is essential.

Management Styles and Structural Considerations

The dominant organizational structure within the collegial culture is the *collegium* (Birnbaum, 1991). One can think of this type of organizational configuration as a circle (vastly different from the traditional pyramid structure of a bureaucracy). Collegia commonly exist among faculty, but administrators in institutions with collegial cultures also embody collegial characteristics. All are involved in and value the community of scholars. Leaders, including the college president, are "first among equals."

Because collegial culture proponents look to the past for their models of organizational functioning, administration is expected to be established and routine. Strategic planning, rational decision making, and tried-and-true management systems are valued. Innovation, risk taking, and new approaches to administrative and academic practice are discouraged. Emulating the specialization of the academic disciplines, student affairs departments and professional areas are divided into their respective areas of expertise.

The primacy of the disciplines, importance of faculty consultation, and role of history must be considered as one makes an argument for change. When student affairs professionals approach the faculty to gain approval for a policy change, they must do so with an understanding of the collegial culture. If not, the initiative will certainly fail.

Roles in the Collegial Culture

Students, according to the collegial culture frame, are burgeoning scholars who are part of a long tradition. Reading and writing are paramount; lecturing is common. Respect for faculty, academic tradition, and institutional history are vital. Faculty are at the center in the collegial culture because they fulfill the primary mission of the institution: the academic education of students within their chosen disciplines. Administrators in a collegial culture support the academic mission.

Managerial Culture

Terrel, a five year veteran of the student affairs field, recently changed roles at his institution. After five years as a programmer in student activities, he accepted a position as the manager of the student center. Although he worked in the same building, his job was surprisingly different. His people skills, honed through managing volunteers, were now used in staff supervision. His problem-solving skills, well practiced from the unavoidable dilemmas that accompany activities planning, came in handy during conference and meeting planning. The big change for Terrel was the increased emphasis on e-mail, budget forms, and requisitions. He felt like he had entered another career.

Origins of Managerial Culture

As higher education in the United States grew and expanded in the twentieth century, so did its administrative functions. Budgeting, human resources, physical plant, and hundreds of other areas expanded with the increased size and complexity of colleges and universities. Out of this growth came the managerial culture. With efficiency and effectiveness as the organizational objectives, this cultural form had its most notable expression in colleges serving underserved populations: community and junior colleges and Catholic institutions (Bergquist & Pawlak, 2008). Kerr's multi-university embodied the vision of the managerial culture: a myriad of services, amenities, and functions under one roof (2001).

Characteristics of Managerial Culture

Effective management exists to advance undergraduate education. Unlike the collegial culture's research focus, teaching is central within managerial culture. Serving a population often new to higher education, students within the managerial culture are taught the knowledge, skills, and attitudes to become successful, responsible learners (Bergquist & Pawlak, 2008).

Meaning is created in the managerial culture through the organization, implementation, and evaluation of work (Bergquist & Pawlak, 2008). In a managerial culture, tradition counts less than administrative effectiveness. Assessment assists institutional members in making sense of the environment and determining future directions. The meaning of a policy or decision is found in its practical application. Managerial culture institutions are goal and purpose driven, with fiscal responsibility, effective supervision skills, and high-quality service as both the ends and the means.

Management Techniques and Structural Considerations

The organizational structure within managerial culture institutions is bureaucratic, complete with the time-honored elements of hierarchy, span of control, one person–one boss, efficiency, use of information, and competence. The managerial culture perspective adds strength to student affairs in several ways. Sound financial management and budgeting functions assist student affairs professionals in developing a solid resource base. High-quality practice in personnel and supervision functions enable senior student affairs officers (SSAOs) to avail students of the finest educational practices possible. An understanding of how the organization works helps student affairs professionals to be coordinated and connected across their divisions and the larger institution. Finally, centralization and coordination with other personnel and functions enable student affairs to have a "voice at the table" concerning how students are affected by institutional decisions.

Roles in Managerial Culture

In the managerial culture, students are customers or clients. Some colleges and universities employing this approach look to Disney and other customer-service oriented organizations for insight on how best to serve students. Faculty are seen as employees with the means to deliver the product—education. They certainly carry the privileges of tenure, control of the curriculum, and other traditional functions explicit in collegial culture. But their traditional faculty roles are tempered with a businesslike demeanor that guides a student-centered rather than faculty-centered approach. Administrators are expected to be expert managers with the credentials, experience, and training necessary for these complex roles. The managerial culture dictates a more formal approach to administrative work, with official policies, procedures, and practices.

Developmental Culture

Malika is a newly appointed residence hall director at a large state university. Her previous work in student affairs took place in smaller, private institutions. She was surprised to discover how many decisions and practices at her new institution are based on locally and nationally developed theory. Unlike any division of student affairs she had experienced previously, her current division has a research staff. They conduct surveys, exit interviews, focus groups, and nationally normed studies. In staff meetings it was not unusual for someone to ask, "What do we know from the research? What does it tell us about student growth and development?" She was not used to residence life practice being so research based. Malika was grateful that her master's program had prepared her well in how to apply theory to practice.

Origins of the Developmental Culture

The developmental culture is arguably the most familiar perspective to student affairs professionals. This culture, arising from student activism long practiced in colleges and universities, has a considerable history within higher education generally and student affairs specifically. The student affairs field shares two significant connections to the developmental culture's origins: counseling and discipline.

Early master's programs in student affairs often began as concentrations in counseling departments. The "personnel" name in the field's original title came from the human resource and military processes of testing, guidance, and advising (Appleton, Briggs, & Rhatigan, 1978). In fact, several authors of the founding documents of student affairs (American Council on Education, 1937, 1949) were counselors and counselor educators. The functions of advising, career development, mental health counseling, discipline, placement, and assessment were outlined in the revised *Student Personnel Point of View* (American Council on Education, 1949). Service-learning, community service, and learning communities emphasize growth and learning, goals of the developmental culture.

In addition to the links to counseling illustrated above, early student affairs approaches embraced the challenge and support philosophy of counseling (Sanford, 1966, 1968). This philosophy, an early precursor to later theories regarding identity, moral, social, and cognitive development, is still widely practiced by student affairs professionals. Cognitive, behavioral, emotional, and spiritual growth are possible through student affairs practices. According to the principles of the developmental culture, growth entails personal openness and service to others—principles that are deeply integrated into student affairs practices (Bergquist & Pawlak, 2008).

Characteristics of Developmental Culture

In the developmental culture, personal and professional growth are primarily achieved through training and education. Currently integrated into all aspects of student affairs, training occurs throughout the division and among staff, students, and administrators. Training, institutional research, and principles of organizational development frame the developmental culture (Bergquist & Pawlak, 2008). At the core of the activities within this culture is the belief that the organization has a responsibility to train its people. Treated as people with the potential to learn, faculty, staff, administrators, and students are availed of opportunities to acquire new techniques, obtain the resources necessary to be successful in their roles, and advance through the organization in personally and professionally fulfilling ways.

Management Techniques and Structural Considerations

Senge (2006) translated developmental principles into organizational structure when he wrote about learning organizations. He defined these as "organizations where people continually expand their capacity to create the results they truly desire, where new and expansive patterns of thinking are nurtured, where collective aspiration is set free, and where people are continually learning how to learn together" (p. 3). These organizations are generative, change oriented, reflective, and inquiry based. Higher education institutions that adhere to a developmental culture rely on collaboration and innovation as ways to organize their work and achieve their goals.

Student affairs divisions within a developmental culture institution emphasize learner-centered education as reflected in the *Student Learning Imperative* (1994) and *Learning Reconsidered* (Keeling, 2004). From this perspective, learning occurs everywhere and can be created within student-centered communities, such as residence halls, student unions, and governance structures. With such a learning focus, academic and student affairs collaboration is possible.

Roles in Developmental Culture

In a developmental culture, students are viewed as full participants in the learning process with as much to teach as they have to learn. In keeping with a rich developmental perspective, faculty are involved in the education of students in the classroom and collaborate with student affairs professionals out of class. Administrators are educators who use managerial and organizational tools to encourage developmental changes in students.

Advocacy Culture

Two years ago, Chris enrolled at his state school. As the first openly transgender student on campus, he knew he would face significant challenges during his four years on campus. Quickly, however, Chris learned that the Lesbian, Gay, Bisexual, Transgender, Queer, and Ally (LGBTQA) Services Office was a powerful ally and advocate in his journey for recognition and respect at the university. LGBTQA services, in collaboration with the Queer Student Union, lobbied the administration to have gender identity added to the university's nondiscrimination clause. Chris found powerful allies in several faculty members, and they have been working with the registrar's office to have a "preferred name" category added to the student information management system. Before college, Chris did not envision himself as an activist. Today, he is hopeful that the changes he is fighting to create will improve campus climate for other transgender students.

Origins of the Advocacy Culture

The advocacy culture is one that finds balance in opposition and meaning by creating more equitable campus environments. This culture emerged as faculty grew discontented with the managerial culture's governance of the academy. Concerns over job security and compensation were the driving forces for the growth of the advocacy culture, which resulted in collective bargaining and other joint actions. The advocacy culture is well established in community colleges, at which faculty collective bargaining originated. With close ties to elementary and secondary education, two-year college faculty borrowed bargaining methods from the teachers from those educational levels. By the mid 1980s the advocacy culture had found a place at public institutions; private institutions have yet to embrace this cultural model.

Characteristics of the Advocacy Culture

Students, faculty, and staff immersed in the advocacy culture are particularly sensitive to issues of fairness, equity, and justice. As individuals and groups they are attentive to policies and practices that contradict institutional or individual commitments to these values. Although their willingness to act on behalf of a belief or cause may vary, adherents to the advocacy culture seek to expose and undermine injustice in the academy. This is not to say that every individual involved in the advocacy culture is concerned with equity or justice for all. Faculty may come to the advocacy model for many reasons, including their desire to maintain the status quo and defend themselves against what they see as radical or disadvantageous institutional change.

Faculty who are heavily involved in advocacy efforts often seek to broaden their scope and extend their influence beyond the campus community. Service-learning provides a method for committed faculty to both promote unique learning opportunities for students as well as positively impact those beyond the traditional confines of the academy. Assuming leadership roles off campus, some faculty find the ideological support they lacked on campus. Students and communities, too, benefit from this learning model. Students become fully engaged as they address critical community problems, and communities gain valuable support from committed individuals.

Student affairs has a strong and consistent legacy of advocacy. Offices that advocate for underrepresented students (such as LGBTQA services, women's centers, offices for students with disabilities, and multicultural centers) have long fought to improve campus climates. These offices serve as mediators, conveying students' demands and needs to administrators and faculty who may be viewed as impediments to justice and equity.

All members of the advocacy culture are keenly aware of the various power dynamics that affect their positions within their institutions. Although students, faculty, and staff can find powerful allies and advocates on campus, they are also wary of the powerful forces that often mobilize against their collective and individual interests. For this reason, bargaining and mediation serve as vital catalysts for progress. Outside mediators, such as professional organizations, national associations, and labor unions, may become involved in local struggles for power and control.

Management Techniques and Structural Considerations

Change in the advocacy culture occurs through a reciprocal process by which multiple constituencies seek to protect and advance their interests. Throughout this process, the decision making of upper administrators is closely observed by faculty, staff, and student groups. This approach promotes a culture of accountability and distributes power more broadly. In this environment, committee work with representation from various campus groups is a critical way for institutional constituents to advocate for their interests. Diverse committees often skillfully and effectively collaborate to author policies and generate ideas that are more acceptable and equitable for a greater portion of the community. These groups play a critical role in shaping the future of the institution. With faculty, staff, and students at the table, institutional planning has a more comprehensive scope. Because the advocacy culture views conflict as an inevitable and important part of the academy, faculty and administrators in this culture may find that the easiest way to effect change is to collaborate from the beginning.

Roles in the Advocacy Culture

Although conflict is a foundational component of the advocacy culture, all members of the academy are also potential allies. In this environment, faculty fiercely defend the academic realm against administrative encroachment. Among themselves, faculty find both solidarity and dissension, so they must organize effectively and identify strategic methods to protect their interests. Administrators may spend considerable time forging strategic relationships and forming representative committees to ensure effective decision making. Like faculty alliances, collective student movements assume an important role in that their demands shape institutional priorities and direction.

Virtual Culture

Joshua has just completed his third semester of online education at an institution approximately two thousand miles away. Unlike many of his high school peers, Joshua was accepted to a prestigious public residential college. He attended for one year before his mother fell ill and he was forced to withdraw to care for her. Lacking the financial means to return to his first school, Joshua was excited to learn that he could obtain his degree from an accredited university without ever stepping foot on its campus. Online education not only granted him the flexibility to work and care for his mother while getting a college education but also gave him the opportunity to use advanced networking and computing technologies. In fact, his new institution's virtual presence has allowed him to meet and interact with peers from around the world. This chance to tailor his learning to the realities of his life means that Joshua reaps the benefits of higher education while also fulfilling familial responsibilities. The possibilities are limitless.

Origins of the Virtual Culture

The virtual culture is solidly rooted in postmodernism. *Virtual* refers not only to the important role of technology in this culture but also to the dynamic nature of higher education organization and management. Unlike the previously mentioned cultures, the virtual culture emerged and exists outside the academy. It arose as rapidly developing technologies influenced the lives of individuals—as children and educators encountered computers and the Internet, these technologies increasingly became integrated into their educational experiences. The Internet's ability to instantly communicate and its limitless configurations have been the driving forces behind this technological revolution. Virtual education became integrated into higher education just as it did at the lower educational levels. With global implications, the emergence of these technologies not only changed the way students learn but redefined the role of the teacher and the very nature of knowledge.

Characteristics of the Virtual Culture

As mentioned before, the virtual culture is more than the technology that makes computers and the Internet a reality. It consists of a highly responsive, open, and shared organizational structure. Institutions steeped in this culture do not have clearly defined boundaries, in part because virtual relationships are far-reaching and dynamic. The virtual institution is in many ways a cosmopolitan one, in which colleges and universities form a global learning network. Relationships with other institutions, economies, and individuals are limitless, and an institution's identity becomes closely linked with its virtual presence.

The virtual culture is in some ways a response to postmodernism where meaning is dynamic and ambiguous. The loose structure and undefined boundaries of the virtual culture are particularly adept at responding to the emerging complexities of this environment. The virtual culture also answers the call from many to increase the accessibility and openness of higher education. Linking local institutional resources with international networks, the virtual culture carries the dissemination of knowledge to the extreme. In virtual cultures, information is so widely available that faculty gain prestige from their ability to skillfully employ technology in their teaching and synthesis of new ideas rather than from their vast knowledge of obscure topics. Here, meaning is made by connecting information and ideas within an interconnected relationship and network of peers and colleagues.

Management Techniques and Structural Considerations

The primary tool of virtual institutions is the computer. Within these institutions, computers perform many functions, including teaching and testing, running complex simulations, managing data, and aiding research. Increasingly, student service providers are turning to the Internet as a site of service and program delivery. Within this virtual setting, administrators develop a dynamic Web presence that allows them to efficiently and accessibly deliver services. In addition to the formal, institutionally sanctioned Web presence that has permeated today's campuses, social networking sites (e.g., Facebook.com) have changed the experiences of many students. As these technologies sweep across the globe, administrators must react with policies that reflect this changing higher education landscape.

Social networks not limited to student use are influencing faculty and administrators as well. Sites like Facebook make it easier to disseminate ideas and seek support from a diverse array of colleagues. Administrators are discovering that social networking sites are effective ways to connect with students. The flexible virtual culture and its accompanying technologies also have important implications for the schedules and work lives of administrators: blogs, wikis, and Web sites are ubiquitous inside and outside the academy. As these online technologies increasingly supplement or even replace in-person interactions, staff may find that their schedules are more flexible, and supervisors may discover new ways to manage employees, workload, and information.

Roles in the Virtual Culture

In the virtual culture, students, faculty, and staff are rewarded for their technological competence. In the classroom, tech-savvy faculty are adept at locating and manipulating data. They are responsible for teaching students how to obtain information from the far reaches of the virtual environment and synthesize it into relevant knowledge. Similar to faculty domains, student affairs offices are wired for near- and far-service delivery. They are highly dynamic structures that respond to student and faculty needs with a variety of delivery means. Functional silos and power gleaned through control of information cannot exist, because knowledge is readily shared by and accessible to many across all locations. Here, administrative management monitors employees and information using a vast network of highly developed technologies, which allow for efficient operation and continual reorganization. Students are campus community members perhaps most familiar with the virtual environment. Computers and the Internet have been a continuous presence throughout their young lives. Everything, from personal relationships to how they undertake their education, is underscored by interactions with a virtual environment. Faculty, staff, and administrators miss a significant opportunity for interaction with students when they fail to keep up with this virtual environment.

Tangible Culture

For the past year, Alexis has held the role of assistant dean of students at an elite public university, and has been a member of the university community for the past twelve years. Completing her undergraduate and doctoral degrees on the grounds of the university, she had only a brief experience away while getting her master's degree. Alexis feels strongly connected to not only her students and colleagues but also the architecture and landscape of this campus. The progressive teachings of her master's program are tempered by the traditional, conservative ethos of her alma mater. Over the years, Alexis has found great professional satisfaction in taking part in and perpetuating the traditions and rituals that have long been a part of this university's culture. When Alexis imagines her future career, she knows that her greatest professional (and perhaps personal) pleasure would be to see several generations of university students enjoy the same college experience she did.

Origins of the Tangible Culture

Members of today's universities often look back to higher education's origins to find comfort in the stability of the premodern ideas and virtues (e.g., progress and logic) upon which the academy was founded. Indeed, the fast-paced and dynamic environment of postmodernism may cause uneasiness for some members of the academy.

In times of uncertainty and change, higher education leaders often call upon idyllic images and values of ancient academic communities. These somewhat distorted visions reflect premodern values and ideals that still have a great impact on campus communities. These ideals—a strong, unified, and homogeneous campus community; a focus on the local community and environs; excellent teaching; a strong ethic of service; and a perfectly coiffed landscape—were established by some of the first universities founded. As the oldest of the cultures discussed by Bergquist and Pawlak (2008), the tangible culture was the way of life in the earliest institutions. Over centuries of development, this culture continues to permeate higher education.

Characteristics of the Tangible Culture

In a tangible culture, faculty and staff derive great pleasure from the preservation of the college or university's traditions. In this culture, community members often point to venerated customs and rites of passage as significant personal and communal elements of these institutions. In the classroom, educators measure success not by the amount that students learn but rather by the time they spend learning. Unlike in the collegial culture, faculty in the tangible culture seek personal engagement with students. This closeness allows them to monitor students' progress in pursuits both within and outside the academic realm. Faculty also have strict expectations regarding the space and practices devoted to teaching and learning: mandatory attendance policies, study halls, and residential learning opportunities are several ways faculty in the tangible culture manage when and where learning occurs.

The sometimes-ancient artifacts of the modern, tangible university continue to play an important role in representing today's institutional values. Grand graduation ceremonies with elaborate regalia and mysterious rites are significant events for tangible culture communities. These rituals and ceremonies, which provide insight into an institution's values and history, are grounded in the heavily symbolic, traditional campus architecture.

The tangible culture's emphasis on space is most dramatically exhibited through the grandeur of the institution's imposing buildings and perfectly manicured lawns. Temporal boundaries are reinforced by the physical confines created by courtyards and the often rural locales of these universities. As these institutions grew, significant emphasis was (and continues to be) placed on capital improvements and renovations. New construction does not stray far from the aesthetic of the campus's earliest buildings, as planners seek to create a visually cohesive campus that perpetuates the established architectural mode and traditional feel.

Faculty and staff working in these institutions share a desire for solidarity and integration, both of which are created through tradition, history, and long-standing cultural practices. Prestige is enhanced by activities that reinforce reputation, status, and hierarchy within the institution.

Managerial Techniques and Structural Considerations

As members of these communities, faculty and staff find great satisfaction in fulfilling the roles of their predecessors. Their goals are often unstated and certainly unquestioned, because they are doing the work that has always been done. This work is completed in the context of unspoken spatial and temporal boundaries.

Faculty members in the tangible culture value face-to-face contact and expect others do the same. Carefully constructed residence halls and student centers promote community as well as offer students and faculty places where face-to-face interactions occur. In this vein, educators gain status on campus by building their reputation with various community members. The most respected faculty members and administrators are known by many *and* know many. Meaning is created through personal interaction, community participation, and learning about and recitation of the institution's history and heritage.

New community members who come from institutions at which technology was highly integrated may find the emphasis on physicality and in-person interaction outmoded. Technological inroads of the sort valued in the virtual culture may be possible insofar that they promote community or enhance the quality of teaching. Strategic planning in this environment may be heavily focused on capital improvements and preservation of the status quo. Here, change occurs slowly and with deliberate attention to institutional reputation, community, and heritage.

Student affairs offices at these institutions are highly integrated into the traditions and daily life of the campus. Their work must operate within the temporal and spatial boundaries established by the tangible culture. Often, student affairs administrators may feel the "weight" of history on their shoulders as they face fierce resistance to change from a variety of constituencies, including loyal alumni/ae and long-standing faculty. Success rests with those administrators who forge purposeful relationships with faculty and other constituencies while respecting the institution's distinct heritage.

Roles in the Tangible Culture

As in the collegial culture, students, faculty, and administrators in the tangible culture are part of a distinct lineage. However, unlike in the collegial culture, students and faculty in the tangible culture enjoy intimate contact with one another. All individuals are expected to be active community members, earning respect through individual interaction and contact. Faculty members are teachers; mentors; and, in some sense, parents to their students. Students are successful when they engage in the community and follow the paths of the generations that came before them.

Conclusion

This chapter outlined six cultural lenses through which to view student affairs administration. There is no "right and wrong" when it comes to the cultures shared here.

Cultures that work for one institution may be completely out of place for another. The presence of a culture and the practices accompanying that approach are dependent on the nature of the community members within the institution, the unique history of the institution, practices that have evolved over time, and the values community members hold. Successful student affairs practice and administration depend on a deep understanding of the cultural values within an institution and the practices that define that institution's unique way of being.

References

American College Personnel Association. (1994). *The student learning imperative: Implications for student affairs*. Washington, DC: Author.

American Council on Education. (1937). *The student personnel point of view, 1937*. Washington, DC: Author.

American Council on Education. (1949). *The student personnel point of view, 1949*. Washington, DC: Author.

Appleton, J., Briggs, C., & Rhatigan, J. (1978). *Pieces of eight: The rites, roles, and style of the dean by eight who have been there*. Portland, OR: National Association of Student Personnel Administrators.

Bergquist, W. H., & Pawlak, K. (2008). *Engaging the six cultures of the academy*. San Francisco: Jossey-Bass.

Birnbaum, R. (1991). *How colleges work*. San Francisco: Jossey-Bass.

Keeling, R. P. (Ed.). (2004). *Learning reconsidered: A campus-wide focus on the student experience*. Washington, DC: American College Personnel Association & National Association of Student Personnel Administrators.

Kerr, C. (2001). *The uses of the university* (5th ed.). Cambridge, MA: Harvard University Press.

Manning, K. (1993). Rethinking the introduction to student affairs course. *NASPA Journal, 30*, 196–202.

Sandeen, A. (1991). *The chief student affairs officer*. San Francisco: Jossey-Bass.

Sanford, N. (1966). *Self and society: Social change and individual development*. New York: Atherton.

Sanford, N. (1968). *Where colleges fail: A study of student as person*. San Francisco: Jossey-Bass.

Senge, P. (2006). *The fifth discipline*. New York: Doubleday.

University of Oxford. (2010). *A brief history of the university*. Retrieved July 6, 2010 from www.ox.ac.uk/about_the_university/introducing_oxford/a_brief_history_of_the_university/index.html.

CHAPTER SIXTEEN

STRATEGY AND INTENTIONALITY IN PRACTICE

Shaun R. Harper

The problem was that formal planning did not seem to do what proponents said it should. Campuses first tried one approach and then, when it failed, another. . . . [T]he fundamental failure of strategic planning, in business or education, was the implicit assumption that the analytic processes of planning can lead to the synthesizing process of strategy. (Birnbaum, 2000, pp. 73–74)

In *Management Fads in Higher Education*, Birnbaum (2000) identifies strategic planning as one of seven management processes that higher education leaders have adopted from other sectors, namely business and government. He offers a chronological account of the emergence, evolution, and eventual decline of intensive, campuswide planning processes between 1972 and 1994. Birnbaum critiques such prescriptive processes as those that require twelve to eighteen months of effort to produce a rigid five-year action plan. Other scholars (for example, Dickeson, 1999; Kezar, 2001) have similarly observed that strategic planning as a formal exercise has been largely ineffective in American higher education. However, Dooris (2002) offers a case study of one university's productive use of strategic planning over a twenty-year period. The process reportedly enabled the institution to reduce costs by shifting resources from the least effective to the most promising programs; eliminate duplication in services and operational activities; and enhance academic quality as evidenced by a range of indicators. And notwithstanding its critiques, the existence of a strategic plan has been used by the Southern Association of Colleges and Schools and other academic accreditation entities as a sign of institutional effectiveness (Alstete, 2004).

Although the relative strengths and shortcomings could be further debated, there are two reasons why this chapter is not about formal strategic planning processes. First, graduate students and early-career professionals in student affairs, the primary readers of this book, are not typically engaged in high-level strategic planning exercises. Most of their time is spent working with students, not on institutional change endeavors. Second, most published scholarship on strategic planning suggests it typically occurs in a linear fashion that entails scanning the environment, crafting a strategic response to external forces, implementing the strategy, and then assessing its impact—tasks mostly undertaken by campus leaders, often with the goal of positioning the institution differently in a competitive marketplace (Bess & Dee, 2008; Chaffee, 1984). Birnbaum (2000) notes that this linear process is inconsistent with how most college and university educators do their work, and Eckel and Kezar (2003) argue that engagement in formal strategic planning of this design is not requisite for strategic change. Thus the focus of this chapter is on being thoughtful, systematic, and intentional in one's own educational practice, emphases that seem more appropriate for the predominant readership of this book. In other words, it is about personally organizing student affairs work for the deliberate and strategic production of educational outcomes.

Those who wish to know more about writing and implementing formal strategic plans in higher education should consult books that have been published on the topic—for example, Rowley and Sherman (2001); Dooris, Kelley, and Trainer (2004); and Norris and Poulton (2008). Jerry Price's (2009) chapter in the third edition of the *Handbook of Student Affairs Administration* focuses specifically on the strategic development of student affairs facilities plans. Perhaps Matney and Taylor's (2007) description of how the student affairs division at the University of Michigan engaged in strategic planning might prove useful. Furthermore, the National Association of College and University Business Officers provides several resources related to the strategic planning process, including two guidebooks (Sanaghan, 2009; Tromp & Ruben, 2004). Additionally, the Society for College and University Planning also offers practical planning instruments, organizes workshops and conferences, and publishes *Planning for Higher Education*, a peer-reviewed journal that routinely contains scholarly articles on strategic planning.

Intentionality—defined herein as reflectively and deliberately employing a set of strategies to produce desired educational outcomes—is used throughout this chapter to explain how student affairs educators can be strategic thinkers and doers. Harper and Quaye (2009) posit that those who act with intentionality "are conscious of every action they undertake and are able to consider the long-range implications of decisions" (p. 7). In the next section, the link between intentionality and effective student affairs practice is explicated and substantiated with examples. The focus then shifts to a discussion of strategically enhancing student learning and development through the co-curriculum, followed by a synthesis of the benefits associated with data-driven and mission-centered educational practice. The chapter concludes with a description of ways in which student affairs educators might respond with intentionality to three contemporary issues in American higher education: male student disengagement in campus activities, inequitable outcomes in community college transfer rates, and effectively preparing undergraduates for social justice and participation in a diverse democracy. In lieu of step-by-step process models and inflexible five-year plans that focus on institutional change, a set of student-centered and self-reflective strategic practices are advocated throughout this chapter.

Intentionality: An Enabler of Good Practice

Blimling, Whitt, and Associates (1999) offer these seven principles of "good practice" in student affairs: engaging students in active learning, helping students develop coherent values and ethical standards, communicating high expectations, using systematic inquiry to improve performance, aligning resources with institutional goals and mission, forging partnerships, and creating inclusive communities. Noteworthy are the active verbs contained in each, signifying action from educators in their work with college students. These authors make clear in each chapter how employing these practices could help foster student learning in college. In his interviews with senior student affairs administrators, Hartley (2001) found that institutions were beginning to embrace the concept of student learning but that programming offered in student affairs divisions was essentially the same as it had always been. Concerning student learning through diverse interactions, Chang, Chang, and Ledesma (2005) contend that many educators engage in "magical thinking"—an erroneous assumption that powerful educational outcomes will be automatically manufactured through student-initiated engagement with peers who are different.

Few would dispute the importance of students' learning as much as they can, inside and outside the classroom, during the college years. Therefore, to maximize learning, educators (including those who work in student affairs) must replace magical thinking with deliberate strategies that bring the seven principles of good practice to fruition on their campuses. Intentionality entails reading Blimling et al.'s (1999) book and reflectively asking oneself, What *specifically* can I do to ensure I am employing these practices in my work? Or critically examining one's actions vis-à-vis the ideals conveyed in *Learning Reconsidered 2* (Keeling, 2006); the practical implications offered in the most recent issue of the *Journal of College Student Development* and other publications; and the innovative approaches presented in sessions at professional conferences. Occasionally revisiting the institution's mission statement and strategically contemplating ways to organize one's professional work around the values espoused therein is another example of intentionality. Despite the hectic nature of student affairs work, intentionality requires honest and ongoing reflection on how professional practice can be improved. And one's *actual* contribution to student learning, diversity, and other institutional priorities is constantly examined. Conversely, engaging in student affairs work without reflecting, reading, and deliberately aligning actions with effective practices and important philosophical stances in the profession constitutes negligence and is likely to lead to educational malpractice.

As noted previously, intentionality is both reflective and actionable. Strange and Banning (2001) call for campus environments that are "intentionally designed to offer opportunities, incentives, and reinforcements for growth and development" (p. 201). In the magical-thinking paradigm, one would wrongly presume that such environmental conditions already exist and are being nurtured by other educators on the campus—that student development is somehow occurring on its own. Those who are intentional in their work are constantly engaged in formal and informal assessment activities. They frequently employ a range of techniques, such as those presented by Schuh, Upcraft, and Associates (2001), to determine how diverse populations of students interact with and experience various aspects of the campus environment. Data and insights from students then compel intentional educators to first reflectively consider and then strategically adjust their practices in response to student needs.

Kuh (2008) names a set of "high-impact" educational experiences that necessitate active learning and sustained engagement, including study abroad programs, service-learning opportunities, undergraduate research programs, summer internships are among them. Accordingly, these experiences afford students deeply reflective opportunities to clarify their personal values and better understand themselves in relation to others; challenge them to interact in educationally purposeful ways with professors and peers, including those who are different from them; and provide situations in which students receive substantive feedback on their performance. Despite their significance, however, Kuh acknowledges the existence of racial disparities in these experiences, with White undergraduates being cumulatively more engaged in such opportunities than are students of color. Intentionality would compel a student affairs educator to determine the extent to which such disparities exist on her or his campus, and then respond with what Harper (2009) calls "race-conscious student engagement practices" (p. 41)—a set of calculated steps that shift the weight of responsibility for engagement from students who are attempting to succeed in environments in which they are underrepresented and often stereotyped to educators who possess expertise on student success. This is just one example of intentionality in practice.

Another example of intentionality might be, for example, a hall director's making time to deliberately partner with colleagues in the Lesbian, Gay, Bisexual, and Transgender (LGBT) Center to offer a series of collaborative programming on sexual orientation for residents in her building. Or the new professional, immediately after reading Strange and Banning's (2001) book on campus environments, might walk across campus to digitally photograph barriers to accessibility for students with physical disabilities, later forwarding the pictures and a memo to colleagues in the division. Also exemplifying intentionality is the academic advisor who uses a portion of advising sessions to ask commuter and part-time students how they would prefer to receive information about out-of-class engagement opportunities, and who then communicates this information in a systematic way to the campus activities office and later checks the database to ensure that each individual advisee is receiving information in ways she or he requested. The career services professional who attends a conference, takes copious notes in every session, and thoughtfully begins implementing innovative lessons learned upon returning to campus provides an additional example of intentionality. Central to the practical dimension of intentionality is going beyond routine, one-size-fits-all programming and service models. Comfort, habit, and minimalism are exchanged for an application of principles that guide the profession, the thoughtful implementation of practices proven effective in similar institutional contexts, and a reliance on data collected from students.

Perhaps most important, intentionality demands seeing oneself as an *educator* rather than a practitioner, staff member, advisor, director, or some other title commonly assigned to those responsible for student learning and development outside the classroom. Like their faculty counterparts, these educators understand the effort required to facilitate student learning and take seriously the strategic design of situations that confer upon students the outcomes necessary for success in post-college endeavors. They are also fascinated by learning, as evidenced through reading, actively taking notes at conferences, and exploring experiential and explanatory insights from students. There is recognition that effective educators—regardless of where their work is done on the campus—reflect, plan, commit themselves firmly to the production of outcomes, thoughtfully select strategies to enhance student learning, and ground their educational approaches in published literature and research. Described in the next section is a formal method for approaching intentionality that extends beyond the work of individual student affairs educators.

Co-Curriculum as a Strategic Resource

Harper and antonio (2008) argue, "Effective professors who want students to learn and master a certain concept plan classroom activities designed to yield desired outcomes; student affairs educators who seek to be intentional must treat such work like curricular planning" (p. 11). They further note that at some point in the 1990s, *extracurricular*—a popular term inherently suggesting that learning occurring outside the classroom is "extra"—was replaced by *co-curricular*. Despite this semantic shift, Harper and antonio contend that formal, written curricular plans analogous to those developed by faculty in academic schools and departments do not exist in most student affairs divisions. That is, the out-of-class side of the co-curriculum is usually informal at best. They give an example of how faculty in a sociology department met at some point to determine what students in the major should know: faculty selected and strategically sequenced classes, they probably made certain agreements about books students would read, and most professors were purposefully assigned to teach specific sociology courses in which they possessed expertise. Harper and antonio call for a similar approach to curriculum development in student affairs.

Formalizing the co-curriculum is a deliberate and strategic way for individual student affairs educators who approach their work with intentionality to collaborate with others to enhance student learning. An effective alternative to offering fragmented programs and meaningless experiences is the implementation of a curricular model that is constructed around a set of desired educational outcomes, that identifies the programs and experiences necessary for the actualization of these outcomes, that strategically sequences them and assigns responsibility for implementation to expert educators in the division, and that lays out a multifaceted set of assessment activities to measure student learning and development. Such a curricular model should document what students ought to know and the competencies they should possess from one year to another through graduation. The use of curricular planning in student affairs as recommended here is consistent with approaches advocated in *Learning Reconsidered 2* (Keeling, 2006).

Curricular planning techniques can be used to organize student learning efforts for an entire student affairs division or a specific office. For instance, Kerr and Tweedy (2006) describe a curricular approach to residential education at the University of Delaware. Their efforts moved the institution beyond the popular approach of determining program effectiveness merely by the number of residents who attended. "While we knew that motivating students to attend programming by providing pizza increased attendance, we did not know whether or how that programming affected learning. Program statistics made us look good and kept our budget healthy, but did not necessarily prove that any learning directly resulted from our efforts. We realized that our model for delivering educational programming, despite its success by certain measures, was not the most effective means of delivering education in our residence halls" (p. 9).

Their work began with the following questions: "What should every individual student learn as a result of living in a residence hall; what must a student do in order to learn this; and what must *we* do to engage each and every one of our students in this learning?" (p. 11). Educators in residence life then worked collaboratively to develop a curriculum focused on citizenship education for 7,200 students who lived on campus. Guided by several of the institution's general education goals, the University of Delaware's curricular model emphasized self-awareness and the examination of one's values, one's connection and engagement with diverse peers, and the exchange of ideas in a safe and inclusive community.

Across the three areas, twenty-eight competencies for students were identified and lesson plans were developed. The curriculum also specified which competencies a student was to develop during her or his first residential year through the senior year. In one hall for first-year students, three major learning outcomes were pursued: (1) each student will understand the obligations that membership in a society requires; (2) each student will understand the obligations a democratic society owes the individual; and (3) each student will understand the obligation to pursue change when democracy is not working. Seventeen educational activities were listed under these learning outcomes (see Kerr & Tweedy, 2006).

Recognizing that curriculum writing is unfamiliar to most student affairs educators, administrators in residence life at the University of Delaware provided tremendous support and guidance, but also held colleagues accountable by reviewing their curricular plans (Kerr & Tweedy, 2006). Much like academic curriculum approval processes at departmental, school, and institution levels, a Residence Life Curriculum Review Committee was established to scrutinize learning plans developed for the halls. Unfortunately, the University of Delaware abandoned its model in October 2007 after a free-speech group wrote a letter to the president that accused the program of "systematic thought reform," claiming it promoted specific views on race, sexuality, and morality (Hoover, 2007). Notwithstanding its discontinuation, the structure of this institution's model serves as an excellent example of how student affairs educators can develop and formally implement curriculum.

Curriculum as a strategic resource should not be confused with a strategic plan. Although a written document is required, the out-of-class curriculum must be flexible enough for educators to respond to evolving student needs and capitalize on unanticipated opportunities for learning. Although a professor typically arrives with notes and a plan for what is to be accomplished in a class session, it is sometimes necessary for her or him to depart from the agenda to better explain a particular concept or allow students to benefit from rich perspectives offered by their peers. Similarly, student affairs educators should use the curriculum as a guide, recognizing when certain lessons are worthy of reinforcement or when current events may stimulate student learning in ways not previously envisioned. Determining what to include in a curriculum that resides outside the academic domain should be informed in large part by the institution's mission as well as various data sources related to student characteristics, attitudes, behaviors, experiences, and outcomes.

Data Driven and Mission Centered

> Mission refers to the overarching purposes of the institution—what it is and stands for as well as what it aspires to be. The mission establishes the tone of a college and conveys its educational purposes, whether based on religious, ideological, or educational beliefs, giving direction to all aspects of institutional life, including the policies and practices that foster student success. (Kuh, Kinzie, Schuh, Whitt, & Associates, 2005, p. 25)

Conceivably, every person hired to work at a college or university should be expected to contribute in some way to the actualization of its mission. The book *Student Success in College: Creating Conditions that Matter* (Kuh et al., 2005) is based on the Documenting Effective Educational Practice (DEEP) project, a study of twenty institutions of varying size and type at which student engagement and graduation rates were high. Common among these institutions were two characteristics: (1) a clearly articulated mission and set of educational purposes; and (2) a well-understood cultural philosophy of how things were done on the campus concerning teaching, learning, engagement, and student success. The authors distinguish an espoused mission (what the institution publicly claims to be about) from the enacted mission (what educators and administrators actually do in their daily practices to make good on educational promises). Accordingly, the colleges and universities they studied were "quite vigilant about making certain the institution is doing what it claims to do, and doing it at the highest level of effectiveness possible" (p. 60). Similarly, Hartley (2002) studied three liberal arts colleges that previously faced significant financial and operational turmoil. A renewal of their mission commitment and revitalization of educational purposes sustained them. Hartley deemed these institutions *purpose centered*, whereas the practices commonly employed on campuses in the DEEP study were called *mission driven*.

Consistent with principles advocated in Blimling et al.'s (1999) book, intentional student affairs educators read and routinely revisit mission statements to reacquaint themselves with the aims, purposes, and educational philosophies that supposedly govern their institutions. Their own practices are then juxtaposed with these ideals to determine the extent to which personal and collaborative efforts lead to mission enactment. Such examination is important, especially as evidence of educational effectiveness is being increasingly demanded. For example, in recent years student learning has been placed at the forefront of institutional accreditation processes (Alstete, 2004), and accreditation entities are now using mission statements to measure certain aspects of institutional effectiveness (Hartley, 2002). Thus, as student affairs educators claim their share of responsibility for student learning, they must ensure that the approaches they use and the curricular models they create are mission driven. Practices designed around the mission, learning outcomes, and students' needs are likely to help advance the institution, as was the case at the DEEP schools (Kuh et al., 2005).

Also necessary is a dependency on data and insights from students. Designing a co-curriculum without student input is unlikely to be successful, as will any attempt to be educationally purposeful in the absence of important contextual information concerning what students do, who they are, how they perceive and respond to the environment, what conditions facilitate productive learning, and a host of other related topics. Strategy without data is sure to be flawed. In Chapter Eighteen of this book, Marilee Bresciani offers several ideas for gathering and utilizing data in student affairs practice. Others are presented and discussed by Schuh et al. (2001), as well as by Harper and Museus (2007). Additionally, Banta, Jones, and Black (2009) furnish examples of student affairs divisions that employed effective assessment practices and used data to guide their strategic efforts.

Data-driven decision making, a concept recently made popular in K–12 education (Kowalski & Lasley, 2009), is unlikely to qualify as one of the "management fads" Birnbaum (2000) describes. This kind of decision making is a strategic approach to determining which programs and services are worthy of fiscal investment and human resources and which activities are most likely to lead to mission alignment, student learning, and the equitable distribution of important developmental outcomes. Despite its commonsensical nature, many student affairs educators organize and perform their work in the absence of data. For example, programs are annually repeated merely because they were done the year before, although it is entirely possible that institutional self-assessment would reveal outcomes disparities that might in turn signal the urgency of redirecting resources to programming of a more purposeful design. Furthermore, it is common to go through a semester, or even an entire school year, without systematically interviewing individual students about what they are learning, conducting focus groups to better understand needs and navigational challenges in the campus environment, or requesting key available data from the office of institutional research to guide educational efforts.

Harris and Bensimon (2007) argue that data are useless "without people who have the willingness to become engaged with the data and have the know-how to unpack data tables by asking questions, looking for patterns, forming hunches, challenging interpretations, and putting a story to those data" (p. 78). Similarly, Dowd (2005) writes that "data don't drive" but practitioners do. Instead of operating in a culture of evidence, in which the emphasis is simply on collecting data to demonstrate effectiveness, she advocates a culture of inquiry in which educators constantly seek answers and insights into matters regarding student learning, engagement, and achievement. Dowd further states that this approach requires "sustained professional development and dialogue about the barriers to student achievement. A culture of inquiry depends on the capacity for insightful questioning of evidence and informed interpretation of results" (p. 5). Dowd goes on to describe *Equity for All: Institutional Responsibility for Student Success*, a project that brought together teams of educators and administrators for institutional self-assessment. Team members examined data regarding outcomes inequities on their campus, collectively interpreted and ascribed meaning to the data, and then used insights garnered from the data to reshape their educational practices. This is just one example of how data can be strategically used to organize student affairs work; others are offered in the next section.

The Strategic Confrontation of Contemporary Issues

Student affairs educators who are strategic and intentional in their work are more likely to effectively mediate some of the most complex issues in American higher education than are less thoughtful and deliberate colleagues. Three illustrations of effectiveness are presented in this section. These are in no way intended to be viewed as the most urgent or enduring challenges on college and university campuses, but instead are offered as three examples (among many) of situations that require strategic responses from educators. Models of how student affairs educators can strategically organize their work in an integrated fashion are presented. In each scenario, educators are engaged in what Birnbaum (2000) calls the "synthesizing process of strategy," meaning their efforts are multifaceted, simultaneous, and reflective of several strategic approaches described throughout this chapter.

Where the Men Aren't: Understanding Before Acting

In his third year as a campus activities advisor at a large public university, Kmao finally decided to do something about a troubling trend he had seen in the student government and other major organizations on campus: hardly any men were involved, particularly in leadership positions. These gender disparities had seemed to worsen each year since Kmao took the job. Interested in learning more about this phenomenon, he first consulted the student affairs literature to see what insights had been offered by others. His search immediately led him to Sax's (2008) book *The Gender Gap in College*, in which the author presents trend data on gender differences in engagement at colleges and universities across the country. Much to his surprise, findings reported in the book very much mirrored what was occurring on Kmao's campus. He also consulted other books (for example, Cuyjet & Associates, 2006; Harper & Harris, 2010; and Kellom, 2004) for additional explanatory insights and practical ideas for increasing the engagement of male students.

Intrigued by survey results reported in Sax's (2008) book, Kmao became interested in corroborating his personal observations with official data concerning male engagement trends on his campus. Therefore, he wrote an e-mail to the vice president for student affairs asking if he could see a copy of the institution's National Survey of Student Engagement (NSSE) data disaggregated by gender. The vice president contacted colleagues in the Office of Institutional Research, who quickly supplied the requested NSSE data report. These data further confirmed what Kmao had seen in his work with student organizations, but offered no contextual details to explain the social undercurrents of engagement differences between women and men on campus. Hence Kmao was not yet comfortable enough to launch a campaign to increase the participation of male students in enriching educational experiences. He wondered how colleagues on other campuses were addressing this problem, which promoted him to join the National Association of Student Personnel Administrators (NASPA) Men and Masculinities Knowledge Community (MMKC). There he found a helpful dialogue and exchange of ideas among men's studies scholars in student affairs and other educators who were similarly concerned about male student outcomes and developmental experiences in higher education. Resources provided in the MMKC quarterly newsletter also proved useful.

Months before embarking on his intentional journey toward closing gender gaps in engagement on his campus, Kmao got approval from his supervisor to attend the American College Personnel Association (ACPA) Annual Convention. Instead of waiting until he arrived at the convention to arbitrarily select a set of sessions to attend, he accessed the program booklet online a few weeks prior to traveling. Kmao deliberately built a schedule that included sessions on men, masculinities, and gender, because he suspected expert colleagues would have useful program models and research findings that would help him craft a more dynamic set of strategic efforts. In each session he took notes, posed several questions, and afterward asked presenters for their business cards and advice on addressing particular aspects of the male disengagement dilemma. On his flight home from the convention, Kmao consolidated his notes and constructed a list of innovative approaches he intended to test on his campus. On the first day back in the office, he shared with colleagues in the campus activities office what he learned at the convention as well as some ideas he hoped they could collaboratively implement to close gender gaps in engagement.

Presenters in one ACPA session had shared findings from a qualitative research study in which they sought a more nuanced understanding of environmental factors leading to engagement disparities reflected in NSSE data at their institution. This inspired Kmao to do the same upon returning to his campus. In fact, within three weeks after the ACPA convention he organized a series of focus groups with diverse populations of male undergraduates. The goal of these focus groups was to gain a deeper understanding of why men found leadership and engagement opportunities unappealing. A separate group was held with male student leaders who were actively engaged, wherein the focus was on understanding what compelled them to spend their out-of-class time in such purposeful ways, especially given that their same-sex peers were not similarly engaged. Kmao digitally recorded these focus group interviews (with the students' permission), had them transcribed, and thoughtfully reflected on what the men were saying as he carefully studied each transcript.

Although the focus group data were extremely insightful, Kmao was left with an insufficient understanding of what men were doing on campus instead of participating actively in clubs, organizations, and leadership development experiences. He recalled Sax's (2008) finding that men devote considerably more time to playing video games, watching television, exercising, drinking beer, and partying than do their female counterparts, yet Kmao wanted to know more about time-spending trends among men on his specific campus. Therefore, at the beginning of fall semester, he befriended fourteen first-year male students on Facebook and routinely visited their sites to analyze their status updates (wherein students normally report what they are doing) and peruse their photo albums (which typically include pictures from events in which students participate). Additionally, following a group of eight sophomores and juniors on Twitter enabled Kmao to receive updates throughout the day (sometimes hourly) on how these men were spending their time outside the classroom. Eventually, Kmao invited the twenty-two students with whom he had been virtually engaged to his office for individual interviews about the expenditure of their time; half agreed to talk with him.

Kmao's efforts reflect the intentionality required for effective, data-driven educational practice. Before attempting to initiate any programmatic solutions to an important problem on his campus, he first sought understanding—his focus was on learning before doing. He deliberately sought valuable insights from men on his campus, from scholars who have written about college men and masculinities, and from colleagues from other campuses who were working to close gender gaps in student engagement. Consequently, Kmao was able to thoughtfully organize his work with male students in a way that is much more likely to lead to effectiveness than would have been the case had he hastily approached the problem with insufficient understanding.

Troubling Transfer Trends: Toward Strategic, Collaborative Change

Last year, Keisha was hired as coordinator of student retention and transfer initiatives at a community college. In her job interview, colleagues described the institution's transfer rate—meaning the number of students who enter the college, declare transferring to a four-year institution as their goal, and then actually do so within three years—as "better than at most" community colleges of similar size. This information excited Keisha on a personal level, because she began her own postsecondary educational journey at a technical college and then transferred to the university at which she earned bachelor's and master's degrees in engineering. After a few weeks in the position, she noticed that claims made in the interview were indeed true: transfer rates, overall, were not bad. However, a closer look at the data revealed that *certain* students, who upon entry expressed a desire to transfer, were not doing so at rates comparable to others'. Similar to Kmao, Keisha first took time to understand the problem before attempting to solve it. She was especially intrigued by one particular process model, the Equity Scorecard.

Harris and Bensimon (2007) provide a thorough explanation of the Equity Scorecard process. First, a team comprising educators (staff, faculty, and administrators) is formed on a campus with the ultimate goal of identifying, deeply understanding, and strategically addressing inequities in college student outcomes. A team's collaborative work entails "making sense of easily accessible institutional data that are disaggregated by race and ethnicity. During the meetings, team members collaborate by examining the disaggregated data collectively, raising questions about the data, deciding what additional data they should look at to answer their questions, and challenging others' assumptions and interpretations about the data" (p. 81).

Harris and Bensimon further assert that the collaborative identification of educational disparities usually strengthens individual team member's commitment to enacting necessary efforts to achieve equity in their respective courses, programs, and departments. Keisha believed this process would help her colleagues understand that the college's transfer achievements were not equitably distributed. She strategically selected this particular process because she knew her colleagues would not believe there was a problem with transfer rates unless they discovered it themselves. She also suspected that direct involvement would engender among team members a stronger vow to alter their own educational practices and challenge their colleagues to recognize themselves as culprits in the cyclical reproduction of outcomes inequities.

Keisha was right. After spending nearly one year engaged in the Equity Scorecard process, team members identified disparities not only in transfer rates but also in a host of other outcomes and achievement indicators. Having sufficient data enabled the team to strategically target its efforts and institutional resources. Subsequently, the team wisely proposed a set of strategic initiatives for populations who were transferring at lower rates as well as corrective efforts in specific courses that routinely stifled transfer progress for certain students. Keisha's deliberate introduction of a collaborative process model on her campus is an excellent example of strategic practice. She knew there was no way she could have single-handedly closed transfer gaps, convinced her colleagues there was a problem, or fully understood all the environmental factors that reproduced outcomes inequities. But Keisha was also aware that good practice entails the strategic cultivation of collaborative partnerships for student success, (Blimling, Whitt, & Associates, 1999), and she recognized the Equity Scorecard to be an effective process worthy of trial on her campus.

Remediation for Social Justice: Using Curriculum to Educate Educators

Karina and Kyle were recently hired to work in the student affairs division at a small, private liberal arts college. Coincidentally, both graduated from the same student affairs master's program. In graduate school, Karina and Kyle committed themselves to being agents for social justice; they pledged to act deliberately in their future roles as student affairs educators. For them this entailed raising consciousness about power; privilege; oppression; and the inequitable distribution of resources, fairness, and opportunities. They took away their own right to remain silent about justice issues in interactions with colleagues and in their educational work with students. Both were eager to advance a social justice agenda in their new roles and considered themselves lucky to have landed on the same campus.

Kyle and Karina found appealing the college's public declaration of commitment to preparing students for participation in a diverse democracy, which was repeatedly touted in admissions brochures; in several places on the Web site; and, most important, in the mission statement. This articulation of educational purpose resonated with these two new professionals because they felt strongly that environmental conditions should be deliberately fostered that enable students to critically examine flawed assumptions they bring to college concerning people who are different from themselves. Karina and Kyle were inspired by Sylvia Hurtado's scholarship on linking diversity outcomes with educational mission, especially her 2005 presidential address to the Association for the Study of Higher Education (see Hurtado, 2007). When deciding between multiple job offers, they felt that this particular college would be an ideal space in which to advance many of the principles Hurtado conveyed. They were wrong.

Within the first few weeks, Karina and Kyle quickly encountered "magical thinking" among their colleagues. They saw little evidence of strategic effort in the student affairs division toward the actualization of the college's mission. It also became clear to them that several student affairs educators who claimed to be agents for social justice were clueless about what such work entailed—apparently it had become a popular yet empty buzzword in the division. Kyle and Karina wondered how students were supposed to learn about justice, democracy, and diversity when the majority of educators with whom they interacted outside the classroom were insufficiently prepared to teach them. In conversations, several colleagues admitted they were uncomfortable facilitating difficult dialogues with students on justice-related topics. Most said they had received insufficient instruction in graduate school on how to teach college students about power, privilege, oppression, and assorted "-isms" (racism, sexism, heterosexism, ageism, and so on).

Although they entered with hopes of working collaboratively with other student affairs colleagues to develop a curriculum similar to the one described by Kerr and Tweedy (2006), it became immediately apparent to Karina and Kyle that such efforts would fail if student learning was to be facilitated by educators who themselves were in need of remediation. Given this, they asked the dean of students for support and resources to develop a curriculum that would better prepare student affairs educators to effectively teach for social justice. They strategically aligned their justification for this effort with values conveyed in the mission statement. The dean enthusiastically agreed. In fact, she volunteered to join Kyle and Karina as a collaborative partner and recommended five other colleagues who would likely make valuable contributions to the development of a curriculum for the student affairs division.

The team of eight professionals began its collaborative work with a survey that measured how sufficiently prepared student affairs educators felt teaching and programming on social justice topics. They also conducted individual interviews to explore more deeply the nature of their colleagues' discomfort. In addition, team members facilitated a series of focus groups in which undergraduates were invited to critique the effectiveness of student affairs educators in preparing them for participation in a diverse democracy. Data and insights from these efforts were helpful as the team developed objectives and learning outcomes for the curriculum. One of their many findings was that several colleagues were struggling to effectively address resistant students—those who were opposed to learning about diversity, oppression, power inequities, and so on. Before attempting any sort of curricular solution, Karina suggested that the team read Dr. Jones's book chapter on student resistance (see Jones, 2007). Intrigued by strategies offered therein, team members recommended inviting the author to campus for an educational session with colleagues across the division. This was just one of several ideas the team wrote into its curricular plan.

Once team members completed their initial sketch of the curriculum, a draft was unveiled at the annual student affairs retreat. Their colleagues were invited to offer feedback, and key persons were identified to assume responsibility for executing educational activities associated with goals and learning outcomes documented in the curriculum. Within the first two years, the curriculum received tremendous praise from people across the campus, within and beyond the student affairs division. By their own admission, several professionals (especially those who had worked at the institution a long time) felt better prepared to help the college truly advance its mission of preparing students for participation in a diverse democracy. Formal assessment data also confirmed the division's forward movement and educational effectiveness. Kyle, Karina, and the dean of students eventually presented their curricular model at ACPA and NASPA conferences, and, like Kerr and Tweedy (2006), they coauthored an article on their strategic and collaborative work for *About Campus*. The vision for intentionality in social justice teaching—originally proposed by two new professionals—ultimately earned this institution recognition as a national model of excellence. More important, its well-designed curriculum enabled the student affairs division to contribute to the realization of educational purposes espoused and promises made in the college's mission statement.

Conclusion

In similar but varied ways, Kmao, Keisha, Karina, and Kyle approached their work with strategy and intentionality, both as individuals and in collaboration with other student affairs colleagues on their campuses. Their efforts and others advocated throughout this chapter are urgently necessary if student affairs educators are to contribute in the most robust ways to student learning and development. However, attempting to do this work without the guidance of principles for good practice, data and ongoing inquiry, and a commitment to institutional mission will yield, at best, only a fraction of the educational outcomes that students are expected to accumulate inside and outside the classroom. Magical thinking must be replaced with strategic thinking, curriculum, and deliberate efforts to organize one's own professional practice around the ideals conveyed in this chapter. Anything less would constitute bad practice.

References

Alstete, J. W. (2004). *Accreditation matters: Achieving academic recognition and renewal* (ASHE Higher Education Report, Vol. 30, No. 4). San Francisco: Jossey-Bass.

Banta, T. W., Jones, E. A., & Black, K. E. (2009). *Designing effective assessment: Principles and profiles of good practice.* San Francisco: Jossey-Bass.

Bess, J. L., & Dee, J. R. (2008). *Understanding college and university organization: Theories for effective policy and practice.* Sterling, VA: Stylus.

Birnbaum, R. (2000). *Management fads in higher education: Where they come from, what they do, why they fail.* San Francisco: Jossey-Bass.

Blimling, G. S., Whitt, E. J., & Associates. (1999). *Good practice in student affairs: Principles to foster student learning.* San Francisco: Jossey-Bass.

Chaffee, E. E. (1984). Successful strategic management in small private colleges. *Journal of Higher Education, 55(2)*, 212–241.

Chang, M. J., Chang, J. C., & Ledesma, M. C. (2005). Beyond magical thinking: Doing the real work of diversifying our institutions. *About Campus, 9*(2), 9–16.

Cuyjet, M. J., & Associates. (2006). *African American men in college.* San Francisco: Jossey-Bass.

Dickeson, R. C. (1999). *Prioritizing academic programs and services: Reallocating resources to achieve strategic balance.* San Francisco: Jossey-Bass.

Dooris, M. J. (2002). Two decades of strategic planning: Is strategic planning a useful tool or a counterproductive management fad? *Planning for Higher Education, 31*(2), 26–32.

Dooris, M. J., Kelley, J. M., & Trainer, J. F. (Eds.). (2004). *Successful strategic planning* (New Directions for Institutional Research No. 123). San Francisco: Jossey-Bass.

Dowd, A. C. (2005). *Data don't drive: Building a practitioner-driven culture of inquiry to assess community college performance.* Indianapolis, IN: Lumina Foundation for Education.

Eckel, P. D., & Kezar, A. J. (2003). *Taking the reins: Institutional transformation in higher education.* Westport, CT: Praeger.

Harper, S. R. (2009). Race-conscious student engagement practices and the equitable distribution of enriching educational experiences. *Liberal Education, 95*(4), 38–45.

Harper, S. R., & antonio, a. l. (2008). Not by accident: Intentionality in fostering environments for learning and cross-cultural engagement. In S. R. Harper (Ed.), *Creating inclusive campus environments for cross-cultural learning and student engagement* (pp. 1–18). Washington, DC: National Association of Student Personnel Administrators.

Harper, S. R., & Harris III, F. (2010). *College men and masculinities: Theory, research, and implications for practice.* San Francisco: Jossey-Bass.

Harper, S. R., & Museus, S. D. (Eds.). (2007). *Using qualitative methods in institutional assessment* (New Directions for Institutional Research No. 136). San Francisco: Jossey-Bass.

Harper, S. R., & Quaye, S. J. (Eds.). (2009). *Student engagement in higher education: Theoretical perspectives and practical approaches for diverse populations.* New York: Routledge.

Harris, F., III, & Bensimon, E. M. (2007). The Equity Scorecard: A collaborative approach to assess and respond to racial/ethnic disparities in student outcomes. In S. R. Harper & L. D. Patton (Eds.), *Responding to the realities of race on campus* (New Directions for Student Services No. 120, pp. 77–84). San Francisco: Jossey-Bass.

Hartley, M. (2001). Student learning as a framework for student affairs: Rhetoric or reality? *NASPA Journal, 38*(2), 224–237.

Hartley, M. (2002). *Call to purpose: Mission-centered change at three liberal arts colleges.* New York: Routledge.

Hoover, E. (2007, November 16). U. of Delaware abandons sessions on diversity: Effort to teach tolerance in dormitories attacked as 'thought reform.' *Chronicle of Higher Education, 54*(12), A1.

Hurtado, S. (2007). Linking diversity with the educational and civic missions of higher education. *Review of Higher Education, 30*(2), 185–196.

Jones, S. R. (2007). Student resistance to cross-cultural engagement: Annoying distraction or site for transformative learning? In S. R. Harper (Ed.), *Creating inclusive campus environments for cross-cultural learning and student engagement* (pp. 67–85). Washington, DC: National Association of Student Personnel Administrators.

Keeling, R. P. (Ed.). (2006). *Learning reconsidered 2: Implementing a campus-wide focus on the student experience.* Washington, DC: American College Personnel Association, Association of College and University Housing Officers-International, Association of College Unions International, National Association for Campus Activities, National Academic Advising Association, National Association of Student Personnel Administrators, & National Intramural-Recreational Sports Association.

Kellom, G. (Ed.). (2004). *Developing effective programs and services for college men* (New Directions for Student Services No. 107). San Francisco: Jossey-Bass.

Kerr, K. G., & Tweedy, J. (2006). Beyond seat time and student satisfaction: A curricular approach to residential education. *About Campus, 11*(5), 9–15.

Kezar, A. J. (2001). *Understanding and facilitating organizational change in the 21st century: Recent research and conceptualizations* (ASHE Higher Education Report, Vol. 28, No. 4). San Francisco: Jossey-Bass.

Kowalski, T. J., & Lasley, T. J. (2009). *Handbook of data-based decision making in education.* New York: Routledge.

Kuh, G. D. (2008). *High-impact educational practices: What they are, who has access to them, and why they matter.* Washington, DC: Association of American Colleges and Universities.

Kuh, G. D., Kinzie, J., Schuh, J. H., Whitt, E. J., & Associates. (2005). *Student success in college: Creating conditions that matter.* San Francisco: Jossey-Bass.

Matney, M. M., & Taylor, S. H. (2007). Transforming student affairs strategic planning into tangible results. *NASPA Journal, 44*(1), 165–192.

Norris, D., & Poulton, N. (2008). *A guide to planning for change.* Ann Arbor, MI: Society for College and University Planning.

Price, J. (2009). Facilities planning and development. In G. S. McClellan & J. Stringer (Eds.), *The handbook of student affairs administration* (3rd ed., pp. 565–585). San Francisco: Jossey-Bass.

Rowley, D. J., & Sherman, H. (2001). *From strategy to change: Implementing the plan in higher education.* San Francisco: Jossey-Bass.

Sanaghan, P. (2009). *Collaborative strategic planning in higher education.* Washington, DC: National Association of College and University Business Officers.

Sax, L. J. (2008). *The gender gap in college: Maximizing the developmental potential of women and men.* San Francisco: Jossey-Bass.

Schuh, J. H., Upcraft, M. L., & Associates. (2001). *Assessment practice in student affairs: An applications manual.* San Francisco: Jossey-Bass.

Strange, C. C., & Banning, J. H. (2001). *Educating by design: Creating campus learning environments that work.* San Francisco: Jossey-Bass.

Tromp, S. A., & Ruben, B. D. (2004). *Strategic planning in higher education: A guide for leaders.* Washington, DC: National Association of College and University Business Officers.

CHAPTER SEVENTEEN

FINANCING STUDENT AFFAIRS

John H. Schuh

The fiscal environment in which higher education operates continues to experience stress, according to a variety of observers. Rising costs are one example of this stress. From 1929–1930 through 1995–1996, for example, educational and general expenditures per student rose faster than the consumer price index (a measure of inflation) (Snyder, Dillow, & Hoffman, 2008, Table 347). From 1985 through 2007, the higher education price index, a measure of inflation specifically calibrated to the costs experienced by institutions of higher education, has increased at a rate greater than the consumer price index in twenty out of the twenty-three years (Commonfund Institute, 2008). Costs have escalated, state support as a percentage of institutional revenues for higher education has diminished (Snyder et al., 2008, Table 337); doubts and concerns about college costs have been raised (Vedder, 2007); and those inside and outside the academy have posed questions about affordability (NACUBO, 2002). Even after discounting for student grant aid, net prices continue to rise faster than inflation (Wellman, 2001; Baum & Ma, 2008). In part because of increasing costs, higher education faces a murky future: "Public concern about rising costs may ultimately contribute to the erosion of public confidence in higher education" (U.S. Department of Education, 2006, p. 10).

This chapter is designed to provide a primer on financing student affairs. It will provide a conceptual way of thinking about the costs of higher education, and then will move into sources of revenue and expenditures in student affairs. It will include approaches to managing financial resources through various methods of budgeting. A number of books and other resources have been written about higher education finance, and these will be highlighted throughout. I encourage you to consult with these materials for a more in-depth treatment of the topic.

Thinking Conceptually About Finance

As previously discussed, one of the pressing issues in higher education is rising costs, particularly those paid by students (and their parents). Archibald and Feldman (2008) describe the situation this way: "Opinion surveys consistently find that how much one has to pay for a college education is a serious national issue" (p. 268). They identify two approaches to explaining why higher education costs have increased rapidly. The first of these approaches was originally developed by Bowen (1996), who identified certain "laws" that govern higher education costs. Among Bowen's laws are that institutions of higher education have virtually no limit on the amount of money they can spend on "seemingly fruitful education ends" (p. 123); that each institution raises all the money it can; and that each institution spends all it raises. As a consequence, these systemic "laws," which illustrate the fiscal environment in which higher education operates, are an approach to explaining why higher education has experienced rapidly increasing costs.

The other approach posited by Archibald and Feldman (2008) has to do with rapidly increasing costs of services provided by highly educated workers, among them health care providers, lawyers, statisticians, actuaries, and faculty members in higher education (pp. 285–286). The underlying concept is that higher education is no different from industries that rely on highly educated people who deliver services and, consequently, that "cost per student in higher education follows a time path very similar to the time path of other personal service industries that rely on highly educated labor" (p. 289). Regardless of which approach one subscribes to, however, the fact is that the cost of attendance for students has increased rapidly, and pressure is being put on institutions of higher education to contain their costs (U.S. Department of Education, 2006).

Leslie and Fretwell (1996) developed an excellent taxonomy of reasons why higher education is facing fiscal stress. Contributing external reasons include periodic economic recessions, changing student demographics, more complex and problematic budgeting as a consequence of increasingly wide variety of sources of support, macropolitical tax-limitation politics, micromanagement by state governments, political disaffection by voters, and increased legal requirements. Institutions also are suffering from internal sources of stress, according to these authors, including deferred maintenance, lack of incentives to change, management problems, and tuition discounts for students (Redd, 2000).

In the final analysis, those who have budgetary responsibilities in student affairs will have to make sure that their organizations are efficient, use resources wisely, and can demonstrate to stakeholders that their interests are central in financial decisions. Sandeen and Barr (2006) described the situation this way: "If student affairs leaders are to achieve their goals on their campus, it is essential that they become expert fiscal managers, articulate advocates for their programs, creative resource procurers, and knowledgeable contributors to their institution's overall budget processes" (p. 106). For that to occur, a good place to start is with an examination of the sources of revenue and categories of expenditures in student affairs, to which we now turn.

Revenue Sources

Although it may seem simplistic, revenue for student affairs comes from three main sources: the institution's general fund, student fees, and fees for service. Student fees are charged to all students as part of the cost of attendance while fees for service are specific fees students pay and are optional, such as a fee they might pay to park a car. Only those who have cars pay parking fees. The commentary that follows is very general in nature and makes no attempt to cover the universe of institutions of higher education since many colleges and universities have different approaches to funding student affairs that are idiosyncratic due to their institutional missions, histories, cultures, and customs. The examples given below are designed to be illustrative only and are not representative of any specific institution. The term *student services* here represents the broad array of programs, activities, and services that may be assigned to the portfolio of the division of student affairs and is the common way of referring to student affairs in the Integrated Postsecondary Education Data System (IPEDS, 2008).

General Fund Revenue

Depending on an institution's form of governance, general fund revenue will represent different categories of revenue. An institution is either "public," meaning that its "programs and activities are operated by publicly elected or appointed school officials and which is supported primarily by public funds" (IPEDS, 2008, n.p.), or "private," meaning that it is "controlled by a private individual(s) or by a nongovernmental agency, usually supported primarily by other than public funds, and operated by other than publicly elected or appointed officials. These institutions may be either for-profit or not-for-profit" (IPEDS, 2008, n.p.). The major difference is that the general fund typically represents tuition and state appropriations at public universities. At private institutions, the general fund could very well represent virtually all income, including tuition and fees as well as other revenue sources that will vary widely from institution to institution such as endowment income. Some student services at public institutions may be funded by the general fund, such as judicial affairs, services for students with disabilities, senior administrative oversight, and academic advising.

Student Fees

Some institutions charge students mandatory fees for student services that are paid as part of the students' semester (or quarter) bills. Examples of mandatory student fees are student health fees, campus recreation fees, and computer fees. These are fees that students pay whether or not they use the associated facilities or services. The primary difference between mandatory student fees and tuition is that the proceeds from the collection of mandatory fees go directly to the operation they support.

Other student fees may be optional. That is, a student does not have to pay the fee but may choose to do so when paying the institutional bill for tuition and mandatory fees. These fees might, for example, go toward a bus passes, subscriptions to the campus newspaper, or parking if students are permitted to keep cars on campus.

Fees for Service

Finally, fees for service may fund some student services. These are fees that are paid for the use of various services, often using a metric of usage, such as a monthly meal pass or rental of an apartment on campus for a month. Examples of these could include day care centers, student housing, dining services, and tickets to campus entertainment and sporting events. And, of course, a blended approach often is used. For example, student fees might fund recreational services' facilities, but then users might pay a fee to rent a locker or to participate in a specific activity such as a camping or sailing trip.

At private institutions it is less common for students to pay a substantial number of fees in addition to tuition. Tuition charges very well may cover almost the entire cost of all student services, although students may pay additional fees for such experiences as study abroad or alternative spring breaks dedicated to service-learning. The approach to charging additional fees will vary from institution to institution.

Institutional Differences in Funding Student Affairs

There are two common ways of measuring institutional support of student affairs: by the amount of revenue per student that is devoted to student affairs and by the percentage of institutional budget that is devoted to student affairs. Regardless of the measure used, public institutions tend to devote less funding to student affairs than do private, not-for-profit institutions (Snyder et al., 2008). The current taxonomy of expenditure categories for private, for-profit institutions, however, is such that it is not possible to draw broad conclusions about their level of support for student affairs (Snyder et al.).

As reported in the *Digest of Education Statistics 2007* (Snyder et al., 2008), in the most recent year reported, academic year 2004–2005, two-year public institutions devoted 9 percent of their budgets to student services and spent $913 per student on student services (Table 348). Four-year public institutions allocated 3.6 percent of their budgets and spent $1,091 per student on student services (Table 348). Private, not-for-profit institutions spent considerably more on student services: two-year, private not-for-profits spent 14.98 percent of their budgets on student services, or $2,629 per student (Table 351). Four-year, private, not-for-profit institutions spent 7.38 percent of their budgets, or $2,858 per student (Table 351).

Expenditures

The categories for expenditures range widely in student affairs. All student services have expenditures for personnel costs (salaries and fringe benefits); office operations (for example, office supplies and such communication devices as telephones and fax machines); and perhaps support for hourly employees, including students. Units may also spend money on travel for staff and in some cases students, and for capital items, which sometimes include furniture, computing equipment, and other nonconsumable goods. The definition of *capital* will vary from institution to institution, but often a specific expenditure amount will define what is considered a capital item. For example, this amount might be $500 or more for some institutions, while at others the minimum expenditure might be $1000 or even $5000. Institutions often have a detailed procedure for purchasing capital items, and may require that such bids from vendors be secured before capital items may be purchased, also, contracts with specific vendors may require that capital items be purchased from them.

Besides these fundamental costs, the cost of operations will also vary considerably from unit to unit. For example, some student services are strictly office operations, such as judicial affairs, whereas others have significant commitments to supporting facilities. Housing, student unions, and recreational services are examples of facilities-intensive operations, for which the cost of utilities, maintenance, and housekeeping can be significant. In addition, some units have facilities that have been financed through a borrowing program in the form of bonds. In these cases each unit is responsible for making periodic repayments to bondholders. Student housing and student unions are examples of operations that sometimes make significant expenditures dedicated to repaying their debt.

While the following list is not comprehensive, it illustrates some of the unique aspects of expenditures in student affairs units, recognizing that on some campuses these units might be assigned to an administrative unit other than student affairs:

- Food services have large expenditures for raw food items and kitchen and dining equipment.
- Health services have expenditures related to health care, including, in some cases, pharmaceutical and laboratory supplies and equipment.
- Intensive English language centers and international student admissions offices will have significant expenditures for international travel, as may be the case for study abroad programs.
- Recreational programs will have considerable expenditures for the consumable supplies needed to support their various activities.
- Campus housing may have potentially large expenditures for utilities.
- Services for students with disabilities may experience large costs for various services designed to assist students with disabilities.

This list illustrates that many student affairs offices have idiosyncratic expenses that may not occur anywhere else in an institution. Budget managers need to be familiar with the unique nature of their unit's expenditures and conversant in explaining the nature of the unit's expenditures to stakeholders.

Budgeting Approaches

Institutions have budgets for several reasons. Budgets provide a guide to unit leaders so that they can track their revenues and expenditures over the course of a fiscal year (commonly, but not always, from July 1 through June 30). With real-time budgeting, unit managers can access information at any time to determine the relative status of the revenues and expenditures for which they are responsible and make adjustments accordingly. Budgets also serve as planning documents. Over the course of several years unit managers can provide additional funds to support initiatives that are aligned with the unit's strategic plan. For example, if the housing department has set a goal of expanding learning communities, over time the department's budget officer can dedicate additional funds to the learning communities program. Or, in times of fiscal stress, the budget may be reduced in ways that are consistent with the strategic plan. Finally, budgets also provide departmental leaders with a transparent tool for describing the priorities of the department, for the reasons that are described above. A useful way to determine a unit's priorities is to review budgets over time, say for a period of five years. Over that period of time, one can learn the unit's priorities since where resources are allocated clearly represent organizational priorities.

This section will begin by discussing line item budgets, which are a common way of depicting revenue sources and expenditures. Discussion then turns to several budgeting approaches, including incremental, program, responsibility center, and capital budgeting. Most institutions of higher education utilize one or a combination of these approaches. Two other budgeting approaches, formula and zero-base budgeting, are not discussed since they are not used commonly. Readers seeking more information about these approaches should consult Woodard and von Destinon (2000). Dickmeyer (1996) also provides more information about other forms of budgeting, including alternate-level, quota, investment, and incentive budgeting or intramural funding.

Line Item Budgeting

Line items are used to depict revenue sources and expenditures categories in a wide variety of budgets. Line item expenditures are often divided into personnel and nonpersonnel categories. Personnel categories can have a line for every salaried position funded by a budget, along with fringe benefits and wages for hourly employees. Nonpersonnel items may include office supplies, telecommunications, equipment rental, utilities, and others depending on the nature of the department or program's expenditures funded by the budget. In some institutions, expenditures for travel and capital items also are discrete categories.

Why are line item budgets used? First, they are easy to understand. It does not take much of an accounting background to understand the concepts underlying these budgets. Second, they are easy to construct. New resources are added to a department's budget whenever possible, perhaps without serious questions being raised about the efficacy of the programs and activities the department provides. Third, they provide for good budgetary controls, in that the budget manager can determine on a line-by-line basis the extent to which revenues are meeting projections and expenditures are in line with expectations.

Incremental Budgeting

Incremental budgeting, which is often represented by line items, "is based on the previous year's allocation, and . . . is adjusted based on guidelines provided by the budget office" (Woodard & von Destinon, 2000, p. 332). It is a widely used approach to budgeting in higher education. This type of budget often is depicted by line items. Put simply, this approach takes the previous year's budget and makes a percentage or incremental change to it. For example, the total amount of money allocated to salaries may be increased by 3 percent, or funding for supplies might be cut by 2 percent. According to Barr (2002), "An incremental approach to budgeting is based on the assumption that both needs and costs vary only a small amount from year to year" (p. 37). In the end, budget managers adjust their budgets accordingly, and the work of budgeting is accomplished.

Incremental budgeting has some disadvantages. Perhaps foremost among these is that it "does not force the institution to examine priorities in a way that encourages annual reallocation, reductions, and elimination of programs" (Woodard & von Destinon, 2000, p. 333). Dickmeyer (1996) adds, "Responsibility for setting assumptions and priorities may be shirked with incremental budgeting" (p. 544). This type of budgeting assumes, moreover, that all aspects of a budget category can be increased or decreased at the same rate, which may not be the case. For example, in the category of insurance, annual increases in the cost of employee health insurance premiums may be much greater than annual increases in employee life insurance premiums. Remember that strategic planning challenges an institution to develop a vision of what it might become, thus at times requiring dramatic changes in organization and programs. Incremental budgeting does not lend itself well to making major changes in an institution's educational program and services.

Program Budgeting

According to Steiss (1972), a program is a "group of interdependent, closely related services or activities which possess or contribute to a common objective or set of allied objectives" (p. 157). Program budgeting, moreover, which "emphasizes the idea that budgets flow from ideas," (Dickmeyer, 1996, p. 545), consists of five tasks: identifying goals, examining current programs, developing a multiyear plan, analyzing and selecting alternative programs, and evaluating the programs.

Douglas (1991) maintains that program budgeting allows the overall cost associated with a program to be examined. But Schmidtlein (1981/2001) observes that academics generally do not favor program budgeting: "Faculty jealously protect their academic freedom and professional autonomy. As a consequence, they do not welcome the 'uninformed' opinion of budget staff and lay policy makers into the substance of their fields" (p. 422). Program budgeting provides a big-picture approach to budgeting and planning and identifies the path and direction of programming for the next several budget cycles.

Responsibility Center Budgeting

The next budgeting approach discussed here is responsibility center (or cost center) budgeting (Balderston, 1995). This form of budgeting also has been referred to as responsibility center management, value center management, and revenue center management, among other titles (Lang, 2001). Finney (1994) defined a *cost center* as "a unit of an organization for which costs are budgeted and collected, implying measurable characteristics of performance and responsibility" (p. 174). Responsibility center budgeting, according to Woodard and von Destinon (2000), is "a way to extend centralized planning and decision-making and to make each instructional unit financially responsible for its activities" (p. 335). "Under a responsibility centered model, each unit is financially responsible for activities and is held accountable for expenditures" (Barr, 2002, p. 41). Lee and Van Horn (1983) point out that this approach works best with self-contained units, such as an institution's hospital or athletic department. It is more difficult for units that support the activities of the entire campus, such as the registrar's office. It also may engender competition among units for students. For example, students may not be encouraged to change majors if such an action has revenue implications.

According to Stocum and Rooney (1997, p. 51), an advantage of this form of budgeting is that "it allows deans to shift funds from one spending category to another, depending on need, with accountability only for the total." On the other hand, they point out that this responsibility center budgeting can mean that "academic programs can become driven entirely by financial entrepreneurship" (p. 51). Adams (1997, p. 61) asserts that this form of budgeting results in "pressure to reduce the number of professors, for professors to teach more courses, to recognize only funded research and contracted service, and to eliminate majors and graduate programs with small enrollments, regardless of their importance for the culture." About this form of budgeting, Strauss, Curry, and Whalen (2001, p. 607) observe, "Can responsibility center budgeting work at a public institution of higher education? Of course, it can. What is required is leadership and the ability of an institution to earn income and retain unspent balances. And of the two, leadership is by far the most important."

Another advantage of this approach to budgeting is that units may be permitted to carry funds forward from one fiscal year to the next if they realize a surplus. However, any deficits ". . . must be made up the following fiscal year from allocated budget resources to the unit" (Barr, 2009, p. 498). In some respects, this form of budgeting applies the concepts used by auxiliary services, such as campus housing or the student union, to units that formerly did not have to be concerned with revenue sources, since funding was provided out of the institution's general fund. That is, units supported by the institution's general fund received an allocation at the beginning of the fiscal year and simply had to be careful not to overspend over the course of the fiscal year. In this approach, unit leaders also have to be accurate in estimating and realizing their revenue, because even if expenditures are in line with budgetary projections, if revenue is not realized according to plan, serious budget problems can result. "It has the major disadvantage of encouraging competition between units and concentrating on unit goals to the exclusion of institutional goals and objectives" (Barr, 2002, p. 41).

Capital Budgeting

One other form of budgeting that student affairs units may be engaged in on an occasional basis is capital budgeting. Capital budgets are designed for facility development or renovation, or other major expenditures that may extend over several years, and may be paid for through the issuance of bonds. The renovation of a student union is an example of a capital project. Typically, institutions have guidelines for this type of budgeting, and the process will involve the senior officers of the institution as well as its governing board in the approval process. Barr (2002) provides a framework for understanding capital budgeting and Price (2003) describes facility development projects in detail.

Accounting Methods

Depending on the kinds of accounts a student affairs office manages, two different forms of accounting—cash or accrual—are commonly used. Cash accounting is a form of bookkeeping in which "revenue, expense, and balance sheet items are recorded when cash is paid or received" (Finney, 1994, p. 174). Accrual accounting is a system in which "revenue is recorded when earned and balance sheet account charges are recorded when commitments are made" (p. 173), regardless of when funds are actually received or disbursed. "In other words, the accrual basis attempts to determine the real economic impact of what has occurred during a given period of time rather than simply determining how much cash was received or disbursed" (Meisinger & Dubeck, 1996, p. 469).

What are the implications of different accounting approaches for student affairs budget managers? Cash accounting may be used for accounts supported by the institution's general fund (supplied by tuition or state revenues). The accounting process may include encumbrances (commitments for expenditures), but for the most part it is not dramatically different from balancing a checkbook. Funds are deposited in various accounts at the beginning of the fiscal year (or, at some schools, more frequently). Expenses are deducted on a monthly basis, and the account manager must make sure that expenditures do not exceed budgeted amounts. Coupling cash accounting with line item budgeting helps protect budgets from overdrafts. The quality of spending is not an important issue in this approach; the real concern, rather, is making sure the budget is balanced at the end of the fiscal year.

With accrual accounting, which is frequently used for programs and services funded without state revenues or tuition dollars (such as student housing, the bookstore, or the student union), the account manager has to make sure revenue projections are realistic and expenditures are kept within the realized revenue level. This form of accounting is more complicated than cash accounting, in that not all revenues appearing on a budget statement will actually be collected. In fact, accrual accounting forces the budget manager to approach the budgeting cycle more like a manager of a for-profit business. Delving into the subtleties of accounting practices is beyond the scope of this chapter; however, it bears mention that budget managers in institutions of higher education must understand the distinctions between cash and accrual accounting and realize that the accrual basis, although providing a more accurate financial picture than cash accounting, also has additional risks, such as not collecting all the income that is credited to an account at the beginning of the semester or checks not clearing because of insufficient funds.

It is also important to understand the difference between restricted and unrestricted accounts. Unrestricted accounts include funds that can be spent in any way that is allowed by the institution. An example of an unrestricted account might be one that is supported by a public institution's general fund (tuition and state appropriation). In this case, the student affairs division's senior budget officer might be able to transfer funds from one office supported by the general fund (for example, the office of the dean of students) to pay for office supplies in the office of student activities (also supported by the institution's general fund). A restricted account, alternately, manages funds that may only be used to support the purposes for which they were originally received. For example, student fees directed to the office of career services to support an online resume system could not typically be transferred to the department of recreation to pay for repairs to the campus swimming pool. Restricted accounts commonly are found in scholarship programs; for example, donors might have made restricted gifts to support outstanding sophomores to study abroad during their junior years.

Preparing Budgets

Budgeting in higher education can be very accommodating. Fincher (1986) observes that "the budgeting process in institutions of higher education is successful because it has many accommodating features. Within hours after the arrival of a new fiscal year, budgeting-in-amendment begins" (p. 76). That is, changes to the adopted budget for the fiscal year begin almost as soon as the budget goes into effect.

Regardless of how accommodating budgeting procedures may be, student affairs staff need to pay close attention to the budgeting process. They need to avoid what Woodard, Love, and Komives (2000) asserted: "Student affairs professionals do not place a premium on understanding the financial and budgeting structure and processes of their institutions" (pp. 71–72). Remember this admonition as the process of preparing a budget for a discrete department within a student affairs division is described. Much of what follows in this section is based on Robins's excellent discussion of unit budgeting (1986) and incorporates a combination of the features of incremental budgeting.

Budget forms are distributed by the institution's budget office to department heads, usually during the spring. These forms, along with guidelines concerning percentage adjustments to salaries and operating expenditures, provide the basis for the department head's work. The guidelines often provide an acceptable range for salary increases and guidance on how budgets for supplies and services may be amended for the next year. Salary guidelines also might indicate whether salary adjustments should include awards for meritorious service. In some instances merit must be recognized. In other cases, merit awards may be added to a basic cost-of-living increase.

The materials provided by the budget office address many of the following expense categories: personnel costs, which include salaries and wages; operating expenses, which encompass costs associated with office supplies, telecommunications, postage, and perhaps utilities; capital, which includes equipment purchases; fringe benefits, which include such items as retirement, insurance, and social security costs; and travel expenses. Different institutions organize these categories in different ways, but all these items are typically found in the budget preparation material. The information the budget office supplies for personnel costs tends to be quite detailed; such information as position number, rank or grade, percentage of time worked, and length of appointment—along with current salary information—may be provided for every position.

The unit head's job is to apply the budgetary guidelines to the various categories of the budget. Guidance usually is provided for this task. The budget office prepares estimates for the next fiscal year for the cost of such items as postage, telephone rental, office supplies, and the like. The unit head must merely apply the necessary adjustments to the budget items within these categories. In the area of salaries, as mentioned earlier, cost-of-living and merit increases may be recommended for each salary grade. Merit increases should be linked to performance reviews; if they are not, the unit head will have a difficult time explaining to the unit's employees why some of them received larger increases than others. Merit increases should not be awarded unless unequal increases can be validly justified.

After completing the unit budget, the unit head forwards the budget material to the division head for review. This review examines such factors as compliance with the guidelines prepared by the budget office, internal consistency, and compatibility with budgetary plans prepared by other unit heads. The division head has to be concerned with all of the same issues as the unit heads, but he or she also needs to make sure that the budget plans fit nicely with one another. If one department consistently receives larger increases (or smaller decreases) than do other units, the division head will have to explain why, not only to his or her supervisor but also to disgruntled employees. When the division head completes work on the budget, the budget is then forwarded through normal channels for review by appropriate campus offices.

Woodard and von Destinon (2000) offer some additional budgeting recommendations, including determining the contribution of the unit to the divisional and institutional mission; measuring the workload of staff in individual units; trying to provide measurable outcomes for a unit; determining if most activities help students do things for themselves; protecting services designed to maintain ethical, health, and safety standards; and identifying new sources of revenue. Adding to this list of suggestions, the Pew Higher Education Research Program (1996) recommends that across-the-board cuts be resisted, concluding: "Democratic [budget] cutting represents not just a failure of will, but, more significantly, a failure to understand that maintaining quality in some areas will require a reduction or elimination of others" (p. 515). For example, if an institution downsizes one unit and assigns a number of its activities to another unit that does not have adequate staff or expertise to take on the additional responsibilities, institutional decision makers are engaging in self-deception: funds might be saved, but students will be poorly served, and little good will result. Please see Barr (2002); Woodard (1993, 1995); and Woodard and von Destinon (2000) for additional discussions of the budget development process in general.

Budgeting for Auxiliary Services

Auxiliary services, are "those essentially self-supporting operations which exist to furnish a service to students, faculty, or staff, and which charge a fee that is directly related to, although not necessarily equal to, the cost of the service. Examples are residence halls, food services, college stores, and intercollegiate athletics" (Snyder & Dillow, 2010, p. 665). According to Ambler, they can represent "as much as eight percent or more of a chief student affairs officer's fiscal responsibility" (Ambler, 2000, p. 131). Indeed, the size of auxiliary budgets can be enormous. For example, the auxiliary budget at Purdue University in 2007–2008 was $231 million, or just under 15 percent of the university's total budget of $1,550.9 million. To be sure, auxiliaries often include intercollegiate athletics at public institutions, but this budget category was the second largest of the university's total budget, surpassed only by expenditures for instruction and departmental research (Purdue University, 2008).

Building a budget for an auxiliary service incorporates some of the principles described above, but it also includes several additional features. Primary among these features is that unit leaders in auxiliary services must be able to forecast revenues accurately. For housing directors, that means estimating net revenues realized from room and board payments as well as income from summer conferences housed on campus. For student union directors, estimating income from various revenue sources such as food service, room rental, program fees, and perhaps the bookstore is central to the financial health of their operations. Many units in student affairs at public colleges and universities, such as student health services or counseling centers, can be operated as quasi-auxiliary services in that they receive no support from the institution's general fund other than overhead (including office space and perhaps utilities). Rather, all of their revenues come from student fees and fees for service. Their fiscal health depends on accurate revenue projections for student fees and the services provided for which revenue is received.

Auxiliaries must include such additional factors as changes in debt service, utilities, and institutional overhead charges in the development of their budgets. Auxiliary budgets are segregated from other institutional budgets and are designed to be operated without institutional subsidy, meaning that they must generate sufficient revenue to fund their operations. In fact, Lennington (1996) asserts that auxiliary enterprises "provide an opportunity to generate revenues that can be used to subsidize" the institution's academic mission (p. 87).

Once an auxiliary service budget is developed, consultation should be arranged with appropriate constituent groups. Auxiliaries may have budget committees that include students, faculty, or graduates. The role of these committees can range from acting in an advisory capacity to actually having to approve changes in fee charges before these are submitted for governing board approval. In some states, such as

Indiana, Iowa, and Kansas, approval of room and board rates by the state's governing board is scheduled much earlier in the academic calendar than is the approval process for adjustments to other fees or tuition. As a consequence, the budget manager may have to forecast costs for as long as eighteen months or more. This requires great skill and good luck, because an intervening external circumstance, such as an oil embargo or crop failure, can have a major, negative impact on the auxiliary service's budget.

Auxiliary unit heads should heed the same advice given for other unit heads regarding personnel expenditures. For example, the director of the student union typically cannot award employees 6 percent raises, even if the money is available, if the average increase for all staff at the institution is 4 percent. Nor can fringe benefits be adjusted differently, such as by providing a better retirement package or more vacation days for auxiliary unit staff. Auxiliary services generally function within the budgeting framework of their institution, even if they must generate their own operating revenues.

Trends in Finance and Budgeting

This section describes current trends in budgeting and finance, including downsizing and reallocation, outsourcing of services and programs, increasing revenues, securing grants and contracts, and fundraising.

Downsizing and Reallocation

One unpleasant aspect of budgeting in the past few years has been dealing with institutional mandates to downsize many operations. Downsizing refers to eliminating positions or, in some cases, entire units; it results from institutions' simply not having sufficient revenue streams to support all the activities and services they would like to provide. Determining which essential programs and services need to be provided and which can be eliminated is a difficult exercise that senior leaders and department heads are forced to undertake. Downsizing will usually result in fundamental changes in programs and services as well as many unhappy staff, faculty, and students. Involving students and faculty in the process is crucial.

Outsourcing of Services and Programs

One strategy related to downsizing—outsourcing or privatization—involves entering into contracts with enterprises outside the institution to provide services that have become quite expensive for the institution itself to offer. Food service operations, for example, have been outsourced for years. One institution went from losing about $100,000 per year when the college operated its own food service to gaining an annual rebate from a contractor of $168,000 (Angrisani, 1994). Although such savings are not always possible, outsourcing represents one attractive scenario for senior administrators looking for ways to cut expenditures.

Moneta and Dillon (2001) point out that the "prospect of turning over a college or university administrative service to a private provider continues to generate anxiety, resistance and fear among many of us who have directly managed one or more of those services" (p. 31). They believe, however, that outsourcing can be wise if circumstances so indicate: "Nonetheless, it is likely and in many cases desirable, to convey management responsibility for some campus service to a private partner where the benefits derived from those relationships outweigh risks of continued self operation or are likely to enhance service quality or reduce costs" (Moneta & Dillon, p. 31).

Rush, Kempner, and Goldstein (1995) have developed six categories of factors that need to be taken into account when deciding whether or not to outsource a service or operation: financial considerations, human resources, mission and cultural factors, management control and efficiency, the quality of services, and legal and ethical components. They argue that "regardless of the size, location or affiliation of the institution, and no matter what functional area is under consideration, campus decision makers need to use a structured methodology that supports efficient and effective decision making" that can withstand the scrutiny of various campus constituencies (p. 6).

One should not assume that outsourcing is a panacea, however. When a bookstore, for example, is outsourced, employees can be affected—private companies may not have pay scales or fringe benefit packages similar to those of the higher education institution. Even if the employees do not lose their jobs in an outsourcing arrangement, there is an excellent chance that their total compensation will be affected negatively. This presents quite an ethical dilemma for the student affairs officer faced with solving a budgetary problem.

Another issue that may be influential in an outsourcing decision is the contemporary interest of many students in issues related to the environment and worker rights. Levine and Cureton (1998) have described a resurgence in student activism; if outsourcing is conducted without a sensitivity to the environment and worker rights, student dissent may result. It is therefore important to remember that even when outsourcing appears to be the only solution to a problem, it may come at a cost.

Increasing Revenues

Whereas outsourcing and downsizing are used to reduce costs, two recent trends have emerged in higher education to help raise additional revenues. One is to apply substantial overhead charges, such as a percentage of gross revenue, to auxiliary units for services provided by general administrative units on campus, including purchasing, accounting, providing security, and the like. As discussed earlier, auxiliaries at public institutions typically are expected to pay their way without subsidies from the campus general fund, and at some private institutions auxiliaries are designed to subsidize the institution's general fund. At some institutions, contributions from auxiliaries actually exceed the value of the services provided to them by the institution. Situations exist where some units, such as health services, are charged rent for the space they occupy in a campus building. In other circumstances, charges are assessed for custodial and maintenance services without the auxiliary's being given the option of hiring its own staff or contracting with a private firm. The consequence of levying overhead charges is that additional funds are provided for other needs on campus, such as faculty salaries, library support, and other activities charged to an institution's general fund.

Another option is to charge students dedicated fees or activity fees for student affairs units. These might include a special fee to pay the debt on student affairs buildings (such as the student union) or a dedicated health services or counseling fee. These fees reduce the pressure on the general fund and allow the institution to take the political position that tuition increases have been slowed. Quite obviously, dedicated, mandatory fees represent additional costs to students. Sandeen and Barr (2006) assert, "Critics of the student fee approach to funding student services may assert that it may cause resentment toward student affairs because of its 'privileged funding position' and may even result in accusations that student affairs leaders manipulate students in order to obtain their support for new or increased student fees" (p. 101). Nevertheless, given the lack of fiscal health in higher education over the past decade, it is quite possible that more fees will be charged to students.

Grants and Contracts

Still another source of funding that is likely to play an increasingly important role in the future is external grants or contracts. Grants can be sought from not for profit sources for such activities as supporting start up costs for new programs, or for support for students. An example of this might be finding support to develop a resource center for historically under represented groups of students. The grant would support the development of the program and securing appropriate space. In turn, the institution would have to promise to sustain the program once it is up and running.

Some aspects of student affairs have been engaged in contract work for years. Campus residence halls, for example, can work with youth groups to provide housing on campus for a summer program, or can provide housing for conferences on campus during the academic year if space is available. Union facilities often are available for rental to individuals or groups who wish to hold events on campus, such as a service club's banquet or a wedding reception. Other student affairs units will be pressed in the future to similarly secure contracts and grants to support their work.

Fundraising

Fundraising is a fairly recent development in the area of generating additional revenue for student affairs. Annual giving, such as yearly fundraising drives that focus on gifts from alumni and institutional friends, can be directed toward routine operations, whereas campaigns may help secure larger gifts, often for specific purposes, such as assisting scholarship programs, providing seed gifts for the development of new facilities, or aiding in the significant renovation of facilities that are becoming obsolete (see Barr, 2002; Jackson, 2000).

Graduates who served in significant roles in certain student groups as undergraduates are excellent prospects as donors. These graduates might have served as resident assistants, student government officers, union board members, and leaders of campus recreation programs. Student affairs needs to carefully coordinate fundraising efforts through the institution's fundraising arm, because other elements of the institution, such as the students' academic major departments, also will consider these graduates to be good prospects.

Some aspects of student affairs have excellent potential for fund raising. Among these are facilities for students, such as recreation facilities, student unions, and residence halls. Another is programming for students, which can include leadership development activities, travel to student conferences, or support for speakers to come to campus. Finally, there are some aspects of fundraising in student affairs that have a long history of success, a primary example of which is student scholarship support. Most campuses are actively engaged in scholarship development, and if financial aid is part of the student affairs portfolio, fundraising for student scholarships will be an important divisional activity. Jackson (2000) is optimistic about fundraising in student affairs: "Student affairs programs now have the opportunity to help their institutions finance projects that may not have been funded by external sources a decade ago" (p. 610). He urges student affairs staff to "gain support for programs in a manner similar to deans, faculty and staff in academic departments" (pp. 610–611).

Conclusion

Financial pressure on student affairs units will continue to rise in the future: states are running short of funds, and the federal government cannot be considered a dependable source of revenue. Student fees will likely increase at a faster rate than tuition, and the use of downsizing and outsourcing will increase in frequency. Given this unpleasant scenario, student affairs managers and leaders have no choice but to develop strong financial management skills or face dire consequences. This chapter examined some of the more salient issues related to these topics. Well-developed financial management skills are central to success in the contemporary financial environment of higher education. A high level of expertise will serve all student affairs officers well, helping them develop programs that provide important learning opportunities for students while simultaneously meeting the administrative and organizational needs of their institution.

References

Adams, E. M. (1997, September/October). Rationality in the academy: Why responsibility center budgeting is a wrong step down the wrong road. *Change, 29,* 59–61.

Ambler, D. A. (2000). Organizational and administrative models. In M. J. Barr, M. K. Desler, & Associates, *The handbook of student affairs administration* (2nd ed., pp. 121–134). San Francisco: Jossey-Bass.

Angrisani, C. (1994). Students' needs dictate contract decision. *On-Campus Hospitality, 16*(4), 22–26.

Archibald, R. B., & Feldman, D. H. (2008). Explaining increases in higher education costs. *Journal of Higher Education, 79*(3), 268–295.

Balderston, F. E. (1995). *Managing today's university: Strategies for viability, change, and excellence.* San Francisco: Jossey-Bass.

Barr, M. J. (2002). *Academic administrator's guide to budgets and financial management.* San Francisco: Jossey-Bass.

Barr, M. J. (2009). Budgeting and fiscal management for student affairs. In G. S. McClellan, J. Stringer & Associates, *The handbook of student affairs administration* (3rd ed.) (pp. 481–504). San Francisco: Jossey-Bass.

Baum, S., & Ma, J. (2008). *Trends in college pricing 2008.* Washington, DC: College Board.

Bowen, H. R. (1996). What determines the cost of higher education? In D. W. Breneman, L. L. Leslie, & R. E. Anderson (Eds.), *ASHE Reader on finance in higher education* (pp. 113–127). Needham Heights, MA: Simon & Schuster.

Commonfund Institute. (2008). *2007 HEPI (Higher Education Price Index).* Wilton, CT: Author.

Dickmeyer, N. (1996). Budgeting. In D. W. Breneman, L. L. Leslie, & R. Anderson (Eds.). *ASHE reader on finance in higher education* (pp. 539-561). Needham Heights, MA: Simon & Schuster.

Douglas, D. O. (1991). Fiscal resource management: Background and relevance for student affairs. In T. K. Miller, R. B. Winston Jr., & Associates (Eds.), *Administration and leadership in student affairs* (pp. 615–641). Muncie, IN: Accelerated Development.

Fincher, C. (1986). Budgeting myths and fictions. In L. L. Leslie & R. E. Anderson (Eds.), *ASHE reader on finance in higher education* (pp. 73–86). Lexington, MA: Ginn Press.

Finney, R. G. (1994). *Basics of budgeting.* New York: AMACOM.

Integrated Postsecondary Education Data System (IPEDS). (2008). *Glossary.* Washington, DC: National Center for Education Statistics. Retrieved August 14, 2008, from http://nces.ed.gov/ipeds/glossary/index.asp?id=511\.

Jackson, M. L. (2000). Fund-raising and development. In M. J. Barr, M. K. Desler, & Associates, *The handbook of student affairs administration* (2nd ed., pp. 597–611). San Francisco: Jossey-Bass.

Lang, D. W. (2001). A primer on responsibility centre budgeting and responsibility centre management. In J. L. Yeager, G. M. Nelson, E. A. Potter, J. C. Weidman, & T. G. Zullo (Eds.), *ASHE reader on finance in higher education* (2nd ed., pp. 568–590). Boston: Pearson.

Lee, S. M., & Van Horn, J. C. (1983). *Academic administration.* Lincoln: University of Nebraska Press.

Lennington, R. L. (1996). *Managing higher education as a business.* Phoenix, AZ: ACE/Oryx.

Leslie, D. W., & Fretwell, E. K., Jr. (1996). *Wise moves in hard times: Crafting and managing resilient colleges and universities.* San Francisco: Jossey-Bass.

Levine, A., & Cureton, J. S. (1998). *When hope and fear collide.* San Francisco: Jossey-Bass.

Meisinger, R. J., Jr., & Dubeck, L. W. (1996). Fund accounting. In D. W. Breneman, L. L. Leslie, & R. E. Anderson (Eds.), *ASHE reader on finance in higher education* (pp. 465–491). Needham Heights, MA: Simon & Schuster.

Moneta, L., & Dillon, W. L. (2001). Strategies for effective outsourcing. In L. Dietz & E. Enchelmayer (Eds.), *Developing external partnerships* (New Directions for Student Services No. 96, pp. 31–49). San Francisco: Jossey-Bass.

Muston, R. A. (1980). Resource allocation and program budgeting. In C. H. Foxley (Ed.), *Applying management techniques* (New Directions for Student Services No. 9, pp. 79–92). San Francisco: Jossey-Bass.

Pew Higher Education Research Program. (1996). The other side of the mountain. In D. W. Breneman, L. L. Leslie, & R. E. Anderson (Eds.), *ASHE reader on finance in higher education* (pp. 511–518). Needham Heights, MA: Simon & Schuster.

Price, J. (Ed.). (2003). *Planning and achieving successful student affairs facilities projects* (New Directions for Student Services No. 101). San Francisco: Jossey-Bass.

Purdue University. (2008). *Purdue University data digest 2007–2008.* West Lafayette, IN: Author.

Redd, K. E. (2000). *Discounting toward disaster: Tuition discounting, college finance, and enrollments of low-income undergraduates* (USA Group Foundation New Agenda Series, Volume 3, No. 2). Indianapolis: USA Group Foundation.

Robins, G. B. (1986). Understanding the college budget. In L. L. Leslie & R. E. Anderson (Eds.), *ASHE reader on finance in higher education* (pp. 28–56). Lexington, MA: Ginn Press.

Rush, S. C., Kempner, D. E., & Goldstein, P. J. (1995). Contract management: A process approach to making the decision. In *Peterson's contract services for higher education* (pp. 5–9). Princeton, NJ: Peterson's.

Sandeen, A., & Barr, M. J. (2006). *Critical issues for student affairs.* San Francisco: Jossey-Bass.

Schmidtlein F. A. (1981/2001). Why linking budgets to plans has proven difficult in higher education. In J. L. Yeager, G. M. Nelson, E. A. Potter, J. C. Weidman, & T. G. Zullo (Eds.), *ASHE reader on finance in higher education* (2nd ed.) (pp. 415-424). Boston, MA: Pearson.

Snyder, T. D., Dillow, S. A., and Hoffman, C. M. (2008). *Digest of education statistics 2007* (NCES 2008–022). Washington, DC: National Center for Education Statistics, Institute of Education Sciences, U.S. Department of Education.

Snyder, T.D., and Dillow, S.A. (2010). *Digest of Education Statistics 2009.* National Center for Education Statistics, Institute of Education Sciences, U.S. Department of Education. Washington, DC.

Steiss, A. W. (1972). *Public budgeting and management.* Lexington, MA: Heath.

Stocum, D. L., & Rooney, P. M. (1997, September/October). Responding to resource constraints: A departmentally based system of responsibility center management. *Change, 29*(5), 51–57.

Strauss, J., Curry, J, & Whalen, E. (2001). Revenue responsibility budgeting. In J. L. Yeager, G. M. Nelson, E. A. Potter, J. C. Weidman, & T. G. Zullo (Eds.), *ASHE reader on finance in higher education* (2nd ed., pp. 591–607). Boston: Pearson.

U. S. Department of Education. (2006). *A test of leadership: Charting the future of U.S. higher education.* Washington, DC: Author.

Vedder, R. (2007). *Over invested and over priced.* Washington, DC: Center for College Affordability and Productivity. Retrieved September 18, 2008, from www.collegeaffordability.net/research.php.

Wellman, J. V. (2001). *Looking back, going forward: The Carnegie Commission policy.* Washington, DC: The Institute for Higher Education Policy, The Ford Foundation, and the Education Resources Institute.

Woodard, D. B., Jr. (1993). Budgeting and fiscal management. In M. J. Barr, M. K. Desler, & Associates, *The handbook of student affairs administration* (pp. 242-259). San Francisco: Jossey-Bass.

Woodard, D. B., Jr. (1995). *Budgeting as a tool for policy in student affairs* (New Directions for Student Services no. 70). San Francisco: Jossey-Bass.

Woodard, D. B., Jr., Love, P., & Komives, S. R. (2000). *Leadership and management issues for a new century* (New Directions for Student Services No. 92). San Francisco: Jossey-Bass.

Woodard, D. B., Jr., & von Destinon, M. (2000). Budgeting and fiscal management. In M. J. Barr, M. K. Desler, & Associates, *The handbook of student affairs administration* (2nd ed., pp. 327–346). San Francisco: Jossey-Bass.

CHAPTER EIGHTEEN

ASSESSMENT AND EVALUATION

Marilee J. Bresciani

The ability to incorporate assessment and evaluation into day-to-day practices is emerging as a necessary competency for student affairs practitioners (Flowers, 2003; Gayles & Kelly, 2007; Herdlein, 2004; Hickmott & Bresciani, in press; Strange, 2001; Waple, 2006; Young & Elfrink, 1991; Young & Janosik, 2007). This chapter first defines assessment and evaluation. Then, focusing primarily on outcomes-based assessment, I explain the importance of this kind of assessment, describe key components of the practice, and illustrate how assessment results can be used to inform planning and budgeting decisions. I also include questions to consider in implementing the practice of outcomes-based assessment at your campus.

Definitions of Assessment and Evaluation

Although assessment and evaluation have been in practice in the profession for quite some time, definitions of each concept have varied (Astin, 1993; Ewell, 1997; Kuh, Schuh, Whitt, & Associates, 1991). Upcraft and Schuh (1996) define *assessment* as "any effort to gather, analyze, and interpret evidence which describes institutional, divisional, or agency effectiveness" (p. 18). They define *evaluation* as "any effort to use assessment evidence to improve institutional, departmental, divisional, or institutional effectiveness" (p. 19). Suskie (2004) also considers evaluation as part of the assessment process, in that evaluation requires the use of "assessment information to make an informed judgment on such things as whether students have achieved the learning goals we've established for them" (p. 5).

The authors listed in the previous paragraph do differentiate the meaning of assessment from evaluation. However, Palomba and Banta (1999) do not differentiate between assessment and evaluation, and define assessment as "the systematic collection, review and use of information about educational programs undertaken for the purpose of improving student learning and development" (p. 4). Maki (2004) also does not distinguish between assessment and evaluation, describing assessment as a systematic means to satisfy educators' innate intellectual curiosity about how well their students learn what educators expect them to learn.

The earlier definitions do vary in their meaning and thus "confusion" is present for some. To cause further confusion, there are also many types of assessment. Borrowing definitions from Bresciani, Moore Gardner, and Hickmott (2010), types of assessment can be divided into five main categories: (1) needs assessment, (2) utilization assessment, (3) assessment of satisfaction, (4) assessment based on Astin's Input-Environment-Outcome (I-E-O) Model, and (5) outcomes-based assessment of student learning and development (Bresciani, Zelna, & Anderson, 2004).

Needs assessment focuses on determining the types of services and programs that students indicate they would like or need. Some of these needs could be indirectly identified from such instruments as the Beginning College Survey of Student Engagement (BCSSE), which looks at the activities in which students hope to participate when they enter college. You might choose to do a needs assessment prior to offering services or programs, or you could articulate the outcomes of a planned service or program and ask students to comment on whether those intended outcomes meet their needs or desires.

Utilization assessment focuses on which of your services students are using—and how they are using them. Information gathered in utilization assessment can include the number of students using a particular service; the "type" of student using that service (for example, assessing age, ethnicity, standing, and so on); and details about when and how the service is used. Capturing students' use of services can be accomplished through such methods as using sign-in sheets, identification-card swipe systems, and data-gathering software. Utilization information can inform facilities management, personnel workload discussions, and the timing and placement of programs. In addition, you can use utilization data to help interpret the meaning of results generated from outcomes-based assessment, which will be discussed later in this section.

Assessment of satisfaction explores students' satisfaction with a particular service or a service entity as a whole. National standardized assessment tools include the Educational Benchmarking (EBI) Surveys and the Noel-Levitz Satisfaction Survey. Assessment of satisfaction can be an important component of the assessment of student learning and development because students who express higher levels of satisfaction with services at an institution tend to excel at higher rates (Kuh, Kinzie, Buckley, Bridges, & Hayek, 2006). However, satisfaction surveys on their own do not tell us why students were or were not satisfied. Therefore, we gain no information to improve the programs with which students were dissatisfied.

Astin's I-E-O Model (Astin, 1993) of assessment provides a framework for examining the inputs (e.g., a student's background characteristics and the knowledge with which they entered the experience); environment (e.g., the college experience); and outcomes (e.g., knowledge the student possesses upon graduation) associated with a student's transition through college. This assessment approach is associated with a quasi-experimental methodology, and thus is most readily measured with pre- and post-test methodology. The pre-test will account for a student's knowledge and stage of development upon entering an environment. The post-test, administered after the student has experienced the environment, will measure what the student has gained through participating in that environment while accounting for the student's initial inputs. This is the most sophisticated assessment approach, in that it intends to measure the value-added of the experience with which the student engaged. In other words, with this type of assessment, you will discover how much knowledge the student gained from the experience. It is also the most time consuming, if it is conducted well. To be implemented well, Astin's I-E-O requires attention to sampling and other variables that may influence the measurement of the experience.

For the purpose of this chapter, I will focus on one type of assessment in particular, *outcomes-based assessment* (OBA). Also, for the sake of consistency, I will adapt Suskie's definition (2004): outcomes-based assessment is the ongoing, systematic practice of (1) establishing succinct, identifiable, expected outcomes or end results of student learning, development, or services; (2) ensuring through proper planning and resource allocation that students have opportunities to achieve those expected outcomes or end results; (3) intentionally gathering, analyzing, and interpreting evidence to determine whether and to what extent students have met those expected outcomes or end results; and (4) using the resulting information to (a) celebrate or advertise successful achievement of outcomes, (b) inform the planning processes that will improve the expected outcomes, (c) reallocate resources to the improvement of those outcomes, or (d) revisit the strategic plan to determine whether all of the expected outcomes can continue to be met (Bresciani et al., 2009).

Through OBA we are simply trying to ask and answer the following questions.

- What are we trying to do and why? *or*
- What is my program supposed to accomplish? *or*
- What do I want students to be able to do and/or know as a result of my course/ workshop/orientation/program?
- How well are we doing it?
- How do we know?
- How do we use the information to improve or celebrate successes?
- Do the improvements we make contribute to our intended end results? (Bresciani et al., 2004, p.10)

The Purpose of Assessment

The public demand for accountability in higher education has progressively increased since the beginning of the 1990s (Donald & Denison, 2001). This increasing demand for accountability is discussed throughout much of the higher education assessment literature (Bresciani, 2006; Bresciani et al., 2009; Palomba & Banta, 1999; Schuh, &

Associates, 2009; Upcraft & Schuh, 1996). Increases in college costs, decreases in evidence of students' general learning, and the inability to explain the intended end results of particular services contribute to a growing suspicion and misunderstanding of what it is that we actually do in higher education and what our actual results are (Bresciani; Bresciani et al.; Palomba & Banta; Schuh & Associates; Upcraft & Schuh).

Although the purposes of higher education may be debated, the agreed-upon expectation is that students will be able to graduate with a set of knowledge and skills (Bresciani, 2006; Bresciani et al., 2009; Palomba & Banta, 1999; Schuh & Associates, 2009; Upcraft & Schuh, 1996). The questions that remain, however, are: How well do all the parties involved in facilitating the creation of that set of knowledge and skills actually do the work that is intended? and How well does each program designed to support or contribute to student learning and development do what it is intended to do? Outcomes-based assessment can help answer those questions by not only providing a body of evidence that informs needed improvements but also demonstrating when intended outcomes have been accomplished.

The *Student Learning Imperative* (American College Personnel Association [ACPA], 1996) posits that effective and enriching student affairs policies and programs should stem from research on student learning and institutional assessment data. Student learning research provides a general knowledge base from which to draw conclusions about and gain insight for decision making, programming, and planning. Institution-specific assessment data provide information about institutional culture and context, and about the impact of these on how policies, procedures, and programs are manifested on a particular college or university campus. Combining both research and assessment data provides a comprehensive foundation of information that may be used to inform policymaking and develop meaningful, learning-centered programming.

Upcraft and Schuh (1996) assert that assessment can assist student affairs professionals with decisions regarding the type and scope of programs and services to provide and may also yield information about how much student learning results from particular services or initiatives. With regard to strategic planning, assessment helps identify goals and objectives and highlights any issues in need of resolution before such goals and objections can be realized (Upcraft & Schuh). Assessment data yield information about potential strengths and weaknesses in planning, programming, and policymaking, and provide a systematic means for effective decision making. Such data may also help create priorities in strategic planning efforts by identifying areas that are performing well or that are in need of improvement. The data also may inform the design of action plans within specific units. Assessment is, demonstrably, a very useful component of departmental, divisional, and institutional program review. By utilizing the results of assessment in developing programs, services, and policies, student affairs professionals can ensure student learning remains at the core of their work (Bresciani et al., 2009).

Research conducted on why OBA is not systematically practiced has demonstrated that it may be because OBA is not clearly articulated to professionals within institutions (Bresciani, 2006; Bresciani, 2010; Palomba & Banta, 1999). It therefore becomes imperative, before requiring professionals to participate in OBA, that its purpose be understood by all. For example, it may be helpful to explain to professionals that OBA does not exist for its own sake or for the sake of appeasing an accreditation body. The purpose of OBA is to reflect on the end result of our day-to-day doing. OBA is the process of taking what most of us already do on a daily basis and making it systematic. We simply need to ask and answer this question: Are we accomplishing that which we say we are (Bresciani, 2006; Bresciani et al., 2004; Bresciani et al., 2009)?

Strategic and action planning are incorporated into OBA. Strategic planning informs the mission statements and goals that in turn inform program design (through action planning) (Freeman, Bresciani & Bresciani, 2004; Palomba & Banta, 1999; Upcraft & Schuh, 1996). Furthermore, strategic planning helps prioritize the strategic initiatives or goals that programs may be assessing. For example, assume that your institution values diversity and has determined that designing programs that support students with diverse learning styles is not only an institutional goal but also a high strategic priority; and imagine that engagement of students with diverse learning styles is a program goal of yours that links to the institutional strategic initiative. Therefore, when planning a program designed to support engagement of students with diverse learning styles, you use OBA to assess outcomes that link to this goal, you will have evidence of how well this program links to the institutional strategic initiative—or you may have evidence of what needs to be improved so that your program can better contribute to the institutional strategic initiative.

OBA is not only intended to suggest areas for improvement, but it is also designed to inform decisions about how resources can be reallocated (for example, through budgeting) so that program improvements can be made. Returning to the example in the previous paragraph, imagine that you are now the leader of your division. You know that the institution values programs that support students with diverse learning styles. You therefore encourage your professional staff to design programs that align with this goal and to evaluate how well those programs are contributing to the achievement of this goal.

As OBA results pour in, you realize that there are several resource requests for improving the multiple programs that are contributing to the achievement of this institutional goal. Some of the resources can be reallocated internally—your team of professionals can reallocate resources from less-valued or less-effective programs within their own departments. However, in some programs, there are no internal resources to be reallocated. Now you must determine whether the improvements recommended in those programs are "worth" your reallocating division-level resources. In some cases you may determine that the intended improvements are worth the investment of divisional resources; in others, you may find that program-level performance cannot be improved without your securing external resources. Thus OBA integrates tightly with strategic planning and budgeting.

OBA can be used to evaluate the effectiveness of services and programs. With today's increasing focus on student learning, it is important to use OBA to evaluate how well your program is contributing, either directly or indirectly, to student learning. If some of your colleagues within your division are having difficulty identifying how their services are contributing to student learning, remind them that they are a part of the institution for a reason—to contribute to the learning environment (Maki, 2004); then ask them to examine their programs and reflect on the following questions:

1. Do you directly contribute to student learning and development? If so, how? What is it that your service or program intends to teach students so they can become more successful?
2. Do you indirectly contribute to student learning and development? If so, how? What is it that your service or program intends to teach others, such as parents, instructors, or student affairs professionals, so that they can help students become more successful? What services do you provide that are necessary for student success, such as financial aid, dining services, custodial services, giving directions, or answering student questions? And how well do you do that work?
3. Does your service or program interfere with student learning and development? If so, how?

After reflecting on these three areas of questions, many professionals can begin to see how they directly or indirectly contribute to student learning and development. Sometimes it is helpful to reflect from the perspectives of those for whom our programs are designed to serve. If we have designed effective programs for internal audiences such as business services of effective financial aid practices for our internal office use, rather than the students or other colleagues that we serve, then, we may need to reassess the design.

Typical Components of an Outcomes-Based Assessment Plan and Report

Bresciani (2006) introduced typical components of outcomes-based assessment plans and reports that were drawn from a multi-institutional case study analysis. The components of that outline are listed here along with a description for each element. Where appropriate, I further identify components that assist in linking assessment to resource reallocation and strategic planning.

Program Name

The program name of the program that is being assessed helps indicate the scope of your assessment project. For example, are you planning to assess a series of workshops within the leadership development center or are you planning to evaluate the entire leadership development center? It is often difficult to determine what to include within the scope of an assessment plan (Schuh & Associates, 2009). When in doubt, organize your assessment plan around programs that have autonomous outcomes (outcomes that are not shared by other programs). Be sure to list the program name and contact information of any person who can answer questions about the plan and report (Bresciani et al., 2004, 2009).

Program Mission or Purpose

List the program mission or statement of purpose. It may also be helpful to provide a one- to two-sentence explanation of how this program mission or purpose aligns with the mission of the student affairs department or division—or that of the institution—within which it is organized. Doing so will help explain how the program aligns with institutional and/or the student affairs division's values and priorities.

Program Goals

Goals are broad, general statements that include (1) what the program wants students to be able to do and know and (2) what the program will do to ensure that students attain these abilities and this knowledge. Goals are not directly measurable. Rather, they are evaluated directly or indirectly by measuring specific, related outcomes, which will be discussed in the next section (Bresciani et al., 2004, 2009). The further alignment of each program goal with the goals and strategic initiatives of the department, division, or institution assists with the communication of priorities and allows a program to show how it is operating within stated priorities. In addition, the alignment of each goal with professional accreditation standards, if applicable, allows you to determine how this program intends to meet higher-level organizational goals and strategic planning initiatives. Once data are collected on the outcomes that align with these goals, you can illustrate how well the program is contributing to meeting higher-level organizational goals and strategic planning initiatives.

Outcomes

Outcomes, which are detailed statements derived from program goals, outline specifically what you want the end result of your program efforts to be. In other words, What do you expect the student to know and do as a result of your one-hour workshop, one-hour individual meeting, Web site instructions, or series of workshops? Outcomes do not describe what you are going to do to the student as part of your program but rather they delineate how you want the student to demonstrate what he or she knows or can do (Bresciani et al., 2004, 2009). In this section, you want to list not only the outcomes associated with student learning and development in this program but also broader outcomes associated with student services, program processes, enrollment management, research, fundraising and development, alumni outreach, and other practices.

In addition, you want to be able to align each outcome with a program goal. This alignment allows you to link the outcomes of the program you are assessing with the goals of the department, the student affairs division, and the institution and enables you to evaluate them alongside professional accreditation standards. Once you have collected data on the outcomes that are aligned with these goals, you can illustrate how well the program is contributing to meeting higher-level organization goals and strategic planning initiatives.

Planning for Delivery of Outcomes

This is where the action planning comes into the process; this is the illustration of the planning of through what means the student will learn what is expected of him/her. Here is where you describe or simply draw a diagram that explains how you plan for the student to learn what you expect the student to learn in order for the outcome to be met—for example, from a workshop, from one-on-one consultation, or from the Web site. Indicate all the ways in which you provide students with opportunities to obtain the expected knowledge. It is helpful to include a curriculum alignment matrix or an outcome delivery alignment matrix. Exhibit 18.1 illustrates what an outcome delivery alignment matrix looks like. In the first column of Exhibit 18.1, you would list all your program outcomes, and in the rows across, you would list how you have designed the opportunity for students to learn the outcome. In the cells, you would simply place an "X" for each opportunity provided to learn each specified outcome. Exhibit 18.2 provides an example of a outcome delivery alignment matrix.

When you identify where the opportunity for the outcome to be taught or for the service to be delivered resides, you can better determine whether the outcomes will be met by the opportunity that you have purposefully provided. This also ensures that you have actively provided an opportunity for the outcome to be learned or met, rather than just expecting for the outcome to be met without actually planning for it to be met. Many institutions may be able to refer to action planning documents for more details of the resources required in order for specific outcomes to be met.

EXHIBIT 18.1.   OUTCOME DELIVERY ALIGNMENT MATRIX.

Outcomes	Course/Activity/ Project 1	Course/Activity/ Project 2	Course/Activity/ Project 3	Course/Activity/ Project 4
List outcome a				
List outcome b				
List outcome c				
List outcome d				
Etc.				

Source: Bresciani et al., 2004, p. 29.

Evaluation Methods and Tools

Often, the evaluation methods and tools section of the assessment plan can be very intimidating to practitioners. This section is not intended to include detailed research methodology, but rather to simply describe the tools and methods you will use to evaluate the outcomes of participants in a given program (for example, making observations using a criteria checklist, distributing a survey to program participants, assigning an essay with a rubric, or role playing with a criteria checklist). Because you are using the results for program improvement, you do not need to employ the rigor you would if you wanted the results to be applicable to populations outside the program (Bresciani et al., 2004, 2009). In this section, you want to identify the sample or population you will be evaluating, identify an evaluation method or tool for each outcome, and include the criteria you will use to determine whether each outcome has been met. For example, if your tool to measure an outcome is a survey or test, you should specify which questions in the survey or test are measuring that outcome. If your method involves making observations, you should explain what criteria you are applying to your observations in order to identify whether each outcome has been met.

If necessary, discuss the limitations of your evaluation methods or tools. Documenting such limitations will prove advantageous when considering how to improve the assessment process the next time around, and will demonstrate to the reviewer of the report that you are aware of this assessment's shortcomings. In addition, select other institutional, system, or national data (e.g., enrollment numbers, faculty-student ratios, retention rates, graduation rates, utilization statistics, satisfaction ratings, and National Survey of Student Engagement [NSSE] scores) that will be used to help you interpret how and whether each outcome has been met. For example, you may complement your own evaluation of the effectiveness of an advising process with the use of your institution's existing student satisfaction data about advising to explain how the effectiveness of a practice may have influenced an increase in student satisfaction. Similarly, when evaluating critical thinking, you may use enrollment

EXHIBIT 18.2. OUTCOME DELIVERY ALIGNMENT MATRIX.

Outcomes	5-Minute Class Presentation	Career Services Workshop	One-on-One Counseling	College Workshop
Students will be able to explain the purpose of an internship	X	X	X	E
Students will be able to identify the steps to apply for an internship		X	X	E
Students will be able to determine whether they need an internship in order to meet their academic and career goals		X		E

X = outcome met
E = outcome evaluated

patterns to illustrate that 50 percent of the students in your program had transferred from another program in which critical thinking was taught and evaluated differently. Such an enrollment pattern may explain why your students' critical thinking scores are lower than you would like.

Implementation of the Assessment Process

This is the planning section for the implementation of the assessment process. Remember that you don't have to evaluate everything you do every year. You can simply evaluate two to three outcomes each year, thus creating a multiyear assessment plan. Identify who is responsible for undertaking each step in the evaluation process. Outline the timeline for implementation, explaining which outcomes will be evaluated during which years. Also include which year you will be reviewing all prior outcomes data for a holistic program review discussion.

In addition, identify other programs that are assisting with the evaluation and note when they will be involved. Include timelines, for example, for external reviewers (including professional accreditation reviewers, if applicable) and timelines for communication across departments. Also identify who from these other programs will be participating in interpreting the data and making recommendations and decisions. Finally, be sure to explain how lines of communication will flow: Who will see the results? When will they see the results? and Who will be involved in determining whether the results are acceptable?

Results

Summarize the results for each outcome as well as the process to verify the accuracy of the results. This section may include how results were discussed with students, alumni, other program faculty and administrators, or external reviewers. Link the results generated from this outcomes-based assessment to any other applicable program, divisional or institutional performance indicators.

Reflection, Interpretation, Decisions, and Recommendations

In this section, you will summarize the decisions and recommendations made for each outcome. Illustrate how you determined whether or not the results for each outcome were satisfactory, making sure to describe how the level of acceptable performance was determined and why it was determined to be acceptable or unacceptable. Further demonstrate how decisions and recommendations may be contributing to the improvement of higher-level goals and strategic initiatives. Identify the groups who participated in the reflection, interpretation, and discussion of the evidence that led to the recommendations and decisions, and summarize any suggestions for improving the assessment process, tools, criteria, and outcomes. Also be sure to identify when each outcome will be evaluated again (if the outcome is to be retained). Finally, identify those responsible for implementing the recommended changes and the resources required to do so; if making a recommendation, moreover, identify both to whom the recommendation needs to be forwarded and the action required from that person or organization.

Documentation of Higher-Level Feedback

This section is designed to document how results are used and how discussion of results moves throughout the division or institution. It is the place to document conversations and collaborations that are being implemented in order to systematically improve student learning and development in your program. Indicate to whom the recommendations or decisions must be sent if you require resources, policy changes, or other information outside of the scope of your program. For example, if the decisions you and your students recommended required the approval of the department director, you need to indicate this here. Similarly, if the recommendation requires the approval of another department director or division head, you should also indicate here that the decision must flow through those constituents. Include any responses already obtained from those decision makers. Note any changes that needed to be made to the program goals, outcomes, evaluative criteria, planning processes, and budgeting processes as a result of higher-level feedback.

Appendices

Include any appendices that may help further illustrate the manner in which you evaluate your program. For example, you may want to include the outcome-delivery map or the tools and criteria you used to evaluate each outcome. You may also choose to include your results, along with any external review of your plan and the decisions from that external review.

Questions to Consider When Implementing Outcomes-Based Assessment

The following are questions to consider as you move to implement OBA on your campus (Bresciani, 2006).

1. Have you acknowledged and explained to all why you are engaging in outcomes-based assessment in a manner that will make the process sustainable? (Engaging in OBA to appease an accreditation body does not in itself lead to sustainable practice of evidence-based decision making. However, engaging in OBA in a manner that leads to evidence-based decision making is sustainable as long as the results from OBA are used to inform decisions.)

2. Have you acknowledged and explained the scope of what you want to assess? Do you want professionals to assess programs in order to gather data to improve programs? Or are you wanting to conduct assessment that will lead to the identification of trends over time and upon which you can base your decisions?

3. Have you acknowledged your political environment? Has it been made clear how the institutional leadership views OBA and how they plan to use the process and results from the process?

4. Have you acknowledged your institutional and divisional strategic priorities? Have you, to the best of your ability, included these in your OBA process?

5. Do you have an agreed-upon definition—a shared conceptual understanding—of *assessment* and all of its components? (In other words, is there a common language for assessment?)

6. Have the expectations for engaging in assessment been communicated to everyone? Does everyone know what will happen if they don't engage in OBA?

7. Has it been made clear how OBA results will be used?

8. Have expectations for filing OBA plans with the institutional review board or other relevant committee been made clear?

9. Have you identified what you have already done that constitutes evaluation, assessment, or planning (both formal and informal)? Have you made the connections between what has previously been done to what is currently expected?

10. Have you identified easy-to-access resources (such as data, assessment tools, people, and technology) to aid you in the process?

11. Have you articulated everyone's role in this process? For example, will one assessment committee be evaluating the quality of results from OBA while another evaluates the quality of the OBA process? How much of the process will be centralized? How much will be controlled by departments?

12. Have you established a professional development plan for each step in the OBA process?

13. Have you established a communication plan that illustrates how OBA results and the ensuing decisions will flow through the system? How will plans and reports go through the departments to the senior student affairs officer? To the budgeting officers? To the strategic planning committee? How will recommendations for decisions flow?

14. Have you identified short-range and long-range goals as well as a timeline for implementation?

15. Have you determined how constituencies will be engaged in the OBA process (for example, students, faculty, parents, community members, and other student affairs professionals)?

Conclusion

Although the definitions of assessment and particularly that of outcomes-based assessment may continue to change, the practice of assessment is here to stay, especially as resources grow ever tighter, and demands for excellence increase. In this chapter I have intended to assist readers with the implementation of outcomes-based assessment by presenting definitions of OBA, explaining the purpose of OBA, and describing an outline for an assessment plan and report. In addition, this chapter highlighted connections between OBA and planning and budgeting. It also posed questions to consider when implementing OBA. This chapter is by no means a comprehensive guide to implementing OBA; further resources on this subject, however, can be found in the References below.

References

American College Personnel Association (1996). The student learning imperative. *Journal of College Student Development, 37*(2), entire issue.

Astin, A. W. (1993). *What matters in college? Four critical years revisited.* San Francisco: Jossey-Bass.

Bresciani, M. J. (2006). *Outcomes-based academic and co-curricular program review: A compilation of institutional good practices.* Sterling, VA: Stylus.

Bresciani, M. J. (2010). Understanding barriers to student affairs professionals' engagement in outcomes-based assessment of student learning and development. *Journal of Student Affairs, 14,* p. 81–90.

Bresciani, M. J., Moore Gardner M., & Hickmott, J. (2009). *Demonstrating student success in student affairs.* Sterling, VA: Stylus.

Bresciani, M. J., Zelna, C. L., and Anderson, J. A. (2004). *Assessing student learning and development: A handbook for practitioners.* Washington, DC: National Association of Student Personnel Administrators.

Donald, J. G., & Denison, D. B. (2001). Quality assessment of university students. *Journal of Higher Education, 72*(4), 478–502.

Ewell, P. T. (1997, December). Organizing for learning—A new imperative. *American Association for Higher Education Bulletin, 50*(4), 3–6.

Flowers, L. A. (2003). National study of diversity requirements in student affairs graduate programs. *NASPA Journal, 40*(4), 72–82.

Freeman, J. P., Bresciani, M. J., & Bresciani, D. L. (2004, February 10). Integrated strategic planning: bringing planning and assessment together. Retrieved on March 10, 2004 from www.naspa.org/membership/mem/nr/article.cfm?id=1327.

Gayles, J. G., & Kelly, B. T. (2007). Experiences with diversity in the curriculum: Implications for graduate programs and student affairs practice. *NASPA Journal, 44*(1), 193–208.

Herdlein, R. J., III. (2004). Survey of chief student affairs officers regarding relevance of graduate preparation of new professionals. *NASPA Journal, 42,* 51–70.

Hickmott, J., & Bresciani, M. J. (in press). Examining learning outcomes in student personnel preparation programs. *Journal of College Student Affairs.*

Kuh, G. D., Kinzie, J., Buckley, J., Bridges, B., & Hayek, J. C. (2006). *What matters to student success: A review of the literature* (Final report for the National Postsecondary Education Cooperative and National Center for Education Statistics). Bloomington: Indiana University Center for Postsecondary Research.

Kuh, G. D., Schuh, J. H., Whitt, E. J., & Associates. (1991). *Involving colleges: Successful approaches to fostering student learning and personal development outside the classroom.* San Francisco: Jossey-Bass.

Maki, P. L. (2004). *Assessing for learning: Building a sustainable commitment across the institution.* Sterling, VA: Stylus.

Palomba, C. A., & Banta, T. W. (1999). *Assessment essentials: Planning, implementing, and improving assessment in higher education.* San Francisco: Jossey-Bass.

Schuh, J. H., & Associates (2009). *Assessment methods for student affairs.* San Francisco: Jossey-Bass.

Strange, C. C. (2001). *Spiritual dimensions of graduate preparation in student affairs* (New Directions for Student Services No. 95, pp. 57–67). San Francisco: Jossey-Bass.

Suskie, L. (2004). *Assessing student learning: A common sense guide.* Bolton, MA: Anker.

Upcraft, M. L., & Schuh, J. H. (1996). *Assessment in student affairs: A guide for practitioners*. San Francisco: Jossey-Bass.

Waple, J. N. (2006). An assessment of skills and competencies necessary for entry-level student affairs work. *NASPA Journal, 43*, 1–18.

Young, D. G., & Janosik, S. M. (2007). Using CAS standards to measure learning outcomes of student affairs preparation programs. *NASPA Journal, 44*, 341–366.

Young, R. B., & Elfrink, V. L. (1991). Values education in student affairs graduate programs. *Journal of College Student Development, 32*, 109–115.

PART FIVE

ESSENTIAL COMPETENCIES

The effectiveness of any student affairs division or student services operation hinges on its people. Without competent people, student learning is likely to be stifled, habitual ways of doing are likely to be preferred over more innovative programs and practices, and student affairs educators are likely to be continually misperceived as "the fun and games people who babysit students outside of class." With competence comes credibility. But what makes an effective student affairs educator or administrator? Although there is likely to be some disagreement on this question, authors who have contributed chapters for Part Five of this handbook have written about ten particular areas of competence. These are neither intended to be exhaustive nor indisputable. Instead, they are considered areas in which professional growth and the development of expertise are likely to lead to the enactment of institutional missions, increased gains in student learning and development, and greater legitimacy for student affairs work on college and university campuses. Even

though the competencies they discuss are distinct, many authors thoughtfully address some of the following themes in their chapters: diversity and social justice, collaboration, assessment, and technology.

In Chapter Nineteen, Raechele Pope and John Mueller present models and strategies for developing multicultural competence in student affairs. They maintain that educators must address issues on personal and professional levels before claiming multicultural competence. Susan Komives writes in Chapter Twenty about developing one's leadership capacity. Among the strengths of this chapter is the author's clear delineation of various forms of leadership and practices associated with them. Staffing practices—specifically, recruitment and selection, orientation, supervision, evaluation, professional development, and separation—are discussed in Chapter Twenty-One. Authors Joan Hirt and Terrell Strayhorn explain why each aspect of staffing is important, describe the duties associated with that staffing task, and illustrate how those duties may vary depending on context. Shaun Harper indicated in Chapter Sixteen that those who work with students outside the classroom are educators—not staff, practitioners, or personnel workers—a point that Peter Magolda and Stephen John Quaye also emphasize throughout Chapter Twenty-Two. In this chapter, they talk about the teaching role of student affairs educators, relying on relevant theories and research to stress the importance of creatively utilizing resources to enhance student learning outside the classroom.

In Chapter Twenty-Three, Amy Reynolds describes the awareness, knowledge, and skills necessary for student affairs educators to become competent and ethical helpers, caregivers, and counselors. Reynolds uses models of helping, counseling theory, and assessment approaches to frame conceptualizations of competence throughout the chapter. Patrick Love and Sue Maxam coauthor Chapter Twenty-Four, which focuses on advising groups of students. They discuss students' needs in advising relationships and conclude the chapter by describing several consultant roles (as an alternative to invasive advising) that student affairs educators can play on their campuses. Conflict, the focus of Chapter Twenty-Five, is inevitable, even among professionals who are well intentioned and among students who are working collaboratively on a project or living together in a residence hall. In this chapter, Larry Roper and Christian Matheis offer an overview of conflict, conflict theory, conflict management skills, and strategies and processes for productively engaging conflict.

In Chapter Twenty-Six, Dennis C. Roberts grapples with three important questions: (1) Considering the complexity of the world in which we live, how might we define *community* for a contemporary college or university setting? (2) Is agreement achievable at institutions in which the diversity of thought, background, and purpose is so great? and (3) If there were an agreed-upon, meaningful, and shared definition, could the process of how educators might foster a greater sense of community be prescribed? Throughout the chapter, Roberts offers philosophical perspectives on community, differentiates programming from community building, and furnishes practical examples of how student affairs educators can build community through program implementation.

Jan Arminio presents in Chapter Twenty-Seven the general characteristics that define a profession, professionals, and professionalism, as well as specific attributes of professionalism in the context of student affairs. And in Chapter Twenty-Eight, Elizabeth Whitt examines calls for student affairs partnerships with academic affairs; weighs the advantages and disadvantages of such collaborations; and offers some practical suggestions for academic and student affairs professionals who seek to form productive partnerships for student learning. Whitt warns, however, that her chapter is not a recipe for approaching the cultivation of academic and student affairs partnership programs, nor does she supply simple answers to questions about how to sustain effective partnerships.

CHAPTER NINETEEN

MULTICULTURAL COMPETENCE

Raechele L. Pope and John A. Mueller

Several articles published in the *Chronicle of Higher Education* and *Inside Higher Ed* confirm the ongoing need for multicultural competence on college and university campuses. Seemingly endless examples of racism or racial insensitivity, homophobia or hetero-sexism, sexism, religious intolerance, ableism, and classism are reported. These incidents range from what have been described as microaggressions—daily slights, minor insults, and insensitivity that diminish the target's self-esteem and identity (Ceja, Solórzano, & Yosso, 2000; Sue et al., 2007)—to racial, ethnic, religious, or cultural epithets, graffiti, and vandalism, to harassment and assault. However, even in the absence of these types of negative incidents, multicultural competence is necessary simply to appropriately respond to the growing presence of traditionally underrepresented groups on campuses.

This increasingly diverse community on college campuses presents both opportunities and challenges. Among the opportunities, student diversity generates more positive and robust learning communities (Gurin, 1999; Gurin, Dey, Hurtado, & Gurin, 2002; Hurtado, 2007; Sleeter & Grant, 1994); promotes increased interaction with diverse others (Chang, 1996; Gurin et al., 2002; Pascarella, Edison, Nora, Hagedorn, & Terenzini, 1996); and is positively related to a variety of educational outcomes (Hu & Kuh, 2003; Umbach & Kuh, 2006). Challenges arise, however, when student affairs and higher education professionals are ineffective in managing and responding to this diversity. This chapter focuses on developing multicultural competence as a way to increase effectiveness in student affairs work.

Dynamic Model of Multicultural Competence

Over the years many scholars have proposed that student affairs educators and faculty need to demonstrate greater multicultural sensitivity and responsiveness (for example, Barr & Strong, 1988; Cheatham, 1991; Harper, 2008; Howard-Hamilton, Richardson, & Shuford, 1998; Manning & Coleman-Boatwright, 1991; Pope, 1995; Pope, Reynolds, & Mueller, 2004). Despite these authors' proposals, however, practitioners have received minimal training in multicultural issues, and even fewer have had their work performance evaluated using effectiveness in dealing with diversity as a performance criterion (McEwen & Roper, 1994; Mueller, & Pope, 2001; Pope & Reynolds, 1997; Talbot, 1996; Talbot & Kocarek, 1997). Perhaps it is because of the absence of comprehensive multicultural education and training that campuses continue to use "multicultural experts" to address issues of diversity rather than requiring multicultural competence of all practitioners. Or it may be due to a lack of institutional support or rewards for multicultural competence. Or perhaps it is because practitioners simply do not see multicultural work as their responsibility. Whatever the reason, Pope and Reynolds assert "that multicultural competence is a necessary prerequisite to effective, affirming, and ethical work in student affairs" (p. 270), and thus proposed a specific framework for training professionals to work effectively with diverse student populations and with multicultural issues (Pope, Reynolds, & Mueller, 2004).

The theoretical underpinnings of multicultural competence in student affairs were adapted from the field of counseling psychology by Pope and Reynolds (1997). The seminal multicultural work in counseling psychology by Sue et al. (1982) and Pedersen (1988) identified the tripartite model of multicultural awareness, knowledge, and skills as the foundation of multicultural competence. They defined *multicultural competence* as the awareness, knowledge, and skills needed to work with others who are culturally different from one's self. These three areas have become central in our understanding of what constitutes multicultural competence. Building upon these constructs, Pope and Reynolds proposed a model of core competencies for student affairs professionals that includes multicultural competence as an essential component. In an effort to specify and understand the core competencies that were needed to successfully advise, counsel, mentor, supervise, teach, and interact with all students, Pope and Reynolds developed the Characteristics of a Multiculturally Competent Student Affairs Practitioner, which outlined thirty-three specific multicultural attitudes, knowledge, and skills that were essential for all student affairs practitioners.

Multicultural awareness, the first element in the tripartite model, consists of the attitudes, values, beliefs, and assumptions that shape our understanding of other individuals who are culturally different from us. Being self-aware and understanding the impact that one's upbringing, life experiences, and cultural worldview have on perceptions and interpersonal interactions are central to multicultural awareness. Evaluating any stereotypes, biases, or culturally based assumptions is necessary to determine what, if any, inaccurate or inappropriate views we hold of particular cultures or persons. In order to be multiculturally sensitive, individuals must be open to challenging any misinformation they have absorbed and unlearning any flawed assumptions and beliefs.

Multicultural knowledge, the second part of the tripartite model, is focused on both background information of distinct cultural groups and content knowledge about important cultural constructs. Having cultural group knowledge is essential to multicultural competence, particularly because such information is typically missing from most educational experiences. Whether in primary, secondary, or higher education, most individuals are inadequately exposed to the history, experiences, and realities of various cultural groups, such as American Indians, Latino/a Americans, African Americans, and Asian Americans. In addition, there is a lack of accurate information shared about other groups whose voices are often lost in the mainstream, such as Jews; Muslims; nonbelievers; people with disabilities; immigrants; and lesbian, gay, bisexual, or transgender individuals. Such knowledge can help us contextualize what we observe, deepen our understanding, and enhance our ability to work with others who are culturally different from us. It is important to highlight that there is a risk in learning such group knowledge, in that it can be used in ways that ultimately stereotype and minimize within-group differences. There are many reasons why individuals may differ from their cultural groups in regard to their values, experiences, or identities, so it is vital that professionals not assume that all members of a particular cultural group are the same. Knowing background information about different cultures can, however, raise awareness of all of the diverse and complex factors to be considered when working with others.

In addition, there are important cultural constructs that are useful to know. Knowledge of cultural constructs can increase our understanding of some of these important within-group differences. Examining constructs such as acculturation, identity development, oppression, or cultural encapsulation is vital for multicultural competence. Acculturation and identity development underscore the idea that it is not a person's membership in a cultural group that is essential but rather what meaning that membership has for her or him. The realities, values, and life experiences of a third-generation Korean American, for example, are very different from those of a new Korean immigrant. Or the beliefs, expectations, and relationships with others might be very different for a lesbian who has just come out compared to one who is in an open, long-term relationship. It is also essential that oppression and its effects be fully understood, whether by realizing the impact that internalized self-hatred might have on a Muslim American or comprehending how the heavy weight of racism and classism limit the opportunities for Native Americans living on a reservation. At times the amount of information required to be multiculturally competent seems overwhelming: it is clearly impossible to know everything. However, it is possible to immerse ourselves in understanding the diverse cultures and communities that are in our immediate environment so that as student affairs professionals we can best serve them.

Multicultural skills are the third component of the tripartite model and consist of the behaviors used to effectively apply the multicultural awareness and knowledge previously internalized. Central to multicultural skills is the ability to communicate across cultural differences and an appreciation of how culture influences every aspect of verbal and nonverbal communication. How we use silence, humor, touch, physical space, and eye contact, as well as the content of our conversations, are highly influenced by gender, culture, and upbringing. Designing and implementing culturally appropriate interventions, being comfortable with cultural conflict, consulting with cultural experts, and recovering from cultural errors are just a few of the specific skills needed to be culturally sensitive and relevant in our actions. Many practitioners report that they feel less confident about their skills or ability to translate their multicultural awareness and knowledge into practice, so it is vital that multicultural skills receive ample attention.

Although the tripartite model of multicultural competence has remained a constant, the conceptualization of multicultural competence within the field of counseling has expanded and evolved during the past twenty-five years, leading to the growth and evolution of multicultural research critical to the counseling profession. A similar progression has occurred within the field of student affairs. Pope et al. (2004) built upon and refined the earlier work of Pope and Reynolds (1997), developing the Dynamic Model of Student Affairs Competence to intensify understanding and further integrate the construct of multicultural competence into foundational theoretical and applied understandings of the profession (see Figure 19.1).

FIGURE 19.1. DYNAMIC MODEL OF STUDENT AFFAIRS COMPETENCE.

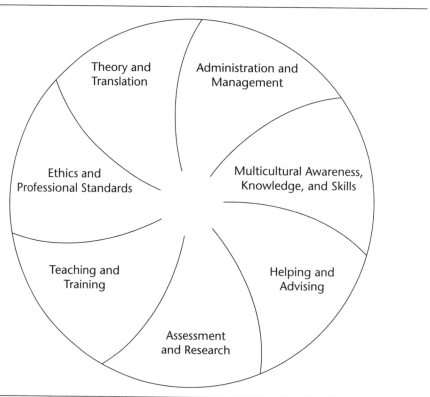

Source: Reprinted from Pope, R. L., Reynolds, A. L. & Mueller, J. M. (2004). *Multicultural Competence in Student Affairs.* San Francisco: Jossey-Bass.

The Dynamic Model of Student Affairs Competence is a more parsimonious conceptualization of the requisite qualities and abilities for efficacious student affairs practice. The visual representation of the model underscores some important philosophical assumptions. The open hub at the center of the wheel suggests a dynamic and fluid nature to multicultural competence. Proficiency in one area may influence one's competence in another area. Nowhere is such influence more important than in the area of multicultural competence. The Dynamic Model also conceptualizes multicultural competence as both a distinctive category of awareness, knowledge, and skills and as an area that needs to be effectively integrated into each of the other six core competencies. All practitioners need a basic level of competence in all of these areas in order to be effective and ethical professionals; however, some will develop expertise in certain areas, depending on their job requirements, expectations, and personal interests. Such differing strengths are adequate as long as individuals can meet key requirements for quality service.

The first core competency is administration and management. It incorporates the awareness, knowledge, and skills needed to complete the tasks that are commonly found in most practitioner positions, such as budgeting, strategic planning, resource allocation, supervision, and delegation. Understanding how the core assumptions, theories, and practices of administration have not always effectively incorporated cultural concerns and realities is fundamental to being a culturally competent administrator. Being aware of the limitations of the literature; seeking out alternative literature, such as the work on multicultural organization development (see Jackson & Holvino, 1988; Pope, 1993); and understanding how cultural worldviews and stages of identity development may influence the interpersonal components of human resource management are just a few of the necessary components of multicultural competence in administration and management.   .

Theory and translation, the second area of competence, incorporates the theory, research, and practical knowledge that inform the entire field of student affairs. Although there are many theories that influence the field, some of the most vital are student development, leadership, organization development, and many of the process models that prescribe the translation of theory to practice. It is important to challenge the cultural relevancy of some of the core assumptions of these foundational theories, such as the view that gaining independence from one's parents is necessary for mature development or the view that assertion and independence are the hallmarks of effective leadership.

The third area of competence, helping and advising, involves the diverse set of components necessary for most student affairs positions, such as communication, crisis intervention, group advisement, and conflict management. In reality, all interactions involve diverse worldviews, values, realities, and experiences, and being aware of how cultural similarities and differences can have a significant impact on all helping relationships is very important. Cultural realities also need to be integrated into our understanding of the fourth area of the model, ethics and professional standards. The multicultural nature of higher education is at the center of many ethical challenges and requires that we make ethical principles more culturally meaningful and appropriate for all individuals.

The fifth area of competence, teaching and training, emphasizes the importance of integrating multicultural awareness, knowledge, and skills into preparation programs and professional development within the field of student affairs. Without multiculturalism, our educational interventions may be incomplete, inaccurate, or irrelevant, so it is essential that we incorporate multicultural issues and dynamics into all types of teaching and training. Assessment and research, the sixth competence area, requires that student affairs professionals infuse multicultural knowledge, skills, and awareness into all aspects of assessment and research. That means being aware of the assumptions and cultural variables that influence research and assessment and being familiar with culturally sensitive research designs and techniques and diverse instruments.

Finally, the seventh competence area, multicultural awareness, knowledge, and skills are viewed as a unique competence that may assist student affairs practitioners in creating and sustaining diverse and inclusive campuses. Because all professionals need to be able to provide services, intervene, and address the needs of all students, it is incumbent upon them to ensure that they have the insight, knowledge, and tools necessary for multiculturally sensitive practice. And although the field of student affairs is increasingly attending to multicultural issues, it is still necessary for each professional to take responsibility for the development of his or her own multicultural competence.

Assessment

Developing multicultural competence is a challenging task with many fronts, one of which is assessment. Assessment of multicultural competence can facilitate the development of an individual's competence, the implementation of effective educational interventions, and the examination of factors that are related to and influence multicultural competence (Reynolds, 2008). Assessment occurs in both informal and formal ways; the key is to define the goal of the assessment in order to select which approach is most feasible and appropriate. Both the Dynamic Model of Multicultural Competence (Pope et al., 2004) and the Characteristics of a Multiculturally Competent Student Affairs Practitioner (Pope & Reynolds, 1997), while serving as useful means to describing the breadth and depth of multicultural competence in student affairs practice, can be (and have been) used in the informal and formal assessment of multicultural competence.

Informal Assessment

Pope et al. (2004) suggested that the Dynamic Model, although not a measurement instrument itself, could be used informally in self-assessment, goal setting, and supervision. This can be accomplished by considering each of the competence areas and, starting from the middle and moving toward the perimeter, shading in the area to indicate the extent of one's competence in that area. A more fully shaded area would indicate a higher degree of competence. Even though this technique does not yield a numerical score or a valid or reliable measurement, it can illustrate the relative strength of each competence area. Professionals are likely to note that they have greater expertise in some areas than in others, although there should be a level of basic competence in each area (Pope et al., 2004). This self-assessment can provide a deeper level of competence if one considers the degree to which multicultural awareness, knowledge, and skills are infused across each of the competencies. The Characteristics of a Multiculturally Competent Student Affairs Practitioner (Pope & Reynolds, 1997), a checklist of more detailed and nuanced descriptions of the multicultural awareness, knowledge, and skills required for multicultural competence, similarly can be used as an assessment device. These informal forms of assessment can be useful in identifying and developing goals to promote multicultural competence in staff evaluation procedures and staff development programs.

Formal Assessment

Before the construct of multicultural competence was introduced to the student affairs profession, there was a call for the profession to operationalize and assess the cultural competence of practitioners and the effectiveness of programs designed to address diversity (Ebbers & Henry, 1990). Several instruments exist within the counseling psychology profession, including the Multicultural Counseling Inventory (MCI), developed by Sodowsky, Taffe, Gutkin, & Wise (1994); the Multicultural Counseling Awareness Scale: Form B-Revised (MCAS:B), developed by Ponterotto et al. (1996); the Multicultural Awareness Knowledge-Skills Survey (MAKSS), developed by D'Andrea, Daniels, and Heck (1991); and the Cross-Cultural Counseling Inventory-Revised (CCCI-R), developed by LaFromboise, Coleman, and Hernandez (1991). The first comparable instrument developed for use in the student affairs profession was the Multicultural Competence in Student Affairs–Preliminary 2 (MCSA-P2) Scale, developed by Pope and Mueller (2000).

Using the Characteristics of a Multiculturally Competent Student Affairs Practitioner (Pope & Reynolds, 1997) as a framework, Pope and Mueller (2000) developed the MCSA-P2. The instrument, comprised of thirty-four items arranged on a Likert-type self-report scale, measures the single construct of multicultural competence rather than the three components of awareness, knowledge, and skills. A number of studies have been conducted with the instrument, identifying relevant demographic, experience, and educational variables that are related to multicultural competence and that have expanded our understanding of the construct (King & Howard-Hamilton, 2000; Martin, 2005; Miklitsch, 2006; Mueller & Pope, 2001; Weigand, 2005). Additionally, these studies have consistently provided evidence of the instrument's strong psychometric performance (i.e., its reliability and validity). In its current format, this instrument is most appropriate for research purposes and is not intended for staff evaluation or training purposes (Pope & Mueller, 2000).

A more recent addition to the measurement of individual multicultural competence in student affairs is the Multicultural Competence Characteristics of Student Affairs Professionals Inventory (MCCSAPI), developed by Castellanos, Gloria, Mayorga, and Salas (2007). Using the actual statements from the Characteristics of a Multiculturally Competent Student Affairs Practitioner (Pope & Reynolds, 1997), the designers of the MCCSAPI developed this thirty-two-item instrument. Although no factor analysis was reported and there are high interscale correlations, the designers of the MCCSAPI propose that the instrument measures three subscales. The authors also report high internal reliability coefficients. Because it has only recently been introduced, however, there is limited evidence of the psychometric properties of the MCCSAPI.

Although there is growing interest in assessment of multicultural competence in student affairs, there is a great deal yet to be done. The MCSA-P2 currently has the most evidence to support its psychometric performance, but it has limitations in that it measures a construct in the context of a profession with many dimensions and functional areas. A review of the literature in the counseling profession shows both how approaches to assessment of multicultural competence have grown and how they can inform our own assessment strategies given the breadth and depth of the student affairs profession. Using the counseling literature as a guide, we as student affairs researchers and practitioners may begin looking at assessment of multicultural competence through use portfolios (Coleman & Hau, 2003) or observer reports (Ponterotto, Mendelsohn, & Belizaire, 2003); attention might also be directed to how we can focus our assessments on supervision (Pope-Davis, Toporek & Ortega-Villalobos, 2003), training and development environments (Toporek, Liu & Pope-Davis, 2003), and teaching approaches (D'Andrea, Daniels, & Noonan, 2003).

Becoming Multiculturally Competent

Multicultural competence is important as a theory and construct, but its greatest value arguably comes in its application to everyday work in student affairs. It is vital that through professional preparation, professional development, and individual super-vision, adequate attention is focused on the "how to" of multicultural competence. That being said, it is also important to acknowledge that there is no definitive cookbook, recipe, or checklist for multiculturally sensitive practice. Becoming multiculturally competent means enhancing awareness, expanding knowledge and engaging in new behaviors, and translating those competencies to new and different settings. The process can be exciting, stimulating, provocative, rewarding, and exhausting. Although it is very much a process that takes place from within, it is facilitated by an environment that challenges our ways of thinking and behaving and supports the risks we take and the efforts we make. Given these two dimensions, the internal and the external, developing multicultural competence can be facilitated at both the professional and individual levels.

Professional Level

Developing multicultural competence needs support and commitment at the professional level of student affairs, evidenced in our institutions, departments, professional associations, and graduate preparations programs. Institutions and departments, for example, can establish multicultural competence as both a guiding principle and an expectation. Pope's Multicultural Change Intervention Matrix (1993, 1995) proposed intentional programmatic and policy interventions at the individual, group, and institution levels. Further, Grieger's Multicultural Organizational Development Checklist (1996) specifies nearly 60 short-term and long-term initiatives of student affairs divisions in the areas of goal setting, policy development, staff recruitment, training and development, and program evaluation. Finally, Reynolds, Pope, and Wells (2002) offer a model for developing institutional and departmental diversity plans that are based in multicultural competence, particularly in the areas of mission statements, policies, and training. On a more individual level, there is growing support in the literature for the effectiveness of supervisory relationships in enhancing multicultural competence (Miklitsch, 2006; Mueller & Pope, 2001; Weigand, 2005) particularly where open, candid, and inquisitive conversations about multiculturalism take place between the supervisor and the supervisee about student and staff concerns, programming ideas, and policy considerations.

Because professional organizations provide ongoing professional development and leadership training, discussions about contemporary issues, standards of professional practice and ethical guidelines, and opportunities to influence the course of the profession, they can be key to enhancing multicultural competence among practitioners. Many student affairs professional organizations, including the National Association of Student Personnel Administrators (NASPA) and the American College Personnel Association (ACPA), have now incorporated the essential concepts and principles of multicultural competence into their professional development priorities and initiatives. Professional associations can also enhance multicultural competence of their members by infusing and modeling principles of social justice in their governmental and leadership structures as well as in policymaking and decision-making activities.

Graduate preparation programs, moreover, can become a significant starting point for developing multicultural competence among student affairs professionals. McEwen and Roper (1994) highlighted this assertion in a set of recommendations for integrating multiculturalism in student affairs preparation programs: they suggested incorporating multicultural content and experiences into core courses in student affairs preparation programs that address theory, profiles of college students, assessment and evaluation, individual and group helping skills, and management and administration. Also, students can develop greater multicultural competence through observing these skills from supervisors in their assistantship, practicum, and internship sites as well as from their professors (Pope et al., 2004).

Individual Level

Although the professional contexts noted previously can provide meaningful, challenging, and supportive environments for developing multicultural competence, an individual's own desire, commitment, and effort are just as essential. Developing multicultural competence requires an investment in lifelong learning, a willingness to engage in self-exploration, and a readiness to expand one's multicultural settings and interactions. More specifically, as noted by Pope et al. (2004), it involves a personal call to action, a process, a paradigm shift, a multifaceted approach to learning, and a deliberate act. By *a personal call to action* we suggest that multicultural competence becomes part of our daily experiences, not just at work but in the many spheres of our lives, including our families, neighborhoods, and faith communities and that is not just intellectually consequential but also personally, interpersonally, politically, and even spiritually. Developing multicultural competence is a *process*, and not an "end point" that only a few experts will reach. Any activity that involves developing an integrated and complex set of abilities, insights, and understandings will require risk taking, openness to challenges, patience, and appreciation of small accomplishments along the way. It is a *paradigm shift* in that it requires us not only to learn about other cultures and develop culturally sensitive and appropriate programs and policies but also to seek ways and opportunities to examine and deconstruct our assumptions and worldviews. It involves recognizing, managing, and moving beyond guilt, resentment, and obligation, toward establishing genuine relationships with students and colleagues in multicultural settings. Developing multicultural competence on the individual level requires tapping into *multiple sources of learning* beyond reading, attending workshops and seminars, and consulting with experts. We enhance our multicultural competence when we take advantage of the learning that comes from increased and intentional relationships with our colleagues, supervisors, supervisees, and students. Creating and maintaining genuine contacts with others and legitimizing them as sources of knowledge about our assumptions, privileges, blind spots, and biases can yield many positive dividends. Finally, it is important to think of developing multicultural competence as a *deliberate act* that will not become a natural part of our practice simply because we have learned about the concept; it is an act of risk taking, meaning making, crossing borders, and placing ourselves in (sometimes uncomfortable) positions to explore, reflect, examine, and challenge our ways of seeing and being in the world.

Considerations in Developing Multicultural Competence

As discussed throughout this chapter, developing multicultural competence requires commitment and a supportive environment to nurture that commitment. Developing multicultural competence also requires ongoing education; an openness to examine one's assumptions, biases, and privileges; and the willingness to try new behaviors in new settings. Embracing the concept of multicultural competence is sometimes easier than engaging in the act of developing it, because there may be some attitudes and behaviors that can sabotage our own efforts. We propose that there are certain factors, several of which we address below, that might undermine or interrupt our best efforts. We address several of these below.

Resistance and Defenses

Much has been said about the significance of being aware of one's own assumptions, biases, and privileges. Doing so is not as easy as it sounds; it often raises feelings of guilt, shame, discomfort, resentment, and anxiety. Resistance to learn more, or to apply what has been learned, is one way to mitigate these feelings (Goodman, 2001). Failure to acknowledge and manage these feelings can make it a struggle to move forward in developing multicultural competence; and employing any of several defense mechanisms may become tools of that resistance. Watt (2007) labels a number of these defense mechanisms (including denial, deflection, minimizing, rationalization, and false envy) and urges practitioners and educators to "sit with discomfort, to continuously seek critical consciousness, and to engage in difficult dialogues" (p. 115) that address these defense mechanisms and, ultimately, the resistance to continued growth and change.

Cultural Mistakes

Part of developing multicultural competence is expanding our circle of multicultural relationships and interactions. This does not come without considerable risk. As the volume of these interactions increases, so does the likelihood that we will make cultural mistakes. These mistakes are inevitable. We need to be open to these potential mistakes, lower our defenses when we encounter them, see them as learning opportunities, and make an effort not to make these mistakes again. An easier but less effective response is to deny the mistakes or, worse yet, to withdraw from these relationships and interactions in the hope of avoiding the possibility of mistakes altogether. It is important to realize, as Johnson (2006) notes, that these mistakes are not about our goodness or badness as people. Instead, we should attempt to recover and learn from our mistakes. Being more open and genuine about who we are and our own personal journeys will increase our personal growth and credibility.

Unsupportive Environments

Some of us may find ourselves in work environments that do not support our efforts to become multiculturally competent or to promote multicultural organizations. Working in these environments may require that we intensify our efforts to share the responsibility of developing supportive environments in the following ways: identifying those who share similar goals and building alliances with them; intentionally joining with individuals who are the target of oppression; openly supporting the efforts of those who are attempting to make or who are making a difference, no matter how small that effort or accomplishment may seem; and extending our own efforts to develop multicultural competence on our campuses by becoming involved with student or faculty and staff groups that are focused on issues of race, gender, sexual orientation, or other aspects of diversity. Joining with others and becoming part of a growing effort to create affirming communities of justice can build supportive environments where none existed previously.

Personal Work

As Pope et al. (2004) note, "Developing multicultural competence does not begin and end when we are in our offices" (p. 227). Instead, it is a transformational process with the potential to affect all aspects of our lives, not just our professional lives. The multiple roles, identities, and responsibilities we possess provide many opportunities to explore and examine racism, sexism, heterosexism, and other systems of privilege in our schools, neighborhoods, faith communities, and families. Making multicultural competence a goal in our personal lives makes the effort more authentic.

The Need to Act

Krumboltz (1966) observed, "The way we think about problems determines to a large degree what we will do about them" (p. 4). However, as practitioners in an applied profession, we are often more eager to find solutions to and act on problems than to understand them. Practitioners—those preparing for the profession in particular—can become impatient with learning about and understanding the complexities of racism, sexism, and other forms oppression to the point that their frustration leads to inaction or to premature or poorly guided action. Indeed, there are crises and issues on campus that require immediate responses, but we must bear in mind that multicultural competence involves the ongoing knowledge, awareness, and skill building that can inform our immediate and long-term interventions.

Our Multicultural Selves

Bula (2000) identifies two trends in the multicultural competence literature: assessment of competencies and acquiring those competencies. Citing the work of Knefelkamp, Bula argues that the "multicultural self" is not emphasized enough, and that it is awareness of our multicultural selves that can influence our work with those who share (and do not share) group membership with us. Bula urges practitioners to consider the many aspects of their multicultural selves—including race, gender, age, socioeconomic status, sexual orientation, religion, abilities, and language—and to examine how each of these influences their beliefs, attitudes, values, knowledge, and understandings of oppression and privilege. This self-examination and understanding can become a strong foundation for multicultural competence; it echoes the observation made by Myers (1988) that "self-knowledge is the basis of all knowledge" (p. 3).

Conclusion

Multicultural competence is an integral component of student affairs work. Professionals at every level of each position are faced daily with multicultural issues, concerns, and dynamics that affect their work. By focusing on multicultural competence, we ensure that practitioners have the concrete multicultural awareness, knowledge, and skills needed for efficacious and culturally relevant practice. And although developing multicultural competence is a lifelong process through which individuals make goals, take risks, and change the ways they think about and interact with people both culturally similar and dissimilar, it cannot happen by chance.

For practitioners to become multiculturally competent, they must address these issues on both personal and professional levels. On the personal level, each individual must make multicultural competence a part of his or her daily life. That means making intentional choices to pursue life experiences and professional opportunities to expand multicultural awareness, knowledge, and skills. It is also essential that student affairs professionals consider the importance of integrating multicultural issues into every aspect of their professional lives, from which programs they choose to attend at conferences to the ways they address the needs of underserved and underrepresented students on their campuses. Joining with others on campus who are committed to multicultural issues will help to build a stronger and more unified effort: collaboration and consultation are the cornerstones of effective multicultural interventions. Developing systemic and systematic efforts toward integrating multicultural issues into every aspect of one's work is essential, because there are endless opportunities every day to embrace multicultural competence in ways that will truly make a difference.

References

Barr, D. J., & Strong, L. J. (1988). Embracing multiculturalism: The existing contradictions. *NASPA Journal, 26*(2), 85–90.

Bula, J. F. (2000). Use of the multicultural self in effective practice. In M. Baldwin (Ed.), *The use of self in therapy* (2nd ed., pp. 167–189). New York: Haworth Press.

Castellanos, J., Gloria, A. M., Mayorga, M., & Salas, C. (2007). Student affairs professionals' self-report on multicultural competence: Understanding awareness, knowledge, and skills. *NASPA Journal, 44*, 643–663.

Ceja, M., Solórzano, D., & Yosso, T. (2000). Critical race theory, racial microaggressions, and campus racial climate: The experiences of African American college students. *Journal of Negro Education, 69*, 60–73.

Chang, M. (1996). *Racial diversity in higher education: Does a racially mixed student population affect educational outcomes?* Unpublished doctoral dissertation, University of California, Los Angeles.

Cheatham, H. E. (1991). *Cultural pluralism on campus.* Alexandria, VA: American College Personnel Association.

Coleman, H.L.K., & Hau, J. M. (2003). Multicultural counseling competency and portfolios. In D. B. Pope-Davis, H.L.K. Coleman, W. M. Liu, & R. L. Toporek (Eds.), *Handbook of multicultural competencies in counseling and psychology* (pp. 168–182). Thousand Oaks, CA: Sage.

D'Andrea, M., Daniels, J., & Heck, R. (1991). Evaluating the impact of multicultural counseling training. *Journal of Counseling & Development, 70*, 143–150.

D'Andrea, M., Daniels, J., & Noonan, M. J. (2003). New developments in the assessment of multicultural competence: The Multicultural Awareness-Knowledge-Skills Survey-Teachers Form. In D. B. Pope-Davis, H.L.K. Coleman, W. M. Liu, & R. L. Toporek (Eds.),

Handbook of multicultural competencies in counseling and psychology (pp. 154–167). Thousand Oaks, CA: Sage.

Ebbers, L. H., & Henry, S. L. (1990). Cultural competence: A new challenge to student affairs professionals. *NASPA Journal, 27*, 319–323.

Goodman, D. J. (2001). *Promoting diversity and social justice: Educating people from privileged groups.* Thousand Oaks, CA: Sage.

Grieger, I. (1996). A multicultural organizational development checklist for student affairs. *Journal of College Student Development, 37*, 561–573.

Gurin, P. (1999). Selections from the Compelling Need for Diversity in Higher Education: Expert Reports in Defense of the University of Michigan. *Equity & Excellence in Education, 32*, 36–62.

Gurin, P., Dey, E. L., Hurtado, S., & Gurin, G. (2002). Diversity and higher education: Theory and impact on educational outcomes. *Harvard Educational Review, 72*, 330–366.

Harper, S. R. (Ed.). (2008). *Creating inclusive campus environments for cross-cultural learning and student engagement.* Washington, DC: National Association of Student Affairs Administrators.

Howard-Hamilton, M. F., Richardson, B. J., & Shuford, B. (1998). Promoting multicultural Education: A holistic approach. *College Student Affairs Journal, 18*(1), 5–17.

Hu, S., & Kuh, G. D. (2003). Diversity experiences and college student learning and personal development. *Journal of College Student Development, 44*(3), 320–334.

Hurtado, S. (2007). Linking diversity with the educational and civic missions of higher education. *Review of Higher Education, 30*, 185–196.

Jackson, B. W., & Holvino, E. (1988). Developing multicultural organizations. *Journal of Applied Behavioral Science and Religion, 9*, 14–19.

Johnson, A. G. (2006). *Privilege, power, and difference* (2nd ed.). New York: McGraw-Hill.

King, P. M., & Howard-Hamilton, M. F. (2000). *Becoming a multiculturally competent student affairs professional: Diversity on campus, reports from the field.* Washington, DC: National Association of Student Personnel Administrators.

Krumboltz, J. D. (1966). Promoting adaptive behavior. In J. D. Krumboltz (Ed.), *Revolution in counseling* (pp. 3–26). Boston: Houghton-Mifflin.

LaFromboise, T. D., Coleman, H.L.K., & Hernandez, A. (1991). Development and factor structure of the Cross-Cultural Counseling Inventory-Revised. *Professional Psychology: Research and Practice, 22*, 380–388.

Manning, K., & Coleman-Boatwright, R. (1991). Student affairs initiatives toward a multicultural university. *Journal of College Student Development, 32*, 367–374.

Martin, S. (2005). *A pragmatic exploration of multicultural competence of community college student affairs practitioners.* Unpublished doctoral dissertation, The George Washington University.

McEwen, M. K., & Roper, L. D. (1994). Incorporating multiculturalism into student affairs preparation programs: Suggestions from the literature. *Journal of College Student Development, 35*, 46–53.

Miklitsch, T. A. (2006). *The relationship between multicultural education, multicultural experiences, racial identity, and multicultural competence among student affairs professionals.* Unpublished doctoral dissertation, State University of New York at Buffalo.

Mueller, J. A., & Pope, R. L. (2001). The relationship between multicultural competence and white racial consciousness among student affairs practitioners. *Journal of College Student Development, 42*, 133–144.

Myers, L. J. (1988). *Understanding an Afrocentric worldview: Introduction to an optimal psychology.* Dubuque, IA: Kendall-Hunt.

Pascarella, E. T., Edison, M., Nora, A., Hagedorn, L. S., & Terenzini, P. T. (1996). Influences on students' openness to diversity and challenges in the first year of college. *Journal of Higher Education, 67*, 174–195.

Pedersen, P. (1988). *A handbook for developing multicultural awareness*. Alexandria, VA: American Association for Counseling and Development.

Ponterotto, J. G., Mendelsohn, J., & Belizaire, L. (2003). Assessing teacher multicultural competencies, self-report instruments, observer report evaluations, and a portfolio assessment. In D. B. Pope-Davis, H.L.K. Coleman, W. M. Liu, & R. L. Toporek (Eds.), *Handbook of multicultural competencies in counseling and psychology* (pp. 191–210). Thousand Oaks, CA: Sage.

Ponterotto, J. G., Rieger, B. P., Barrett, A., Harris, G., Sparks, R., Sanchez, C. M., & Magids, D. (1996). Development and initial validation of the Multicultural Counseling Awareness Scale (MCSA). In G. R. Sodowsky & J. Impara (Eds.), *Multicultural assessment in counseling and clinical psychology* (pp. 247–282). Lincoln, NE: Buros Institute of Mental Measurement.

Pope, R. L. (1993). Multicultural-organization development in student affairs: An introduction. *Journal of College Student Development, 34,* 201–205.

Pope, R. L. (1995). Multicultural organizational development: Implications and applications in student affairs. In J. Fried (Ed.), *Shifting paradigms in student affairs: Culture, context, teaching and learning* (pp. 233–250). Washington, DC: American College Personnel Association.

Pope, R. L., & Mueller, J. A. (2000). Development and initial validation of the Multicultural Competence in Student Affairs–Preliminary 2 Scale. *Journal of College Student Development, 41*(6), 599–608.

Pope, R. L., & Reynolds, A. L. (1997). Student affairs core competencies: Integrating multicultural awareness, knowledge, and skills. *Journal of College Student Development, 38,* 266–277.

Pope, R. L., Reynolds, A. L., & Mueller, J. A. (2004). *Multicultural competence in student affairs*. San Francisco: Jossey-Bass.

Pope-Davis, D. B., Toporek, R. L., & Ortega-Villalobos, L. (2003). Assessing supervisors' and supervisees' perceptions of multicultural competence in supervision using the multicultural supervision inventory. In D. B. Pope-Davis, H.L.K. Coleman, W. M. Liu, & R. L. Toporek (Eds.), *Handbook of multicultural competencies in counseling and psychology* (pp. 211–224). Thousand Oaks, CA: Sage.

Reynolds, A. L. (2008). Helping college students: Developing essential support skills for student affairs practice. San Francisco: Jossey-Bass.

Reynolds, A. L., Pope, R. L., & Wells, G. V. (2002). *Creating a student affairs diversity action plan: Blueprint for success*. Paper presented at the meeting of the American College Personnel Association, Long Beach, CA.

Sleeter, C. E., & Grant, C. A. (1994). *Making choices for multicultural education: Five approaches to race, class, and gender*. New York: Maxwell Macmillan International.

Sodowsky, G. R., Taffe, R. C., Gutkin, T. B., & Wise, S. L. (1994). Development of the Multicultural Counseling Inventory (MCI): A self-report measure of multicultural competencies. *Journal of Counseling Psychology, 41,* 153–162.

Sue, D. W., Bernier, J. E., Durran, A., Feinberg, L., Pederson, P., Smith, E. J., & Vasquez-Nuttall, E. (1982). Position paper: Cross-cultural counseling competencies. *Counseling Psychologist, 10,* 45–52.

Sue, D. W., Capodilupo, C. M., Torino, G. C., Bucceri, J. M., Holder, A.M.B., Nadal, K. L., & Esquilin, M. (2007). Racial microaggressions in everyday life: Implications for clinical practice. *American Psychologist, 62,* 271–286.

Talbot, D. M. (1996). *Multiculturalism*. In S. R. Komives & D. B. Woodard (Eds.), *Student services: A handbook for the profession* (3rd ed., pp. 380–396). San Francisco: Jossey-Bass.

Talbot, D. M., & Kocarek, C. (1997). Student affairs graduate faculty members' knowledge, comfort, and behaviors regarding issues of diversity. *Journal of College Student Development, 38*(3), 278–287.

Toporek, R. L., Liu, W. M., & Pope-Davis, D. B. (2003). Assessing multicultural competence of the training environment: Further validation for the psychometric properties of the multicultural environment inventory-revised. In D. B. Pope-Davis, H.L.K. Coleman, W. M. Liu, & R. L. Toporek (Eds.), *Handbook of multicultural competencies in counseling and psychology* (pp. 183–190). Thousand Oaks, CA: Sage.

Umbach, P. D., & Kuh, G. D. (2006). Student experiences with diversity at liberal arts colleges: Another claim for distinctiveness. *Journal of Higher Education, 77*(1), 169–192.

Watt, S. K. (2007). Difficult dialogues, privilege and social justice: Uses of the Privileged Identity Exploration (PIE) Model in student affairs practice. *College Student Affairs Journal, 26,* 114–126.

Weigand, M. J. (2005). *The relationships between multicultural competence, racial identity, and multicultural education and experiences among student affairs professionals responsible for first-year student orientation programs.* Unpublished doctoral dissertation, State University of New York at Buffalo.

CHAPTER TWENTY

LEADERSHIP

Susan R. Komives

Erica Williams is beginning her new position as assistant director of service-learning and civic engagement at Middle State University. She began this newly created position right out of graduate school. The position was designed to facilitate academic and community outreach to enhance civic engagement through service-learning experiences. Pam Johnson, the director of the office, identified several academic units as a priority for Erica, including the College of Psychology and Behavioral Sciences (CPBS) and the College of Public Health.

At the first meeting of the newly formed provost's civic engagement committee, Erica was pleased to meet Mark Washington, chair of the committee and the long-time associate dean and director of academic advising in CPBS. They talked before the meeting started and enjoyed a fun conversation about their fantasy football team picks for the year. Mark gave Erica background on the provost's initiative and logged in on his laptop to send her a campus senate report on the initiative from the previous year, which had resulted in this committee and her new position. When the meeting started, Mark made a point of asking members to share their personal interests in the topic and identify how their offices connected to the goals of the committee. He asked the group to brainstorm what activities and involvements might promote civic engagement outcomes for all students. The group had a lively and uplifting meeting.

Mark responded positively to Erica's invitation for coffee the next week to brainstorm ways to enhance specific service-learning initiatives in CPBS. At that coffee, they found they were like-minded on the values and benefits of service-learning as a pedagogy and identified ways her office could partner with his work in the college. Mark seemed particularly interested in challenging others on the dean's council to become involved in the initiative. Erica shared these ideas with her student advisory board, and the students added several superb suggestions to the list. Upon hearing all the committee plans, Pam told Erica this indeed seemed to be a committee that was going to get things done this year; that she would be replacing Erica as their office representative; and further, that she would let Erica know what initiatives to follow up on as the committee progressed.

What climate has the provost set up on this shared agenda? What practices does Mark seem to be using to create that climate?

What principles does Erica seem to be using in her leadership? Why might she and Mark relate so well?

What values does Pam bring to her leadership?

This chapter reviews historic and conventional understandings of organizational leadership, before moving to a discussion of contemporary relational approaches valued in complex, networked organizations (see Chapter Twelve for further understanding of dynamics of organizations). Grounded in scholarship from psychology, sociology, business, identity studies, and education, this chapter challenges you to think of leadership not only as holding a positional role but also as the behaviors of any individual working with others toward shared goals as well as a process within organizational units (i.e., a committee, work group, or department). The chapter includes a socially responsible, values-based approach to leadership and presents the Social Change Model of Leadership Development (Higher Education Research Institute [HERI], 1996) as a framework to discuss key dimensions of integrity, authenticity, inclusion, meaning making, and collaboration. The goal of the chapter is to synthesize a vast amount of scholarship addressing leadership studies so that you can explore how to develop your own leadership capacity.

Perspectives on Leadership

Leadership is socially constructed. One cannot touch, taste, or see leadership. Common views of leadership evolve with shifting social perspectives of such constructs as relationships, gender roles, power, and social capital. Rost (1991) examined these historical shifts to paint a big picture of the evolution of the construction of leadership. Twenty years ago he labeled early- to mid-twentieth-century perspectives as *industrial* and late-twentieth-century perspectives as *postindustrial*, reflecting the mind-sets of the eras in which they developed. It is critical to realize that as perspectives or constructions on leadership have evolved, all previous perspectives have continued—they do not disappear. Postindustrial, emergent perspectives concurrently exist alongside previous perspectives, even within the same group or organization. An overview of the evolution of leadership perspectives appears in Exhibit 20.1.

Perspectives on leadership and views of organizational dynamics interact and have changed over time. Understanding the evolving construction of leadership is

EXHIBIT 20.1.   SUMMARY OF LEADERSHIP APPROACHES.

Approach	Time Period	Major Assumptions	Major Criticisms
Great Man	Mid-1800s to early 1900s	• Leadership development is based on Darwinistic principles • Leaders are born, not made • Leaders have natural abilities of power and influence	• Scientific research has not proved that leadership is based on hereditary factors • Leadership was believed to exist only in a few individuals
Trait	1904 to 1947	• A leader has superior or endowed qualities • Certain individuals possess a natural ability to lead • Leaders have traits which differentiate them from followers	• The situation is not considered in this approach • Many traits are too obscure or abstract to measure and observe • Studies have not adequately linked traits with leadership effectiveness • Most trait studies omit leadership behaviors and followers' motivation as mediating variables
Behavioral	1950s to early 1980s	• There is one best way to lead • Leaders who express high concern for both people and production or consideration and structure will be effective	• Situational variables and group processes are ignored; studies failed to identify the situations in which specific types of leadership behaviors are relevant
Situational Contingency	1950s to 1960s	• Leaders act differently depending on the situation • The situation determines who will emerge as a leader • Different leadership behaviors are required for different situations	• Most contingency theories are ambiguous, making it difficult to formulate specific, testable propositions • Theories lack accurate measures
Influence	Mid-1920s to 1977	• Leadership is an influence or social exchange process	• More research is needed on the effect charisma has on the leader-follower interaction
Reciprocal	1978 to present	• Leadership is a relational process • Leadership is a shared process • Emphasis is on followership	• Research is lacking • Further clarification is needed on similarities and differences between charismatic and transforming leadership • Processes of collaboration, change, and empowerment are difficult to achieve and measure
Chaos or Systems	1990 to present	• Attempts to describe leadership within a context of a complex, rapidly changing world • Leadership is a relational process • Control is not possible, so leadership is described as an influence relationship • The importance of systems is emphasized.	• Research is lacking • Some concepts are difficult to define and understand • Holistic approach makes it difficult to achieve and measure

Source: Komives, S. R., Lucas, N., & McMahon, T. R. (2007) *Exploring leadership: For college students who want to make a difference* (2nd ed.). San Francisco: Jossey-Bass. Reprinted with permission.

critical to understanding why others may hold different views of what is important
in leadership.

What is your individual perspective on leadership?

What perspectives are valued or practiced by peers with similar social identities?

*What perspectives predominate in your organizations (i.e., division, office, volunteer site,
academic program, or classroom)?*

Conventional, Industrial Views of Leadership

Western views of leadership were shaped in the mid-1800s and early 1900s by the
great man theories of leadership. The word *leader* was common and widely used to refer
to those born to leadership, such as royalty, or those in visible leadership roles, such
as generals, government leaders, or the clergy. In the great man theories, leadership is
an exclusive property of the positional leaders, who are almost exclusively men. This
elite view of who could be a leader excluded most people, certainly most men, all
women, and anyone who was not White. Those espousing this perspective were not at
all concerned with followers or the dynamics of a positional leader's engagement with
followers. The prevailing question was whether leaders were born or could be made.
Current examples of this perspective are those who believe heroic leaders bring truth
and wisdom to their roles, such as do college presidential search committees that look
for the perfect leader to solve a university's problems.

The rise of psychology as a field of study in the early 1900s and the concurrent
interest in the military in identifying those officers who had the potential to be effective
if promoted to generals shifted the emphasis in the construction of leadership. The
growing awareness that leaders were needed at the top of all kinds of organizations
moved the study of leadership to examine what traits or characteristics are possessed
by an effective positional leader. *Trait theory* identified such traits as intelligence, decisive-
ness, and aggressiveness (Stogdill, 1974). If a person demonstrated those traits or could
learn to exhibit these traits, then he must surely be a capable leader. The masculine traits
valued in this early part of the twentieth century established a normative expectation
of what was considered "leaderly." Over time, however, it became clear that even
those with these designated traits might not always be effective leaders.

The failure of traits to identify leaders led to the speculation that perhaps it was
not the traits possessed by a leader but the behaviors in which leaders engaged that
determined that leader's effectiveness. *Behavioral theory* led to the examination of such
behaviors as decision making and leadership styles. Lewin, Lippitt, and White's (1939)
classic study of leadership styles examined whether those exhibiting democratic,
autocratic, or laissez-faire styles were most effective with their followers and in
accomplishing their groups' goals or tasks. Other classic studies at The Ohio State
University (Stogdill & Coons, 1957) and the University of Michigan (Northouse, 2007)
established that behaviors that attended to both tasks and relationships were critical for
effective leadership. Such two-factor theories examining the balance between *tasks*
and *relationships* led to a conclusion that there was no fixed set of behaviors that, if used

consistently, would work in every situation. Indeed, the situation or context emerged as an important consideration in the behaviors practiced by the leader. Behavioral theories were the first to consider the essential role of followers in understanding leadership. Although still a leader-centric approach emphasizing how leaders could influence followers, behavioral theories acknowledged the follower role.

Situational or contingency theory differentiated the leader's behavior based on the situation that included the nature of the followers as part of the situational dynamic. Situations range from newly formed groups in which members are not used to working together (called immature groups) to highly functional, mature groups who have worked together for some time. Newly formed groups might best respond to high-task, low-relationship leadership when they are seeking clear focus and direction. As the group matures and members share group responsibilities, the leader may emphasize both tasks and relationships. Fully mature groups may need the leadership to be high in relationship orientation, keeping the motivation and morale thriving, but low in task orientation; or they may need little formal leadership (low task, low relationship). Some leaders appear to fit best with certain types of organizations. With the growth of business management programs in the 1960s and 1970s, two-factor situational theory models, such as the Managerial Grid (Blake & Mouton, 1964) and situational leadership theory (Hershey & Blanchard, 1969), brought forward the importance of followers in shaping the behaviors of the leader that determine the leader's effectiveness. These models are still prevalent in the corporate world and are conveyed through management training programs.

Although leadership theories were still leader-centric, the growing value of the role of followers shifted emphasis to *influence theories* that examined the nature of the leader-follower relationship. This influence might derive from an authority position; might come from the power base of the leader like the power of expertise; or might involve some personal characteristic of the positional leader, such as charisma (Conger, Kanungo, & Associates, 1988). The perspective of leadership as an influence relationship led to the recognition that anyone who is effective at influencing others might well be a leader—or at least is exhibiting leadership behaviors. This notion, which implies that leadership could come from someone other than only the person in authority (the positional leader), opened up conventional thinking to a new social construction of leadership that included those in both positional and nonpositional roles.

Transition Perspectives

The changing role of the positional leader was powerfully affirmed by Greenleaf's (1977) concept of *servant leadership*. Former AT&T executive Robert Greenleaf described the importance of the positional leader's serving the group and empowering individuals in the group to make their highest possible contributions. This servant leadership approach accentuated the importance of the positional leader as facilitator and the essential role of all group members working toward shared goals and vision. The key question Greenleaf asked was, Are those whom the leader serves better off through their engagement with the servant leader, and do they rise to leadership themselves? Greenleaf's vision of the leader as servant led to new expectations for the leader to exhibit authenticity, integrity, and trustworthiness.

The emerging emphasis on followers or on group members led some scholars to advance the development of followership skills (Kelley, 1991), while other theorists believed that anyone engaging in leadership, whether in a positional or nonpositional role, was also a leader (Komives, Lucas, & McMahon, 1998). Kouzes and Posner's (2007) research published in *The Leadership Challenge*, identified five practices of effective leaders in positional or nonpositional roles. These practices—model the way, challenge the process, inspire a shared vision, encourage the heart, and enable others to act—inspired many to engage in new relational orientations in organizations (Kouzes & Posner).

> *How does Mark's leadership reflect these five practices?*
>
> *How does Pam's leadership reflect these practices, or does it?*

Emergent, Relational, Postindustrial Views of Leadership

In the same decade as Greenleaf's (1977) rethinking of positional leadership, noted historian James MacGregor Burns (1978) published his seminal, Pulitzer-prize-winning book *Leadership*. Burns observed and advocated for *transforming leadership*—leadership that transforms followers into leaders themselves. Burns acknowledged that all relationships include transactions, and that those transactions are akin to management practices (i.e., transactional leadership). Burns thought that leadership, however, focuses on improving and bettering the human condition and advocated that transforming leadership is grounded in modal and end values. In this perspective, both the means and the ends of leadership need to be ethical and morally grounded. Actions intended to harm or hurt others—or done by underhanded or coercive means—would not be defined as leadership but rather considered to be tyranny, dictatorship, or manipulation. These postindustrial views of leadership shifted the emphasis on organizational leadership, originally perceived only as hierarchical, top-down modes of influence, to encompass dynamic relationships among people working together for shared objectives.

Relational views of leadership reflect the reciprocal nature of the influence shared between and among those working together in groups and organizations. In these models, leadership is "a relational and ethical process of people together attempting to accomplish positive change" (Komives et al., 2007, p. ix). Komives et al. (2007) advocated relational leadership as purposeful, inclusive, empowering, ethical, and process oriented. Viewing leadership as a process emphasizes that all group members, regardless of their roles, are responsible for and fully engaged in the shared leadership experience. These relational perspectives value collaborative practices and view the group as a community working together for shared outcomes.

> *How did the way Mark organized the first meeting support building inclusive and empowering relationships among members?*

In these relational views, beliefs such as the value of diversity, traits such as integrity, and skills such as active listening or teamwork become critical. Avolio and

Gardner (2005) and their colleagues examined all these postindustrial perspectives and concluded that the root construct of these views is *authentic leadership*. Authentic approaches emphasize self-awareness, relational integrity, congruent behavior, and a commitment to capacity building in all organization members.

Chaos theory (Wheatley, 2006) and views of organizations as networked environments continued to elevate the role of relational leadership in complex organizations. Allen and Cherrey (2000) studied the networked era of the information age and concluded contemporary fast-paced times require new ways of relating, new ways of learning together, new ways of changing, and new ways of leading. These postindustrial views both seek to promote leader-full organizations, not just leader-led organizations, and recognize the informal networks in organizations in which much leadership occurs.

How do the connections Mark and Erica made in the opening scenario reflect leadership?

Although Rost (1991) described this evolution from industrial to postindustrial views as a paradigm shift, for many people nothing shifted—the presumed move reflected their approaches to leadership all along. The supposedly newer postindustrial leadership perspectives valuing relationships, teams, and collaboration were the enacted leadership practices of many women and others in collectivist cultures (Bordas, 2007; Komives & Dugan, 2010). These perspectives were less valued in earlier times in dominant, Western culture, so were not socially constructed to be perceived as leadership; the emergence of the value of these perspectives, now described as postindustrial, could be viewed as a recognition and embracing of the perspectives of many who led from the margins with these relational styles (Komives & Dugan). How these changing perspectives exclude or include diverse social identities is a complex part of the construction of leadership.

Contemporary leadership is concerned with authentic relationships among people working together toward shared purposes and with how people work together for meaningful change. These theories particularly encourage outcomes dedicated to improving the human condition and of social value. Expanding individuals' capacity to engage in this approach to leadership is critical in the pluralistic contexts on college campuses (Roberts, 2007).

Socially Responsible Leadership

Student affairs professionals must build their own capacity to engage in leadership with others and concurrently promote the leadership capabilities of groups and organizations of which they are members. Of the dozens of emergent leadership theories and models in the postindustrial paradigm, the Social Change Model of Leadership Development (SCM) has proven to apply concurrently to individuals, groups, and communities or organizations (HERI, 1996). Although not yet widely known outside of student affairs work in higher education, it is the most used model in co-curricular programs for student leadership since the mid-1990s (Kezar, Carducci, & Contreras-McGavin, 2006) and serves as a useful model to guide student affairs practice (HERI; Komives, Wagner, & Associates, 2009; Outcalt, Faris, & McMahon, 2001).

The SCM approach to leadership is "a purposeful, collaborative, values-based process that results in positive social change" (Komives et al., 2009, p. xii). The model is congruent with professional values in student affairs and affirming of a social justice commitment to professional practice. Whether their work is framed as leadership for social change or socially responsible leadership, those engaged in the knowledge, skills, and attitudes reflected in these values are engaging responsibly in the leadership process.

The SCM identifies three dimensions that interact for responsible social change—individual, group, and society-community all organized around the hub of change. Individual values in the model are consciousness of self, congruence and commitment (see Exhibit 20.2). These individual values are reflected in other models in their affirmation of authenticity, character, integrity, and mindfulness. Group values are collaboration, common purpose, and controversy with civility. These group values encompass what other models identify as shared vision, interdependence, respect for diversity, and teamwork. The society-community value in the model is citizenship, or what other models identify as engagement and becoming a responsible member of one's communities of practice.

EXHIBIT 20.2.   VALUES OF THE SOCIAL CHANGE MODEL OF LEADERSHIP DEVELOPMENT (SCM).

Value	Definition
Change	As the hub and ultimate goal of the SCM, change gives meaning and purpose to the other Cs. Change means improving the status quo, creating a better world, and demonstrating a comfort with transition and ambiguity in the process of change.
Consciousness of self	Consciousness of self requires an awareness of personal beliefs, values, attitudes, and emotions. Self-awareness, conscious mindfulness, introspection, and continual personal reflection are foundational elements of the leadership process.
Congruence	Congruence requires that one has identified personal values, beliefs, attitudes, and emotions and acts consistently with these. A congruent individual is genuine and honest and "walks the talk."
Commitment	Commitment requires an intrinsic passion, energy, and purposeful investment toward action. Follow-through and willing involvement through commitment lead to positive social change.
Collaboration	Collaboration multiplies a group's effort through collective contributions, capitalizing on the diversity and strengths of the relationships and interconnections among individuals involved in the change process. Collaboration assumes that a group is working toward a common purpose with mutually beneficial goals; it serves to generate creative solutions as a result of group diversity, requiring participants to engage across difference and share authority, responsibility, and accountability for the group's success.
Common purpose	A common purpose necessitates and contributes to a high level of group trust, involving all participants in shared responsibility toward collective aims, values, and vision.
Controversy with civility	Within a diverse group, it is inevitable that differing viewpoints will exist. When a group is working toward positive social change, open, critical, and civil discourse can lead to new, creative solutions and is an integral component of the leadership process. Multiple perspectives need to be understood and integrated to bring value to a group.
Citizenship	Citizenship occurs when one becomes responsibly connected to the community and society in which one resides by actively working toward change to benefit others through care, service, social responsibility, and community involvement.

Source: Adapted from Astin, 1996; HERI, 1996; Wagner, 2007.

**FIGURE 20.1.   THE SOCIAL CHANGE MODEL OF LEADERSHIP
DEVELOPMENT.**

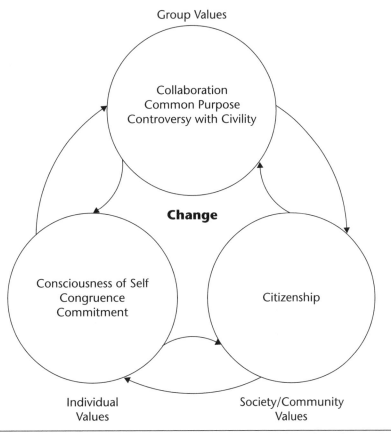

Group Values

Collaboration
Common Purpose
Controversy with Civility

Change

Consciousness of Self
Congruence
Commitment

Citizenship

Individual
Values

Society/Community
Values

Source: A Social Change Model of Leadership Development (3rd ed., p. 20) by Higher Education Research
Institute (HERI). Copyright © 1996, National Clearinghouse for Leadership Programs. Reprinted
with permission of the National Clearinghouse for Leadership Programs.

As illustrated in Figure 20.1, each dimension of the model is in dynamic reciprocity
with the other dimensions. If a group is unable to come to common purpose (group
dimension), it might examine how committed the individuals are to the group (individual dimension) and ask individuals to examine why they are exhibiting resistance
(individual dimension) if they cannot come to common purpose.

The SCM can become a diagnostic process model to explore how an organization
functions or an individual assessment model to examine personal capacity building.

*What might Mark and Erica's apparent collaboration and agreement on common purpose
indicate about their individual values or their community values?*

What did Mark do to get the group to come to common purpose?

How does the SCM inform an understanding of Pam's approach to leadership?

Leadership is not an episodic phenomenon (Rost, 1991). Leadership is happening in every gathering of any group of people everywhere on a daily basis—friendship groups, families, project groups, car pools, pick-up basketball games, classrooms, and staff meetings. The SCM and any of the relational models of leadership apply to all groups of people, whether loosely organized like friendship groups or highly structured like a division of student affairs. The purpose of this book is to explore professional practices in student affairs work; this chapter largely focuses, therefore, on leadership within an organizational context—called organizational leadership.

A Focus on Organizational Leadership

Western culture perspectives on leadership are largely developed from such organizational leadership settings as hierarchical work environments. In these settings,

- Leadership is typically perceived as the directives and actions of supervisors filtered down through the organizational hierarchy; it relates to authority and control.
- Leadership is exhibited by individuals as professionals in their offices, divisions, and universities; on committees; and in professional associations.
- Leadership processes are visible when it becomes evident that some offices get a lot accomplished and are loyal to each one another whereas others struggle to make effective decisions and distrust one another.

It is useful to examine a distinction between management and leadership and to explore how leadership is framed within the dynamics of diverse organizations.

Management and Leadership

When considering organizational leadership, many people often confuse management and leadership (Zaleznik, 1977). In the industrial era of conventional leadership constructions grounded in organizational leadership settings, the terms *management* and *leadership* were often used as synonyms. In the postindustrial era, however, the distinction between management and leadership has become clearer, and current perspectives view them as distinct yet essential processes in any organization. Catchy phrases like "leaders know *why* and managers know *how*" or "management is about doing things right, and leadership is about doing the right things" distinguish management's essential role of getting things done in smooth, effective, efficient, and often transactional ways from leadership's meaning-making role of establishing and working toward a shared vision that upholds the values and moral purpose of the group. It takes leadership to accomplish change through innovation and approaching new solutions to old problems, but it takes management to adopt the innovations and make them work smoothly within the organizational system (Kirton, 1978). Management and leadership are often presented as dualisms—management versus leadership. Today's complex organizations require that professionals instead perceive this as a "both/and" and not "either/or" (Komives, 2001; Love & Estanek, 2004). Each perspective or role is essential for the organization's goals. Management may work best in the hierarchical scaffolding of the organization, but leadership comes from all around. Student affairs professionals need to be both good managers and good leaders. Furthermore, each student affairs professional needs to have the individual capacity to contribute to the leadership process of any group in which he or she is engaged, including committees, and work effectively with others toward shared goals.

Frameworks for Leadership Perspectives

Another way to view the social construction of leadership is to examine the way individuals view organizations. As an application of situational leadership theory, organizational cultures reflect shared views of what approaches to leadership are effective in their organizational setting. Chapter Twelve identifies the four organizational frames of Bolman and Deal (2008) as helpful in understanding organizations and the leadership perspectives in those organizations. As illustrated in Exhibit 20.3, leaders who predominately use a *structural* frame view themselves as social architects designing the organizational system to meet goals. Leaders who use a *human resource* frame see themselves as serving and supporting others in the organization. Those using the *political* frame form coalitions and seek partners to advocate in the organization. And leaders who use the *symbolic* frame bring a cultural lens to their leadership, seeking to make meaning for others and inspire shared work. Research on the use of the four frames indicates that student affairs practitioners predominately bring a human resource frame to their leadership (Kane, 2001; Maitra, 2007) and may lack understanding of the benefits of the other frames. People who can view an organization from multiple frames are more effective in their leadership and are trusted by others as understanding diverse perspectives (Bensimon, Neumann, & Birnbaum, 1989; Kuh, 2003).

What frame or frames might Erica be using?

How about Mark or Pam?

EXHIBIT 20.3.   REFRAMING LEADERSHIP IN BOLMAN AND DEAL'S FRAMES.

Frame	Leadership Is Effective When:		Leadership Is Ineffective When:	
	Leader is:	Leadership Process is:	Leader is:	Leadership Process is:
Structural	Analyst, architect	Analysis, design	Petty bureaucrat, tyrant	Management by detail and fiat
Human resource	Catalyst, servant	Support, empowerment	Weakling, pushover	Abdication
Political	Advocate, negotiator	Advocacy, coalition building	Con artist, thug	Manipulation, fraud
Symbolic	Prophet, poet	Inspiration, meaning making	Fanatic, charlatan	Mirage, smoke and mirrors

Source: Bolman & Deal, 2008, p. 356. Reprinted with permission of John Wiley & Sons, Inc.

Implementing Effective Leadership

How does one come to be effective in his or her personal leadership? Leadership can be learned (Lord & Hall, 2005). It is not born in each person but rather is made based on how one engages his or her talents and identity to build the capacity to work effectively with others. There are challenges in developing leadership and implementing leadership in real-life and cyber groups.

Challenges to Effective Leadership

Individuals encounter numerous challenges and barriers to exhibiting their leadership potential, and organizations experience challenges in promoting effective leadership among group members. A few of these challenges are highlighted here.

Philosophical Confusion. *Leadership* is such a common word that there are hundreds of definitions and frames that construct its meaning. At the end of the 1980s, in the midst of the paradigm shift between the industrial and postindustrial models, a colleague observed that we were lost in the leadership forest, looking for pathways out of the woods. In the years since that observation, those pathways have become clearer, and one can identify schools of thinking about leadership that fit one's personal philosophy. Those who cannot articulate their own approaches to leadership may still be lost in the leadership forest and would find it helpful to examine the assumptions in the pathways that best connect with their professional and personal philosophies. For example, those who believe it is the positional leader's role to get the job done and motivate and supervise followers toward that end may use more industrial, managerial practices; those who believe the group shares the leadership responsibility probably utilize more relational, collaborative practices.

Lack of Self-Empowerment. Each professional needs confidence in his or her role and preparation to know he or she has a voice in any group endeavor. Self-empowerment is claimed; no one delegates empowerment to others. Some professionals, however, hold constraining or disempowering beliefs that affect their sense of empowerment. Scholars who expanded on the social change model in *Leadership Reconsidered* (Astin & Astin, 2000) identified individual qualities of effective leadership (for example, commitment, empathy, competence, authenticity, and self-knowledge) and group qualities of effective leadership (for example, shared purpose, collaboration, division of labor, disagreement with respect, and a created learning environment). Further, they identified disempowering beliefs and empowering beliefs of key campus constituent groups. Identifying the disempowering beliefs that rob one of self-empowerment is useful. For students these disempowering beliefs include such individual internal thoughts as "I don't have time to get involved" and "I can't 'lead' because I don't hold a formal leadership title," and such group beliefs as "This campus doesn't care about students" or "Students do not have enough experience to lead major campus-change efforts" (Astin & Astin, p. 25). For faculty, individual constraining or disempowering beliefs include such statements as "My colleagues will never change their way of doing things" or "It is not my role to initiate but rather 'to transfer disciplinary knowledge,'" and such group beliefs as "Nothing can be changed because of administrative attitudes" or "Faculty and staff have nothing in common" (p. 42). Exhibits 20.4 and 20.5 contain the complete analysis of student affairs professionals from *Leadership Reconsidered* (Astin & Astin). The constraining beliefs include how an individual may act in the external environment and related implications for individual and group leadership development.

Although empowerment is claimed, professionals can create empowering environments to make it more possible for individual members to fully exercise their leadership.

How might Erica's behaviors be understood in the empowering beliefs?

EXHIBIT 20.4. CONSTRAINING BELIEFS IN STUDENT AFFAIRS.

Individual Internal Beliefs	Individual External Actions	Implications for Individual Leadership Development
• My perspectives and ideas would not be taken seriously by others at this institution • The work I do is not appreciated within the institution • I'm a second-class citizen within the institution	• Individual staff members do not speak their mind or share their perspectives at meetings • Staff members do not ask to participate in institutional decisions or institutional forums • Individual staff members do not attempt to influence the institution's values, future plans, or goals	Individual members lose opportunities to model and develop individual qualities of leadership: • *Self-knowledge* is distorted by constraining beliefs • *Commitment* becomes difficult because one is suppressing one's passion and not sharing perspectives • Opportunities to develop *competence* and *empathy* are diminished

Group Internal Beliefs	Group External Actions	Implications for Group Leadership Development
• The work of student affairs is peripheral to the main work of the academy • Student affairs professionals are "service providers" rather than educators • Learning happens mainly in the classroom	• Student affairs staff are generally not included in discussions of "academic" issues • Resource allocation does not reflect the contribution of the student affairs division • The administrative structure leaves student affairs out of the academic "loop"	Implications for group qualities of leadership: • *Collaboration* is diminished • Opportunities to develop *shared purpose* and to *disagree with respect* are reduced • The *learning environment* is hindered because individual knowledge is not shared with group

Source: Astin & Astin, 2000, p. 57. Reprinted with permission of the W. K. Kellogg Foundation.

EXHIBIT 20.5.   EMPOWERING BELIEFS IN STUDENT AFFAIRS.

Individual Internal Beliefs

- I can make a difference in individual students' lives
- Student learning and development should be viewed holistically and individuallyI can be creative and innovative in my work with students and colleagues
- I am a full partner with faculty in facilitating student development

Individual External Actions

- Individual staff members are proactive in their work with students and colleagues
- Student affairs staff regularly promote an integrated/holistic perspective in their dealings with faculty
- Student affairs staff take the initiative to promote student learning by proposing and trying out new approaches

Implications for Individual Leadership Development

Promotes the following individual leadership qualities:

- *Self-knowledge* (i.e., of one's capabilities)
- *Commitment* (i.e., to making a difference in students' lives and to serving as institutional leaders)
- *Authenticity* (i.e., by modeling core values to students and faculty)
- *Collaboration* (i.e., reaching out to faculty and staff colleagues)

Group Internal Beliefs

- Student affairs are partners with faculty in promoting the holistic development of students
- Student learning occurs outside the classroom, as well as within. Education should be student-centered
- Equity and diversity are high priorities
- Community is a critical part of effective education

Group External Actions

- Institutional mission statements articulate the importance of holistic development
- Teaching and mentoring receive significant weight in the faculty reward system
- Student affairs sponsors workshops, seminars, and classes on diversity and equity for students and staff
- Student affairs builds collaboration into its work with students and other employees in the institution
- Student affairs creates learning opportunities and experiences that facilitate holistic development of students

Implications for Group Leadership Development

The following group leadership qualities are modeled and reinforced:

- *Collaboration* and *division of labor* (i.e., in working actively with faculty and staff to implement a holistic approach to student learning)
- *Shared purpose* and *commitment* (i.e., in the consistent support shown for a holistic approach and for the values of diversity, equity, and community)
- *Group learning* is enhanced when faculty, staff, and students work together

Source: Astin & Astin, 2000, p. 64. Reprinted with permission of the W. K. Kellogg Foundation.

The Reality of Bad, Dysfunctional Leadership. Americans are unfailingly optimistic about promoting high expectations of leadership. Even this chapter is written from the perspective of that aspiration. Sadly, there are many examples of managers at the top of organizational hierarchies who are unethical, exploitative, or incompetent. In her book *Bad Leadership*, Kellerman (2004) identified seven different types of bad leadership: incompetent, rigid, intemperate, callous, corrupt, insular, and evil. It is, unfortunately, easy to identify recent public and corporate figures whose greed or self-aggrandizement led to their downfalls and irreparably harmed their companies or other entities in their care. The *Chronicle of Higher Education* contains too many stories of college presidents who refurnish their offices in a year when staff are experiencing furloughs or no raises, of scholars who have plagiarized material in their books, and of staff who did not address campus issues before they became crises (Hellmich, 2007; Kelley & Chang, 2007). In her book *The Allure of Toxic Leaders*, Lipman-Blumen (2005) goes one step further and challenges followers and group members to examine why they put up with such toxic behaviors on the part of others in their organizations and in their positional leadership in particular. Even though in hierarchical management structures it is often hard for a "subordinate" to challenge the toxic behaviors of a bad manager, staff and group members must be vigilant in order to question practices that lead to toxic or dysfunctional behaviors. Any staff member or group member could help the group set healthy norms ("Before we move on, could we all check in on how we feel about this decision?") or make values-based comments that shape group behaviors ("I think it is essential that we reach out to that other department and include them before we make a final decision"). Indeed, vigilantly supporting and upholding an ethical climate is critical to prevent organizational dysfunction.

How might Erica approach Pam before this situation unfolds further?

Developing Enhanced Capacity for Leadership

Organizations are social entities designed for specific purposes. Developing the leadership capacity of individuals in those organizations and designing processes for groups of individuals to work effectively together are critical for dynamic, renewing, effective outcomes. Individuals must be concerned about their own leadership development and the leadership capacity of the various organizational entities with which they engage, called their *communities of practice* (Wenger, 1998).

Individual Capacity. Just how does an individual develop his or her leadership approach? There is little research examining leadership development across the life span (Day, 2000; Drath, 1998; Lord & Hall, 2005). The Leadership Identity Development Model (LID) (Komives, Longerbeam, Owen, Mainella, & Osteen, 2006) provides insights applicable to professional leadership development. In this six-stage model, organizational leadership is typified in the leader-centric stage (stage three: "leader identified"), in which the hierarchical beliefs that the positional leader is the only leader in the group and that others are followers predominate. Even when caring and empowering, the positional leader in this stage feels the responsibility to "get the job done" and works to motivate and involve followers in that endeavor. Individuals in this stage believe that leadership is a behavior of the leader, whereas followers engage in followership.

When individuals come to recognize the profound interdependence of group members (perhaps what Kegan [1994] calls a stage of consciousness shift), leadership is seen as more complex (stage four: "leadership differentiated") and is differentiated as nonpositional and as a process. Positional leaders using stage-four thinking practice shared leadership; view their roles as facilitative; and design empowering, inclusive environments for group members. Group members in stage four feel responsible for their groups, and each practices a philosophy that he or she can be *a* leader even if not *the* leader of the group. They recognize they can be leaders without titles.

> *What did you previously think leadership was?*
> *What do you think it is now?*

Individuals are ultimately responsible for developing their own capacities for leadership (Komives & Carpenter, 2009; Kruger, 2000). Look back at Exhibits 20.4 and 20.5 to examine the constraining and empowering beliefs that you yourself might hold. Individuals might examine how their leadership identities intersect with their other social identities (Aguirre & Martinez, 2007; Sanchez-Hucles & Sanchez, 2007). How do those social identities reveal what approaches may be most comfortable, how one views differences in others, and what orientations one brings to understanding organizations? How skilled is one at being purposeful, inclusive, ethical, empowering of others, and process orientated in group settings? How capable is one at seeing other perspectives on any issue, actively listening to others, engaging in teamwork, and helping the group make meaning? How might one's personality preferences shape one's approach to leadership?

Group Capacity. Individuals must accept their roles in shaping and developing the ability of their groups and communities of practice to engage in the process of leadership. A keen process orientation ensures that the group is constantly building and revisiting the process used to ensure they are ethical, inclusive, and empowering of all involved. Using the values of the SCM gives a focus that assists the group in staying committed to a common purpose, engaging in collaborative practices, and handling any controversies with civility. It is helpful to understand groups and recognize that groups go through predictable stages of forming, storming, norming, and performing (Tuckman, 1965; Tuckman & Jensen, 1977) so that in times of storming groups can show the care and attention needed to establish normative expectations that value inclusion, empowerment, and ethical practices.

LID findings shed light on how an individual's leadership identity might intersect with the group's predominant ways of functioning (Komives et al., 2006; Komives et al., 2007). A professional who identifies as *a* leader even when not *the* leader, and who feels responsible for the interdependence in the group (i.e., holding LID stage-four beliefs), may feel stifled and frustrated in a hierarchical organization in which the positional leader claims the control and authority of the role. The positional leader practicing this authority-based leadership (i.e., holding LID stage-three beliefs) may indeed feel threatened by this staff member's thinking him or her to be seeking power and may even consider the staff member insubordinate. Conversely, a stage-three professional who looks to the leader for guidance and direction may judge a stage-four leader to be indecisive, when actually that leader is practicing shared, participative leadership and seeking highly involved group solutions (Komives, Owen, Longerbeam, Mainella, & Osteen, 2005; Komives et al., 2006; Komives et al., 2007).

Cyberleadership. Many leadership interactions in contemporary organizations occur in cyberspace (Zaccaro & Bader, 2003). Technology such as wikis, video conferencing, webinars, Web sites, and even e-mail make it possible for groups to share comments on draft documents, engage in dialogue before or after formal meetings, and link organization needs to a myriad of resources. These technologies become valuable new vehicles for implementing the organization's values of inclusion and empowerment, and must reflect the highest of ethical practices.

Conclusion

In the scenario that opened this chapter, Mark's leadership demonstrated the relational, collaborative, interdependent beliefs that would build an empowering environment for those involved in the provost's committee. Erica was thriving and empowered by his approach to leadership and shut down and disempowered by Pam's intervention.

Professionals need new ways of learning, relating, changing, and leading in today's pluralistic, complex organizations (Allen & Cherrey, 2000). While seeking to be effective managers, professionals must concurrently develop their leadership capacity and seek to create leader-full organizations. Developing one's individual capacity for authentic, values-based leadership that reflects the values of the SCM (HERI, 1996), engages the individual in the intrapersonal, interpersonal, and community commitments needed to work in today's complex colleges and universities. Whether in positional or non-positional roles, leaders who are dedicated to practicing socially responsible leadership are essential in creating ethical campus environments.

As a final note, I think it is important to acknowledge that this approach to leadership honors the essential role of serving as models for students when they learn by observing professionals in action. Indeed, as Bart Giamatti (1988), former president of Yale and baseball commissioner, observed, "An educational institution teaches far, far more, and more profoundly, by how it acts than by anything anyone within it ever says" (pp. 191–192). Students should observe student affairs professionals being collaborative, empowered, ethical leaders.

References

Aguirre, A., Jr., & Martinez, R. O. (2007). *Diversity leadership in higher education* (ASHE Higher Education Report, Vol. 32, No. 3). San Francisco: Jossey-Bass.

Allen, K. E., & Cherrey, C. (2000). *Systemic leadership: Enriching the meaning of our work.* Washington, DC: American College Personnel Association & National Association of Campus Activities.

Astin, A. W., & Astin, H. S. (2000). *Leadership reconsidered: Engaging higher education in social change.* Battle Creek, MI: W. K. Kellogg Foundation.

Astin, H. S. (1996, July/August). Leadership for social change. *About Campus,* 4–10.

Avolio, B. J., & Gardner, W. L. (2005). Authentic leadership development: Getting to the roots of positive forms of leadership. *Leadership Quarterly, 16,* 315–338.

Bensimon, E. M., Neumann, A., & Birnbaum, R. (1989). *Making sense of administrative leadership* (ASHE-ERIC Higher Education Report, No. 1). San Francisco: Jossey-Bass.

Blake, R. R., & Mouton, J. S. (1964). *The managerial grid.* Houston, TX: Gulf.

Bolman, L. G., & Deal, T. E. (2008). *Reframing organizations: Artistry, choice, and leadership* (4th ed.). San Francisco: Jossey-Bass.

Bordas, J. (2007). *Salsa, soul, and spirit: New approaches to leadership from Latino, Black, and American Indian communities.* San Francisco: Berrett-Koehler.

Burns, J. M. (1978). *Leadership.* New York: Harper & Row.

Conger, J. A., Kanungo, R. N., & Associates. (Eds.). (1988). *Charismatic leadership: The elusive factor in organizational effectiveness.* San Francisco: Jossey-Bass.

Day, D. V. (2000). Leadership development: A review in context. *Leadership Quarterly, 11,* 581–613.

Drath, W. H. (1998). Approaching the future of leadership development. In C. D. McCauley, R. S. Mosley, & E. Van Velson (Eds.), *Handbook of leadership development* (Center for Creative Leadership, pp. 403–432). San Francisco: Jossey-Bass.

Giamatti, A. B. (1988). *A free and ordered space: The real world of the university.* New York: W. W. Norton.

Greenleaf, R. K. (1977). *Servant leadership.* New York: Paulist.

Hellmich, D. H. (2007). *Ethical leadership in the community college: Bridging theory and daily practice.* Bolton, MA: Anker.

Hershey, P., & Blanchard, K. H. (1969). Life-cycle theory of leadership. *Training and Development Journal, 23,* 153–170.

Higher Education Research Institute (HERI). (1996). *A social change model of leadership development: Guidebook version III.* College Park, MD: National Clearinghouse for Leadership Programs.

Kane, S. D. (2001). *Mid-level student affairs administrators' organizational "frame" orientations and perceptions of their effectiveness by senior student affairs officers.* Unpublished doctoral dissertation, University of Maryland-College Park, AAT 3035847.

Kegan, R. (1994). *In over our heads: The mental demands of modern life.* Cambridge, MA: Harvard University Press.

Kellerman, B. (2004). *Bad leadership.* Cambridge, MA: Harvard Business School Press.

Kelley, P. C., & Chang, P. L. (2007). A typology of university ethical lapses: Types, levels of seriousness, and originating location. *Journal of Higher Education, 78,* 402–429.

Kelley, R. E. (1991). *The power of followership.* New York: Doubleday Currency.

Kezar, A. J., Carducci, R., Contreras-McGavin, M. (2006). *Rethinking the "L" word in higher education: The revolution in research on leadership* (ASHE Higher Education Report, Vol. 31, No. 6). San Francisco: Jossey-Bass.

Kirton, M. (1978). Adopters and innovators: A description and measure. *Journal of Applied Psychology, 61,* 622–629.

Komives, S. R. (2001). Both/and not either/or: Viewing the gap as social construction. *Journal of College Student Development, 42,* 338–341.

Komives, S. R., & Carpenter, S. (2009). Professional development as life-long learning. In J. Stringer & G. McClelland (Eds.), *The handbook of student affairs administration* (3rd ed., pp. 371–387). San Francisco: Jossey-Bass.

Komives, S. R., & Dugan, J. P. (2010). Contemporary leadership theories. In R. A. Couto (Ed.), *Handbook of political and civic leadership* (pp. 109–125). Thousand Oaks, CA: Sage.

Komives, S. R., Longerbeam, S., Owen, J. O., Mainella, F. C., & Osteen, L. (2006). A leadership identity development model: Applications from a grounded theory. *Journal of College Student Development, 47,* 401–418.

Komives, S. R., Lucas, N., & McMahon, T. R. (1998). *Exploring leadership.* San Francisco: Jossey-Bass.

Komives, S. R., Lucas, N., & McMahon, T. R. (2007). *Exploring leadership* (2nd ed.). San Francisco: Jossey-Bass.

Komives, S. R., Owen, J. E., Longerbeam, S., Mainella, F. C., & Osteen, L. (2005). Developing a leadership identity: A grounded theory. *Journal of College Student Development, 46,* 593–611.

Komives, S. R., Wagner, W., & Associates. (2009). *Leadership for a better world: Understanding the social change model of leadership development.* A publication of the National Clearinghouse for Leadership Programs. San Francisco: Jossey-Bass.

Kouzes, J. M., & Posner, B. Z. (2007). *The leadership challenge.* (4th ed.). San Francisco: Jossey-Bass.

Kruger, K. (2000). New alternatives for professional development. In M. J. Barr, M. K. Desler, & Associates, *The handbook of student affairs administration* (2nd ed., pp. 535–553). San Francisco: Jossey-Bass.

Kuh, G. D. (2003). Organizational theory. In S. R. Komives, D. B. Woodard Jr., & Associates (Eds.), *Student services: A handbook for the profession* (3rd ed, pp. 269–296). San Francisco: Jossey-Bass.

Lewin, K., Lippitt, R., & White, R. K. (1939). Patterns of aggressive behavior on experimentally created social climates. *Journal of Social Psychology, 10,* 271–299.

Lipman-Blumen, J. (2005). *The allure of toxic leaders.* New York: Oxford University Press.

Lord, R. G., & Hall, R. J. (2005). Identity, deep structure and the development of leadership skill. *Leadership Quarterly, 16,* 591–615.

Love, P. G., & Estanek, S. M. (2004). *Rethinking student affairs practice.* San Francisco: Jossey-Bass.

Maitra, A. (2007). *An analysis of leadership styles and practices of university women in administrative vice presidencies.* Unpublished doctoral dissertation, Bowling Green State University. Retrieved from www.ohiolink.edu/etd/view.cgi?acc_num=bgsu1178711590.

Northouse, P. G. (2007). *Leadership theory and practice* (4th ed.). Thousand Oaks, CA: Sage.

Outcalt, C. L., Faris, S. K., & McMahon, K. N. (Eds.). (2001). *Developing non-hierarchical leadership on campus: Case studies and best practices in higher education.* Westport, CT: Greenwood Press.

Roberts, D. R. (2007). *Deeper learning in leadership: Helping college students find the potential within.* San Francisco: Jossey-Bass.

Rost, J. C. (1991). *Leadership for the twenty-first century.* Westport, CT: Praeger.

Sanchez-Hucles, J., & Sanchez, P. J. (2007). From margin to center: The voices of diverse feminist leaders. In J. L. Chin, B. Lott, J. K. Rice, & J. Sanchez-Hucles (Eds.), *Women and leadership: Transforming visions and diverse voices* (pp. 211–227). Malden, MA: Blackwell.

Stogdill, R. M. (1974). *Handbook of leadership: A survey of theory and research.* New York: Free Press.

Stogdill, R. W., & Coons, A. E. (Eds.). (1957). *Leader behavior: Its description and measurement* (Research Monograph No. 88). Columbus: Ohio State University, Bureau of Business Research.

Tuckman, B. W. (1965). Developmental sequence in small groups. *Psychological Bulletin, 63,* 384–399.

Tuckman, B. W., & Jensen, M. C. (1977). Stages of small group development revisited. *Group and Organizational Studies, 2,* 419–427.

Wagner, W. (2007). The social change model of leadership: A brief overview. *Concepts & Connections, 15*(1), 8–10.

Wenger, E. (1998). *Communities of practice: Learning, meaning, and identity.* Cambridge, England: Cambridge University Press.

Wheatley, M. J. (2006). *Leadership and the new science: Discovering order in a chaotic world* (3rd ed.). San Francisco: Berrett-Koehler.

Zaccaro, S. J., & Bader, P. (2003). E-leadership and the challenges of leading e-teams: Minimizing the bad and maximizing the good. *Organizational Dynamics, 31,* 377–387.

Zaleznik, A. (1977). Managers and leaders: Are they different? *Harvard Business Review, 55*(5), 67–78.

CHAPTER TWENTY-ONE

STAFFING AND SUPERVISION

Joan B. Hirt and Terrell L. Strayhorn

In most instances, student affairs professionals work with others—student employees, paraprofessionals, support staff, and professional colleagues, to name a few. Administrative units, in turn, are led by supervisors who teach employees new skills, counsel those who report to them, and assess the performance of their staff members. In short, supervision is a function that requires professionals to use many of the other competencies described in this handbook. Supervision goes beyond the daily management of personnel and activities, however. It involves a full spectrum of duties, from recruiting and hiring new staff to training them, providing them with developmental opportunities, and evaluating their performance. Furthermore, the separation (or termination) of employees is a supervisory responsibility. Collectively, these duties are best described as staffing practices, and they form the focus of this chapter.

We begin by looking at the importance of staffing practices for both individuals and organizations. Next, we describe models of supervision and staffing practices, including the Winston and Creamer (1997) model that is the nexus of the chapter. We then go on to discuss each of the elements in that model: recruitment and selection, orientation, supervision, evaluation, professional development, and separation. We explain why each element is important, describe the duties associated with that element, and illustrate how those duties may vary depending on context (e.g, the level of the position, the type of institution, available technology). We conclude by discussing how staffing practices contribute to the vitality of the student affairs profession.

Why Staffing Practices Are Important

Personnel matters can be viewed from two perspectives: the organizational and the individual. In 2008 there were 4,314 colleges and universities in the United States, which enrolled 15.2 million undergraduates and 2.6 million graduate and professional students (Chronicle of Higher Education, 2009). There are thousands of student affairs administrators managing programs for and delivering services to those students. Nearly all of these practitioners possess bachelor's degrees, and many have earned postbaccalaureate degrees in student affairs or higher education administration at one of the approximately 130 graduate preparation programs across the country (Cilente, Henning, Skinner Jackson, Kennedy, & Sloan, 2006; Renn, Jessup Anger, & Hodges, 2007). Given the rising cost of postsecondary education, millions of dollars have been expended educating the student affairs professional workforce.

This investment in the preparation of practitioners is compounded when the costs of recruiting, training, supervising, and developing staff are considered. Arguably, colleges and universities invest heavily in their student affairs professionals. Valuations reveal that 75 to 85 percent of most institutional budgets are personnel related (Winston & Miller, 1991). Yet estimates also suggest that 50 to 60 percent of new practitioners leave the student affairs profession within the first five years of their careers (Bender, 1980; Berwick, 1992; Evans, 1988; Lorden, 1998; Tull, 2006). In short, campuses expend precious resources on staff members whose contributions to the institution are essential but may be fleeting. Managers have a compelling interest in protecting their investment in personnel.

The individual perspective in staffing matters is just as important as that of the organization. Aspiring professionals invest time, energy, and money earning degrees that serve as passports to a career in campus administration. Surely they do not undertake such an arduous trek with the intent of abandoning that career after just a few years, yet many do just that. Job satisfaction and staff morale influence student affairs administrators' intent to leave their jobs or the profession altogether (Johnsrud & Rosser, 1999). *Job satisfaction* is a measure of how people feel about their jobs, whereas *morale* assesses people's sentiments about the institutions for which they work. Supervisors can influence both satisfaction and morale (Johnson & Johnson, 2006; Rosser & Javinar, 2003; Rosser, 2004) hence they play an important role in staff retention.

Beyond organizational and individual arguments, there are philosophical reasons undergirding our contention that staffing practices are important. The guiding ethic of the student affairs profession is the development of the whole person (American Council on Education 1937; 1949): those who aspire to careers in the profession are committed to promoting intellectual, social, psychological, physical, and moral development among the students they serve. Managers who expect staff members to care about the holistic development of their students must be concerned about the holistic development of those staff members (Blackhurst, Brandt, & Kalinkowski, 1998; Dalton, 2003; Nuss, 2003). Collectively, these organizational, individual, and philosophical interests offer persuasive evidence that staffing practices are important.

Models of Staffing Practices

Although definitions of supervision are abundant, the research on supervision and staffing practices in student affairs, surprisingly, is relatively sparse (Carpenter,

Torres, & Winston, 2001; Cooper, Saunders, Howell, & Bates, 2001; Saunders, Cooper, Winston, & Chernow, 2000). Some, like Dalton (1996), adopt a human resource approach and emphasize how supervisors can hone the talents of their staff members. Others (for example, Mills, 2000) concentrate on the role of supervision in achieving organizational objectives. In this context the supervisor's job is to relay the institution's goals to staff members and harness employee talents to achieve those goals. Both of these methods capture certain essential elements of supervision, but neither addresses the full array of responsibilities associated with personnel management in postsecondary education (Janosik & Creamer, 2003).

Winston and Creamer (1997) delineated a comprehensive model that encompasses the many components of staffing practices. Their model originally consisted of five interactive elements. The cornerstone, recruitment and selection, is more complex than it may seem at first blush and requires supervisors to analyze the staffing needs of the unit, design a position description that captures the essential duties of the job, conduct a recruiting campaign that attracts candidates from a broad spectrum of backgrounds, and hire the right person for the position. Orientation, the second element of the model, facilitates the transition to the position for the newly hired staff member. As such, it often precedes a new hire's first day on the job (Saunders & Cooper, 2009) and may continue throughout the incumbent's first year in the position or even longer.

The next three elements in the model include the activities that professionals typically associate with the personnel function. Supervision entails a relationship between manager and staff member that aims to facilitate the attainment of both organizational and individual objectives. Performance appraisal serves as a mechanism to both evaluate employee performance and identify future professional development needs (Winston & Creamer, 1997). The final element, staff development, involves purposefully designed, multifaceted activities that enable staff members to address gaps in their knowledge and to gain new skills that promote individual growth and institutional advancement. The original model was modified to include a sixth element, separation, when Conley (2001) pointed out the varied reasons that cause staff members to leave a position. Supervisors have obligations to both the person leaving and to other employees in their unit when a departure occurs.

Collectively, these six elements encapsulate the building blocks of staffing practices. We caution readers, however, not to consider these elements as either discrete or sequential. They operate synergistically, at times overlapping and interacting. Supervision, for instance, likely takes place while orientation is occurring. Performance appraisal, when done right, uncovers areas that should be addressed in ongoing professional development. The very essence of the model is the evolutionary nature of staffing practices. Both individuals and institutions are constantly changing as they adapt to growth and environmental shifts. Staffing, then, is a process and must be thought of as an ongoing activity in which supervisors routinely engage (Janosik & Creamer, 2003; Winston & Creamer, 1997). Some further elaboration may illuminate the importance of each element of the model.

Recruitment and Selection

Clearly, the success of any administrative unit rests in large part upon the people who work to accomplish the organization's goals. As Winston and Creamer (1997) note: "There are no equivalent substitutes for talented and professionally competent staff. . . . The first commandment for student affairs administrators, therefore, is to hire the right people. The second commandment is to do it the right way" (p. 123). There are multiple reasons why recruiting and hiring are important, but three are most relevant to this discussion. First, selecting the candidate who is best suited for a position ensures that the incumbent is prepared to carry out his or her job responsibilities and increases the probability that the organization can achieve its goals. Second, bringing the right candidate to campus maximizes the potential for individual employee development. Third, recruiting is the single most fertile opportunity to expand organizational perspectives by attracting people with diverse backgrounds and skill sets who will bring something new to the unit.

To achieve these outcomes, recruiting and hiring need to be done right. To start, administrators who strive to attract a diverse pool of applicants have to design a diversified recruiting plan. This may entail such traditional actions as listing the job in the *Chronicle of Higher Education* or through placement centers at regional or national professional conferences. Administrators should go beyond these efforts, however, to reach out to other potential applicant pools. For example, advertising jobs in *Diverse Issues in Higher Education*, the *Hispanic Outlook in Higher Education*, or similar publications might reach some potential applicants who otherwise might not learn of the vacancy. In the same vein, *how* a position is advertised is as important as *where* it is advertised. In this sense, technology can be quite useful: Web sites, electronic bulletin boards, discussion forums, and listservs are all economical and efficient ways to announce job opportunities. Social networking sites (e.g., Facebook, Twitter, and LinkedIn) are increasingly being used to inform potential applicants of job vacancies and encourage them to peruse information about the administrative unit that is hiring, the campus, and the local community.

Recruiting efforts directly influence the hiring process. Selected candidates should be interviewed by representative stakeholders, including students, support staff, and professional colleagues, as well as by the supervisor. Deciding among several competitive candidates is the desired end state in a hiring process. It is alternative scenarios that are troublesome. When the recruiting process fails to produce a pool of qualified applicants or yields a pool that is not sufficiently diverse, the manager must decide whether to proceed with interviews. Likewise, if candidates are interviewed but none is a good fit for the job, a supervisor must decide whether to make an offer. In either of these eventualities, administrators are well served to remember that hiring a less-than-qualified applicant serves neither the institution's nor the individual's needs. It is almost always better to start the search process over again than to deal with the individual and organizational consequences of hiring someone who is not right for the job.

Regardless of how well conceived the plan or meticulously executed the process, recruitment and selection are influenced by contextual issues, some of which are organizationally driven. All colleges and universities, for example, have policies and procedures that guide hiring and may shape the process in unintended ways. The campus setting also plays an important role. Urban institutions may have difficulty attracting applicants for entry-level jobs, for instance, if salaries are low and the cost of living in the city is high. Campuses in rural settings may have difficulty when recruiting candidates because they cannot offer some of the cultural and commercial attractions available to those at urban institutions. Specialized institutions, such as religiously affiliated, single-sex, or minority-serving colleges and universities, have other filters through which candidates are evaluated that pose unique challenges in the hiring process (Hirt, 2006). All sorts of circumstances shape interest in positions; qualifications of applicants; and, ultimately, the success of the search process.

No circumstances, however, can diminish Winston and Creamer's (1997) admonition about hiring the right person and doing it the right way. Employing a staff member who is qualified for the job, who stands to benefit personally and professionally from the position, and who can contribute to the organization allows the supervisor to address the second element of the model, orientation.

Orientation

Recently hired staff members and experienced staff members with newly assigned roles need guidance from supervisors and other staff peers to enable them to work effectively immediately upon starting a new job (Janosik & Creamer, 2003; Strayhorn, 2009). Orientation is one mechanism through which supervisors provide the necessary guidance and knowledge to increase the likelihood of staff members' success. Providing information about the position, unit or division, institution, and surrounding community offers staff members a sense of history, an understanding of how work gets done, and even practical advice about insurance options and retirement plans. Orientation is important for other reasons, as well. The way in which staff members are oriented to a job, unit, or institution influences whether they can manage their personal and professional transitions effectively, whether they will understand the importance of professional development and therefore engage in it regularly, whether they will achieve individual and institutional goals in terms of productivity, and whether they will remain in the student affairs profession (Conley, 2001; Saunders & Cooper, 2003).

Student affairs professionals, especially those new to the field, cite orientation as critical to their success during the first few years of professional service (Winston & Creamer, 1997). Yet all new (and even newly reassigned) staff members need certain information to carry out their duties. For instance, supervisors should talk with staff members about behavioral norms (e.g., what to wear to work); political realities (e.g., how shrinking budgets affect travel); procedures for performance appraisal (i.e., standards by which work will be judged); and everyday practices (e.g., where to find office supplies and how to access e-mail) that affect the nature of work. Doing so will enable professionals to succeed and lessen the chances for role ambiguity or confusion. An effective orientation program eases initial concerns about adjustment and tries to reduce, if not eliminate, the trepidation that many new administrators feel about their roles. Additionally, well-designed orientation programs socialize new members to the values, traditions, and culture of an organization; foster their sense of belonging; and build their confidence to carry out job tasks (Saunders & Cooper, 2003).

Responsibilities for orienting new and newly reassigned staff members to the institution, unit, or job function falls to supervisors and experienced staff peers, although supervisors, by virtue of their position, generally assume the lion's share of the work in designing and implementing a formal orientation process. Additionally, because the nature of student affairs work varies by institution size, racial composition, and mission, contextual factors influence orientation practices. On the one hand, small colleges, such as private liberal arts colleges, are characterized by units composed of generalists; therefore, orientation plans at such campuses might emphasize the "multiple hats" that staff members wear. On the other hand, at large, urban universities, student affairs functions are carried out by specialists. This may require highly technical, individualized training approaches. Just as the work differs in various settings, so too must the orientation processes that socialize professionals to the unit and institution for which they work (Hirt, 2006).

The use of technology can help facilitate orientation. Electronic messages can introduce new and newly reassigned professionals to the office before their first day on the job (Strayhorn, 2009). Discussion board forums and online social networking sites offer mechanisms for new staff members to engage with their peers; such forums may even be used to teach staff members about unit policies and procedures and to elicit their feedback about the orientation process (boyd & Ellison, 2007). Increasingly, campus administrators make use of audience response systems (i.e., "clickers") to receive real-time feedback (Virginia Commonwealth University, 2008). In similar fashion, supervisors might use clickers to identify staff members' strengths and weaknesses, or their expectations and anxieties, during the orientation process.

Attending to the knowledge, skills, and abilities of staff members early on (during orientation) should enable managers to identify areas in which additional supervision may be needed. Supervision is another core element of Winston and Creamer's (1997) model, to which we now turn.

Supervision

Supervision may seem like the most straightforward element of staffing practices. After all, most professionals supervise others—paraprofessionals, entry-level administrators, support staff, or other professionals—and all college and university administrators report to someone in the organizational hierarchy. However, supervision is far more complex than it initially appears (Tull, 2009) and requires both an understanding of human dynamics and an appreciation for human differences (Arminio & Creamer, 2001). Done right, supervision leads to individual accomplishment, organizational achievement, and professional advancement.

Good supervision enables employees to accomplish their job tasks, appreciate the responsibilities of others, gain new knowledge, and acquire skills to advance their careers (Amey & Ressor, 2002). When individuals thrive in their jobs, they contribute to the success of the administrative units in which they work; and achievement at the unit level contributes to institutional accomplishment (Rebore, 2001). In addition to its individual and institutional benefits, good supervision serves the student affairs profession overall by promoting the retention of talented and committed colleagues. Student affairs administrators, particularly those new to the field, cite supervision as key to their decision to remain in the field (Renn & Hodges, 2007).

Because the ability to supervise others is relatively important, it is surprising that so few administrators are trained in the art of managing people. There is an abundance of literature identifying the characteristics of good supervisors (e.g., Tull, 2006; Winston & Hirt, 2003) that those interested in the topic ought to study. In general, however, these characteristics can be conceptualized in three categories. First, supervisors are teachers who instruct staff members about the organizational environment and institutional culture. Second, supervisors are communicators who serve as conduits. They transmit information from superiors to those they manage and communicate needs of their staff members to unit and institutional managers. Third, good supervisors are able to motivate their employees in a variety of ways, not only through formal rewards but also through leadership and the ways in which they conduct themselves on a daily basis.

Looking beyond personal skills, supervision can be enhanced through technology. Personnel management software can organize records, track evaluations, and monitor professional development programs. Cell phones make supervisors more available to staff members. Communications through text messages, e-mail, listservs, and electronic distribution lists ensure that important news is uniformly relayed in an efficient and effective manner. Discussion boards enable supervisors to elicit employee opinions; they can even be used to teach staff members about new policies or procedures. Finally, inventive supervisors might use podcasts to transmit information or wikis to develop new programs and services. As the demands on supervisors increase, technology can help meet those demands.

Technology can never replace the human dimension of supervision, however, and there are contextual circumstances that have an impact on that dimension. It is imperative that managers understand and appreciate how their sex, race, ethnicity, sexual orientation, religion, socioeconomic background, and other characteristics and experiences influence their perceptions of others and others' perceptions of them. Learning how to effectively supervise people who differ from oneself is essential to employee success. In turn, effective supervision and employee success are at the core of performance appraisal.

Performance Appraisal

By now the interactive nature of the Winston and Creamer (1997) model should be relatively clear: the recruitment and selection process identifies areas that may need to be addressed in the orientation process, and the orientation process allows supervisors to assess the assets that staff members bring to the job as well as areas in which ongoing direction might be warranted. It may be assumed that all these elements lead up to what is commonly referred to as employee evaluation. The term *evaluation*, however, implies some sort of summative rating. Performance appraisal is a process through which employee productivity is assessed in light of both individual and institutional objectives.

There are eight essential elements that characterize the performance appraisal process. First, although the procedure typically evaluates employee productivity, it should also lay the groundwork for staff development. Development efforts may address deficiencies in performance, but should also identify future directions for employees and suggest ways to acquire the knowledge, skills, and experiences that will enable them to move forward. Second, dual purposes of evaluation are tied to rewards: those who contribute to organizational success are recognized for their achievements, whereas underperformers are not rewarded. Third, the context must be considered. Jobs tend to change over time, as do employees. Environmental factors, moreover, can contribute to the circumstances under which a job is performed. For example, a career services administrator should not be held accountable if the job placement rate for graduates drops precipitously due to an economic downturn, an event well beyond the employee's control (Creamer & Janosik, 2003; Winston & Creamer, 1997).

The next two elements of the procedure are inextricably linked. The fourth element is that personnel who are affected by the appraisal process should be involved in designing that process. Staff buy-in is critical if performance appraisal is to be successful. Staff engagement links directly to the fifth element: the appraisal process should be transparent, open, and equitable. Although this may appear patently obvious, achieving clarity can be challenging. To a large extent, transparency, the sixth element, is facilitated when appraisal is ongoing (the sixth element of the process) rather than episodic. If supervisors are routinely providing feedback to staff members, the seventh element of effective performance appraisal, the process should reveal no major surprises. Such ongoing evaluation relies on good leadership. Supervisors should serve as models for employees and offer praise and constructive criticism in an effort to promote employee growth and organizational success (Creamer & Janosik, 2003; Winston & Creamer, 1997).

The eighth and final element of the performance appraisal process provides for contextual differences in systems. That is, no single system of appraisal works better than others. The nature of the administrative unit, the mission of the institution, the type of employee involved, and related characteristics should all be considered when designing an appraisal process. The key is to develop a method that works and avoids systemic unfairness. Processes that lead supervisors to assign equal ratings to all employees or that prohibit any staff member from excelling are destined to fail. Processes that habitually lead to lower ratings for certain groups of employees (e.g., women or people of color) are particularly invidious. When the other elements are built into the design of the performance appraisal process, however, systemic bias is unlikely. Indeed, a solid appraisal process will inherently identify opportunities for professional development (Creamer & Janosik, 2003; Winston & Creamer, 1997).

Professional Development

Conventional wisdom suggests that great people are not born but rather made. Similarly, practitioners become highly productive, effective administrators through professional development. Professional development is crucial to increasing the performance and enhancing the growth of new, newly reassigned, and even experienced staff members (Winston & Creamer, 1997).

Professional development has two primary purposes: professional and personal growth of individual staff members (human development) and facilitation of institutional effectiveness (organization development) (Janosik & Creamer, 2003). Activities that foster individual growth fall along the lines of what Dalton (1996) called "talent development." Widely used strategies for human development include participating in workshops; reading recent publications; bringing experts to campus for in-service programs sponsored by the division; attending national, state, and regional conventions (e.g., ACPA and NASPA); and undertaking advanced course work in such areas as budgeting, management, and Web authoring. When professional development programs encourage involvement among all staff members, supervisors can improve functioning across the unit, which in turn enhances overall effectiveness by clarifying roles, expanding capacity, and renewing commitments to the overarching mission. These two purposes must be well integrated in practice to be most effective.

DeCoster and Brown (1991) outlined six goals that make up a curriculum for professional development: (1) facilitating interaction among staff peers, (2) developing specific skills and competencies, (3) promoting self-awareness and achievement of predetermined objectives, (4) encouraging staff participation in programs and workshops, (5) nurturing staff renewal, and (6) sharing knowledge based on theory and research. Although there is considerable agreement about the goals of staff development, technological advances provide exciting new opportunities to achieve these goals. Increasingly, webinars, e-courses, and online training modules can be used to learn about new legislative and federal reporting requirements (e.g., FERPA); best practices in learning outcomes assessment; and such contemporary issues as campus safety and sustainability. As state investments in higher education continue to decrease and conference fees and travel costs soar, technology may become the preferred method of delivering professional development—that is, it will become the rule rather than the exception.

Whether provided through face-to-face, structured learning opportunities or facilitated through Web-based technology, all professional development activities should attend to the contextual issues that shape the nature of student affairs work at various campuses. For instance, historically Black colleges emphasize an abiding commitment to racial uplift and social justice in their missions (Hirt, Strayhorn, Amelink, & Bennett, 2006), whereas community colleges educate large numbers of nonresidential, part-time adult learners. Because most graduate preparation programs are situated in large, public research universities, recent graduates may be unfamiliar with the unique contexts of other institutions. Extensive, consistent, and long-term professional development should prove useful for familiarizing recent hires with the institutions for which they work. Further, intentionally designed professional development programs significantly improve job satisfaction and the ability to perform job tasks successfully, which in turn is likely to reduce the likelihood of involuntary separation.

Separation

Throughout this chapter we have identified many of the crucial needs of student affairs professionals—such as orientation and professional development—which also are key elements of Winston and Creamer's (1997) model of staff practices. Failure to attend to the needs of staff members can undermine job performance in terms of productivity; compromise achievement of individual and departmental goals; and lead to dissatisfaction, which is an immediate precursor to departure from the job, or separation (Burns, 1982; Conley, 2001). Whether measured in time spent training a new hire or in actual dollars, a tremendous loss of resources occurs when workers depart prematurely. Separation is thus an important and costly matter for supervisors.

Conley (2001) identified five reasons why staff members leave their positions or the field of student affairs entirely: (1) professional reasons; (2) personal reasons; (3) retirement; (4) involuntary separation; and (5) incapacitation, illness, or death. Subsequently, Hirt and Janosik (2003) reduced these into voluntary and involuntary reasons for employee departure. Voluntary reasons can be further divided into three major groups: professional reasons, personal reasons, and issues related to retirement. Professional reasons for departure range from opportunities for advancement (i.e., promotion) to changing functional areas (e.g., moving from housing to career services), and from pursuing further training to low salaries. The last of these reasons is important, given that 16 to 20 percent of those who leave the profession do so because of low earning potential (Burns, 1982). Alternately, an employee's departure may be the result of a commitment to a spouse or partner; family responsibilities, such as child rearing; or relocation, all of which are examples of personal reasons for temporary or permanent departure from one's position or institution. Finally, staff members may leave a position to retire.

Involuntary reasons for employee separation include illness or death and job termination. Departures caused by death, especially unexpected deaths (e.g., fatal accidents or medical complications), can evoke serious emotional responses within the unit or division. As a result, supervisors must handle the loss both personally and professionally, perhaps while fulfilling administrative duties such as documenting the death, sharing information with insurance companies, and processing final paychecks (Hirt & Janosik, 2003). Staff members may be terminated for any number of reasons, including poor performance, insubordination, downsizing, or criminal or unethical behavior. We are all too familiar with the scenario of an administrator who mismanages fiscal resources by authorizing inappropriate expenditures (e.g., exotic trips for personal pleasure) or hiring a less-than-qualified applicant yet offering a higher-than-expected salary. In all cases, supervisors play important roles when staff members separate from an institution or leave a position in student affairs.

Just as the reasons for separation differ in terms of locus of control (i.e., voluntary versus involuntary), contextual issues may influence the reasons why staff members leave positions or the profession altogether. For instance, student affairs practitioners at large, public universities tend to work individually rather than with teams. Individuals who prefer to work closely with others may become dissatisfied at a large institution and pursue new opportunities—perhaps at small liberal arts or comprehensive institutions— that afford them collaborative experiences. Work environments that are unwelcoming, hostile, or socially isolating for women and people of color, for example, also influence decisions to leave a job. Supervisors must understand and appreciate how these factors influence the nature of work in a unit, employees' subjective evaluations of their jobs, and employees' decisions to stay with or separate from an institution.

Conclusion

Staffing is a synergistic process. The recruiting and selection procedure lays the groundwork for determining what should be covered when orientating new staff members. It can also reveal areas in which professional development may be merited. Ongoing supervision offers employees regular feedback on their accomplishments and enables supervisors to appraise performance as well as note areas for future professional development. When employees are promoted or leave an administrative unit, supervisors have an opportunity to assess the personnel needs of the organization as well as those of the remaining staff members. Administrators who master the skills associated with staffing practices are certain to manage individuals who succeed in their personal aspirations. Furthermore, staff members who achieve their ambitions are more likely to remain in the field, which in turn ensures the viability and vitality of the student affairs profession.

References

American Council on Education. (1937). *The student personnel point of view.* Washington, DC: Author.

American Council on Education. (1949). *The student personnel point of view* (Rev. ed.). Washington, DC: Author.

Amey, M. J., & Ressor, L. M. (2002). *Beginning your journey: A guide for new professionals in student affairs.* Washington, DC: National Association of Student Personnel Administrators.

Arminio, J., & Creamer, D. G. (2001). What supervisors say about quality supervision. *College Student Affairs Journal, 21*(1), 35–44.

Bender, B. E. (1980). Job satisfaction in student affairs. *NASPA Journal, 18*(2), 3–9.

Berwick, K. R. (1992). Stress among student affairs administrators: The relationship of personal characteristics and organizational variables to work-related stress. *Journal of College Student Development, 33*, 11–10.

Blackhurst, A. E., Brandt, J. E., & Kalinkowski, J. (1998). Effects of career development on the organizational commitment and life satisfaction of women student affairs administrations. *NASPA Journal, 36*(1), 19–34.

boyd, d. m., & Ellison, N. B. (2007). Social network sites: Definition, history, and scholarship. *Journal of Computer-Mediated Communication, 13*(1), 210–230.

Burns, M. (1982). Who leaves the student affairs field? *NASPA Journal, 20*, 9–12.

Carpenter, D. S., Torres, V., & Winston, R. B. (2001). Staffing the student affairs division: Theory, practice, and issues. *College Student Affairs Journal, 21*(1), 2–6.

Chronicle of Higher Education (2009). *Chronicle of Higher Education Almanac 2008–09*. Washington, DC: Chronicle of Higher Education

Cilente, K., Henning, G., Skinner Jackson, J., Kennedy, D., & Sloan, T. (2006). *Report on the new professional needs study*. Washington, DC: American College Personnel Association. Retrieved December 11, 2006, from www.myacpa.org/research/newprofessionals.php.

Conley, V. M. (2001). Separation: An integral aspect of the staffing process. *College Student Affairs Journal, 21*(1), 57–63.

Cooper, D. L., Saunders, S. A., Howell, M. T., & Bates, J. M. (2001). Published research about supervision in student affairs: A review of the literature 1969–1999. *College Student Affairs Journal, 20*(2), 82–92.

Creamer, D. G., & Janosik, S. M. (2003). Performance appraisal: Accountability that leads to professional development. In S. M Janosik, D. G. Creamer, J. B. Hirt, R. B. Winston, S. A. Saunders, & D. L. Cooper (Eds.), *Supervising new professionals in student affairs: A guide for practitioners* (pp. 123–151). New York: Brunner-Routledge.

Dalton, J. C. (1996). Managing human resources. In S.R. Komives, D.B. Woodard Jr., & Associates (Eds.), *Student services: A handbook for the profession* (3rd ed., pp. 494–511). San Francisco: Jossey-Bass.

Dalton, J. C. (2003). Managing human resources. In S. R. Komives, D. B. Woodard Jr., & Associates (Eds.), *Student services: A handbook for the profession* (4th ed., pp. 397–419). San Francisco: Jossey-Bass.

DeCoster, D. A., & Brown, S. S. (1991). Staff development: Personal and professional education. In T. K. Miller, R. B. Winston Jr., & Associates (Eds.), *Administration and leadership in student affairs: Actualizing student development in higher education* (2nd ed., pp. 563–613). Muncie, IN: Accelerated Development.

Evans, N. J. (1988). Attrition of student affairs professionals: A review of the literature. *Journal of College Student Development, 29*, 19–24.

Hirt, J. B. (2006). *Where you work matters: Student affairs administrators at different types of institutions*. Lanham, MD: University Press of America.

Hirt, J. B., & Janosik, S. M. (2003). Employee separation: The role of supervisors. In S. M. Janosik, D. G. Creamer, J. B. Hirt, R. B. Winston Jr., S. A. Saunders, & D. L. Cooper (Eds.), *Supervising new professionals in student affairs: A guide for practitioners* (pp. 153–174). New York: Brunner-Routledge.

Hirt, J. B., Strayhorn, T. L., Amelink, C. T., & Bennett, B. R. (2006). The nature of student affairs work at historically Black colleges and universities. *Journal of College Student Development, 47*(6), 661–676.

Janosik, S. M., & Creamer, D. G. (2003). Introduction: A comprehensive model. In S. M Janosik, D. G. Creamer, J. B. Hirt, R. B. Winston, S. A. Saunders, & D. L. Cooper (Eds.), *Supervising new professionals in student affairs: A guide for practitioners* (pp. 1–16). New York: Brunner-Routledge.

Johnson, D. W., & Johnson, F. P. (2006). *Joining together: Group theory and group skills* (9th ed.). Boston: Pearson Education.

Johnsrud, L. K., & Rosser, V. J. (1999). College and university mid-level administrators: Explaining and improving their morale. *Review of Higher Education, 22*(2), 121–141.

Lorden, L. P. (1998). Attrition in the student affairs profession. *NASPA Journal, 35*, 207–216.

Mills, D. B. (2000). The role of the middle manager. In M. J. Barr, K. Dessler, & Associates (Eds.), *The handbook of student affairs administration* (2nd ed., pp. 135–153). San Francisco: Jossey-Bass.

Nuss, E. M. (2003). The development of student affairs. In S. R. Komives, D. B. Woodard Jr., & Associates (Eds.), *Student services: A handbook for the profession* (4th ed., pp. 65–88). San Francisco: Jossey-Bass.

Rebore, R. W. (2001). *Human resources administration in education: A management approach.* Boston: Allyn & Bacon.

Renn, K. A., & Hodges, J. P. (2007). The first year on the job: Experiences of new professionals in student affairs. *NASPA Journal, 44(2),* 367–391.

Renn, K. A., Jessup Anger, E. R., & Hodges, J. P. (2007, April). *First year on the job: Themes from the National Study of New Professionals in Student Affairs.* Paper presented at the American College Personnel Association/National Association of Student Personnel Administrators Joint Meeting, Orlando, FL.

Rosser, V. J. (2004). A national study on midlevel leaders in higher education: The unsung professionals of the academy. *Higher Education: The International Journal of Higher Education and Planning, 48*(3), 317–337.

Rosser, V. J., & Javinar, J. M. (2003). Midlevel student affairs leaders' intentions to leave: Examining the quality of their professional and institutional worklife. *Journal of College Student Development, 46*(6), 813–830.

Saunders, S. A., & Cooper, D. L. (2003). Orientation: Building the foundations for success. In S. M. Janosik, D. G. Creamer, J. B. Hirt, R. B. Winston Jr., S. A. Saunders, & D. L. Cooper (Eds.), *Supervising new professionals in student affairs: A guide for practitioners* (pp. 17–41). New York: Brunner-Routledge.

Saunders, S. A., & Cooper, D. L. (2009). Orientation in the socialization process. In A. Tull, J. B. Hirt, & S. A. Saunders (Eds.), *Becoming socialized in student affairs administration: A guide for new professionals and their supervisors.* Sterling, VA: Stylus.

Saunders, S. A., Cooper, D. L., Winston, R. B., & Chernow, E. (2000). Supervising staff in student affairs: Exploration of the synergistic approach. *Journal of College Student Development, 4*(2), 181–191.

Strayhorn, T. L. (2009). Staff peer relationships in the socialization process. In A. Tull, J. B. Hirt, & S. A. Saunders (Eds.), *Becoming socialized in student affairs administration: A guide for new professionals and their supervisors.* Sterling, VA: Stylus.

Tull, A. (2006). Synergistic supervision, job satisfaction, and intention to turnover of new professionals in student affairs. *Journal of College Student Development, 47,* 465–477.

Tull, A. (2009). Supervision and mentorship in the socialization process. In A. Tull, J. B. Hirt, & S. A. Saunders (Eds.), *Becoming socialized in student affairs: A guide for new professionals and their supervisors.* Sterling, VA: Stylus.

Virginia Commonwealth University. (2008, October). Using clickers for small-group social norming with athletes and first-year students. Retrieved November 1, 2008, from www.yourstrategy.org/clickers/index.html.

Winston, R. B., Jr., & Creamer, D. G. (1997). *Improving staffing practices in student affairs.* San Francisco: Jossey-Bass.

Winston, R. B., & Hirt, J. B. (2003). Activating synergistic supervision approaches: Practical suggestions. In S. M. Janosik, D. G. Creamer, J. B. Hirt, R. B. Winston, S. A. Saunders, & D. L. Cooper (Eds.), *Supervising new professionals in student affairs: A guide for practitioners* (pp. 43–83). New York: Brunner-Routledge.

Winston, R. B., & Miller, T. K. (1991). Human resource management: Professional preparation and staff selection. In T. K. Miller, R. B Winston Jr., & Associates (Eds.), *Administration and leadership in student affairs: Actualizing student development in higher education* (2nd ed.). Muncie, IN: Accelerated Development.

CHAPTER TWENTY-TWO

TEACHING IN THE CO-CURRICULUM

Peter M. Magolda and Stephen John Quaye

As the U.S. population continues to grow, demographic changes will influence postsecondary enrollments (Day, 1996). Colleges that have experienced growth tend to enroll students who are increasingly diverse in regard to social class, race, gender, ethnicity, age, and sexual orientation. Collegiate demographers expect future enrollment gains to be the greatest for middle- and lower-income students as well as historically underrepresented racial and ethnic minorities (College Board, 2005). Collectively, these prospective students are less prepared academically and financially to attend college than were previous generations. These demographic trends, which indicate an overall increase in diverse learners from various cultures with varied learning preferences, have far-reaching educational implications for both faculty members and student affairs educators as they modify the curriculum and co-curriculum, respectively, to optimally support student learning.

In this chapter we focus on how student affairs educators can facilitate student learning in the co-curriculum. Given the aforementioned changes occurring across higher education institutions, it is critical that student affairs educators develop their competencies in working with learners with varied learning styles, backgrounds, and needs. We begin this chapter with a discussion of institutional influences on student learning, followed by an argument that student affairs professionals should understand their roles as educators. We then use the Learning Partnerships Model (Baxter Magolda, 2004) to illustrate practical ways to foster learning in the co-curriculum and recommend that these practice-oriented strategies be grounded in relevant theoretical knowledge. Our chapter concludes with an acknowledgement of those who might disagree with our position by highlighting essential responses to stimulate dialogue with persons who hold differing opinions. Throughout the chapter we incorporate relevant theories, research, and literature to enact our espoused belief in the importance of using relevant resources to enhance student learning.

Institutional Influences on Student Learning

Societal issues, such as demographics, influence students' educational experiences inside and outside the classroom. So, too, do institutional factors, such as institutional learning outcomes for students (what students need to know) and organizational structures. Student affairs educators intent on optimizing the co-curriculum must clarify learning outcomes and realign departmental organizational structures to achieve these outcomes.

Learning Outcomes

What do contemporary college students need to know? Answering this seemingly straightforward question is more difficult than it appears. In 2007, the Association of American Colleges & Universities (AAC&U) published a report that included this astute observation: "Across all the discussion of access, affordability, and even account-ability, there has been near-total public and policy silence about what contemporary college graduates need to know and be able to do" (p. 3). Although no universally agreed-upon collegiate learning outcomes exist—nor should they exist—Guskin (1994) identified specific undergraduate learning outcomes to which many higher education institutions subscribe or aspire:

> Student learning at the undergraduate level is very complex, both in our aims and in what is achieved, whether directly or indirectly. We want students to learn about a lot of things. We want them to accumulate information and knowledge in a host of fields, with depth in at least one. We expect students to develop skills not only in writing and communication but in the use of quantitative and scientific methods and in the learning of a foreign language. Even more importantly, we have strong expectations regarding students' conceptual learning—the development of conceptual, intellectual tools that enable them to compare and contrast the material they are acquiring and to make judgments about its relevance to other issues of concern. (p. 19)

Ten years later, AAC&U (2004) introduced a more contemporary list of widely endorsed collegiate learning outcomes, which include disciplinary knowledge, practical skills, and values: "Strong analytical, communication, qualitative, and informa-tional skills . . . deep understanding of and hands-on experience with the inquiry practices of disciplines that explore the natural, social, and cultural realms . . . inter-cultural knowledge and collaborative problem-solving skills . . . a proactive sense of responsibility for individual, civic, and social choices . . . [and] habits of the mind that foster integrative thinking and the ability to transfer skills and knowledge from one setting to another" (pp. 5–6).

A purposeful and responsive co-curriculum, a foundation for education, must align with predetermined and prioritized institutional learning outcomes.

Organizational Structures

The organizational structure of the academy has a profound influence on students. Colleges are complex organizations comprising hundreds of loosely coupled subcultures (e.g., students, faculty, alumni, staff, trustees); so, too, are divisions of student affairs. Often, campus subcultures and organizational structures do not optimally support students.

An examination of the traditional division of labor between student affairs and academic affairs illuminates higher education's insular, fragmented, and antiquated organizational structure. Historically, faculty members have overseen students' cognitive and intellectual development, a high institutional priority. Student affairs educators have become the de facto campus resource for affective, personal, social, and vocational dimensions of students' development, which typically are of secondary importance within the academy. This separate and unequal organizational structure, rooted in a fragmented approach to serving students, artificially separates cognitive and affective dimensions of students' lives, which is counter to the way students organize their lives and counter to what student affairs educators know about the integration of intellectual, identity, and relational development (Baxter Magolda, 2009).

Author and activist bell hooks (1994), in *Teaching to Transgress*, recognizes the liabilities of fragmented organizations as they relate to learning and urges members of these discrete enclaves to cross borders, navigate differences, and interact with *the other* to enhance students' learning. hooks suggests: "Talk to one another, collaborate in a discussion that crosses boundaries and creates a space for intervention. It is fashionable these days, when 'difference' is a hot topic in progressive circles, to talk about . . . 'border crossing,' but we often have no concrete examples of individuals who actually occupy different locations within structures, sharing ideas with one another, mapping out terrains of commonality, connection, and shared concern with teaching practices" (p. 130). Encouraging border crossings, as hooks recommends, invites those from within and beyond student affairs (e.g., academic affairs) to interact and negotiate integrated visions of the academy (Kuh, 1996; Pascarella & Terenzini, 2005).

Ill-defined learning outcomes and bifurcated organizational silos that breed provincial divisions of labor must yield to clearly defined learning outcomes and collaborative organizational structures and alliances. These new outcomes, structures, and collaborations will enable students to interconnect the multitude of learning opportunities across the curriculum and co-curriculum.

In the remainder of this chapter, we introduce a series of teaching issues for student affairs educators to consider as they revise their college or university's co-curriculum and modify the ways they educate students outside the classroom. Our aim is to introduce educational possibilities without being overly prescriptive in the hope that each reader will take into consideration his or her institution's demographics, learning outcomes for students, and organizational structures before adopting and adapting any of these recommendations.

Student Affairs Professionals as Educators

Historically, three distinct approaches to student affairs work—student services, student development, and student learning (Ender, Newton, & Caple, 1996)—have influenced the degree to which student affairs professionals view themselves as *educators* in the co-curriculum.

Student Services

The *student services* tradition defines the roles of student affairs professionals as administrators responsible for supporting the academic mission of the university by providing high-quality services to students in nonacademic functional areas, such as admissions, financial aid, housing, and counseling. Conventional wisdom from within this tradition suggests that providing quality services to students allows them ultimately to concentrate on and excel in academic pursuits (Ender et al., 1996).

Student Development

Over time, the academy recognized that many noncognitive student development issues occurring outside the classroom—such as students' personal, emotional, and identity development needs—complicated students' learning inside the classroom. This realization spawned a movement to alter student affairs professionals' primary roles from service providers to specialists in noncognitive human development. Conventional wisdom from within this tradition suggests that if student affairs professionals administer to students' noncognitive needs, students' cognitive capacities will improve.

Student Learning

The *Student Learning Imperative* (American College Personnel Association [ACPA], 1994); *Powerful Partnerships* (American Association for Higher Education [AAHE], ACPA, & National Association of Student Personnel Administrators [NASPA], 1998); and "Learning Reconsidered" (Keeling, 2004), three position papers drafted by national higher education and student affairs associations, all advocated for a holistic approach to learning that challenged this pervasive, separate, and unequal mind-body dichotomy as well as this segregated student affairs–academic affairs division of labor. "Learning Reconsidered" contributors (Keeling, 2004), concerned about the fragmented systems and the co-curriculum's lack of emphasis on learning, redefined learning as "a comprehensive, holistic, transformative activity that integrates *academic learning* and *student development*, processes that have often been considered separate, and even independent of each other" (p. 4).

As a result, a third student affairs tradition emerged that situated learning at the epicenter of the co-curriculum, with development and service as its foundation. Conventional wisdom from within this tradition suggests that students' experiences inside and out of the classroom as well as individually and collectively influence their learning (Baxter Magolda, 1996; Kuh, Douglas, Lund, & Ramin-Gyurnek, 1994; Terenzini, Springer, Pascarella, & Nora, 1995). Scholars have recommended that faculty and student affairs educators integrate student learning and development, deemphasizing in-class–out-of-class and cognitive-noncognitive dichotomies (e.g., Ender et al., 1996; King & Baxter Magolda, 1996).

This learning-centered philosophy redefines the roles of student affairs professionals as those of educators. If learning is to become the centerpiece of the co-curriculum, then it is essential for student affairs professionals to view themselves as educators. Answers to an all-important question, moreover, should guide all student affairs educators' actions—How does what I am doing or proposing to do enhance student learning?

Consistent with the learning-centered philosophy we propose here is Rhoads and Black's (1995) notion that student affairs educators should think of themselves as transformative educators. This belief is based on "theories of educational practice most often described as critical pedagogy, which is grounded in a critical cultural perspective that focuses attention on the role teachers might play in creating democratic classrooms in which students struggle to understand how culture and social structure have shaped their lives" (p. 413).

Given the demographic shifts discussed at the outset of this chapter, it makes sense for student affairs educators to work with learners in considering the roles of cultures and subcultures in their lives. With issues of diversity and multiculturalism at the forefront of institutional mission statements, those who subscribe to a critical cultural perspective place students at the epicenter of the learning enterprise (Rhoads & Black, 1995).

Rhoads and Black (1995) advocate that student affairs educators foster conditions that enable diverse constituents (students and educators) to interact together in ways that are participatory and build community. This necessitates different notions of what constitutes learning—learning involves holism, inclusion, and action beyond the classroom. For instance, a residence hall director might work with her resident advisors to develop strategies for building community within the hall, a process that could include finding ways to support learners in connecting their in-class learning to their relationships with peers.

Shifting from Techniques to Purposes and Outcomes

When outsiders ask student affairs professionals to describe their roles as educators, responses tend to center on instructional *processes* or *techniques* (e.g., we conduct workshops, supervise staff, or sponsor service-learning trips). Seldom do educators explicitly discuss the *purposes* or *outcomes* associated with these techniques. What is the purpose of the educational workshop? What are the desired outcomes of weekly staff supervision meetings? What do students learn as a result of their involvement in service-learning outings?

Barr and Tagg (1995) introduce an analogy that illuminates important distinctions between educational *processes* and *purposes* and offer a rationale for favoring purposes rather than processes. Understanding their arguments is important for student affairs educators who are serious about the act of teaching in the co-curriculum: "To say that the purpose of colleges is to provide instruction is like saying that General Motors' business is to operate assembly lines or that the purpose of medical care is to fill hospital beds. We now see that our mission is not instruction but rather that of producing learning with every student by whatever means work best" (p. 13).

Within the academy, faculty and students frequently debate what constitutes effective instruction, for example, pondering the merits of large lectures versus small seminars. Proponents and opponents of these pedagogies focus their attention on instructional *processes* or *techniques*. Some faculty and students favor lectures because they allow faculty to efficiently and unambiguously transmit knowledge to students. Conversely, some faculty and students prefer seminars, because they afford faculty and students opportunities to discuss and debate knowledge. In determining the goodness of a pedagogical technique—be it lecture or seminar in this example—one must look beyond the technique or method and carefully examine the purposes and the intended outcomes of the educating act.

"Often, faculty members' disciplinary expertise can lure them into mechanically performing their teaching duties without a high degree of mindfulness or self-reflection. This autopilot mode often leads instructors to ignore how their values shape classroom practices" (Magolda & Connolly, 2002, p. 77). Too often, educators (inside and outside the classroom) fixate on the teaching methods, seldom scrutinizing whether a particular teaching method helped students to achieve the desired purpose or learning outcomes.

The self-reflection that we advocate is not a technique or a set of procedures or a learned skill or competency. Instead it is an idiosyncratic, personal process of identifying and questioning internal assumptions about learning (Brookfield, 1995). Serious self-reflection reveals that the most appropriate pedagogy (i.e., lecture or seminar) is the one that best helps students achieve the espoused learning goals.

Rather than starting with the technique—the workshop, supervision meeting, or service-learning opportunity—why not focus on the purpose of the educating act as well as the outcome? We urge student affairs educators to heed Barr and Tagg's (1995) advice and worry less about instructional methods or processes and concentrate more on selecting methods that yield the desired learning outcomes. This should ensure the educator never losing sight of the goal of "producing learning with every student by whatever means work best" (Barr & Tagg, p. 13).

If student affairs educators believe the purpose of the co-curriculum is to enhance student learning, they must shift away from what Barr and Tagg (1995) have termed an *instructional* paradigm (i.e., educators transmit information to students and expect them to receive, master, and utilize the content) toward a *learning* paradigm. In this learning paradigm, educators encourage students to become active, engaged, reflective partners in learning and codesign with students active learning environments that they will use to achieve specific learning outcomes.

A university judicial officer, when meeting with a student accused of a campus code violation, wants the student to learn as a result of his or her involvement in the judicial process. Yet America's litigious society has elevated the importance of judicial *instruction*—meeting with a student found guilty of a violation to unambiguously clarify acceptable and unacceptable behaviors and then render an appropriate sanction. This instruction-centered, "teaching as telling pedagogy" (Christensen, Garvin, & Sweet, 1991, p. 3) situates the judicial officer as the ethics expert and the student as the ethics apprentice. Although efficient, fair, and transparent, this instructional process does not ensure that the student achieved the desired learning outcomes as a result of judicial intervention.

A judicial officer who subscribes to a learning-centered pedagogy might, for example, identify learning outcomes (e.g. by helping the student think differently about what it means to be to be a university citizen) and codesign an appropriate sanction with not only the student violator but also those students negatively affected by the violation. This co-constructed sanction, for example, might require the policy violator to interview peers harmed by the action to solicit their views about the incident; post a blog on the Internet documenting what the student learned as a result of the interviews and interactions with the judicial officer; and invite peers to respond to the blog through a virtual discussion.

The purpose of this co-constructed judicial exemplar, rooted in a learning paradigm, is to encourage the policy violator to become a community member committed to acting in a humane and responsible manner. This learning-centered intervention: (1) takes into consideration the learner's characteristics and the learning context; (2) focuses on learning outcomes, not learning procedures; (3) extends learning beyond the classroom; (4) necessitates that all stakeholders—the policy violator, the judicial officer, and those affected by the policy violation—act as both teachers and learners; (5) blurs cognitive and noncognitive aspects of the student's development; (6) encourages student interaction based on difference; and (7) makes use of new technologies (i.e., the Internet) for teaching and learning. A good first step toward infusing this learning paradigm into the co-curriculum is to ask a key question—What do we want students to learn (desired outcomes) and be? We focus on this question and other important questions in the next section.

Student Affairs Professionals as Learning Partners

A distinctive feature of this learning paradigm is the relationship between the educator and student. Nontraditional learning partnership supplants the traditional sage-apprentice relationship, in which the educator teaches and the student learns. A primary reason for this new form of partnership is to promote self-authorship (i.e., the process of developing internal authority) and learning. Baxter Magolda's (2004) Learning Partnerships Model (LPM) posits that educators support learners in developing internal authority by validating them as knowers, situating learning in their experiences, and defining learning as mutually constructing meanings. These three approaches involve:

- Respecting students' thoughts and feelings, thus affirming the value of their voices
- Helping learners view their experiences as opportunities for learning and growth
- Collaborating with students to analyze their own problems, engaging in mutual learning with them (Baxter Magolda, 2009)

Simultaneously, educators challenge learners to develop internal authority by portraying knowledge as complex and socially constructed, emphasizing self as central to knowledge construction, and sharing authority and expertise with learners. Inherent in the LPM are the following actions:

- Drawing participants' attention to the complexity of their work and life decisions and discouraging simplistic solutions
- Encouraging participants to develop their personal authority by listening to their own voices in determining how to live their lives
- Encouraging participants to share authority and expertise and work interdependently with others to solve mutual problems (Baxter Magolda, 2009)

As learning partners, educators support students by accepting their current meaning-making structures and perspectives about learning and simultaneously challenge them to strive for more complex learning processes. Learning partnerships in the co-curriculum require students to invest in the process of formulating their belief systems and to share teaching and learning responsibilities with educators. The aim of these partnerships is transformative learning.

Learning partnerships necessitate that educators relinquish power and invite students to join in thinking about and implementing new processes that enable students to recognize their own valuable insights and freely express them. Given that students are accustomed to seeing themselves in a passive manner (Freire, 1970), educators should model for students ways to critically analyze and build on the work of their peers; set high expectations and work with students to reach those expectations; and provide specific feedback to students, noting strengths and weaknesses as well as soliciting feedback from students.

Learning partnerships require that educators *situate learning in students' experiences*. Doing so entails welcoming students' experiences and meaning making into the learning process and helping them recognize the relevancy of their past experiences in current teaching-learning environments. When educators share authority with students, they encourage students to identify meaningful problems or questions to pursue related to the learning context and invite them to continually monitor whether their co-curricular involvement aligns with their own values and aspirations. Most important, situating learning in students' experiences provides ample opportunities for students to apply their new and old knowledge to meaningful contexts (Baxter Magolda, 2004, 2009).

Learning partnerships involve *mutually constructing meaning and learning* with students. Educators engage in dialogues with students that take their voices into consideration and offer opportunities to mutually construct knowledge by teaching students key processes, then asking them to implement these processes to address authentic problems, questions, or needs. Mutual construction also implies conceiving of students and educators as partners in students' development. This principle does not mandate that educators abdicate their expertise or knowledge; rather, educators infuse their knowledge and expertise in the context of students' perspectives, bringing this expertise to the dialogue but not imposing it unilaterally (Baxter Magolda, 2004, 2009).

Educators must challenge learners to become independent authorities through *portraying knowledge as complex and socially constructed*, for example by drawing learners' attention to the complexity of their work and life decisions and discouraging simplistic solutions to complex problems. Educators must also *emphasize self as central to knowledge construction*, for example by encouraging learners to recognize the value of their own views. Finally, educators should encourage learners to *share authority and expertise* and work interdependently with others to solve mutual problems (Baxter Magolda, 2004). The LPM is a conceptual, not prescriptive, model that prompts educators to think differently about learning and challenge conventional roles of educators and students.

Student Affairs Professionals as Theoretically Informed Connoisseurs and Critics

Thus far we have attempted to lay a blueprint for student affairs educators as they revise the co-curriculum at their institutions and reconsider their roles as educators in the co-curriculum. If one carefully examines our analysis and recommendations, she or he might quickly conclude that enacting this agenda involves more than simply spending time with students; it requires that student affairs educators possess firm theoretical and practical foundations for their work. It necessitates that as a professional one understands and appreciates theories and practices of demography, learning, organizations, student affairs, pedagogy, and learning partnerships.

Theories focusing, for example, on learning partnerships (Baxter Magolda, 2004) or student success (Kuh, Kinzie, Schuh, & Whitt, 2005) have influenced student affairs' practices aimed at supporting student learning. Likewise, everyday practices aimed at enhancing student learning have influenced the refinement of existing theories as well as the development of new theories. In *theory*, as this analysis suggests, the student affairs profession envisions the relationship between theory and practice as symbiotic, yet in *practice* a dichotomy persists in which, too often, practice trumps theory. This divide and collective aversion to theory thwart efforts of student affairs educators to forge a learning-centered co-curriculum.

Student affairs educators often are unaware of the theories that guide their practices. Yet if they are to enact their proposed learning-centered agenda and educate in new and different ways, they must make explicit and bring to the forefront of their collective consciousness both the theoretical and practical influences of the student affairs profession.

Theory usually takes center stage during professionals' graduate studies. Unfortunately, interest in theory quickly dissipates upon graduation, as Barr (1990) notes: "Practitioners who emerge from a strong, theory-based program often experience dissonance between theory and actual practice in their first practitioner setting. . . . What is learned in the classroom at times may not seem relevant or even valued in the new professional setting" (p. 20).

Strange and King (1990) offer further insights into the profession's propensity toward practice and reluctance to fully recognize the value and influences of theory:

> Success in an applied field tends to be gauged in terms of what an individual has done. . . . Claims of expertise, grounded in "what you know" rather than "what you have done," will predictably be met with suspicion in an applied field. This is especially true of a field like student affairs where interaction with people is paramount. Nothing substitutes for experience and maturity in terms of learning about and responding to the complexities of human behaviors. Consequently, a status claim based on "what you know" (e.g., knowledge of current theory) rather than "what you have done" is understandably threatening because it tends to undercut the experiential foundation of the field. (pp. 18–19)

We concur with Strange and King's conclusions, yet remain perplexed about the profession's estrangement from formal, explicit theories, because we posit that it is impossible to be *without theory* (although we readily acknowledge that individuals may not be conscious of the theories that influence their practices).

An admissions counselor reviewing a prospective student's application implicitly draws on attrition-retention theories as well as tacit knowledge when making an admission recommendation. When making a final evaluation, the counselor weights more heavily the student's high school transcript and co-curricular involvement than the student's standardized test scores. Although the counselor may not be conscious of the attrition-retention practice or explicitly describe them to colleagues, theory is influencing and enhancing her practice.

Although beliefs, values, and theories define and influence student affairs educators' actions, these actions may or may not be informed by formal educational theories (Clark & Peterson, 1986). Student affairs educators regularly rely on personal theories about the connections between teaching and learning not only for making everyday decisions (e.g., admissions decisions) but also for making sense of daily interactions and situations. Argyris and Schön (1974) distinguished between theories of action, which the personal theorist (e.g., the admissions counselor) is aware of and can articulate (i.e., espoused theories), and the unarticulated and implicit theoretical frames in one's actions (in other words, theories-in-use). One constructs an implicit theory by, for example, *reading* a person's actions and inferring a system of tacit understandings—the theory-in-use—within which the actions make sense. For example, examining the counselor's decision to minimize the importance of standardized test scores, one might conclude she is using an implicit theory that standardized tests are weak predictors of student success in college. What makes implicit theories problematic, however, is that their relationship to everyday educational practices and decisions can be so transparent that their validity is taken as self-evident, despite the fact that they often are shaped by habit, tradition, and precedent and adopted in an uncritical way (Carr & Kemmis, 1986). From our perspective, personal theories of learning are the kinds of knowledge student affairs educators need to possess in order to serve students. Making implicit theory explicit is essential.

Argyris and Schön (1974) posit that surfacing one's tacit theories-in-use improves practice. That is, one can employ a different and improved plan of action only after first exposing the current (and perhaps flawed) frameworks upon which one unconsciously relies. The key to enhancing practice is to reveal the discrepancies between one's theories of action (i.e., explanations of how to interpret and direct a situation) and one's theories-in-use (inferences from actions in that situation). The goal is to better understand one's implicit beliefs about teaching and learning (Magolda & Connolly, 2002).

The student affairs profession would benefit from more critically self-reflective educators who seriously and systematically contemplate the theoretical assumptions and experiences that guide their practices. Individually reflecting on one's actions and illuminating theoretical and practical influences on one's practice are prerequisites to becoming what Eisner (1998) refers to as educational connoisseurs and critics. Connoisseurship, according to Eisner, centers on the art of appreciation. Connoisseurs see, not simply look. Connoisseurship (something that one naturally develops; it is not a technique) involves building the capability to identify and appreciate various dimensions of situations or experiences and the way they interrelate with one's values and the values of others. To be a connoisseur, according to Eisner, is "to know how to look, to see, and to appreciate" (p. xx). It is less about expertness and more about enthusiasm and appreciation.

If student affairs educators can reveal their implicit and explicit theories, they have taken the first step to becoming enthusiasts—honing their capacities to identify and appreciate various dimensions of matters of importance. These educators continually work to understand their own values and how these values interconnect with those of others.

Eisner (1998) also advocates that individuals become educational critics. Developing connoisseurship, a private act, provides subject matter for critics. Criticism, however, is a public act centering on disclosure—a process of enabling others to see the qualities of an issue or item. The critic, in this public discourse, makes it possible for others less knowledgeable about a particular domain to appreciate the qualities that the critic recognizes. Educators must possess the capacity to understand themselves and the theories that act as the foundations of their practices and perceive themselves as educational connoisseurs and critics.

Student Affairs Professionals as Political Activists

The position that we have put forth throughout this chapter is grounded in relevant literature, makes intuitive sense, and can be carefully translated to any institutional context. Despite the evidence that suggests student affairs professionals regard themselves as educators, some colleagues disagree with our position. For example, the National Association of Scholars (NAS) released a 2008 statement, "Rebuilding Campus Community: The Wrong Imperative," in which the authors argued: "At a recent national conference, residence lifers declared they were now 'equal partners' with faculty in higher education. They characterized residence life in the old days as being concerned merely with 'programming activities,' while under the new 'curricular model,' res lifers, like faculty members, act as teachers. Teachers of what? And by what means? It is much in the interest of faculty members everywhere to begin posing these questions."

We trust that we have answered the NAS questions. Our argument is that by using relevant theories to guide their practices, student affairs educators become connoisseurs and critics of learning centered on the student experience. Despite our attention to the learning focus of this chapter, there are university colleagues who will respond in different ways to our claims. Consequently, student affairs educators must implement these teaching ideals within a political climate where divergent views and goals about the purposes of higher education exist. Student affairs educators, therefore, must be activists with their ideas, ground those ideas in relevant evidence and theories, and know how to communicate their learning purposes to advocates and critics alike. To accomplish these aims, understanding the politics of one's institution and the larger context is essential.

Conclusion

What do student affairs educators need to know and do in order to successfully design and implement a progressive co-curriculum that focuses on learning? At the very least they need to be responsive to the changing demographics of colleges and universities, establish measurable learning outcomes, embrace alternative conceptions of their roles as educators, and think broadly while acting locally. In addition, student affairs educators must situate learning at the epicenter of their practices and work on a daily basis to forge learning partnerships with students. Student affairs educators must understand their own theories of learning before they embark on the task of educating others. They must model lifelong learning by honing their capabilities to identify and appreciate various dimensions of situations or experiences related to themselves, students, and higher education, and make pubic these views (i.e., act as educational connoisseurs and critics). Finally, they should recognize the political struggles associated with these changes and engage in campus political processes to continually define and redefine what it means to teach and learn.

In *Principles of Good Practice for Student Affairs*, the authors write: "The choice of student affairs educators is simple: We can pursue a course that engages us in the central mission of our institutions, or retreat to the margins in the hope that we will avoid the inconvenience of change" (ACPA & NASPA, 1998, p. 1). The world, higher education, and undergraduates are changing; in order to respond appropriately to these changes, student affairs educators must focus their practices on creating environments that facilitate student learning.

References

American Association for Higher Education (AAHE), American College Personnel Association (ACPA), & National Association of Student Personnel Administrators (NASPA). (1998). *Powerful partnerships: A shared responsibility for learning.* Washington, DC: Authors.

American College Personnel Association (ACPA). (1994). *The student learning imperative.* Washington, DC: Author.

American College Personnel Association (ACPA) & National Association of Student Personnel Administrators (NASPA). (1998). *Principles of good practice for student affairs.* Washington, DC: Authors.

Argyris, C., & Schön, D. A. (1974). *Theory in practice: Increasing professional effectiveness.* San Francisco: Jossey-Bass.

Association of American Colleges & Universities (AAC&U). (2004). *Our students' best work: A framework for accountability worthy of our mission.* Washington, DC: Author.

Association of American Colleges & Universities (AAC&U). (2007). *College learning for the new global century.* Washington, DC: Author.

Barr, M. J. (1990). Making the transition to a professional role. In D. D. Coleman & J. E. Johnson (Eds.), *The new professional: A resource guide for new student affairs professionals and their supervisors* (pp. 17–29). Washington, DC: National Association of Student Personnel Administrators.

Barr, R. B., & Tagg, J. (1995, November/December). From teaching to learning: A new paradigm for undergraduate education. *Change, 27*(6), 13–25.

Baxter Magolda, M. B. (1996). Cognitive learning and personal development: A false dichotomy. *About Campus, 1*(3), 16–21.

Baxter Magolda, M. B. (2004). Self-authorship as the common goal of 21st century education. In M. B. Baxter Magolda & P. M. King (Eds.), *Learning partnerships: Theory and models of practice to educate for self-authorship* (pp. 1–35). Sterling, VA: Stylus.

Baxter Magolda, M. B. (2009). *Authoring your life: Developing an internal voice to navigate life's challenges.* Sterling, VA: Stylus.

Brookfield, S. D. (1995). *Becoming a critically reflective teacher.* San Francisco: Jossey-Bass.

Carr, W., & Kemmis, S. (1986). *Becoming critical: Education, knowledge, and action research.* Philadelphia: Falmer Press.

Christensen, C. R., Garvin, D. A., & Sweet, A. (1991). *Education for judgment: The artistry of discussion leadership.* Boston: Harvard Business School Press.

Clark, C. M., & Peterson, P. L. (1986). Teachers' thought processes. In M. C. Wittrock (Ed.), *Handbook of research on teaching* (3rd ed., pp. 255–296). New York: Macmillan.

College Board. (2005). *The impact of demographic changes on higher education: Summary of conference discussions.* New York: Author.

Day, J. C. (1996). *Population projections of the United States by age, sex, race, and Hispanic origin: 1995–2050.* Washington, DC: U.S. Bureau of the Census.

Eisner, E. W. (1998). *The enlightened eye: Qualitative inquiry and the enhancement of educational practice* (2nd ed.). New York: Macmillan.

Ender, S. C., Newton, F. B., & Caple, R. B. (1996). Contributions to learning: Present realities. In S. C. Ender, F. B. Newton, & R. B. Caple (Eds.), *Contributing to learning: The role of student affairs* (pp. 5–17). San Francisco: Jossey-Bass.

Freire, P. (1970). *Pedagogy of the oppressed.* New York: Continuum.

Guskin, A. E. (1994). Reducing costs & enhancing student learning. Part II: Restructuring the role of faculty. *Change, 26*(5), 16–25.

hooks, b. (1994). *Teaching to transgress: Education as the practice of freedom.* New York: Routledge.

Keeling, R. P. (Ed.). (2004). *Learning reconsidered: A campus-wide focus on the student experience.* Washington, DC: American College Personnel Association & National Association of Student Personnel Administrators.

King, P. M., & Baxter Magolda, M. B. (1996). A developmental perspective on learning. *Journal of College Student Development, 37*(2), 163–173.

Kuh, G. D. (1996). Guiding principles of creating seamless learning environments for undergraduates. *Journal of College Student Development, 37*(2), 135–148.

Kuh, G. D., Douglas, K. B., Lund, J. P., & Ramin-Gyurnek, J. (1994). *Student learning outside the classroom: Transcending artificial boundaries.* ASHE-ERIC Higher Education Report (Vol. 23, No. 8). Washington, DC: Graduate School of Education and Human Development, The George Washington University.

Kuh, G. D., Kinzie, J., Schuh, J., & Whitt, E. (2005). *Student success in college: Creating conditions that matter.* San Francisco: Jossey-Bass.

Magolda, P. M., & Connolly, M. (2002). Computing the value of teaching dialogues. In G. Wheeler (Ed.), *Teaching and learning in college* (4th ed., pp. 60–90). Elyria, OH: Info-Tec.

National Association of Scholars (NAS) (2008, July 16). *Rebuilding campus community: The wrong imperative.* Retrieved February 3, 2009, from www.nas.org/polArticles.cfm?Doc_Id=251.

Pascarella, E. T., & Terenzini, P. T. (2005). *How college affects students: A third decade of research.* San Francisco: Jossey-Bass.

Rhoads, R. A., & Black, M. A. (1995). Student affairs practitioners as transformative educators: Advancing a critical cultural perspective. *Journal of College Student Development, 36*(5), 413–421.

Strange, C. C., & King, P. M. (1990). The professional practice of student development. In D. G. Creamer (Ed.), *College student development: Theory and practice for the 1990s.* Alexandria, VA: American College Personnel Association.

Terenzini, P. T., Springer, L., Pascarella, E. T., & Nora, A. (1995). Academic and out-of-class influences on students' intellectual orientations. *Review of Higher Education, 19(2)*, 23–44.

CHAPTER TWENTY-THREE

COUNSELING AND HELPING SKILLS

Amy L. Reynolds

As the associate director of student life, Gail was responsible for the advising of student government and training of student leaders. She had extensive contact with the students and often heard about their classes, crushes, and various adventures. One evening after a student government meeting, she was in her office talking with some students. As one of the students, Julia, reached across the table, Gail noticed that there were scars on her forearms, including some fresh cut marks. It was clear to Gail that Julia had been cutting her arms, but that didn't make sense to her. Julia was a strong leader, was caring toward others, and offered no indication of depression or personal troubles. Gail realized that maybe she didn't know Julia as well as she thought. But what to do? How should she approach her and ask her questions about her arms and her overall well-being? What if Julia were defensive and withdrew? Gail decided that she would call the counseling center the next day to consult.

Attending to the needs of the whole student has been embedded in the core values, philosophy, and literature of the student affairs profession from the very beginning. And although the field of student affairs has become highly specialized (e.g., first-year programs, residence life, career services, the counseling center, and so on), student affairs practitioners act first and foremost as caretakers, educators, and helpers to actively assist students with the emotional and academic demands of college life and to promote their personal development (Creamer, Winston, & Miller, 2001). Student affairs professionals have endless opportunities to support, advise, and help students on a daily basis, from helping students in acute crisis who come to the counseling center to supporting those who struggle with developmental issues that affect them in social and academic arenas. The visibility of student affairs practitioners on campus makes them accessible and approachable to students with a wide range of problems and concerns (Pope, Reynolds, & Mueller, 2004). Many student affairs professionals are not specifically trained as counselors and may not possess the skills, experiences, or desire necessary to provide therapy to students. As a result, it is critical that student affairs professionals never practice beyond their skills and training. However, they often offer support and help students with important life decisions (Winston, 2003). Given the changing reality and demands of higher education, it is important that practitioners respond to the personal needs and concerns of students with sensitivity and effective helping skills.

Every campus has both professional counselors and, in the language of Delworth and Aulepp (1976), "allied professional counselors." The professional counselors typically work in career centers and counseling centers, and have received more advanced training in counseling knowledge and skills through course work and supervised practical experience. They are well equipped to deal with the more serious psychological concerns that many college students experience. While these professionals exist on every campus, the term *helper* is more commonly used for student affairs professionals who work outside of these functional areas.

Okun (2002) used the term *helper* to describe people who help others understand, cope, and deal with their problems. She suggested helper as an umbrella term that includes professional helpers; generalist human service workers; and nonprofessional helpers who vary in terms of their formal training in theory, communication, and assessment skills. In her framework, student affairs practitioners fall within the second category of generalist human service workers who have specialized human relations training at the college level, a team of colleagues and supervisors with whom to consult, and access to professional development and more routine and day-to-day contact with their clients (students). As helpers they need to fully understand the limits of their counseling expertise and utilize their well-developed and practiced helping knowledge and skills in their direct interactions with students.

The primary purpose of this chapter is to examine the specific and unique awareness, knowledge, and skills necessary for student affairs practitioners to be effective and ethical in their roles as helpers and caregivers. Incorporating counseling theory, models of helping, and approaches to assessment and conceptualization of student needs are addressed as part of the core competencies of student affairs professionals. This chapter also will explore some key concerns and challenges facing helpers, such as the importance of self-awareness, ethical demands, and multicultural competence. Finally, I will reconceptualize and expand the role of student affairs practitioners as helpers on campus to include their work as change agents and advocates who assist in the creation of campus communities that truly value and understand students.

Prevalent Mental Health Issues and Concerns on Campus

Because "college student mental health problems are becoming more common, more problematic and a much larger focus on college and university campuses" (Benton, 2006, p. 4), it is vital that all student affairs practitioners understand these concerns and what impact they have on the academic, social, and psychological well-being of students. However, it is not uncommon for practitioners, who are helpers and not professional counselors, to feel unsure about and unprepared to face the mental health concerns of students (Williams, 2005).

Research has shown that mental health symptoms and problems impair functioning in major life domains such as family, work, social life, and school for many college students (Soet & Sevig, 2006). These problems create additional barriers and may make it difficult for students to integrate academically and socially into campus life. Every year the American College Health Association (ACHA) collects data on the significant mental health concerns of all college students, not just those using counseling services. The most recent data from spring 2006 analyzed the results of over 94,000 students and found that almost 18 percent experienced depression and 12 percent reported being anxious (American College Health Association [ACHA], 2006). These students reported that their individual academic performance is affected by alcohol use, depression, anxiety, relationship concerns, stress, and sleep difficulties. They found that 13 percent of students felt very sad, 9.8 percent felt hopeless, and almost 30 percent felt overwhelmed by all they had to do.

The ACHA survey (2006) also reported that almost 10 percent of students surveyed seriously considered suicide during that year and many more (almost 45 percent) stated that it was difficult for them to function at times. In a study by Soet and Sevig (2006), almost 30 percent of college students either had been or currently were in counseling, 14 percent had taken psychotropic medications, and 6.8 percent were currently using such medicine. Other significant mental health problems for college students include substance abuse, violent behavior, bipolar disorders, family problems, sexual victimization, eating disorders, personality disorders, sleep disorders, and impulsive behavior (including sexual promiscuity and self-mutilation) (Grayson & Meilman, 2006; Kadison & DiGeronimo, 2004).

The reasons for this increase in college student mental health concerns include growing financial pressure and parental expectations; early experimentation with drugs, alcohol, and sex; divorce or family dysfunction; physical or sexual abuse; and poor parenting (Kitzrow, 2003). In addition, Keeling (2000) suggested that "earlier diagnosis and treatment, improved drugs, more reasonable social attitudes toward psychological assistance, disability protections, and the availability of more sophisticated services" (p. 2) may contribute. Regardless of the why, some college students will need treatment, medication, consultation, relapse prevention, and support in order to be successful in college; and because the mental health and well-being of college students "is not the sole responsibility of those with titles such as counselor, psychologist, or advisor" (Benton, 2006, p. 19), it is vital that student affairs professionals expand their awareness, knowledge, and skills to work effectively with students with psychological difficulties and concerns.

Helping Awareness, Knowledge, and Skills

Exploration of the core principles, knowledge, and skills of the student affairs profession has occurred over many decades, and a variety of conceptualizations exist (see Lovell & Kosten, 2000). Waple (2006) and Pope et al. (2004) suggested using a competency-based approach as a primary emphasis within student affairs preparation programs. During the past thirty years, empirical studies have examined the skills, knowledge, and personal traits needed for success in student affairs (Burkard, Cole, Ott, & Stoflet, 2005; Waple, 2006). Some suggest that the student affairs profession is not adequately preparing and training new practitioners in their roles as helpers. According to Burkard et al., professionals are expected to have "counseling skills that extend well beyond the basic skills often taught in graduate programs" (p. 298). Counseling courses typically focus on individual counseling and microskills, giving little attention to more advanced helping skills, such as conflict resolution and mediation, crisis intervention, and group facilitation. Increased focus on advanced helping skills, which represents a significant change in what is expected of new professionals, may reflect the changing mental health and emotional needs of students.

In addition, it is essential that multicultural competence be viewed as a core competence necessary for all helpers. Pope et al. (2004) described *multicultural competence* as the awareness, knowledge, and skills needed to ethically and effectively work with others who are both culturally different and similar, as well as the ability to address and integrate multicultural issues into all aspects of student affairs work in meaningful, productive, and relevant ways. Multicultural scholars have suggested that important values, worldviews, and realities of many individuals are ignored, minimized, or viewed as irrelevant (see Reynolds, 1995; Sue & Sue, 2003). Therefore, the unique experiences and perspectives of individuals from diverse cultural, religious, racial, socioeconomic, and sexual orientation backgrounds need to be integrated into helping theories and practices.

There are many risks involved when student affairs practitioners do not adequately understand or address the cultural realities of various groups on campus. Student affairs professionals who are unable to fully comprehend, for example, the struggles that many Native American students feel when they enter a predominantly White campus or the centrality of family to many Latino/a students, may not be able to help those students succeed. If practitioners interact with students based on the assumption that they are all heterosexual or identify as either male or female, they will undoubtedly hurt or disempower lesbian, gay, bisexual, and transgender (LGBT) students and increase their isolation. These examples just scratch the surface of the breadth of multicultural awareness, knowledge, and skills needed by student affairs professionals as they interact with and help college students. It is vital that student affairs practitioners increase their multicultural helping competence in order to provide the most affirming, effective, and ethical services possible.

In order to understand the levels and types of competence required to effectively help students, several areas will be briefly addressed in this section: the roles of counseling and helping theories, the centrality of the helping relationship, models for helping interactions, and conceptualizing student issues and concerns. It is important to highlight that student affairs practitioners are often the first contact with students who are troubled, upset, or unsure, and thus they need to be able to respond in supportive and constructive ways.

The Roles of Helping and Counseling Theories

Theory has always been fundamental to the student affairs profession, and the field is largely interdisciplinary in its use of theories (e.g., organization development, leadership, student development). Helping and counseling theories are varied and serve different purposes when being used by professional counselors and therapists. There is rich diversity among psychodynamic, cognitive-behavioral, humanistic, feminist, and multicultural theories; however, these theories are not always appropriate or effective in the context of student affairs helping relationships. Nevertheless, they may still offer ways to conceptualize the concerns of college students. For example, humanistic theories, such as client-centered or gestalt approaches, focus on the potential for growth and the need for self-awareness and responsibility, emphases that are very consistent with those of the student affairs profession (Mueller, 2008). Another example of a counseling theory is the psychodynamic perspective, as postulated by Freud, Jung, and others, which is not always viewed as typically relevant in a student affairs context. However, these theories do offer great insight into the role of the unconscious and early childhood influences on the development and insight of young adults.

These counseling and helping theories provide student affairs practitioners with insight into human nature and mechanisms for change and growth. By understanding the histories, philosophies, and key concepts of counseling and helping theories, along with their associated goals and techniques, we are better prepared to evaluate their effectiveness and determine their value for student affairs practice. Once practitioners have a strong understanding of helping theories, they can develop their own philosophies and integrated theories that will guide their helping efforts. According to Mueller (2008), cultivating a personal theory can guide our actions and behaviors, particularly in interpersonal relationships (such as counseling). Mueller also suggested that individualized theories are affected by one's cultural and social identities (e.g., race, gender, sexual orientation); family background; life experiences; education level; socioeconomic status; and other significant variables. Student affairs professionals need to develop their own unique helping voices that will allow them to effectively support and assist their students.

Centrality of the Helping Relationship

Most counseling theories support the notion that the helping relationship is central to the success of those important interpersonal interactions (Mueller, 2008). Carl Rogers (1995) is best known for his emphasis on building a trusting relationship as the key to successful counseling. Through his client-centered counseling theory, he suggested that there were several key conditions for therapeutic change: contact, empathy, client and counselor congruence, and unconditional positive regard. Making direct personal contact can help students feel important and reassure them that they are not alone. Such connection encourages them to be more open. The same is true for empathy, which is the ability of helpers to understand students' internal frames of reference. The helping relationship is more effective when both helpers and students are fully present; are aware of their thoughts, feelings, and beliefs; and express these in ways that are genuine, consistent, and appropriate. When a helper is real, the relationship is strengthened. Without a doubt, unconditional positive regard, or the helper's genuine acceptance of the student's feelings, behaviors, experiences, and attitudes, is a necessary condition for trust and connection. Furthermore, if students are worried about being judged, they hold back and are unable to benefit from the helping relationship. Conversely, if students believe that their helpers will accept them even when they have made bad choices or are struggling, then they will be more open and able to grow in self-awareness. When students experience "genuine acceptance and empathy, therapeutic change is most likely to occur" (Mueller, p. 102).

Helping Models

Within the counseling field there are many models of the helping process; however, many experts agree that helping is typically a multi-stage process. Through a synthesis of the counseling literature, Roe Clark (2008) offered a three-phase model of helping for the student affairs practitioner based on the work of Okun (2002) and Hill and O'Brien (1999) among others. The three phases are (1) establishing rapport with the student and exploring the dilemma, (2) gaining insight into the dilemma and focusing, and (3) taking action. Each phase suggests particular skills needed for the helper to be successful.

The first phase highlights the importance of building rapport. Student affairs practitioners often enjoy ongoing relationships with the students they help. Through those connections, professionals have multiple opportunities to reach out to students and encourage mutual concern and respect. Being welcoming, learning background information, initiating contact, and spending time together are just some of the ways that practitioners build rapport and help students feel safe and comfortable. This initial bonding becomes the foundation for the rest of the working relationship (Okun, 2002). Taking the earlier example of Gail and Julia, it would be important for Gail to actively reach out to Julia and ask her how she has been doing. The conversation can begin casually and eventually build to asking more personal questions. If a positive relationship has already been established, this initial phase is much easier. Another goal during this initial phase is to help students share their stories and express their thoughts and feelings. Dilemmas or problems often are imbedded in students' stories. The specific microskills to enhance rapport and encourage student openness typically emphasized during this phase include listening, reflecting, and summarizing.

With the second phase of helping, gaining insight into the dilemma and focusing, helpers center attention on the core of students' concerns. Many individuals seeking help need support in sharing their true concerns, often beginning by talking casually or identifying concerns that are less central. During this phase student affairs practitioners can reframe or reinterpret students' dilemmas or encourage students to explore how they contribute to their dilemmas. Through ongoing, deeper conversations, students can uncover their true thoughts and feelings—and the meanings behind their actions. Similarly, by gently asking probing questions about what areas of Julia's life are going well and what areas are creating stress, Gail may be able to help Julia see her problems and feelings more clearly. Sometimes just shining a different light on a problem can help a student see it in a new way and access alternative solutions and approaches to his or her concerns. According to Roe Clark (2008), the helper is more active during phase two, and several new skill clusters are added: questioning, clarifying, interpreting, and confronting.

In the final phase of helping, taking action, helpers assists students in setting goals and making action plans. Insight without action is unlikely to have much effect on a student's life, so this phase is quite important. Using the opening scenario, Gail could facilitate taking action by encouraging Julia to reach out to others when she is struggling, and suggesting that she consider counseling to help her with her problems. Action can occur on the inside (changing one's self-image or worldview) or on the outside (altering specific behaviors). This phase tends to be the most concrete of the three in that the helper encourages the student to act in measurable ways. It is essential to follow up with additional support to help the student implement and maintain any changes. As the helper gathers more information and gains a greater understanding of the student's underlying concerns, it may become clear that the student should meet with a professional counselor. In these circumstances, an appropriate referral must be made. Making referrals and developing goals and action plans are the skill clusters commonly used in this final phase of helping.

The three phases of helping proposed by Roe Clark (2008) can occur in a one-time interaction or across several meetings. They can be initiated by the student or the helper. Each phase has its own unique challenges, such as learning to be patient with silence, helping a student get unstuck, or dealing with intense emotions. Developing the necessary skills to be an effective helper will take time and practice. New helpers, in particular, who have minimal training will struggle with some temptations and fears as identified by Roe Clark: excessive questioning and fact finding, premature problem solving, and worrying about saying the "right" thing. According to Roe Clark, "Effective helping is not accidental, but rather the intentional result of a skilled and structured interaction intended to foster rapport, self-understanding, and positive action" (p. 167).

Conceptualizing Student Issues

When working with college students with mental health and other personal issues, it is important to consider how we conceptualize their concerns. Students' being in treatment or having emotional or psychological issues may or may not be relevant to our interactions with them. What is important to consider is how their concerns influence them and their academic or social environments. Some students may be depressed or anxious, but have learned how to manage their mood disorders through psychotherapy, medicine, or social support. Using the example of Julia, the cuts on her arm are likely an indication that she is not coping well. However, if she gets additional support and becomes more able to effectively address her problems, then such prior behavior and struggles are no longer important. In general, if a student's behavior or performance is not problematic, then his or her diagnosis or mental health history should be irrelevant. Making decisions or acting in ways that show bias against someone with mental health difficulties or a history of such problems may be discrimination, based on the Americans with Disabilities Act (Dickerson, 2006). Undoubtedly some students are unable to effectively manage their mental health and create difficulties for other students. However, it is important to state that even in those circumstances it is their behavior, not their diagnoses, that should be considered and addressed.

Delworth (1989) developed the AISP (Assessment-Intervention of Student Problems) model, which highlighted the importance of viewing problematic students in multidimensional ways to provide more just, effective, and appropriate services and interventions. Being able to distinguish between behaviors that have a negative effect on others and those that result from serious underlying psychological issues is essential to effective helping. Student affairs practitioners may not always know if a student has underlying psychological issues, or whether he or she is simply immature. However, by identifying specific problematic behaviors and consulting others, including professional counselors, helpers can determine the most appropriate and necessary response. In order to accomplish this, student affairs professionals need active and collaborative relationships with health staff, counselors, and staff from the students with disabilities office.

In order to ascertain which students need what types of assistance, it is important to be able to effectively conceptualize students' concerns. Many practitioners spend a lot of time addressing the needs and concerns of a few students who have negative effects on the larger campus community; however, it is also important to reach out to those students who are not extremely distressed or who do not disturb the campus environment. Spooner (2000) suggested that campuses evaluate what impact the environment is having on students and their behavior, rather than assuming that all difficulties come from the students themselves. When the campus is experienced as being distressing or oppressive, for example, it can create psychological difficulties or intensify ones that already exist. This has become increasingly important as many campuses struggle with policies and procedures regarding students with mental health and behavioral issues. Recent events in which the mental health difficulties of a few students had a negative and traumatic impact on the campus community—such as with the tragedies at Virginia Tech and Northern Illinois—highlight the need to proactively address these issues.

Concerns and Challenges for Helpers

The role and responsibility of counselor and helper is challenging and demanding. Personal and ethical concerns and challenges may emerge to which the helper must attend and draw upon his or her own skills and talents. An important part of being a helper is having the tools and insights to handle the complex issues that come the way of student affairs practitioners.

Personal Concerns and Challenges

Personal concerns or challenges need to be considered by student affairs practitioners when acting in the role of helper. One challenge is for helpers to be continually engaged in the process of self-awareness. Effective helpers are insightful and self-critical. Being in touch with their feelings and comfortable with themselves are ways that helpers can set positive examples for students. This does not mean that helpers need to be fully self-actualized; however, it is vital that they are engaged in their own development and self-improvement. A second potential challenge for those who want to be helpers is avoiding burnout. Dealing with students' strong emotions, hearing their painful stories, and setting appropriate boundaries can make helpers feel drained and emotionally overwhelmed. Corey and Corey (1998) explored the effect of stress on helpers. Individual sources of stress include self-doubt, perfectionism, emotional exhaustion, or taking on too much responsibility for those being helped. Environmental challenges include having too many demands and not enough time or resources to deal with them, leading to frustration with institutional bureaucracy and sometimes making it difficult to help others. To be effective helpers, it is necessary for us to attend to our own needs and ask for help when needed.

Ethical Concerns and Challenges

Student affairs professionals have often been the voice of ethical reasoning—the conscience—of their campuses (Brown, 1985; Talley, 1997). There are many complex and demanding ethical challenges inherent in the helping role (see also Chapter Six in this volume). Increasingly, multicultural competence is viewed in the student affairs profession as part of an ethical mandate necessitating that practitioners be adequately trained and prepared to meet the needs of all students. Because complex cultural dynamics are embedded in every corner of higher education, from training to admissions to core curriculum to programming, student affairs professionals must be capable of addressing multicultural issues and working effectively with culturally diverse populations (Pope & Reynolds, 1997). Nowhere is this need for multicultural competence stronger than in the helping interactions that occur on college campuses every day.

According to Janosik, Creamer, and Humphrey (2004), despite the availability of professional codes of ethics, many practitioners are unsure about how to respond to ethical challenges. Because many ethical issues grow out of helping relationships, it is crucial that student affairs professionals understand the unique dilemmas and circumstances that arise when engaged in helping, advising, or counseling relationships. Being aware of potential ethical dilemmas is the first step to becoming an ethical student affairs professional.

Among the primary ethical issues that affect helpers are competence, dual relationships, confidentiality, and the duty to warn. Competence means not practicing outside our areas of expertise. Well-meaning helpers must not be so overtaken by the desire to help that they forget that they are not therapists. The number-one ethical guideline is to do no harm, and when we work outside our areas of competence it is possible to do more harm than good. A second ethical area pertains to the dual relationships that often occur on college campuses. It is not uncommon for student affairs professionals to serve multiple roles with students (supervisor-friend, counselor–committee member) which can lead to conflicts of interest for either the students or the helpers. Sometimes, through the course of helping, practitioners can learn information on which they may feel some pressure to report or act. Although there are legal requirements protecting the privacy of students' educational records (e.g., the Family Education Rights and Privacy Act [FERPA] of 1974), the primary reason for helpers to maintain confidentiality is that it increases students' trust in the helping process. However, this can become complex based on the policy, procedures, or expectations of a particular department. Professional codes for counselors state that they are unable to break confidentiality unless their clients are threatening suicide, homicide, or are endangering the well-being of a child. Although student affairs practitioners do not follow the same rules, it is likely that students will not disclose to practitioners if they do not believe that their privacy and confidentiality are being protected. Furthermore, students' expectations can be complicated at times. A student may disclose to her hall director that she is being stalked and expect that she has control over that information. Although a student does not have to file a police report in such circumstances, sometimes residence hall policy requires that internal reports be made to protect the safety and well-being of the residents. In order to effectively manage such ethical dilemmas, it is essential that student affairs practitioners anticipate and discuss how to address some of these prominent ethical challenges before they actually happen.

The issues of suicidal and homicidal ideation and behavior have become heightened concerns in recent years. What is the liability for practitioners who learn of a student's feelings of despair or rage? The mandate of doing no harm is still central to the responsibility of professionals, but balancing the rights of individual students with the safety and well-being of the larger campus community is typically an ethical dilemma with no right or wrong answers (Archer & Cooper, 1998; Fried, 2003). Student affairs professionals need to be prepared to directly deal with and respond to these types of issues on a regular basis.

Dickerson (2006) suggested that institutions must review relevant laws and ethical codes, train staff, and provide adequate information and informed consent to all students. There are many resources available to assist campuses in these efforts. For example, the Bazelon Center for Mental Health Law (2007) has created a model policy in its efforts to "help colleges and universities navigate these complex issues and develop a nondiscriminatory approach to a student who is in crisis because of a mental health problem" (p. 2). According to Dickerson, these policy and educational efforts "balance privacy concerns against the health and safety of students and the campus in general" (p. 60). Ultimately, learning how to navigate this balancing act will help student affair professionals manage the complicated ethical demands of being both helpers and administrators.

Helpers as Change Agents on Campuses

Typically, helping is conceptualized in the context of a one-on-one relationship in which one helper (student affairs professional) assists one college student. Although often very important, these interactions are only a small subset of the actual and potential opportunities for helping. Further, such interventions rarely focus on addressing how the larger environment (family, campus, community, or society) may contribute to students' difficulties. Many multicultural experts view this type of individualistic helping as not always culturally relevant and meaningful (Sue & Sue, 2003). The role of helper may be expanded to include that of change agent and advocate.

Expanding the Helping Role

The need for student affairs practitioners to act as helpers and guide students through their college experiences is unquestioned. Every day provides new opportunities for student affairs professionals to listen, give support, and offer feedback to students who are struggling to understand themselves, others, and their futures. And although most of these interactions are not therapy, providing both challenge and support to students can be therapeutic and increase the likelihood of their personal and academic success.

Embracing the role of helper as central to the mission and goals of student affairs allows practitioners to not only contribute to the growth, development, and well-being of students but to also benefit the larger campus community. By espousing a helping orientation and broadening our conceptualization of the helping role, we as professionals not only honor our past but also create additional opportunities to build more responsive campuses that can benefit everyone. Recent and ongoing campus events have demonstrated that the emotional and psychological concerns of students are having an impact on our communities. Through our role as helpers we can make significant contributions to our campus. Our knowledge of student development and insight into who college students are and what they need in order to learn, grow, and develop as students and human beings can only help humanize our institutions. In order to achieve such lofty goals, it is essential that the profession, through its preparation programs and professional development efforts, effectively train all student affairs professionals to be helpers.

Importance of Social Change and Advocacy

Many in the counseling profession are giving increased attention to the value of social advocacy, conceptualizing helping as occurring in the broader realm of social change. Lewis, Arnold, House, and Toporek (2003) suggested that helpers should view student or client empowerment and community collaboration as essential to all helping interactions. Identifying the strengths and resources of students and assisting them with self-advocacy aligns with a commitment to social justice based in the historical and philosophical foundations of the field of student affairs (Evans & Reason, 2001). According to Reynolds (2008):

> By making a commitment to advocacy and placing it as a primary goal of the helping enterprise, we are able to help others twice. Once, by addressing their individual concerns and needs, and twice by encouraging the development of self-advocacy skills whereby they are empowered to make meaning of their own world and create changes that will benefit them and the larger world around them. This speaks to the larger professional imperative of incorporating multicultural competence so that we are fully able to help all students. Advocacy, empowerment, and community collaboration are the tools of tomorrow; they are the gifts that keep on giving because they create the strategies and tools in individuals to affect their environment and create change. (pp. 260–261)

By developing compassionate and affirming environments, student affairs professionals—in their helping roles—will better serve their campuses, acting as change agents to ensure students' personal and academic success.

Summary

Student affairs professionals are frequently placed in the roles of helpers; and many students rely on them for compassion, support, and guidance. In order to be effective helpers, practitioners need to develop essential awareness, knowledge, and skills to guide their efforts. Being self-aware, developing an understanding of counseling and helping theories and models of helping, and cultivating important skills and interventions are necessary for ethical practice. Furthermore, reconceptualizing and expanding the helper role to focus on a broader range of both helping skills and opportunities to act as student advocates is truly needed in order to create campus environments that value and understand students.

References

American College Health Association (ACHA). (2006). Reference group executive summary. Retrieved August 10, 2007, from www.acha-ncha.org.

Archer, J., & Cooper, S. (1998). *Counseling and mental health services on campus: A handbook of contemporary practices and challenges.* San Francisco: Jossey-Bass.

Bazelon Center for Mental Health Law (2007). Supporting students: A model policy for colleges and universities. Retrieved August 12, 2007, from www.bazelon.org/pdf/SupportingStudents.pdf.

Benton, S. A. (2006). The scope and context of the problem. In S. A. Benton & S. L. Benton (Eds.), *College student mental health: Effective services and strategies across campus* (pp. 1–14). Washington, DC: National Association of Student Personnel Administrators.

Brown, R. D. (1985). Creating an ethical community. In H. Canon & R. Brown (Eds.), *Applied ethics in student services* (New Directions for Student Services No. 30, pp. 67–80). San Francisco: Jossey-Bass.

Burkard, A., Cole, D. C., Ott, M., & Stoflet, T. (2005). Entry-level competencies of new student affairs professionals: A Delphi study. *NASPA Journal, 42*, 283–309.

Corey, M. S., & Corey, G. (1998). *Becoming a helper.* Pacific Grove, CA: Brooks/Cole.

Creamer, D. G., Winston, R. B., & Miller, T. K. (2001). The professional student affairs administrator: Roles and functions. In R. B. Winston, D. G. Creamer, & T. K. Miller (Eds.), *The professional student affairs administrator: Educator, leader, and manager* (pp. 3–38). New York: Brunner-Routledge.

Delworth, U. (1989). The AISP model: Assessment-Intervention of Student Problems. In U. Delworth (Ed.), *Dealing with the behavioral and psychological problems of students* (New Directions for Student Services No. 45, pp. 15–30). San Francisco: Jossey-Bass.

Delworth, U., & Aulepp, L. (1976). *Training manual for paraprofessionals and allied professionals programs.* Boulder, CO: Western Interstate Commission for Higher Education.

Dickerson, D. (2006). Legal issues for campus administrators, faculty, and staff. In S. A. Benton & S. L. Benton (Eds.), *College student mental health: Effective services and strategies across campus* (pp. 35–120). Washington, DC: National Association of Student Personnel Administrators.

Evans, N. J., & Reason, R. D. (2001). Guiding principles: A review and analysis of student affairs philosophical statements. *Journal of College Student Development, 42*, 359–377.

Fried, J. (2003). Ethical standards and principles. In S. R. Komives, D. B. Woodard Jr., & Associates (Eds.), *Student services: A handbook for the profession* (4th ed., pp. 107–127). San Francisco: Jossey-Bass.

Grayson, P. A., & Meilman, P. W. (Eds.). (2006). *College mental health practice.* New York: Routledge.

Hill, C. E., & O'Brien, K. M. (1999). *Helping skills: Facilitating exploration, insight, and action.* Washington, DC: American Psychological Association.

Janosik, S. M., Creamer, D. G., & Humphrey, E. (2004). An analysis of ethical problems facing student affairs administrators. *NASPA Journal, 41*, 356–374.

Kadison, R., & DiGeronimo, T. F. (2004). *College of the overwhelmed: The campus mental health crisis and what to do about it.* San Francisco: Jossey-Bass.

Keeling, R. (2000). Psychological diversity and the mission of student affairs. *NetResults, 20.* Retrieved October 1, 2007, from http://www.naspa.org/netresults/article.cfm?ID=62&category=Feature)

Kitzrow, M. A. (2003). The mental health needs of today's college students: Challenges and recommendations. *NASPA Journal, 41*, 167–181.

Lewis, J., Arnold, M. S., House, R., & Toporek, R. (2003). Advocacy competencies. Retrieved April 22, 2008, from www.counseling.org/Publications.

Lovell, C., & Kosten, L. (2000). Skills, knowledge, and personal traits necessary for success as a student affairs administrator: A meta-analysis of thirty years of research. *NASPA Journal, 37*, 553–572.

Mueller, J. A. (2008). Underlying and relevant helping theories. In A. L. Reynolds (Ed.), *Helping college students: Developing essential support skills for student affairs practice* (pp. 75–108). San Francisco: Jossey-Bass.

Okun, B. F. (2002). *Effective helping: Interviewing and counseling techniques* (6th ed.). Pacific Grove, CA: Brooks/Cole.

Pope, R. L., & Reynolds, A. L. (1997). Multicultural competencies in student affairs: Integrating multicultural knowledge, awareness, and skills. *Journal of College Student Development, 38*, 266–277.

Pope, R. L., Reynolds, A. L., & Mueller, J. A. (2004). *Multicultural competence in student affairs.* San Francisco: Jossey-Bass.

Reynolds, A. L. (1995). Multiculturalism in counseling and advising. In J. Fried (Ed.), *Shifting paradigms in student affairs: A cultural perspective* (pp. 155-170). Washington, DC: ACPA Media.

Reynolds, A. L. (2008). *Helping college students: Developing essential support skills for student affairs practice.* San Francisco: Jossey-Bass.

Roe Clark, M. (2008). Microcounseling skills. In A. L. Reynolds (Ed.), *Helping college students: Developing essential support skills for student affairs practice* (pp. 131–167). San Francisco: Jossey-Bass.

Rogers, C. (1995). *A way of being.* New York: Mariner Books.

Soet, J., & Sevig, T. (2006). Mental health issues facing a diverse sample of college students: Results from the College Student Mental Health Survey. *NASPA Journal, 43,* 410–431.

Spooner, S. E. (2000). The college counseling environment. In D. C. Davis & K. M. Humphrey (Eds.), *College counseling: Issues and strategies for a new millennium* (pp. 3–14). Alexandria, VA: American Counseling Association.

Sue, D. W., & Sue, D. (2003). *Counseling the culturally diverse: Theory and practice* (4th ed.). New York: Wiley.

Talley, F. J. (1997). Ethics in management. In J. Fried (Ed.), *Ethics for today's campus: New perspectives on education, student development, and institutional management* (New Directions for Student Services No. 77, pp. 45–66). San Francisco: Jossey-Bass.

Waple, J. N. (2006). An assessment of skills and competencies necessary for entry-level student affairs work. *NASPA Journal, 43,* 1–18.

Williams, L. B. (2005). My medicated students: I'm not that kind of doctor. *About Campus, 10,* 27–29.

Winston, R. B. (2003). Counseling and helping skills. In S. R. Komives, D. B. Woodard Jr., & Associates (Eds.), *Student services: A handbook for the profession* (4th ed., pp. 484–506). San Francisco: Jossey-Bass.

CHAPTER TWENTY-FOUR

ADVISING AND CONSULTATION

Patrick Love and Sue Maxam

Advising may be the universal task in student affairs, because it exists at the foundation of much of the work we do. This is, of course, the case for academic advising, career advising, and student organization advising. But advising is an important competency for most other positions as well, including those in financial aid, judicial affairs, residence life, international student affairs, commuter affairs, and new student orientation. Advising "is perhaps the only structured campus endeavor that can guarantee students sustained interaction with a caring and concerned adult who can help them shape such an experience" (Hunter & White, 2004, p. 20). Advising is the practice through which a student's learning and development can be directly encouraged. It is the strategy used most often to increase student success and retention (Habley & McClanahan, 2004; Pascarella & Terenzini, 2005; Smith, 2007), and "the quality of academic advising is the single most powerful predictor of satisfaction with the campus environment for students at four-year schools" (Kuh, 2008a, p. 73).

Advising is not merely providing advice. Providing advice is a unidirectional relationship in which a person who "knows better" tells another person what to do. Rather, advising is a helping relationship between two people and a dynamic process of mutual discovery and self-determination. An advisor helps individuals identify choices and take responsibility for the choices they make. While the advisor may indeed have more knowledge and experience than the advisee and be aware of the "bigger picture," the goal of advising is to generate learning, growth, empowerment, and self-authorship, in addition to sharing information, opinion, and one's accumulated wisdom. Nutt (2004) emphasizes that advising is integral to the success of students: through this experience "they learn specific skills and strategies necessary to navigate their educational experiences, and make effective decisions concerning their goals, choices and needs."

Since advising goes beyond the one-on-one relationships, this chapter also focuses on advising groups. The sections on individual and group advising are followed by a discussion of current issues facing individual and group advisors, including challenges facing today's students, the growing role of technology in advisement, and assessment. The chapter concludes with a focus on a different type of advising relationship, that is the issue of serving as an organizational consultant (an institutional advisor).

Advising Individuals

Most research regarding advising has focused on academic advising, but the information presented in this section applies to any position that involves advising individual students. The topics addressed are the core values of advising; goals and learning outcomes of advising; and the skills and competencies of advising, including interpersonal skills, problem solving, and understanding and applying developmental and learning theory.

Core Values of Advising

The National Academic Advising Association (NACADA) has developed a set of core values to highlight the importance of advising and its impact on individuals, institutions, and society. These core values, listed below, serve as a framework to guide advisors as they interact with students both individually and in groups (Gordon, Habley, & Grites, 2008, pp. 525–532):

- Advisors are responsible to the individuals they advise;
- Advisors are responsible for involving others, when appropriate, in the advising process;
- Advisors are responsible to their institutions;
- Advisors are responsible to higher education in general;
- Advisors are responsible to their educational community; and
- Advisors are responsible for their professional practices and for themselves personally.

Adhering to these core values provides advisors with opportunities to promote student success in terms of academic achievement, engagement, satisfaction, global citizenship, personal growth, and attainment of educational and career goals.

Goals and Learning Outcomes of Advising

The goals for academic advising (Habley, 2000), as created by a NACADA task force and incorporated into the work of the Council for the Advancement of Standards (CAS) for Academic Advising, include:

- Assisting students in self-understanding and self-acceptance;
- Assisting students in considering their life goals by relating their interests, skills, abilities, and values to careers, the world of work, and the nature and purpose of higher education;
- Assisting students in developing an educational plan consistent with their life goals and objectives;
- Assisting students in developing decision-making skills;
- Providing accurate information about institutional policies, procedures, resources, and programs;
- Referring students to other institutional or community support services;
- Assisting students in evaluating or reevaluating progress toward establishing goals and educational plans; and
- Providing information about students to the institution, college, academic departments, or some combination thereof (pp. 40–41).

While these have been promulgated as goals of academic advising, these goals fit virtually any individual advising relationship in higher education. Systems must be in place to measure whether advising goals have been achieved, so it is important that learning outcomes be developed to complement them. CAS, in conjunction with the authors of *Learning Reconsidered 2* (Keeling, 2006), has developed a learning outcomes model that defines six learning outcome domains:

- Knowledge acquisition, construction, integration, and application (e.g., connecting knowledge to ideas and experiences)
- Cognitive complexity (e.g., critical and reflective thinking, creativity, and reasoning)
- Intrapersonal development (e.g., realistic self-appraisal, identity development, and commitment to ethics and integrity)
- Interpersonal competence (e.g., meaningful relationships, collaboration, and effective leadership)
- Humanitarian and civic engagement (e.g., understanding cultural and human differences, social responsibility, and global perspectives)
- Practical competence (e.g., goal planning, communication and technology skills, and career development)

There are numerous ways in which learning outcomes can be measured, including quantitative approaches (e.g., standardized instruments like the National Survey for Student Engagement or a homegrown questionnaire); qualitative assessments (e.g., observing student behavior, interviewing people, or reviewing documents); and learning portfolios. Advisors can then use these tools to help students have the most successful college experiences possible.

According to Nutt (2004) and Macaruso (2004), learning outcomes of advising must be guided by the mission, philosophy, goals, and curriculum of each institution.

These outcomes articulate what students will demonstrate, know, understand, value, and do as a result of participating in individual or group advising.

Skills and Competencies of Advising

Effective advising involves a complex set of skills, competencies, and knowledge bases. Academic advisors must begin advising relationships with clear knowledge of institutional academic programs and curricular and co-curricular requirements. Other advisors need to know the policies and procedures governing their advising relationships with students. Important skills and competencies for individual advisors include interpersonal skills, problem solving, and understanding and applying developmental and learning theory.

Interpersonal Skills. Interpersonal skills are made up of active listening, questioning, and referral skills (Nutt, 2000). Active listening skills are the foundation of any effective interpersonal interaction and include:

- Establishing and maintaining appropriate eye contact
- Not interrupting with solutions before students have fully explained their ideas or problem;
- Being aware of body language that indicates lack of attention or discomfort on the part of the advisor and unexpressed feelings on the part of the advisee
- Being wary of emotional involvement or reactions, which can distract and reduce ability to listen
- Focusing on both the content and tone of students' words
- Acknowledging what students are saying through verbal and nonverbal feedback
- Reflecting on or paraphrasing what has been said (Burley-Allen, 1995; Nutt, 2000)

The key to effective questioning is focusing on the concerns of the student, not the concerns of the advisor (Nutt, 2000). This involves using both open-ended and close-ended questions. Open-ended questions often uncover additional insights, problems, concerns, and issues that might not otherwise have been addressed. Questions also communicate appropriate role expectations. In an effective advising relationship, there is mutual responsibility for guiding the discussion. For example, rather than asking, "How can I help you?" (which implies that an advisor's role is to solve students' problems), advisors can ask "What questions should we discuss today?" (which promotes a shared responsibility in problem solving, with the student taking the lead role in shaping the agenda for the meeting).

Effective referrals depend on an advisor's listening and questioning skills, because the first step in referring a student is to determine the student's concerns. The advisor also needs knowledge of appropriate referral services and their availability. The probability of an effective referral is enhanced when the advisor has already taken the time to visit possible referral services and has established relationships with specific individuals to whom students can be referred (Nutt, 2000). The advisor also needs to be able to explain in a clear, open, and sensitive manner why there is a need for a referral to another source of assistance. A referral should involve direct communication with the service to which the student is being referred. There should be a sensitive transfer of the student from the present advising relationship to the new helping relationship. This can involve working with the student to set up an appointment or actually walking the student to the new office. Finally, effective referrals include following up with students about the referral and the assistance they received to ensure that their needs were met (Nutt, 2000).

Problem Solving. Effective problem solving requires a partnership between advisor and advisee. Just as advising is not solely providing advice, problem solving is not merely supplying solutions. The role of the advisor is to work with the student in the problem-solving process. Obviously, the interpersonal skills described above are prerequisites to effective problem solving. Advisors must also avoid establishing premature boundaries that might restrict the ability to see creative solutions. "This means overcoming our personal predispositions, defenses, and habits" (Napier & Gershenfeld, 1987, p. 341) while looking at the problem or issue from a different perspective to yield as many choices as possible.

There are both rational and intuitive elements to problem solving. One typical example of a rational system of problem solving is as follows:

- Problem identification—Working together to define the problem at hand and exploring beneath the surface of the presenting problem (e.g., choice of major) in order to discover possible root problems (e.g., fear of disappointing parents).
- Diagnosis—Gathering data about the problem, including the degree of urgency and stress, other underlying factors, the degree to which this problem is affecting others, and the degree to which the student "owns" the problem (as opposed to believing the problem actually lies somewhere else).
- Generating alternatives—Identifying the possible solutions to the problem. Upon doing so, additional data may need to be gathered.
- Selecting solutions—Evaluating alternatives for potential effectiveness and consequences, selecting a solution, creating a plan of action, and discussing obstacles to implementing the plan (e.g., internal resistance on the part of the student).
- Implementation—Putting the plan into action.
- Evaluation and adjustment—Evaluating the implementation for effectiveness and making necessary adjustments. (Napier & Gershenfeld, 1987)

As any effective problem solver has discovered, relying only on a rational process is problematic because it implies that all necessary information is available and interpretable, and that is rarely the case. It is thus important that intuitive aspects of problem solving are also incorporated into the advising relationship. Advisors need to encourage students to listen to, explore, understand, and trust their instincts and hunches as well. For example, when deciding upon a major or career, a student can utilize interest or personality inventories, interview people in the careers, and list pros and cons of pursuing a particular career. These tend to be rational elements of the problem-solving process. Intuitive aspects include reflecting on a visit to a work site related to the career, and exploring with one's advisor how it felt to be there or imagining what a future in that career would be like. Both rational and intuitive elements interact and contribute to the effectiveness of the problem-solving process. Freije (2008) maintains that all of these interactions and skills send the message to the student that advising is "not just about checking off the correct boxes. It is about personal and intellectual development" (p. 21).

Understanding and Applying Developmental and Learning Theories. Student developmental and learning theory can help in explaining many of the complicated issues facing students. Effective advising requires knowledge of a wide array of developmental and learning theories (Creamer, 2000); the ability to discover levels of development through the advising relationship; and the ability to provide appropriate challenges to stimulate reflection and action that may lead to further development. While some scholars (e.g., Gordon & Steele, 1995) argue for knowledge of an exhaustive set of developmental and developmentally related theories, Creamer (2000) suggests the most important areas of focus should be on identity theory; meaning-making theory (i.e., cognitive-structural theories); and typology or personality theories. Many of these theories are reviewed in Part Three of this volume.

Creamer (2000) holds that students' advising needs change as they progress in their development. It is therefore important that advisors be able to assess the developmental status of the students with whom they work. Formal assessment involves the use of validated and reliable structured interviews or paper-and-pencil instruments. While such instruments can be effective for persistent personality type assessment (e.g., the Myers Briggs Typology Indicator), Love and Guthrie (1999) argue that "rarely are the time, opportunity, or resources available to conduct formal assessments" (p. 86). Instead, they suggest that professionals develop the skill of intentional informal assessment, which requires knowledge and understanding of theory and qualitative data techniques (i.e., observation and clinical interviewing), identification of one's own biases and assumptions, being able to look for evidence of developmental levels in the experiences of students, and self-reflection and self-evaluation of one's abilities in this area. Intentional informal assessment requires a mind-set different from typical advising relationships, and it requires practice.

Advising Groups

The types of student groups on campus that use staff as advisors are numerous, and they range widely in size, purpose, and degree of formality and structure. Formal groups include student government, Greek organizations, residence hall associations, academic clubs and organizations, honors societies, on-campus military groups, and advocacy and support organizations, such as those for students of color, or lesbian, gay, bisexual, and transgender (LGBT) students. Many of the same skills and knowledge sets that underlie effective individual advising apply to group situations; however, additional skills sets and considerations are involved. As with individual advising, it is important to be aware of institution-specific expectations for the role of group advisor. There are also functions and roles for group advisors. The knowledge bases and skills addressed later in this section are group motivation, group dynamics, and group development.

Group Advisor Functions and Roles

Bloland (1967) identified three related functions of the group advisor: maintenance, group growth, and program content. Maintenance functions are those that help to continue and protect the group, such as preserving the history of the group, and guarding against rule, policy, or ethics violations. Group growth functions are described below in the group development section and focus on helping the group improve its performance and work toward its goals. The program content functions are those through which the advisor appropriately shares her or his expertise in the areas of group focus, such as by conducting Robert's Rules of Order workshops for student government leaders.

Dunkel and Schuh (1998) identify a number of essential roles for advisors of student groups: mentor, supervisor, teacher, leader, and follower. Additional roles of a group advisor not covered in this section include educator, counselor, role model, programmer, communicator, ambassador, accountant, and manager (Riordan, 2003). Dunkel and Schuh cite DeCoster and Brown's (1982) definition of a *mentor* as a more experienced person in a relationship with a less experienced person based on modeling behavior and on an extended, shared dialogue. A mentor relationship is also one in which both people choose the relationship; a mentoring relationship cannot be assigned or forced on one individual by the other. The advisor of a student organization, therefore, may have the opportunity to serve as a mentor to the students in the organization. Dunkel and Schuh (1998) identify supervision as one of the skills of a group advisor, in that supervision and group advising both involve team building, performance planning, individual and group communication, recognition and documentation of individual and group actions, encouraging self-assessment on the part of group members, and evaluating individual and group performance.

Group advising also involves the role and skills of teacher. For an advisor of a student group, the focus and content of the teaching role center on such topics as group roles and responsibilities, meeting facilitation, leadership, and group problem solving (Dunkel & Schuh, 1998). While the advisor attempts to encourage the development of effective leadership and followership among the members of the group, the advisor also will serve in the roles of leader and follower. A person attempting to influence others toward the accomplishment of a task or goal is exerting leadership (Hersey & Blanchard, 1988), so the very nature of an advising position includes the notion of leadership. The advisor is attempting to influence the development of leaders within the student group and to influence positive group development and functioning. Dunkel and Schuh (1998) caution group advisors to be aware of their bases of influence as they teach students about appropriate and effective uses of power. In order to be most effective, the group advisor also needs to play the role of follower. That is, the advisor will need to "get out of the way" and allow the group to function, strive, and sometimes fail. Individual and organizational failure can be an important learning tool, if handled in a caring and sensitive way. There are also events that may be too important to allow the group to fail. In these instances, it may be appropriate for the advisor to "rescue" the group, but then use the situation as a teachable moment after the event has been completed.

Group Motivation

According to Dunkel and Schuh (1998, p. 77), "Understanding what motivates students may be [the] single most desirable skill" for a group advisor. Motivation exhibited by group members can range from no initiative to an obvious, innate desire to contribute and participate. Comprehending the range of motivation levels in the group and the factors that influence them is a vital competency. This requires being able to identify and assess the needs, wants, and drives (Hersey & Blanchard, 1988) of the students involved in the group. A common mistake of inexperienced advisors is making the assumption that the motivations of the group match their own motivation, or match the initial motivation espoused by group members, or match the motivation of the most involved students. Assessment of motivation levels needs to be ongoing, especially in the development of a new group. It can be conducted informally and intentionally through conversations with group members or with formal exercises done as a part of ongoing group development.

Group Dynamics

Group dynamics is the study of the interpersonal processes that occur in groups that affect individual group members and overall group functioning. Group dynamics includes such concepts as group cohesion, group conflict, power and influence variation, leader emergence and effectiveness, group effectiveness, and the influence of groups on individuals. An understanding of basic concepts of group dynamics contributes to the effectiveness of a group advisor and to the success of the group.

Johnson and Johnson (1991) indicate that an effective group is one that accomplishes its goals, maintains good working relationships among its members, and adapts to shifting conditions in ways that improve its effectiveness. They also provide a nine-point model of group effectiveness:

1. Group goals must be clearly understood, be relevant to the needs of group members, highlight the positive interdependence of members, and evoke from every member a higher level of commitment to their accomplishment.
2. Group members must communicate their ideas and feelings accurately and clearly.
3. Participation and leadership must be distributed among members.

4. Appropriate decision-making procedures must be flexible in order to match them with the needs of the situation.
5. Conflicts should be encouraged and managed constructively.
6. Power and influence need to be approximately equal throughout the group.
7. Group cohesion needs to be high.
8. Problem-solving adequacy should be high.
9. The interpersonal effectiveness of members needs to be high. (as cited in Dunkel & Schuh, 1998, p. 84)

It is the understanding and effective facilitation of group dynamics that contribute to the process of group development.

Group Development

Group development can be seen as the subset of group dynamics that focuses on the processes related to the growth; development; maturation; transitions; and, sometimes, decline of group functioning. Napier and Gershenfeld (1987) propose five interacting phases of group development: (1) the beginning; (2) movement toward confrontation; (3) compromise and harmony; (4) reassessment; and (5) resolution and recycling. The beginning is the formative phase of group development—the time period when group members come together, establish goals and expectations for the group, share and learn about similarities and differences among group members, experience the discomfort and optimism of a new group, and establish some basic ground rules of group functioning. The advisor can assist in helping the group work through this phase by conducting appropriate icebreakers, facilitating training in group functioning, and assisting the group with goal identification and planning. In the "movement toward confrontation" phase, initial feelings of discomfort continue to be worked through, the optimism of starting something new begins to wane, leadership and power relationships emerge and unfold, subgroups may form around distinctions and divisions in the group, and conflict among members may emerge. The advisor can best help groups in this phase by bringing areas of difference to the surface and suggesting clarification, conducting training in conflict identification and resolution, and facilitating leadership development activities.

Most groups then tend to enter a "compromise and harmony" phase, in which differences are resolved and working relationships grow in effectiveness. It is possible that excessive harmony can actually reduce the efficiency of the group if any lingering or new conflict is repressed, potentially resulting in passive resistance or passive-aggressive behavior. As an advisor, identifying possible instances of repressed conflict can help the group continue to develop. This is also the phase where groups can be strongly encouraged and pushed in their work, given increased levels of strength and resilience. Then, as groups continue their work and experience some accomplishments, they enter the "reassessment" phase of functioning. Goals, expectations, and plans are revisited and revised. This may also be the time when the group is amenable to greater self-assessment of their performance, which the advisor can help to facilitate. Finally,

Napier and Gershenfeld (1987) identify a "resolution and recycling" phase of group development. If the group is at a high level of maturity and functioning, conflict tends to be more open, constructive, and accepted as an important element of creative group performance. Depending on the group, the advisor can assist with appropriate concluding activities, if it is planned that the group will cease to function, or with issues of leadership transition for groups that experience cyclical turnover.

Issues in Individual and Group Advising

Whether someone is involved in the process of individual advising or group advising, advisors will face a number of similar issues. This section provides information on the needs of today's students, the impact of technology on advising, and the role of assessment in advising.

The Needs of Today's Students

Every advisor has the challenge of treating students as unique individuals while using knowledge about any of the number of subgroups to inform the advising relationship. Examples of such subgroups include adult students, first-generation college students, students with learning disabilities, LGBT students, students of color, international students, student athletes, and graduate or professional students. In addition to published resources, the NACADA Web site (www.nacada.ksu.edu) provides up-to-date information on advising various student subpopulations. Beyond the variety of subpopulations that exist on campus, there are other changes in the overall student population that are important for any advisor to understand. Some of these changes are addressed in Chapter Three, so only those most related to advising are addressed here: underpreparedness, shifts in attitudes, shifts in family dynamics, and increases in psychological and emotional damage.

Underpreparedness. College students have been identified as increasingly underprepared (Hansen, 1998; Levine & Cureton, 1998; Upcraft & Stephens, 2000). Many high school students report that they do not engage in the types of educational activities that will prepare them for success in college (McCarthy & Kuh, 2006); and in 2000, 28 percent of freshmen signed up for at least one remedial college course (National Center for Education Statistics [NCES], 2003). Remedial course work and the needs of underprepared students are expected to continue expanding, despite attempts by some systems of higher education to eliminate remedial courses from their curriculum (Woodard, Love, & Komives, 2000).

Shifts in Attitudes. Hurtado and Pryor (2006) found that college students were becoming more polarized politically, noting increases in percentages of both students who identified themselves as liberal and those who identified themselves as conservative. Large-scale problems that students identified as troubling in the late 1990s (Levine &

Cureton, 1998), including poverty, racism, crime, and global conflict, continue to resonate today. Given increasing concerns related to environmental sustainability and social justice, the global economic crisis that emerged during 2008, and a potentially transformative presidential election in November of that year, advisors will need to be sensitive to possible influences on college students and their attitudes toward the world around them.

Shifts in Family Dynamics. Approximately one-quarter of freshmen in 1997 came from divorced families (Hansen, 1998), and almost one-third of all children lived in single-parent situations. This represents a 300 percent increase from 1972 (Hansen, 1998). Additionally, "students who themselves are divorced or single parents make up a significant part of our adult learner population" (Upcraft & Stephens, 2000, p. 77). In addition to evolving forms of families, this past decade has seen an increase in the propensity for and intensity of parental involvement in the college student experience (i.e., helicopter parents); and, specifically, some parents may want to be included in advising sessions with their children (Kennedy & Crissman Ishler, 2008).

Increases in Psychological and Emotional Damage. Gannon (1989) points out that physical violence, sexual abuse, and alcohol and drug abuse within families continue to increase. Hansen (1998) remarks that violence among children and adolescents remains extremely high, and that more than 25 percent of adult women report having been sexually assaulted during their childhood or as young women. Sixty percent of campuses surveyed by Levine and Cureton (1998) reported record use of psychological services, and increases in eating disorders, drug abuse, alcohol abuse, and suicide attempts. Today's student population is dealing with significant levels of psychological and emotional damage. Kennedy and Crissman Ishler (2008) also highlight increases in self-injury, anxiety, depression, and eating disorders during this past decade. Additionally, students who are military veterans of multiple tours of duty in Iraq and Afghanistan are enrolling in college in greater numbers and face significant transition issues as well as emotional and psychological challenges (Calvan, 2007; Paulson & Krippner, 2007). Advisors need to be aware of and prepared for this, since on most campuses advisors are the only professionals with whom students have one-on-one contact (Nutt, 2000).

Obviously, not all students are affected by these trends; however, individual and group advisors need to be sensitive to the fact that in addition to traditional developmental and learning needs, they may be working with some students who are struggling with additional problems. The ability to make appropriate and sensitive referrals becomes that much more important.

Technology and Advising

Technology is playing an increasingly important, even integral role in advising. It has been used to support both advising systems (such as degree audit programs, advising Web sites, and transfer articulation systems) and the actual delivery of advising (such as through social networking, blogs, and instant messaging) (Leonard, 2008). Using both synchronous and asynchronous technology appropriately allows for effective planning, preparation, information sharing, record keeping, and follow-up while facilitating ongoing communication with students. Because it is convenient, instantaneous (in many cases), user-friendly, and accessible for most, technology can actually enhance advisor-advisee relationships by providing additional ways to communicate while building a sense of community and even school spirit. Therefore, it is incumbent upon advisors to stay up-to-date on the effective use of technology. Carter (2007) notes that this is especially vital because students increasingly prefer using technology-driven communication to more traditional modes.

A continually growing number of technologies support delivery of academic and student organization advising:

Instant messaging (IM) provides a means of instantaneous communication for simple and quick questions, answers, updates, or comments.

E-mail and listservs allow advisors to reach out to one, selected, or all advisees quickly, easily, and efficiently.

Social networking sites, such as Facebook (www.facebook.com) and MySpace (www.myspace.com), are online communities that allow users to create and customize their own profiles with photos, videos, and information about themselves, while linking to other members of each site. This has become the preferred method of communication among today's students, more so than traditional e-mail (Leonard, 2008). Advising offices can set up pages, and advisors can use social networking sites to post such pertinent information as office hours, advising philosophies, news, programs, policies, procedures, upcoming events, and frequently asked questions. These sites are also used to create discussion groups.

Blogs are online commentaries on a particular subject that allow readers to respond to their authors' writings. Advisors can use blogs to post academic information, viewpoints, and notes from meetings on a rolling basis, while also engaging students in discussions of relevant academic topics.

Wikis are collections of work designed to enable different authors to contribute to, edit, delete, or modify the content. Like blogs, wikis allow advisors to promote discussion of pertinent issues.

Really simple syndication (RSS) feeds are automatic announcements that there is something new on the Web that may be of interest to subscribers. Advisors can use RSS feeds to provide updates on academic policies or procedures, registration information, and upcoming events.

Podcasts are audio or video files that can be played or downloaded or to which users subscribe. Advisors can use podcasts to address academic topics such as registration instructions and academic progress information.

Skype is a software program that allows users to make inexpensive or free voice and video calls, do instant messaging, and transfer files, all from the user's computer. This is a very useful tool, especially for distance advising.

Course management systems, such as Blackboard (www.blackboard.com) or Moodle (www.moodle.com), although typically course driven, can be used to create a community among a group of individuals who share a common interest or bond. Student organizations and academic advisors use these online communities for discussions, postings, information sharing, online chats, and e-mail exchanges.

Electronic portfolios (e-portfolios) are Web-based collections of evidence assembled and managed by users. Such documentation, which is maintained dynamically, can include electronic files, multimedia, blog entries, hyperlinks, images, and so on. E-portfolios provide students with opportunities to showcase their course work, achievements, and professional growth. They facilitate students' reflection on their own learning, leading to more awareness of the connections among their curricular, co-curricular, and other relevant experiences. E-portfolios can be an important advising tool, helping students stay on track, understand how their experiences fit together, and prepare for their careers.

Twitter (www.twitter.com) is a free social networking and microblogging service that enables users to send and read short messages known as "tweets." Advisors can use Twitter to provide students with brief but important information and news as quickly as possible.

Second Life (www.Secondlife.com) is a free, online virtual world that enables its users to network and interact with each other using avatars. Colleges sometimes use this system to set up virtual campuses mimicking their own as a means of sharing information, running seminars, holding advising sessions, and so on.

Mobile computing describes the use of small, portable, and wireless computing and communication devices, such as laptops, mobile phones, wearable computers, personal digital assistants (PDAs) with Bluetooth or IRDA interfaces, and USB flash drives. Fuelled by the increasing availability of mobile devices among students, advisors, and faculty, mobile computing is gaining popularity because it can be accessed anytime, anywhere, while promoting a collaborative and open learning environment.

Although students often expect immediacy in communication and tend to prefer using technologies such as those listed above, it is important to employ a multifaceted communication approach in advising, combining these tools with face-to-face communication. The personal relationship that develops from one-on-one contact cannot be replicated online. Important nonverbal and subverbal elements of advising relationships are missing in many technology-based interactions. In addition, there are lost opportunities for discussions about other issues that may inadvertently arise during face-to-face conversations. Technologies such as instant messaging, e-mail, podcasts, and blogs tend to deal with the specific issues at hand, whereas personal exchanges can reveal so much more than was originally intended, providing additional insights and information that advisors can use to better serve and connect with students. Further, Carter (2007) maintains that advisors must also be cognizant of the fact that some students may not have immediate access to technology (possibly due to their socioeconomic backgrounds), and others may be reluctant to use it for a variety of reasons. Thus technology is not a substitute and should be used in conjunction with personal contact so that advisors and advisees can build and maintain meaningful relationships.

Technology has taken advising to a new level by simplifying, expediting, and increasing access to information while allowing advisors to enhance relationships with their advisees through online dialogues. Technology, when used properly, frees up an advisor's time for more long-term educational planning and mentoring with their advisees. Advisors need to realize that technology can never replace personal, face-to-face interactions, but rather can supplement them.

Assessment of Advising

The effectiveness of advising must be assessed both on an individual and programmatic level and include delivery and learning outcomes. Specifically, student perceptions of and satisfaction with the delivery process are key elements of assessment, enabling the advisor to glean information regarding effectiveness of both the delivery model and his or her own skills, service orientation, knowledge base, and approach. It is equally important, however, to assess the actual student learning outcomes of advising, which, Campbell and Nutt (2008) emphasize, must reflect the institution's mission and philosophy. Institutions must determine in advance exactly what they want the students to learn, and then formulate the learning outcomes accordingly. Some examples from the learning outcomes domains described earlier are:

- Students will articulate the role and importance of the core curriculum.
- Students will craft a comprehensive, personalized educational plan based on their abilities, goals, interests, and values.
- Students will be able to accurately assess their academic progress.
- Students will use self-knowledge to make decisions related to course, major, and career selection.
- Students will effectively demonstrate the ability to guide or assist a group, organization, or community in meeting its goals.

Once the learning outcomes are established, the advising experiences should be clearly mapped to ensure that students will work toward these outcomes during their tenure at the institution. Nutt (2004) contends that the outcomes mapping must communicate to students, staff, and faculty that learning is strengthened from a long-term advising relationship rather than from one or two advising sessions. It is essential that multiple measures of assessment be used to determine whether or not students are achieving learning outcomes. Quantitative approaches, such as homegrown questionnaires or surveys, as well as standardized instruments, can be particularly effective in that they can be used to develop data sets, which can then be compared with national or regional norms and internally over time. Qualitative approaches, such as observing student behavior and interviewing individuals or groups, can also be used. Other methods include using learning portfolios (traditional or electronic), offering freshman and senior seminar courses, implementing required advisee assignments, and tracking students' use of campus services and resources.

Ultimately, effective and ongoing assessment must demonstrate that advising goes beyond student satisfaction and measures actual learning and engagement (Macaruso, 2004; Nutt, 2004). Knowledge gleaned from comprehensive assessment plans can be used to further enhance advisors' individual abilities as well as advising programs, services, and resources.

Advising the Institution: Internal Consultation

There are some similarities between advising groups and advising the institution in that the institution is a large, complex group, and internal consultants most often work with subgroups within the institution. Many of the same skills that underlie effective advising practices with student groups apply to the role of internal consultant. In fact, student organization advisors often act as consultants to groups, as experts in providing training, and as process consultants when working with groups to diagnose, analyze, and address dysfunctional group processes. A significant difference is an internal consultation tends to be issue or problem driven, rather than being driven by long-term commitment to the growth and development of a particular group.

Consultation is a process that uses "experts" who employ their knowledge, advice, and expertise to assist organizations in addressing organizational problems. The types of problems typically addressed are those that inhibit organizational functioning or detract from student learning and development. Although the use of external consultants in higher education is a growing phenomenon (Kuh, 2008b), it is important not to overlook the vital source of consultants already within the organization. Perhaps the most obvious reason to use internal consultants is the cost savings involved. Internal consultants also are familiar with the organization and may be aware of the concerns being addressed. Drawbacks to using internal consultants include the fact that organization members are sometimes more open and frank with people from outside the organization, and there may be political dynamics that influence the ability of the consultant to assist with the issue at hand. It is, therefore, wisest to use external consultants if there is a significant, intractable, systemic problem (e.g., racial conflict), while internal consultants can best assist in areas of organizational development, improvement, and problem solving.

The art and science of consulting have evolved during the past several decades. Two related and often overlapping forms of consulting have emerged as powerful tools to assist institutions: collaborative consultation and process consultation. It is these forms of consulting that most conform to the descriptions, assumptions, and practices of individual and group advising described earlier in this chapter.

Collaborative Consultation

Models of collaborative consultation have emerged from mental health consultation (Caplan, Caplan, & Erchul, 1994); primary and secondary education (Kampwirth, 2006); special education (Idol, Nevin, & Paolucci-Whitcomb, 1993; Kampwirth, 2006); and other educational fields. The basic assumption in collaborative consultation is that an interdisciplinary team of professionals, which includes internal staff members but can include external professionals as well, must address institutional problems. Professionals are selected for the team because of particular content or process expertise they hold. Responsibility is shared, and various talents and strengths are brought to bear on the issue at hand. Idol, Paolucci-Whitcomb, and Nevin (1987) defined collaborative consultation as "an interactive process that enables people with diverse expertise to generate creative solutions to mutually defined problems . . . and produces solutions that are different from those that the individual team members would produce independently" (p. 1). An advantage of collaborative consultation is that multiple members of the institution help to shape strategies and are invested in the success of the results of the consulting effort and in helping to overcome institutional resistance. Crego (1996) points out that collaborative consultation is a way to transcend the traditional boundaries between departments, divisions, and roles that often block change from being implemented.

Process Consultation

Process consultation is the building of a helping relationship between the consultant and the members of the organization in which the consultant involves members of the organization in defining and analyzing the problem at hand, developing a range of possible solutions, analyzing the solutions for value and potential obstacles, and identifying a solution. An important element of process consultation is the active part that the members of the organization take in solving the problem at hand. Process consultation is often used in combination with collaborative consultation. One of the underlying assumptions of process consultation is that many of the problems in organizational functions (e.g., issues of motivation, conflict, lack of teamwork, and failure to produce desired outcomes) are the result of problematic or dysfunctional interpersonal communication and group processes (Schein, 1998). One of the goals of process consultation is to solve the current problem while uncovering the dynamics of the problem so that the members of the organization can identify for themselves how the problematic situation developed and persisted (Schein, 1998). Another goal is to have the consultation experience be an organization learning experience so that the members can come together, identify, and solve any related future problems that may arise.

The role of the consultant in process consultation is to observe the interactions that occur in the organization as they relate to the problems at hand. The consultant then provides feedback aimed at teaching group members to identify, analyze, and diagnose the behaviors that either help or hinder the group's success and to take steps to correct the problems.

Skills and Competencies of Consultation

While the skills required of the different approaches to consultation vary, there are some competencies that are required of all consultants. These include the interpersonal skills and problem-solving skills mentioned in the individual advising section, as well as the skills related to motivation, group dynamics, and group development needed by group advisors. The skills reviewed in this section are working with fellow organization members and data collection.

Working with Organizational Members. The internal organizational consultant has certain advantages over external consultants, the most significant being insider knowledge of the organization and initial access to organizational members. However, internal consulting is fraught with danger. The internal consultant must be able to engender trust on the part of members. For example, if the consultant is viewed as a pawn of the administration, the staff's willingness to be open and honest will be compromised. Trust building includes the ability to keep confidences (even after the period of consulting is finished), to maintain the integrity of the process, and to treat organizational members with respect. Working with organizational members also requires sensitivity to and knowledge of political processes occurring within the organization. The skills of negotiation, persuasion, and diplomacy become that much more important in a politicized environment.

Data Collection: Interviews and Observation. Schein (1998) suggested a combination of interviewing and observation in the early part of any consulting process. Process consultation interviews can either be individual interviews or focus groups. They have an explicit purpose that is described to the participant(s), provide explanations about the purpose of the questions and the overall interview, and ask descriptive, structural, and contrast questions.

Observation used as data collection is different from merely watching something, which is often a passive experience (e.g., watching a sporting event). Consultation-related observations are conducted with a focus and purpose. The consultant needs to look beyond the content of conversations and surface action of meetings and activities to the processes mentioned earlier. Observation "demands a complete commitment to the task of understanding" the group and its dynamics (Reeves Sanday, 1983, p. 20). The consultant must become part of the situation being observed and focus on observing as an outsider and on trying to understand the situation from the perspective of an insider. It is an awkward dynamic of trying to identify with those being observed and at the same time trying to maintain an objective distance (Reeves Sanday, 1983). Thus, while being able to empathize with those being observed is important, it is not enough. The consultant needs to be able to "record, categorize, and code what is being observed" (Reeves Sanday, 1983, p. 21). It is this information—and the analysis of the information gathered from interviews and observations—that the internal consultant brings to the group in order to analyze the problem at hand and work together to identify solutions and learn from the overall process.

Conclusion

Advising is a skill that is utilized by many different student affairs professionals and in a variety of contexts. No matter what the advisor's role and no matter which individuals or groups are being advised, the practice of advising involves a focus on learning. Academic advisors encourage learning on the part of their advisees; group advisors encourage learning on part of the members of the groups they advise; and institutional advisors, or consultants, encourage learning on the part of institution members. Quality advising requires individuals with appropriate skills and knowledge sets, and the willingness and ability to continually upgrade their skills and enhance their knowledge sets.

References

Bloland, P. A (1967). *Student group advising in higher education* (Student Personnel Series No. 8). Washington, DC: American Personnel and Guidance Association.

Burley-Allen, M. (1995). *Listening: The forgotten skill.* New York: Wiley.

Calvan, B. C. (2007). *Veterans face tough transition to college.* Retrieved December 7, 2009, from www.sacbee.com/101/story/403546.html.

Campbell, S. M., & Nutt, C. L. (2008). Academic advising in the new global century: Supporting student engagement and learning outcomes achievement. *Peer Review, 10*(1), 4–7.

Caplan, G., Caplan, R. B., & Erchul, W. P. (1994). Caplanian mental health consultation: Historical background and current status. *Consulting Psychology Journal: Practice and Research, 46,* 2–12.

Carter, J. (2007). Utilizing technology in academic advising. *NACADA Clearinghouse of Academic Advising Resources* www.nacada.ksu.edu/Clearinghouse/AdvisingIssues/Technology.htm#tech.

Creamer, D. G. (2000). Use of theory in academic advising. In V. N. Gordon & W. R. Habley (Eds.), *Academic advising: A comprehensive handbook* (pp. 18–34). San Francisco: Jossey-Bass.

Crego, C. A. (1996). Consultation and mediation. In S. R. Komives, D. B. Woodard Jr., & Associates (Eds.), *Student services: A handbook for the profession* (3rd ed., pp. 361–379). San Francisco: Jossey-Bass.

DeCoster, D. A., & Brown, R. D. (1982). Mentoring relationships and the educational process. In R. D. Brown and D. A. DeCoster (Eds.), *Mentoring-transcript systems for promoting student growth* (New Directions for Student Services No. 19). San Francisco: Jossey-Bass.

Dunkel, N. W., & Schuh, J. H. (1998). *Advising student groups and organizations.* San Francisco: Jossey-Bass.

Freije, M. (2008). Advising and the liberal arts: It takes a college. *Peer Review, 10*(1), 21–23.

Gannon, J. R. (1989). *Soul survivors: A new beginning for adults abused as children.* Englewood Cliffs, NJ: Prentice Hall.

Gordon, V. N., Habley, W. R., & Grites, T. J. (2008). *Academic advising: A comprehensive handbook* (2nd ed.). San Francisco: Jossey-Bass.

Gordon, V. N., & Steele, G. E. (1995). *Toward a theory of academic advising.* Paper presented at the National Academic Advising Association annual meeting, Nashville, TN.

Habley, W. R. (2000). Current practices in academic advising. In V. N. Gordon & W. R. Habley (Eds.), *Academic advising: A comprehensive handbook* (pp. 35–43). San Francisco: Jossey-Bass.

Habley, W. R., & McClanahan, R. (2004). *What works in student retention? All survey colleges.* Iowa City, IA: ACT.

Hansen, E. J. (1998). Essential demographics of today's college students. *American Association of Higher Education Bulletin, 51*(3), 3–5.

Hersey, P., & Blanchard, K. H. (1988). *Management of organizational behavior.* Englewood Cliffs, NJ: Prentice Hall.

Hunter, M. S., & White, E. R. (2004). Could fixing academic advising fix higher education? *About Campus, 9*(1), 20–25.

Hurtado, S., & Pryor, J. H. (2006, April). *Looking at the past, shaping the future: Getting to know our students for the past 40 years.* Paper presented at the annual meeting of the National Association of Student Personnel Administrators and the American College Personnel Association, Orlando, FL.

Idol, L., Nevin, A., & Paolucci-Whitcomb, P. (1993). *Collaborative consultation* (2nd ed.). Austin, TX: Pro-Ed.

Idol, L., Paolucci-Whitcomb, P., & Nevin, A. (1987). *Collaborative consultation.* Rockville, MD: Aspen.

Johnson, D. W., & Johnson, F. P. (1991). *Joining together group theory and group skills.* Needham Heights, MA: Allyn & Bacon.

Kampwirth, T. J. (2006). *Collaborative consultation in the schools.* Upper Saddle River, NJ: Merrill.

Keeling, R. P. (Ed.). (2006). *Learning reconsidered 2: A campus-wide focus on the student experience.* Washington, DC: American College Personnel Association & National Association of Student Personnel Administrators.

Kennedy, K. & Crissman Ishler, J. (2008). The changing college student. In V. N. Gordon, W. R. Habley, & T. J. Grites (Eds.), *Academic advising: A comprehensive handbook* (pp. 123–141). San Francisco: Jossey-Bass.

Kuh, G. D. (2008a). Advising for student success. In V. N. Gordon, W. R. Habley, & T. J. Grites (Eds.), *Academic advising: A comprehensive handbook* (pp. 68–84). San Francisco: Jossey-Bass.

Kuh, G. D. (2008b, December 12). Diagnosing why some students don't succeed. *Chronicle of Higher Education, 55*(16), A72.

Leonard, M. J. (2008). Advising delivery: Using technology. In V. N. Gordon, W. R. Habley, & T. J. Grites (Eds.), *Academic advising: A comprehensive handbook* (2nd ed., pp. 292–306). San Francisco: Jossey-Bass.

Levine, A., & Cureton, J. S. (1998). *When hope and fear collide: A portrait of today's college students.* San Francisco: Jossey-Bass.

Love, P. G., & Guthrie, V. (1999). *Understanding and applying cognitive development theory* (New Directions for Students Services No. 88). San Francisco: Jossey-Bass.

Macaruso, V. (2004). Resources and challenges in the assessment of advising. *Academic Advising Today, 27*(4). Retrieved from www.nacada.ksu.edu/AAT/NW27_4.htm#1.

McCarthy, M. M., & Kuh, G. D. (2006). Are students ready for college? What student engagement data say. *Phi Delta Kappan, 87*, 664–669.

Napier, R. W., & Gershenfeld, M. K. (1987). *Group theory and experience.* Boston: Houghton Mifflin.

National Center for Education Statistics (NCES). (2003). *Remedial education at degree-granting postsecondary institutions in fall 2000: Statistical analysis report* (NCES 2004–010). Washington, DC: U.S. Department of Education.

Nutt, C. L. (2000). One-to-one advising. In V. N. Gordon & W. R. Habley (Eds.), *Academic advising: A comprehensive handbook* (pp. 220–227). San Francisco: Jossey-Bass.

Nutt, C. L. (2004). Assessing student learning in academic advising. *Academic Advising Today, 27*(4). Retrieved from www.nacada.ksu.edu/AAT/NW27_4.htm#6.

Pascarella, E. T., & Terenzini, P. T. (2005). *How college affects students: A third decade of research.* San Francisco: Jossey-Bass.

Paulson, D., & Krippner, S. (2007). *Haunted by combat.* Westport, CT: Praeger Security International.

Reeves Sanday, P. (1983). The ethnographic paradigm(s). In J. Van Maanen (Ed.), *Qualitative methodology* (pp. 19–36). Beverly Hills, CA: Sage.

Riordan, B. G. (2003). The fraternity advisor: Roles, responsibilities, and resources. In D. E. Gregory & Associates (Eds.), *The administration of fraternal organizations on North American campuses: A pattern for the new millennium* (pp. 319–347). St. Johns, FL: College Administration.

Schein, E. H. (1998). *Process consultation revisited: Building the helping relationship.* Reading, MA: Addison, Wesley, Longman.

Smith, J. H. (2007). Using data to inform decisions: Intrusive advising at a community college. *Community College Journal of Research and Practice, 31,* 813–831.

Upcraft, M. L., & Stephens, P. S. (2000). Academic advising and today's changing students. In V. N. Gordon and W. R. Habley (Eds.), *Academic advising: A comprehensive handbook* (pp. 73–83). San Francisco: Jossey-Bass.

Woodard, D. B., Jr., Love, P. G., & Komives, S. R. (2000). *Leadership and management issues for the new century* (New Directions for Students Services No. 92). San Francisco: Jossey-Bass.

CHAPTER TWENTY-FIVE

CONFLICT RESOLUTION

Larry Roper and Christian Matheis

College and university environments are dynamic settings, serving a wide range of internal and external constituents. We attract students, faculty, and staff who represent diversity in all its forms to fulfill our broad missions and the unique social responsibilities we undertake. College campuses invite diversity of opinions, lifestyles, worldviews, values, personal expressions, and beliefs, which makes conflict and controversy inevitable features of campus life but is also essential to our vitality. Because there are numerous contexts in which teaching, learning, and exploration of ideas take place, conflict may arise from all dimensions of campus life—the research agendas of some faculty, our policies and professional practices, and invited speakers or other student activities. At the same time, campus leaders aspire to create campus communities that model positive relationships, harmony, and cooperation. Although it may appear that the goal of inviting controversy is incompatible with a desire to build community, the two dynamics actually build on each other. Genuine community building requires authentic interaction, which includes encouraging members to share their most deeply held feelings, cultivating an appreciation of diversity, and acknowledging and managing conflict or points of tension (Peck, 1987).

Effective communication is at the heart of any well-functioning community. Whether through face-to-face interaction or mediated communication, campus participants need the ability to express themselves effectively and understand the perspectives of others. The development and use of communication technology (e.g., e-mail, the Internet, Web pages, chat rooms, and blogs), and the capacity for broad and rapid communication technology brings, add to the complexity of our communication challenge. Technology allows extensive and immediate communication of positive and negative messages. Individuals from dissimilar cultures are able to be in constant contact with one another, increasing the importance of cultivating effective intercultural communication (Ting-Toomey & Oetzel, 2001).

Possessing conflict management skills allows student affairs professionals to effectively pursue their core responsibilities of building campus community, constructing effective organizations, nurturing positive learning environments, and alleviating barriers to student participation and success (Taylor, 2003). When conflict arises, student affairs leaders must have the ability to view conflict as a potentially positive dynamic, convene key individuals, assess the dynamics of the situation, identify the appropriate process, and facilitate towards a successful outcome.

When we bring conflict or controversial issues to the surface we create opportunities to air important issues, produce new thinking and express creative ideas, and ease tension. As we address conflict, we enhance the ability to build more positive relationships, increase goal and mission alignment, and improve the capacity of individuals and groups to pursue shared values (Folger, Marshall, & Randall, 2008). When we fail to address conflict, we affect the productivity of the organization and place the mental health and physical well-being of members at risk (Ting-Toomey & Oetzel, 2001).

This chapter offers readers an introduction to and overview of conflict, conflict theory, conflict management skills, strategies and processes for engaging conflict, and general observations to support effective leadership.

Understanding Conflict

Seldom do we embrace conflict as an opportunity for learning and change. More often we prefer to avoid it because of the negative way conflict has been framed historically. However, conflict and its successful resolution can open up many possibilities for organizations and free us to more deeply explore issues that matter to the campus community. But in order to seize the positive potential that conflict offers we need to reframe our view of conflict, moving from a negative connotation to a perspective of conflict as an opportunity-enhancing dynamic (Cupach & Canary, 1997).

Conflict occurs within relationships and arises through interaction of two or more people, making it relational. Messages regarding how we view ourselves and interact with others are acquired through cultural formation, giving conflict a cultural dimension (LeBaron, 2003). Recognizing conflict as a social and cultural phenomenon and understanding how it plays out in diverse organizations will enhance our leadership in achieving campus and organizational goals and will enable diversity to be a positive factor in institutional life. Effective leadership in a diverse environment enables: (1) full use of the organization's human capital; (2) enhanced knowledge and mutual respect; (3) increased commitment among diverse community members across all levels of the organization; (4) greater innovation and flexibility as others are able to participate more constructively in problem-solving teams; and (5) improved productivity, given that more energy is able to be committed to achieving organizational goals, and less energy is dedicated to dealing with cultural miscommunication (Ting-Toomey and Oetzel, 2001).

Defining Conflict

Conflict can be viewed as occurring along cognitive (perception), emotional (feeling), and behavioral (action) dimensions. Conflict generally arises when a person (or group) believes that his or her needs, interests, wants, and values are incompatible with those of another. Additionally, the person experiencing conflict may have an emotional reaction to a particular situation or interaction, and then act out or verbalize in order to communicate those perceptions (Mayer, 2000). Pruitt and Kim (2004) reinforce the view that conflict most often begins with perception—in particular, the belief that one's interests or aspirations are incompatible with another's. In addition to perception, interdependence is another key aspect of conflict. Interdependence brings competition and cooperation dynamics into the interaction of those who find themselves at odds (Folger et al., 2008). Wilmot and Hocker (2007) define conflict as "an expressed struggle between at least two parties who perceive incompatible goals, scarce resources, and interference from others in achieving their goals" (p. 27). Runde and Flanagan (2007) slightly expand the definition of conflict as "any situation in which people have incompatible interests, goals, principles, or feelings" (p. 19). Finally, LeBaron (2003) offers a simple and elegant definition of conflict, describing it as "difference that matters" (p. 11). Conflict is multidimensional, a factor that requires leaders to understand aspects of culture, identity, power, values, and many other variables.

Nature and Causes of Conflict

Human needs can be found at the foundation of all conflicts. People engage in conflict because of a desire to fulfill their needs, live out their values or fulfill their wishes and desires (Mayer, 2000). Most conflicts can be described as "mixed-motive" interactions in which the parties involved are interdependent and share both competitive and cooperative interests (Deutsch, 1991). Deutsch (2006) further explains that the type of interdependence among goals will greatly influence the likelihood of conflict. In situations in which there is positive interdependence ("I succeed if they succeed" and vice versa), there is greater motive to cooperate and support the success of others. When there is negative interdependence ("I succeed if they fail" and vice versa), there is a greater motive to compete and see others fail. Conflict can occur either because people do not see clearly the value of cooperation or because they perceive scarcity or obstacles to their goals, engaging in competition—even if competition is unwarranted—in order to achieve their desired outcomes.

The identities of the players involved add a distinctive cultural flavor to conflict. Members of a campus community possess varying cultural orientations, which are manifested by individuals possessing different *starting points* and *currencies*. Some members' starting point is to view themselves as individuals, whereas others view themselves primarily as group members. As a result, conflict may result from the challenge of negotiating individualistic and collectivist orientations in interpersonal and intergroup relationships. At the same time, diversity brings with it different ways of being and acting in the world, which make up one's currency. When we fail to cultivate awareness of different starting points and currency, the ensuing miscommunication and misunderstanding can produce conflict. Student affairs professionals need to be mindful of the ways individual-oriented and group-oriented outlooks influence values, expectations, and behaviors. Awareness of how identities are formed and preserved, moreover, helps us understand how a person's worldview informs her or his ways of being and the attitudes she or he brings to conflict (LeBaron, 2003).

Theories, Skills, and Strategies for Approaching Conflict

It is almost always the case that practitioners will need to draw upon different frameworks at different times in order to address the various complexities surrounding conflicts. Taken collectively or individually, the following five models—organizational psychology, values theory, conflict mediation, human relations theory, and restorative justice—can serve as practical, conceptual devices for engaging conflict in relevant, imaginative, and educational ways.

Organizational Psychology

Some dimensions of organizational psychology assess conflict by delineating two different forms that it takes in organizations: beneficial conflict and competitive conflict (Muchinsky, 2000). *Beneficial conflict* refers to dynamics in which parties who are in conflict are motivated to understand different positions and interests, with the ultimate goal of seeking common understanding. Even when views are considered to be opposing, this method of approaching conflict is one in which parties seek mutually satisfactory decisions. A likely outcome of taking a beneficial approach is that relationships will ultimately be strengthened as a result of experiencing and resolving conflict. Moreover, this view takes a hopeful approach by predicting that future conflicts will be also be resolved in correlation with the successes of previous conflict resolution.

Organizational psychologists also articulate a converse form of conflict, *competitive conflict*, which refers to scenarios in which parties to a conflict vehemently reject the motivations, positions, and interests held by those with whom they are not in agreement. From this position, one takes up defensive postures in order to *win* in a competition of ideas, facts, ideologies, etc. on the basis of other conceptual and evidentiary claims. Whether as a reflex or as a well-thought-out strategy, individuals responding from a competitive paradigm will seek real and imagined weaknesses in others. Some weaknesses that may be targeted potentially include issues directly related to a conflict, or peripheral character issues about a particular person, personality characteristics, belief systems, etc. Under this mode, it is often the case that some individuals will take a "by any means necessary" approach, even at times using superior authority to impose their solutions upon others.

Values Theory

Values theory proposes that we understand conflicts as emerging from the likelihood that multiple, equally valid principles exist as bases for our choices and for evaluating the real or imagines consequences of those choices. Moreover, values theory encourages us to look at our judgments as either descriptive or normative (MacKinnon, 1998). We can think of values, in a traditional sense, as the bases for our choices; values comprise the ideas and beliefs that account for what we may decide is good, bad, right, wrong, neutral, and so on. A conflict of values (or values conflict) is one in which we are faced with choices between values that are potentially equal—for example, *honesty* and *confidentiality* (MacKinnon). Values conflicts can also emerge when people do not have a shared understanding of the different kinds of values that may be unstated or under-stated when addressing issues. When approaching conflicts of values, it may be important to determine the kinds of judgments that are being made by the people involved.

Descriptive judgments are empirical in that they rely on evidence or data as a way to decide which values are more or less valid in a given conflict. In this situation one might ask, "What can the facts tell us to address in order to resolve this conflict?" In a related mode, normative judgments are moral claims about whether or not a particular course of action is justifiable. What outcomes should we attempt to achieve that adhere to or change our standards as a community? Under values theory, all judg-ments are evaluative. This is an important point for understanding conflict. Though a person might claim to be free of judgment, perhaps as a self-reflective character assessment, the reality is that as humans we are evaluative beings. We make judgments, and that is a fundamentally important part of our rational, intellectual, and emotional capacities. What deserves more attention is the quality and validity of those judg-ments. In and out of conflict, it is our responsibility to justify the ideological positions we take based upon our evident or undisclosed values. Practitioners must be prepared to articulate and sometimes adapt their values in relationships with others who may hold similar or different values in any given situation.

Conflict Mediation

Conflict Mediation strategies draw from a variety of theories and disciplinary practices, and apply them to the tasks of conflict resolution (Davis, 1989). As a body of knowl-edge based in application and practice, conflict mediation theories may differ greatly depending upon the unique skills and talents of each mediator. However, some basic tenets are commonly found in most mediation practices. Conflict mediation tends to identify individual parties to a conflict, and seeks to bring these parties into a mutually beneficial exchange regarding several important factors. Mediators facilitate dialogue—one-on-one and between parties—in attempts to illuminate each party's ownership of the conflict. This ownership is sometimes referred to as a party's *interest*, which may refer to basic concerns, desires, fears, or needs that inform a person's investment in a conflict situation. The fundamental is this question: What interest, or stake, does each person have in each situation?

Mediators assist parties in disclosing and coming to shared understandings of respective interests. From an understanding of different interests, conflict mediation encourages disclosure of positions, which are each party's respective proposed solutions that would satisfy their interests (Davis, 1989). Further, a mediation method draws upon the competencies that parties already have, and brings those to the fore in order to develop mutually beneficial—or at least mutually agreeable—solutions. In these processes, mediators take conflict to be a normal fact of human life. Conflict is a natural tension arising from oppositional differences, whether real or perceived. Mediation theories will often portray conflict as an opportunity for collaboration; thus it is a mediator's role to support parties in gaining a sense of the possibility for collaborative outcomes.

Human Relations Theory

Conflict is often defined and analyzed from an individualistic perspective that situates one or a few atomistic persons as the ideal subjects of theory and practice. Human relations theories take a different approach by contextualizing conflict in terms of two leading elements of groups, communities, and social settings: communication and culture. Conflict can be attributed to different patterns or styles of communication, including resistance to communication and avoidance of situations in which one may find communication challenging or impossible (Law, 1995; Isaacs, 2002). Cultures, and more specifically differences between cultures, are an important element of understanding conflict as well (DuPraw, 2002). For human relations theorists, differences between cultures are not the sources of conflict. Rather, conflict stems from lack of understanding about differences, limited opportunities to encounter differences, and disparate meanings usually stemming from incomplete or ineffective communication.

In social settings, conflicts emerge as a result of the absence of shared meaning or shared understanding about cultural phenomena, as well as challenges to establishing effective communication. Put into practice, human relations theory emphasizes the use of dialogue, often in group or community settings, as the method for building relationships and developing shared meaning about individual and collective cultures (Palmer, 1989). Dialogue itself has inherent value in helping us discover and at times create new capacities for understanding and lasting relationships.

Restorative Justice

Models of restorative justice address conflicts as matters of harm or wrongdoing (Zehr, 2002; Sue, 2006). Adherents to principles of restorative justice point out that many conflicts emerge from a sense of injustice. Therefore, responding to conflict involves acting to restore a state of justice in interpersonal and societal contexts. When people believe that a person or group has committed a harmful or unjust act, theories of restorative justice encourage those involved to view conflict surrounding the wrongdoing and harm with an immutable commitment to conflict transformation and peacebuilding. This is quite different from most conventional models of justice that view offenders or perpetrators as inherently flawed and beyond repair; that kind of "lock them up and throw away the key" method falls within a framework called retributive justice. On the contrary, restorative methods see all persons as deserving of human treatment and healing. Those who have been identified as acting to cause conflict or harm are primarily responsible, but they are not alone in their responsibility. Restorative justice requires that we acknowledge one another as sharing in common social and community processes that give rise to the actions of individuals. Our social and communal influences may prohibit or permit, discourage or encourage, diminish or enhance the likelihood that certain individuals or groups will commit just or unjust acts. Engaging conflict through a restorative approach involves working to restore the dignity of those who have been victims or survivors of wrongdoing *as well as* restoring the humanity of those who carried out harmful acts. Zehr (2002) explains three guiding principles that can provide practical reference points for addressing conflict. First, there must be opportunities for a wrong to be articulated by victims and acknowledged by offenders. Second, through an apology, often involving work to make restitution, equity needs to be restored to all persons involved. This often requires empowering people by compensating for disparities of power and influence. Third, there must be a creative plan for the future, addressing key questions surrounding commitments to the future of the community.

Styles and Levels of Conflict

There is rich and varied research on the topic of conflict, which has resulted in studies that look at conflict through a range of disciplinary lenses: for example, psychologists focus on intrapersonal conflict; social psychologists emphasize interpersonal and intergroup conflict; sociologists place stress on social, role, status, and class conflict; economists focus on game theory and decision making; and political scientists place emphasis on political and international conflict (Deutsch, 1991). Although scholars present findings on conflict in the frames of their particular disciplines, there are common and consistent patterns to how people engage in conflict (Ting-Toomey & Oetzel, 2001). Conflict styles reflect individuals' orientations toward conflict and are distinguished by two dimensions, *assertiveness* and *cooperation*. Assertiveness pertains to the degree to which a person's conflict style is characterized by concern for self, whereas cooperation indicates concern for the needs of the other person (Folger et al., 2008).

Cupach and Canary (1997) describe three different levels of conflict that people may experience with others: specific behaviors, relational norms and roles, and personal characteristics and attitudes. Interpersonal conflicts regarding specific behaviors generally entail disputes over the desire to coordinate or achieve common behaviors among or between individuals. It is not uncommon to see conflict of this type when members of an office staff try to achieve alignment in how certain processes are carried out. At the same time, conflict may arise when members of an organization cannot reach agreement on what they expect of their relationships with one another. The absence of shared relational norms may lead to miscommunication over what is expected of one's role. Finally, conflicts ensue because people who are in interdependent relationships find fault with each other's personal qualities, which might include criticizing faults, motives, personality, or general disposition.

Ting-Toomey & Oetzel (2001), summarizing the research of others, identified five styles of conflict: dominating, avoiding, obliging, compromising, and integrating. Each of these styles is displayed along two dimensions, the degree (high to low) to which the person is concerned with meeting his or her own interests or face needs, and the degree (high to low) to which he or she desires to incorporate the needs of others. Each style is characterized by specific tactics: *dominating* (or *competitive/controlling*), pushing for one's own interest above and beyond the interests of the other person; *avoiding*, eluding the conflict topic, the other party in the conflict or the conflict situation; *obliging* (or *accommodating*), being concerned with the other person's conflict interest above and beyond one's own; *compromising*, give-and-take to reach a middle ground agreement; and *integrating* (or *collaborative*), high concern for self and high concern for others. Individuals may vacillate between engagement and avoidance strategies.

The challenge leaders must deal with when looking at the various conflict styles is to manage their own cultural assumptions as they observe the behavior and attitudes of those involved. For example, typical Western perspectives often portray avoiding and obliging styles negatively. However, in group-oriented or collectivist cultures, maintaining face for self and others and preserving relationships is often more highly valued than prevailing over others. Face-saving can allow one to preserve honor and a sense of self-regard. If we fail to look at the behavior through the appropriate cultural lens, we can bring unfair judgment to the person displaying the behavior (LeBaron, 2003).

Strategies for Approaching Conflict

There is no specific or universal approach to resolving interpersonal or intergroup conflict. However, there are particular skills needed by third parties (mediators, conciliators, process consultants, facilitators, or counselors) to assist in resolving conflict. Among those skills are establishing an effective working relationship with the conflicting parties that engenders trust in the third party; establishing a cooperative problem-solving attitude toward the conflict among the conflicting parties; developing a creative group process; and developing sufficient background on the issues involved to function as a viable resource (Deutsch, 1991). Conflict-competent leaders will manifest skills and apply appropriate strategies to help their organizations address conflict situations (Runde and Flanagan, 2007). We discuss possible approaches throughout this section.

Hospitality

Philip Hallie (1981) describes an important tenet of moral philosophy for a world that struggles with conflicts that emerged from the study of ethics through personal narratives. He argues that we make a mistake if we think that peace is the opposite of hate and war, because peace is only the absence of hostility, violence, and harm. Instead, he asks us to think about our capacity to demonstrate hospitality, which he calls "unsentimental efficacious love" (Hallie, 1981, p. 27). Freedom from a hostile, negative, or degrading relationship is not the opposite of harm, it is merely the absence of harm. Hospitality refers to actions that not only remove harm but also that seek to heal the harms that have been done and, most important, prevent further harms from occurring. In engaging with conflict, how can you show hospitality in these ways? What is your capacity to help foster healing among those experiencing conflict? Recognizing that conflict will continue to occur, what can you do to help create the kinds of relationships and communities in which conflict does not involve the degradation of one's humanity? What can you do to foster hospitality amid conflict that will allow creativity and interpersonal insight to flourish?

Critical Thinking

The phrase "critical thinking" is widely used throughout postsecondary education, but it is rarely defined with any practical import. What does critical thinking mean, and what does it have to do with conflict? Critical thinking as a practical philosophy emerged out of the writings of Karl Marx, and was later advanced by theorists at the Institute for Social Research, sometimes called the Frankfurt School, founded in 1923 in Frankfurt, Germany (Bronner & Kellner, 1989). Critical thinking is an important skill for not only academic study and research but also for application in daily life outside of traditional studies. A substantial amount of academic and social learning emphasizes three general modes of thinking about subjects and issues, each from one of three general perspectives: (1) how a relationship or situation has been (in the past); (2) how a situation or relationship is right now (in the present); and (3) how a particular situation or relationship is likely to be (in the future) (Matheis, 2006).

When engaging in critical thinking, we consider at least two additional perspectives on a given subject or situation. Beyond the three modes mentioned above, thinking critically means (4) that we consider how society or issues could be (potentially), and (5) arguing substantially for how a relationship or situation ought to be (ethically, morally, and practically) (Matheis, 2006). This level of insight requires that persons provide substantial arguments for why a given relationship or situation should be one way as opposed to another. When engaging with conflict, practitioners may ask questions based in critical thought, such as:

1. How should we understand a particular situation (or relationship), and why?
2. How should we treat people who are involved in a conflict, and why?
3. What should we do in order to foster and sustain the kinds of relationships in which conflict is positively and effectively engaged, and why should we do so?

Charity—The Principle of Fairness

The Principle of Fairness, sometimes also called the "Principle of Charity," is important not only for effectively engaging conflict but also for building and sustaining healthy relationships, as well as for making effective judgments (Kiersky & Caste, 1995). Adhering to this principle means that we choose to interpret others with the most generous assumptions—about their motives, interests, ideas, and so on. It is easy to diminish the arguments and character of another person by attributing flawed premises to his or her ideas. However, in order to think clearly and make valid judgments, one must be willing, if not eager, to attribute the assumptions that will provide the greatest strength one would expect from another critical thinker. To be able to successfully criticize or evaluate the view of another person, one must be both willing and able to understand and defend that view to its fullest extent prior to attempting to critique it. Otherwise you are criticizing a weakened version of the idea that you have made up solely for the purpose of discrediting the other person. Charity also involves a self-critical willingness to recognize where your perspectives are accurate and also where they may need to be modified if given more information. Charity may mean taking away from an experience those things that you find to be useful and leaving the rest—rather than seeing any particular idea or approach as entirely good or entirely bad; charity means discerning positive qualities from negative qualities in a careful and critical manner. When engaging conflict, are you motivated by charity in giving the strongest interpretations to another person's meaning and intentions? Are you making thoughtful evaluations, or are you applying broad and sweeping judgments without care? What does it mean to demonstrate charity and the principle of fairness for others who are observing and learning from your leadership?

Welcoming and Experiencing Dynamic Tension

Conflict cannot be resolved through avoidance of certain kinds of tension that are natural and important elements of social life. *Dynamic Tension* refers to ongoing changes in comfort and discomfort experienced by people to the extent that some positive response or reaction may be evoked or provoked as an intended or unintended result (Matheis, 2006; Matheis & Sue, 2007). In other words, tensions experienced in a safe environment can positively influence our abilities to work and think creatively. For example, on many occasions classroom discussions in postsecondary education will focus on or touch on historical and contemporary approaches to addressing and resolving important social issues, such as racism, sexism, heterosexism, ageism, ableism, socioeconomic disparities, and religious persecution. It is reasonable to assume that differences of opinion will arise as people think through these and other concepts. With an understanding of the value of dynamic tension, practitioners can facilitate engagement in which conflicts, mistakes, and inevitable divergence in thoughts and ideas do not place relationships in jeopardy. With this in mind, conflict can be engaged such that tension can exist between and among people with different perspectives without fear of losing substantial access to equitable rewards and fair support from instructors, administrators, and peers (Matheis & Sue, 2007; Rankin, Roosa-Millar, & Matheis, 2007).

Understanding Nuances of Justice: Distributive Justice, Social Justice, and Restorative Justice

When conflict arises due to values and perspectives surrounding justice, perhaps surrounding social justice, it may be important to understand some of the ways that "justice" can be understood. Three particular views of justice may be relevant to engaging conflict, specifically by understanding some of the tensions between these concepts. Distributive justice is arguably the most common construct, influencing a majority of people. When justice is viewed as distributive, problems and solutions are generally conceived in terms of the distribution of goods and resources, such as land, money, and supplies. Although attention to economic disparities is important, this emphasis on material solutions is incomplete without addressing intangible matters of human dignity that are important matters of justice (Young, 1990). Social justice is often discussed in regard to material disparities; Young argues, however, that social justice also accounts for self-respect, dignity, recognition, rights, and opportunities—real social patterns that are impossible to quantify. Finally, as discussed earlier, restorative justice amends both distributive and social justice by displacing hegemonic domination and depersonalization, attempting to resolve conflict and respond to wrongdoing through restoration of dignity for all people involved (Sue, 2006; Zehr, 2002). Focusing too narrowly on any single conception of justice is unlikely to resolve conflict in a manner consistent with creating and sustaining communities. Conflicts surrounding justice, then, may be more carefully navigated by taking a nuanced understanding of these different paradigms and bringing them into view as frameworks for analyzing individual, group, and community interests in engaging conflict.

LeBaron (2003) suggests that because all conflict is relational, finding effective ways to relate to each other is our primary task during resolution, regardless of the issues or precipitating event. The goal of the conflict resolution leader is increased relationship effectiveness through implementation of the appropriate process. The success of the process is influenced by four activities: *naming*, what we call the conflict; *framing*, giving the conflict boundaries by defining where it begins and ends; *blaming*—assigning shared responsibility and accountability in a way that does not put the burden of solution solely on one party; and *taming*—bringing the conflict to some kind of closure.

Engaging with Conflict Situations

As a subject for academic study and discourse, conflict may be approached as an abstract concept or set of concepts. Analyzing conflict as a set of ideas, definitions, and theoretical frameworks is only one way to understand this fundamental component of human relationships. Practitioners soon learn that deep and useful understandings of conflict often emerge from a conceptual understanding of the ideas illuminated through personal exploration of one's own knowledge and direct experiences of conflict. Theory, experience, and application are all necessary for the development and maintenance of relevant skills and attitudes pertaining to conflict. The case study that follows may be useful to contextualize theories, concepts, and strategies for engaging with conflict.

Case Study—Theory to Practice

This case study and questions are provided for practical examination of conflict resolution. Advance preparation for engaging conflict can be achieved in part by reflecting on common conflict themes and patterns emerging in postsecondary education, such as those evident and implied in the scenario below.

Early on Friday morning in mid-January, the vice president for student affairs (VPSA) at a medium-size public university received a call from the university's legal advisor informing him that a group of seven individuals were illegally occupying the office of the dean of veterinary medicine. When he arrived on campus, the VPSA met with the provost, the vice president for finance and administration, the legal advisor, and the vice provost for research. At this point they did not know whether or not the protesters were students, and they engaged in a far-ranging conversation concerning alternatives depending on whether the occupants were students or nonstudents. Shortly into the conversation, the VPSA was called out of the room to take a call. The call was from the protesters, asking the VPSA if he would come to the dean's office to join them for a conversation. When the VPSA arrived at the office of the dean of veterinary medicine, he found seven women locked together in a device called a "lazy dragon." The device required anyone attempting to remove them to remove the entire group at once, because they were bound together. The protesters also included a person with a cell phone and a person with a video camera. Outside the building were others with cell phones and food for the protesters. The group was a mixture of students and nonstudents who belonged to a group named the Vegetarian Resource Network (VRN). The protesters were in the office to challenge the teaching of VM 757, a course in small animal surgery. The protesters were concerned by the fact that approximately seventy cats and dogs were euthanized in the process of teaching the course. There had been protests to the course annually for at least the past five years, but none involving the occupation of the dean's office.

The protesters and other university officials engaged in a daylong discussion in an attempt to end the occupation and avoid arrests. At one point the protesters were allowed to unchain themselves in order to negotiate around a table. Through the conversation, several issues emerged: USDA documents provided by the protesters showed that the source of the animals for the course raised ethical and legal questions; the protesters felt they were limited from talking to veterinary students to determine their reactions to the course; the vice provost for research felt uninformed about the procurement procedures for the animals; there was little awareness by the provost about how the course was reviewed; and the faculty of the veterinary school felt under siege concerning the course. When their desires were not satisfied, the protestors were allowed to return to their "lazy dragon." Finally, after eleven hours of conversation, university administrators were confronted with how to secure the building for the weekend.

Case Study—Questions for Consideration

1. How can you go about assessing conflict dynamics?
   a. One of the things we might do in this situation is to ask: in this situation, is conflict positive or negative?
   b. Who might be viewing the conflict differently depending on their values and interests?
   c. Thinking broadly, who are all of the individuals and groups who may be affected positively or negatively in this situation?
2. Who "owns" the issues?
   a. Who are the people with the most to gain or lose if this situation is not resolved effectively?
   b. Traditionally, who has been empowered to make decisions that are relevant to the situation?
   c. Thinking creatively, how might decision making become a shared responsibility for all parties involved?
3. How do you interpret the range of factors in the situation and make effective judgments about conflict?
   a. What are the key interests (needs, wants, hopes) of those involved?
   b. What are the positions (preferred solutions) held by those involved?
   c. What are the competencies (talents, resources, expertise) of those involved?
   d. What role can you take in bringing these questions forward for charitable consideration by everyone who is involved?
4. What are some appropriate models or frameworks to use as reference points in thinking about and acting to engage with conflict?
   a. What is it that will make this conflict either destructive or creative?
   b. What are the outcomes you hope to achieve? What are the outcomes desired by those involved? Where are there consistencies and differences between these desires?
5. What are some appropriate and effective strategies for engaging?
   a. What methods will meet the needs of those involved?
   b. What information will you need in order to project or predict the length of time and amount of energy that you will dedicate? Is this something you can limit, if so what factors inform those limitations.
   c. How will you be open and direct about your recommendations for taking particular courses of engagement and action?
6. What kinds of broad environmental dynamics need to be considered?
   a. What are the roles of stakeholders who are affected, but who are not directly involved or "on the sidelines"?
   b. Are there institutional or historical inequalities that put particular parties at an unearned or unfair advantage or disadvantage?
   c. How will you account for the roles of media and media coverage?
   d. What kinds of political consequences and opportunities exist that affect broader, systemically connected functions of your institution?

7. How will you sustain your capacity for leadership through different self-care strategies?
   a. What are the resources you need in order to bring about an effective process for engaging conflict?
   b. What kinds of mental, emotional, intellectual, and community support do you need in order to effectively engage conflict?
   c. How and when do you become aware of your own capacities? How and when do you become aware of your own limitations?

(*Authors' note:* Details on resolution on this issue can be found in Roper, 2004.)

Conclusion

Conflict resolution may be one of the most important activities we pursue to achieve our organizational and professional goals. Enhancing conflict management skills not only elevates one's professional effectiveness but also provides a means through which a student affairs leader can promote student development. When we help students and colleagues more effectively manage interpersonal conflict, we contribute to their personal growth. Whether mediating minor disputes or large-scale conflicts, leaders need the skills and knowledge to move parties toward reconciliation. Finally, conflict and conflict mediation are central to our quest for community. Our ability and willingness to embrace conflict and its positive potential will directly influence our ability to facilitate community development. Conflict-competent leaders will successfully reconcile our goals of inviting controversy and building community.

References

Bronner, S., & Kellner, D. (1989). *Critical theory and society*. New York: Routledge.

Cupach, W. R., & Canary, D. J. (1997). *Competence in interpersonal conflict*. Long Grove, IL: Waveland.

Davis, A. M. (1989). The logic behind the magic of mediation. *Negotiation Journal, 5*, 17–24.

Deutsch, M. (1991). Subjective features of conflict resolution. In R. Vayrynen (Ed.), *New directions in conflict theory: Conflict resolution and conflict transformation* (pp. 26–56). London: Sage.

Deutsch, M. (2006). Cooperation and competition. In M. Deutsch, P. T. Coleman, & E. C. Marcus (Eds.), *The handbook of conflict resolution: Theory and practice* (2nd ed., pp. 23–42). San Francisco: Jossey-Bass.

DuPraw, M. E. (2002). Working on common cross-cultural communication challenges. In L. Sneddon (Ed.), *Facilitator training manual: National Conference for Community & Justice*. Portland, OR: National Conference for Community & Justice.

Folger, J. P., Marshall, S. P., & Randall, K. S. (2008). *Working through conflict: Strategies for relationships, groups, and organizations*. Boston: Pearson.

Hallie, P. (1981). From cruelty to goodness. *Hastings Center Report, 11*(3), 23–28.

Isaacs, W. (2002). Dialogue. In L. Sneddon (Ed.), *Facilitator training manual: National Conference for Community & Justice*. Portland, OR: National Conference for Community & Justice.

Kiersky, J., & Caste, N. (1995). *Thinking critically*. Belmont, CA: West.

LeBaron, M. (2003). *Bridging cultural conflicts: A new approach for a changing world.* San Francisco: Jossey-Bass.

MacKinnon, B. (1998). *Ethics: Theory and contemporary issues.* Belmont, CA: Wadsworth.

Matheis, C. (2005). *Critical theory, intersubjectivity and community.* Unpublished essay, Oregon State University, Corvallis, OR.

Matheis, C. (2006, October). *Who needs hierarchy? Revolutionary leadership for diverse groups.* Paper presented at the Pennsylvania College Personnel Association annual conference, Stroudsberg, PA.

Matheis, C., & Sue, R. (2007). Difference, power, and discrimination and graduate education: Earning an advanced degree in a fragmented curriculum. In J. Xing, J. Li, L. D. Roper, & S. M. Shaw (Eds.), *Teaching for change: The difference, power, and discrimination model.* Lanham, MD: Lexington Books.

Mayer, B. (2000). *The dynamics of conflict resolution: A practitioner's guide.* San Francisco: Jossey-Bass.

Muchinsky, P. (2000). *Psychology applied to work.* Belmont, CA: Wadsworth.

Palmer, J. (1989). Diversity: Three paradigms for change leaders. *Journal of the O.D. Network.*

Peck, M. S. (1987). *The different drum: Community making and peace.* New York: Simon & Schuster.

Pruitt, D. G., & Kim, S. H. (2004). *Social conflict: Escalation, stalemate, and settlement.* Boston: McGraw-Hill.

Rankin, S., Roosa-Millar, L., & Matheis, C. (2007). Safe campuses for LGBTQA students: Systemic transformation through re(a)wakened senior leaders. In M. Terell (Ed.), *Creating and maintaining safe college campuses: A sourcebook for evaluating and enhancing safety programs.* Sterling, VA: Stylus.

Roper, L. D. (2004, May/June). Helping move from controversy and confrontation to collaboration. *Change, 36*(3), 34–39.

Runde, C. E., & Flanagan, T. A. (2007). *Becoming a conflict competent leader: How you and your organization can manage conflict effectively.* San Francisco: Jossey-Bass & Center for Creative Leadership.

Sue, R. (2006). *Sexual harassment and restorative justice: A transformational approach to addressing sexual harassment claims.* Unpublished master's thesis, Oregon State University, Corvallis.

Taylor, S. L. (2003). Conflict resolution. In S. R. Komives, D. B. Woodard Jr., & Associates (Eds.), *Student services: A handbook for the profession* (4th ed., pp. 525–538). San Francisco: Jossey-Bass.

Ting-Toomey, S., & Oetzel, J. G. (2001). *Managing intercultural conflict effectively.* Thousand Oaks, CA: Sage.

Wilmot, W. W., & Hocker, J. L. (2007). *Interpersonal conflict.* Boston: McGraw-Hill.

Young, I. M. (1990). *Justice and the politics of difference.* Princeton, NJ: Princeton University Press.

Zehr, H. (2002). *The little book of restorative justice.* Intercourse, PA: Good Books.

CHAPTER TWENTY-SIX

COMMUNITY DEVELOPMENT

Dennis C. Roberts

Klaus Schwab, founder of the World Economic Forum in 1971, defined what he believed to be essential to the welfare of the global community when he proposed that the world economy should be driven by one idea: the partnership or stakeholder view (2008). That this idea was reinforced by the global recession that followed immediately after his September 22, 2008, remarks demonstrated its relevance. He said, "The stakeholder concept means that whatever our individual differences may be, we are all interdependent and we have to act together if we want to succeed . . . solutions always require dialogue and often compromises, realistically addressing diverging interests of different stakeholders" [p.1]. These remarks sound as much like those of an educator or humanitarian as they do of someone who has shaped world economic policies and practices, and, this perspective reflects a new form of community for the twenty-first century.

Schwab went on to define five objectives that should provide the foundation for global affairs: (1) delivering environmentally and socially sustainable economic growth; (2) reducing poverty and improving equity; (3) addressing the core sources of global and national vulnerability, and promoting security; (4) sharing the core norms and values that enable global coexistence, and working to reconcile cultural differences; and (5) improving the quality of global cooperation and governance, and the performance of our global institutions (Schwab, 2008, pp. 3–5). As we begin to conceive of community in the twenty-first century, I can find no other shortlist of objectives that so completely captures the challenges and opportunities of the days ahead. These are the core issues of the interdependent and global community for which we must help students prepare. Furthermore, these five objectives may even provide a new, global social justice framework about which we should inform ourselves and our students.

Considering the complexity of the world in which we live and the challenges noted by Schwab (2008), how might we define community for a contemporary college or university setting? Is agreement achievable at institutions where the diversity of thought, background, and purpose varies so greatly? If there were an agreed-on, meaningful, and shared definition, could the process of how educators might foster a greater sense of community be prescribed? These questions have been a major part of student affairs administrators' struggle from the founding days of the field (Lloyd-Jones, 1989).

No matter how imperfect the concepts and models, the frameworks propose aspirations that are essential to our campuses. As has been conveyed in previous chapters, student affairs work is educational work, and the role of student affairs professionals is unique and purposeful in the context of higher education. While some of the curriculum of student affairs grants credit hours and grades, the majority of learning is in the noncredit experiences of students throughout the campus environment. Learning is seen in the encounters each student has with opportunities and programs designed to influence his or her learning. Student affairs programs have a profound impact on students' collegiate experiences, and it is the community that can be created through such programs that is the subject of this chapter.

The starting place for this chapter is a focus on the founding philosophy and theories of student affairs work and how this philosophy embraces the ideal of community. Different ideas of community will then be related to what we have come to recognize as "programming." A distinction will be made between conventional program development and community-building programming that serves other educational purposes. The outcomes one might expect are different, and it is important to recognize this in design, delivery, and evaluation. Once these purposes are defined, I will use examples of programming in practice to demonstrate what student affairs administrators might expect as they embark on or renew their work in community building through program implementation.

Origins of Community Building

As presented in Chapters Four and Five, the founders of student personnel work were very interested in the environment of higher education and how it fostered learning and development. Early student personnel workers sought to complement or complete the educational experiences of students. They viewed students' educational experiences as including the acquisition of information or knowledge as well as maturational development. They would never have thought of themselves as standing apart from or being in competition with the curriculum. Exploration of the historical context and documents at the time when student personnel work emerged reveals some important philosophical underpinnings. Dewey (1923) was very instrumental in the thinking of trailblazers such as Esther Lloyd-Jones (Evans & Reason, 2001). Lloyd-Jones's view of the emerging field of student personnel work was that it should be very innovative and particularly attuned to the environment and culture of a campus as well as to the experiences of students. Lloyd-Jones was far ahead of her contemporaries at the time and remains as a source of innovative thinking among current student affairs professionals (Roberts, 1998). She saw student personnel work much like that of a cultural anthropologist, seeking to understand the dynamics of a living and working community. Along with her colleague Margaret Ruth Smith (1954), Lloyd-Jones advocated that student personnel workers should be attentive to student interests, should seek to connect to learning opportunities throughout the campus environment, and should intervene only to the extent that learning and personal development were enhanced. In essence, this description is indicative of a commitment to creating community among all those affiliated with the college or university.

The early twentieth century was dominated by the emergence of scientific method and positivist views of learning. Dewey (1923) saw this and countered with his views of democratic education. Lloyd-Jones and some of her colleagues followed Dewey by asserting that the emergence of specialization and objectification of learning would irreparably harm the holistic learning environments that had so powerfully shaped higher education in the United States up until that point. Lloyd-Jones likened the move toward specialized functions in education and student personnel work to that of industrial-era assembly lines; even while industrialization was at its zenith, Lloyd-Jones asserted that the transference of an assembly line mentality to learning would be disastrous. In the place of specialization and compartmentalization, Dewey and Lloyd-Jones advocated that education should be more experiential and inquiry based—democratic in its process and outcome.

Ultimately, Dewey's perspective was marginalized (Ehrlich, 1997) and the philosophy derived from him by Lloyd-Jones was abandoned when student personnel workers moved to the "student services" focus of the 1950s and 1960s (Evans & Reason, 2001). This resulted in a split in student affairs practice between the engaged and collaborative learning philosophy derived from Dewey and the service-provider view characteristic of the burgeoning campuses of the mid-twentieth century.

How programs are used to create community will vary depending on whether one endorses a positivist and service emphasis or more of the environmental and cultural view of student affairs administration.

Contrasting Philosophies and Purposes of Programming

The student service view, characteristic of the 1950s, 1960s, and beyond, was predictably bound in a historical context that made many student personnel professionals believe that learning was essentially a process of providing for students and treating them as if they were receptacles for knowledge. During this period, one might reasonably conclude that community was somewhat less important and that student service programming was something that was done for students, with professionals initiating programs conveying an expert notion of learning.

The cultural or democratic philosophy of learning that preceded the student services movement would exploit the relationships among faculty, staff, and students, and would seek to use the grounded experiences of students as stimuli for learning. A program within this view could be one responding to a phenomenon on campus or in the community, it could be a program that students initiate with the support of staff, or it could be an experience deliberately designed to provoke reflection and learning among student participants. In this programmatic view, community could be the stimulus or the end product of the program and would have primary importance to student affairs administrators.

The schism of these two program models in student affairs lives on in today's practice. Neither view of programming is superior to the other. While historical analysis provides evidence that the origin of student affairs work is more aligned with democratic and engaged learning, there was, and continues to be, an appropriate role for more prescriptive programs in students' experiences. Understanding that there is a difference will have a profound impact on how programming is offered to students: a service approach will provide information, and an engaged learning perspective will involve students in the process of determining what should be learned and how. The point is that the latter has a much higher likelihood of fostering community among students.

Defining "Program"

Programming frameworks and processes are available throughout a variety of functional specialties in student affairs work. What one might do as a student affairs professional in new-student orientation, residence education, commuter affairs, fraternal organization advising, or services to adult or special needs students will vary depending on the context and the need. However, some advice is available through generalizable models such as the one advocated by Saunders and Cooper (2001).

Program Development Model

In this generalized schema, programming "is a planned activity with individuals or student groups that is theoretically based and has as its intent the promotion of personal development and learning" (Saunders & Cooper, 2001, p. 310). Note that this definition makes no reference to an environmental or community outcome. The community outcome was not a concentration for Saunders and Cooper as it is in this chapter.

A programmatic intervention may include students in planning and implementation or it may not. In crises or other situations where an immediate response is essential, the number of faculty and staff involved in planning may be limited as well. The point is that these circumstances require the dissemination of information that is critical to others. Community-building is not anticipated, or may not even be desired, as an outcome.

A specific example that may immediately spring to mind as an exception is the case of a campus crisis like an assault, fire, or death of a student. Many times campuses pull together in times like these to offer an immediate and soothing response, and this may look like "community." The positive and selfless responses of others is more likely a representation of the community that was present before the incident even occurred. If there were no sense of connection or community, it would be highly unlikely that individuals would jump to fulfill one another's needs.

Programming is an intervention that requires integrating theory into planning and implementation, and it involves a number of steps and conditions (Saunders & Cooper, 2001).

Planning

1. Select a planning team
2. Identify conditions and constraints
3. Obtain agreement on pedagogies
4. Review the skills and preferences of facilitators
5. Create or select activities
6. Create an agenda for program sessions
7. Identify referral resources

Implementation

1. Define responsibilities for implementation
2. Make arrangements
3. Establish the terms of collaboration
4. Recognize that perfection is impossible
5. Evaluate and redesign, if appropriate [pp. 333–335]

The above conditions may inadvertently help to develop community among participants but there is no focused intent to do so. Community-building programming might involve the very same end-result program. However, learners would be involved from the start. They would help shape the process, the promotion, and they would acquire reflective learner attributes and leadership abilities in the process.

Community-Building Program Model

Building community necessitates that those in the community are involved. One has only to think of moments in one's own experience to realize that true community cannot be imposed or acquired from someone or something else. An example that may be instructive would be the moment when the campus is swept up in a thrilling athletic contest that results in winning the championship; students may or may not have been part of a true community under these circumstances. Those on the team, who had prepared, strategized, and played the game, were likely part of a community. On the other hand, just being swept up in the exhilaration of victory would result in students being a part of campus spirit but perhaps not a true community. Community involves elements of responsibility, struggle, and sustainability (Peck, 1987).

In essence, the difference between program development and community-building programming is much like the distinction made by many contemporary theorists in regard to leadership (see also Chapter Twenty). The industrial-era paradigm of leadership or management in the twentieth century assumed that leaders led because they knew what was in the best interest of the group and had special gifts that justified their taking charge. This is a prescriptive and expert view of leading. Most contemporary leadership theorists advocate a view of leadership that is very different (Rost, 1991). Heifetz (1994) describes leadership as adaptive work among those seeking to address a mutual problem. Leadership then becomes a process of engaging with others to discover processes and knowledge required to resolve a specific dilemma. Applying the adaptive leadership model to programming on campus, the educator seeking to foster community-building programs will be a resource for and participant with other learners rather than directing and controlling the process. By engaging students and involving them in addressing their own concerns not only enhances the capacities of the individuals in the group but also builds community among those working together (Komives, Lucas, and McMahon, 2007). A community-building program model includes

Planning

- Those interested in an idea join in the effort.
- Challenges and opportunities are identified.
- Multiple and related strategies are analyzed.
- Current capability and learning potential for planners are assessed.
- Resources are compiled from the network of extended supporters.
- Opportunities are prioritized based on the human, fiscal, and other material resources available.
- Responsibilities are distributed among the planners based on mutual agreement.

Implementation

- Initiators take responsibility for getting things started and engage others as they are available.
- Resources are confirmed, reservations made, and tasks distributed.
- Collaboration and mutual work are expected.
- Participants recognize that perfection is impossible and rework as necessary.
- Evaluate and refine.
- Reflect and survey the learning acquired by those involved.

Outcomes

- Those involved see themselves as responsible for what happens.
- The capacity of the community and the leadership to deal with issues it confronts is enhanced.
- Problem-solving becomes a natural and sustainable part of the community environment.
- Community health and vitality are created and maintained. [Roberts, 2007]

The above community-building program model is similar, yet different in important ways, from the previous model of Saunders and Cooper (2001). It bears significant similarity to the learning organization model of Senge (1990) and its translation to modern campuses (Brown, 1997). The point of the community-building program model is not to compete with other program development and delivery models but to draw explicit attention to a type of program that has the additional outcomes of leadership development, community capacity building and sustainability.

Understanding community building as part of student affairs work and incorporating a focus on it as we design programs, is only increasing in its importance. The growing diversity of student populations, the increasing presence of international students, and the transparency and permeability of all our communities require us to understand the new global community more fully. Previous learning communities, which may have been relatively homogeneous, simply did not reflect the reality of the world, nor did they help students learn how to welcome and negotiate the new kind of global community that includes so many sharp contrasts. Learning to acknowledge the differences and growing more comfortable in navigating through divisive territory will enhance college graduates' effectiveness in the workplaces of the future. Few if any graduates in the coming decades will work in environments where the cultural, political, religious, and other perspectives can be assumed to be the same or even complementary to one another. These workplaces, and hopefully the higher education settings that prepare students for them, will be packed with fascinating encounters. If welcomed and handled in culturally appropriate ways, these communities can be even stronger than the homogenous communities that educators previously assumed were working to students' advantage.

Now that some philosophy is established as a foundation, what theories are available to help a student affairs administrator understand how to build community through programming?

Theories to Inform Community Development

A number of student development, cultural, and personality theories are addressed elsewhere in this book. This chapter relies on theories that may be less familiar and less used by student affairs professionals. They are, nevertheless, important as one seeks to devise programs that build community. The theories that are included in the following brief synopses come from the study of group behavior, human development and inclusion, healthful communities, and leadership.

Primarily as the result of a rapidly shrinking and flattening world, our views and insights about community have undergone profound changes in recent years. These dynamics sometimes drive our communities apart at the same time as they draw them together. Environmental issues, the effects of terrorism, and interlocked economies are only three examples that demand our attention on a global scale. On the one hand, environmental issues result in divisive and critical judgments across socioeconomic, cultural, and national borders, sometimes voiced by postindustrial nations that blighted the environment and now warn of the developing world's use of increasingly scarce resources. On the other hand, these same emerging environmental concerns have spawned numerous community-based efforts to reduce use, recycle, and renew natural resources. The reaction to the terrorism of 9/11 struck a chord of fear and suspicion at many people's core. Yet 9/11 also stimulated many gatherings and face-to-face interactions that allowed communities to express mutual support they previously took for granted. Finally, the global economic crisis that began in 2008 resulted in deep fissures between financial sector workers, political parties, and the general public. The globe shrank as the earth rotated and revealed the spread and breadth of volatile financial market conditions. These three examples of the post-9/11 world demonstrate that there are both centrifugal and centripetal forces in our communities. The point for student affairs and other educators is to learn how these conditions can actually be used to demonstrate our common humanity and need to reach out to each other.

Lewin's Theory of Group Behavior

Lewin (1952) conducted some of his earliest studies on group process in an experiment designed to encourage housewives to consider alternative food sources in the family diet. The experiment was simple and straightforward; the willingness to change was measured among a group that was informed through a lecture from an expert as compared to a group of participants who were mutually informed and discussed their views. The outcome was dramatic and this led to much of the wisdom espoused today when the phrase "people support what they create" is used. Not only are participants more likely to accept change if they are part of conceiving it, the change that occurs is also much more sustainable over time.

The implication of this research is that programs that are simply informative, no matter how authoritative, are less likely to impact behavior, and they will last for a shorter duration. The lessons:

- If an urgent issue needs attention, and long-term impact is unnecessary, conventional programming is the best fit.
- If the change desired is to be embraced by a broad number of participants, and if the hope is to sustain the change, community-building programming is the best fit.

Schlossberg's Model of Mattering and Marginality

Schlossberg's model (1989) of mattering and marginality defines how individuals respond to divergent experiences in their lives. The concept of mattering and marginality helps provide insight about students who, for whatever reason, see themselves as outside of the circle of acquaintances with whom they would like to affiliate. The conditions Schlossberg suggests are critical in establishing environments that generate a belief that we matter include attention, importance, ego extension, dependence, and appreciation. Students feel marginalized when these conditions are not present; when they feel marginalized, they are less responsive to learning; they are preoccupied with belonging; and they are vulnerable to dropping out of a living group, organization, or of learning entirely. The lessons to learn from Schlossberg are:

- If the information or idea advocated in a program is nonspecific, or the need to know is not clearly understood, conventional programming is the easiest strategy.
- If the idea needs to be embraced deeply by individuals who seek or need to know, community-building programming is necessary to pull participants from potentially marginalized to mattering status.

Boyer's Model of a Learning Community

Boyer (1990) provided a very influential model of community when he challenged higher education to create communities that are purposeful, open, just, disciplined, caring, and celebrative. The Carnegie Foundation and Boyer believed that learning would be significantly enhanced if these attributes were present. In essence, these attributes define community. McDonald (2002) and his associates applied these conditions of community in several helpful case examples. These examples demonstrate that community building is possible and, indeed, very powerful. In his "Afterword" (McDonald, 2002) Parker Palmer proposed five experiential markers that can help determine whether real community exists or not:

- I feel in community when I believe that I play a meaningful role in a shared educational mission, and others see me doing so.
- I feel in community when I am affirmed for the work I do on behalf of the shared mission if it contributes to that mission.
- I feel in community when I know that I can take creative risks in my work and sometimes fail.
- I feel in community when I am trusted with basic information about important issues relating to the shared mission.
- I feel in community when I have a chance to voice my opinion on issues relating to the shared mission or my part of it. (pp. 182–183)

Additional lessons derived from Boyer's seminal work include:

- If community connection is only coincidental to learning, programs may be designed and implemented without attention to attributes such as purposefulness, openness, and caring.
- If a college or university seeks to deepen the connections among its students, faculty, and staff, specific initiatives should be undertaken to make sure that the community embraces and seeks to personify these same commitments.

Peck's Progression of Community

Peck (1987) provides invaluable insight on the progression of collections of people toward real community. While most groups resist the notion that building community is a difficult and arduous process, Peck retold persuasive stories of how groups with which he had worked moved through stages of pseudocommunity, chaos, emptiness, and community. The natural tendency is for human beings to want to be in community with one another but to be unwilling to do the work to get there. The lessons:

- Community does not have to be part of every program initiative and may be a distraction from easier goals that require less substantive attention.
- Communities that accept and embrace diversity are, in many ways, stronger and more critical to our learning environments than those that are supportive and nurturing.
- Real community, although challenging and taxing to build, creates in the members deeper personal awareness, appreciation for each other, and tolerance for the chaos and uncertainty of life experience.

Keeling and Berkowitz's Concept of a Healthy Community

Keeling (1998) and Berkowitz (1997, 1998) espouse essential ideas related to the healing potential in communities. Research is emerging that unhealthy environments result in individual marginalization, psychological distance, refusal to take responsibility for one's own actions, and ultimately a variety of illnesses. In two areas of deepest concern—the spread of HIV/AIDS infection and substance abuse—Keeling and Berkowitz suggest that the only way to counter the deep and systemic causes of these problems is to create open, healthful, and healing communities. The lessons provided by this powerful research and theory building are:

- If maintenance of existing systems and views is acceptable, conventional programming is the quickest and easiest way to achieve results.
- When deep and systemic solutions are needed, engaging students in creating healthy communities may be the primary, and perhaps the only, way to address the concern.

Leadership Reconsidered

Pursuing a model of creating a healthy community requires another essential element: community-building programs must engage a broad segment of the student community in order to build the leadership capacity necessary to bring about change. A team of leadership educators worked with Astin and Astin (2000) over an extended period of time to conceptualize a shared and value-based commitment to leadership. *Leadership Reconsidered: Engaging Higher Education in Social Change* (Astin & Astin) encouraged students, faculty, and staff to rethink how they view themselves and to consider the possibility that leadership must be accepted by all if the lofty objectives of higher education are to be achieved. The lessons:

- Conventional programs will convey knowledge that is knowable and that requires adherence in order for the information to be effective.
- Community-building programs require participants to consider the barriers and opportunities that are encountered when everyone assumes that they are equally capable of leadership. Participants are also encouraged to challenge the assumptions that others have of themselves, shifting toward a belief that they are effective and influential agents of change.

Pope, Reynolds, and Mueller's Approach to Multicultural Competence in the Global Century

Pope, Reynolds, and Mueller (2004) advocate that multicultural awareness, knowledge, and skills are critical to success for student affairs educators and essential to all students' learning. How much more important will multicultural comfort and insight become in the new global century? Putting ourselves in settings in which the experiences, education, and cultures of others may be different from our own may be challenging in a North American context but it becomes even more difficult when students' and colleagues' religions, political perspectives, and worldviews are perhaps ones we may never have encountered or even heard about. Students in the new global universities may not even recognize race as a valid concept, and they may become impatient with U.S.-based concerns that neglect to recognize the dynamics of other nations in South America, Africa, the Middle East, and Asia.

The lessons from global multiculturalism include:

- Conventional programs will educate students about the broad differences that they are likely to encounter in the workplaces and communities of the future.
- Community-building programs will involve students in direct encounters with international students or will take students themselves to other countries, allowing them to develop as global citizens who seek to understand and consistently expand their horizons through study abroad, technology-based exchanges, and deeper encounters with national and historical culture.

Special Conditions That Influence Community Development

There are any number of special conditions that might impact or influence efforts to build community. Three that might have particular importance on the modern college or university campus are the degree of involvement among its constituents, technology, and expectations of community.

Involvement

Astin (1993) and his various associates have contributed some of the finest and most salient research and literature about the conditions that impact learning in higher education. His decades of research led to the conclusion that one of the most important variables is the degree to which students and other campus constituents are involved in the life of the campus. Spending time on tasks in learning and engaging with one's peers were found to be positively and strongly related to students' satisfaction with the college experience and with significant measures of educational attainment. The lesson is that if learning is to be maximized, students have to be available to access the learning placed before them, and they have to have the time to reflect on and integrate those experiences.

Technology

Anyone who works in higher education would have to admit that one of the most important, if not the most important, aspects of their changing experiences with others has been technology. The prevalence of computers and other forms of technology both draws people together as well as pushes them apart. Though able to stay in contact through e-mail with peers and colleagues involved in study abroad throughout the world on a daily basis, roommates debate their living conditions from the opposite sides of small rooms using laptop computers. While cell phones provide easy and immediate access to friends and loved ones, their presence in the hands of students in transit from class to class prohibits the exchange of casual hellos, smiles, and other human gestures. Technology can create cyber, networked, and microwave communities, but it can also divide those who share the same physical and learning spaces.

Community Expectations

One of the things that can positively influence community, especially related to the desire to increase the breadth, depth, and quality of involvement for all, is shared expectations. Whether implicitly or explicitly understood, models such as Boyer's (1990), Peck's (1987), and Schlossberg's (1989) all require some sharing of common expectations. Standards of how others are included or treated will heavily influence the degree to which all the members believe they are valued and benefit from their association. These influences must be recognized and fostered among those seeking to become a community.

When it comes to building community, we can inadvertently become our own worst enemies. Our complex organizations are difficult to navigate because they include numerous competing perspectives, many of which vie for financial support, time, or other resources. It is all too easy for us to become impatient or disgruntled in the give-and-take of resource competition. This is when, using Jaworski's (1998) analogy, we wake up behind enemy lines. We get so caught up in the competitive discourse that we neglect the commitments we've made to being respectful, being open to hearing others' perspectives, and seeking the greater good. We have become the others that we may have vilified in order to advance our own arguments. When this happens, the community suffers and opportunities to build community as a shared resource are undermined.

Competencies Required

What competencies must student affairs administrators possess in order to work with theories and concepts like those described above? Effective programming of the kind described by Saunders and Cooper (2001) requires professional preparation in assessment, interpretation, planning, resource identification and utilization, and administration. This kind of programming also requires expertise in group communication and facilitation.

It is important to recognize that program and community development are integral to any student affairs administrators' responsibilities. And one of the key issues required to enhance effectiveness is being able to determine when direct programming is the easiest and most expedient way of addressing an issue. Particularly given that program development that can be done by an individual or small group is easier to complete, a discerning judgment about the necessity to move quickly could preserve important resources for use in other initiatives.

In addition to the abilities identified above, the professional interested in engaging in community-building programming must have advanced skills in reflection, conceptualization, and collaboration. Probably above all insights or skills, student affairs professionals committed to community building must see themselves as full partners in the collegiate setting, and must be comfortable with serving as catalysts for the learning and involvement of others. The capabilities named above related to community-building are different from those possessed by the conventional programmer. While harder to cultivate, the community-building attributes can have tremendous payoff in the capacity and potential that can be added to the community through their use.

The difficulty with community-building programs is that work is much less applied than one might be used to pursuing. There would likely be less direct involvement and less action-oriented behavior. However, serving in a more indirect and catalytic role is likely to help student affairs professionals relate more fully and meaningfully to the broader educational objectives of their college or university. By doing this, student affairs professionals augment the learning process so that all can experience powerful, holistic learning. The final implication is that the community-building professional is more likely to share many resources and stimulate changes in the environment that will become more long-standing and permanent, regardless of the direct involvement by the individual over time. The shared ownership protects the initiative so that it becomes internalized and can be maintained. If a true learning organization approach is adopted, the subsequent students and educators who work on related issues will also see the need for and promise of change when the time comes to pursue new and different approaches.

The community-building programmer becomes a somewhat unconventional and new kind of educator who works with and through faculty and students to achieve critical learning goals for the institution, as Lloyd-Jones and Smith (1954) suggested.

Examples in Practice

There are innumerable examples to illustrate how conventional and community-building programs would be conceived and implemented. It is also important to recognize that, for purposes of distinction, the following examples will be described as if they are discrete. Actual program implementation is seldom clearly either conventional or community-building in its orientation. Most often there is overlap. Indeed, the overlap will hopefully increase as professionals become more aware of the educational potential and differences in design of each.

Community Service and Service Learning

One of the fastest growing areas of interest on many college campuses today is community service and service learning. For years young and mature citizens have engaged in fundraising for economically depressed families, for illnesses that require more funding for research, and for funds to bolster the services of various community organizations. Today's college-age population is even more interested, with 83 percent of them arriving on campus having completed some form of service in high school (Koch, 2008). It is only natural that these students would want to continue their service involvement while they pursue collegiate studies. The question is, What can a campus do to reinforce and encourage this natural commitment among students?

A programmatic approach to supporting students' interest in service would include establishing an office to serve as a collection place and clearinghouse between agencies in the community needing help and students who are seeking to be of service. The role would primarily be one of assessing student interest, matching it with the needs, establishing cooperation with the community agency, and supporting the logistics necessary for students to get involved. In this programmatic approach, the staff and faculty serve as the experts in identifying the needs of the community, and they offer helpful assistance to students as they find a good fit for their interests. Students in such a model can make a tremendous difference by raising funds (charity and philanthropy) and by volunteering (performing necessary tasks for an agency) to assist agencies that otherwise would not have the resources to get the job done. In this program model, students are satisfied, communities benefit through cheap or free labor, and the institution fulfills its civic mission by placing students in service to the community.

In the community-building program approach to a similar need, the institution and student play very different roles. If community-building were the intent of involving students in the community, students would be more involved in determining the critical needs that begged for their involvement. Students would work with student affairs program staff to assess both campus and external community capacity and then decisions would be made about strategic initiatives that would be undertaken. Students would provide guidance to each other about how to get involved, issues to watch out for, how to establish respectful working relationships, and coaching that would help students begin to understand the deeper issues behind the problem. Today's college campuses are exploding with interest in community service and service learning. Faculty who are eager to engage students more deeply in learning know that going where students' interests and hearts are will reap great benefits in learning. This form of service involvement builds the capacity of the individual, it informs the institution through being involved in the community, and it expands the potential of the community to remedy its own problems. Faculty, students, and community are mutual learners in the process of discovering solutions to persistent public problems.

Leadership Development

Most colleges and universities have noted developing leadership or promoting civic participation as part of their institutional missions from their very founding. As leadership learning has grown in popularity as a critical educational outcome, the press to provide explicit leadership development opportunities has grown dramatically. Advocacy for comprehensive leadership program design (Roberts, 1981, 2007) calls for the provision of more than just an annual student leadership conference, workshop, or other isolated event. It challenges designers to cast the net wider to include a variety of other possibilities.

Any comprehensive leadership development program will begin with the institutional mission as it relates to developing leadership among students. The specific views of leadership as reflected in the institutional mission statement, subsequent planning documents, and critical constituent opinions would be considered. Once such an analysis of leadership development has been undertaken, planners would likely look at existing and potential new leadership development opportunities that could be orchestrated within a framework of serving multiple populations through multiple strategies and with multiple purposes being served. In many college and university settings, staff will conceive the comprehensive plan, even though student input may be solicited. If this is true, and it is coupled with a focus on students' acquisition of abilities and insights, the leadership development program is likely to be conventional in design and should be planned and implemented according to Saunders and Cooper's (2001) criteria.

A community-building approach to comprehensive leadership programs would include critical aspects of design such as establishing institutional context and commitment just like that above. In addition, a community-building approach will include institutional culture as a powerful dimension of leadership learning. When a broad array of offerings are included in a series or framework, consistent and repeated messages will help to unify and will reinforce the common lessons communicated through the different activities and initiatives of the comprehensive program. In addition, a leadership program that develops community would establish ongoing ways for participants to see one another and support one another's work, and would allow reflective time for participants to discern insights about leadership learning from their experiences. As these reflection opportunities are repeated and deepened over time, students begin to understand the enhanced contributions they can make when they act on the convictions that emerge through their experiences.

Living-Learning Experiences

There are several different models for living-learning programs in residence halls on campuses that have at least a portion of their students living in residence. Possibilities include residential colleges, theme learning halls, first-year student interest groups, cluster courses, and others. Again, living-learning programs can be pursued either as conventional programs, or they may embrace a community-building purpose.

In a conventional living-learning program approach, a planning team would be assembled and would likely include multiple constituencies, such as students, faculty, and staff. The presumed purpose would be to enhance the climate in the residence halls by providing students with opportunities to focus on common purposes and educational goals. A living-learning program would allow students to have a choice in place of residence, and it would encourage participation in a mutual set of curricular and co-curricular experiences. Through placing students together around common interests and engaging them in working together, students would be much more likely to establish relationships and important connections with each other.

A community-building approach to living-learning would rely more on identification of mutual needs and interests of a variety of stakeholders. While students, faculty, and staff are likely to be involved in the conventional program approach, the community-building strategy would exploit the critical interests of a variety of those involved. The presumption of what themes or issues are attractive to students would be supplemented by an analysis of the institution's core concerns and the personal and social change concerns of students, faculty, and staff. The staff role in a community-building program would be different than in a conventional program. If students are expected to engage fully and take responsibility for their own learning within the residential community, the residence staff would focus more on the group process and network of resources. There is considerable evidence (e.g., Kuh, Kinzie, Schuh, & Whitt, 2005) that faculty on campuses are increasingly concerned about active engagement of students and that they are eager to enhance learning through partnerships that take learning into environments beyond the classroom. What is important in this kind of scenario is that faculty express their interests, couple them with student aspirations for living in a high-quality and comfortable environment, and utilize the expertise of student affairs staff in planning and overseeing the initiative. A community-building approach to living-learning would be different in the depth of engagement, the inclusion of multiple concerns and interests, and it would define all working to enhance the to deal with the real living issues that they face on a daily basis.

Campus Partnerships and Their Impact on Community

There are also many opportunities that fall outside the boundaries of what is typically seen as student affairs work, and these connective opportunities may be some of the most influential in fostering community. One unlikely but effective partnership focused on educating students about ethical acquisition and use of intellectual resources (Swartz, Carlisle, & Uyeki, 2007). In this example, library staff at the University of California, Los Angeles, reached out to the student affairs staff to develop an information campaign to help students understand the importance of careful use of library and other academic resources when working on projects, papers, and other course assignments. The result was an effective educational intervention that unified administrative areas and built a stronger community of scholars.

The physical environment is another resource for community building. New construction can create visual approaches that invite community members to join with others. Lounges, art, or pleasing exterior views encourage pauses as we move from place to place. Exceptional architectural design can cause passers-by to stop to soak in the beauty, dimension, color, and relationship among the design elements. Although many older campuses are somewhat confined by their buildings and landscapes, modest, intentional redesign can enhance any setting. The addition of park benches and gathering places and the inclusion of small gardens can create opportunities for pause in what is normally a very fast-paced academic life. Placement of convenience services, such as bookstores, cleaners, recreation facilities, and entertainment centers, can either draw the community together or divide it into separate enclaves and territories. The appearance of these gathering places can be designed to invite people either to linger or to move on as quickly as possible. In the specific case of recreation, having healthy food alternatives in an area contiguous to exercise facilities can encourage spontaneous interaction, relaxation, and encounters with others that demonstrate the value of all.

These examples were selected to demonstrate two major themes that are characteristic of many of the programs provided through student affairs—ethics and social justice and establishing environments that provide opportunities for deeper engagement in learning for all students. They may also provide primary opportunities for cooperation among academic and other colleagues.

Service, study abroad, and leadership learning each has the potential to introduce students to previously unrecognized aspects of themselves, thus drawing attention to issues of social justice. Students' insight about the inherent and natural strengths of communities can be a profound revelation that reinforces the worth and dignity of those they serve. Immersing themselves in a country where language, culture, and patterns of human interaction can jar students into examining assumptions about others that they harbored based on language, religious, or other differences. The inevitable experience of getting lost in foreign environments results in students' reaching out for help from others whom they might never have encountered otherwise, and it has the potential to demonstrate the universal goodness and willingness to help among others. Leadership learning can help students realize that leading is not the purview of a privileged few but, given the opportunity, exists as a shared behavior among all human beings. These are social justice questions—questions that are not easily raised through reading texts or discussing abstract concepts in the absence of an experiential base.

Living-learning programs, the library intellectual property example, and the architecture and landscape of our campuses are strategies that can be used to spur deeper engagement in learning. Living-learning experiences and enhancing the focus on academic integrity through a library–student affairs partnership have specific content that increase the potential for students to acquire knowledge and understanding. The architecture and landscape of our environments present symbols of community and provide places to stop, connect with others, and reflect on our learning. Each of these elements has high probability of enhancing student learning, even though no academic credit is required to validate it.

Summary

Schwab's (2008) partnership or stakeholder commitment for global community proposed that "it is in everyone's enlightened interest to stick together to tackle the real global problems, such as nuclear proliferation, terrorism, crime, the destruction of our limited groundwater, crop and grazing land, marine life, biodiversity, pandemics or our life-enabling atmosphere" (p. 7–8). These challenges have no borders, and graduates throughout global higher education will need to recognize them as problems we face in concert rather than in competition with others.

Student affairs practice has a long history of attention to the complex dynamics that enhance learning and development among students in higher education. One stimulus for student learning is what we have come to recognize as extracurricular or co-curricular programs, but different student affairs professionals may approach these programs in very different ways. The purpose of this chapter was not to advocate any one approach to programming but to identify the different philosophical roots, the processes, and the purposes involved in two different models. Both approaches can be effective and can enhance learning, but it is important to know which is most likely to be appropriate to the specific circumstances one encounters.

Criteria for the design and implementation of conventional programs are provided using the work of Saunders and Cooper (2001). By contrast, the community-building model is offered as a way to convey information as well as establish common aspirations, and build communities to support these purposes. Informed professionals will look carefully at the opportunities and purposes they seek to achieve as they determine which model is more appropriate for their specific situations. Examples have been provided throughout this chapter to illustrate how one might approach various programs using each of these models.

The program versus community-building program analysis may seem as if it is only common sense. However, how often do professionals actually analyze the degree to which the goal is simply providing a program versus fostering community on the campus? If the circumstances suggest that community building may be critical for the campus—and that the time can be taken— then what are the determining factors that enhance the potential for community-building success?

The changes that we see in the global community tie our destinies together in ways that make the need for learning across cultures, politics, religions, and nations more important than ever before. By being more intentional in the design of programs, student affairs professionals are more likely to contribute to student experiences that help them embrace a broader global perspective, that demonstrate the power of community, and that draw students to create a sustainable future for us all.

References

Astin, A. W. (1993). *What matters in college? Four critical years revisited.* San Francisco: Jossey-Bass.

Astin, A. W., & Astin, H. S. (Eds.). (2000). *Leadership reconsidered: Engaging higher education in social change.* Battle Creek, MI: W. K. Kellogg Foundation.

Berkowitz, A. D. (1997). From reactive to proactive prevention: Promoting an ecology of health on campus. In P. C. Rivers & E. R. Shore (Eds.), *Substance abuse on campus: A handbook for college and university personnel* (pp. 119–139). Westport, CT: Greenwood Press.

Berkowitz, A. D. (1998). The proactive prevention model: Helping students translate healthy beliefs into healthy actions. *About Campus, 3*(4), 26–27.

Boyer, E. L. (1990). *Campus life: In search of community* (Carnegie Foundation for the Advancement of Teaching). Lawrensville, NJ: Princeton University Press.

Brown, J. S. (1997). On becoming a learning organization. *About Campus, 1*(6), 5–10.

Dewey, J. (1923). *Democracy and education.* New York: Macmillan.

Ehrlich, T. (1997). Dewey versus Hutchins: The next round. In R. Orrill (Ed.), *Education and democracy: Re-imagining liberal learning in America* (pp. 225–262). New York: College Entrance Examination Board.

Evans, N. J., & Reason, R. D. (2001). Guiding principles: A review and analysis of student affairs philosophical statements. *Journal of College Student Development, 42*(4), 359–377.

Heifetz, R. A. (1994). *Leadership without easy answers.* Boston: Harvard University Press.

Jaworski, J. (1998). *Synchronicity: The inner path of leadership.* San Francisco: Berrett-Koehler.

Keeling, R. P. (1998). HIV/AIDS in the academy: Engagement and learning in a context of change. *NASPA Leadership for a Healthy Campus Newsletter, 1.*

Koch, W. (2008, March 12). Internet spurs upswing in volunteerism. *USA Today.*

Komives, S. R., Lucas, N., and McMahon, T. R. (2007). *Exploring leadership for college students who want to make a difference* (2nd ed.). San Francisco: Jossey-Bass.

Kuh, G. D., Kinzie, J., Schuh, J. H., & Whitt, E. J. (2005). *Student success in college.* San Francisco: Jossey-Bass.

Lewin, K. (1952). Group decision and social change. In G. E. Swanson, T. M. Newcomb, & E. L. Hartley (Eds.), *Readings in social psychology* (2nd ed., pp. 459–473). New York: Holt.

Lloyd-Jones, E. M. (1989). Foreword. In D. C. Roberts (Ed.), *Designing campus activities to foster a sense of community* (New Directions for Student Services No. 48, pp. 1–3). San Francisco: Jossey-Bass.

Lloyd-Jones, E. M., & Smith, M. R. (1954). *Student personnel work as deeper teaching.* New York: HarperCollins.

McDonald, W. M. (2002). *Creating campus community: In search of Ernest Boyer's legacy.* San Francisco: Jossey-Bass.

Peck, M. S. (1987). Stages of community-making. In M. S. Peck (Ed.), *The different drum: Community making and peace* (pp. 86–106). New York: Simon & Schuster.

Pope, R. L., Reynolds, A. L. & Mueller, J. A. (2004). *Multicultural competence in student affairs.* San Francisco: Jossey-Bass.

Roberts, D. C. (1981). *Student leadership programs in higher education.* Washington, DC: American College Personnel Association.

Roberts, D. C. (1998). Student learning was always supposed to be the core of our work—what happened? *About Campus, 3*(3), 18–22.

Roberts, D. C. (2007). *Deeper learning in leadership.* San Francisco: Jossey-Bass.

Rost, J. (1991). *Leadership for the twenty-first century.* New York: Praeger.

Saunders, S. A., & Cooper, D. L. (2001). Programmatic interventions: Translating theory to practice. In R. B. Winston, D. G. Creamer, & T. K. Miller (Eds.), *The student affairs administrator: Educator, leader, and manager* (pp. 309–340). New York: Brunner-Routledge.

Schlossberg, N. K. (1989). Marginality and mattering: Key issues in building community. In D. C. Roberts (Ed.), *Designing campus activities to foster a sense of community* (New Directions for Student Services No. 48, pp. 5–15). San Francisco: Jossey-Bass.

Schwab, K. (2008, September). *Innovation, collaboration and new forms of global governance.* Speech given at the World Economic Forum, Foreign Affairs University Beijing.

Senge, P. M. (1990). *The fifth discipline: The art and practice of the learning organization.* New York: Doubleday.

Swartz, P. S., Carlisle, B. A., & Uyeki, E. C. (2007). Libraries and student affairs: Partners for success. *Reference Services Review, 35*(1), 109–122.

CHAPTER TWENTY-SEVEN

PROFESSIONALISM

Jan Arminio

Having been employed in student affairs for over twenty years in the same position after completion of a master's degree, Pat directs the office in a well-defined, structured way. Pat attends the same association conference year after year and does not adopt "fads." New professionals and graduate students complain that Pat is inflexible. Weekly reports and inventories are due every Monday by 9:00AM regardless of any unexpected campus events or crises the previous day or week. For example, Pat expected an inventory of a campus lounge space, including ping pong table equipment, even though supervisees had been dealing with the aftermath of a campus fight that morning. Moreover, applicants for open positions must have specific experiences—"none of this transferrable skills stuff."

Chris has served in several positions in student affairs over the course of ten years. With each position came increasing and new responsibilities. Contemplating entering a doctoral program, Chris not only attends conferences but is a leader in a national professional association. Constantly adapting what is discussed at conferences and in the literature to practice, Chris appears to others as creative. For example, Chris is implementing a restorative justice philosophy in student conduct programs. Employees in Chris's area have job swap days to learn more about each other's work.

Pat and Chris are meant to represent polar opposites. Often, in student affairs, professionals are judged along a Pat-and-Chris–like continuum. Is Pat a professional? Is Chris more professional than Pat? Where might each of us stand along such a continuum? In reality, do most of us represent a professional life somewhere between Pat's and Chris's? This chapter covers the general characteristics that define a profession, professionals, and professionalism, as well as specific characteristics of professionalism in the context of student affairs. Given the connection of occupation to personal and social identity and the critical nature of student affairs work to student success, the exploration of professionalism is significant to the intent of this volume. What is it we should know, How should we perform, and How are we to be with others? To encourage discussion and reflection, questions about Pat and Chris in relation to professionalism pepper this chapter.

What Is It to Be a Professional?

The word *professional* comes from the root *profess*, meaning to declare openly or affirm allegiance to knowledge claims (Hoad, 1986). Whereas the liberal arts are grounded in a philosophy of broad knowledge and transferable skills (Association of American Colleges and Universities, 2008), being a professional necessitates a commitment to a more specific knowledge base and particular skill sets, and values. Choosing a profession assumes a commitment to not only an occupation but also to principles that guide a professional and the profession itself. In essence, professionals make public their selections by being seen in the context of their work and by doing their work. This public affirmation is not to be taken lightly, but should be made with serious sincerity. Being a professional requires being concerned with the generativity of the profession by preparing the profession for the future; who will future professionals be, and how should they be prepared for professional work?

In what ways are the terms *professional* and *career* related? According to Zunker (2006) historically, a career was understood as a pattern of associated jobs undertaken across a lifetime of work. Currently, however, one's career is more likely to be experienced through "multiple career choices" (p. 9). These career choices could be in the same profession (as when student affairs professionals shift to become graduate faculty and teach about student affairs) or in different professions (as when student affairs professionals leave the profession to work in human resources). A professional may make several career choices during a lifetime.

Defining a Profession and Professionalism

Although a profession is an occupation, not all occupations are professions. Professions can be differentiated from occupations in that professions have:

- A systematic theory and body of knowledge on which the work is based
- Work that is relevant to the values of society
- A significant amount of required specialized training that involves the manipulation of ideas and symbols rather than or in addition to physical objects
- An understanding of the values, norms, and conceptions of the workplace subculture
- An emphasis on service and public good as primary work goals
- Autonomy in dictating qualifications for entrance and how performance is judged
- Full-time work group members who possess long-term commitments and compelling interests in the profession

- A community, common identity, and common destiny, including agreed-upon role definitions for members, a common language of the profession that is only partly understood by nonmembers, some power over members, and a system for socialization of new members into the profession
- A code of ethics (Pavalko, 1971; Penney, 1972; Rhoades, 2007; Wilensky, 1964)

The more an occupation possesses the above features, the more likely it is to be considered a profession. A substantial literature base exists verifying that "higher education scholarship and teaching are considered a profession" in that the above criteria are met (Rhoades, 2007, p. 120).

A critical process in the professionalization of a work group is the socialization of new members. Tull (2006) defined professional socialization as the introduction and assimilation to work. In student affairs, graduate programs provide initial introduction and assimilation functions. Because people are often selective about the cultural norms they acquire, occupational socialization must be omnipresent and occur both in formal training programs (such as graduate programs) and informally through actual work (Pavalko, 1971). Reference groups are a primary source of the informal socialization process. Mentors, peers, and colleagues serve as reference group participants from which new work group members arrive at a judgment about the extent to which they have mastered their own professional knowledge and skills. This comparison is important in that it serves to "encourage self selection out of the occupation as well as induce a change in orientation toward the occupation itself" (Pavalko, 1971, p. 98). Such an orientation is often referred to as "identification with the profession." Continuation of the socialization process to reinforce group norms and deepen professional identification can also occur through codes of ethics, certification or licensing procedures, collegial evaluations, doctoral programs, and memberships in occupational associations.

Occupational (or professional) associations serve as sources of identity through their association meetings, rites, and traditions, which minimize competition and emphasize unity (Pavalko 1971; Wilensky, 1964). Subsequently, associations are able to exert at least some control over members by determining criteria of initial and continued membership. Pavalko acknowledged that this can instigate torn loyalties between the employee and an employer. In fact, he specifically noted higher education as a place where fractured identities and loyalties are particularly recognized. Nonetheless, "Associations function as a source of identity, a way of maintaining a conception of oneself as a member of a particular organization" (Pavalko, 1971, p. 107).

In essence, then, a professional is a member of a profession who has been trained to accomplish the work of the profession, follows the norms and ethics of that profession, identifies with the profession through a professional association, and has a long-term commitment to the profession (Pavalko). How does this relate to Pat and Chris? What if Pat's reference group (mentors, peers, colleagues) behave similarly to Pat? Perhaps Pat compares and contrasts behaviors, but views those of some colleagues as faddish. Although both are members of professional associations, Chris serves in a leadership role and implements knowledge gained from professional meetings and current literature. Therefore, Chris can be seen as exhibiting an identity more congruent with the profession, gained through socialization with professional reference groups. How might specific characteristics of student affairs as a profession within the context of higher education more specifically relate to Pat and Chris?

Student Affairs as a Profession

Other chapters of this volume describe the history of student affairs and its movement from an occupation to an emergent profession (see Chapter Four). However, it is important that those entering the profession understand in what ways student affairs meets the criteria of a profession and how student affairs struggles as a profession because it is future professionals who must address these limitations. What follows is a discussion of the degree to which student affairs possesses the characteristics of a profession.

Knowledge and Theory Base

Guiding documents in student affairs, such as the *Student Personnel Point of View Statements*, *Principles of Good Practice*, *Statements of Students Rights and Freedoms*, and others described in this volume, offer guidance for the profession's knowledge base. This volume is itself evidence that the student affairs profession has a theoretical foundation and body of knowledge on which student affairs work is based. There are significant quantity and quality of research by noted and emerging scholars who study the profession of student affairs (Rhoades, 2007). This research includes studies, conducted through a variety of methodologies, of student development theory, educational practices, campus environments, social justice, student characteristics, assessment in higher education, and socialization of the student affairs profession. A number of national journals provide opportunities for the distribution of knowledge and theory (e.g., the *Journal of College and University Housing Officers-International*, *Journal of Student Affairs Research and Practice*, *Journal of Higher Education*, and *Review of Higher Education*). Prominent regional and state journals also exist (e.g., the *College Student Affairs Journal*, *Vermont Connection Journal*, and *Georgia Journal of College Student Affairs*) as well as special-topic journals (e.g., the *Journal About Women in Higher Education* and *Michigan Journal of Community Service Learning*). These also include a premier academic national journal, the *Journal of College Student Development* published by the American College Personnel Association (ACPA) College Student Educators International. A number of magazines promote effective practice, including those that are of national, general interest, such as *About Campus;* those of special interest to student affairs leaders, such as the *Leadership Exchange;* and trade magazines geared toward those employed in particular functional areas, such as *Programming Magazine* and the *Bulletin*. Chris reads current professional literature, incorporating what is learned into practice. There is no evidence that Pat does. Perhaps Pat is overwhelmed with work responsibilities or with the amount of professional literature available. According to Hirt and Creamer (1998), associations "bombard" members with literature, creating an additional source of stress as members try to find time to "read, digest, and operationalize so much information" (p. 56).

Work Valued by Society

American society not only values education and higher education (U. S. Department of Education, 2006) but also values the philosophy of educating the whole person, a foundation of student affairs work. However, it is also true that though valued, public financial support has decreased for higher education so that the responsibility for funding higher education has fallen more on students and private sources. Simultaneously, stakeholders are requiring increased evidence that students gain from higher education what institutions say they will gain (Rhoades, 2007; U.S. Department of Education). Furthermore, it is also the case that the education occurring in classrooms is still more highly regarded than that occurring outside the classroom. Both Pat and Chris believe that what they do is valued by their institutions and that they are competent. How might they find evidence that this is the case? Comparing their work to professional standards is one way.

Specialized Training

The existence of professional standards is an important criterion for determining whether a burgeoning field is a profession (Miller, 1984; Paterson & Carpenter, 1989). Standards in student affairs are written by a consortium of nearly forty professional associations called the Council for the Advancement of Standards in Higher Education (CAS)), which was formed in 1979 and has established standards in over thirty areas of higher education(CAS, 2009a). One of those areas is graduate education in student affairs. These standards require that graduate programs offer course content in foundational studies (i.e., history, philosophy, ethics, culture, and research in higher education and particularly student affairs),); course content in professional studies (i.e., basic knowledge of the profession, such as student development theory, student characteristics and effects of college on students, individual and group interventions, organization and administration of student affairs, assessment, evaluation, and research); and three hundred hours of supervised practice. This practice provides opportunities for the application of foundational and professional studies and student affairs values and norms, as well as for the conceptualization of workplace subcultures. Obviously, graduate programs play a significant role in preparing new professionals for work in higher education.

Receiving a graduate education in student affairs from a program that complies with CAS standards at an accredited institution is the best means to prepare for entrance into student affairs (Janosik, Carpenter, & Creamer, 2006). Currently there are 140 master's programs and 57 doctoral programs listed in the American College Personnel Association's (ACPA) graduate program directory (see www.myacpa.org/c12/directory.cfm). However, it is possible to acquire positions in student affairs without graduating from a program that meets these standards or without any graduate education. And even with a student affairs–related degree, there is continuous training necessary to maintain professional competence (Janosik et al., 2006). Increasingly, the doctoral degree functions as a gatekeeper to positions of advancement and leadership in student affairs (Hamrick & Hemphill, 2009). Both Pat and Chris have graduated from graduate programs that comply with CAS standards. Pat finds contentment in work, so has no desire for more education or more responsibilities. Chris finds rejuvenation in discussing "big ideas" with others, initiating change, and taking risks. With what we now know about Pat and Chris, how might the profession judge their performances?

Judging Qualifications and Performance

Rhoades (2007) included the autonomy to dictate qualifications and how performance is judged as an important feature in identifying professions. He argued that although student affairs professionals have many of the characteristics of faculty, they lack academic freedom and intellectual property rights. Also, employment falls under the category of work for hire, meaning that typically, student affairs educators are hired, fired, and reviewed by supervisors, not peers. Nonetheless, CAS standards describe in qualitative terms professional qualifications and guidelines for quality practice in student affairs. It is through standards made autonomously and in accordance with laws and statutes that professionals can compare and judge the quality of their work. From this comparison to standards, professionals set development goals and achieve those goals for continuous improvement. Standards also serve as guides that explain expectations to new professionals and inform professionals when initiating new programs, enhancing existing programs, and accepting new responsibilities (Arminio, 2009). How might Pat and Chris behave in relation to standards? Pat appreciates standards and benchmarks as they provide structure, but is less likely to create innovative programs. Appreciating the insight assessment can offer, Chris considers nuances of how standards are to be translated to the mission of the institution and the organization.

Full-Time Work Group That Has a Long-Term Commitment

The Bureau of Labor Statistics (2009) estimated that there are roughly 443,000 people in the United States employed as education administrators. However, it does not differentiate academic affairs from student affairs. ACPA boasts 9,000 members, and the National Association of Student Personnel Administrators—Student Affairs Administrators in Higher Education (NASPA) has 11,000 members (though many student affairs professionals belong to both). The notion that nearly every U.S. institution employs student affairs educators justifies the claim that student affairs is a national profession. Interestingly, however, undergraduate students, who represent a major market for recruiting student affairs professionals, are largely unaware of the profession (Phelps Tobin, 1998). Unfortunately, as Ortiz and Shintaku (2004) wrote, there is a lack of racial diversity in student affairs—a point with which Taub and

McEwen (2006) concurred—noting that the percentage of student affairs professionals of color is less than that of college graduates of color.

Simultaneously, the reasons people enter the profession are varied. Phelps Tobin (1998) noted that people enter by accident, as a result of recruitment efforts and the influence of role models, and as a natural extension of the undergraduate experience. Taub and McEwen (2006) found that graduate students had entered graduate programs in student affairs because they were encouraged by a specific person and found working on a college campus personally fulfilling. Even so, there is concern regarding the apparent high attrition rate of professionals leaving the student affairs profession (Hamrick & Hemphill, 2009; Renn & Jessup-Anger, 2008; Rosser & Javinar, 2003; Tull, 2006), even though Lorden (1998) questioned this concern. Although recent and accurate documentation of the attrition rate is difficult to find, historical data indicate that anywhere from 33 to 65 percent of graduate students with student affairs–related degrees had left the student affairs profession in one to ten years (Burns, 1982, as cited in Hamrick & Hemphill, 2009; Holmes, Verrier, & Chisholm, 1983, as cited in Hamrick & Hemphill, 2009; Richmond & Sherman, 1991). In contrast, Taub and McEwen found that current master's students felt confident about staying in the profession. In any case, more recent research focuses on reasons that people leave the profession. These reasons include inadequate or inexperienced supervision (Renn & Jessup-Anger, 2008; Rosser & Javinar, 2003; Tull, 2006); the relatively flat nature of student affairs organizations, which limits upward mobility (i.e., large numbers of entry-level positions with fewer mid-level and senior-level opportunities) (Hirt & Creamer, 1998; Lorden, 1998); and role ambiguity (Ward, 1995). There is mixed evidence as to whether perceived low pay is a factor in attrition rates in student affairs (Lorden, 1998; Rosser & Javinar, 2003). Consequently, it is unclear whether or not student affairs meets the professional criterion of its members' demonstrating a long-term commitment. What can be said of Pat and Chris's long-term commitment? Pat has been in the profession twenty years. But is being organized, remaining in one's occupation, and attending conferences yearly sufficient to be a professional? Chris has held several positions within a ten-year span. Are these shorter-term commitments to various positions a concern?

Community, Common Identity, and Control Over Members

Carpenter (1991) identified three roles of a professional community: (1) sharing knowledge, goals, and objectives with clarity and coherence so that they can be discussed and examined by members; (2) creating policies regarding professional behavior and enforcing them; and (3) offering means of socializing and regenerating new members. Attending an opening session of a national conference provides ample opportunity to experience the professional community, common identity, and common destiny of student affairs professionals. There are a number of professional associations within the profession of student affairs. Usually these are differentiated as generalist organizations and organizations that represent specialist or functionalist aspects of student affairs work (Hirt & Creamer, 1998). Generalist organizations include ACPA and

NASPA. Functionalist associations include the Association of College and University Housing Officers-International (ACUHO-I), the National Association for Campus Activities (NACA), the Association for Fraternity and Sorority Advisors (AFA), the Association of College Unions-International (ACUI), as well as many others. Although membership in professional associations is highly recommended, Hirt and Creamer (1998) wrote that professional associations place additional demands on professionals because much of an association's work is accomplished by members who are employed full-time. Members manage committees and task forces; edit, review, and disseminate scholarship and other information; and sponsor conferences, trainings, and meetings for professional associations. On the other hand, student affairs professional associations conduct critical work on behalf of the profession. Besides promoting professional socialization, development, and a common sense of identity, they advocate on behalf of members on issues such as government policy decisions (Moore & Neuberger, 1998). Due to a concern for resources, there has been discussion regarding the consolidation of the general professional associations (Coomes, Wilson, & Gerda, 2003). In 2008, ACPA and NASPA formed a joint task force to contemplate the future of the student affairs profession and to address joint efforts.

Several authors have stressed the important connection between a professional and his or her profession. Case study analysis reveals that congruence between who one is, what is valued, and how one works is "paramount to job effectiveness and personal satisfaction" (Ortiz & Shintaku, 2004, p. 167). Ortiz and Martinez (2009) implored new student affairs professionals to develop professional identities and then enact these in coherent and consistent ways. Ortiz and Shintaku wrote, "Identity and work are intertwined, primarily due to a society that often equates identity with occupation" (p. 163). How might Pat and Chris's social identities influence their identification with the profession? Chris is younger and at times still misidentified as a student, whereas Pat is older and recently returned to work after recuperating from illness. Chris grew up in a small town, raised by working-class parents, and was the first in his family to attend college. Pat's parents were school teachers. They moved frequently once Pat's father became a principal. How might these experiences influence their professional lives? "The importance of one's family background, personal identity, educational history, and interests cannot be overstated" (Magolda & Carnaghi, 2004, p. 205). Yet a professional identity should not overwhelm the personal self. Collins (1991) reminded readers that due to past discrimination White people are more likely to "be" their careers whereas people of color *have* careers. When oppression limits professional opportunities to certain people, an integrated identity with a profession is difficult. "The integration of identity into the work environment proves to be most challenging for students who have social identities that are historically disenfranchised. . . . Identity influences professional lives" (Ortiz & Shintaku, p. 170).

Because student affairs professional associations are predominately self-regulatory, and because the socialization of new and current members into the profession is primarily voluntary, professional associations do not have significant power over members (Rhoades, 2007). Although ACPA (2007) has created a professional competencies document, there is no process to certify or license student affairs professionals or graduate programs. Hence the gatekeepers to the profession are employers rather than professional associations or certifying bodies. Returning to Pat and Chris, there are few requirements from the profession that would prevent them from keeping their positions. Therefore, their own expectations and those of their supervisors are most critical to their professional growth and continued employment.

Code of Ethics

Most student affairs professional associations have ethical statements or codes of ethics (see Chapter Six). CAS created a statement identifying common elements of its members' codes of ethics (2009b). These commonalities dictate that professionals:

- Take responsibility for their actions and support other people's freedom of choice
- Pledge to do no harm
- Engage in actions that contribute to the heath and well-being of others
- Promote human dignity and endorse fairness
- Are faithful to obligations
- Convey truth
- Promote relationships among people and foster community

Codes of ethics in student affairs stress self-regulation and self-consultation. They typically do not impose sanctions on members who act unethically. Both Pat and Chris believe they practice ethically. They are honest and responsible stewards of institutional resources. Also, both abide by institutional policies, laws, and statutes. Nonetheless, the ACPA code of ethics stated that "student affairs professionals will maintain and enhance professional effectiveness by continually improving skills and acquiring new knowledge" (2006, p. 2). Although Pat attends conferences, we do not know if new knowledge is gained or utilized; but we do know this of Chris. Overwhelming work is not an excuse for failing to continually improve skills and knowledge.

As the above discussion demonstrates, the student affairs profession meets some of the criteria for being a profession, but not all. For example, people can enter the profession without formal training. Current and future professionals will need to address this concern. In what ways does the lack of formal training and subsequent development influence professional competence? How are we to judge the competence of Pat and Chris?

Characteristics of the Competent Student Affairs Professional

Competencies are features that define a professional as capable. They include not only what one knows but also what one can perform and how one is with others. Competencies are often defined in relation to knowledge, awareness, and skills (Pope, Reynolds, & Mueller, 2004). Being competent is relevant to all student affairs educators.

What One Knows and What One Can Do

A number of authors have proposed competencies necessary to effectively serve as a student affairs professional (e.g., Janosik et al., 2006; ACPA Professional Competencies Task Force, 2007; Pope, Reynolds, & Mueller, 2004). Exhibit 27.1 provides details for three articulations of core competencies in student affairs. It is important to note that there is a lack of definitional clarity in relation to competencies. However, each of the conceptualizations in Exhibit 27.1 provides guidance related to areas in which student affairs professionals should be competent.

Basic competencies can lead to more complex capacities. To illustrate the depth of knowledge and skills necessary for a lifetime of student affairs work, the Professional Competencies Task Force of the ACPA (2007) identified basic, intermediate, and advanced competencies. Beyond simply demonstrating skills, a defining feature of a professional is the ability to know when and how to act, using judgment or instinct. Wilensky (1964) acknowledged the role of tacit knowledge, subliminal perceptions, and the "aura of mystery" (p. 149) in professional work. Professionals know how to make a decision from "a complex pattern of things without being able to specify by what features" (p. 149). How might Pat or Chris know when an exception to a policy should be made? Should Pat allow exceptions to due dates depending on campus crises? How do they decide when a student is a threat to others or when a student is ready for a leadership position? Certainly data, policy, and procedures help determine these decisions, but so too does professional judgment. Tacit insight requires a breadth

EXHIBIT 27.1.   STUDENT AFFAIRS COMPETENCIES.

Categories of Competencies	Pope, Reynolds, and Mueller (2004)	APCA (2007)	Janosik, Carpenter, and Creamer (2006)
Foundations			History, values, and philosophy
Leadership, management, and administration	Administration and management	Leadership, management, and administration	Management, administration, technology, and organizational development
Pluralism	Multicultural awareness, knowledge, and skills	Pluralism and inclusion	Culture, diversity, and multiculturalism
Helping skills	Advising and helping	Advising and helping	
Assessment and research	Assessment and research	Assessment, evaluation, and research	Assessment and research practices
Teaching	Teaching and training	Teaching	
Ethics and the law	Ethics and professional standards	Ethics and legal foundations	Law, legislation, and policy
Students	Theory and transitions	Student learning and development	Student development, characteristics, environment, and learning

and depth of knowledge and experience that includes the ability to grasp nuances. As Hamrick and Hemphill (2009) noted, "Mere accumulation of years does not necessarily yield maturity, years of experience provide opportunities to test and refine one's skills, capabilities, and instincts" (p. 153). Such testing and refinement can lead to readiness for positions of increasing responsibility. These positions demand expertise in supervision, policy and procedure development and enforcement, budgeting (Hamrick & Hemphill, 2009), managing crises, (Zdziarski & Watkins, 2009), and being proficient in using technology as an educational and administrative tool (Engstrom & Kruger, 1997; Renn & Zeligman, 2005).

Extending Boyer's (1990) work that promoted a broader view of what scholarship is in academia, Carpenter (2001) urged professionals to reconsider scholarly practice in student affairs. He proposed that student affairs scholarly practice should be intentional, theory and data based, peer reviewed, collaborative, unselfish, open to change, careful and skeptical, tolerant of differing perspectives, attentive to regeneration, and autonomous within institutional contexts. Scholarly practice fulfills obligations to students, colleagues, the employing institution, and the profession. Carpenter (2001) wrote, "Student affairs workers owe it to their clients to have engaged in appropriate professional education and preparation and to continue this education as long as they practice" (p. 311). Being a scholarly professional means having the courage to act ethically and competently. When professionals do not know how to proceed, they should engage in a period of careful thought, seeking guidance from scholarly literature, colleagues, and current data. In what ways has either Pat or Chris recognized that consultation with others, including scholarly literature, is warranted? Recognizing what one does not know and understanding that others can offer ideas for improved work are critical to professional life. It appears that Pat is lacking in these areas.

How One Is with Others

What one knows, what one can perform, and how one is with others are not mutually exclusive. Those with whom we work and live experience us as integrated selves. For this reason, and due to past inequities of access to higher education, authors have advocated that student affairs professionals be competent in multiculturalism. Pope, Reynolds, and Mueller (2004) advocated integrating multicultural competencies into all other necessary skills, including administration and management, helping and advising, and assessment and research. As is covered in Chapter Nineteen of this volume, becoming multiculturally competent is a part of a developmental process that necessitates taking risks in exploring others and the self to create a "culture of integrity" in which one behaves according to one's values (Chavez, Guido-Dibrito, & Mallory, 2003, p. 459). Ultimately the professional must be able to "interact effectively and interdependently with diverse others" which assumes "engage[ing] in relationships with others in ways that show respect and understanding of others' perspectives and experiences, but that are also true to one's beliefs" (King & Baxter Magolda, 2005, p. 579). How do Pat and Chris encourage a culture of integrity? Pat's rigid deadlines may indicate a lack of respect by expecting others to adapt to a strictly predetermined structure. Should not Pat consider others' work styles in managing the workplace?

Self-evaluation instruments can identify areas of needed growth in how professionals are with others (CAS, 2009a; McAdams, Foster, & Ward, 2007). The CAS Characteristics of Individual Excellence can be used as such an instrument. It identifies trustworthiness, modeling, fair treatment, and self-reflection as some of the important ways that professionals are to be with others. Which of these elements are areas of needed growth for Pat and Chris? What about areas of strength? How might your evaluation compare with their self-assessments? Who else should be involved in determining professional development needs for Pat and Chris? Tornow, London, and CCL Associates (1998) believed that professionals must initiate feedback from a variety of constituents. What would be an appropriate means for new professionals and graduate students to offer their concerns to Pat, which were mentioned at the beginning of this chapter?

Summary: What Are the Implications of Professionalism?

This chapter examined student affairs in relation to characteristics of a profession and discussed competencies that define professionals. Analysis of professionalism was also provided, and professionalism was considered as it pertains to adhering to the standards of the profession, achieving the competencies of the profession, and working to advance the profession. Professionalism means committing to the profession, students, and institutions with whom we work and being competent and engaged in the work we do. Committing to the profession requires that we as professionals address its deficits. What should the student affairs profession do about people who enter the profession without formal training, the lack of persons of color in the profession, people leaving the profession prematurely, undergraduates who know little of the career opportunities in student affairs, and inadequate supervision? These are our responsibilities now. Ultimately, the tasks of seeking professional development and demonstrating professionalism fall on the professional, with support from professional associations, supervisors, and colleagues. How have Pat and Chris honored their commitment to students, their institutions, and the profession? Do they honor this commitment by having entered the profession through specialized, dictated training that promulgated values, norms, and conceptions of student affairs? Is their performance continually judged by how they apply the current body of knowledge and their compelling interests in conducting work that is valued by society? Do they emphasize the public good as a primary work goal? Are aspects of their identities connected to the profession? How might we answer these questions about ourselves and our colleagues? What will we do about it? All of us take responsibility in promoting the profession by practicing as professionals and demonstrating professionalism.

References

American College Personnel Association (ACPA): College Student Educators International (2006). *Statement of ethical principles and standards.* Retrieved from http://www.myacpa.org/au/documents/EthicsStatement.pdf

American College Personnel Association (ACPA). (2007). *Professional competencies: A report of the steering committee on professional competencies.* Washington, DC: Author.

Arminio, J. (2009). Applying professional standards. In G. S. McClellan & J. Stringer (Eds.), *The handbook of student affairs administration* (3rd ed., pp. 187–205). San Francisco: Jossey-Bass.

Association of American Colleges and Universities (2008, December). Liberal education. Retrieved December 12, 2008, from www.aacu.org/resources/liberaleducation/index.cfm.

Boyer, E. L. (1990). *Scholarship reconsidered: Priorities of the professoriate.* Princeton, NJ: The Carnegie Foundation for the Advancement of Teaching.

Bureau of Labor Statistics, U.S. Department of Labor. (2009, January). Occupational outlook handbook, 2008–09 edition. *Education Administrators.* Retrieved January 9, 2009, from www.bis.gov/oco/ocos007.htm.

Carpenter, D. S. (1991). Student affairs professional: A developmental perspective. In T. K. Miller, R. B. Winston Jr., & Associates (Eds.), *Administration and leadership in student affairs* (pp. 253–278). Muncie, IN: Accelerated Development.

Carpenter, S. (2001). Student affairs scholarship (re?) considered: Toward a scholarship of practice. *College Student Affairs Journal, 42,* 301–318.

Chavez, A. F., Guido-DiBrito, F., & Mallory, S. L. (2003). Learning to value the "other": A framework of individual diversity development. *Journal of College Student Development, 44,* 453–469.

Collins, P. H. (1991). *Black feminist thought: Knowledge, consciousness, and the politics of empowerment.* New York: Routledge.

Coomes, M. D., Wilson, E., & Gerda, J. J. (2003). *Of visions, values, and voices: Consolidating ACPA and NASPA.* Unpublished paper. Bowling Green State University.

Council for the Advancement of Standards in Higher Education (CAS). (2009a). *CAS professional standards for higher education* (7th ed.). Washington, DC: Author.

Council for the Advancement of Standards in Higher Education (CAS). (2009b, January). *Thirty years of professional service.* Retrieved January 12, 2009, from www.cas.edu.

Engstrom, C. M., & Kruger, K. W. (1997). Editors' notes. In C. M. Engstrom & K. W. Kruger (Eds.), *Using technology to promote student learning: Opportunities for today and tomorrow* (New Directions for Student Services No. 78, pp. 1–3). San Francisco: Jossey-Bass.

Hamrick, F. A., & Hemphill, B. O. (2009). Pathways to success in student affairs. In M. J. Amey & L. M. Ressor (Eds.), *Beginning your journey* (3rd ed., pp. 147–171). Washington, DC: National Association of Student Personnel Administrators.

Hirt, J. B., & Creamer, D. G. (1998). Issues facing student affairs professionals: The four realms of professional life. In N. J. Evans & C. E. Phelps Tobin (Eds.), *The state of the art of preparation in student affairs: Another look* (pp. 47–60). Washington, DC: American College Personnel Association.

Hoad, T. F. (Ed.). (1986). *The concise Oxford dictionary of English etymology.* Oxford, NY: Oxford University Press.

Janosik, S. M., Carpenter, S., & Creamer, D. G. (2006). Beyond professional preparation programs: The role of professional associations in ensuring a high-quality workforce. *College Student Affairs Journal, 25,* 228–237.

King, P. M., & Baxter Magolda, M. B. (2005). A developmental model of intercultural maturity. *Journal of College Student Development, 46,* 571–582.

Lorden, L. P. (1998). Attrition in the student affairs profession. *NASPA Journal, 35,* 207–216.

Magolda, P. M., & Carnaghi, J. E. (2004). Preparing the next generation of student affairs professionals. In P. M. Magolda & J. E. Carnaghi (Eds.), *Job one: Experiences of new professionals in student affairs* (pp. 201–228). Lanham, MD: University Press of America.

McAdams, C. R., III, Foster, V. A., & Ward, T. J. (2007). Remediation and dismissal policies in counselor education: Lessons learned from a challenge in federal court. *Counselor Education and Supervision, 46(3)*, 212–229.

Miller, T. K. (1984). Professional standards: Whither thou goest? *Journal of College Student Development, 25*, 412–416.

Moore, L. V., & Neuberger, C. G. (1998). How professional associations are addressing issues in student affairs. In N. J. Evans & C. E. Phelps Tobin (Eds.), *The state of the art of preparation in student affairs: Another look* (pp. 47–60). Washington, DC: American College Personnel Association.

Ortiz, A. M. & Martinez, C. R. (2009). Developing a professional ethic. In M. J. Amey & L. M. Ressor (Eds.), *Beginning your journey* (3rd ed., pp. 39–60). Washington, DC: NASPA.

Ortiz, A. M., & Shintaku, R. H. (2004). Professional and personal identities at the crossroads. In P. M. Magolda & J. E. Carnaghi (Eds.), *Job one: Experiences of new professionals in student affairs* (pp. 163–178). Lanham, MD: University Press of America.

Paterson, B. G. & Carpenter, S. D. (1989). The emerging student affairs profession: What still needs to be done. *NASPA Journal, 27*, 123–127.

Pavalko, R. M. (1971). *Sociology of occupations and professions*. Itasca: IL: F. E. Peacock.

Penney, J. F. (1972). *Perspective and challenge in college personnel work*. Springfield, IL: Charles C. Thomas.

Phelps Tobin, C. E. (1998). Recruiting and retaining qualified graduate students. In N. J. Evans & C. E. Phelps Tobin (Eds.), *The state of the art of preparation and practice in student affairs: Another look* (pp. 83–104). Washington, DC: American College Personnel Association.

Pope, R. L., Reynolds, A. L., & Mueller, J. A. (2004). *Multicultural competence in student affairs*. San Francisco: Jossey-Bass.

Renn, K. A., & Jessup-Anger, E. R. (2008). Preparing new professionals: Lessons for graduate preparation programs from the national study of new professionals in student affairs. *Journal of College Student Development, 49*, 319–335.

Renn, K. A., & Zeligman, D. M. (2005). Learning about technology and student affairs: Outcomes of an online immersion. *Journal of College Student Development, 46*, 547–555.

Rhoades, G. (2007). The study of the academic profession. In P. J. Gumport (Ed.), *Sociology of higher education: Contributions and their contexts* (pp. 113–146). Baltimore, MD: Johns Hopkins University Press.

Richmond, J., & Sherman, K. J. (1991). Student-development preparation and placement: A longitudinal study of graduate students' and new professionals' experiences. *Journal of College Student development, 32*, 8–16.

Rosser, V. J., & Javinar, J. M. (2003). Midlevel student affairs leaders' intentions to leave: Examining the quality of their professional and institutional work life. *Journal of College Student Development, 44*, 813–830.

Taub, D. J., & McEwen, M. K. (2006). Decision to enter the profession of student affairs. *Journal of Counseling Development, 47*, 206–216.

Tornow, W. W., London, M., & CCL Associates. (1998). *Maximizing the value of 360 degree feedback: A process for successful individual and organizational development*. San Francisco: Jossey-Bass.

Tull, A. (2006). Synergistic supervision, job satisfaction, and intention to turnover of new professionals in student affairs. *Journal of College Student Development, 47*, 465–480.

U. S. Department of Education. (2006). *A test of leadership: Charting the future of U. S. higher education*. Washington, DC: Author.

Ward, L. (1995). Role stress and propensity to leave among new student affairs professionals. *NASPA Journals, 33*, 35–44.

Wilensky, H. L. (1964). The professionalization of everyone? *American Journal of Sociology, 2*, 137–158. Retrieved January 13, 2009, from http://www.jstor.org/stable/2775206.

Zdziarski, E. L., & Watkins, D. (2009). What is the crisis management plan at my institution? Crisis management for new professionals. In M. J. Amey & L. M. Ressor (Eds.), *Beginning your journey* (3rd ed., pp. 173–184). Washington, DC: National Association of Student Personnel Administrators.

Zunker, V. G. (2006). *Career counseling: A holistic approach* (7th ed.). Belmont, CA: Thompson.

CHAPTER TWENTY-EIGHT

ACADEMIC AND STUDENT AFFAIRS PARTNERSHIPS

Elizabeth J. Whitt

Only when everyone on campus—particularly academic affairs and student affairs staff—shares the responsibility for student learning will we be able to make significant progress in improving it.

AAHE, ACPA, & NASPA, 1998, P. 1

Not all partnerships are virtuous.

MANNING, KINZIE, & SCHUH, 2006, P. 131

Both of these quotations, one asserting that academic and student affairs collaborations are necessary for fostering student learning and the other a caveat about such collaborations, are relevant to the topic of creating and sustaining academic and student affairs partnerships. This chapter examines the context for calls for such partnerships, considers evidence of their advantages and disadvantages, and offers some practical suggestions for academic and student affairs staff and leaders who seek to form effective partnerships for student learning. Offering advice to leaders facing complex and unpredictable challenges within and outside their organizations, psychologist Karl Weick said, "Refuse to simplify reality . . . [and] leap while looking" (as cited in Coutu, 2003, pp. 86–88). A similar request is appropriate for the reader of this chapter: do not approach this text seeking a recipe for creating academic and

---

This chapter is based on the substantial contributions of Becki Elkins Nesheim, Melanie Guentzel, Angela Kellogg, William McDonald, and Cynthia Wells.

student affairs partnership programs or simple answers to questions about how to create and sustain effective partnerships. Do approach it with a sense of your context and culture and how they might influence applying the information provided here to facilitate partnerships on your campus.

Partnerships for Learning

The beginning of the twenty-first century offers higher education myriad challenges, including shifting student demographics, new competitive demands, complex technological advancements, globalization, and insufficient—and shrinking—funding (Colby, Ehrlich, Beaumont, & Stephens, 2003; U.S. Department of Education, 2006). At the same time, the importance of higher education increases as undergraduate education verges on a "requirement of a fully expressed citizenship" in contemporary society (Shapiro, 2005, p. 8). In a recent address, in fact, President Barack Obama asserted "this country needs and values the talents of every American. That is why we will provide the support necessary for you to complete college and meet a new goal: by 2020, America will once again have the highest proportion of college graduates in the world." (Speech to the Joint Houses of Congress, February 24, 2009)

Nevertheless, evidence of a lack of confidence in higher education's ability and willingness to prepare effective and productive citizens is long-standing and plentiful. Critiques from outside and within the academy have been a consistent feature of the landscape of higher education in the United States for more than two decades (see AAC&U, 2002; ACPA, 1994; Boyer Commission, 1998; Chickering & Gamson, 1987; National Association of State Universities and Land-Grant Colleges [NASULGC], 1997, 1999, 2000; Study Group on the Conditions of Excellence in American Higher Education, 1984; U.S. Department of Education, 2006). Throughout these twenty years of calls for change and accountability for student learning, the message has remained much the same: "[The list of] fissures between higher education's rhetoric and its performance is long, and it is growing. . . . All this has led to a significant gap between the needs of society that should be met by universities and colleges and the actual performance of these institutions" (Newman, Couturier, & Scurry, 2004, p. 67).

Among the perceived barriers to achieving the purposes of higher education is fragmentation of campuses and curricula. For many years, reformers have charged that colleges and universities have become too divided by organizational structure, disciplinary priorities, and competing missions to educate students effectively. Indeed, research on college impact is unequivocal: student success (learning, development, persistence) is associated with seamless learning environments, which are characterized by coherent educational purposes and comprehensive policies and practices designed to achieve those purposes (Kuh, 1996; Kuh, Kinzie, Schuh, Whitt, & Associates, 2005; Pascarella & Terenzini, 1991, 2005).

Research on the impact of college also points to engagement as the primary means by which students learn, develop, and persist in college (Astin, 1993; Kuh et al., 2005; Pascarella & Terenzini, 1991, 2005). Engagement has two key components: (1) the amount of time and effort students put into their studies and other education-related activities, and (2) the allocation of institutional resources for services and learning opportunities that encourage students to participate in and benefit from such activities. Educational practices and conditions, such as purposeful student-faculty contact; active and collaborative learning strategies; and collaboration among faculty, academic affairs units, and student affairs units to produce programs and services, have been associated with high levels of student learning. Summarizing thirty years of research on college impact, Pascarella and Terenzini (2005) noted: "The greatest impact [of college] appears to stem from students' total level of campus engagement, particularly when academic, interpersonal, and extracurricular involvements are mutually reinforcing. [Therefore], the holistic nature of learning suggests a clear need to rethink and restructure highly segmented departmental and program configurations" (p. 647).

Partnership programs between academic and student affairs units have been advocated as one means to create seamless learning environments and foster student engagement. Academic and student affairs partnerships have the potential to create such environments by calling on those who work most closely with students—in class and out of class, and in curricular, co-curricular, and extracurricular activities—to collaborate in designing, implementing, and improving student learning.

The benefits of academic and student affairs partnerships for addressing concerns about fragmentation and effective undergraduate education have been extolled in student affairs literature for many years (AAHE, ACPA, & NASPA, 1998; Blimling, Whitt, & Associates, 1999; Colwell, 2006; Cook & Lewis, 2007; Kezar, 2001, 2003; Kezar, Hirsch, & Burack, 2001; Kolins, 2000; Kuh, 1996; Kuh & Banta, 2000; Kuh et al., 2005; Kuh, Schuh, Whitt, & Associates, 1991; Manning, Kinzie, & Schuh, 2006; Martin & Samels, 2001; Pascarella & Terenzini, 1991, 2005; Schroeder, 1999a, 1999b, 2004; Schuh & Whitt, 1999). A recent publication, for example, compared fully developed academic and student affairs partnerships to Dante's ninth circle of heaven (Cook & Lewis, 2007).

Two aspects of most of this body of literature—with a few exceptions (e.g., Kezar, 2001; Kuh & Banta, 2000; Kuh et al., 1991; Kuh et al., 2005; Manning et al., 2006; Pascarella & Terenzini, 1991, 2005)—are notable here. First, the literature is mainly exhortative rather than based on evidence; most assertions about the effectiveness of partnerships for learning are made without reference to empirical evidence. Second, it seems to assume that partnerships between academic and students affairs are, almost always and almost everywhere, an appropriate response to challenges in facilitating undergraduate success. One could argue that academic and student affairs partnerships have become an all-purpose response to a wide variety of campus issues and student concerns, an end ("Let's create a partnership") rather than a means ("Let's address our students' needs for meaningful community involvement by a sustained, programmatic collaboration between academic and student affairs") (Bourassa &

Kruger, 2001; Kezar et al., 2001). The next section provides a brief overview of the limited research about academic and student affairs partnerships.

Research on Partnership Programs

This section includes a discussion on the benefits of developing partnerships between academic and student affairs. It also includes some of the challenges related to developing such partnerships.

Benefits of Partnerships

As noted above, much of the writing on the value of academic and student affairs partnerships is based on anecdotes and hope, rather than on evidence. A considerable body of literature has emerged, however, on how partnerships are enacted (that is, how they are created and maintained as opposed to how they influence student success). Although most of this work is based on descriptions—rather than studies—of examples of partnerships, when examined holistically it illustrates some of the salient issues that partnerships are intended to address, including improving student access and retention, providing evidence of learning outcomes, coping with financial constraints, and meeting the needs of changing student populations. Examples of the uses of partnerships include assessment and research on students (Kuh & Banta, 2000); early-academic-warning systems (Kuh et al., 2005; Schroeder, 1999a, 1999b); first-year experiences (Kezar, 2001; Schroeder, Minor, & Tarkow, 1999); learning communities (Gabelnick, MacGregor, Matthews, & Leigh Smith, 1990; Kurotsuchi Inkelas & Weisman, 2003; McHugh Engstrom, 2004; Pike, 1999; Shapiro & Levine, 1999; Zheng, Saunders, Shelley, & Whalen, 2002); service learning (Jacoby, 1999); and sexual assault prevention (Yeater, Miltenberger, Laden, Ellis, & O'Donohue, 2001).

One of very few examples of research focused on the creation of academic and student affairs partnerships was a national study conducted by Kezar (2001, 2003). Her survey in 2000 of senior student affairs officers asked about the role of student affairs in collaboration; structural models facilitating collaboration; successful strategies for collaboration; and obstacles to, and outcomes of, collaboration. The respondents to the survey noted that collaborative initiatives were occurring on each of their campuses and identified cooperation, student affairs attitudes, common goals, and personalities as important factors in creating effective partnerships. These data provided insights into the use and success of both cultural and structural strategies in developing and maintaining academic and student affairs partnerships. Cultural strategies were identified as cross-institutional dialogue, staff development, common vision development, common language development, communication strategies, cooperation, faculty attitudes, personalities, redefining mission, student affairs attitudes, and generating enthusiasm. Structural strategies included combined fiscal resources, promotion and tenure requirement changes, reassignment of duties, restructuring, planning, setting expectations, accountability, a modified reward system, and systematic change. The student affairs leaders involved in the study preferred cultural strategies but asserted that structural strategies were similarly effective. Kezar (2003) concluded that partnership development was complex, multifaceted, and somewhat context dependent.

Moreover, recent research on educational effectiveness has fueled the notion that forming partnerships may be a productive strategy. The Documenting Effective Educational Practices (DEEP) project, a comprehensive study of educationally effective colleges and universities (Kuh et al., 2005), highlighted the importance of shared responsibility for undergraduate learning to enhance student success. At the DEEP institutions, "Effective partnerships among those who have the most contact with students—faculty and student affairs professionals—fuel the collaborative spirit and positive attitude of these campuses" (Kuh et al., 2005, p. 157). Partnerships may thus have a positive impact on learning and the educational climate.

Not All Partnerships Are Virtuous

Although the results of an academic and student affairs partnership might be positive, and although the intentions of parties entering into an academic and student affairs partnership are generally good, partners face many challenges to developing and sustaining partnership. Many partnerships fail as a result of competing assumptions about student learning (Kezar, 2001; Kuh, 1997; Schroeder, 2004); different cultural assumptions of faculty and staff (Arnold & Kuh, 1999; Kuh & Whitt, 1988); communication gaps generated by differing personalities, differing academic preparation, differing values, and differing purposes (Blake, 1979); loosely coupled systems favoring independent action (Weick, 1982); lack of shared vision; and tightly bound organizations that limit innovation (Schroeder, 1999a).

The historical separation within the institution between the formal curriculum, provided by faculty, who address the in-class cognitive development of students, and the informal curriculum, provided by student affairs professionals responsible for the out-of-class and psychosocial development of students, has also contributed to the barriers that limit collaboration (Manning et al., 2006). Enhancing these difficulties are organizational characteristics of IHEs, including loosely coupled systems favoring independent action and separate and distinct governance structures for academic and student affairs (Kuh & Banta, 2000; Wehlburg, 2008).

This historical focus on separate aspects of student life has allowed for the formation of divergent perspectives on student learning (Kezar, 2001; Schroeder, 2004). Partnerships are "not virtuous," for example, "when student and academic affairs do not view themselves as equally vital to student learning" (Manning et al., 2006, p. 131). Amid calls to bridge the gaps between academic affairs and student affairs and to refocus their mutual work as educators on student learning, these divisions continue (National Association of Student Personnel Administrators and American College Personnel Association, 2004; Schroeder, 1999b).

In a 2005 *About Campus* article about academic and student affairs partnerships, Peter Magolda queried, "Is collaboration inherently a good deed?" (p. 17). He answered his question, in part, by noting, "I remain unconvinced that all such efforts to reorganize the way individuals and offices work together are worthwhile. 'Just because' does not meet the prima facie test" (p. 17). In Magolda's view, the "all-important question [is] 'Is collaboration a good idea?'" (p. 17). He asserted that academic and student affairs have, instead, become "a bandwagon . . . because it is fashionable and sounds right, [adopted] often without purposefully and carefully considering whether a particular partnership has merit" (p. 17).

Boyer Partnership Assessment Project

As noted above, research about the effectiveness of academic and student affairs partnerships is in its infancy. Whereas literature advocating their use—even asserting their benefits—is easy to find, research about the extent to which they are "a good idea," and in what forms, under what circumstances, in what ways, and for which students, is scarce. Little empirical guidance exists for persons or institutions interested in deciding if a partnership program is a good idea in their particular contexts. The promise of partnership programs is clear, but empirically grounded, comprehensive assessment of the outcomes of partnership programs—for students, educators, and institutions—is required. The Boyer Partnership Assessment Project (BPAP) sought to address this need.

The Boyer Partnership Assessment Project (BPAP) was a FIPSE-funded study coordinated by the Ernest L. Boyer Center at Messiah College and conducted by the author of and contributors to this chapter. The study used qualitative research methods to examine academic and student affairs partnership programs at eighteen institutions: four community colleges and fourteen four-year institutions, including six public universities, three private universities, and five private colleges (see Table 28.1). Types

TABLE 28.1.   BOYER PARTNERSHIP ASSESSMENT PROJECT— INSTITUTIONAL PARTICIPANTS.

Barnard College (NY): In-Residence Seminar	Portland Community College, Cascade Campus (OR): Multicultural Awareness Council
Brevard Community College (FL): Center for Service Learning	Prince George's Community College (MD): Developmental Math Program
Carson-Newman College (TN): Boyer Laboratory for Learning	Saint Mary's College (CA): Catholic Institute for Lasallian Social Action
DePaul University (IL): Chicago Quarter	Siena College (NY): Franciscan Center for Service and Advocacy
DePauw University (IN): DePauw Year One	University of Arizona: Faculty Fellows and Student-Faculty Interaction Grants
William Rainey Harper College (IL): Learning Communities	University of Maryland: College Park Scholars
George Mason University (VA): New Century College	University of Missouri: Freshman Interest Groups
Messiah College (PA): External Programs	Villanova University (PA): Villanova Experience
North Carolina State University: First-Year College Living-Learning Community	Virginia Tech University: Residential Leadership Community

of partnership programs represented were first-year transitions, service learning and community service, living-learning communities, academic support, interdisciplinary courses, cultural programming, and leadership development.

Data were collected via site visits to each institution by teams of researchers (Whitt, Elkins Nesheim, Guentzel, Kellogg, McDonald, & Wells, 2008). The primary data collection method was individual and group interviews with institutional and partnership program leaders as well as student, faculty, and staff program participants (Merriam, 1998). We also reviewed relevant institutional documents and attended program events. Following each site visit, we prepared a detailed report of the partnership program. To ensure trustworthiness (Lincoln & Guba, 1985), we sent the initial site report to the institution for wide distribution and review. These reports formed the basis for inductive analysis of data across the sites.

We began this research with the goal of discovering and describing the elements of effective partnership programs. Could we identify practices common to these programs? Did they, in fact, create seamless learning environments? What learning—what outcomes for students, for educators, and for institutions—occurred as a result of the partnership programs? What, as we looked across our sample, accounted for those positive outcomes? And what lessons might others take from these elements in thinking about creating effective partnership programs? The following sections offer brief responses to these questions about student outcomes and common (what we called "good") practices.

Student Outcomes

The BPAP research yielded information and insights about outcomes of partnership programs for students, educators, and institutions. Detailed descriptions of these outcomes and the conditions associated with them are provided elsewhere (Elkins Nesheim, Guentzel, Kellogg, Whitt, & Wells, 2006; Elkins Nesheim, Guentzel, Kellogg, McDonald, Wells, & Whitt, 2007; Wells, Kellogg, Elkins Nesheim, Guentzel, McDonald, & Whitt, 2007). What follows is a brief summary of the results about partnership program outcomes for students (Elkins Nesheim et al., 2007).

As a result of involvement in the BPAP partnership programs, students became acclimated to college life and to their particular colleges or universities, and engaged in meaningful ways in a variety of academic and nonacademic experiences. Participation in the programs facilitated students' adjustment to the academic and social demands of postsecondary education, in part by helping students acquire the sense that they were important members of a community of students, faculty, and staff. Participation also facilitated involvement in educationally purposeful activities on and off campus, which also assisted in acclimation to college. Effective transitions, in turn, facilitated persistence.

Perhaps most important, involvement in partnership programs yielded a wide range of learning outcomes, encompassing curricular and co-curricular experiences as well as in-class and out-of-class endeavors. Educators and students noted a variety of student learning outcomes, including helping students to (1) make connections between in-class and out-of-class experiences, (2) think critically, and (3) understand themselves and others.

Students involved in Freshman Interest Groups (FIGs) at the University of Missouri, for example, noted that "what happened on the floor tied into every aspect of your life" and commented that FIGs include "all the aspects of what directly affect your life once you come to college—where you live and your classes" (personal communication). The FIGs also provided an academic foundation for student inter-actions in the dorm. A hall coordinator said, "I hear them in the bathrooms in the morning talking about what they had to do for class that day. . . . It's really neat" (personal communication).

Good Practices for Academic and Student Affairs Partnerships

One of the purposes of the BPAP was to seek to identify "good practices" in academic and student affairs partnerships. To do so, we analyzed data across the sites inductively. At the end of this process, we had identified seven "good practices" and created operational definitions of each that were consistent with and reflected the weight of evidence from the eighteen sites. Note that we do not characterize these as "best practices." One of the overarching results of the study was an emphasis on the significance of institutional context in determining whether particular approaches to creating and sustaining partnerships were effective. To describe a practice as "best" is to assert its usefulness across contexts—an assertion that cannot be accurate when it comes to academic and student affairs partnerships. What follows, then, is a brief description of good partnership practices, based on the BPAP study (more information can be found in Whitt et al., 2008).

1. Good Practice for Partnership Programs Reflects and Advances the Institution's Mission.
Effective partnership programs are grounded in and extend the institution's mission in their purpose, design, implementation, and assessment. In the process, partner-ship programs demonstrate and enhance institutional commitments to students and their learning. The importance of clear connections between institutional mission and institutional policies, practices, and programs for creating educationally effective opportunities for students has been well established in other research about college impact (see, Kuh et al., 1991; Kuh et al., 2005; Pascarella & Terenzini, 2005). What is noteworthy here is evidence of these connections in a wide range of partnership programs in a wide range of institutions.

The mission of George Mason University (GMU), a public research university in Virginia, asserted that the university "will respond to the call for interdisciplinary research and teaching, not simply by adding programs but by rethinking the traditional structure of the academy" (George Mason University Mission Statement, http://www.gmu.edu/resources/visitors/vision/mission.html). One example of GMU's commitment to interdisciplinary teaching and "rethinking" traditional structures is New Century College, an interdisciplinary curricular unit that integrates academics with experiential learning. The program offers majors in integrative studies, including a comprehensive first-year curriculum and learning communities. An academic administrator at GMU commented that, as the research mission of the institution has expanded, "[our] challenge is to make sure that we continue to develop emphases on and rewards for-high quality and innovative teaching. . . . New Century fits solidly in here. They contribute greatly to our educational climate."

2. Good Practice for Partnership Programs Embodies and Fosters a Learning-Oriented Ethos. Effective partnership programs foster learning, in and out of classrooms, in formal and informal settings, and for students as well as educators. Florida's Brevard Community College developed the Center for Service Learning (CSL) in 1988 to involve students systematically in educational and public-service experiences. The mission of CSL is to make service an integral part of students' educational experiences and to prepare students to be lifelong learners, responsible community members, and productive citizens. Service activities are both credit- and non-credit-bearing and aim to link community service and academic study.

3. Good Practice for Partnership Programs Builds on and Nurtures Relationships. Effective partnerships grow out of existing relationships between and among academic and student affairs professionals. Such relationships—often based on mutual interests or shared experiences—cross organizational and cultural boundaries to blur distinctions between academic and student affairs. In every case, the partnerships we studied evolved from informal and formal relationships based on common interests.

Relationships were essential to the success of the Developmental Math Program at Prince George's Community College in Maryland. Counselors from the college's Student Development and Counseling Office are paired with faculty who teach developmental mathematics. An advisor described her partnership with a faculty member: "We were cooperating right from the very beginning. He comes down and gives me a list of students who miss his class. . . . I visit class and we've done several workshops with students in class on goal setting, learning styles, study skills, that kind of thing. . . . I see our work as a partnership" (personal communication).

4. Good Practice for Partnership Programs Recognizes, Understands, and Attends to Institutional Culture. Recognition of the institutional culture in which the partnership program exists is paramount to success. Partnerships comprehended and heeded institutional subcultures; organizational structures; and the unique characteristics of students, faculty, staff, and administrators. The Multicultural Awareness Council (MAC) at the Cascade Campus of Portland Community College (PCC) in Oregon is a committee of academic and student affairs staff members and students that develops creative programs for student populations typically underserved by campus activities. The council aims "to create a multicultural event calendar that will honor the diverse cultures, perspectives, and ethnicities of the PCC student body and community"; "to emphasize the immigrant experience in the United States"; and "to provide PCC students, faculty, and staff with a forum to discuss multicultural issues." A number of faculty, staff, and students described the culture of PCC as "a family." One educator affirmed, "We are very tight-knit. We're all part of the Cascade family—it's a culture that's been there since the beginning, conversations about values and our relationships. When it's nurturing, people want to be together no matter what it takes. People can put up with a lot of stress if they're in a supportive environment." And a student noted that MAC is "a partnership—that's what it is. It brings together the key components of the college, like a marriage."

5. Good Practice for Partnership Programs Values and Implements Assessment.
Whether responding to an external funding application or an institutional concern, effective partnership programs have a clear understanding of what they intend to accomplish and identify means to evaluate their accomplishments. Multiple assessment strategies and data (e.g., participation rates, retention rates, satisfaction, and learning outcomes) were used to guide and improve the programs. One of the benefits of assessment for Virginia Tech University's Residential Leadership Community (RLC) was its very existence. During budget cuts, the vice president for student affairs made "an early decision [to] preserve the programs that were most effective." "How did we know [what was effective]? We had assessment processes in place. We knew what we were doing well and we could continue the things we knew we were doing well." The RLC "survived the budget cuts [because] we had evidence of its effectiveness."

6. Good Practice for Partnership Programs uses Resources Creatively and Effectively.
Effective partnership programs thrive in both resource-rich and resource-limited contexts. They capitalize on existing financial, human, and environmental resources and generate additional resources as necessary. Programs we studied differed in size and resources, but they shared a willingness to think creatively about using resources to support student learning.

One example of this principle in a limited-resource context is the FIG partnership program at the University of Missouri. An administrator noted, "We're kind of running full speed ahead but on empty." One way the program has managed to be "successful on a shoestring" and "both inexpensive and effective" is by establishing partnerships with campus units beyond academic and student affairs. For example, "Campus Dining is another partner that has been supportive. They have provided dining cards for [FIGs faculty] and feed all the FIGs students a day early"—that is, a day before the regular dining contract begins for residence hall students.

7. Good Practice for Partnership Programs Demands and Cultivates Multiple Manifestations of Leadership.
Effective partnership programs not only require strong organizational leadership but also draw upon and foster principles of shared leadership. In addition, the programs we studied facilitated leadership development for students and educators. From the beginning, the Chicago Quarter (CQ) at DePaul University had "the full support of University leaders. They were visionary people who saw that the people involved were really committed" to the program. As a consequence, CQ "was very much top-down in its inception. . . . [Leaders in liberal arts]

said 'let's go for it.'" The early leaders "had a collective vision—and authority—that made it practical to go ahead with sweeping change."

Conclusions

We embarked on the Boyer Partnership Assessment Project (BPAP) with the assumption that academic and student affairs partnerships are a "good idea." In fact, five years of study and interaction with the partnership program sites taught us that such collaborations can be a wonderful idea, yielding positive outcomes—anticipated and unanticipated—for students, educators, and institutions. At the same time, we have modified our initial assumptions to acknowledge that partnerships are a good idea when they reflect and respect their contexts. In addition, partnerships can be a good idea if they are created and implemented for reasons and in ways that serve the interests of students and the partners. Most important, they are a good idea if they are consistent with the partners' individual and collective values about learning and teaching and reflect the various cultural contexts of the partnership accurately. To be effective and meaningful, then, collaborations between academic and student affairs should be approached "cautiously, purposefully, and honestly" (Magolda, 2005, p. 21).

To facilitate thinking about how to proceed to use all of this information, this chapter concludes with a few lessons or points for the reader to ponder. They are offered in the hope that they can be instructive to readers who seek to understand or create effective academic and student affairs collaborations.

- Effective partnerships "grow where they are planted." That is, in collaborations, as in so many other aspects of higher education, context is everything. They cannot be created without clear understanding of their cultural roots, including the cultures of the institution, of academic and student affairs, and of students.
- Effective partnerships are in the eye of the beholder. In fact, we found that our understandings of the terms *partnership, academic affairs*, and *student affairs* were meaningless in many of the programs we studied. We abandoned attempts to develop a clear and concise definition of *partnerships* early on as we came to appreciate that partners are engaged in a partnership if they think they are.
- Effective partnerships require some planning, quite a lot of nurturing, and a bit of serendipity. The partners we studied gave a great deal of credit for their success to good timing, risk taking in the face of unexpected opportunities, and fortuitous relationships. At the same time, they acknowledged that partnerships are hard work. Tending to the health of relationships, assessing whether the partnerships are achieving their goals, sustaining the programs despite and in response to changes and challenges—in all cases, two or more individuals made the partnership and the partnership program a priority for time and effort.
- Effective partnership programs are, in many ways, about belief: belief in shared responsibility and shared effort in improving students' learning, as well as

belief in the capacity of the participants to create something meaningful. We found little discussion about equal responsibilities and resources, but a lot of discussion about the importance of communication, openness to change, and willingness to work hard. We found less attention to management of partnership details than we expected, and a lot more attention to inspiration, creativity, and fun.

• Effective partnership programs do not eliminate politics or territoriality. Deciding to collaborate does not constitute the waving of a magic wand that eliminates messiness and conflict. Instead, deciding to collaborate seems to involve creating a sense of community that includes willingness to stay present in the partnership and to remain dedicated to its goals, despite conflicts within or external to the partnership.

References

American Association for Higher Education (AAHE), American College Personnel Association (ACPA), & National Association of Student Personnel Administrators (NASPA). (1998). *Powerful partnerships: A shared responsibility for learning*. Washington, DC: American College Personnel Association.

American College Personnel Association (ACPA). (1994). *The student learning imperative: Implications for student affairs*. Washington, DC: Author.

Arnold, K., & Kuh, G. D. (1999). What matters in undergraduate education? Mental models, student learning and student affairs. In E. J. Whitt (Ed.), *Student learning as student affairs work: Responding to our imperative*. Washington, DC: National Association of Student Personnel Administrators.

Association of American Colleges and Universities (AAC&U). (2002). *Greater expectations: A new vision for learning as a nation goes to college*. Washington DC: Author.

Astin, A. (1993). *What matters in college? Four critical years revisited*. San Francisco: Jossey-Bass.

Blake, E. S. (1979). Classroom and context: An educational dialectic. *Academe, 65*, 280-291.

Blimling, G. S., Whitt, E. J., & Associates (1999). *Good practice in student affairs: Principles to foster student learning*. San Francisco: Jossey-Bass.

Bourassa, D. M., & Kruger, K. (2001). The national dialogue on academic and student affairs collaboration. In A. Kezar, D. J. Hirsch, & C. Burack (Eds.), *Understanding the role of academic and student affairs collaboration in creating a successful learning environment* (New Directions for Higher Education No. 116, pp. 9–38). San Francisco: Jossey-Bass.

Boyer Commission on Educating Undergraduates in the Research University. (1998). *Reinventing undergraduate education: A blueprint for America's research universities*. Stony Brook: State University of New York.

Chickering, A. W., & Gamson, Z. F. (1987). Seven principles for good practice in undergraduate education. *AAHE Bulletin, 39*(7), 3–7.

Colby, A., Ehrlich, T., Beaumont, E., & Stephens, J. (2003). *Educating citizens: Preparing America's undergraduates for lives of moral and civic responsibility*. San Francisco: Jossey-Bass.

Colwell, B. W. (2006). Partners in a community of learners: Student and academic affairs at small colleges In S. B. Westfall (Ed.) *The small college dean* (New Directions for Student Services No. 116, pp. 53–66). San Francisco: Jossey-Bass.

Cook, J. H., & Lewis, C. A. (Eds.). (2007). *Student and academic affairs collaboration: The divine comity*. Washington, DC: National Association of Student Personnel Administrators.

Coutu, D. L. (2003). Sense and reliability: A conversation with noted psychologist Karl E. Weick. *Harvard Business Review, 81*(4), 84–90.

Elkins Nesheim, B. S., Guentzel, M. J., Kellogg, A. H., McDonald, W. M., Wells, C., & Whitt, E. J. (2007). Outcomes for students of Student Affairs-Academic Affairs Partnership Programs. *Journal of College Student Development, 48*, 435–454.

Elkins Nesheim, B. S., Guentzel, M. J., Kellogg, A. H., Whitt, E. J., & Wells, C. (2006, November). *Outcomes for educators of student and academic affairs partnership programs.* Paper presented at the Annual Meeting of the Association for the Study of Higher Education, Anaheim, CA.

Gabelnick, F., MacGregor, J., Matthews, R. S., & Leigh Smith, B. (1990). Faculty responses to learning communities. In F. Gabelnick, J. MacGregor, R. S. Matthews, & B. Leigh Smith (Eds.), *Learning communities: Creating connections among students, faculty, and disciplines* (New Directions for Teaching and Learning No. 41, pp. 77–87). San Francisco: Jossey-Bass.

George Mason University. (2010). *Mission statement.* Fairfax, VA: Author. Retrieved June 23, 2010 from http://www.gmu.edu/resources/visitors/vision/mission.html.

Jacoby, B. (1999). Partnerships for service learning. In J. H. Schuh & E. J. Whitt (Eds.) *Creating successful partnerships between academic and student affairs* (New Directions for Student Services no. 87, pp. 19–35). San Francisco: Jossey-Bass.

Kezar, A. (2001). Documenting the landscape: Results of a national study on academic and student affairs collaborations. In A. Kezar, D. J. Hirsch, & C. Burack (Eds.), *Understanding the role of academic and student affairs collaboration in creating a successful learning environment* (New Directions for Higher Education No. 116, pp. 39–52). San Francisco: Jossey-Bass.

Kezar, A. (2003). Achieving student success: Strategies for creating partnerships between academic and student affairs. *NASPA Journal, 41*, 1–22.

Kezar, A., Hirsch, D. J., & Burack, C. (Eds.). (2001). *Understanding the role of academic and student affairs collaboration in creating a successful learning environment* (New Directions for Higher Education No. 116). San Francisco: Jossey-Bass.

Kolins, C. A. (2000, Winter/Spring). An appraisal of collaboration: Assessing academic and student affairs officers at public two-year colleges. *Student Development in the Two-Year Colleges, 14*, 9–12.

Kuh, G. D. (1996). Guiding principles for creating seamless learning environments for undergraduates. *Journal of College Student Development, 37*, 135–148.

Kuh, G. D. (1997, June). *Working together to enhance student learning inside and outside the classroom.* Paper presented at the annual AAHE Assessment and Quality Conference, Miami, FL.

Kuh, G. D., & Banta, T. W. (2000). Faculty–student affairs collaboration on assessment: Lessons from the field. *About Campus, 4*(6), 4–11.

Kuh, G. D., Kinzie, J. I., Schuh, J. H., Whitt, E. J., & Associates. (2005). *Student success in college: Creating conditions that matter.* San Francisco: Jossey-Bass.

Kuh, G. D., Schuh, J. H., Whitt, E. J., & Associates. (1991). *Involving colleges: Successful approaches to fostering student learning and development outside the classroom.* San Francisco: Jossey-Bass.

Kuh, G. D., & Whitt, E. J. (1988). *The invisible tapestry: Culture in American colleges and universities* (ASHE-ERIC Higher Education Report No. 1). Washington, DC: Association for the Study of Higher Education.

Kurotsuchi Inkelas, K., & Weisman, J. L. (2003). Different by design: An examination of student outcomes among participants in three types of living-learning programs. *Journal of College Student Development, 44*(3), 335–368.

Lincoln, Y. S., & Guba, E. G. (1985). *Naturalistic inquiry.* Beverly Hills, CA: Sage.

Magolda, P. M. (2005). Proceed with caution: Uncommon wisdom about academic and student affairs partnerships. *About Campus, 9*(6), 16–21.

Manning, K., Kinzie, J., & Schuh, J. H. (2006). *One size does not fit all: Traditional and innovative models of student affairs practice.* New York: Routledge.

Martin, J., & Samels, J. E. (2001). Lessons learned: Eight best practices for new partnerships. In A. Kezar, D. Hirsch, & C. Burack (Eds.), *Understanding the role of academic and student affairs collaboration in creating a successful learning environment* (New Directions for Higher Education No. 116, pp. 39–52). San Francisco: Jossey-Bass.

McHugh Engstrom, C. (2004). The power of faculty–student affairs for promoting integrative learning experiences in learning communities. In S. N. Hurd & R. Freerman Stein (Eds.),

Building and sustaining learning communities: The Syracuse University experience (pp. 59–75). Bolton, MA: Anker.

Merriam, S. B. (1998). *Qualitative research and case study applications in education* (2nd ed.) San Francisco: Jossey-Bass.

National Association of State Universities and Land-Grant Colleges (NASULGC). (1997). *Returning to our roots: The student experience.* Washington, DC: Author.

National Association of State Universities and Land-Grant Colleges (NASULGC). (1999). *Returning to our roots: A learning society.* Washington, DC: Author.

National Association of State Universities and Land-Grant Colleges (NASULGC). (2000). *Returning to our roots: Toward a coherent campus culture.* Washington, DC: Author.

National Association of Student Personnel Administrators and American College Personnel Association (NASPA and ACPA). (2004). *Learning reconsidered.* Washington, DC: Authors. Retrieved June 21, 2010 from www.myacpa.org/pub/documents/learningreconsidered.pdf.

Newman, F., Couturier, L., & Scurry, J. (2004). *The future of higher education: Rhetoric, reality, and the risks of the market.* San Francisco: Jossey-Bass.

Pascarella, E. T., & Terenzini, P. T. (1991). *How college affects students.* San Francisco: Jossey-Bass.

Pascarella, E. T., & Terenzini, P. T. (2005). *How college affects students: Vol. 2. A third decade of research.* San Francisco: Jossey-Bass.

Pike, G. R. (1999). The effects of residential learning communities and traditional residential living arrangements on educational gains during the first year of college. *Journal of College Student Development, 40*(3), 269–284.

Schroeder, C. (1999a). Partnerships: An imperative for enhancing student learning and institutional effectiveness. In J. H. Schuh & E. J. Whitt (Eds.), *Creating successful partnerships between academic and student affairs* (New Directions for Student Services No. 87, pp. 5–18). San Francisco: Jossey-Bass.

Schroeder, C. (1999b). Forging educational partnerships that advance student learning. In G. S. Blimling & E. J. Whitt (Eds.), *Good practice in student affairs: Principles to foster student learning* (pp.133–156). San Francisco: Jossey-Bass.

Schroeder, C. C., Minor, F. D., & Tarkow, T. A. (1999). Freshman interest groups: Partnerships for promoting student success. In J. H. Schuh & E. J. Whitt (Eds.), *Creating successful partnerships between academic and student affairs* (New Directions for Student Services no. 87, pp. 37–49). San Francisco: Jossey-Bass.

Schroeder, C. (2004). Collaborative partnerships: Keys to enhancing student learning and success. In J. Gardner & L. Upcraft (Eds.), *Challenging and supporting the first-year student.* San Francisco: Jossey-Bass.

Schuh, J. H., & Whitt, E. J. (Eds.). (1999). *Creating successful partnerships between academic and student affairs* (New Directions for Student Services No. 87). San Francisco: Jossey-Bass.

Shapiro, H. (2005). *A larger sense of purpose: Higher education and society.* Princeton, NJ: Princeton University Press.

Shapiro, N. S., & Levine, J. H. (1999). *Creating learning communities: A practical guide to winning support, organizing for change, and implementing programs.* San Francisco: Jossey-Bass.

Study Group on the Conditions of Excellence in American Higher Education. (1984). *Involvement in learning: Realizing the potential of American higher education: Final report.* Washington, DC: National Institute of Education.

U.S. Department of Education. (2006). *A test of leadership: Charting the future of U.S. higher education.* Washington DC: Author.

Wehlburg, C. M. (2008). *Promoting integrated and transformative assessment: A deeper focus on student learning.* San Francisco: Jossey-Bass.

Weick, K. E. (1982). Administering education in loosely coupled schools. *Phi Beta Kappan, (63)*10, 673–676.

Wells, C., Kellogg, A. H., Elkins Nesheim, B. S., Guentzel, M. J., McDonald, W., & Whitt, E. J. (2007). *Institutional outcomes of academic and student affairs partnership programs.* Paper presented at the annual meeting of the Association for the Study of Higher Education, Louisville, KY.

Whitt, E. J., Elkins Nesheim, B. S., Guentzel, M. J., Kellogg, A. H., McDonald, W. M., & Wells, C. A. (2008). "Principles of good practice" for academic and student affairs partnership programs. *Journal of College Student Development, 49,* 235–249.

Yeater, E. A., Miltenberger, P., Laden, R. M., Ellis, S., & O'Donohue, W. (2001). Collaborating with academic affairs: The development of a sexual assault prevention and counseling program within an academic department. *NASPA Journal, 38,* 438–450.

Zheng, L. J., Saunders, K. P., Shelly, M.C.I., & Whalen, D. F. (2002). Predictors of academic success for freshmen residence hall students. *Journal of College Student Development, 43*(2), 267–283.

PART SIX

THE FUTURE

Two important questions are thoughtfully considered in this final section of the handbook: Where is the student affairs profession going? and What's in its future? Linda Sax and Casandra Harper emphasize in Chapter Twenty-Nine the importance of relying on decades of published research on students, their development, and their learning outcomes to guide current and future student affairs practice. Specifically, they highlight the literature on "conditional effects"—ways in which college environments, such as classrooms, peer culture, and out-of-class engagement affect students differently on the basis of race, class, gender, or other unique characteristics. Sax and Harper provide several examples of how this research can be utilized in practice. Similarly, in Chapter Thirty, Ana Martínez Alemán and Katherine Wartman discuss the present and future effects of changing technologies on higher education in general and student affairs practice specifically. They consider how students form identities online; how technology will continue to reshape communication norms and campus culture; and technological influences on

students as these relate to such factors as race, class, gender, and sexual orientation. Martínez Alemán and Wartman conclude their chapter with several suggestions for how student affairs educators and administrators might respond to students' use of technologies.

In the last chapter, the editors of this fifth edition of *Student Services* describe pressing societal issues and trends influencing higher education and student affairs at this moment in history. Financial and economic forces, shifting demographics and access to higher education, globalization, and unanticipated technological advancements are among the general higher education concerns we highlight. Future developments for student affairs include the profession's continued quest for legitimacy amid other academic priorities, the necessary expansion of campus mental health resources and psychological services, the need for increased cross-cultural engagement, the emergence of new programs and services, and documenting learning outcomes to demonstrate educational effectiveness. We conclude the book with some advice for those responsible for shaping the future of student affairs.

CHAPTER TWENTY-NINE

USING RESEARCH TO INFORM PRACTICE: CONSIDERING THE CONDITIONAL EFFECTS OF COLLEGE

Linda J. Sax and Casandra E. Harper

Imagine you have been given the responsibility to design a program or service aimed at enhancing "success" for a specific population of undergraduates at your institution. Perhaps it is a residential experience designed to improve college adjustment for first-generation college students. Or an initiative aimed at increasing academic engagement among male students. Or maybe it is a peer tutoring program designed to boost retention rates for racial and ethnic minority students. An important aspect of your planning should be consulting research to find out what seems to work on other campuses, so that you can emulate successful practices at your own institution. You might read books and published research articles, or perhaps attend scholarly conferences, all in an attempt to learn from others and gain insights about what practices are most successful in promoting adjustment, engagement, degree attainment, or whichever markers of success your institution hopes to realize for its students.

The good news is that you have a vast scholarly literature from which to draw, because decades of research have examined how college affects a broad range of student outcomes. You will undoubtedly find dozens, if not hundreds, of studies indentifying college student experiences that favorably influence your particular outcome of interest. Indeed, studies conducted across numerous disciplines have examined the effects of a wide range of college environments, spanning the residential, the curricular, and the co-curricular aspects of the student experience.

The problem, however, is that much of the research on the impact of college reveals what works for students *in general*, not necessarily what works for particular subgroups of students. As noted by Pascarella and Terenzini (1991, 2005) in their

Portions of this chapter appear in Sax (2008) and are reprinted with permission from John Wiley & Sons, Inc massive reviews of the college impact literature, research on how college affects students often is based on large, aggregated samples of college students, revealing little or nothing about which different *types* of students stand to benefit most or least from a particular college experience. However, the fact is that the college student population is highly diverse in terms of gender, race, ethnicity, social class background, sexual orientation, religion, and numerous other characteristics. It seems logical that what works for *some* students may not work for *all* students. If you seek to determine best practices for a particular subpopulation of students—such as first-generation students, underrepresented minority students, or male students—you might question whether the findings reported in previous research are relevant to the population you are trying to serve.

This chapter is designed to help student affairs professionals identify and use research that addresses the "conditional effects" of college, or the ways in which college environments—such as classroom climate, peer culture, or out-of-class involvement—might affect students differently on the basis of their race, class, gender, or other unique characteristics. Research on the conditional effects of college is a critical frontier in the expansive literature on the impact of college, especially as educators engage with an increasingly diverse population of college students. The chapter begins by discussing the importance of examining conditional effects to improve our understanding of the student experience. Next, we provide guidance for professionals who want to know how to identify and understand research on conditional effects. The chapter then offers concrete examples from selected studies on conditional effects of college that will be relevant for student affairs educators. The overall goal of the chapter is to engender motivation to use and confidence in using findings from conditional effects studies in our everyday work with students.

Why Should Educators Consider the Conditional Effects of College?

Over the past several decades, the field of higher education has experienced a proliferation of research on the impact of college. This body of research is synthesized in major reviews (e.g., Feldman & Newcomb, 1969; Pascarella & Terenzini, 1991, 2005); large-scale inquiries published as books (e.g., Astin, 1977, 1993; Bowen & Bok, 1998; Kuh, Kinzie, Schuh, Whitt, & Associates, 2005; Sax, 2008; Trent & Medsker, 1968); as well as hundreds of published research studies, appearing in journals such as the *Review of Higher Education*, *Research in Higher Education*, the *Journal of Higher Education*, the *Journal of College Student Development*, and the *Journal of Student Affairs Research and Practice* (formerly *NASPA Journal*).

This expansive body of research has revealed the many ways in which students change and develop as the result of their college experiences. Broadly speaking, research demonstrates that students who establish meaningful connections on campus—with peers, faculty, the curriculum, and so on—stand to benefit most from college. The value of student involvement (Astin, 1999); engagement (Harper & Quaye, 2009;

Kuh, 2001); and integration (Tinto, 1987; Weidman, 1989) is well understood by both researchers and student affairs professionals. These concepts are central to a wide range of curricular and co-curricular initiatives that have been shown to confer academic and personal benefits to students, including first-year seminars (Upcraft, Gardner, & Barefoot, 2005); service-learning opportunities (Astin, Vogelgesang, Ikeda, & Yee, 2000; Eyler & Giles, 1999); and living-learning programs (Gabelnick, MacGregor, Matthews, & Smith, 1990; Inkelas, Vogt, Longerbeam, Owen, & Johnson, 2006; Inkelas & Weisman, 2003). There is no doubt that the vast scholarly literature on college effects has been critical to improving practice and enhancing the importance and visibility of the field of student affairs.

However, scholars have long argued for more research that considers how different types of students might be affected in unique ways by their experiences, or the conditional effects of college. There is, in fact, a growing body of literature demonstrating what we can learn by examining the impact of college separately for different student populations (Harper & Quaye, 2009; Stage, 2007). Research that disaggregates students on the basis of race and ethnicity is particularly common (see, for example, Carter, 1999; Cabrera, Nora & Terenzini, 1999; Flowers & Pascarella, 2003; Hurtado, Han, Saenz, Espinosa, Cabrera, & Cerna, 2007; Pascarella, Wolniak, Pierson, & Flowers, 2004; Saenz, Ngai, & Hurtado, 2007; and St. John, Hu, Simmons, Carter, & Weber, 2004). Studies have also examined how the impact of college is conditioned by a student's gender (see, for example, Bryant, 2003; Harper, 2008; Harper, Carini, Bridges, & Hayek, 2004; Harper & Quaye, 2007; Kezar & Moriarty, 2000; Pascarella, Whitt, et al., 1997; Sax, 1994a, 1994b, 1994c, 1996, 2008; Sax, Bryant & Gilmartin, 2004; Smith, Morrison, & Wolf, 1994; and Whitt, Pascarella, Nesheim, Marth, & Pierson, 2003). Fewer studies examine conditional college effects as they vary by students' socioeconomic statuses (e.g., Walpole, 2003; Kim & Sax, 2009). Despite the existence of studies that demonstrate differential effects of college for students of various demographic backgrounds, however, the practice of higher education is largely driven by an aggregate view of how college affects students.

The premise behind the study of conditional effects is that because students differ from each other in numerous ways when they arrive at college, they may react in unique ways to their experiences during college. This is especially important given the growing diversity of the college student population, because we cannot assume that the directions and magnitudes of college influences are going to be consistent for all students (Harper & Quaye, 2009; Pascarella & Terenzini, 1991, 1998, 2005; Perna & Thomas, 2008; Sax, 2008; Stage, 2007; Stage & Anaya, 1996).

For example, imagine that we are interested in knowing how college students are influenced by participating in service-learning—a community service experience accompanied by student reflection aimed at enhancing intellectual understanding or civic engagement (Bringle & Hatcher, 1995). We might simply compare service-learning participants with nonparticipants in terms of some aspect of development, such as leadership ability, humanitarianism, or academic achievement. However, in considering whether service-learning makes a difference for students, we might be inclined to think, "Well, it *depends*." Perhaps it depends on gender, whereby women and men would be affected in different ways by the service-learning experience. Or perhaps it depends on students' racial and ethnic backgrounds, whereby the impact of service-learning would be stronger or weaker for students of particular racial and ethnic groups. Maybe the impact of service-learning depends on students' majors, with students in some majors more or less likely to make important connections between the service experience and academic course content. The point is that we have reason to suspect that the impact of service-learning may vary across the different types of students engaged in the service-learning experience. The same is true for practically *any* college experience: We cannot assume that all students will be affected in the same ways by their participation in common college experiences. Pascarella (2006) points out that in practice "limiting one's vision to general effects can frequently be misleading and mask dramatic differences in the impact of an intervention or experience for different kinds of students" (p. 512).

Visualizing Conditional College Effects

It may be useful to consider the conditional effects of college using a visual aid. Consider the many models of college impact provided in the higher education literature, such as Astin's Input-Environment-Outcome (I-E-O) Model (1993), Pascarella's General Model for Assessing Change (1985), Tinto's Model of Student Departure (1987), and Weidman's Model of Undergraduate Socialization (1989). In general, these models provide a framework for considering the impact of college while taking into account students' characteristics and predispositions prior to college. Perhaps the most straightforward of these is Astin's I-E-O model, which is shown in Figure 29.1. The model is divided into three blocks representing the "I" (inputs), "E" (environments), and "O" (outcomes). Inputs are defined as the characteristics of students at the point of college entry, including educational and family backgrounds, skills, abilities, goals, aspirations, and values. Environments include characteristics of the institution as well as students' behaviors, such as academic engagement, interactions with family and friends, employment, and extracurricular activities. Outcomes, finally, include measurable characteristics of the student after exposure to the college environment.

FIGURE 29.1.   ASTIN'S INPUT-ENVIRONMENT-OUTCOME (I-E-O) MODEL OF COLLEGE IMPACT.

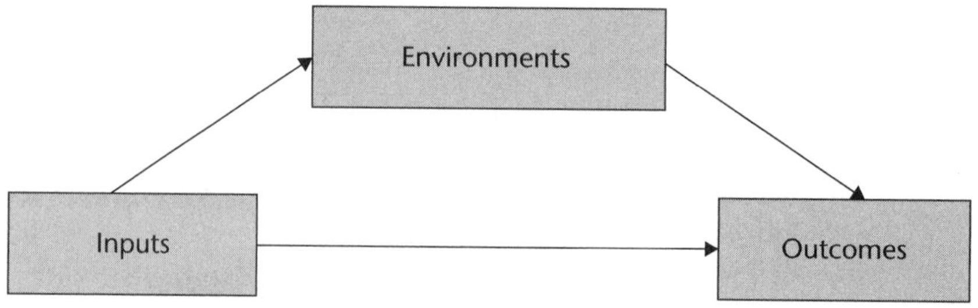

Source: Astin (1993). Used with permission.

Other major college impact models are rooted in the basic structure of the I-E-O model. Central to this model is the notion that the impact of college is dependent upon the characteristics of students before they step foot on campus. Accounting for background factors, or inputs, is critical because the characteristics and predispositions that students bring with them to college lead them to select certain environments when they arrive on campus. If these background factors are not accounted for, it is impossible to determine the extent to which student characteristics at the end of college are attributable to what the students did *during* college versus what the students were like *before* they enrolled in college.

Because existing college impact models encourage us to consider student characteristics prior to college, they are useful here in our consideration of the conditional effects of college. Although they do not explicitly address whether the nature of college impact *depends* on student characteristics, they certainly do not preclude that possibility. Indeed, one might visualize unique I-E-O models for different groups of students (e.g., one model for women and another for men). However, an alternative way to visualize this concept is through a conditional model of college impact, as represented in Figure 29.2. This model is similar in structure to Astin's I-E-O model but differs by visually depicting the relationships between the various blocks as *unique* for different groups of students. For example, two arrows—one for women and one for men—could connect "College Environments and Experiences" with "College Outcomes." Or one might have several arrows, each reflecting the impact of college for students of particular racial and ethnic groups. The possibilities are endless, given variations among students based on race, ethnicity, class, sexual orientation, or any number of characteristics. The model can also be used to study conditional effects of college that are dependent on various factors, such as major, place of residence, or type of institution.

Certainly, as the number of subgroups increases, so do the number of arrows between boxes; at some point this may become unwieldy from a visual perspective. However, from a practical standpoint, it is important to be mindful of the variety of student traits—and combinations of traits—that may shape the dynamics of college

FIGURE 29.2.   CONDITIONAL MODEL OF COLLEGE IMPACT.

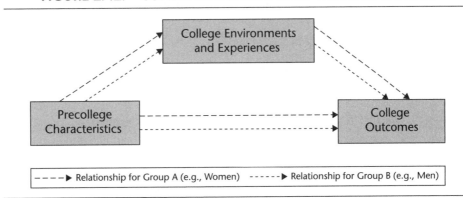

Source: Reprinted from Sax (2008) with permission of John Wiley & Sons, Inc.

impact. This mind-set may be intuitive for many campus personnel, but unfortunately the research community has not responded quickly enough to the need for information on the extent and nature of conditional college effects. Thus student affairs educators and administrators are limited in their ability to make informed decisions about which students will benefit most from which programs and services.

Identifying and Understanding Research on Conditional Effects

In order for research on conditional effects to be useful to practice, student affairs professionals who may not be trained as researchers need to know what they are looking for in research studies and how to interpret what they find.

Determining if Conditional Effects Are Addressed

Usually, whether or not a study takes conditional effects into account will be clear from the title or abstract. Although not always referring to "conditional effects" by name, authors will almost always justify their explorations of differential college effects in the introduction or literature review. They typically make the case that their subpopulations are worthy of study in their own right, as opposed to being subsumed into the larger population of college students.

Various Conditions That Might Be Addressed

The majority of studies examining the conditional effects of college have focused on how the impact of college depends on the student's race and ethnicity or gender. This information has been useful in documenting the prevalence of conditional effects across a range of college outcomes. However, we ought to have a better understanding of how college influences are dependent on other student characteristics, such as socioeconomic status, (dis)ability, religion, age, sexual orientation, academic preparation, learning styles, first-generation status, transfer status, and so forth. We also need to consider how the impact of college differs for students based on college experiential factors, such as major, place of residence, and full- or part-time enrollment.

How Are Conditional Effects Detected?

Conditional effects of college may be studied both qualitatively and quantitatively. Because qualitative research inherently considers the uniqueness of each participant being studied, the notion of conditional college effects is generally consistent with the qualitative approach to studies of college students. An understanding of conditional effects may be gleaned from a variety of qualitative methods, including interviews or observations of students that are analyzed in terms of students' gender, race, or other factors.

When it comes to quantitative research, there are a variety of approaches that also can be used to examine conditional effects of college. One way is to examine college impact separately for two or more groups of students, as defined by race and ethnicity, gender, or other student characteristics. In this case, separate analyses would be conducted for each subgroup in order to see whether the impact of college (or some particular aspect of college) is *different* for any particular group or groups. This may be accomplished through a variety of methods, including multiple regression, structural equation modeling, or hierarchical linear modeling. Whichever method is used, the researcher's goal is to see if the influence of college for different student populations is the same (suggesting general effects) or different (suggesting conditional effects).

Another approach commonly taken in research on conditional effects is to include all students in one analysis but to test for conditional effects using "interaction" or "cross-product" terms. For example, if the researcher is interested in whether the impact of a peer tutoring program differs for male and female students, the analysis would first control for the main effects of two variables (gender and participation in peer tutoring), and would then test for the significance of a new cross-product variable, gender × peer tutoring, which reflects the interaction between gender and tutoring. Often researchers will use this "combined sample" approach as a first test for the presence of conditional effects and, if these are found, will proceed by running separate analyses for the different student subgroups.

Using Information on Conditional Effects

To make the best use of research and effectively incorporate the findings into practice, there are a number of questions you can ask yourself to help determine the relevance of specific results to your own institutional context. These questions include: How do the students you work with in your institution differ from those studied in the article? To what extent does your institution already consider these sorts of conditional effects in its planning? Are there resources available on your campus that were not available in the study? Do your professional experiences resonate with the findings in the study? Would you make changes as a result of these findings, and, if yes, would they be appropriate given the mission of your institution and the students it serves? Can you look at your environment in a new way given these findings? The bottom line is that although conditional effects may be detected in research, student affairs professionals will need to act judiciously in determining if the findings are relevant to the students on their particular campuses.

Examples from Research on Conditional Effects of College

As noted above, there are a variety of ways to approach conditional effects. As you search for studies that might have practical relevance to your own work or interests, your approach might vary according to the information you seek. A closer look at a handful of recent studies will help illustrate some of the conditional effects that have been detected in research; these also include discussions of how their results might best be used to inform practice. Examining conditional effects allows scholar-practitioners to be more strategic when analyzing the impact of college on students and when advising particular students interested in achieving specific outcomes. Astin's (1977, 1993) I-E-O model provides a natural framework to help organize these examples, because your own search for studies on conditional effects may be driven by your interests in particular student input characteristics, specific student environments, or desired college outcomes.

Inputs

One way to approach conditional effects is to consider students' individual characteristics or inputs. There are a fair number of higher education professionals whose work is focused on certain subgroups of students, each of which shares a common characteristic. This characteristic might include gender, race, sexual orientation, major, ability, socioeconomic status, year in school, and so on. Individuals working with or researching a certain group of students might be most interested in approaching conditional effects from this input-based lens. These educators and researchers might want to know whether experiences of college are the same for different types of students. Examples follow of studies examining key student characteristics that are of particular relevance to student affairs.

Socioeconomic Status. Walpole (2003) studied whether the effects of the college environment on graduate school attendance depended on students' socioeconomic status (SES). Her analysis revealed aspects of the college environment that increased the odds of students' deciding to attend graduate school, and found more support for the positive influence of college on low-SES students than on high-SES students. Specifically, Walpole found that the likelihood of attending graduate school was significantly greater among low-SES students who worked with faculty on research, spoke with faculty outside of class, and participated in intercollegiate sports. Even though low- and high-SES students reported similar rates of participation in each of these activities, the benefits of participation on graduate school attendance were evident only among low-SES students. In fact, Walpole's analysis revealed that the college environment did little to "significantly increase the odds of graduate school attendance for high SES students" (p. 64).

The clear evidence of the benefit of certain college experiences on graduate school attendance among students from low-SES backgrounds suggests the need for additional efforts targeted at these students. Walpole noted that the low-SES students may not be able to participate in these experiences due to constraints in time and money, which often cause them to work a substantial number of hours, perhaps off campus. The implications for policy and practice regarding students from low-SES backgrounds are, therefore, to increase financial aid, create and encourage students to pursue work-study opportunities—particularly those involving working with faculty on research, and to encourage these students to increase their contact with faculty outside of class and their involvement in student clubs and groups.

Race and Ethnicity. Pascarella, Wolniak, et al. (2004) examined whether the effects of certain college environments or experiences on the development of graduate school aspirations depended on race. For example, among African American students, graduate school plans were positively influenced by full-time enrollment and attendance at a historically Black college or university, but were negatively influenced by work responsibilities. The effects of full-time enrollment and work were not significant among Hispanic or White students. Among Hispanic students, graduate plans were influenced by "study time, exposure to arts and humanities courses, and . . . intercollegiate athletic participation" (p. 310). These positive influences found among Hispanic students were unique in that similar effects were not found among the samples of African American or White participants.

The research also revealed certain environments that positively influenced graduate degree aspirations among some students and inhibited such aspirations among others. For example, "Years living on campus had a significant, negative impact on graduate degree plans for both African American and Hispanic students, but a significant positive effect on White students' plans to earn a graduate degree" (Pascarella, Wolniak, et al., 2004, p. 310). The authors note that the complexity revealed by examining the conditional effects creates even more questions about the true nature of such findings, which are masked when simply examining general college effects.

Although further research is needed to delve more deeply into the relationships explored between environments and outcomes for these students of various racial groups, the results suggest an added layer of nuance to the general effects scholarship. This study indicates that the same environment or experience can lead to different outcomes for different types of students. It is worth questioning why some students were positively influenced, others were negatively influenced, and some were not significantly influenced at all by certain experiences. Examining just this small subset of conditional effects research begins to demonstrate how complex the findings and implications can be when taking a more nuanced approach.

Environments

Another way to approach conditional effects is to consider the college environment. College is replete with opportunities to engage with and potentially transform students. There are a number of programs, services, and involvement opportunities available to college students on any given college campus. Individuals working in certain areas of student life might be most interested in approaching conditional effects from this environmental perspective. They might want to know, for example, whether the offices or programs they work for have any effects on students and, if so, whether the effects vary for different types of students. The following are examples of studies examining key college environments that are of particular relevance to student affairs.

Living-Learning Programs. Inkelas, Daver, Vogt, and Leonard (2007) examined the conditional effects of certain student and institutional characteristics and experiences on first-generation college students' academic and social transitions to college. They conducted research among students in living-learning (L-L) programs versus students in traditional residence halls (TRH). The authors found that among first-generation students participating in an L-L program, their academic transition positively related to "course-related faculty interaction" and "usage of co-curricular residence hall resources (such as hall workshops, peer counselors, and social activities)" (p. 419). Faculty interaction was also a positive predictor among first-generation students living in a TRH, as were college grades; however, involvement in community service was a uniquely negative predictor among TRH students and was not significant among L-L participants.

Students' social transition to college was also examined in this study and revealed the unique effects of aspects of the college environment. Among first-generation students participating in an L-L program, use of co-curricular residence hall resources emerged as a uniquely positive predictor, as did the perception that the residence hall climate was academically supportive, whereas faculty mentorship was a uniquely negative predictor. The only other college-level variable that emerged as a significant predictor of students' social transition—the perception that the residence hall climate was socially supportive—emerged for both L-L and TRH participants.

Overall, the relative contribution of L-L programs to students' transition to college was found to be low to moderate, but still noteworthy given this preliminary evidence among an at-risk population. The recommendations for practice based on these findings were primarily focused on expanding access to L-L programs among first-generation college students through targeted recruitment by practitioners and by allowing students living off-campus to participate (because first-generation students are more likely to live off campus).

Honors Program Participation. Seifert, Pascarella, Colangelo, and Assouline (2007) considered the differential effects of participation in honors programs by gender, race, parental income, and whether the student was attending his or her first-choice college on a variety of individual outcomes. Their results revealed the uniquely positive effect of participating in an honors program on reading comprehension among students of color and those attending their first-choice college; the effect was not significant among White students, nor among students who were attending a college that was not their first choice. Similarly, students' cognitive skill development was positively predicted by honors participation among men and students from families with above-median incomes, and was not significant among women and students from families with below-median incomes. The authors noted that the benefits of participating in an honors program was evident among "those students whose access to and persistence in higher education has been of great interest," such as students of color and men—because of their lower college-going rates and longer time-to-degree rates in comparison to women (p. 71).

Student-Faculty Interactions. Sax, Bryant, and Harper (2005) tested separately for women and men the effects of student-faculty interactions on a variety of academic and psychosocial outcomes. The results revealed a strong mix of the effects of interactions with faculty: some effects were significant for both genders, others were stronger for one gender, and yet others had opposite effects—positive for one gender and negative for the other. Student-faculty interactions were positively associated with "scholarly self-confidence, leadership ability, degree aspirations, and retention" among both genders (p. 653). Among men, interactions with faculty were positively related to "gains in political engagement, social activism, and liberalism," as well as "more egalitarian views on gender roles" (pp. 653–654). Among women, an interesting pattern emerged with respect to feedback from faculty: "Women who felt that faculty did not take their comments seriously reported greater than average declines in self-rated physical health, math ability, and degree aspirations. Conversely, women who reported receiving honest feedback from faculty reported gains in their sense of physical and emotional health, academic performance, and overall drive to achieve" (p. 654).

Finally, working with faculty on research was associated with more egalitarian gender role views among men and traditional gender role views among women. Also, challenging a professor's ideas in class lead women to feel more overwhelmed and men to feel less overwhelmed. The implications for faculty and counselors are to not only be cognizant of and therefore hopefully minimize the deleterious effects that certain student-faculty interactions can produce but also to strategically encourage—according to gender—the types of interactions that are associated with positive gains.

Living on Campus. Pike's (2002) article "The Differential Effects of On- and Off-Campus Living Arrangements on Students' Openness to Diversity" found that living on campus was a significant predictor of openness to diversity, even after accounting for differences in students' background characteristics (including race, gender, and ACT scores). This relationship was particularly strong among students living in freshman interest groups (FIGs). Pike found these results to be generally consistent with previous research, at least in terms of the benefits of living on campus. The effects of living on campus were attributed to the types of relationships students establish in such an environment and the expanded worldview that this opportunity creates. These results are perhaps most encouraging to educators working in residence life, because this provides further validation of the benefits gained as a result of intentional programming and planning.

Outcomes

Another way to organize your search is according to the outcomes of interest, an approach that might be useful for those seeking to take a big-picture approach to improving the student experience overall. Professionals involved in assessment and institutional research, for example, might be most interested in understanding the effectiveness of the college experience on certain key outcomes determined by the mission of the institution and perhaps by accreditation requirements. The following are examples of studies examining key student outcomes commonly addressed in higher education.

Identity Development. In a study of the differential impact of various "contextual influences (events, experiences, and relationships)" on college men and women's identity development, Moran (2003) noted that, overall, men's identity development tended to be positively influenced by contextual influences, whereas women were much more likely than men to be hindered by contextual influences. Knowing this, might we, as educators, consider a more targeted approach to our advice to students about engaging in these and other seemingly innocuous activities? Would these results cause us to consider different processing activities for students who participate in these activities?

This is not to suggest that we should dissuade students (particularly women, in this example) from engaging in such experiences. More research on multiple campuses with a larger sample aimed at understanding the direct relationship between these activities and identity development would be required before drawing such a conclusion. Further, a study might suggest a negative relationship between an experience and one outcome, whereas another study might positively relate the same experience to a different outcome. Therefore, we would not want to act hastily and deprive students of the benefits of such involvement, but we would want to be proactive about understanding and potentially avoiding the negative effects. Let's illustrate this idea with another example from the same study.

Moran (2003) found that "male participants were often nourished as a result of 'challenging' contextual influences, while females' identity dimensions were often thwarted when faced with such challenges" (p. 128). She further clarified that the dimension of identity most affected by challenges among women was racial and ethnic identity. Given these results, how can we restructure or reframe programs and discussions centering on racial and ethnic issues to account for gender differences? As educators, how can we change the nature of classroom and out-of-class interactions in a way that addresses the disparate needs of women and men? Are there strategies women can employ to counteract the negative effects of being challenged? Moran's suggestions for educators and administrators include assisting students to develop the ability to reinterpret conclusions they have drawn from negative experiences.

Academic Achievement. Fischer (2007) examined racial differences in students' academic gains in college (defined by college GPA) and found that higher grades were predicted by different individual characteristics and college experiences across racial groups. One theme that emerged among the findings was the role of students' social ties, both on- and off-campus, formal and informal. For example, having higher grades was associated with "having more extensive formal ties on-campus" such as being involved in clubs and organizations, among Asian, Hispanic, and Black students but was unrelated to GPA among White students (p. 141). In contrast, having off-campus social ties was negatively associated with grades among White and Black students, but was not significantly associated with grades among Asian or Hispanic students. Having "own-group ties" was positively related to GPA among Asian students, whereas "informal social ties were negatively related to college grades" among Hispanic students (p. 141).

Overall, Fischer's (2007) results provide added support for the benefits of getting involved and establishing connections on campus. Fischer recommends targeting students according to their admissions applications as well as during orientation in order to emphasize the benefits of involvement and the specific opportunities available on campus to become involved.

Another measure of academic achievement is persistence. St. John et al. (2004) examined the conditional effects of students' college majors on persistence among African American and White students. Persistence was positively predicted by majoring in health, business, and engineering and computer science among African American sophomores, but was not significant among their White peers. The authors suggest that making connections between choice of major and future employment opportunities is particularly salient for African American students, given that their persistence was found to be most likely in the majors that arguably had the greatest economic potential.

A final example of academic achievement outcomes is illustrated by the results of Flowers and Pascarella's study (2003), which examined the conditional effects of college on cognitive outcomes by race. The results revealed a number of aspects of the college environment that were significant predictors for African American students but were not significant for White students. For example, reading comprehension was negatively related to the number of social science courses taken in college among African American students, whereas these courses were unrelated to reading comprehension among White students. Another outcome, writing skills, was found to be positively associated with volunteer work among African American students, but this association was not a significant predictor for White students. Similarly, college grades were a significant and positive predictor of critical thinking among African American students but was not significantly related to this outcome among White students.

Conclusion

As the above examples illustrate, understanding and serving our diverse population of college students requires more than just knowing how students differ from one another in their incoming characteristics, such as in gender, race, class and other defining traits. It necessitates knowing that these different characteristics may result in unique reactions to the college environment. In other words, we cannot assume that the effects of college can be generalized across different student populations. This chapter has presented a rationale for considering the conditional effects of college and has provided tools to identify and learn from some published studies on conditional effects. Fortunately, research examining the conditional effects of college is on the rise, especially as the diversification of the student population demands that scholars and administrators recognize the need to revisit existing assumptions about effective educational practice. As our understanding of college impact extends from a generalized notion to more specific understandings for different student subgroups, student affairs educators and administrators will be better able to develop programs and services that are designed to maximize the benefits of college for all students.

References

Astin, A. W. (1977). *Four critical years: Effects of college on beliefs, attitudes, and knowledge.* San Francisco: Jossey-Bass.

Astin, A. W. (1993). *What matters in college? Four critical years revisited.* San Francisco: Jossey-Bass.

Astin, A. W. (1999). Student involvement: A developmental theory for higher education. *Journal of College Student Development, 40*, 518–529.

Astin, A. W., Vogelgesang, L. J., Ikeda, E. K., & Yee, J. A. (2000). *How service learning affects students.* Los Angeles: Higher Education Research Institute, University of California.

Bowen, W. G., & Bok, D. C. (1998). *The shape of the river: Long-term consequences of considering race in college and university admissions.* Princeton, NJ: Princeton University Press.

Bringle, R. G., & Hatcher, J. A. (1995). A service-learning curriculum for faculty. *Michigan Journal of Community Service Learning, 2*, 112–122.

Bryant, A. N. (2003). Changes in attitudes toward women's roles: Predicting gender-role traditionalism among college students. *Sex Roles, 48*, 131–142.

Cabrera, A. F., Nora, A., & Terenzini, P. T. (1999). Campus racial climate and the adjustment of students to college: A comparison between White students and African American students. *Journal of Higher Education, 70*(2), 134–160.

Carter, D. F. (1999). The impact of institutional choice and environments on African American and White students' degree expectations. *Research in Higher Education, 40(1)*, 17–41.

Eyler, J., & Giles, D. (1999). *Where's the learning in service-learning?* San Francisco: Jossey-Bass.

Feldman, K. A., & Newcomb, T. M. (1969). *The impact of college on students.* San Francisco: Jossey-Bass.

Fischer, M. (2007). Settling into campus life: Differences by race/ethnicity in college involvement and outcomes. *Journal of Higher Education, 78*(2), 125–161.

Flowers, L. A. & Pascarella, E. T. (2003). Cognitive effects of college: Differences between African American and Caucasian students. *Research in Higher Education, 44*(1), 21–49.

Gabelnick, F., MacGregor, J., Matthews, R. S., & Smith, B. L. (1990). *Resources on learning communities* (New Directions for Teaching and Learning No. 41, pp. 95–102) San Francisco: Jossey-Bass.

Harper, S. R. (2008). Realizing the intended outcomes of Brown: High-achieving African American male undergraduates and social capital. *American Behavioral Scientist, 51*(7), 1029–1052.

Harper, S. R., Carini, R. M., Bridges, B. K., & Hayek, J. C. (2004). Gender differences in student engagement among African American undergraduates at historically Black colleges and universities. *Journal of College Student Development, 45*(3), 271–284.

Harper, S. R., & Quaye, S. J. (2007). Student organizations as venues for Black identity expression and development among African American male student leaders. *Journal of College Student Development, 48*(2), 133–159.

Harper, S. R., & Quaye, S. J. (Eds.). (2009). *Student engagement in higher education: Theoretical perspectives and practical approaches for diverse populations.* New York: Routledge.

Hurtado, S., Han, J. C., Saenz, V. B., Espinosa, L. L., Cabrera, N. L., & Cerna, O. S. (2007). Predicting transition and adjustment to college: Biomedical and behavioral science aspirants' and minority students' first year of college. *Research in Higher Education, 48*(7), 841–887.

Inkelas, K. K., Daver, Z. E., Vogt, K. E., & Leonard, J. B. (2007). Living-learning programs and first-generation college students' academic and social transition to college. *Research in Higher Education, 48*(4), 403–434.

Inkelas, K. K., Vogt, K. E., Longerbeam, S. D., Owen, J., & Johnson, D. (2006). Measuring outcomes of living-learning programs: Examining college environments and student learning and development. *Journal of General Education, 55*(1), 40–76.

Inkelas, K. K., & Weisman, J. L. (2003). Different by design: An examination of student outcomes among participants in three types of living-learning programs. *Journal of College Student Development, 44*, 335–368.

Kezar, A., & Moriarty, D. (2000). Expanding our understanding of student leadership development: A study exploring gender and ethnic identity. *Journal of College Student Development, 41*, 55–69.

Kim, Y. K., & Sax, L. J. (2009). Student-faculty interaction in research universities: Differences by student gender, race, income, and first-generation status. *Research in Higher Education, 50(4)*, 437–459.

Kuh, G. D. (2001). Assessing what really matters to student learning: Inside the National Survey of Student Engagement. *Change, 33*, 10–17.

Kuh, G. D., Kinzie, J., Schuh, J. H., Whitt, E. J., & Associates (2005). *Student success in college: Creating conditions that matter.* San Francisco: Jossey-Bass.

Moran, C. (2003). Nourishing and thwarting effects of contextual influences upon multiple dimensions of identity: Does gender matter? *NASPA Journal, 40*, 113–131.

Pascarella, E. T. (1985). College environmental influences on learning and cognitive development: A critical review and synthesis. In J. C. Smart (Ed.), *Higher education: Handbook of theory and research* (Vol. 1, pp. 1–61). New York: Agathon Press.

Pascarella, E. T. (2006). How college affects students: Ten directions for future research. *Journal of College Student Development, 47*(5), 508–520.

Pascarella, E. T., & Terenzini, P. T. (1991). *How college affects students: Findings and insights from twenty years of research.* San Francisco: Jossey-Bass.

Pascarella, E. T., & Terenzini, P. T. (1998). Studying college students in the 21st century: Meeting new challenges. *Review of Higher Education, 21*, 151–165.

Pascarella, E. T., & Terenzini, P. T. (2005). *How college affects students: Vol. 2. A third decade of research.* San Francisco: Jossey-Bass.

Pascarella, E. T., Whitt, E. J., Edison, M. I., Nora, A., Hagedorn, L. S., Yeager, P. M., et al. (1997). Women's perceptions of a "chilly climate" and their cognitive outcomes during the first year of college. *Journal of College Student Development, 38*, 109–124.

Pascarella, E. T., Wolniak, G. C., Pierson, C. T., & Flowers, L. A. (2004). The role of race in the development of plans for a graduate degree. *Review of Higher Education, 27*, 299–320.

Perna, L. W., & Thomas, S. L. (2008). *Theoretical perspectives on student success: Understanding the contributions of the disciplines* (ASHE Higher Education Report, Vol. 34, No. 1). San Francisco: Jossey-Bass.

Pike, G. (2002). The differential effects of on- and off-campus living arrangements on students' openness to diversity. *NASPA Journal, 39*, 283–299.

Saenz, V. B., Ngai, H. N., & Hurtado, S. (2007). Factors influencing positive interactions across race for African American, Asian American, Latino, and White college students. *Research in Higher Education, 48*(1), 1–38.

Sax, L. J. (1994a). Mathematical self-concept: How college reinforces the gender gap. *Research in Higher Education, 35*(2), 141–166.

Sax, L. J. (1994b). Predicting gender and major-field differences in mathematical self-concept during college. *Journal of Women and Minorities in Science and Engineering, 1*, 291–307.

Sax, L. J. (1994c). Retaining tomorrow's scientists: Exploring the factors that keep male and female college students interested in science careers. *Journal of Women and Minorities in Science and Engineering, 1*, 45–61.

Sax, L. J. (1996). The dynamics of "tokenism": How college students are affected by the proportion of women in their major. *Research in Higher Education, 37*, 389–425.

Sax, L. J. (2008). *The gender gap in college: Maximizing the developmental potential of women and men.* San Francisco: Jossey-Bass.

Sax, L. J., Bryant, A. N., & Gilmartin, S. K. (2004). A longitudinal investigation of emotional health among male and female first-year college students. *Journal of the First Year Experience and Students in Transition, 16*(2), 39–65.

Sax, L. J., Bryant, A. N., & Harper, C. E. (2005). The differential effects of student-faculty interaction on college outcomes for women and men. *Journal of College Student Development, 46*(6), 642–659.

Seifert, T. A., Pascarella, E. T., Colangelo, N., & Assouline, S. (2007). The effects of honors program participation on experiences of good practices and learning outcomes. *Journal of College Student Development, 48*(1), 57–74.

Smith, D. G., Morrison, D. E., & Wolf, L. E. (1994). College as a gendered experience: An empirical analysis using multiple lenses. *Journal of Higher Education, 65,* 696–725.

Stage, F. K. (Ed.). (2007). *Answering critical questions using quantitative data* (New Directions for Institutional Research No. 133, pp. 5–16). San Francisco: Jossey-Bass.

Stage, F. K., & Anaya, G. (1996). A transformational view of college student research. In F. K. Stage, G. L. Anaya, J. P. Bean, D. Hossler, & G. D. Kuh (Eds.), *College students: The evolving nature of research* (pp. xi–xxii). Needham Heights, MA: Simon & Schuster.

St. John, E. P., Hu, S., Simmons, A., Carter, D. F. & Weber, J. (2004). What difference does a major make? The influence of college major field on persistence by African American and white students. *Research in Higher Education, 45*(3), 209–232.

Tinto, V. (1987). *Leaving college: Rethinking the causes and cures of student attrition.* Chicago: University of Chicago Press.

Trent, J. W., & Medsker, L. L. (1968). *Beyond high school.* San Francisco: Jossey-Bass.

Upcraft, M. L., Gardner, J. N., & Barefoot, B. O. (2005). *Challenging and supporting the first-year student: A handbook for improving the first year of college.* San Francisco: Jossey-Bass.

Walpole, M. (2003). Socioeconomic status and college: How SES affects college experiences and outcomes. *Review of Higher Education, 27,* 45–73.

Weidman, J. C. (1989). Undergraduate socialization: A conceptual approach. In J. C. Smart (Ed.), *Higher education: Handbook of theory and research* (Vol. 5, pp. 289-322). New York: Agathon Press.

Whitt, E. J., Pascarella, E. T., Nesheim, B.S.E., Marth, B. P., & Pierson, C. T. (2003). Differences between women and men in objectively measured outcomes, and the factors that influence those outcomes, in the first three years of college. *Journal of College Student Development, 44,* 587–610.

CHAPTER THIRTY

STUDENT TECHNOLOGY USE AND STUDENT AFFAIRS PRACTICE

Ana M. Martínez Alemán and Katherine Lynk Wartman

College and university students inhabit and populate hybrid worlds. Whether commuting to campus or living on campus in residence halls, students readily navigate and travel both real-world and online environments. Living in a century in which technological advances enable easy, quick, and highly developed computer-mediated communication, our students effortlessly execute the many functions of their academic and social lives in and through online spaces that are informed by and affect their real-world experiences. Whether students are completing academic course work or consuming and producing information on social networking sites, college and university student life is regulated by technology. Consequently, the unique challenge of student affairs professionals in this century is to understand and interpret student cultures and behaviors that arise from the merging of their real and digital environments.

In this chapter we present a broad overview of some current technologies that particularly influence the relationships between students and student affairs professionals, and that as a consequence have a bearing on student affairs practice. The focus of this chapter is on recent work intended to explain the meaning that college students make of social networking sites, Facebook in particular. Although currently the most popular social networking site generally and among college students particularly, given the essential nature of technology—its developmental velocity and propensity for social transformation—we cannot be certain that Facebook will continue to hold dominance in college and university campus cultures. However, what is clear is that interactive, social online spaces will continue to be a fundamental component of campus culture, whatever their form or iteration. The sociocultural transformation of college student culture set in motion by the development of user-friendly, interactive online spaces will continue to evolve. Given the diachronic character of technology, this chapter is but an opening view of the current landscape of college student online spaces and of what this technology suggests for student affairs practice.

Computer-Mediated Communication

Our understanding of the role of technology in the lives of twenty-first-century college students begins with the realization that these are generations whose access to digital media is historically unprecedented. Since the late 1990s, traditional-age students (eighteen- to twenty-four-year-olds) for whom information is not just *consumed* but *produced* across various technological platforms with ever-increasing sophistication have enrolled in our colleges and universities. In *Growing Up Digital: The Rise of the Net Generation* (1998), Tapscott correctly forecasted that the rise of this historically unique "Net generation" would render technology "transparent" and effectively change how new generations communicate. Indeed, technological growth and increased capability in the last decades have enabled generations of adolescents and young adults to understand computer-mediated communication as natural and authentic; as ordinary and routine; and as ever present and immediate. Most important, as generations for whom relationships are often and in varying ways realized online, their developmental arcs will be unmistakably influenced by technology use. Consequently, how self and community are assumed and shaped will be characteristic of college students' computer-mediated communication.

Already browsing the Internet by the 1990s, college and university students became more expert and eager users of technologies than were those who preceded them. The introduction of Mosaic, a user interface that enabled embedding of images in text (instead of appearing in a separate window), ensured the rapid increase of college students' Internet use (Reid, 1997) and the subsequent popularity of social networking sites like Facebook, which allows the easy uploading of digital photos and images. The introduction of search engines, improved downloading capabilities of multiple media, and the refinement of portable laptops and wireless communication all contributed to the fast enculturation of the relevance of interactive technology for users, especially for younger generations. As suggested by demographic data, by the end of the twentieth century, 20 percent of college students had used computers as children, all had used computers as teenagers, and half were experienced Internet users (Jones, 2002). As a result, students entering college at the beginning of this century were informed, experienced users of fast, efficient, and graphically loaded technology. As Tapscott (2008) has observed in his update on the Net Generation, these are students who have grown up in the digital world. Consequently, college and university students are well versed in the culture and capabilities of personal computing and take for granted technology as "their way of life" (Martínez Alemán & Wartman, p. 16, 2009). In sum, new traditional-age college and university entrants have lived in a hybrid world of interaction between real and online experiences and relationships.

Since the 1990s, then, college and university students have been high-volume online users. More than any other demographic, college students are likely to communicate with family, friends, and faculty online (Jones, 2002). In 2007, college and university students in the United States spent an average of eighteen hours every week online, typically communicating on social networking sites and on Instant Messenger. Predictably, almost all undergraduates (99.9 percent) consider technology as central to communicating with friends on-campus and off-campus and do so through social networking sites, especially sites like Facebook (Salaway, Katz, Caruso, Kvavik, & Nelson, 2007). College and university students residing on campus are regular users of social networking sites, and recent data show that Facebook is now the online site most favored by college students (College Students: Facebook Top Site, 2009). The largest age group of active Facebook users in the U.S. are eighteen- to twenty-five-year-olds (Number of US Facebook Users, 2009), a demographic concentrated on our residential college and university campuses.

As consumers and producers of digital information knowledge, college and university students engage in technologies that simulate real-world activities and associations. As students, they make use of learning technologies, both to fulfill course requirements and as part of a broader social, recreational scheme. For example, students may join a multi-user virtual environment (MUVE), such as Second Life, either as an online gaming exercise or as course-work requirement. Virtual worlds and online gaming, whether single-user platforms or massively multiplayer online role-playing games (MMORPGs), are part of the technological landscape that engages college students in hybrid learning activities requiring decision making, group participation, and knowledge acquisition (Brown, 2006; Van Eck, 2006). Often these learning technologies have been a part of many of our students' K–12 educational experiences; and if not, their generational context certainly predisposes them to virtual environments in which they can use new models of teaching and learning. In contrast to linear faculty-student instruction, these and other forms of online learning are active and interactive and come from multiple sources. Engaging the whole student in the sense that multiple aspects of cognition, behavioral, and affective domains are exercised, learning technologies, digital game-based learning (DGBL), and current and future MUVEs are compatible with the neo-millennial learner's communal learning styles (Dede, 2005). Because these learning technologies appeal to generational learning characteristics—experiential learning with mentorship (whether by faculty, student affairs professionals, peers, or experts) and communal contemplation and deliberation—student affairs administrators face and will continue to confront the effects of technology on student development and student culture (Dede, 2005).

Together with the accelerating rise in learning and information technologies on campuses, general-use technologies not specific to the college community have migrated to the campus. Students, faculty, administrators, and staff use text messages to communicate in both their personal and professional lives. Each of these groups participates in online blogging in the campus context or in the broader online world; takes part in webinars; consumes and contributes to online wikis; and utilizes interactive

Web applications for professional networking. Since 2003, LinkedIn has been used by student affairs professionals, faculty, other administrators, and even students to make links within professional communities. Finally, launched in 2006, Twitter makes micro-blogging possible across Internet-connected smartphones, extending the reach of the Internet and its social networking capacities beyond user computers, thus effectively changing the geography of the campus and the sociology of its constituents.

Online Social Networking: The Facebook Phenomenon

The most significant transformation of the sociology of campus communication and community through technology can be seen in the development and expansion of social networking sites, especially the now-dominant social networking site Facebook and the business-oriented, professional social networking site LinkedIn. Social networking sites like Facebook have unmistakably altered communication on campus. Their nearly effortless use and fast graphic user interface]exchanges appeal to generational dispositions and expectations common to traditional-aged college students as well as to generations of older students who are now acclimated social networking site users. New data on Facebook user demographics show a rapid increase in the number of users ages thirty-five to forty-five, most of them women (Number of US Facebook Users, 2009). Consequently, for reentry or adult students, typically over age twenty-five, Facebook can also present a means for campus integration and socialization.

Early research on Internet use did not capture the effects of the interactive nature of such social networking sites as Facebook, especially the ways in which social networking sites can be used as platforms for producing self-presentation. Viewing Internet use as a source of social isolation, early research ignored the role that real-life relational experiences play in the digital communication of identity and the social value that users derive from these communications (Katz & Rice, 2002). In their Syntopia Project, Katz and Rice attended to the character of online identity and social bonding, and rightly assessed that the production of online self-representation was not disjointed or lacking coherence. This suggested that online use had positive effects on identity—in particular, that these spaces had a propensity for enabling users to unify self and identity rather than engendering dissociated or fractured notions of self (p. 283).

Not so surprisingly, social networking sites like Facebook also serve as a means for the accrual of social capital by users. As Donath and boyd (2004) note, the most prominent and significant feature of online social networking sites is the ability to present one's relationships, associations, and friendships, implied in which is the authentication of identity. But researchers also argue that such public displays of associations can lead some users to accumulate superficial associations as well as encourage self-promotion and egotism (Rosen, 2007; Walther et al., 2008). The accumulation of "friends" on Facebook, for example, can be understood as commodifying relationships, rendering social networking the accretion of social capital and power (Marwick, 2005). Displayed publicly on the site, the user's social graph signals important information about the user—who his or her friends are, what groups he or she belongs to—effectively suggesting an identity to the viewer. According to boyd (2007), this property of social networking sites like Facebook and MySpace functions as a guide for the viewer about who and what the user is and, in doing so, validates the user. This validation is indispensable for social capital in that online connections are verified and then likely to be traded upon in the real world. Ellison, Steinfeld, and Lampe (2007) argue that Facebook does help undergraduates accrue and direct social capital but does not advance "bonding social capital." Social capital may certainly multiply for users of Facebook as a consequence of an increase in connections, but these often are not profound relationships.

Since its development in 2004, Facebook has captured the cultural relevance of "trust-based" or "friendship-based" communication, in which connections are vetted through known relationships (like other friends or relatives) within a particular social context (such as a college campus, residence hall, or academic course) (boyd & Ellison, 2007; Lampe, Ellison, & Steinfield, 2007). Like other social networking sites that predated it, Facebook's premise is that an individual's direct and indirect social contacts and relationships (the individual's "social graph") are significant, and that a connection with a known "friend" provides some measure of safety, security, and cultural relevance. The network of friendships and associations comprises primary social bonds as well as secondary bonds and beyond. Users can trust and give varying levels of importance to communications based on connections that they have validated within a specific social context. Identifying with and knowing the background of the Facebook connection appears to give users a measure of security that they consider important (boyd, 2004).

In such niche communities as college and university campuses, this is a considerably vital feature. Trust-based or friendship-based social networking sites like Facebook give students the platforms on and through which they can present themselves as both autonomous, independent beings and as members of various communities and groups. Simultaneously "egocentric" (boyd & Ellison, 2007) and communal, trust-based sites like Facebook rely on an assortment of real-world structures, such as group identification and purposes, temporal structures, system infrastructures, and user characteristics (Jones, 1998), to enable the exchange of culturally important and user-specific information.

As a unique niche community or "walled garden," the college campus is oftentimes developmentally distinctive and organized by students' shared interests and norms. Online, the traditional-age college user reproduces real-world and campus conventions but also engages in the active production of new group norms shaped and informed by their developmental positions. On Facebook, college students engage in a reproduction of their social geography, in which the signs and symbols of college cultures have significance and consequently communicate meaning. A distinction of the "postmodern condition" (Lyotard, 1984), computer-mediated communication through Facebook appears to be a means to engage with the meta-narrative of identity salient with Net generations. Through this digital platform, students consume and produce narratives of identity because the technology enables them to use language—so central to social bonds—to create meaning. On Facebook, language and image—another generationally important sign—are used to construct representations of self and identity and group membership that often challenge modernist assumptions (Lyotard). The challenge to modernist norms comes from the realization that social networking sites are spaces in which users tolerate unpredictable and incongruent signaling, especially with regard to self-presentation. The production and consumption of stable and alterable self-presentation marks the space generationally as well as developmentally.

Social Networking and Identity

Facebook and other social networking sites are places of "hyper-reality" (Baudrillard, 1983) in which composed and conditional self-identity goes beyond real and online space at the same time. Identity construction on Facebook is about using new forms of expression and exploring potential other identities. On Facebook, college students' identities—exhibited through their the "profiles"—are fluid, variable versions of what and who the student user is and is not. Facebook profiles can be counterfeit, but they are not inauthentic; students create profiles that are playful, paradoxical, or honest. But because users often share campus and generational culture, and because signals are predictable within the digital and real-world niches, the communication of identity on Facebook is understood by users as authentic and trustworthy (Lampe, Ellison, & Steinfeld, 2007). Students understand Facebook as a hyper-reality, as a space in which real and imagined properties of self can be put on display to trusted associations. Despite the extension of Facebook to users outside a student's campus network, students nevertheless interpret Facebook profiles as hyper-real—expressions of a fluid identity grounded in real-world and online contexts (Martínez Alemán & Wartman, 2009).

Identity construction on Facebook is characterized by an online practice that boyd and Ellison (2007) termed "impression management"—how students control and execute the presentation of self online through their social networking site profiles. On social networking sites, information is a signal that indicates user characteristics. Self-presentation on Facebook through the user profile and applications is thus a function of the language and images posted, the intent of the user-owner in the postings, and the perception of the audience-users. Facebook profiles, then, are "user portrayals" of students' self-understandings and "how it is that they want to be seen by others" (Martínez Alemán & Wartman, 2009, p. 39). College students vary in their consciousness relative to these signals, but all users have some awareness of the signaling effects of profile construction and postings (Martínez Alemán & Wartman, 2009).

Student affairs professionals, consequently, can correctly discern that student use of social networking sites has implications for student identity development and, further, for students' understanding, presentation, and perception of gender, race and ethnicity, and social class. Although very little empirical research has been conducted to learn about and determine the logically complex and specific sociocultural effects of gender, race, ethnicity, and class on student identity online, social scientists have identified the salience of these cultural constructions in online behavior and identity presentation (boyd, 2004, 2007; DeVoss & Selfe, 2002; EDUCAUSE, 2007; Ellison et al., 2007; Valkenburg & Schouten, 2006). From this research, we know that impression management is marked by gender, race and ethnicity, and social class consciousness (Hargittai, 2007; Martínez Alemán & Wartman, 2009). Our students are also participants in online sites dedicated to racial and ethnic identity groups. AsianAvenue, BlackPlanet, and MiGente provide our students with more opportunities to negotiate and contemplate identity with others.

Recent empirical work on the meaning that college students make of their Facebook use confirms that students do explore forms of self-expression that are informed by race and ethnicity, class consciousness, and gender (Martínez Alemán & Wartman, 2009). Students of color in this study were very aware of the differences between their profile constructions and those of White students. They were deliberate in their decisions about photographs posted that could suggest to faculty and White students that they did not "belong" on campus. Noting the double standard that exists between perceptions of majority and minority student behavior, students of color did not want to be photographed drinking alcohol or in party scenes that would imply illicit behavior. African American women intentionally posed for Facebook photos, carefully selecting attire and aesthetics that would be perceived as professional, qualified, and aligned with normative standards of femininity. Whereas students of color were very conscious of how their profiles (and identities) would be read—especially by faculty, administrators, and White students, White students were generally unaware of race and ethnicity distinctions in self-presentation. Although White students in this study recognized that race and ethnicity are factors that matter to identity and that these are sociocultural factors affecting campus life, they were unable to articulate the differences in online identities or profiles between students of color and White students. Generally, White students could not "see" racial and ethnic differences on Facebook profiles (Martínez Alemán & Wartman).

Expressing gender on social networking sites is also a relevant concern of students and is thus important for student affairs professionals to understand. On Facebook, for example, women are the more active users, taking and uploading more photographs than their male peers (Martínez Alemán & Wartman, 2009). Men's photo albums typically comprise photos of travel or parties, whereas women's albums include a much broader range of activities and contain presentations of family and friends. On Facebook, college women appear to attend to online identity more than do college men, actively engaging in self-authorship through self-presentation online, all the while "adhering to traditional real-world gender conventions about communication and self-presentation" (p. 86). Among men, normative conventions of masculinity are common in Facebook use; men seem to be less concerned with conformity and perception, and more about registering autonomy publicly online. Bravado as well as playfulness characterize men's online identities.

Embedded in a student's presentation of gender is the performance of sexuality. On social networking sites, college and university students make public "cultural narratives of normative and counter-normative behavior" (Martínez Alemán & Wartman, 2009, p. 85). College students often prepare profiles to signal claims about normative student identity by portraying that they are heterosexual. Yet they also perform counter-normatives by explicitly identifying as gay, lesbian, or transgender, and by subverting Facebook's "relationship status" through ritualized student coding. There is also, typically, a degree of playfulness in the depiction of sexuality by heterosexual women, which is not common among heterosexual men: whereas heterosexual college women will publicly post that they are "in a relationship with" another woman, heterosexual men rarely do the same. Cultural, campus, and generational norms still inform these decisions for college students; accordingly, the conscious and intentional weight of homophobia will mark such postings, making heterosexual men less likely to (even in jest) appear gay. In general, choices about relationship status on Facebook run along normative gender lines.

We are not very clear about the effects of social class consciousness on students' use of social networking sites. College students do read and perceive cultural signals and cues on Facebook, so it stands to reason that social class is both an interpretable dimension and constitutive element of use. Research bears this out to some extent in that college students do admit that there are indicators of social or economic class status on Facebook profiles. For example, first-generation college students spent more time on MySpace communicating with friends who did not attend college or who were at local colleges in their hometowns (Martínez Alemán & Wartman, 2009). This makes sense given that MySpace users tend to come from lower income levels, 12 percent of whom earn $60,000 or less per year (Tancer, 2007). Facebook, although now the dominant social networking site, still captures more affluent and highly educated users (Number of US Facebook Users, 2009). Concerned with student engagement and the potential for student disaffection, student affairs administrators should take this aspect of student social networking site use into account. How students do and don't perceive themselves to be a part of college culture now includes their performances on and reactions to online spaces.

It is also imperative to note that there appears to be a "developmental curve that characterizes Facebook use" among college and university students (Martínez Alemán & Wartman, 2009, p. 53). The nature and purpose of college students' use across their undergraduate years appears to reflect their developmental positions and evolving self-awareness. First- and second-year college students have higher rates and frequency of use than third-year and graduating students. Students in the early years of residential college life, furthermore, appear to have fewer concerns about impression management, and their use consciousness is characterized by fewer concerns about privacy and user control (Martínez Alemán & Wartman, 2009). As student affairs practitioners begin to shape policies on campus online social networking, it is important for them to consider this developmental difference among early-adult students.

Student Affairs and Students' Technology Use

Students on today's college campuses live their lives in hybrid environments that include face-to-face as well as online interactions. To students, their behavior in online communities is real and intertwines with their everyday lives on their bricks-and-mortar campuses (Martínez Alemán & Wartman, 2009). The challenge for student affairs administrators is to maintain their roles in student culture while understanding and adapting their work to suit these new student environments. Student affairs administrators must come to understand how students use various forms of popular online technology, such as social networking sites and instant messaging applications, to interact with others, and then adapt their practice to include this understanding. This may entail using these forms of technology themselves. Student affairs administrators must find a way to provide students with the right balance of challenge and support (Sanford, 1962), engage students in active learning, build supportive and inclusive communities (Principles of Good Practice for Student Affairs, 1996), and support students' identity development in these new environment. Student behavior online is still student behavior, and the time has passed when administrators can simply ignore such activities, considering them to be outside of the realm of their responsibilities. If student behavior is a function of the person and the environment (Evans, Forney & Guido-DiBrito, 1998; Lewin, 1936), how does this change when the environment includes both real and online elements?

One reason that understanding students' learning and development in this hybrid context can be complicated and challenging is that student affairs administrators strive to consider the development of the whole student (American Council on Education, 1994). Students may have certain identities that play out more online, and they may also present different identities to different people depending on the context, such that their identities appear fragmented. Student affairs administrators typically look at student identity development from a modernist perspective; a postmodern perspective would account for these different identities. For example, a student who is president of a prominent organization on campus can also be someone who engages in binge drinking on weekends, and sometimes photos of these escapades appear online on social networking sites.

Student affairs administrators have a unique vantage point when it comes to student culture. They are intimately familiar with student culture and even help to shape it through their work with students, but they are not the ones who dictate its standards, simply because they are not students. Students themselves are the ones who ultimately contribute to the formation of student culture. This is true for student culture on campus and online, including on social networking sites. In fact, students believe that the online communities they create on spaces like Facebook are ultimately and fundamentally about college students (Martínez Alemán & Wartman, 2009). Just as with "real" campus culture, some students (most likely student leaders) will gladly welcome student affairs administrators to participate, whereas some will consider their presence invasive. Student affairs administrators need to remember this when working with students in the context of students' use of technology. Even if student affairs administrators engage in online activity on social networking sites themselves, they need to respect the cultures and spaces that students create there.

Understanding the way students use online media to communicate with one another and explore identity will help administrators be better able to support the whole student (including the student's multiple selves). For example, if a student affairs administrator who works in residence life is familiar with how students converse using

Instant Messenger, and a roommate conflict arises over content posted through this medium, she may be better able to counsel and advise the students in this situation. Similarly, a student affairs administrator in career development may be able to coach seniors entering the job market about self-presentation on online social networking sites if he is familiar with how students use these sites. How can student affairs administrators learn about online campus culture and how students are most currently using technology if they are not students and technically outsiders to this campus culture, especially as these usage trends may shift and change so rapidly? One way is to learn from the students themselves, especially student leaders, who are in a unique position between student affairs administrators and the greater student body, and who may serve as "cultural translators" (Martínez Alemán & Wartman, 2009).

When student affairs administrators understand how students use technology to express themselves and to communicate with one another as well as to form communities, they can both effectively react to student conduct online and educate students in order to support their development in the online context. Even though some student behaviors do technically take place online rather than on campus, this does not mean that the information posted there is private. Student affairs administrators' must still encourage active student learning (Principles of Good Practice for Student Affairs, 1996) and, according to the principles in *Learning Reconsidered* (Keeling, 2004), the most transformative learning occurs within the active context of students' lives—which includes both real and online elements.

Reactive Approaches: Student Conduct

Students' use of online social networking sites has received primarily negative attention. For example, administrators as well as the popular media have expressed concern over students' lack of privacy, exposing too much information about themselves publicly, most often through photos of questionable behaviors. We believe that students' use of online social networking sites is a campus reality and that social networking sites, rather than representing a cause for alarm and concern, can be used in a positive way to help students build community.

Student affairs administrators are free to react to any behavior that occurs online and violates college policy. It is the responsibility of student affairs administrators who work in judicial affairs to enforce these standards of conduct (Council for the Advancement of Standards in Higher Education, 1996). This does not necessarily mean that student affairs administrators or campus police should search online for student behavior that violates college policy, in the same way that a dean of students would not likely stand outside a campus party checking students' identification cards to ensure that everyone there is at least twenty-one years of age. However, this does mean that student affairs professionals are justified in reacting when these sorts of instances come to their attention, whether through their own use of social networking sites or through another source, such as students themselves. Students should understand student affairs administrators' reactions to their behavior online, because to students the hyper-reality (Baudrillard, 1983) that they live in and the behavior they exhibit online are "real" (Martínez Alemán & Wartman, 2009). Because students perceive the online campus community as a "walled garden," they may not understand how administrators come across information about questionable behaviors. Behavior of concern that relates not only to general student conduct but also to student well-being may come to administrators' attention. For example, a student might notice a statement of self-harm on a roommate's Facebook page, or a student might become concerned about another student's mental health during an exchange that is taking place on Instant Messenger. These instances may then be brought to the attention of a student affairs administrator. In fact, because of the ease of student-to-student communication that technology allows, and because sites like Facebook serve as hubs for identity development and self-expression, it may be the case that students (and thus also administrators) have more access to information about students' well-being than they have had in the past.

The same protocols that apply to student conduct and safety in general also apply in this new context. For example, if there is a chance that a student could inflict harm on himself or others, and if administrators have prior knowledge of this and can foresee that something harmful might occur, the institution could be liable if something bad happens to a student. Student affairs administrators have a responsibility to consider safety as a central aspect of student life (Bickel & Lake, 1999). If cases concerning safety arise online, administrators should follow their college policies as if they had learned of this information in another way, such as a face-to-face disclosure from a student. In addition to responding to online information about students' potential self-harm or harm to others, student administrators also want to take seriously students' concerns about their own safety in the online environment and work with campus security and police departments to do so. Student affairs administrators and campus police should establish protocols to respond to students who are concerned about their personal safety online. Preventing these incidents can also be the subject of educational sessions for students, especially new students.

The most worrisome student conduct online should be enforceable under policies that institutions already have in place, such as those governing technology use and student conduct. However, student affairs administrators should consider how they will handle behavior that occurs online, whether it is on Facebook or elsewhere, and then communicate these policies to students in order to best educate them about the potential consequences of their online behavior. Some colleges and universities have posted these policies and discussions of principles for responsible use of social networking sites on their Web sites as general guidelines and suggestions that are more specific than those in place addressing campus computer use or student conduct. Students may need education to discern what behaviors constitute a violation of campus policy. In particular, students may need education about consequences for posting information online that could defame or be libelous. The first student to be expelled from a university as a result of an online posting on Facebook was found to have written comments on his page that defamed a campus police officer (Schweitzer, 2005). There may be opportunities for student affairs administrators to collaborate with information technology staff in order to educate students about these policies. First-year orientation may be a good time to conduct a session educating students.

When a student affairs administrator encounters worrisome student behavior, on Facebook or another online site, that does not directly violate campus policy or pose a safety threat, this can provide the student affairs administrator with an opportunity to have an educative conversation with the student that might give him or her a chance for active learning from his or her contextual environment (Keeling, 2004) and help the student to reflect upon his or her expression of identity. Such interventions can be particularly important for students in public leadership positions on campus, such as athletes, resident advisors, and officers in student organizations.

Proactive Approaches: Education and Training

It is important that student affairs administrators educate students about their use of online technologies, not just so that students are aware of campus policies but also so that student affairs administrators can help students best manage their self-presentation online and encourage student development and engagement. Student affairs administrators should help to facilitate educational sessions and trainings regarding students' communication and self-presentation management in the online sphere.

As previously mentioned, student leaders are in a unique position to help educate others about online student culture. As students themselves, they understand the social norms and inner workings of online campus culture. They serve as cultural translators, teaching student affairs administrators about online campus culture and helping to reach the greater student body with messages about self-presentation and impression management in this environment (Martínez Alemán & Wartman, 2009). Student leaders should be trained so that they may serve as resources for other students seeking to learn about Facebook and other online social networking domains. Who should conduct these trainings for student leaders? Student affairs administrators who are well versed in online campus culture could do so, although it would be best to conduct the trainings alongside other students. It is important to have student representation because students are the true authorities on online campus culture.

In the trainings, student leaders should also have the chance to reflect on their own use of these technologies and how they manage their communication and self-presentation online. Most student leaders have a high level of consciousness about this (Martínez Alemán & Wartman, 2009). They should also be trained in how to react when they come across an image or message in an online forum that causes concern. Do the student leaders confront the student themselves or first report the incident directly to a supervisor in student affairs? What types of behavior should be of concern for student leaders? For example, what are the different possible responses to a photo in which an underage student appears to be holding an alcoholic drink at an off-campus party, or to a message a student posts to her online profile indicating that she might be suicidal? What are the protocols when student leaders are concerned about a student's safety, or when a student comes to a student leader concerned about his or her own safety? These policies and procedures should be established and communicated to student leaders ahead of time rather than dealt with on strictly a reactionary basis.

The focus of the educational sessions for the general student body should be on navigating privacy settings and controlling what information is seen and by whom on Facebook and other online applications. Some students have a certain naïveté when it comes to managing their privacy online and do not understand the full range of control they have over the content that they share (Martínez Alemán & Wartman, 2009). Through these trainings, administrators use student leaders, such as sports team captains, orientation leaders, and resident advisors as proxies to educate students and raise their consciousness about the level of control they can have over what they post online. As students use certain technologies at younger and younger ages, more will be coming to college aware of different privacy functions for managing their multiple identities. However, it is likely that they will need to be educated in the context of both college policy and online social norms established by college students. In addition, it is important to educate students about safety online, reminding students not to post contact information in places where people whom they might not want to have this information could potentially access it. Because of the "walled garden" effect, students often feel safe within their online communities and need help differentiating between what is public and what is private.

Student affairs administrators not only support individual student learning and development but also help to build supportive and inclusive communities (Principles of Good Practice for Student Affairs, 1996). Student affairs administrators can focus on educating students about their individual online activity and also help students use online social networking sites to facilitate campus community development. Because online campus culture is such a strong reality on college campuses today, administrators do need to respond to and work within the context of this new culture. However, when doing so, they must remember that there are students who choose not to play an active role in this aspect of campus life and do not engage with others in the online social world of their peers. When helping students to use different media as tools to communicate with others and build community, student affairs administrators must remember that there are students who may not be a part of these online communities. Some commuter students or students who do not have their own computers and do most of their computing in campus labs may have more limited access to these resources than do residential students who have computers in their residence hall rooms. Some students, moreover, may simply choose not to be on social networking sites. There are some specific ways in which different areas of student affairs might want to think about supporting student development and community engagement in the context of the new campus reality.

Athletics

Athletes are student leaders who may require special training. It is particularly important to educate athletes about impression management because they are public figures on and off campus. As representatives of their college or university, student-athletes need to reflect on how they present their identities online. They should also be made aware of specific consequences, imposed by the athletic department, for their actions on social networking sites. Many colleges and universities have established specific guidelines for athletes in regard to their performance in the online social world, and have specific policies about what athletes can and cannot post online, often managing student profiles within the athletic department. However, as previously mentioned, the strongest messages about self-representation norms come from other students. Therefore, team captains or students on an athletic council, for example, may be the best candidates to train other athletes on these topics.

Campus Activities

Student affairs administrators who work in campus activities may be best positioned to help students advertise campus events through online venues, a process that will increase attendance at these events and therefore help build campus community. Because online social networking sites are central to how students communicate information and are often the primary form of peer-to-peer communication (Martínez-Alemán & Wartman, 2009), they can be useful for informing the broader campus community of college- and university-sponsored events. It is important, however, for student affairs administrators to keep in mind that not every student has access to online social networking sites and that even though they can be a very effective tool for disseminating news about campus goings-on quickly and widely, alternative methods of communication and advertising should also be used in order to ensure that all students hear about these events and are provided with the opportunity to attend them.

Career Services

Increasingly, employers are researching candidates by looking at their online social networking site profiles. Conducting educational sessions and speaking with students individually about managing their professional identities online are areas to which student affairs administrators working in career services could contribute. For example, they could discuss impression management in this context. In addition, offices like career services that provide regular workshops for students may want to use online social networking sites in order to advertise these events to students.

Orientation

Student affairs administrators are typically prepared to orient students to campus culture once the students actually arrive on the physical college campus. However, students are orienting themselves to campus culture well before they ever arrive at new-student orientation sessions on their bricks-and-mortar campuses. The online social world of college students allows access to incoming students, and the connections that these students first make to campus culture occur in this online environment (Martínez

Alemán & Wartman, 2009). Incoming students network with their peers online in the spring and summer before matriculating at their chosen colleges and universities. This may help students with adjustment and contribute to student engagement. Student affairs administrators who work with orientation and first-year programs will want to make sure that this communication between new students online is not unregulated, because this can lead to the promulgation of misinformation. Administrators should work with orientation leaders and other student leaders in order to understand the ways in which students may have already been acquainted with campus culture before arriving on campus. Administrators will also want to make sure that online forums for prospective students are not unregulated. Administrators don't need to be part of these conversations themselves, but should make sure that student leaders are reading the information posted in order to correct any misinformation that circulates and also to help new students negotiate campus culture online.

Orientation leaders are also student leaders who should receive specific training in online social networking, in regard to both impression management and the use of privacy settings, so that they are best positioned to help incoming students navigate the online social world at college. In addition, orientation is an ideal time to hold educational sessions for incoming students to discuss these topics. Preferably, these sessions would be facilitated by orientation leaders or other student leaders.

Residential Life

Like administrators in campus activities, those who work in residential life can assist students in using Facebook to advertise community-building events and provide residents with an online space to get to know and communicate with one another. Student leaders in residential life, such as resident advisors, will need training on responses to student behavior of concern that arises in the online social world. They will also need to be aware of how interactions between students may be complicated by the use of technology for peer-to-peer communication. For example, a simple roommate conflict could be complicated by an exchange between the two roommates that takes place online: if the students are communicating primarily online rather than face-to-face, there is a greater likelihood that miscommunication will occur.

Administrators' Use of Online Social Networking Sites

As discussed earlier, student affairs administrators may want to become members of online social networking sites that are frequented by college students. This will likely happen more and more as sites like Facebook broaden to include more users from outside of college. In addition, growing numbers of people who had online social networking accounts as undergraduate students will become student affairs administrators. Finally, student affairs administrators may want to join the online campus community in order to learn more about student culture.

Do administrators belong in students' online social world? Student affairs administrators, even though they are very close to the center of campus life, are actually on the periphery of the online social world at their colleges. They may open accounts, explore the online social campus, and even have communication exchanges with students, yet students don't necessarily consider administrators to be members of their online niche community (Martínez Alemán & Wartman, 2009). Therefore, when present in the online social world of college students, student affairs administrators must be cautious and be mindful that the online campus culture is essentially shaped and managed by college students rather than professionals.

Student affairs administrators' boundaries on online social networking sites like Facebook and their roles in the online social world are really not that different from those in the real world of college student culture. Administrators are both insiders and outsiders in relation to student life. Although they may come to intimately understand the inner workings of student campus culture as they work to promote community and individual student development, they are not quite part of the culture because they are not students. Administrators need to be mindful of their unique insider-outsider position in regard to student culture (Martínez -Alemán & Wartman, 2009).

Administrators may join the online social community, but it is not necessary that they do so. It is important, if administrators wish to communicate with students through online social networking sites and have access to each other's information, that they let students initiate these contacts. Student affairs administrators should let students dictate the terms of their online social worlds and decide whether or not to invite the administrators to be part of their virtual networks. In general, student affairs administrators should not initiate requests to see student information by communicating with students through these media—even though a student affairs administrator may consider what they post online "public space," to students, asking to see their profiles or information that is only accessible with their permission can be seen as invasive. Other students will gladly welcome student affairs administrators to the online social world and happily share information and communicate with them through this forum.

Administrators also need to be conscious of their own impression management online and learn how to navigate the privacy settings, which allow the user to control what information is shared, and with whom. Some student affairs administrators may also exhibit some degree of naïveté as new users of online social networking sites. Impression management, how to control one's privacy, and how to limit the information that one shares with students are topics that could be featured in training sessions—sponsored by student affairs organizations—for graduate students, new professionals, and any administrator joining the online social community for the first time.

Conclusion

In this chapter we have highlighted the nature of technology use among college and university students, in particular their use and understanding of online social networking sites. We featured student use and the meaning they make of Facebook, the most popular social networking site among college students today. We present this discussion in order to inform student affairs educators about the many ways in which technology intersects with college student development, especially students' construction of identity as racial, ethnic, and gendered selves in early adulthood. Even if Facebook loses its popularity prior to the publication of the sixth edition of *Student Services*, we are certain that it will be replaced with a new social networking option that college students find appealing.

The new campus reality for students is a hybrid world of online and real-world experiences, and student affairs professionals are uniquely positioned to educate and assist them in negotiating this terrain. Student affairs educators are charged with overseeing student growth and development, student engagement and well-being, and the general social and cultural health of student life. Given the remarkable impact that social networking sites and other online spaces have had on new and upcoming generations of college students, student affairs practice must now include an awareness of student life online and must build a competence for its care and support.

References

American Council on Education. (1994). The student personnel point of view. In A. L. Rentz (Ed.), *Student affairs: A profession's heritage.* Lanham, MD: American College Personnel Association.

Baudrillard, J. (1983). *Simulations.* Cambridge, MA: MIT Press.

Bickel, R. D., & Lake, P. F. (1999). *The rights and responsibilities of the modern university.* Durham, NC: Carolina Academic Press.

boyd, d. m. (2004, April). *Friendster and publicly articulated social networks.* Paper presented at the Conference on Human Factors and Computing Systems (CHI 2004), Vienna.

boyd, d. m. (2007). Why youth (heart) social network sites: The role of networked publics in teenage social life. In D. Buckingham (Ed.), *MacArthur Foundation series on digital learning—Youth, identity, and digital media volume* (pp. 119–142). Cambridge, MA: MIT Press.

boyd, d. m., & Ellison, N. (2007). Social network sites: Definition, history, and scholarship. *Journal of Computer-Mediated Communication, 13*(1), article 11.

Brown, J. S. (2006). New learning environments in the 21st century: Exploring the edge. *Forum Futures 2006.* Cambridge, MA: Forum for the Future of Higher Education. Retrieved July 30, 2009, from www.educause.edu/ELI/LearningTechnologies/Games SimulationsandVirtualWorld/11263.

College students: Facebook top site, social networking really hot. (2009). Retrieved July 12, 2009, from www.mediabuyerplanner.com/entry/35928/college-students-facebook-top-site-social-networking-really-hot/.

Council for the Advancement of Standards in Higher Education. (1996). CAS self-assessment guide for student conduct programs. Retrieved July 29, 2009, from www.usu.edu/studentconduct/CASassesment.pdf.

Dede, C. (2005). Planning for neomillennial learning styles. *EDUCAUSE.* Retrieved August 26, 2007, from http://connect.educause.edu/Library/EDUCAUSE+Quarterly/Planningfor NeomillennialL/39899.

DeVoss, D. N., & Selfe, C. L. (2002). This page under construction: Reading women shaping online identities. *Pedagogy: Critical Approaches to Teaching Literature, Language, Composition and Culture, 2*(1), 31–48.

Donath, J., & boyd, d. m. (2004). Public displays of connection. *BT Technology Journal, 22*(4), 70–82.

EDUCAUSE (2007). *EDUCAUSE core data survey.* Retrieved July 30, 2009, from www.educause .edu/ir/library/pdf/pub8004e.pdf.

Ellison, N. B., Steinfeld, C., & Lampe, C. (2007). The benefits of Facebook "friends": Social capital and college students' use of online social network sites. *Journal of Computer- Mediated Communication, 12*(4), article 1. Retrieved December 8, 2007, from http://jcmc.indiana.edu/ vol12/issue4/ellison.html.

Evans, N. J., Forney, D. S., & Guido-DiBrito, F. (1998). *Student development in college: Theory, research, and practice.* San Francisco: Jossey-Bass.

Hargittai, E. (2007). Whose space? Differences among users and non-users of social network sites. *Journal of Computer-Mediated Communication, 13*(1), article 14. Retrieved January 2, 2008, from http://jcmc.indiana.edu/vol13/issue1/hargittai.html.

Jones, S. G. (Ed.). (1998). *Cybersociety 2.0: Revisiting computer-mediated communication and community.* Thousand Oaks, CA: Sage.

Jones, S. G. (2002). The Internet goes to college: How students are living in the future with today's technology. *Pew Internet & American Life Project.* Retrieved August 16, 2007, from www .pewInternet.org/.

Katz, J. E., & Rice, R. E. (2002). *Social consequences of Internet use: Access, involvement, and interaction.* Cambridge, MA: MIT Press.

Keeling, R. P. (Ed.). (2004). *Learning reconsidered: A campus-wide focus on the student experience.* Washington DC: American College Personnel Association & National Association of Student Personnel Administrators.

Lampe, C., Ellison, N., & Steinfeld, C. (2007). A familiar Face(book): Profile elements as signals in an online social network. *Proceedings of Conference on Human Factors in Computing Systems (CHI 2007)* (pp. 435–444). New York: ACM Press.

Lewin, K. (1936). *Principles of topological psychology.* New York: McGraw-Hill.

Lyotard, J. (1984). *The postmodern condition: A report on knowledge.* Minneapolis: University of Minnesota Press.

Martínez Alemán, A. M., & Wartman, K. L. (2009). *Online social networking on campus: Understanding what matters in student culture.* New York: Routledge.

Marwick, A. (2005). *"I'm a lot more interesting than a Friendster profile": Identity presentation, authenticity, and power in social networking services.* Paper presented at Internet Research 6.0, Chicago.

Number of US Facebook users over 35 nearly doubles in last 60 days. Retrieved July 26, 2009, from www.insidefacebook.com/2009/03/25/number-of-us-facebook-users-over-35-nearly-doubles-in-last-60-days/.

Principles of good practice for student affairs. (1996). Retrieved July 29, 2009, from www.acpa .nche.edu/pgp/principle.htm.

Reid, R. H. (1997). *Architects of the Web: 1000 days that built the future of business.* New York: Wiley.

Rosen, C. (2007). Virtual friendship and the new narcissism. *New Atlantis, 17,* 15–31.

Salaway, G., Katz, R. N., Caruso, J. B., Kvavik, R. B., & Nelson, M. R. (2007). The ECAR study of undergraduate students and information technology, 2007. *EDUCAUSE Center for Applied Research.* Retrieved July 12, 2009, from http://connect.educause.edu/Library/ECAR/ Highlightsofthe2007ECARSt/45912.

Sanford, N. (1962). *The American college.* New York: Wiley.

Schweitzer, S. (2005, October 6). Fisher College expels student over Website entries. *Boston Globe.* Retrieved July 29, 2009, from www.boston.com/news/local/articles/2005/10/06/fisher_college_expels_student_over_website_entries/.

Tancer, B. (2007, October 24). MySpace v Facebook: Competing addictions. Retrieved November 27, 2008, from www.time.com/time/business/artilce/0,8599,1675244,00.html.

Tapscott, D. (1998). *Growing up digital: The rise of the Net generation.* New York: McGraw-Hill.

Tapscott, D. (2008). *Grown up digital: How the Net generation is changing your world*. New York: McGraw-Hill.

Valkenburg, P. M., & Schouten, P. J. (2006). Friend networking sites and their relationship to adolescents' well-being and social self-esteem. *Cyberpsychological Behavior*, *9*(5), 584–590.

Van Eck, R. (2006). Digital game-based learning: It's not just the digital natives who are restless. *EDUCAUSE Review*, *41*(2).

Walther, J. B., Van Der Heide, B., Kim, S. -Y., Westerman, D., & Tom Tong, S. (2008). The role of friends' appearance and behavior on evaluations of individuals on Facebook: Are we known by the company we keep? *Human Communication Research*, *34*(1), *28–49*.

CHAPTER THIRTY-ONE

SHAPING THE FUTURE

Susan R. Jones, Shaun R. Harper, and John H. Schuh

A recent article in the *Chronicle of Higher Education*, titled "Will Higher Education Be the Next Bubble to Burst?" (Cronin & Horton, 2009), conveys the tenor of present times. We write and prepare this fifth edition of *Student Services* during unprecedented economic, political, social, and cultural change. The economy has experienced (and we along with it!) the worst economic downfall in seventy years; the first biracial President of the United States was elected, which brings both cause for great hope and risk of a false sense of complacency in a "postracial" world; unprecedented violence from which campuses are no longer protected; and, particularly in urban areas, American public secondary education's struggling under the weight of a crumbling infrastructure and the pressures of No Child Left Behind. However, all is not bleak. We witnessed historic numbers of college students voting in the last presidential election and engaging in community service in record numbers as the "9/11 generation" (Dote, Cramer, Dietz, & Grimm, 2006, p. 4); and we saw higher education respond to the these historical, cultural, economic, and social pressures with innovation and creativity.

As reflected in the content of the chapters in this fifth edition of the "Green Book," there is very little in our work as student affairs educators, including the theories that guide our thinking and the competencies and skills central to our practice, not affected by the larger, contemporary societal landscape in which higher education exists. However, a question raised in 1954 by two pioneering scholars in student affairs, Esther Lloyd-Jones and Margaret Smith, is pertinent as we turn our attention in this final chapter to the future of student affairs. They wrote: "How is education to gain

The authors would like to acknowledge and thank vice presidents for student affairs who helped to generate the topics discussed in this chapter: Dr. Gregory Blimling, Dr. Linda Clement, and Dr. Larry Roper.

from student personnel work the full values that it offers? Must student personnel work continue in education as a collection of special services designed ostensibly to correct the mistakes of educators or, at best, to do what the rest of education cannot do in a system that is frankly dualistic? Is there some better way to conceive of student personnel work—perhaps of education itself—that will eventuate in greater growth and development of each student for life in a society that he [*sic*] will by his living improve?" (Lloyd-Jones & Smith, 1954, p. 12).

The questions posed by Lloyd-Jones and Smith (1954) in their book *Student Personnel Work as Deeper Teaching* are essentially the same as those taken up in subsequent reform documents in higher education and student affairs (Jones, 2007). Perhaps admirably, we are a profession in a continuous process of self-improvement, always seeking *some better way to conceive of student personnel work—perhaps of education itself*. With each reform document, we as professionals are offered a slightly different perspective and set of marching orders in conceiving the central focus of our work. These reform documents also illuminate that the very roots of our profession are well anchored in the pedagogical notion of *deeper teaching*. The foundational philosophical documents of the field (and the many reform documents that followed) are steadfast in their communication of core principles that center on a commitment to the education of the whole student, the role of student affairs educators in promoting student development and learning, and active engagement in civic life with a sense of responsibility for larger social issues as an intended outcome (Evans & Reason, 2001; e.g., *The Student Personnel Point of View* [1937], *The Student Learning Imperative* [1996], and *Principles of Good Practice for Student Affairs* [1997]).

Despite an abiding commitment to these noble ideas, student affairs educators continue efforts to pursue these goals and tend to current student-life quandaries that are as vexing now, if not more so, than ever. Such issues as alcohol and substance abuse, serious mental health problems, campus violence and incivility, reduced state support of higher education, budget shortfalls, access and retention, high-profile scandals, responding to legislative mandates and parents' demands, and competition among institutions for students predominate the work of student affairs educators today, as they have for a number of years. The delivery of the Commission on the Future of Higher Education's final report, "The Spellings Commission Report" (U.S. Department of Education, 2006), asserts that public perception is that higher education is not meeting the demands of contemporary times, a sentiment echoed by McPherson and Shulenberger (2008). The commission's report claimed, "Too many Americans just aren't getting the education they need. There are disturbing signs that many students who do earn degrees have not actually mastered the reading, writing and thinking skills we expect of college graduates" (U.S. Department of Education, 2006, p. xii).

Yet, we have no shortage of language in the historical and current guiding documents of the profession emphasizing student learning, our integral relationship with the academic mission and faculty, and the nature of the practice of student affairs educators (Jones, 2007). The learning imperative, learning partnerships, learning-centered environments, learning communities, learning outcomes, evidence-based learning, and transformational learning all situate student learning as central and at the core of our work. If we are to *learn* one thing from these documents it is that the commitment to student learning and development has been an abiding one. However, how these noble ideas get translated to practice is still a work in progress. Indeed, *Learning Reconsidered* (Keeling, 2004), the most recent of the "reform" documents (with its companion piece *Learning Reconsidered 2* [Keeling, 2006]) captured this dilemma:

> Our educational practice has . . . emphasized information transfer without a great deal of thought given to the meaning, pertinence, or application of the information in the context of a student's life. Likewise, student affairs educators have often not intentionally or systematically focused on abstract or transferable learning derived from the out-of-classroom experiences they have designed. But few of the assumptions on which our educational structures and processes were based remain intact in the world of today's students. The degree of this disconnection is profound and has serious implications for both teaching processes and the structures institutions use to help students learn. [Keeling, 2004, pp. 9–10]

This was the very disconnect against which Lloyd-Jones and Smith (1954) cautioned, and was the impetus for their conceptualization of student personnel work as deeper teaching. Is there *some better way to conceive of student personnel work* as we anticipate and shape the future of student affairs? We ask the reader to keep this question in mind as we offer our own thinking about those pressing societal issues and trends influencing higher education and, in particular, about student affairs at this moment in history. We also focus on directions and advice for those responsible for shaping the future of student affairs.

Societal Trends

It is difficult to forecast the future with certainty, but several societal forces at work now seem likely to persist into the immediate future. In this section, we offer our thoughts regarding these trends and the issues they pose for higher education.

Financial and Economic Forces

The fallout from the economic collapse in the United States in 2008–2009 no doubt will be experienced for many years. Already suffering from the decline of state and federal support of American higher education, colleges and universities are asking questions about typical ways of organizing and conducting business in an effort to reinvent themselves. So, too, is the American public. With the cost of higher education unreachable for many, and with financial aid allocations not keeping pace with increases in tuition, parents, students, and other stakeholders are exhibiting "a growing sense among the public that higher education might be overpriced and under-delivering" (Cronin & Horton, 2009, n.p.). The consequences of such financial pressures are many for higher education.

The decline in public confidence in higher education brings not only greater calls for accountability but also increasing government intrusion in higher education. For example, in a number of states, state legislators are calling for regulation of textbook pricing, learning outcomes associated with college attendance, campus safety measures, and the kinds of movies or other entertainment students bring to the campus. Since 1980, the percentage of revenues from state governments of public degree-granting institutions has declined (Snyder, Dillow, & Hoffman, 2009, Table 349). During this same period of time, governmental oversight for higher education increased (Thelin, 2004).

Demographic Trends and Access

Economic forces, in addition to other trends at work, will have a deep impact on access to higher education and on *who* is able to afford and attend colleges and universities. The dual dilemma of institutions increasingly dependent upon student tuition coupled with students' inability to afford these rising tuitions will force higher education to deliver the curriculum, programs, and services through alternative means. Whether this involves online courses (it was not long ago that many in higher education scoffed at the now highly successful, for-profit enterprise of the University of Phoenix); renting out facilities and bringing retail to campuses to generate revenue; or hiring greater numbers of part-time faculty to deliver the curriculum, colleges and universities must figure out ways to reduce costs and increase enrollments, particularly of those most vulnerable to tuition increases.

Students enrolling in institutions of higher education continue to be increasingly diverse. For example, the number of students in all age categories is projected to grow through 2017 (Snyder, Dillow, & Hoffman, 2009, Figure 13), although the growth (or in some cases, decline) will vary from state to state, as is pointed out below. Women will continue to outnumber men in baccalaureate degree programs as well as some graduate and professional degree programs. All indications are that the demographics of college attendance will continue to shift. As the U.S. Department of Education reports, "The percentage of American college students who are minorities has been increasing. In 1976, 15 percent were minorities, compared with 32 percent in 2007" (Snyder et al., 2009, p. 270). However, the crisis in secondary education, particularly in urban areas, greatly affects higher education and the preparation of high school students for college. Achievement gaps persist between White and Black high school students and White and Latino populations. In Washington, DC, for example, only 9 percent of students graduate from high school (3 percent in the most troubled areas of the city), and only 8 percent are on grade level in math (M. Rhee, personal communication, May 1, 2009). This injustice not only has an impact on enrollments in colleges and universities but also raises the larger issue of a need for an educated citizenry that reflects the demographics of the United States. Further, as Cronin and Horton (2009) point out, "The numbers of college-aged students in the 'baby-boom echo,' which crested with this year's high-school senior class, will decline over the next decade. Certain Great Plains and Northeastern states may lose 10 percent of the 12th-graders eligible for college. Vermont is expected to lose 20 percent by 2020" (n.p.).

These demographic trends will only exacerbate the economic pressures experienced by colleges and universities and further bolster the pattern of increased enrollments at community colleges. In addition, the future is likely to bring increases in older students, those with careers in need of retooling after they were laid off during the recession, and student veterans returning to school after military service in Iraq and Afghanistan. College and universities are already receiving large numbers of soldiers who are returning from the experience of combat and transitioning to higher education with a unique set of needs for support (Ackerman, DiRamio, & Garza Mitchell, 2009). Other societal trends, such as the visible dialogue and debate surrounding same-sex marriage (e.g., Proposition 8 in California); immigration laws; reasonable accommodation for persons with disabilities; students from foster families; and the nomination of the first Latina as a U.S. Supreme Court justice, are likely to raise awareness of and increase activism for greater equality and justice.

Globalization

Problems and challenges that student affairs professionals face in the United States are common around the world. In Asia, for example, working collaboratively with stakeholders is a central challenge and absolutely necessary to ensure student success (Ho, 2007). In regard to assessment, expectations that student affairs professionals demonstrate their efficacy can be found in Europe and Asia, as well as in North America. The increasing emphasis on accountability in Europe and the United States, according to Huisman and Currie (2004) (professors from the Netherlands and Australia, respectively), has resulted from several global trends:

- Changing relationships between governments and universities
- Concerns about efficiency and adequate value for money expended
- Internationalization of higher education and globalization
- Information and communication technology developments

Huisman and Currie add, "[Accountability's] role will differ depending on the historical context and the way national governments decide to implement accountability mechanisms and how they are approaching globalization as a neo-liberal ideology" (2004, pp. 533–534).

Technology

We are reluctant to write anything about technology because almost as rapidly as the ink dries on this paper (which in itself may soon be an outmoded delivery), technology will change. However, the influence of technology on society is undeniable and consequential. The telephone and the "interoffice memo" are now nearly obsolete means of communication and, as our students remind us, "E-mail is for old people." Where the current reliance on Facebook, Twitter, and other social networking tools will lead, it is difficult to say. What does seem clear is that technology will continue to influence communication in multiple and diverse settings: among friends and colleagues, in the classroom (or in lieu of the classroom), and between institutions and students. We don't yet know the consequences associated with such reliance on technology. For example, does the efficiency of the "paperless" campus mean that students, faculty, and administrators can conduct all their institutional business without ever leaving their homes? What is lost as students communicate with one another entirely through Facebook or Twitter? How is learning augmented or deterred through use of technology? These questions are likely to persist into the future, although the technology will probably be different by the time we get there. Consider this example. Teamwork previously entailed gathering in one place and working to achieve a common goal. Technological advances now mean that members of a work team do not have to be in the same city, or even on the same continent, to work together to achieve a common end. Given this context, how will student affairs facilitate collaborative learning?

Student Affairs Themes and Issues

The image of higher education as the "ivory tower" was long ago dropped as a useful way for a college or university to thrive. Many examples may be found to demonstrate the influence of societal and world events on higher education (world wars and the GI bill, Vietnam and student protests, economics and access, to name a few). As in the past, societal trends exert pressure on higher education to respond and adapt. Student affairs is no exception and in this section we highlight several areas where societal trends are most keenly influencing student affairs practice.

Student Affairs' Identity and Role

Before we move to more specific themes and issues related to student affairs, we think it important to once again revisit an age-old discussion about the identity and role of student affairs within higher education. This is not meant to be a comment about our "second-class citizen" status, because all the chapters in this text point to the integral and vital role that student affairs plays, both in the lives of students and in contributing to the enterprise of higher education. However, as student affairs educators we must remain vigilant about our roles and assertive in communicating the ways in which we contribute to the primary mission and purpose of higher education as well as to the specific missions and goals of the institutions with which we are affiliated (see Kezar & Lester, 2009). As economic forces continue to bear down, this will only increase in importance. This means we need to foreground our commitment to student learning in relation to the "curriculum" student affairs delivers, the learning outcomes developed to anchor that curriculum, and the measures created to assess and document the results of participation. Moreover, student affairs will have to be increasingly self-reliant in generating the necessary resources to offer programs, services, and learning experiences for students. What this trend suggests is that relying on an institution's general fund for support is likely to be a phenomenon of the past. Student affairs will be financed to a great extent by student fees and fees for service, thereby resulting in a growing reliance on meeting student needs.

Greater focus on student learning also means engaging more meaningfully with faculty and academic affairs. Blake (1979, 1996) offered a provocative, if not amusing, caricature highlighting the differences between student affairs educators and faculty. She noted:

> The successful student affairs professional is apt to enjoy people, taking pleasure in their diversity and individuality. He or she is often drawn to the subjective, experiential aspects of life, toward events and problems in their particularity, and toward accomplishing things through others, frequently by organizing people into groups. . . . Faculty, on the other hand, are typically oriented to ideas and reflection; to working with books, experiments, and schema of various kinds; to valuing reason and proof, detached judgment, aesthetic sensibility, [and] exactitude. . . . It does no harm to a scholar's reputation if he or she is somewhat ill at ease socially, impractical or compulsive, or a less than active public citizen. [Blake, 1996, pp. 5–6]

An emphasis on student learning should place student affairs educators in closer contact and dialogue with faculty, especially as academic departments develop their own set of learning outcomes (due to the same pressures for accountability to which student affairs educators are responding). However, partnerships must be reciprocal, which means that there must be something gained and contributed by all involved in the partnership. This requires that student affairs educators understand the faculty culture and reward system, and that faculty embrace collaboration with student affairs educators who are working toward common and complementary learning goals and outcomes. This student affairs theme may seem more esoteric compared to the more pressing issues discussed below. However, we suggest that this real commitment to student learning and the ability to work effectively and strategically with faculty undergird all else.

Mental Health and Delivery of Psychological and Health Services

As Amy Reynolds discussed in Chapter Twenty-Three on counseling and helping skills, many college students experience challenges to their mental health and exhibit psychological problems that require the attention of skilled clinicians. Long gone are the days when college counseling centers were staffed by student affairs educators with skills in active listening and counseling to assist students in dealing with expected developmental issues. At the far end of the spectrum is the severe psychological distress that results in suicidal or homicidal behaviors evident in the tragedies at Virginia Tech and Northern Illinois. Far more prevalent are the increasing numbers of students treated for depression, suicidal ideation, severe anxiety, personality disorders, and substance abuse. Often these treatments include counseling and medications that must be managed by students; and, if medication is not taken properly, this can result in additional psychological problems.

This scenario will result in the increased demand for counseling and psychological services and the need to manage the delivery of these services. Counseling centers will have to continue to organize themselves in order to both assess the potential threat of students' exhibiting signs of psychological distress and manage crises as they arise. Some colleges and universities may find it necessary to outsource psychological services. Reaching those students who, for cultural or familial reasons, are least likely to access the services and support provided by counseling centers will continue as a challenge.

Health services will also continue to deal with emerging health crises. The future is likely to bring additional strains of flu, just as the last few years found student affairs leaders and health educators responding to threats of pandemics from avian flu, MRSA, and H1N1. Indications are that HIV infections are on the rise for those in the eighteen-to-twenty-four age range, which includes many college students, and the numbers of students with sexually-transmitted diseases and infections remain alarming given the health education occurring on many campuses. Creative educational programming and increased financial resources and staffing will be necessary to deliver effective and high-quality services. However, operating under the same budgetary constraints as other units in student affairs, counseling center and health center staff may find it necessary to be entrepreneurial in garnering increased funding to support the growing needs of students.

Intercultural Engagement

Despite at least a decade of concerted efforts on the part of colleges and universities to diversify the student body and to create and deliver diversity initiatives, campuses remain balkanized by race and ethnicity. Many students continue to come to higher education from relatively homogenous neighborhoods and high schools, having had little opportunity to meaningfully interact with those from different backgrounds (e.g., by race, religion, ethnicity, and social class). Even when in the presence of racially diverse others, most students maintain same-race friendship groups and social networks. As noted in Chapter Three, much research exists to confirm the educational benefits accrued in inclusive learning environments, and student affairs educators must continue to work vigorously to create these. However, as Quaye and Baxter Magolda (2007) pointed out, it is not enough to simply provide services for racial and ethnic minority students; just as important are facilitating the conversations about existing oppression and racism that created the need for this work in the first place.

With the election of Barack Obama as the first biracial president of the United States in 2008, many in America are declaring that racial tensions are behind us and that race no longer matters. The ushering in of what some are calling the "postracial era" will probably influence the "diversity agenda" on many campuses, with some finding new ways to dampen the fire of past work toward promoting campus inclusivity and equity. Student affairs educators, often seen as the champions of such diversity initiatives, will need to maintain vigilance and take a more direct advocacy role to ensure that diversity efforts are not remarginalized on campuses.

New Programs and Services

The future is likely to hold new configurations for facilitating the work of student affairs. Whether the result of budget cuts, new student populations, or other forces, new programs and services—and the delivery of these—are likely on the horizon. For example, as noted earlier, programs and services for veterans are reemerging on many campuses. More deliberate efforts to work with parents and alumni, graduate students, and other student populations are developing. Also gaining importance are collaborative initiatives with intercollegiate athletics, intramural and recreational sports, multicultural affairs and TRiO Programs, and other departments on campus. Programs to increase student awareness of and participation in environmental sustainability efforts are also gaining momentum on several campuses. In addition, educators and administrators are recognizing the important role that community colleges play in educating 36.1 percent of all students in American higher education (U.S. Department of Education, 2008). As such, more programs to ensure the successful completion of certificates and associate's degrees as well as increased transfer rates to four-year institutions are on the horizon at community colleges. The expansion of student affairs and services at for-profit and online institutions is also likely to continue.

Demonstrating Learning Outcomes

The need to document what students are learning as a result of their participation in student affairs programs and services is here to stay. Calls for accountability have at their root the importance of higher education's commitment to accountability and improvement. Ewell (2002) and Gray (2002) have identified assessment for accountability and improvement, but the accountability movement (often described as quality assurance in Europe) is not confined to the United States. Jürgen Kohler (2003), a professor from Germany, describes the purpose of quality assurance this way: "Internally, it [quality assurance] aims at improving the position of the institution in a competitive environment, not to mention the intrinsic academic value of enhancing research and teaching as such. Externally, it is part of the accountability which universities owe to stakeholders, especially students in this context, and society, either as employers or the state as the funding body" (p. 322).

Future Directions and Advice

Many of the issues identified in this chapter are likely to persist into the future. However, new challenges will no doubt emerge. The future of the student affairs profession will be shaped by these external forces, but also by the vision, knowledge, skills, and competencies of those providing leadership in the profession. What follows, then, in the form of advice to emerging professionals, are a few areas in which we believe student affairs educators need to develop skills and dispositions in order to provide the kind of leadership that will enable the student affairs profession to be sustained and thrive well into our future.

Ability to Adapt to Change

As the colloquial phrase suggests, the only thing one can truly count on is change itself. Indeed, the omnipresence of change, and the speed with which the world is changing, necessitate the need for great flexibility and for innovation and creativity in anticipating and responding to changing conditions. This requires the ability to scan both external and internal environments and to truly understand how larger societal trends will necessarily affect higher education and student affairs. The ways in which "we have always done things" will no longer carry the day. Most likely, for example, student affairs educators will need to get more involved in generating funding through development efforts and other entrepreneurial activities.

Ability to Collaborate and Find Connections

Partnerships have long been stressed in student affairs. However, now perhaps more so than ever, our future depends upon our ability to collaborate with multiple stakeholders and constituencies inside and outside higher education. This will require skills in communication, border crossing, and negotiating in order to create meaningful and effective partnerships and manage limited resources. Partnerships with academic affairs will be particularly important, which means demonstrating the ability to connect to the academic mission of the institution in new and creative ways. State legislatures, neighboring communities, and parents are among those with whom student affairs must collaborate and create closer links in the future. Although the discussion of breaking out of organizational silos seems to be a persistent one, the future truly calls for a more holistic organizational and institutional approach to the complex issues higher education is facing and to which student affairs must respond.

Accountability Environment

Newcomer, Hatry, and Wholey (2004) made this observation, which we think applies to assessment across higher education: "The demand for program evaluation information is growing. The U.S. Congress, state legislatures, local legislative bodies, foundations, and other funding agencies are increasingly demanding information on how program funds were used and what those programs produced" (p. xxxvii). We see no reason to believe that institutions will be held less accountable for their activities and outcomes in the future than has been the case in the past. The National Commission on the Future of Higher Education (U. S. Department of Education, 2006) also emphasized that institutions will need to develop more accountability measures in the future. Now, it is true that we have a new administration in Washington, but there is no evidence to suggest that this administration is uninterested in accountability. So, our view is that we in higher education will be held accountable for our collective efforts by the national leadership in Washington. In addition, regional accrediting organizations also are emphasizing accountability on the part of their member institutions seeking reaccreditation (see, for example Middle States Commission on Higher Education, 2002; Southern Association of Colleges and Schools, 2004). Without question, accountability in higher education is here to stay.

Rigorous Preparation for Diversity

As noted earlier in this chapter, demographers predict an increase in the enrollment of racial and ethnic minority students (especially Latinos) in U.S. higher education. Student affairs educators must abandon "one-size-fits-all" programming models and recognize the need to redesign long-standing activities and environments. As campuses become more diverse, so too will the needs, challenges, preferences, and cultural expectations students bring with them upon enrollment. This requires preparation (and in some instances remediation). Educators and administrators who lack expertise in communicating with or fostering supportive environments for students who are not in the majority should constantly work to overcome such shortcomings. Likewise, student affairs professionals must actively work to examine their own stereotypes and assumptions about certain groups (for example, gay and lesbian persons) and seek advice from experienced colleagues who can help them prepare for a more significant presence of these students on campus.

Linking to K–12 Education

It seems like common sense to suggest that the pipeline to higher education begins with elementary and secondary education and that the vestiges of the quality and nature of experiences students have in high school come with them to the collegiate environment. However, perhaps nowhere are outcomes disparities more profound than in secondary education, specifically in large urban areas. Higher education simply must become a more vigorous partner with K–12 education, which means that student affairs educators must link with high schools in new and creative ways. The more traditional bridge programs or upward-bound programs may continue to serve their purposes, but what is needed are more radical notions of partnerships between student affairs and high schools that involve neighborhoods, communities, school guidance personnel, families, and even perhaps religious leaders.

Engaging in Ongoing Personal and Professional Development

Student affairs professional associations offer conferences and institutes, scholarly journals and other published resources, and several opportunities for connectivity with colleagues. Engagement in these organizations is essential for those who wish to remain on the cutting edge of the profession. Simply attending conferences is insufficient—returning from the conference, reflecting on what was learned, and beginning to selectively implement innovative ideas is preferred. Moreover, reading the latest published research and thoughtfully integrating implications offered therein into one's professional practice is important. So too is seeking advice from colleagues who have effectively solved tough student affairs dilemmas at institutions similar to your own. The future of the student affairs profession depends upon expert educators who continuously seek to learn more about students, pursue new approaches to teaching and learning outside the classroom, and constantly ask how they can become more skillful manufacturers of productive educational outcomes.

So, in conclusion, and as we head into the future, is there *some better way to conceive of student personnel work—perhaps of education itself?* This is the question first raised in 1954 by Lloyd-Jones and Smith. And this is the question that we as student affairs educators can continue to ask ourselves every day.

References

Ackerman, R., DiRamio, D., & Garza Mitchell, R. L. (2009). Transitions: Combat veterans as college students. In R. Ackerman & D. DiRamio (Eds.), *Creating a veteran-friendly campus: Strategies for transition and success* (New Directions for Student Services No. 126, pp. 5–14). San Francisco: Jossey-Bass.

American College Personnel Association. (1996). *The student learning imperative: Implications for student affairs.* Retrieved from http://www.acpa.nche.edu/sli.sli.htm.

American College Personnel Association and National Association of Student Personnel Administrators. (1997). *Principles of good practice for student affairs.* Retrieved from http://www.acpa.nche.edu/pgp/principle.htm.

American Council on Education (1994). The student personnel point of view. In A. L. Rentz (Ed.), *Student affairs: A profession's heritage* (American College Personnel Association Media Publication, No. 40, 2nd ed., pp. 66–77). Lanham, MD: University Press of America. (Original work published in 1937)

Blake, E. S. (1979). Classroom and context: An educational dialectic. *Academe, 65,* 280–292.

Blake, E. S. (1996, September/October). The yin & yang of student learning in college. *About Campus,* 4, 4–9.

Cronin, J. M., & Horton, H. E. (2009, May 22). Will higher education be the next bubble to burst? *Chronicle of Higher Education.* Retrieved June 22, 2009, from http://chronicle.com/weekly/v55/i37/37a05601.htm.

Dote, L., Cramer, K., Dietz, N., & Grimm, R., Jr. (2006). *College students helping America.* Washington, DC: Corporation for National and Community Service.

Evans, N. J., & Reason, R. D. (2001). Guiding principles: A review and analysis of student affairs philosophical statements. *Journal of College Student Development, 42,* 359–377.

Ewell, P. T. (2002). An emerging scholarship: A brief history of assessment. In T. W. Banta & Associates (Eds.), *Building a scholarship of assessment* (pp. 3–25). San Francisco: Jossey-Bass.

Gray, P. J. (2002). The roots of assessment: Tensions, solutions and research directions. In T. W. Banta & Associates (Eds.), *Building a scholarship of assessment* (pp. 49–66). San Francisco: Jossey-Bass.

Ho, P. P. (2007). What really matters—Re-conceptualizing "value" in student affairs. *Student Affairs Forum 2007.* Hong Kong: Chinese University of Hong Kong.

Huisman, J., & Currie, J. (2004). Accountability in higher education: Bridge over troubled water? *Higher Education, 48*(4), 529–551.

Jones, S. R. (2007, March). *What ever happened to deeper teaching? (Re)considering process and outcomes.* Paper presented at the ACPA-NASPA Faculty Summit, Orlando, FL.

Keeling, R. P. (Ed.). (2004). *Learning reconsidered: A campus-wide focus on the student experience.* Washington, DC: American College Personnel Association & National Association of Student Personnel Administrators.

Keeling, R. P. (Ed.), (2006). *Learning reconsidered 2: Implementing a campus-wide focus on the student experience.* Washington, DC: National Association of Student Personnel Administrators.

Kezar, A. J., & Lester, J. (2009). *Organizing higher education for collaboration.* San Francisco: Jossey-Bass.

Kohler, J. (2003). Quality assurance, accreditation, and recognition of qualifications as regulatory mechanisms in the European higher education area. *Higher Education in Europe, 28*(3), 317–330.

Lloyd-Jones, E., & Smith, M. R. (Eds.). (1954). *Student personnel work as deeper teaching.* New York: Harper.

McPherson, P., & Shulenberger, D. (2008). *University tuition, consumer choice and college affordability.* Washington, DC: NASULGC.

Middle States Commission on Higher Education. (2002). *Characteristics of excellence in higher education: Eligibility requirements and standards for accreditation.* Philadelphia: Author.

Newcomer, J. S., Hatry, H. P., & Wholey, K. E. (Eds.). (2004). *Handbook of practice program evaluation* (2nd ed.). San Francisco: Jossey-Bass.

Quaye, S. J., & Baxter Magolda, M. B. (2007). Enhancing racial self-understanding through structured learning and reflective experiences. In S. Harper & L. Patton (Eds.), *Responding to the realities of race on campus* (New Directions for Student Services No. 120, pp. 55–66). San Francisco: Jossey-Bass.

Snyder, T. D., Dillow, S. A., & Hoffman, C. M. (2009). *Digest of education statistics 2008* (NCES 2009–020). Washington, DC: U.S. Department of Education, National Center for Education Statistics.

Southern Association of Colleges and Schools. (2004). *Handbook for reaffirmation of accreditation.* Decatur, GA: Author.

Thelin, J. R. (2004). *A history of American higher education.* Baltimore, MD: Johns Hopkins University Press.

U.S. Department of Education. (2006). *A test of leadership: Charting the future of U.S. higher education.* Retrieved January 19, 2007, from www.ed.gov/print/about/bdscomm/list/hiedfuture/reports/final-report.pdf.

U.S. Department of Education. (2008). *Integrated Postsecondary Education Data System: IPEDS spring 2008 compendium tables.* Washington, DC: National Center for Education Statistics, Institute of Education Sciences.

NAME INDEX

A

Abes, E. S., 135–136, 149, 156, 160, 168, 189, 201, 202, 212
Ackerman, R., 72, 538
Adams, E. M., 310
Aguirre, A., Jr., 368
Allen, K. E., 359, 369
Allen, W. R., 33, 36, 46, 247, 249
Allmendinger, D., 8
Alstete, J. W., 287
Altbach, P. G., 31, 71, 253
Ambler, D. A., 314
Amelink, C. T., 380
Amey, M. J., 378
Anaya, G., 501
Ancis, J. R., 249, 253
Anderson, J. A., 92, 322
Anderson, M. L., 173
Angrisani, C., 315
antonio, a. l., 2, 46, 49, 50, 52, 53, 55, 56, 291, 443
Appelbaum, P. S., 127
Appiah, K., 96, 103
Appleton, J., 277
Archer, J., 408
Archibald, R. B., 304

B

Bader, P., 369
Baez, B., 20, 247
Bailey, K. W., 198

Ardiaolo, F. P., 70
Areen, J., 120
Argyris, C., 394, 395
Aristotle, 96, 121, 122, 124
Arminio, J., 158, 336, 377, 468, 473
Arnett, J. J., 155
Arnold, K., 486
Arnold, K. D., 243, 252
Arnold, M. S., 409
Arseneau, J. R., 156, 200, 201
Asch, A., 156
Assouline, S., 508
Astin, A. W., 13, 19, 24, 30, 34, 35, 49, 74, 75, 157, 237, 250, 258, 321, 323, 360, 364, 365, 457, 459, 484, 500, 501, 503, 506
Astin, H. S., 364, 365, 457
Aulepp, L., 400
Avolio, B. J., 358
Axtell, J., 4

Balderston, F. E., 310
Baldridge, J. V., 235
Baldwin, J., 187, 203
Baltes, P. B., 173
Banning, J. H., 88, 157, 244, 245, 248, 249, 250, 252, 253, 289, 290
Banta, T. W., 32, 294, 323, 324, 325, 484, 486
Barber, J. P., 212, 215
Barefoot, B. O., 501
Barr, D. J., 338
Barr, M. J., 68, 69, 97, 304, 309, 310, 311, 314, 317, 394
Barr, R. B., 390
Barratt, W., 69
Bashaw, C. T., 64, 69, 89
Baudrillard, J., 520, 525
Baum, K., 126
Baum, S., 303
Baumgartner, L. M., 173
Baxter Magolda, M. B., 86, 91, 154, 156, 159, 176, 178, 207, 208, 210–211, 212, 213, 216, 217, 218, 219, 222, 385, 387, 389, 391, 393, 478, 541
Beauchamp, T., 101

Beaumont, E., 483

Bebeau, M. J., 176

Beemyn, B., 199

Bekken, B. M., 217

Belenky, M. F., 154, 176, 177, 178

Belizaire, L., 344

Bender, B. E., 373

Bengston, V. L., 173

Bennett, B. R., 380

Bensimon, E. M., 37, 294, 297, 298, 363

Benton, S. A., 400, 401

Berger, J. B., 25, 49

Bergquist, W. H., 232, 233–234, 272, 273, 274, 276, 278, 284

Berkowitz, A. D., 457

Berry, J. W., 192, 193

Berryhill-Paapke, E., 196

Berwick, K. R., 373

Bess, J. L., 236, 288

Beth, A., 173

Bickel, R. D., 70, 525

Bilodeau, B. L., 200, 201

Birnbaum, R., 24, 226, 232, 233, 234, 235, 236, 239, 287, 288, 294, 295, 363

Black, K. E., 294

Black, M. A., 159, 160, 389

Blackhurst, A. E., 373

Blaich, C. F., 31

Blake, E. S., 486, 540

Blake, R. R., 357

Blanchard, K. H., 357, 419, 420

Blimling, G. S., 289, 293, 298, 484

Bloland, P., 68, 81, 91, 93, 419

Bok, D. C., 500, 701

Bolman, L., 154, 157, 226, 227, 229, 230, 231, 232, 239, 363

Bonner, F. A., II, 198

Bourassa, D. M., 484

Bowen, H. R., 24, 304

Bowen, W. G., 71, 500

boyd, d. m., 377, 518, 519

Boyer, E. L., 17, 456, 478

Brandt, J. E., 373

Brawer, F. B., 246

Braxton, J. M., 157, 258

Breneman, D., 75

Bresciani, D. L., 325

Bresciani, M. J., 92, 272, 294, 321, 322, 323, 324, 325, 326, 327, 328, 329, 331

Bridges, B. K., 36, 258, 322

Briggs, C., 277

Briggs, L. R., 63

Brinbaum, R., 275

Bringle, R. G., 501

Brint, S., 13

Britzman, D. P., 160

Broido, E. M., 80

Bronfenbrenner, U., 173, 243, 246, 252

Bronner, S., 441

Brown, J. S., 454, 517

Brown, R., 106

Brown, R. D., 68, 407

Brown, S. S., 380

Brubacher, J. S., 64

Bryant, A. N., 501, 508

Buckley, J. A., 218, 258, 322

Bula, J. F., 348

Burack, C., 484

Burkard, A., 402

Burke, C. B., 7

Burley-Allen, M., 416

Burns, J. M., 358

Burns, M., 381

Bush, G., 33

Butin, D. W., 160

C

Cabrera, A. F., 249, 253

Caffarella, R. S., 173

Calvan, B. C., 423

Campbell, S. M., 426

Canary, D. J., 434, 439

Caplan, G., 428

Caplan, R. B., 428

Caple, R. B., 84, 388

Carducci, R., 359

Carlisle, B. A., 464

Carnaghi, J. E., 475

Carpenter, D. S., 373

Carpenter, S., 89, 368, 478

Carpenter, S. D., 472

Carr, W., 395

Carter, D. F., 30

Carter, J., 425

Carter, K. A., 199

Carter, R. T., 190, 191

Caruso, J. B., 517

Cass, V. C., 156, 200

Caste, N., 442

Castellanos, J., 344

Ceja, M., 337

Chaffee, E. E., 288

Chang, J., 55

Chang, J. C., 289

Chang, M., 337

Chang, M. J., 2, 43, 46, 49, 50, 52, 53, 55, 289

Chavez, A. F., 478

Cheatham, H. E., 338

Checkoway, B., 29

Chen, G. A., 193

Chernow, E., 374

Cherrey, C., 359, 369

Chickering, A. W., 31, 106, 154, 155, 169, 171–172, 175, 483

Childress, J., 101

Chiriboga, D. A., 173

Cho Seung Hui, 112

Choney, S. K., 196

Christensen, C. R., 391

Cilente, K., 136, 373

Clark, B., 14, 15, 21

Clark, B. R., 24, 235, 236

Clark, C. M., 394

Clark, M. C., 173

Clark, R., 404, 405

Clark, T. A., 64

Clarke, C. G., 53, 55

Clayton-Pederson, A., 36, 46, 249

Clinchy, B. M., 176, 177

Clinton, B., 33, 74

Clothier, R. C., 84

Cohen, A. M., 246

Cohen, M., 234

Colangelo, N., 508

Colby, A., 179, 180, 483

Cole, D. C., 402

Coleman, H. L. K., 344

Coleman-Boatwright, R., 338
Coles, R., 150, 151, 152
Collins, D., 69
Collins, J. C., 266
Collins, P. H., 189, 198, 475
Colwell, B. W., 484
Conger, J. A., 357
Conley, V. M., 374, 376, 381
Connolly, M., 390, 395
Contreras, F. E., 37
Contreras-McGavin, M., 359
Cook, D. A., 190
Cook, J. H., 484
Coomes, M. D., 475
Coons, A. E., 356
Cooper, D. L., 189, 374, 376, 377, 451, 452, 454, 460, 462, 465
Cooper, S., 408
Corbin, J., 157
Cosgrove, J., 69
Cottone, R., 115
Couturier, L., 483
Cowley, W. H., 63, 84
Cramer, K., 534
Creamer, D. G., 65, 212, 222, 372, 374, 375, 376, 377, 378, 379, 380, 381, 399, 407, 418, 471, 472, 474, 475, 477
Crego, C. A., 428
Crissman Ishler, J., 423
Cronin, J. M., 534, 536, 537
Cross, P., 19
Cross, W. E., 189, 190
Cross, W. E., Jr., 151, 152
Cruce, T. M., 31, 258
Cupach, W. R., 434, 439
Cureton, J. S., 97, 316, 422, 423
Currie, J., 538
Currivan, J., 97
Curry, J., 310
Curtis, B., 199
Curtis, D. V., 235
Cuyjet, M. J., 295

D

Dalai Lama, 101, 102, 108
Dalton, J. C., 373, 380

D'Andrea, M., 343, 344
Daniels, J., 343, 344
D'Augelli, A. R., 200
Daver, Z. E., 69, 507
Davis, A. M., 437, 438
Davis, M., 199
Davis, T. L., 198
Day, D. V., 367
Day, J., 101
Day, J. C., 385
De Waal, C., 86
Deal, T., 154, 157, 226, 227, 229, 230, 231, 232, 239, 363
DeAngelo, L., 53
Deaux, K., 155
DeBra, E., 34
DeCoster, D. A., 380, 419
Dede, C., 517
Dee, J. R., 288
Delgado Bernal, D., 197
Delgado, R., 156, 160, 196
Delgado-Romero, E., 195
Delworth, U., 400, 406
Denison, D. B., 323
Denson, N., 49, 52
Denzin, N. K., 159
Deutsch, M., 435, 439
DeVoss, D. N., 520
Dewey, J., 84, 85, 86, 88, 89, 93, 215, 449, 450
Dey, E. L., 25, 43–46, 47, 49, 56, 337
Dickerson, D., 406, 408
Dickeson, R. C., 287
Dickmeyer, N., 308, 309
Diener, T., 11
Dietz, N., 534
DiGeronimo, T. F., 401
Dill, B. T., 156
Dillon, F. R., 170
Dillon, W. L., 316
Dillow, S. A., 46, 303, 314, 537
DiRamio, D., 72, 538
Doermann, H., 9
Donald, J. G., 323
Donath, J., 518
Donofrio, K., 237

Dooris, M. J., 287, 288
Dote, L., 534
Dougherty, K. J., 28
Douglas, D. O., 309
Douglas, K. B., 258, 389
Dowd, A. C., 294, 295
Downing, N. E., 156, 197
Drath, W. H., 367
Drewry, H. N., 9
Driscoll, A., 26
Dubeck, L. W., 311
Dugan, J. P., 359
Duhart, D. T., 126
Dungy, G., 61, 82
Dunkel, N. W., 419, 420
DuPraw, M. E., 438
Duster, T., 51

E

Ebbers, L. H., 343
Eckel, P., 229, 288
Ecker, G. P., 235
Edison, M., 337
Edmundson, M., 123
Edwards, K. E., 198
Egart, K., 217
Ehrenberg, R. G., 19
Ehrlich, T., 450, 483
Einstein, A., 97, 112
Eisner, E. W., 395
Elder, G. H., Jr., 173, 174
Elfrink, V. L., 87, 90, 321
Elkins Nesheim, B., 29, 488
Ellis, S., 485
Ellison, N. B., 377, 519, 520
Ender, S. C., 388
Engstrom, C., 262, 478
Erchul, W. P., 428
Erikson, E. H., 154, 155, 169, 170, 172, 187, 188
Estanek, S. M., 362
Evans, N. J., 81, 87, 88, 89, 91, 92, 136, 157, 168, 170, 172, 177, 180, 181, 373, 410, 449, 450, 523, 535
Ewell, P. T., 321, 542
Eyler, J., 501

F

Faris, S. K., 359
Fassisnger, R. E., 156, 200, 201
Feagin, J. R., 249
Fein, R. A., 129
Feldman, D. H., 304, 500
Felix-Ortiz de la Garza, M., 193
Ferdman, B. M., 193
Ferraro, K. F., 173, 175
Field, K., 74
Fincher, C., 312
Fine, M., 156, 158
Finklestein, M., 237
Finney, R. G., 311
Fischer, A. R., 197
Fischer, K. S., 179
Fischer, M., 510, 511
Fiske, M., 173
Flanagan, T. A., 435, 440
Fley, J., 63, 64
Flowers, L. A., 321, 511
Folger, J. P., 434, 435, 439
Forney, D. E., 88, 91, 170
Forney, D. S., 523
Foster, V. A., 479
Fowler, J. W., 155, 176, 182
Fox, M.J.T., 32
Franklin, B., 6
Freeland, R., 13
Freeman, J. P., 325
Freire, P., 217
Fretwell, E. K., Jr., 304
Freud, S., 403
Fried, J., 96, 100, 101, 102, 103, 107, 408
Fuhrman, B., 84, 85, 86

G

Gabelnick, F., 485
Gaff, J. G., 246
Gallegos, P. I., 193
Gamson, Z. F., 483
Gannon, J. R., 423
Gardner, J., 169
Gardner, J. N., 501
Gardner, W. L., 359

Garland, P., 63
Garvin, D. A., 391
Garza Mitchell, R. L., 538
Gasman, M., 2, 3, 20, 21, 247
Gaston-Gayles, J. L., 70, 89
Gayles, J. G., 321
Geiger, R. L., 63
Gerda, J. J., 475
Gershenfeld, M. K., 417, 421, 422
Giamatti, B., 369
Gibson, J., 156
Gilbert, L. A., 197, 200
Giles, D., 501
Gilligan, C., 107, 155, 176, 179, 180–181, 183
Gilmartin, S. K., 501
Gilroy, M., 69
Gioia, D. A., 237
Gladieux, L. E., 70
Gloria, A. M., 344
Goldberger, N. R., 176, 177, 178
Goldstein, P. J., 316
Gonyea, R. M., 258
Goodchild, L., 21
Goodman, D. J., 347
Goodman, J., 173
Gordon, L., 9, 12
Gordon, S. A., 61
Gordon, V. N., 414, 418
Graham, S. W., 173
Grant, C. A., 337
Gray, P. J., 542
Grayson, P. A., 401
Greenleaf, R. K., 357–358
Griffin, K. A., 2, 24, 33
Grimm, R., Jr., 534
Grites, T. J., 414
Grunwald, H. E., 43
Guba, E. G., 158, 159, 488
Guentzel, M., 29, 488
Guideo-Dibrito, F., 478
Guido, F., 170
Guido-Dibrito, F., 88, 91, 523
Guillory, J. P., 32
Gumport, P. J., 29, 237, 253
Gurin, G., 44, 337
Gurin, P., 43, 44, 337
Guskin, A. E., 386

Guthrie, V., 106, 107, 418
Gutkin, T. B., 343

H

Habley, W. R., 413, 414
Hagedorn, L. S., 249, 337
Haidt, J., 133
Hall, R., 248
Hall, R. J., 364, 367
Hallie, P., 441
Halperin, D. M., 201
Halpin, G., 181
Halpin, W. G., 181
Hamrick, F. A., 88, 89, 90, 473, 474, 478
Handlin, M., 5
Handlin, O., 5
Hansen, E. J., 422, 423
Hardiman, R., 189
Harding, T. S., 62
Hargittai, E., 521
Harper, S. R., 46, 48, 49, 56, 71, 272, 287, 288, 290, 291, 294, 295, 336, 338, 497, 499, 500, 501, 508, 534
Harris, F., III, 294, 295, 297, 298
Hartley, M., 289, 293, 294
Harwarth, I., 34
Haskins, C. H., 4
Hatcher, J. A., 501
Hatry, H. P., 543
Hau, J. M., 344
Hayek, J. C., 258, 322
Haynes, C., 217, 218, 219
Healy, M., 217
Heck, R., 343
Heifetz, R. A., 453
Hellmich, D. H., 367
Helms, J. E., 154, 155, 162, 190, 191, 197
Hemphill, B. O., 473, 474, 478
Henning, G., 373
Henry, S. L., 343
Hentoff, N., 124
Herdlein, R. J., III, 321
Hernandez, E., 156, 195, 212
Hersey, P., 419, 420

Hershey, P., 357
Heyle, A. M., 195
Hickmott, J., 321, 322
Hill, C. E., 404
Hirsch, D. J., 484
Hirschy, A. S., 258
Hirt, J. B., 29, 30, 31, 39, 246,
    249, 335, 372, 376, 377, 378,
    380, 381, 471, 474, 475
Hlebowitsh, P. S., 85
Ho, P. P., 538
Hoad, T. F., 469
Hocker, J. L., 435
Hodges, J. P., 373, 378
Hoffman, C. M., 35, 36, 46,
    303, 537
Holland, J., 154, 157, 168
Holmes, L. H., 64
Holvino, E., 341
hooks, b., 156, 217, 387
Hoover, E., 292
Horn, L., 37
Hornak, A., 217
Horowitz, H. L., 9, 12, 63, 250
Horse, P. G., 196
Horton, H. E., 534, 536, 537
House, R., 409
Howard-Hamilton, M., 189
Howard-Hamilton, M. F., 338,
    343
Howell, L. C., 173
Hu, S., 337
Hughes, J. A., 173, 253
Huisman, J., 538
Hume, D., 8
Humphrey, E., 407
Hunter, M. S., 413
Hurtado, S., 2, 24, 30, 36, 37, 43,
    44, 47, 48, 49, 248, 249, 253,
    299, 337, 422

I

Idol, I., 428
Ikeda, E. K., 501
Imani, N., 249
Inglebret, E., 247
Inkelas, K. K., 507

Isaac, C., 63
Isaacs, W., 438

J

Jablonski, M. A., 89
Jackson, B. W., 189, 341
Jackson, M. L., 317, 318
Jacoby, B., 485
Jalomo, R. E., 258
Janosik, S. M., 374, 376, 379,
    380, 381, 407, 472, 473, 477
Javinar, J. M., 474
Jaworski, J., 106
Jefferson, T., 6
Jencks, C., 13
Jensen, M. C., 368
Jessup Anger, E. R., 373, 474
Jewell, J. O., 33, 36
Johnson, A. G., 347
Johnson, D., 501
Johnson, D. W., 420
Johnson, F. P., 420
Johnson, L. B., 70
Johnson, P., 353–354
Johnsrud, L. K., 373
Johnstone, D. B., 253
Jones, C. E., 181
Jones, E. A., 294
Jones, S. G., 516, 517
Jones, S. R., 135, 136, 149, 154,
    156, 158, 162, 168, 187, 189,
    198, 201, 212, 300, 534, 535
Josselson, R., 155, 169, 170,
    171, 197
Jung, C., 157, 403

K

Kadison, R., 401
Kalinkowski, J., 373
Kampwirth, T. J., 428
Kanapaux, W., 131
Kane, S. D., 363
Kanter, M., 69
Kanungo, R. N., 357
Kaplin, W. A., 120
Karabel, J., 12, 13

Kasch, D., 160, 189, 201
Katz, J. E., 518
Katz, R. N., 517
Kauffman, K., 179, 180
Keating, L. A., 68
Keefe, S. E., 193
Keeling, R. P., 73, 86, 87, 92, 109,
    207, 208, 278, 289, 291, 388,
    401, 415, 457, 524, 526, 536
Kegan, R., 156, 187, 188, 207,
    209–210, 215, 217, 367
Kellerman, B., 366
Kelley, J. M., 288
Kelley, R. E., 358
Kellner, D., 441
Kellogg, A. H., 488
Kellom, G., 295
Kelly, B. T., 321
Kemmis, S., 395
Kempner, D. E., 316
Kendall Brown, M., 212, 215
Kennedy, D., 373
Kennedy, K., 423
Keohane, N. O., 31
Keppel, F., 70
Kerr, C., 14–15, 15, 24, 29
Kerr, K. G., 292, 299, 300
Kezar, A., 86, 136, 226, 229,
    234, 235, 287, 288, 484, 485,
    486, 501
Kezar, A. J., 359, 539
Kiersky, J., 442
Kim, S. H., 435
Kim, Y. K., 501
Kimmel, M. S., 156, 198
King, J. E., 70
King, P. M., 91, 155, 176, 179,
    183, 207, 211, 212, 213, 215,
    218, 343, 394, 478
Kinzie, J., 34, 35, 157, 247, 249,
    258, 259, 261, 264, 266, 267,
    293, 322, 393, 463, 482, 483,
    484, 500
Kirst, M. W., 68
Kirton, M., 362
Kitchener, K. S., 98, 100, 114,
    176, 179, 183, 207
Kitzrow, M. A., 401

Klaus, P., 126

Knefelkamp, L. L., 150, 152, 154, 177, 183

Knight-Abowitz, K., 217

Kocarek, C., 338

Kocet, 115

Koch, W., 461

Kodama, C. M., 162

Kohlberg, L., 155, 176, 179–180, 181–182

Kohler, J., 542

Kolb, D. A., 108, 157, 168

Kolins, C. A., 484

Komives, S. R., 19, 92, 244, 312, 353, 355, 358, 359, 362, 367, 368, 453

Korn, W. S., 74

Kosten, L. A., 88, 401

Kouzes, J. M., 358

Kowalski, T. J., 294

Krippner, S., 423

Kroger, J., 187, 188

Kruger, K., 368, 478

Kruger, K., 485

Krumboltz, J. D., 348

Kuh, G. D., 34, 136, 157, 246, 247, 257, 258, 259, 260, 261, 262, 263, 264, 265, 266, 267, 290, 293, 294, 321, 322, 337, 387, 389, 393, 413, 422, 427, 463, 483, 484, 485, 486, 500, 501

Kuhn, T. S., 158, 160

Kurotsuchi Inkelas, K., 485

Kvavik, R. B., 517

L

Laden, R. M., 485

Ladson-Billings, G., 196, 217

LaFromboise, T. D., 195, 196

Lake, P. T., 70, 525

Lampe, C., 519, 520

Lang, D. W., 310

Langdon, E., 35

Lasley, T. J., 294

Lather, P., 160

Law, 438

Lazlo, E., 97

Lears, F., 123

LeBaron, M., 434, 435, 436, 440, 443

Ledesma, M. C., 55, 289

Lee, B. A., 120

Lee, S., 172

Lee, S. M., 310

Lehman, J. S., 44

Lehman, N., 12

Leigh Smith, B., 485

Lennington, R. L., 314

Leonard, E. A., 62, 63, 197

Leonard, J. B., 507

Leonard, M. J., 424

Leslie, D. W., 304

Lester, J., 539

Levine, A., 97, 110, 316, 422, 423

Levine, D., 11, 55

Levine, J. H., 485

Levinson, D. J., 155, 173

Lewin, K., 135, 149, 356, 455, 523

Lewin, K. Z., 88

Lewis, C. A., 484

Lewis, E., 44

Lewis, J., 409

Liang, C. T. H., 172

Liddell, D. L., 181

Lincoln, Y. S., 158, 159, 488

Lindsay, N. K., 212, 215

Lipman-Blumen, J., 367

Lippitt, R., 356

Liu, W. M., 344

Lloyd-Jones, E., 80, 81, 85, 449, 450, 461, 534, 535, 536, 545

Locke, J., 8

Loevinger, J., 188

Lomawaima, K. T., 195

London, H. B., 261

Longerbeam, S. D., 367, 368, 501

Loo, C. M., 49

Lopez, G., 44

Lord, R. G., 364, 367

Lorden, L. P., 373, 474

Love, P. G., 19, 106, 312, 336, 362, 413, 418

Lovell, C. D., 88, 401

Lowe, S. C., 32

Lucas, C. J., 62

Lucas, N., 355, 358, 453

Luna, F. C., 253

Lund, J. P., 258, 389

Lynch, C. L., 179

Lynn, M., 46

Lyons, J. W., 245, 246

Lyotard, J., 156, 519

M

Ma, J., 303

McAdams, C. R., III, 479

Macaruso, V., 415, 427

McCarthy, M. M., 422

McCarty, T. L., 195

McCauley, 115

McClanahan, R., 413

McClellan, G. S., 32

McClendon, S. A., 258

McCormick, A. C., 26

McDonald, W. M., 456, 488

McDoniel, L. J., 69

McEwen, M. K., 135, 151, 152, 154, 155, 156, 161, 162, 172, 188, 201, 212, 345, 474

MacGregor, J., 485

McHugh Engstrom, C., 485

McKeon, R., 96

MacKinnon, B., 437

McLaughlin, A. E., 156

McMahon, K. N., 359

McMahon, T. R., 355, 358, 453

McPherson, P., 535

Madison, J., 6

Magnusson, D., 173

Magolda, P. M., 160, 217, 336, 385, 390, 395, 475, 486–487, 492

Mainella, F. C., 367, 368

Maitra, A., 363

Maki, P. L., 322, 326

Malcolm X, 123

Malcom, L. E., 37

Maline, M., 34

Malley, 102, 103

Mallory, S. L., 478
Manning, K., 89, 249, 272, 273, 338, 482, 484, 486
March, J., 234
Marcia, J. E., 155, 169, 170, 171, 189
Marie, J., 217
Marshall, S. P., 434
Marth, B. P., 501
Martin, J., 267, 484
Martin, S., 343
Martínez Alemán, A. M., 85, 497, 515, 516, 520, 521, 522, 525, 526, 527, 528, 528–529, 530
Martinez, C. R., 475
Martinez, R. O., 368
Marwick, A., 518
Marx, K., 441
Mason, T., 19
Matheis, C., 336, 433, 441, 442, 443
Matney, M. M., 288
Matthews, R. S., 485
Maxam, S., 336, 413
Mayer, B., 435
Mayhew, M. J., 43
Mayorga, M., 344
Meacham, J., 246
Meara, N., 101, 102
Medsker, L. L., 500
Meilman, P. W., 401
Meisinger, R. J., Jr., 311
Mena, S. B., 89
Mendelsohn, J., 344
Mentkowski, M., 209
Merriam, S. B., 173
Meszaros, P. S., 212, 222
Meyer, P. M., 126
Mezirow, J., 208, 215
Miklitsch, T. A., 343, 345
Milem, J. F., 2, 25, 36, 46, 47, 49, 50, 55, 249
Miller, B. A., 200
Miller, T. K., 68, 373, 399, 472
Mills, R., 218
Miltenberger, P., 485
Minor, F. D., 485

Misa, K., 49
Mitchell, R. L., 72
Moffatt, M., 17
Mohatt, G. V., 196
Mohr, J. J., 249
Moneta, L., 316
Moore Gardner, M., 322
Moore, L. V., 151, 475
Moore, M. H., 130
Moos, R. H., 244, 252, 253
Moran, C., 510
Morelon-Quainoo, C. L., 36
Morgan, G., 226, 227, 238, 239
Moriarty, D., 501
Morrison, D. E., 501
Mouton, J. S., 357
Muchinsky, P., 436
Mueller, J. A., 335, 337, 340, 343, 345, 400, 403, 404, 458, 476, 477, 478
Muñoz, F. M., 272, 273
Murphy, J. P., 84
Murty, K. S., 247
Museus, S. D., 294
Myers, H. F., 193
Myers, I. B., 168
Myers, L. J., 348

N

Nagda, B. A., 44
Napier, R. W., 417, 421, 422
Narvaez, D., 176
Nelson Laird, T. F., 36
Nelson, M. R., 517
Nemeth Tuttle, K., 70
Nerad, M., 12
Nesheim, B. S. E., 501
Nettles, M. T., 36
Neuberger, C. G., 475
Neugarten, B. L., 173, 174
Neumann, A., 363
Nevin, A., 428
Newcomb, M. D., 193, 500
Newcomer, J. S., 543
Newman, F., 483
Newton, F. B., 388
Nidiffer, J., 63, 64, 89

Nieves, A. D., 156
Noddings, N., 85, 86, 107
Noonan, M. J., 344
Nora, A., 249, 258, 337, 389
Norris, D., 288
Northouse, P. G., 356
Nunez, A. M., 37
Nuss, E. M., 63, 64, 68, 69, 70, 373
Nutt, C. L., 413, 415, 416, 417, 423, 426, 427

O

Obama, B., 69, 76, 483, 541
O'Brien, K. M., 404
O'Donohue, W., 485
Oetzel, J. G., 434, 440
Okun, B. F., 400, 404
Orrill, R., 85
Ortega-Villalobos, L., 344
Ortiz, A. M., 191, 217, 258, 473, 475
Osei-Kofi, N., 49
Ossana, S. M., 197
Osteen, L., 367, 368
O'Sullivan, E., 109
Ott, M., 402
Outcalt, C. L., 247, 359
Owen, J., 501
Owen, J. O., 367, 368
Ozaki, C. C., 218
Ozer, E. J., 195

P

Pace, C. R., 243
Padilla, A. M., 193
Palmer, A. F., 63
Palmer, J., 438
Palmer, M. M., 34, 247
Palmer, P., 106, 456
Palomba, C. A., 321, 323, 324, 325
Paolucci-Whitcomb, P., 428
Park, J. J., 38
Parker, C., 151, 154
Parker, L., 46

Parks, S. D., 156, 176, 182, 183
Parrott, S. A., 74
Pascarella, E. T., 31, 36, 248, 249, 258, 260, 337, 387, 413, 483, 484, 489, 499, 500, 501, 502, 507, 508, 511
Paterson, B. G., 472
Patterson, C. H., 151, 152
Patton, L. D., 46, 136, 170, 242, 252
Paulson, D., 423
Pavalko, R. M., 470
Pavel, D. M., 247
Pavela, G., 120, 124, 132
Pawlak, K., 272, 273, 274, 276, 278, 284
Peck, M. S., 433, 452, 457, 459
Peck, S., 106
Pedersen, P., 338
Penney, J. F., 470
Perez, R. J., 213
Perna, L. W., 36, 53, 157, 501
Perry, W., 106
Perry, W. G., Jr., 154, 155, 161, 176, 183
Peterson, P. L., 394
Phelps Tobin, C. E., 473
Phinney, J. S., 155, 170, 192, 193
Piaget, J., 155, 175, 176
Pierce, A. E., 64
Pierson, C. T., 501
Pike, G., 509
Pike, G. R., 261, 485
Piper, T. D., 218
Pizzolato, J. E., 212, 218
Plato, 121, 122
Ponterotto, J. G., 343, 344
Pope, R. L., 161, 172, 201, 335, 337, 338, 340, 342, 343, 344, 345, 346, 348, 400, 401, 402, 407, 458, 476, 477, 478
Pope-Davis, D. B., 344
Popp, N., 210
Portnow, K., 210
Posner, B. Z., 358
Poulton, N.., 288
Pratt, D. M., 126
Price, J., 288, 311

Prince, J. S., 68
Pruitt, D. G., 435
Pryor, J. H., 422

Q

Quaye, J., 71, 160, 288
Quaye, S. J., 336, 385, 500, 501, 541

R

Rader, L., 197, 200
Raffel, M., 126
Ramin-Gyurnek, J., 258, 389
Randall, K. S., 434
Rankin, S. R., 253, 443
Raphael, 121, 122
Ratliff, R. C., 70
Reason, R. D., 80, 81, 87, 89, 92, 249, 253, 410, 449, 450, 535
Redd, K. E., 304
Reeves Sanday, P., 429, 430
Reid, R. H., 516
Reisser, L., 31, 155, 169, 171–172, 175
Rendon, L. I., 258
Renn, K. A., 136, 170, 187, 192, 200, 201, 242, 243, 252, 373, 378, 474, 478
Rentz, A. L., 92
Ressor, L. M., 378
Rest, J., 176, 181
Reynolds, A. L., 161, 189, 201, 336, 338, 340, 342, 343, 344, 345, 399, 400, 402, 407, 458, 476, 477, 478, 540
Rhatigan, J. J., 63, 69, 76, 277
Rhee, M., 537
Rhoades, G., 237, 470, 471, 472, 473
Rhoads, R. A., 86, 159, 160, 191, 389
Rice, R. E., 518
Richards, S., 49
Richardson, B. J., 338
Riesman, D., 13

Rifkin, J., 189
Riley, G. L., 235
Riordan, B. G., 419
Robbins, R. R., 196
Roberts, D. C., 336, 448, 453
Roberts, D. R., 359
Rodgers, R. F., 151, 153
Roebuck, J. B., 247
Rogers, C., 403
Rogers, J. L., 217
Rogers, R. R., 80, 81, 83, 87, 92
Rolison, G., 49
Rooney, P. M., 310
Roosa-Millar, L., 443
Root, M. P. P., 192
Roper, L., 248, 336, 433
Roper, L. D., 345
Rosen, C., 518
Rosser, V. J., 373, 474
Rost, J., 453
Rost, J. C., 354, 359, 362
Roush, K. L., 156, 197
Rowley, D. J., 288
Ruben, B. D., 288
Rudolph, F., 4, 8, 34, 63
Rudy, W., 64
Runde, C. E., 435, 440
Rush, S. C., 316

S

Saenz, V., 49
St. John, E. P., 511
Salas, C., 344
Salaway, G., 517
Salinas Holmes, M., 36
Sam, D. L., 193
Samels, J. E., 484
Sanaghan, P., 288
Sanchez, P. J., 368
Sanchez-Hucles, J., 368
Sandeen, A., 304
Sandler, B., 248
Sanford, N., 15, 153, 243, 250, 278
Saunders, K. P., 485
Saunders, S. A., 374, 376, 377, 451, 452, 454, 460, 462, 465

Savoy, H. B., 170, 199
Sax, L. J., 74, 295, 297, 497, 499, 500, 501, 503, 508
Schein, E. H., 428, 429
Schenkel, S., 170
Schlossberg, N. K., 173, 455–456, 459
Schmidt, L., 101
Schmidtlein, F. A., 309
Schön, D. A., 394, 395
Schoper, S., 92
Schouten, P. J., 520
Schroeder, C., 485, 486
Schuh, J. H., 88, 157, 249, 259, 260, 261, 264, 265, 266, 267, 272, 290, 293, 294, 303, 321, 323, 324, 325, 326, 393, 419, 420, 463, 482, 483, 484, 500, 534
Schuster, J., 237
Schwab, K., 448, 449, 465
Schweitzer, S., 525
Scott, W. D., 68
Scurry, J., 483
Seal, M., 237
Sedlacek, W. E., 249
Seifert, T. A., 258, 508
Selfe, C. L., 520
Senge, P. M., 454
Sevig, T., 401
Shapiro, N. S., 485
Shaw, K. M., 261
Shelley, M. C. I., 485
Sherman, H., 288
Shintaku, R. H., 473, 475
Shor, I., 217
Shoup, R., 258
Shuetz, P., 246
Shuford, B., 338
Shulenberger, D., 535
Siegel, B., 123
Siko, K. L., 89
Silverman, M. M., 126, 127
Simpson, J., 121
Skewes-Cox, T. E., 247
Skinner Jackson, J., 373
Sleeter, C. E., 337
Sloan, T., 373

Sloane, F., 126
Slosson, E., 10
Smith, A., 8
Smith, D. G., 36, 49, 247, 501
Smith, J. H., 413
Smith, M. R., 80, 81, 85, 450, 461, 534, 535, 536, 545
Snyder, T. D., 35, 36, 46, 303, 306, 314, 537
Sodowsky, G. R., 343
Soet, J., 401
Solórzano, D. G., 46, 337
Sonnenberg, B., 35, 36
Spellings, M., 73
Spooner, S. E., 406
Sporn, B., 236
Springer, L., 389
Stage, F. K., 501
Stamatakos, L. C., 80, 81, 83, 87, 92
Stanford, N., 523
Steele, G. E., 418
Stefancic, J., 156, 160, 196
Steinfeld, C., 519, 520
Steiss, A. W., 309
Stephens, J., 483
Stephens, P. S., 422, 423
Stern, G. G., 243
Stewart, G. M., 63
Stocum, D. L., 310
Stoflet, T., 402
Stogdill, R. W., 356
Strange, C. C., 88, 157, 244, 245, 248, 249, 250, 252, 253, 289, 290, 321, 394
Strauss, A., 157
Strauss, J., 310
Strayhorn, T. L., 335, 372, 376, 377, 380
Strong, K. L., 218
Strong, L. J., 338
Sue, D., 402, 409
Sue, D. W., 337, 338, 402, 409
Sue, R., 438, 442, 443
Sullivan, N., 156, 160
Super, D. E., 169, 174
Suskie, L., 321
Swartz, P. S., 464

Sweatt, H., 52
Sweet, A., 391
Synnott, M., 12

T

Taffe, R. C., 343
Tagg, J., 390
Talbot, D. M., 338
Talbot, M., 63
Talley, F. J., 407
Tanaka, G., 158
Tancer, B., 522
Tapscott, D., 516
Tarkow, T. A., 485
Tarule, J. M., 176, 177
Tatum, B. D., 152, 189
Taub, D. J., 474
Taylor, H., 84
Taylor, K. B., 212, 213, 218, 219
Taylor, S. H., 288
Taylor, S. L., 434
Teranishi, R. T., 38
Terenzini, P. T., 36, 249, 258, 260, 337, 387, 389, 413, 483, 484, 489, 499, 500, 501
Thelin, J. R., 2, 3, 20, 84, 537
Thoma, S. J., 176
Thomas, A. D., 34, 247
Thomas, J. B., 237
Thomas, S. L., 157, 501
Thompson, 115
Thompson, C. E., 190, 191
Tidball, C. S., 247
Tidball, M. E., 34, 35, 247
Tierney, W. G., 32, 49, 266
Ting-Toomey, S., 434, 440
Tinto, V., 157, 262, 265, 501
Toporek, R. L., 344, 409
Torres, V., 155, 156, 158, 187, 189, 190, 193, 195, 212, 374
Trainer, J. F., 288
Trent, J. W., 500
Treviño, J., 49
Trimble, J. E., 196
Tromp, S. A., 288
Trow, M., 3
Truman, H. S., 13

Tubbs, N. J., 199
Tuckman, B. W., 368
Tull, A., 373, 377, 378, 470, 474
Turner, C. S. V., 20, 49, 247
Tuttle, K. N., 89
Tweedy, J., 292, 299, 300
Twigg, C. A., 263
Twombly, S. B., 70, 89

U

Umbach, P. D., 34, 247, 337
Underwood, R., 38
Upcraft, M. L., 151, 290, 321,
    324, 325, 422, 423, 501
Uyeki, E. C., 464

V

Vaillant, G., 173
Valkenburg, P. M., 520
Van Eck, R., 517
Van Horn, J. C., 310
VanDenHende, M., 247
Vandiver, B. J., 189, 190
VanHecke, J. R., 212
Vedder, P., 193
Vedder, R., 303
Vera, H., 249
Vernaglia, E. R., 170, 199
Villalpando, O., 160
Vogelgesang, L. J., 501
Vogt, K. E., 501, 507
Von Destinon, M., 308, 309, 310,
    313, 314

W

Wadsworth, B. J., 176
Wagner, W., 359, 360
Wakefield, K., 212
Wakelyn, J. L., 7
Walpole, M., 501, 506
Walther, J. B., 518
Waple, J. N., 321, 401, 402

Ward, K., 32, 70, 89
Ward, L., 474
Ward, T. J., 479
Wartman, K. L., 497, 515, 516,
    520, 521, 522, 525, 526, 527,
    528, 529, 530
Washington, B. T., 9
Washington, M., 353–354
Watkins, D., 478
Watt, J. D., 181
Watt, S. K., 347
Weber, L., 156
Wechsler, H., 21
Wehlburg, C. M., 486
Weick, K. E., 233, 235, 482, 486
Weidman, J. C., 501
Weigand, M. J., 343, 345
Weinberg, M., 46
Weiner, E., 121
Weisman, J. L., 485
Wellman, J. V., 303
Wells, C. A., 488
Wells, G. V., 345
Wenger, E., 367
Whalen, D. F., 485
Whalen, E., 310
Wheatley, M. J., 112, 359
White, C. B., 47
White, E. R., 413
White, J., 121
White, R. K., 356
Whitt, E. J., 157, 246, 259, 260,
    261, 264, 265, 266, 267, 289,
    293, 298, 321, 336, 393, 463,
    482, 483, 484, 486, 488, 489,
    500, 501
Wholey, K. E., 543
Widick, C., 151, 154, 177, 183
Wijeyesinghe, C. L., 192
Wilde, O., 12
Wildman, T. M., 218
Wilensky, H. L., 470, 477
Williams, E., 353–354
Williams, J. M., 36
Williamson, E. G., 64, 65

Wilmot, W. W., 435
Wilson, E., 475
Wing, L., 189
Winston, R. B., 372, 373, 374,
    375, 376, 377, 378, 379, 380,
    381, 399, 400
Wise, S. L., 343
Wolf, D., 33
Wolf, L. E., 501
Wolf-Wendel, L. E., 70, 89, 247
Wolniak, G. C., 31, 258, 507
Wood, P. K., 179
Woodard, D. B., 19, 244
Woodard, D. B., Jr., 308, 309,
    310, 312, 313, 314
Wooden, O. S., 46
Worthington, R. L., 170, 199,
    200
Wright, S., 9, 11

Y

Yankelovich, D., 105
Yates, E. L., 247
Yeater, E. A., 485
Yee, J. A., 501
Yon, D., 156
Yonkers Talz, K., 217
Yosso, T. J., 46, 337
Young, I., 98, 105, 106
Young, I. M., 443
Young, R. B., 84, 87, 90, 169

Z

Zaccaro, S. J., 369
Zaleznik, A., 362
Zdziarski, E. L., 478
Zehr, H., 438, 439, 443
Zeligman, D. M., 478
Zelna, C. L., 92, 322
Zhao, C., 26, 262
Zheng, L. J., 485
Zunker, V. G., 469
Zusman, A., 29

SUBJECT INDEX

Page references followed by *fig* indicate an illustrated figure; followed by *t* indicate a table; followed by *e* indicate an exhibit.

A

About Campus (Kerr & Tweedy), 300

Academic-student affairs partnerships: Boyer Partnership Assessment Project (BPAP), 487*t*–492; DEEP project, 293, 294, 486; negative aspects of, 486–487; research on benefits of, 485–486; types of, 483–485

Accountability: increasing demand for student learning, 542; increasing environment of, 543

Acculturation: ethnic identity theory of, 192–193; Health Model Conceptualization of Acculturation, 196

ACPA code of ethics, 109

ACPA-College Student Educators International, 66

Adult development theories: description of, 172–173; life course perspectives, 173–174; life events and transition perspectives, 173; life stage perspectives, 173

Advising: core values of, 414; description and components of, 413; groups, 418–422; individuals, 414–418; internal consultation of the institution, 427–430; issues in individual and group, 422–427; skills and competencies of, 416–418; technology role in, 423–426

Advocacy culture: management techniques and structural considerations of, 280–281; origins and characteristics of, 279–280; roles in the, 281; scenario description of, 279

Afghanistan War veterans, 538

African American students: Black racial identity theory and, 151–152; online networking sites used by, 521

AISP (Assessment-Intervention of Student Problems) model, 406

Alabama State Board of Education, Dixon v., 70

Allegheny College, Mahoney v., 131

The Allure of Toxic Leaders (Lipman-Blumen), 367

American Association of Higher Education (AAHE), 73, 208, 388

American Association of University Women (AAUW), 66

American College Health Association, 126

American College Health Association (ACHA), 401

American College Personnel Association (ACPA): *Developments* (newsletter) of, 115; ethical code of, 98, 109, 113–114, 476; Ethics Committee of, 115; gender disparities presentations during conference of, 296–297; graduate program directory of, 472; *Journal of College Student Development* of, 471; *Learning*

Reconsidered: report by, 73, 87, 92, 208, 278, 536; *Learning Reconsidered 2* report by, 73, 92, 289, 291, 415, 524, 536; on multicultural competence development, 345; origins of, 66; *Principles of Good Practice for Student Affairs* by, 73, 397, 471, 523, 524, 527, 535; Professional Competencies Task Force of the, 477; on roles and functions of student affairs staff, 83; on student affairs principles and values, 87, 88, 89, 90; student learning focus of, 109; *Student Learning Imperative* by, 73, 92, 208, 278, 324, 388, 535

The American College (Sanford), 15

American Council on Education (ACE), 65, 274, 277, 373, 523

American with Disabilities Act, 406

American Indian College Fund, 33

American Indian Higher Education Consortium (AIHEC), 32, 247

American Indian Movement, 32

American Indians. *See* Native Americans

American Psychiatric Association, 127

"American Way" higher education, 3–4, 6–10

Amygdala, 130

Arizona State University (ASU)'s speech code, 124

Asian American Identity Development (AAID) theory, 193

Asian American identity theories, 193

Asian American- and Pacific Islander-Serving Institution program, 38

Asian American-serving institutions, 37–38

Assessment: of advising, 426–427; definition of, 321–323; multicultural competence, 342–344; needs, 322; purpose of, 323–326; satisfaction, 322; student affairs role in, 72–73; utilization, 322. *See also* Evaluation

Assessment tools: AISP (Assessment-Intervention of Student Problems) model, 406; Astin's Input-Environment-Outcome (I-E-O) Model on, 322–323, 502*fig*–503, 506; Beginning College Survey of Student Engagement (BCSSE), 322; Cross-Cultural Counseling Inventory-Revised (CCCI-R), 343; Educational Benchmarking (EBI) Surveys, 322; Multicultural Awareness Knowledge-Skills Survey (MAKSS), 343; Multicultural Change Intervention Matrix, 345; Multicultural Competence Characteristics of Student Affairs Professionals Inventory (MCCSAPI), 344; Multicultural Competence in Student Affairs—Preliminary 2 (MCSA-P2) Scale, 343; Multicultural Counseling Awareness Scale: Form B-Revised (MCAS:B), 343; Multicultural Counseling Awareness Scale, 343; Multicultural Counseling Inventory (MCI), 343; Multicultural Organizational Development Checklist, 345; National Survey of Student Engagement (NSSE), 263, 264, 296, 329, 415; Noel-Levitz Satisfaction Survey, 322; outcomes-based assessment (OBA), 323, 324–332; Pascarella's General Model for Assessing Change, 502; Tinto's Model of Student Departure, 502; Weidman's Model of Undergraduate Socialization, 502

Associate's colleges, 27–29

Association of American Colleges and Universities (AAC&U), 207, 208, 258, 386, 469

Association of College Unions International (ACUI), 66, 475

Association of College and University Housing Officers-International (ACUHO-I), 98, 475

Association for Fraternity and Sorority Advisors (AFA), 475

Astin's Input-Environment-Outcome (I-E-O) Model, 322–323, 502*fig*–503, 506

Athletic department: educating athletes on social networking conduct, 527–528; student affairs relationship with, 113

Authentic leadership, 359

Authority: academic power structures and, 236; four types of, 236

Auxiliary services: budgeting for, 314–315; definition of, 314

B

Baccalaureate colleges, 30–31

Bad Leadership (Kellerman), 366

Bakke, Regents of the University of California v., 71

Basic Educational Opportunity Grants (BEOG) [Pell Grants], 16, 38

Baxter Magolda's self-authorship journey, 210–212

Bazelon Center for Mental Health Law, 408

Beginning College Survey of Student Engagement (BCSSE), 322

Behavioral theory of leadership, 355*e*, 356–357

Beneficial conflict, 436

Bisexual students. *See* LGBT (lesbian, gay, bisexual, and transgender) students

Black culture centers (BCCs), 252

Black identity theories, 190–191

Black racial identity theory, 151–152

Black Student Union, 191

Blackboard, 425

Blind students, 38

Blogs, 424

Bollinger et al., Gratz et al. v., 44

Bollinger et al., Grutter et al. v., 44

Boyer Commission, 29, 483

Boyer Partnership Assessment Project (BPAP): description of the, 487–488; on good practices for academic-student affairs partnerships, 489–492; institutional participants in, 487*t*; student outcomes findings of the, 488–489

Boyer's model of a learning community, 456

Brevard Community College (Florida), 490

Brown v. the Board of Education, 70

Bureau of Labor Statistics, 473

C

Campus climate: applying Dey's framework on, 50–54; definition of, 248; Dey's framework on diversity of, 45–50*fig*; diversity agenda for, 54–56; factors contributing to, 248–249; institutional identities and, 245–249; for LGBT (lesbian, gay, bisexual, and transgender) students, 249; relationship between students and, 43–45. *See also* Campus environment

Campus climate internal forces: behavioral climate, 49; compositional diversity, 47–48; historical legacy of inclusion or exclusion, 48; organizational/structural diversity, 49–50; psychological climate, 48–49

Campus design matrix, 244*fig*–245

Campus ecology: campus design matrix of, 244*fig*–245; definition of, 244

Campus environment: accountability and institutional productivity of, 253; conditional effects of college

and, 507–509; ecology theory applied to, 243–245, 250–252; future directions for research and practice, 252–254; influence of institutional types on, 246–248; institutional types and missions, 245–246; new populations in, 253–254; student affairs practice and, 249–252; theories on, 157, 242–254. *See also* Campus climate

Campus safety: brain's fear system and risk management of, 130–132; campus ecology encouraging, 244*fig*–245; memorandum to faculty on, 125–129; murder rate on, 125–126; suicidal ideation and, 131; Virginia Tech incident (2007), 112, 125, 129–130, 540

Career development theory, 174

Career services, 528

Carlisle School, 9

Carnegie Basic Classifications: associate's colleges, 27–29; baccalaureate colleges, 30–31; description of, 26–27, 245; distribution of institutional types/missions by, 27*fig*; doctorate-granting universities, 29–30; HBCU spanning six of the, 35–36; master's colleges and universities, 30; special focus institutions, 31–32; student enrollment by, 28*fig*; tribal colleges, 32–33. *See also* Higher education institutions

Carnegie Classification of Institutions of Higher Education, 25–26

Carnegie Foundation for the Advancement of Teaching (CFAT), 17, 25, 26, 39, 456

Center for Neural Science (NYU), 131

Chaos theory, 355*e*, 359

Chicago Quarter (CQ) [DePaul University], 491–492

Chronicle of Higher Education, 74, 124, 337, 366, 373, 375, 534

The Chronicle of Higher Education, 74

Civil Rights Act (1964), 14

Civil Rights Movement, 16

Civility: description and meaning of, 121–122; "speech codes" as incivility instead of, 122–124; student affairs role in promoting, 124–125

Co-curriculum: institutional influences, 386–388; as a strategic resource, 291–293; student affairs professionals as educators, 388–391; student affairs professionals as learning partners, 391–393; student affairs professionals as political activists, 396; student affairs professionals as theoretically informed, 393–395

Codes of ethics, 98, 109, 113–115, 476

Cognitive development theories: cognitive-structural perspectives, 175–184; description of, 155

Cognitive-structure perspectives: overview of, 175–176; spiritual development, 182–183; student affairs practice using, 183–184; theories of intellectual and epistemological development, 176–179; theories of moral development, 179–182

Collaborative consultation, 428

College Entrance Examination Board (CEEB), 12

College of William & Mary, 5, 6

Collegiate culture: characteristics of, 274–275; decline of, 20–21; management styles and structural considerations of, 275; origins of the, 274; roles in, 275

Coming of Age in New Jersey (Moffatt), 17

Commonfund Institute, 303

Communication: community development and role of technological, 459; computer-mediated, 516–518; "friendship-based" online, 519; as heart of well-functioning community, 433–434; instant messaging (IM), 424, 524, 525; social networking sites, 375, 424; technology role in, 424–426. *See also* Dialogue; Social networking sites

Community: campus-community partnerships and impact on, 463–465; as context for dialogue on ethics, 105–107; crisis intervention and threats to the, 111–112; development expectations of, 459–460; Keeling and Berkowitz's concept of healthy, 457; professional, 474–476

Community colleges: campus culture of, 246; increasing higher education role of, 542; student services offered by, 68–69

Community development: competencies required for, 460–461; contrasting philosophies and programming for, 450–451; examples in practices of, 461–465; multicultural competence role in, 458; objectives and benefits of, 448–449; origins of community building for, 449–450; programming frameworks for, 451–454; special conditions influencing, 458–460; theories to inform, 454–458

Community development programs: community-building program model of, 452–454; philosophies and purposes of, 450–451; program development model of, 451–452

Community service, 461–462

Community-building program model, 452–454

Competitive conflict, 436

Conditional college effects: examples from research on, 505–511; identifying and understanding research on, 504–505; models for visualizing the, 502*fig*–504; Sax's model of, 503*fig*; why educators should consider the, 500–502

Conflict: beneficial, 436; competitive, 436; conflict mediation approach to, 437–438; defining, 435; engaging with situations of, 443–446; human relations theory on, 438; nature and causes of, 435–436; organizational psychology approach to, 436; restorative justice approach to, 438–439; strategies for approaching, 440–443; styles and levels of, 439–440; understanding, 434; values theory on, 437

Conflict management strategies: case study on practicing, 444–446; charity and Principle of Fairness, 442; critical thinking, 441; demonstrating hospitality, 441; understanding nuances of justice, 443; welcoming and experiencing dynamic tension, 442–443

Conflict mediation, 437–438

Conflict resolution: conflict mediation for, 437–438; mediation for, 437–438; restorative justice models of, 438–439

Constructivism, 159

Consultation: collaborative, 428; description of, 427; process, 426–429; skills and competencies of, 429–430

Contingency theory of leadership, 355*e*, 357

Cosmopolitanism: Ethics in a World of Strangers (Appiah), 96

Council for the Advancement of Standards (CAS) for Academic Advising, 414–415

Council for the Advancement of Standards in Higher Education (CAS), 69–70, 83, 98, 472, 476, 479

Counseling: AISP (Assessment-Intervention of Student Problems) model for, 406; conceptualizing student issues during, 405–406; helpers as change agents, 409–410; helping awareness, knowledge, and skills, 401–406; helping models of, 404–405; helping relationship and, 403–404; prevalent concerns by students, 400–401; roles of counseling theories, 403; student support through, 399–400. *See also* Mental health

Course management systems, 425

Critical race theory (CRT), 162, 196–197

Critical theory, 159–160

Cross-Cultural Counseling Inventory-Revised (CCCI-R), 343

Cultural border crossing, 52–53

Cultural values, student services sensitivity to, 103–104

Culture: advocacy, 279–281; collegial, 20–21, 273–275; developmental, 277–279; student affairs managerial, 275–277; tangible, 283–285; virtual, 281–283

Cyberleadership, 369

D

Dark side of organization, 238–240

Deadly Lessons: Understanding Lethal School Violence report (NRC), 128

Deaf students, 38

Dean of men, 64–65

Dean of women, 64–65

DEEP project, 293, 294, 486

Deeper teaching, 535

Democracy education, 84–85
DePaul University, 491–492
Development: community, 448–466; identity, 187–189, 197–203, 510; professional, 65–67, 113–115, 380–381
Development Instruction Model, 183
Developmental culture: management techniques and structural considerations of, 278; origins and characteristics of, 277–278; roles in, 279; scenario description of, 277
Developmental plasticity, 200
Developmental theories: cognitive, 155; description of, 153; on dissonance or crisis, 154; on epigenetic principle and developmental trajectory, 154–155; psychosocial, 155; on stages, phases, statuses, vectors, 154, 171–172*e*. *See also* Student development
Developmental trajectory, 154–155
Developments (ACPA newsletter), 115
Dialogue: community as context for ethics, 105–107; respectful listening as essence of, 123–124. *See also* Communication
"The Differential Effects of On- and Off-Campus Living Arrangements on Students' Openness to Diversity" (Pike), 509
Digest of Education Statistics 2007 (Snyder et al.), 306
"Dilemma of diversity," 11–12
Directory of Graduate Programs in Student Personnel, 69
Distributive justice, 443
Diverse Issues in Higher Education, 375
Diversity: Dey's legacy on, 45–46; "dilemma of diversity" (early 20th century), 11–12; external forces of, 46–47; framework on campus climate, 45–54; as

increasing higher education trend, 537; internal forces of, 47–50*fig*; reconsidering American higher education, 38–40; rigorous preparation for increasing, 544; special populations served in higher education, 33–38; unique needs defining contemporary student, 71–75. *See also* Student enrollment
Dixon v. Alabama State Board of Education, 70
Do no harm, 100
Doctorate-granting universities, 29–30
Documenting Effective Educational Practice (DEEP) project, 293, 294, 486
Duné College, 32
Dynamic Model of Multicultural Competence: description of the, 337–342; illustrated diagram of student affairs competence, 340*fig*
Dynamic tension: definition of, 442; welcoming and experiencing, 442–443

E

E-mail, 424
Ecology theory: across the campus, 251–252; campus living environments and, 243–245, 250–251
Educational Benchmarking (EBI) Surveys, 322
Educational Testing Service (ETS), 12
EducationDynamics, 264
EDUCAUSE, 520
Ego development theories, 188
Ego identity, 188
Electronic portfolios (e-portfolios), 425
Epigenetic principle, 154–155
Epistemological Reflection Model, 178

Equity for All: Institutional Responsibility for Student Success project, 295
"Ethical affect" concept, 107
Ethical issues: ACPA code of ethics, 98, 109, 113–114, 476; case examples on, 117–118; community as context for dialogue on, 105–107; contemporary campus, 110–113; dark side of organizations and related, 238–240; ethical decision making process, 115–116; fundamental principles and themes, 107–110; helper concerns and challenges related to, 407–408; levels of ethical inquiry, 98; patterns of meaning and ethical perspectives, 102–105; principles, 98–101; professional codes and communities, 113–115, 476; virtues, 101–102
"The Ethics of Argument: Plato's Gorgias and the Modern Lawyer" (White), 122
Ethics Wheel, 103*fig*, 105
Ethnic identity theories: acculturation, 192–193; American Indian-Native American identity theories, 195–196; Asian American identity theories, 193; changing perspectives on, 196–197; commonalities among, 194*t*; Latino identity theories, 193, 195. *See also* Racial identity theories
Evaluation: definition of assessment and, 321–323; performance appraisals, 378–380. *See also* Assessment

F

Facebook: educating students on productive use of, 526–529; "friendship-based" communication of, 519; identity construction on, 520–522; impression management on, 520, 527–528; increasing use of, 538–539; number of active users, 517, 518, 522; as recruitment and selection tool, 375; social capital created through, 518–519; social class and developmental curve characterizing use of, 522; student conduct on, 524–526. *See also* Social networking sites

Fact Sheet: Violence and Mental Illness (APA), 127

Faculty: co-curriculum resource for, 291–293; conditional effects of college and interactions of students and, 508–509; creating sense of community, 264–265; framework for student development and role of, 220*t*–221*t*; memorandum on teaching troubled students to, 125–129

Family Education Rights and Privacy Act (FERPA), 408

Fear system of brain, 130–132

Feedback: conditional effects of college and faculty, 508–509; documenting OBA higher-level, 331

"Fifth dimension," 47–48

Financial issues: ethical management of resources, 112–113; financing student affairs, 303–318; raising concerns over costs of attendance, 75

Foreclosure (identity resolution), 170, 171

Four Critical Years (Astin), 13

Four-frame model: in higher education, 232–235; human resource frame, 227*t*, 228–229; multiframe thinking, 230–231; organizational archetypes in the, 232*t*; overview of the, 227*t*; political frame, 227*t*, 229;

structural frame, 227*t*, 228; symbolic frame, 227*t*, 229–230

Fraternity system, 62

Freedmen's Bureau, 9

Freshman Interest Groups (FIGs) [University of Missouri], 489, 491, 509

G

Gay students. *See* LGBT (lesbian, gay, bisexual, and transgender) students

Gender differences: online social networking site use and, 521; reactions to faculty feedback and, 508–509; understanding disparities of, 295–297. *See also* Men; Women

The Gender Gap in College (Sax), 295

Gender identity theories: men's identity development, 198; transgendered identity, 199; women's identity development, 197–198

George Mason University (GMU), 489–490

German model of education, 10

GI Bill, 12–13, 70, 72, 104, 110

GLB (gay, lesbian, and bisexual) identity, 200–201. *See also* LGBT (lesbian, gay, bisexual, and transgender) students

Global economic crisis (2008), 455

Globalization, 538

Golden Rule, 101

Gratz et al. v. Bollinger et al., 44

Great Awakening, 62

Great man theories of leadership, 355*e*, 356

Great Society, 70

Group behavior theory, 455

Group development, 421–422

Group motivation for advising, 420

Group think, 203

Growing Up Digital: The Rise of the Net Generation (Tapscott), 516

Grutter et al. v. Bollinger et al., 44

H

Hampton Institute, 9

Harvard College (Harvard University), 5, 61

Helper skills: concerns and challenges related to, 406–408; description of, 400; knowledge and related, 401–406; roles of helping theories, 403

Helpers: as campus change agents, 409–410; concerns and challenges, 406–408; description of, 400

Helping models, 404–405

Helping relationship, 403–404

Heterosexual identity, 199–200

Higher education: Carnegie Classification of Institutions of Higher Education, 25–26; conditional college effects of, 500–511; "dilemma of diversity" (early 20th century) faced by, 11–12; German model of, 10; historical overview of U.S., 3–22; institutional variety in U.S., 24–40; linking K–12 education to, 544; Oxbridge model of, 4, 274; Oxford-Cambridge model of, 4, 15; reconsidering diversity in U.S., 38–40; societal value of, 472; specific populations served in, 33–38

Higher Education Act (1965), 14, 20, 33, 37, 70

Higher education history: adjustment and accountability era (1970–1990), 16–18; colonial period of, 4–6; creating "American Way," 3–4, 6–10; "Golden Age" (1945–1970), 12–14; during the 1960s, 14–16; 1990 to 2010, 19–21; post–World War I (1915–1945), 11–12; university building (1880–1914), 10–11

Higher education institutions: Asian American- and Pacific Islander-serving, 37–38;

community colleges, 68–69, 246, 542; Hispanic-serving institutions (HSIs), 20, 33, 35–36; historically Black colleges and universities (HBCUs), 9, 33, 35–36, 247; image as driving behavior in, 237; internal consultation and advising of the, 427–430; predominantly White institutions (PWIs), 35; student affairs-academic partnerships in, 482–493; student learning influences of, 386–388; tribal colleges, 32–33, 247; as value-driven, 235–236; women's colleges, 33–35, 247. *See also* Carnegie Basic Classifications; Student affairs

Higher Education Opportunity Act (2008), 74

Higher Education Research Institute (HERI), 354, 359, 360, 361, 369

Higher Learning Commission, 69

Hippocratic Oath, 100

Hispanic Outlook in Higher Education, 375

Hispanic-serving institutions (HSIs): development of, 35–36; establishment of, 20, 33, 35

Historically Black colleges and universities (HBCUs): campus climate of, 247; development of, 35–36; establishment of, 9, 33

Honors programs, 508

How Colleges Work (Birnbaum), 232

How We Think (Dewey), 85

Human ecology theory, 243–244

Human relations theory, 438

I

Identity: definition of, 187; ego, 188; ethnic, 192–197; gender, 197–199; impression management of, 520, 527–528; multiple, 201–202*fig*; online social networking and,

520–522; racial, 190–194*t*, 196–197; sexual, 199–201; transgendered, 199

Identity achievement, 170, 171

Identity development: conditional college effects and, 510; evolution of theories on, 188–189; GLB (gay, lesbian, and bisexual), 200–201; men's, 198; multiple identity, 201–202*fig*; overview of, 187–188; student affairs practice application of theories, 202–203; women's, 197–198. *See also* Social identity theories; Student development

Identity diffusion, 170, 171

Identity reconstruction process, 189

Images of Organization (Morgan), 238

Impression management, 520, 527–528

In loco parentis notion, 67, 68, 70, 75, 99, 242, 250

Inclusion: encouraging cultural border crossing for, 52–53; institutional history on, 52; recommendations for promoting, 50–51

The Independent (newspaper), 10

Influence theory of leadership, 355*e*, 357

Information, ethical oversight of, 112

Input-Environment-Outcome (I-E-O) Model: overview of, 322–323; visualizing conditional college effects using, 502*fig*–503, 506

Instant messaging (IM), 424, 524, 525

Institutional review boards (IRBs), 114

Integrated Postsecondary Education Data System (IPEDS), 24, 39, 305

Intellectual development: Perry's scheme on, 176–177*e*; in women, 177–178

International students, 9/11 impact on, 47

Involvement in Learning: Realizing the Potential of American Higher Education report (1984), 17

Iraq War veterans, 110, 538

J

Journal of College Student Development (ACPA), 89, 289, 471

Justice: conflict management by understanding nuances of, 443; distributive, 443; restorative, 438–439, 443; social, 298–300, 443; as student affairs principle, 100

K

K-12 education, 544

Kappa Alpha (Union College, 1825), 62

Keeling and Berkowitz's concept of healthy community, 457

Kegan's self-evolution theory, 209–210

Kent State University, 16

Knowledge: helping awareness and, 401–406; self-knowledge as basis of all, 348; student affairs professional, 471–472; women's development of, 177–178

Kohlberg's stages of moral reasoning, 179–180*e*

L

Latino critical theory (LatCrit), 197

Latino identity theories, 193, 195

Latinos/Latinas students: increasing enrollment of, 544; Torres's self-authorship study on, 212

Leadership: authentic, 359; community development and role of, 457–458; constraining beliefs in student affairs, 365*e*; conventional and industrial views of, 356–357; cyberleadership, 369; description of, 354, 356; emergent, relational, postindustrial views of, 358–359; empowering beliefs in student affairs, 366*e*; implementing effective, 364–369; organizational, 362–363*e*; reality of bad or dysfunctional, 366–367; SCM (Social Change Model of Leadership Development), 354, 359–362, 369; servant, 357–358; socially responsible, 359–362; summary of approaches to, 355*e*; tradition perspectives of, 357–358; transforming, 358

Leadership and Ambiguity (Cohen & March), 234

The Leadership Challenge (Kouzes & Posner), 358

Leadership development, 462–463

Leadership Identity Development Model (LID), 367–368

Leadership Reconsidered (Astin & Astin), 364, 365, 457

Learning community model, 456

Learning Partnerships Model (LPM), 216*fig*–219, 391–393

Learning Reconsidered: A Campus-Wide Focus on the Student Experience (Keeling), 73, 87, 92, 208, 278, 536

Learning Reconsidered 2 (Keeling), 73, 92, 289, 291, 415, 524, 536

Learning. *See* Student learning

Learning That Lasts (Mentkowski & Associates), 209

LeDoux Laboratory, 132

Legal cases: *Brown v. the Board of Education*, 70; *Dixon v. Alabama State Board of Education*, 70; *Gratz et al. v. Bollinger et al.*, 44; *Grutter et al. v. Bollinger et al.*, 44; *Mahoney v. Allegheny College*, 131; *Regents of the University of California v. Bakke*, 71; *Shin*

v. Massachusetts Institute of Technology et al., 131

Legal issues: protecting and promoting civility, 121–125; risk management and brain's fear system, 130–132; teaching troubled students, 125–130

Legislation: American with Disabilities Act, 406; Civil Rights Act (1964), 14; Family Education Rights and Privacy Act (FERPA), 408; Higher Education Act (1965), 14, 20, 33, 37, 70; Higher Education Opportunity Act (2008), 74; Morrill Land-Grant Act (1862), 10, 11, 63; National Defense Education Act (1958), 70; No Child Left Behind, 73, 534; Second Land-Grant Act (1890), 9, 11; Section 504 (Vocational Rehabilitation Act), 17; Servicemen's Readjustment Act (GI Bill), 12–13, 70, 72, 104, 110; Title III (Higher Education Act), 33; Title IX, 17, 71; Title VII (Civil Rights Act), 71; Tribally Controlled and University Assistance Act (1978), 33

Lewin's theory of group behavior, 455

LGBT (lesbian, gay, bisexual, and transgender) students: advising groups of, 418–419; campus climate for, 249; counseling and helping provided to, 402; identity development, 200–201; intentionality of offering sexual orientation programs for, 290; online social networking site use by, 521–522; same-sex marriage debate impact on, 47, 538; taking multidimensional approach to, 51; transgendered identity, 199; transgendered identity theory, 199. *See also* GLB (gay, lesbian, and bisexual) identity

LGBTQA (Lesbian, Gay, Bisexual, Transgender, Queer, and Ally) Services Office, 279, 280

Life course perspectives, 173–174

Life events and transition perspectives, 173

Life stage perspectives, 173

LinkedIn, 375, 518

Listening (respectful), 123–124

Listservs, 424

Living-learning experiences, 463, 507–508

M

Mahoney v. Allegheny College, 131

Management Fads in Higher Education (Birnbaum), 287

Managerial culture: management techniques and structural considerations of, 276–277; origins and characteristics of, 276; roles in, 277; scenario description of, 275–276

Managerial Grid model, 357

Massachusetts Institute of Technology et al., Shin v., 131

Master's colleges and universities, 30

Men: identity development, 198; understanding gender disparities of, 295–297. *See also* Gender differences

Men and Masculinities Knowledge Community (MMKC), 296

Mental health: AISP (Assessment-Intervention of Student Problems) model to assess, 406; prevalent campus concerns and related, 400–401; student affairs services related to, 540–541; studies on students and, 126–127. *See also* Counseling

Middle States Commission on Higher Education, 543

Minority students. *See* Diversity

Mobile computing, 425
Model of mattering and marginality, 455–456
Model of Multiple Dimensions of Identity, 162
Moodle, 425
Moral development: Gilligan's theory of, 180–181; Kohlberg's stages of moral reasoning, 179–180*e*; Rest's theory of, 181–182
Moratorium (identity resolution), 170, 171
Morrill Land-Grant Act (1862), 10, 11, 63
Mosaic, 516
Multicultural Awareness Knowledge-Skills Survey (MAKSS), 343
Multicultural Change Intervention Matrix, 345
Multicultural competence: assessment of, 342–344; considerations in developing, 346–348; definition of, 338, 402; development of, 344–346; dynamic model of, 337–342; Pope, Reynolds, and Mueller's approach to, 458
Multicultural Competence Characteristics of Student Affairs Professionals Inventory (MCCSAPI), 344
Multicultural Competence in Student Affairs—Preliminary 2 (MCSA-P2) Scale, 343
Multicultural Counseling Awareness Scale: Form B-Revised (MCAS:B), 343
Multicultural Counseling Awareness Scale, 343
Multicultural Counseling Inventory (MCI), 343
Multicultural Organizational Development Checklist, 345
Multidimensional Identity Model, 201
Multiple identity theories, 201–202*fig*
Multiracial theories, 191–192

Muslim students, 47
MUVE (multi-user virtual environment), 517
Myers Briggs Typology Indicator, 418
MySpace, 519, 522

N

NACADA Web site, 422
NASPA Assessment Knowledge Consortium, 72
NASPA Center for Research, 72
NASPA Graduate Program Directory, 69
A Nation at Risk report (1983), 17
National Academic Advising Association (NACADA), 414
National Association of Appointment Secretaries (NAAS), 66
National Association of Orientation Directors (NODA), 114
National Association of Scholars, 83
National Association of State Universities and Land-Grant Colleges, 245, 483
National Association of Student Affairs Professionals (NASAP), 67, 70
National Association of Student Personnel Administrators (NASPA): *Learning Reconsidered*: report by, 73, 87, 92, 208, 278; membership number of the, 473; on multicultural competence, 345; origins of, 66; *Powerful Partnerships*: by, 73, 208, 388; *Principles of Good Practice for Student Affairs* by, 73, 397, 471, 523, 524, 527, 535; professional ethical code of, 98, 114; on student affairs principles and values, 88, 89, 90
National Center for Academic Transformation, 263

National Center for Education Statistics (NCES), 72, 422
National Commission on the Future of Higher Education, 543
National Defense Education Act (1958), 70
National Orientation Directors Association (NODA), 98
National Research Council (NRC), 128, 129–130
National Survey of Student Engagement (NSSE), 263, 264, 296, 329, 415
Native American-American Indian identity theories, 195–196
Native Americans students: College of William & Mary attendance by, 6; counseling support provided to, 402; Five Categories of Indianness, 196; higher education institutions established for, 9; tribal colleges for, 32–33
Navajo Nation, 32
Needs assessment, 322
New York University, 131
Nichomean Ethics (Aristotle), 124
9/11: community development impact of, 455; impact on Muslim students by, 47
No Child Left Behind, 73, 534
Noel-Levitz Satisfaction Survey, 322
Nontraditional students, 20
Northern Illinois University incident (2008), 112
Number of US Facebook Users (2009), 517, 518, 522

O

On-campus living, 509
One Size Does Not Fit All (Manning, Kinzie, & Schuh), 249
Online social networking. *See* Social networking sites
Organization for Economic Cooperation and Development (OECD), 71

Organizational leadership: Bolman and Deal's framing of, 363*e*; frameworks for, 363; management and, 362–363; reality of bad or dysfunctional, 366–367

Organizational theory: on dark side of organizations, 238–240; description of, 157, 226–227; on distinctive organizational features, 235–238; four frames in higher education, 232*t*–235; four-frame model of organizations, 227*t*–231. *See also* Student organizations

Orientation: online technology for student, 528–529; student affairs staff, 376–377

Outcome delivery alignment matrix, 328*e*–329*e*

Outcomes-based assessment (OBA): components of, 326–331; description of, 323, 324–326; outcome delivery alignment matrix, 328*e*–329*e*; questions to consider when implementing, 331–332

Oxbridge model of education, 4, 274

Oxford-Cambridge model of education, 4, 15

P

Pacific Islander-serving institutions, 37–38

Pascarella's General Model for Assessing Change, 502

Peabody Foundation, 9

Peck's progression of community, 457

Pell Grants (BEOG), 16, 38

People of Color Racial Identity theory, 162

Performance appraisals, 378–380

Perry's intellectual development scheme, 176–177*e*

Pew Higher Education Research Program, 313

Phenomenology, 104

Planning for Higher Education, 288

Podcasts, 424

Portland Community College (PCC), 490–491

Positivism, 158–159

Poststructural theories, 160

Powerful Partnerships: A Shared Responsibility for Learning (1998), 73, 208, 388

Practice. *See* Student affairs practice

Predominantly White institutions (PWIs), 35

Prince George's Community College (Maryland), 490

Principle of Fairness (or Charity), 442

Principles of Good Practice for Student Affairs (1996), 73, 397, 471, 523, 524, 527, 535

Problem solving skills, 417–418

Problem-based learning, 85–86

Process consultation, 428–429

Profession: codes of ethics, 109, 113–115, 476; defining, 469–471; student affairs as a, 471–476. *See also* Student affairs professionals

Professional associations: ethical codes of, 113–115; origins and development of, 65–67

Professional Competencies Task Force (ACPA), 477

Professional development: engaging in ongoing, 544–545; goals and opportunities for, 380–381; professional associations and, 65–67, 113–115

Professional ethical codes, 113–115

Professional philosophies: basic principles of, 81–82; profession's identity component of, 83; roles and functions component of, 82–83; values component of, 82

Professionalism: characteristics of student affairs, 476–479;

defining, 469–471; implications for student affairs professional, 479; socialization of, 470

Program development model, 451–452

Progression of community model, 457

Proposition 8 (California), 538

Psychosocial developmental theories: adult development, 172–174; career development, 174; description of, 155; identity development, 170–171; overview of perspective, 168–169; student affairs practice using, 174–175; vectors of development, 171–172*e*

Purdue University, 314

Q

Queer theory, 160, 201

Questions and Answers on College Student Suicide (Pavela), 132

R

Racial identity theories: Black identity theories, 190–191; changing perspectives on, 196–197; commonalities among, 194*t*; multiracial, 191–192; White identity theories, 191. *See also* Ethnic identity theories

Recruitment/selection practices, 375–376

Reflective Judgment Model, 179

Reframing Organizations (Bolman & Deal), 227

Regents of the University of California v. Bakke, 71

Religion: early higher education and role of, 5; majority of student self-identified as Christian, 72. *See also* Spiritual development

Restorative justice, 438–439, 443

Revolutionary War, 62

Risk management, 130–132
RSS (really simple syndication) feeds, 424

S

Safety issues. *See* Campus safety
Same-sex marriage debate, 47, 538
Scholastic Aptitude Test (SAT), 12
Scholssberg's model of mattering and marginality, 455–456
The School of Athens (Raphael), 121
"School on a hill," 4–5
Scottish Enlightenment, 8
Second Great Awakening, 7
Second Land-Grant Act (1890), 9, 11
Second Life, 425, 517
Section 504 (Vocational Rehabilitation Act), 17
Self-authorship: Baxter Magolda's theory on, 210–212; Kegan's self-evolution theory on, 209–210; research on contemporary college students and, 212–214; as transformative learning foundation, 209–214
Self-evolution theory, 209–210
Separation or termination, 381–382
Servant leadership, 357–358
Service learning, 461–462
Servicemen's Readjustment Act (GI Bill), 12–13, 70, 72, 104, 110
Sexual identity: definition of, 199; heterosexual, 199–200; LGBT (lesbian, gay, bisexual, and transgender), 47, 199, 200–201; online social networking site and role of, 521–522
Sexual orientation: definition of, 199; heterosexual, 199–200; LGBT (lesbian, gay, bisexual, and transgender), 47, 199, 200–201
Sherman School, 9
Shin v. Massachusetts Institute of Technology et al., 131

Situational theory of leadership, 355*e*, 357
Skype, 424
Social Change Model of Leadership Development (SCM): description of, 360, 361–362; illustrated diagram of the, 361*fig*; values of the, 360*e*, 369
Social identity theories: description of, 155–156, 189; ethnic identity theories, 192–197; gender identity theories, 197–199; Model of Multiple Dimensions of Identity, 162; multiple identity theories, 201–202*fig*; People of Color Racial Identity, 162; racial identity theories, 190–192; sexual identity and sexual orientation, 199–201; White Racial Identity, 162. *See also* Identity development
Social justice: conflict management through, 443; using curriculum to educate educators on, 298–300; student affairs personnel advocacy for, 90
Social networking sites: dedicated to racial and ethnic identity groups, 521; educating students on productive use of, 526–529; identity and role of, 520–522; impression management on, 520, 527–528; LinkedIn, 375, 518; MySpace, 519, 522; recruitment and selection using, 375; student affairs administrators' use of, 529–530; student affairs advising and role of, 424–425; student conduct on, 524–526; Twitter, 375, 425, 518, 538, 539. *See also* Communication; Facebook
Societal trends: demographic, 537–538; financial and economic forces, 536–537; globalization, 538; technological advances, 538–539

Society for College and University Planning, 288
Socioeconomic status (SES): graduate school attendance and, 506; online social networking and role of, 522
Southern Association of Colleges and Schools, 9, 543
Special focus institutions, 31–32
"Speech codes" incivility, 122–124
"The Spellings Commission Report" (2006), 535
Spiritual development, 182–183. *See also* Religion
Staffing practices: employee separation, 381–382; importance of, 372–373; models of, 373–374; orientation, 376–377; performance appraisal, 378–380; professional development, 380–381; recruitment and selection, 375–376; supervision, 377–378
Statements of Students Rights and Freedoms, 471
Stewardship, 109–110
The Structure of Scientific Revolutions (Kuhn), 158
Student activism: during the 1950s, 70; during the 1960s, 16; during Revolutionary War, 62
Student affairs: academic partnerships with, 482–493; continuing intercultural engagement by, 541; empirically grounded work of, 88–89; enduring principles and values of, 87–90; federal mandates and stakeholder expectations of, 73–75; financing, 303–318; five ethical principles and virtues of, 98–102; founding and historic development of, 61–6275; future directions and advice for, 542–545; identity and role of, 539–540; philosophical legacy of, 83–86; staffing and supervision practices of, 372–382; student learning

as primary role in, 72–73, 92; themes and issues facing, 539–542; theories related to, 152–157. *See also* Higher education institutions; Student affairs professionals; Student services

Student affairs budgeting: accounting methods used for, 311–312; for auxiliary services, 314–315; capital, 311; incremental, 309; line item, 308; preparing budgets, 312–314; program, 309; responsibility center, 310

Student affairs financing: budgeting approaches to, 307–315; conceptual thinking about, 304; expenditures, 306–307; fundraising trends, 317–318; revenue sources of, 305–306, 316–317; trends in finance and budgeting, 315–318

Student affairs history: contemporary student life (1990-present), 71–75; diversification (1850–1900), 63; expanding student life (1950–1970), 67–71; federal legislation affecting race and gender (1970–1990), 71; founding and early years (1636–1850) of, 61–62; modern developments (1900–1950), 64–67; policy perspectives, legal challenges, and student activism, 70–71

Student affairs practice: advocacy culture context of, 279–281; applications of campus environment theory on, 249–252; co-curriculum as strategic resource for, 291–293; cognitive-structure perspectives used in, 183–184; collegial culture context of, 20–21, 273–275; as data driven and mission centered, 293–295; developmental culture

context of, 277–279; identity development theories used in, 202–203; intentionality as enabler of, 289–291; managerial culture context of, 275–277; psychosocial developmental theories used in, 174–175; relationships of theories to, 161–163; strategic confrontation of contemporary issues of, 295–300; tangible culture context of, 283–285; technology use in, 423–426, 522–530; virtual culture context of, 281–283

Student affairs professionals: characteristics of competent, 476–479; five ethical principles and virtues of, 98–102; implications of professionalism for, 479; *in loco parentis* notion of, 67, 68, 70, 75, 99, 242, 250; multicultural competence of, 337–349, 402; philosophies and values of, 80–93; as political activists, 396; professional associations for, 65–67, 113–115; professional development of, 380–381, 544–545; professional preparation and standards of, 69–70; responsibility to society by, 89–90; separation or termination of, 381–382; shifting from techniques to purposes and outcomes, 389–391; social justice advocacy by, 90; staffing and supervision of, 372–382; stewardship role by, 109–110; *Student Personnel Point of View (SPPV)* report (1937) on, 65, 66, 250, 278, 471, 535; teaching troubled students, 125–130; as theoretically informed connoisseurs and critics, 393–395. *See also* Profession; Student affairs

Student affairs revenue: fees for service, 306; general fund, 305; institutional differences in funding, 306; student fees, 305; trends for increasing, 316–317

Student affairs-academic partnerships: Boyer Partnership Assessment Project (BPAP), 487*t*–492; DEEP project, 293, 294, 486; negative aspects of, 486–487; research on benefits of, 485–486; types of, 483–485

Student development: cognitive-structural perspectives of, 175–184; Facebook use and, 522; foundational philosophy of, 75; framework for, 220*t*–221*t*; learning contexts that promote, 214–221*t*; learning linked to, 207–208; psychosocial perspectives on, 168–175; student affairs philosophy on, 90–92; student affairs professionals' role in, 388. *See also* Developmental theories; Identity development

Student development movement: origins of the, 68; student affairs role in, 91

Student Development Services in Post-Secondary Education (1975), 91

"Student Development in Tomorrow's Higher Education—A Return to the Academy" (Brown), 68

Student enrollment: Carnegie Basic Classifications on, 28*fig*; increasing Latinos/Latinas students, 544; nontraditional, 20. *See also* Diversity

Student learning: accountability for demonstrating, 542; community service and, 461–462; complexity of, 207; contexts that promote development, 214–221*t*; democracy education as part of, 84–85; development linked to, 207–208; DGBL (digital game-based learning), 517;

goals for academic advising and, 414–416; institutional influences on, 386–388; Learning Partnerships Model (LPM) on, 216*fig*–219, 391–393; living-learning experiences for, 463, 507–508; as making meaning, 208–209; as primary focus of student affairs, 72–73, 92; problem-based, 85–86; self-authorship component of, 209–214; student affairs philosophy on, 92; student affairs professionals' educator roles in, 388–391; student affairs professionals as learning partners for, 391–393; student affairs-academic partnerships for, 482–493

Student Learning Imperative (ACPA), 73, 92, 208, 278, 324, 388, 535

Student organizations: leadership of, 362–363*e*; origins and earliest, 62. *See also* Organizational theory

Student Personnel Point of View (SPPV) report (1937), 65, 66, 250, 278, 471, 535

Student Personnel Work as Deeper Teaching (Lloyd-Jones & Smith), 535

Student retention, 53–54

Student services: advising and consultation, 413–430; community colleges, 68–69; continuing intercultural engagement of, 541; counseling and helping, 399–410; definition of, 388; outsourcing of, 315–316; psychological and health, 540–541. *See also* Student affairs

Student success: conditional college effects and academic, 510–511; creating conditions that create, 259–267; student scenarios threatening, 257–259; theories on, 157, 209–221*t*

Student Success in College: Creating Conditions that Matter (Kuh et al.), 293

Student success conditions: 1: feature student success as institutional priority, 259; 2: teach students to use institutional resources, 259–262; 3: make successful programs widely available, 262–263; 4: establish early-warning systems and safety nets, 263–264; 5: help faculty create sense of community, 264–265; 6: focusing on what matters to student success, 265–266; 7: reculture the student affairs division, 266–267

Student success theories: Baxter Magolda's self-authorship journey, 210–212; description of, 157; Kegan's self-evolution, 209–210; on learning contexts promoting development, 214–221*t*; Learning Partnerships Model (LPM) on, 216*fig*–219; self-authorship research on college students, 212–214

Students: advising, 413–427; community service by, 461–462; conditional effects of college on, 500–511; counseling and helping, 399–410; graduate school attendance and SES of, 506; institutions serving deaf and blind, 38; leadership development of, 462–463; needs of today's, 422–423; nontraditional, 20; social networking sites and conduct of, 524–529; teaching troubled, 125–130; underpreparedness of, 422. *See also specific populations*

Students with disabilities, 38

Suicidal ideation, 131–132

Supervision practices, 377–378

Supplementary Educational Opportunity Grants (SEOG), 16

T

Tangible culture: managerial techniques and structural considerations of, 285; origins and characteristics of, 283–284; roles in the, 285; scenario description of, 283

Teacher: The One Who Made the Difference (Edmundson), 123

Teaching to Transgress (hooks), 387

Technology: advising and role of, 423–426; community development and role of, 459; as continuing societal trend, 538–539; DGBL (digital game-based learning), 517; instant messaging (IM), 424, 524, 525; MMORPGs (massively multiplayer online role-playing games), 517; Mosaic, 516; MUVE (multi-user virtual environment), 517; social networking sites, 375, 424, 515, 518–522; student affairs approach to educating students about, 526–529; student affairs concerns related to, 522–524

Temporality, 104

Termination or separation, 381–382

Theories: Black racial identity, 151–152; cognitive developmental, 155, 175–184; community development, 454–458; conflict and conflict resolution, 436–439; constructivism, 159; critical race, 162, 196–197; critical theory, 159–160; description of, 150–152; developmental, 153–155, 168–184; emerging theoretical perspectives, 156; evolution of, 160–161; helping and counseling, 403; holistic development, 156; human ecology, 243–244; organizations and campus environments, 157, 226–240, 242–254; paradigmatic influences on construction/application of, 157–161; positivism, 158–159; poststructural, 160; psychosocial developmental, 155, 168–175; queer theory, 160, 201; relationships to student affairs practice, 161–163; social identity, 155–156, 188–201; student affairs-related, 152–157, 471–476; student learning, 209–222; student success, 157, 257–268; summary of college student-related, 138–148; typology, 157; value of, 149–150

Tinto's Model of Student Departure, 502

Title III (Higher Education Act), 33

Title IX, 17, 71

Title VII (Civil Rights Act), 71

Trait theory of leadership, 355*e*, 356

Transformative learning: Baxter Magolda's self-authorship theory, 210–212; Kegan's self-evolution theory on, 209–210; research on self-authorship and, 212–214; self-authorship foundation of, 209–214

Transforming leadership, 358

Transgender Law and Policy Institute, 199

Transgender students. *See* LGBT (lesbian, gay, bisexual, and transgender) students

Transgendered identity theory, 199

Treat Assessment in Schools: A Guide to Managing Threatening Situations and to Creating Safe School Climates report, 128–129

Tribal colleges: campus climate of, 247; establishment of, 32–33

Tribally Controlled and University Assistance Act (1978), 33

TRiO Programs, 542

Tuskegee Institute, 9

Twitter, 375, 425, 518, 538, 539

Typology models, 157

U

United States: historical overview of higher education in the, 3–22; institutional variety in the, 24–40; societal trends in the, 536–539

United States Military Academy at West Point, 7

United States Naval Academy at Annapolis, 7

University of Missouri, 489, 491

University model (1880–1914), 3–4

University movement (1870–1910), 10–11

University of North Carolina at Pembroke, 9

University of Virginia, 6

U.S. Census, 261

U.S. Department of Education: on campus murder rate, 125; on increasing numbers of minority students, 537; on increasing role of community colleges, 542; Integrated Postsecondary Education Data System (IPEDS), 39; on rising costs of high education, 303; on societal value of higher education, 472; "The Spellings Commission Report" (2006) by, 535

U.S. Department of Health and Human services, 128

U.S. Department of Justice, 126

Utilization assessment, 322

V

Values: advising core, 414; higher education system as driven by, 235–236; professional philosophies and role of, 82; SCM (Social Change Model of Leadership Development), 360*e*, 369; student affairs principles and, 87–90; student

services sensitivity to cultural, 103–104

Values theory, 437

Vectors of development, 171–172*e*

Virginia Commonwealth University, 377

Virginia Tech shooting (2007), 112, 125, 129–130, 540

Virginia Tech University's Residential Leadership Community (RLC), 491

Virginia Youth Violence Project, 126

Virtual culture: management techniques and structural considerations of, 282–283; origins and characteristics of, 281–282; roles in the, 283; scenario description of, 281

Vocational Rehabilitation Act, 17

W

Washington Post ASU's speech code article, 124

Weidman's Model of Undergraduate Socialization, 502

What Matters in College? (Astin), 19

Where You Work Matters (Hirt), 249

White House Initiative on Tribal Colleges and Universities, 32

White identity theories, 191, 162

White Racial Identity theory, 162

wikis, 424

Women: early higher education open to, 8, 11–12; historic development of institutional focus on, 64–65; identity resolution styles by, 171; increasing enrollment during 21st century, 19–20; intellectual development of, 177–178. *See also* Gender differences

Women's colleges: campus climate of, 247; establishment and development of, 33–35

World Economic Forum, 448